The
JOY
of
SECTS

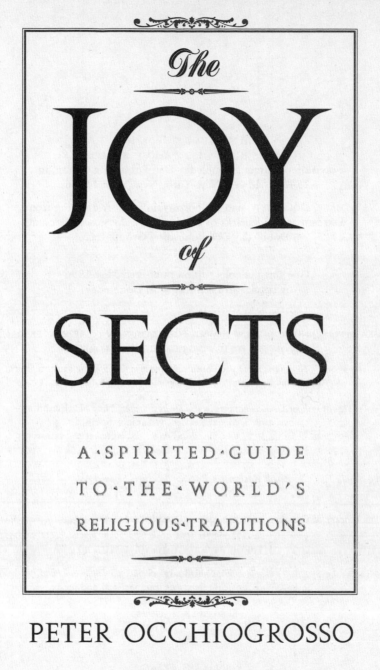

The JOY of SECTS

A·SPIRITED·GUIDE TO·THE·WORLD'S RELIGIOUS·TRADITIONS

PETER OCCHIOGROSSO

A WINOKUR-BOATES BOOK

IMAGE BOOKS
DOUBLEDAY
NEW YORK LONDON TORONTO SYDNEY AUCKLAND

AN IMAGE BOOK
PUBLISHED BY DOUBLEDAY
a division of Bantam Doubleday Dell Publishing Group, Inc.
1540 Broadway, New York, New York 10036

IMAGE, DOUBLEDAY, and the portrayal of a deer drinking from
a stream are trademarks of Doubleday, a division of Bantam
Doubleday Dell Publishing Group, Inc.

First Image Books edition published May 1996
by special arrangement with Doubleday.

GRATEFUL ACKNOWLEDGMENT IS MADE FOR PERMISSION TO REPRINT EXTRACTS
FROM THE FOLLOWING COPYRIGHTED WORKS:

The World's Religions by Huston Smith. Copyright © 1991 by Huston Smith.
Reprinted by permission of HarperCollins Publishers, Inc.

Handbook of Denominations in the United States, New Ninth Edition,
by Frank S. Mead, Revised by Samuel S. Hill.
Copyright © 1985, 1990 by Abingdon Press. Excerpted with permission.

Book design by Patrice Fodero Sheridan

The Library of Congress has cataloged the Doubleday hardcover edition as follows:
Occhiogrosso, Peter.
The joy of sects / Peter Occhiogrosso.
p.   cm.
"A Winokur/Boates book."
Includes bibliographical references (pp. 585–93) and index.
1. Religions.   I. Title.
BL80.2.028   1994
291—dc20   93-48492
CIP

ISBN 0-385-42565-1
7   9   10   8   6

In memory of my mother,
Elvira Morello Occhiogrosso Whittier
1913–1994

And in memory of Lex Hixon,
teacher, friend, and guide
1941–1995

". . . only the open space of awareness
remains."

And to all the secret saints, buddhas,
lamedvovniks, awliya, and ordinary
mystics working in obscurity for the
liberation of all beings

ACKNOWLEDGMENTS

Many thanks to all the people who offered their help without asking anything in return. A number of scholars and advanced practitioners in the great wisdom traditions outlined in this book were kind enough to give me the benefit of their expertise and experience, either by looking over relevant sections of the manuscript, patiently explaining subtle concepts, or answering dumb questions graciously. Any errors or inadequacies of expression regarding these concepts, however, are entirely my own doing. The following includes some but not all of the people who helped me, arranged according to the areas of their expertise.

Swami Atmavratananda of the SRV Retreat Center in Greenville, New York. Ira Schepetin of Vedantic Light in Woodstock, New York.

Reginald Ray of the Naropa Institute, Boulder, Colorado. Robert A. F. Thurman of Columbia University. Helen Harkaspi of Plain Water Zen Practice in Poughkeepsie, New York. Natalie Maxwell-Hauptman of New York City and Kai Mei Marrero of Yonkers, New York.

Dr. J. Wu of the Taoist Center in Washington, D.C. Michael Saso of the Beijing Foreign Language Institute and the University of Hawaii.

Rabbi Jonathan Kligler of the Woodstock Jewish Congregation. Rabbi Ira Eisenstein and Gabe Motola of Woodstock, New York.

Peter Bouteneff and Paul Meyendorff of St. Vladimir's Seminary, Crestwood, New York.

Shaykh Nur al Jerrahi of Masjid al-Farah in New York City.

Various authorities helped to clarify aspects of the New Age, including Roger Woolger, Burrill Crohn, Peter Blum, Howard Finkelson, and

Acknowledgments

John Isaacs; Betsy Stang and Jim Davis of the Wittenberg Center for Alternative Resources; and Dr. Tony Blisko, D.C., of the Mid-Hudson Chiropractic Center.

Mitchell Zucker, Jennifer Dignan, Cassia Berman, and Dave Tapper were a great help in providing connections to some of the people listed here.

Derin Tanyol and Joanne Greenbaum of Art Resource in New York City and Gillian Speeth of Picture This in Philadelphia provided invaluable help in locating artwork and illustrations to accompany and amplify the text.

I couldn't have completed this book without access to a large number of specialized and often hard-to-locate books, and I received a great deal of guidance and generous help in searching for them from Anne Roberts of Mirabai Books in Woodstock and the staff of East West Books in Manhattan. I owe a special thanks to Judy Fischetti of the Woodstock Public Library for her tireless efforts in tracking down countless books and articles through the Interlibrary Loan Program, and for persuading various librarians to let me hold on to many of those books beyond the allotted time.

I'm grateful to Reid Boates and Jon Winocur for coming up with the root idea for this book, along with its title. Reid was especially helpful in seeing the manuscript through the difficult early stages and offering many suggestions to help shape each chapter, as did my agent, Stuart Krichevsky. To Barbara Flanagan, who edited the final version of this manuscript, as she has done with four of my previous books, I offer the appreciative tribute of a writer saved from numerous potential embarrassments. It's an exercise in humility to work with a gifted editor who isn't afraid to point out, with grace, one's solecisms and stylistic lapses.

At Doubleday, I'm thankful to Tom Cahill, who has had faith in this book from the beginning; to David DeCosse and Mike Iannazzi, who were helpful in the early stages of writing; and especially to Trace Murphy, who calmly saw the so-called final manuscript through months of cascading deadlines and ten thousand changes, corrections, additions, and deletions without once flinching (visibly) or telling me to shut up and get on with it. Finally, Marysarah Quinn designed a complicated layout with great skill and equanimity, producing a visually appealing book out of a heap of messy manuscript pages and a pile of photographs. Imagine what she could do with a few loaves and fishes.

CONTENTS

Let brotherly love continue. Do not neglect to show hospitality to strangers, for thereby some have entertained angels unawares. Remember those who are in prison, as though in prison with them; and those who are ill-treated, since you also are in the body.

—HEBREWS, 13:1–3 (REVISED STANDARD VERSION)

Saints and mystics throughout history have adorned their realizations with different names and given them different faces and interpretations, but what they are all fundamentally experiencing is the essential nature of the mind. Christians and Jews call it "God"; Hindus call it "the Self," "Shiva," "Brahman," and "Vishnu"; Sufi mystics name it "the Hidden Essence"; and Buddhists call it "buddha nature." At the heart of all religions is the certainty that there is a fundamental truth, and that this life is a sacred opportunity to evolve and realize it.

—SOGYAL RINPOCHE,
THE TIBETAN BOOK OF LIVING AND DYING

HOW TO USE THIS BOOK

As a reference work for the television and computer age, this book is designed for easy access to names, terms, and boxed tidbits of unusual or illuminative information, and can be browsed just for the fun of it. But the text is also a sequential narrative that can be read from beginning to end, with occasional digressions into related sidebars. (The CD-ROM and video game versions are sure to follow.) In the meantime, a few simple typographical elements should facilitate finding information the old fashioned way—through the Index.

The defining references for most names and terms appear in the text in **boldface.** In the Index, the pages on which those references appear are also in boldface. An asterisk after a name or term in the text means that it is defined in another chapter and can be located through the Index. Some key terms that either need further definition or do not appear in the main text are collected in the COMING TO TERMS section at the end of each chapter. These references are also in boldface in the Index. In addition, each chapter except "The New Age" contains one or more listings of sacred scripture and related texts in sections called THE GOOD

BOOK. Near the end of each chapter is a description of a place of worship representative of one or another branch of that particular tradition, labeled INSIDE A. . . .

Phonetic pronunciation is provided for some words that may be hard to find in most English dictionaries or that may just be convenient to know for those of us who still like to sound words out. The literal meanings of most terms taken from foreign languages are given in quotation marks in parentheses following the term—e.g., **karma** ("action, deed"). Unless otherwise noted, the literal meaning derives from the liturgical or common language for that particular religion (Sanskrit for Hinduism, Hebrew for Judaism, Arabic for Islam, Chinese for Taoism, and so on). Nontypical sources are abbreviated as follows: Ar. (Arabic), Aram. (Aramaic), Ch. (Chinese), Gr. (Greek), Heb. (Hebrew), Jap. (Japanese), Lat. (Latin), Skt. (Sanskrit), Tib. (Tibetan).

INTRODUCTION

✳ THE PERENNIAL PHILOSOPHY

As many lights shine as there are pious pilgrims. If God is infinite, the ways that lead to him must be infinite. . . . Why discuss or debate? What matters is to find God at all costs and not to torture oneself over the choice of the best road to take. Rigid adherence to certain dogmas is not indispensable, at times it can be harmful. If you know God, you will not concern yourself with doctrines. You could have read all the holy books of all the religions, you could believe in all the revealed credos, and yet be incapable of finding God!

> —RAMAKRISHNA OF BENGAL, IN
> *THE GOSPEL OF SRI RAMAKRISHNA*

Had God pleased, he could have made of you one people: but it is His wish to prove you by that which He has bestowed upon you. Vie with each other in good works, for to God you shall all return and He will resolve for you your differences.

> —QURAN 5:49

The doctrine that man is born with a precious jewel in his heart, a "drop of spirit" that unites him to the Way, and yet is not his own possession but held in common by all, is not only widespread but also of great antiquity. None can say when the existence of this jewel was first proclaimed, or, indeed, when and why it first came to be overlooked and forgotten.

—JOHN BLOFELD, *TAOISM: THE ROAD TO IMMORTALITY*

The direct knowledge of the one Absolute and Its projection of the universe is an actual experience common to all seers of all times.

—SWAMI ABHAYANANDA (STAN TROUT),
HISTORY OF MYSTICISM

How odd it seems that in the recorded history of spiritual practice, including over 6,000 years of sectarian conflict, the first formal meeting of the world's religious representatives took place only 100 years ago. The World Parliament of Religions, the centerpiece of the Columbian Exhibition of 1893 in Chicago, gathered 400 men and women representing 41 religions and denominations for 17 days of conferences, speeches, lectures, and discussions. This watershed event not only introduced Hinduism and Buddhism to the West but also presented women and African American religious leaders to the world and began the entry of Judaism and Catholicism into the American religious mainstream.

The century since that historic gathering has brought a vast widening of interfaith dialogue: Buddhism and Hinduism, the *Tao Te Ching* and the *I Ching*, Zen and Yoga and Sufism have become more widely known in the West in those 100 years than they had in the previous 2,000. Christianity and Islam have likewise spread Eastward; the nations of the world appear to know more about each other's religions than perhaps at any time in history. But the last century has also brought ominous escalations of ethnic religious conflict and religious persecution around the globe, in Northern Ireland and the Middle East, in Azerbaijan and the former Yugoslavia, in Kashmir and Tibet. Is there a link between these two trends of growing interconnection and expanding conflict, or are they just relationships passing in the night? Beyond that, is there an intrinsic value to the great religious traditions outlined and explained in this book, or are they more of a drag on human consciousness and evolution than a source of uplift?

Before we can answer that question, we need to do a little research.

Introduction

But examining the broad historical developments of the world's great wisdom traditions necessitates making side journeys into the particulars of minor sects, orders, and philosophical schools. This immersion in the sea of spiritual minutiae might be expected to induce a certain cynicism about the vast universe of religious sects and their inability to coexist peaceably with each other. The Western traditions worship one God, in fact the same God, under at least three different names and through hundreds of different denominations. Why would a universal God require so many and such various forms of worship? The Eastern traditions are even more diverse, and their conceptions of the Deity appear more challenging, if not confounding, to Westerners. Not only do the world's traditions vary greatly from each other in surface ritual and internal construction, but some of them also share long histories of brutal and violent opposition to each other. Is God that perverse, or is humanity that dense?

Yet when one parts the thickets of history, pushing aside the many accounts detailing brutal facts of religious oppression—facts that might generate disquiet in even the most devout—more significant insights begin to emerge. For the careful observer, parallels and cross-references among the great traditions start to come into focus; patterns appear to overlay the map of world religion in a remarkable way. Such overarching patterns are simple to state, but they become endlessly complex when described in depth. And yet they do help to put the great traditions in a perspective that is not always immediately apparent from the viewpoint of a person practicing one religion. These patterns also help to explain how traditions that announce themselves as having essentially the same goals—to help individuals find God or discover their own True Nature while practicing greater love and compassion toward their neighbors—can appear to go about them in such confusing ways and be so antagonistic toward each other.

One of the first realizations to appear is that religions function on many different levels. Some of those levels are designed to help develop a strong ethical basis for life, to satisfy a need for ritual, or to provide an outlet for love and devotion. On still other levels, religions incorporate incrustations of outmoded belief, hierarchical resistance to change, or misguided change for mere expediency. They sometimes develop to serve the specialized purposes of small groups of ethnically or geographically defined people (purposes that may run counter to their professed goal of universality), often through apparently meaningless ancient rituals. Not to denigrate ritual: it can be as transformative and numinous as it can be mechanized and sclerotic. But when the attachment to ritual for its own sake, or to ethnic identification, overcomes the avowed mission of religions to teach compassion and liberation from the limited self, then conflict and persecution may become acceptable options.

Yet there is another, far deeper, level to the great traditions that isn't often spoken of by their mainstream purveyors, probably because from the institutional point of view it appears shadowed by danger. This is the level sometimes referred to as the Perennial Philosophy. The term *philosophia perennis,* first employed by the 17th- and 18th-century German philosopher and mathematician Gottfried Leibnitz, was given wider exposure by Aldous Huxley's 1945 book *The Perennial Philosophy.* Quoting extensively from mystics and spiritual masters mainly of the Hindu, Buddhist, Taoist, Judaic, Christian, and Islamic traditions, Huxley finds and develops several key themes common to all of them, although not always prominent in the institutional versions of those religions.

More recently, the American psychologist and author Ken Wilber, who has sought to integrate Western psychological insights with Eastern spirituality, identified some of the basic tenets of the Perennial Philosophy. In his book *Grace and Grit,* he enumerates what he considers seven of the most salient:

One, Spirit exists, and Two, Spirit is found within. Three, most of us don't realize this Spirit within, however, because we are living in a world of sin, separation, and duality—that is, we are living in a fallen or illusory state. Four, there is a way out of this fallen state of sin and illusion, there is a Path to our liberation. Five, if we follow this path to its conclusion, the result is a Rebirth or Enlightenment, a *direct experience* of Spirit within, a Supreme Liberation, which—Six—marks the end of sin and suffering, and which—Seven—issues in social action of mercy and compassion on behalf of all sentient beings.

The "*direct experience* of Spirit within," which amounts to a union with or absorption in the Divine—called God, Brahman, the

Tao, Reality, or whatever name is applied to It—is generally referred to as mystical experience, or mysticism, and is the key element of the Perennial Philosophy. The identification of sin with duality in the third principle may require a brief explanation; although duality is the central problem to which the Perennial Philosophy addresses itself, it is not clearly understood in Western rational thought. Simply stated, humanity's basic dilemma stems from a split between "I" and "others" which is the beginning of the separative ego. The fact that each of us clings to the belief that we are individual personalities, ultimately separate from all other individuals and even from God and the universe, is held by proponents of the Perennial Philosophy to be responsible for all suffering. The belief in the separative ego is actually a misperception, but it results in various forms of grasping and greed (to shore us up against the rest of the world), in hatred and aggression (toward whatever feels threatening), and ignorance (of whatever is apparently useless to the ego). This belief is made explicit in the teachings of the Buddha, but it underlies all mystical wisdom, which at its root seeks to break down duality and return us to the unitive condition—or to allow us to see that we already *are* one with all existence if we would only realize it. For that reason, adherents of various mystical schools often refer to their principal tenet as nonduality—the firm belief that any sense of a division between oneself and others, between oneself and the material universe, or between oneself and God or the Absolute (in whatever terms one conceives of the Absolute) is an illusion. Once this illusion is comprehended fully, by definition one can no longer suffer the pain of separation or deprivation or be driven by anger, hatred, greed, aggression, or any of the other weapons with which we protect the separative ego from the menacing world of other separative egos. On a relative level, nonduality is implied by the statement of the Golden Rule that appears in several religious traditions: do to others what you would have them do to you. But on the level of absolute Truth, nonduality denies any distinction between "you" and "them": there are no "others" and, besides, there's nothing to do.

Some authors and spiritual teachers have identified nondualism, and the seven principles enumerated by Wilber, as the underpinning of yoga in its many manifestations. The practice of yoga is so ancient that its roots, when traced back in history, disappear in the mists of the Indus River Valley at least 5,000 years ago. The yogic tradition can be followed throughout the many developments of Indian religion, through the further discoveries of the Buddha in the 6th century BC and the subsequent dissemination of Buddhism throughout Asia, and in the mystical practices of the early Taoists of China.

Like a lotus plant whose tubers run underground and send up flowers that bloom above the muck in which they grow, the Perennial Philosophy flourishes again in the deserts of the Middle East around the time of Jesus—who began his ministry after 40 days of solitary meditation in the desert—and in the 4th and 5th centuries with the Desert Fathers, whose silent practices were directly related to the inner realization achieved by Jesus. It crops up in the 7th century in the mystical practices of Islam and Sufism, which in turn travel to Europe and infuse the great saints like Francis of Assisi with the same mystical fire that was in danger of disappearing entirely from the institutional Christian church. And it has been present for more than a millennium in the Judaic tradition of Kabbalah as well as in the Hasidic movement of Eastern Europe in the 18th century.

However they are stated, in whatever language they appear, mystical principles inform all the great traditions, even if they are buried more deeply in some than in others. They appear to be largely obscured in the West, but the East, too, shows a surprising measure of resistance. The Oriental traditions have frequently become overladen with dogmatic excesses, suffered distortion from the selfish interests of the priest class, or become muddled through connection with the political agendas of the hierarchy.

For these reasons, some spiritual teachers and writers have sought to separate two major channels of spirituality—that is, to distinguish the mystical elements of Perennial Philosophy that all great traditions have in common from the specific doctrines, dogmas, and practices of the institutional religions. Ken Wilber goes so far as to differentiate between what he calls "spiritual" leaders and "religious" ones: Gandhi, Emerson, St. Teresa of Avila, and William James fall into the former category; Billy Graham, Fulton Sheen, Pat Robertson, and Cardinal O'Connor are in the latter. Western students of Hinduism, Buddhism, and Taoism generally prefer to focus on the mystical teachings of these religions, ignoring the cultural contexts in which they occur—and which often incorporate large proportions of folk religion, myth, and devotional fervor with unexpectedly rigid moral and social codes.

Tao-chiao, the institutional or Religious Taoism, as opposed to the Philosophical Taoism of Lao-tzu popular in the West, may seem silly and ritualistic to most Americans, as chockablock with superstition and hidebound belief as the most ardently fundamentalist snake handlers of the Ozarks or the Catholic Church of the Inquisition. Modern-day Indian worshipers of Shiva and Vishnu still engage in practices of such devotional frenzy that people regularly perish during their celebrations, sometimes from overexuberance, but often as the result of internecine skirmishes between different sects of the same tradition. None of this has much relevance to Western students of Vedanta, who practice the all-embracing tolerance preached by Ramakrishna and Vivekananda. In short, Eastern religion as practiced by the masses of believers may have more in common with Western religion than its Western proponents prefer to think.

Yet, much as a modern, rational Westerner may sympathize with Wilber's preference for the "spiritual" over the "religious," in the long run it may be neither practical nor desirable to judge the mystical core of religions vis-à-vis their institutionalized, theological contexts. It may not even be possible to separate fully these two aspects—sometimes referred to as the esoteric and the exoteric—of any religious tradition. One would have a hard time imagining the lives and characters of the greatest, most universally admired mystics, whether John of the Cross, Jelaluddin Rumi, or Sri Ramakrishna, removed from the ground of their respective Christian, Islamic, and Hindu belief systems.

In fact, the evidence suggests that it may be dangerous to achieve realization, and the high-level psychic abilities that can come with it (or what the Hindus call *siddhis),* unless one is properly grounded. The spiritual literature and the popular press are full of accounts of so-called spiritual masters and gurus, Eastern and Western, who developed certain esoteric powers without first having established a strong enough ethical, moral, or devotional base and who subsequently gave way to the lures of power and became deluded. The religious scholar Jacob Needleman once compared the esoteric core of a religion to "a very pure, high-octane fuel. Put it into an old Volkswagen," he said, "and the car will go like hell for a mile before it blows apart."

In other words, most people may not be ready just yet to make the move from purely ritualistic and devotional religion to one that combines these exoteric elements with an interior or yogic discipline. Does that mean that they should abandon spiritual practice altogether? Would the world be better off without the grounding in ethical conduct, compassion, and social conscience that most religions can provide, however imperfectly? We have only to look at those moments in recent history where religion has fallen away almost completely—the reigns of Hitler, Stalin, and Pol Pot, or some of the inner-city ghettos of America—to see what a dangerous proposition that can be.

But what about all the evils committed in the name of religion, in the name of an all-loving, all-merciful God called Yahveh, Shiva, Kali, Christ, or Allah? Without doubt, false religion and religious corruption have done their harm, but falsehood and corruption characteristically surround all our most valued institutions, including government, law, and medicine. The practice of devotion, prayer, ritual, and sacrifice should not be confused with the misuse of religion to justify war, persecution, and the pursuit of power. As the English devotional writer William Law noted, these abuses result from "turning to God without turning from the self." Spiritual systems may be flawed, but never so much as the people who administer and transmit them.

We need to make one further distinction within the religions under discussion: between the elite version practiced in the monastic setting or by those who have the time and resources to devote themselves entirely to the study of sacred texts and inner work and the popular version that appeals to the larger working or peasant classes and seeks more proximate goals, such as protection from misfortune and evil spirits, fertility and productivity, and other forms of material happiness. The former usually incorporates both esoteric and exoteric forms, inner practice and outer ritual, whereas the latter is centered on outer practice but may often embody high levels of devotion and faith. One form is not necessarily better than the other, but each may be better suited to different temperaments and needs. In the study of religions in books such as this one, it is easy to overlook the popular aspects of religion because they are not well documented when compared with the abundance of sacred texts and commentaries and historical information relating to monastic and esoteric practice. And I believe that some scholars and enthusiasts especially of Eastern esoteric practice tend to be embarrassed or put off by the popular expression of these religions, which can be informed by narrow-minded local cultures and mores, just as occurs in many areas of Christian practice in the West. But the fact remains that popular Buddhism and Hinduism, for instance, serve many more people than do the more rarefied forms taught in monasteries or by Eastern masters in the West.

Besides, as we have seen, under and through each of the great traditions runs a stream—vastly deeper than the surface waters but somehow also inseparable from them—a single stream that feeds each of those traditions from a single source. This stream of mystical belief and practice, which we are calling the Perennial Philosophy, not only sustains each of the world's religions but also unites them in a subtle way of which those sailing on the surface may not be aware. Both levels—the surface and the underground stream—deserve study because both must be understood in order to apprehend the way each religion functions and because an appreciation of them may help to explain some of the apparent dichotomies and contradictions within the fabric of each religion itself.

If the hidden springs of faith are uniformly profound, the surfaces can be wildly uneven. In his classic work *The World's Religions*, Huston Smith admits that he chose to write about only the best aspects of religion, leaving out "witch hunts in Massachusetts, monkey trials in Tennessee, and snake worship in the Ozarks." Just as a serious survey of the world's great music would be heavy on Bach and Coltrane, extremely light on Mantovani and Como, a guide to religions and religious terminology probably ought to focus on the great achievements of the spiritual traditions, not on the failings of so many of their human purveyors. But the truth is, those very failings often place the rest of religion in a valuable perspective. Besides, bad religion can be as entertaining as bad movies, and far more instructive.

The question remains as to whether some kind of spiritual evolution is in progress, whether large numbers of people gradually taking up meditation and other forms of inner practice will create a critical mass of global enlightenment, or whether we will continue in what could be called the Brazilian rain forest mode. In the past, this theory goes, a small number of mystics, ascetics, monastics, wandering mendicants, and other followers of the Perennial Philosophy were capable of providing the spiritual oxygen that helped the rest of the world to breathe and that sustained the mainstream practice of religion with all its surface anomalies. These days it seems increasingly questionable whether this approach will be sufficient to redeem a crippled planet; on the whole, the evolutionary theory makes more sense. But how long will it take? The Bolivian visionary Oscar Ichazo said some years ago, "In the past eras the mystical trip was an individual matter, or at least a matter of small groups, but no longer. This is what is new in human history. Everybody can now achieve a higher degree of consciousness. . . . The vision of humanity as one enormous family, one objective tribe, may once have been utopian. Now it is a practical necessity."

✻ THE CIRCLE GAME

Within the larger patterns of religious evolution revolve smaller cycles that repeat themselves with astonishing tenacity. Most of the major religions coalesced around genuinely enlightened men whose teachings represented radical departures from the belief systems of their time and place: Moses, Buddha, Lao-tzu, Shankara, Jesus, Muhammad. Their brilliant insights, whether understood as flowing from divine guidance or from inner realization (which some would say amounts to the same thing), led to radically new visions of spiritual laws and beliefs. But those new visions were sometimes flattened out and distorted by disciples in their zeal to universalize and spread the new faith—a tendency that German social scientist Max Weber referred to as "the routinization of charisma."

And so the Israelites occasionally lost focus on the Mosaic law as they became caught up in wars, legalism, and the formalities of Temple worship. Some Buddhist monks treated women in a demeaning fashion that the Buddha never indicated. Some Taoists became enchanted with the notion of prolonging physical life and finding magical elixirs of immortality rather than living with perfect balance in the very moment of daily life, as Lao-tzu suggested. Christians, having survived their early persecution by the Romans, themselves became brutal persecutors and murderers in the name of the Prince of Peace, as their earthly kingdom grew further and further from the Kingdom of God. Muslim caliphs spent more time amassing booty and building an empire than living the simple life of worship and service advocated by the Prophet Muhammad.

After years of accretion it may become clear that a tradition has temporarily lost sight of the initial vision of its founder. Reformers rise up and demand a paring away of fat and corruption, a return to the original vision; new sects develop, new clerical or mystical orders appear. The Old Testament prophets, Bodhidharma, Chu Hsi, Francis of Assisi, Mansur al-Hallaj, the Ba'al Shem Tov, and others like them worked to clarify and redirect the aims and practices of their traditions without rending the fabric. In some cases, their insights gave the tradition a new impetus and vigor that lasted for years or centuries until, inevitably perhaps, the reformed religion itself became bloated and inutile. New visions were called for and the process continued and is continuing still. In fact, the new visions and the resultant transformations of ritual, the constant emergence of new practices or new ways of understanding older practices and beliefs have become an integral part of the traditions as they are lived today. The fact that the great traditions have survived misguided leaders and occasional periods of decadence and yet continue to evolve may be the strongest testimony to their underlying strength.

In other cases, however, the rehabilitation process was so radical that an entirely new religion emerged, even though it may not have been immediately apparent to its earliest adherents. When Martin Luther nailed his 95 Theses to the cathedral door, he was not looking to start a new religion but to open a dialogue with the hierarchy in Rome. The Bahai Faith began as a sect of orthodox Islam but soon split off amid intense persecution and today bears very little connection to its parent tradition.

The notion of divine guidance in the cyclical process of religious evolution is reflected in the often quoted verse from the Hindu holy book the *Bhagavad-Gita,* in which the God-man Krishna, a reincarnation of Vishnu, explains his reappearance in different times, different forms, and, if we wish to interpret it that way, different religious traditions:

When goodness grows weak, when evil increases,
I make myself a body.
In every age I come back to deliver the holy,
To destroy the sin of the sinner, to establish righteousness. (4:7–8)

✳ TWO TRIADS

The Tao that can be described is not the Tao.

—LAO-TZU (CHINA, C. 600 BC)

God cannot be grasped by the mind. If he could be grasped, he would not
be God.

—EVAGRIUS OF PONTUS (EGYPT, AD 345–399)

The sections of this book are arranged roughly in chronological order, moving from East to West. By presenting the material in narrative rather than purely outline form, I hope to show how the major
traditions (and many of the minor ones) developed out of each
other. One further pattern that emerged from studying the six
largest and most influential religious traditions of the world is that
they appear to fall into two somewhat parallel triads: Hinduism,
Buddhism, and Taoism in the East, Judaism, Christianity, and Islam
in the West. Without trying to make too much of this shining sym-
metry, we can at least examine some of the parallels, acknowledging beforehand the potential oversimplification inherent in a reduc-
tion of this sort.

In the East, Hinduism is the most ancient tradition, stretching back to
somewhere between 4000 and 2000 BC, actually combining several different traditions in an evolutionary spiral to which the term *Hinduism*
barely does justice. But even in its earlier forms, it addressed the relationship of the individual soul to the Absolute Godhead, presented a coherent worldview, and developed a strong moral code. Around 500 BC,
Siddhartha Gautama, a historical figure from northern India who came
to be known as the Buddha, fully steeped in the ethos and culture of his
time, departed from the religion of the land. He walked a different path
through the dense forests of northern India, basing his new teachings on

insights radically different from those of the mother tradition, and his new vision quickly took on a life of its own.

Over the next thousand years, Buddhism spread from India to Sri Lanka and Southeast Asia, to China, Tibet, Korea, and Japan. In China, Buddhist missionaries interacted with the ancient tradition of Taoism, which predated the teachings of the Buddha. Taoist principles subtly infiltrated Buddhism and had a lasting effect on the school of Buddhism known in China as Ch'an and in Japan as Zen. Buddhism and Taoism coexisted peacefully in China for hundreds of years, cross-pollinating each other in subtle and overt dimensions. Some observers have further made the case that both Hinduism and Taoism developed from the same yogic tradition based on deep meditative practices. At any rate, the three religious traditions are inextricably interrelated through the medium of Buddhism.

In the West, the oldest active religion is Judaism. Abraham, the father of the Hebrew people, lived around the beginning of the second millennium BC. Moses formulated the law that was to become the foundation of Judaism sometime toward the end of that millennium, perhaps as early as 1200 BC. Then, around AD 30, Jesus of Nazareth, as thoroughly imbued with the Jewish law and worldview of his day as the Buddha had been with Indian culture, began to preach his stunningly simple yet profound vision of the Kingdom of God. Grounded in the Jewish principles of compassion and social justice, his teachings nonetheless signaled a departure from Temple-based Judaism. As with Buddhism, his new vision of existing beliefs and practices assumed its own life. His followers' belief that Jesus was God incarnate forced a break with Judaism, and over the next 2,000 years Christianity traveled across the Mediterranean to Europe and from there to the New World and back to Africa and Asia.

Islam has roots reaching back into both Christianity and Judaism. The traditional progenitors of the Arab people are Abraham and Ishmael, the son of Abraham by his slave-girl Hagar. Islam views Adam, Noah, Abraham, Moses, and Jesus as prophets in a long line that culminated in Muhammad, the "Seal of the Prophets." Some Muslim practices resonate with those of Judaism and Christianity, from the custom of circumcision to the five-times-daily prayer, which is reminiscent of prayer cycles of the Christian monks and anchorites the Prophet Muhammad encountered in the Arabian desert. Other aspects of Islam offer clear alternatives to preexisting elements of Jewish and Christian practice: the Quran as holy book, the mosque as holy place, and Friday as holy day.

Unlike the Eastern triad, the Big Three in the West have been at each other's throats from the beginning, the ferocity of their opposition dwarfing the occasional wars among Eastern believers. Even before the Romans got to the early Christians, the Jewish establishment persecuted them as a dangerous breakaway sect. The Christians, once they came to power, returned the favor a hundredfold, hunting and killing Jews with a brutality that made their initial persecution seem mild. Islam then burst on the scene in the 7th century, and the antagonism among Christians, Jews, and Muslims has hardly abated since.

What, if any, is the significance of these twin triads? Are they, in the currently fashionable language, opposing lobes of the earth's brain—one intuitive, passive, creative, the other analytical, active, destructive? No metaphor is likely to hold up entirely, and various reasons have been advanced for the essential differences between Eastern and Western approaches to spiritual practice. Aldous Huxley in *The Perennial Philosophy* presents a novel theory that might not have occurred to a less creative mind:

> Religions whose theology has been least preoccupied with events in time and most concerned with eternity have been consistently the least violent and the most humane in political practice. Unlike early Judaism, Christianity and Mohammedanism (all of them obsessed with time), Hinduism and Buddhism have never been persecuting faiths, have preached almost no holy wars and have refrained from that proselytizing religious imperialism which has gone hand in hand with the political and economic repression of the colored peoples.

Time is as good a reason as any, apparently, to go hacking your neighbors to pieces over a difference in conception of God. In parts of the Mediterranean, violence has been perpetrated over whether one believes that the Third Person of the Trinity, the Holy Spirit, proceeds from the Father and the Son or from the Father alone. Even today the issues remain so hair-splittingly picayune that church historians have trouble reconciling the vast amounts of blood spilled over such minutiae.

Introduction

From the point of view of the mystics, whose experience of enlightenment typically leads them to see the interconnectedness of all humanity and the Godhead, this hair- and head-splitting is uncalled for. For although mystics often speak in the particular language and terminology of their own religions, they are clearly describing a universal knowledge. As the American-born Swami Abhayananda writes in his *History of Mysticism,* "The experience of the one Reality is the same for all, of course; and in all the declarations of the many prophets, saints, and messiahs, we can hear the attempt to convey a common knowledge based on that common vision."

The same author goes on to make another crucial distinction. In speaking of the Perennial Philosophy, sages and writers often mention the One Reality, knowledge of which derives from what is sometimes called the unitive experience, a merging with God. But according to Abhayananda the One is actually two or, more properly, two-in-One. Each mystical tradition that posits an eternally unchanging Godhead also acknowledges the changing and inconstant worldly manifestation of that Godhead. In the Upanishads, this is represented by Brahman and Maya, in Taoism it is the Tao and the Te; in Greek mysticism it was the One, or Theos (God), and Logos (the Word); in Judaism, Yahveh and Shekhinah; in Christianity, God the Father and God the Son (Jesus Christ).

As a Westerner who has studied under a renowned spiritual master in India, Swami Abhayananda has been able to make this distinction especially evident for other Westerners:

Clearly, we live simultaneously in two frameworks of reality, that of the divisible world of multiple phenomena, and that of the eternal Self, the unbroken Whole. . . . This complementarity of identities necessitates two entirely different mental attitudes, or states of awareness: when we focus on the Self, we become aware, "I am the one infinite Existence-Consciousness-Bliss"; but when we take the attitude of love toward God, we become aware, "I am Thy creature and Thy servant, O Lord." And it is the paradoxical fact that both attitudes are correct and valid which accounts for the confused oscillation many dedicated truth-seekers feel between the attitude of Self-knowledge . . . and devotion to God. . . . I am convinced that, if we are to speak truly and to live realistically, it is necessary to embrace both attitudes, and to relinquish the logic which begs for an either/or approach to identity.

So it turns out that the apparently simple matter of a unitive experience is not nearly so simple as we might wish. Maybe the very complexity of religion in all its forms is what makes it so utterly absorbing. For those who take it seriously, which according to most recent surveys is between 80 and 90 percent of all Americans, it is hardly just another thing to collect and admire, like baseball cards. Religion, in whatever proportion of esoteric and exoteric it may appear for the moment in one individual's practice, remains complex beyond all rational attempts to grasp it and, perhaps ultimately, beyond all imagining as well.

AUTHOR'S NOTE: I set out to write this book not from the position of a religious scholar but as an interested participant who wanted to convey as much information as concisely as possible about the religions of the world. I tried to put myself in the reader's place and ask what I would want to know about a particular tradition, school, denomination, or teacher, including aspects of religion that may not have to do with its practice but that nevertheless satisfy a certain curiosity. From the standpoint of a devout practitioner, this approach may at times appear irrelevant, misguided, or even blasphemous. I'm sorry if I give anyone that impression; however, I'm not writing only for the devout but also for the interested outsider, for the curious unbeliever, for the mystified, and for anyone who ever wondered what the difference is between karma and dharma, samadhi and satori, Talmud and Torah, Methodists and Presbyterians, Sunnis and Shiites, or Eckists and Aricans.

Given that supposedly egalitarian premise, I found it difficult to maintain a genuinely objective stance. My own biases, social predispositions, and religious preconceptions kept getting in the way, forcing me to go back and refocus the lenses through which I viewed the world's religions. In the end I had to acknowledge my presence in a specific time and place; if something about a particular religion struck me as humorous or hypocritical, even after examining my preconceptions and discussing the matter with practitioners of that tradition, I chose to go with my feeling. In many cases, reseeing the religion through further reading or conversations led me to change, delete, or add passages to the text. The responsibility for these expressions, however, including any errors of fact or understanding that may have crept in, is mine and mine alone.

Some readers may quarrel with the use of the word *sect,* which is sometimes given pejorative overtones or mistakenly equated with the derisive term *cult.* A sect can be a dissenting group which has broken away from the main body of a religion, in the sense that the Puritans, say, were a rigorist sect of the Anglican Church, which is itself a branch of Protestant Christianity. But more generally, *sect* is synonymous with *denomination,* meaning any viable subset of a major religion that differs from other sects in interpreting the revelation of that religion. Roman Catholicism and Lutheranism are both sects of Christianity, just as Shiites and Sunnis belong to differing sects of Islam.

Nonetheless, the term developed in a specifically European Christian context, in which members of one sect often believed that all other sects taught serious doctrinal errors that would render salvation impossible. The prevalence of this kind of sectarianism in Europe is what made the search for religious freedom paramount among so many of the early American colonists. But the exclusivist attitude of many Christians is not necessarily shared by their Sufi or Buddhist counterparts. There it is more accurate to speak of *orders,* along the lines of Christian orders of monks and nuns. Orders may differ regarding teaching lineage, monastic rules, and specific orientations and goals, yet they share the same essential beliefs; certainly they hold that all orders are legitimate facilitators of spiritual growth. Often the differences have to do with philosophical orientation, in which case the term *school* would apply as well.

Because of the mind's prejudice in favor of numbers, the larger the religious subgroup, the less likely we are to call it a sect in everyday parlance. So we may tend to think of Orthodox Jews as composing a branch of Judaism, of the Hasidim as a subset of Orthodox Judaism, and the Lubavitchers as a sect of Hasidim. Although individuals may at first refer to themselves as Christian or Buddhist, when pressed they generally become more specific, explaining that they are actually Seventh-Day Adventist or Russian Orthodox or members of the Kagyu Order of Tibetan Buddhism.

This book uses the term *sect* in its broadest sense, with no pejorative connotations. Sects should be distinguished from cults, which are generally excluded from consideration here, because cults have very little to do with genuine religion. Don't look for Jim Jones or Jonestown in the Index. Where members of a legitimate sect have wandered off into the fringes of a cult, like the infamous Branch Davidians of David Koresh who considered themselves a subset of the Davidian sect of Seventh-Day Adventists, they may be included simply to set the record straight.

Since this book is written from an unabashedly Western point of view for the general reader rather than the academic, I've eliminated most diacritical marks in foreign words and retained the conventional system of dating using BC and AD as opposed to the CE (Common Era) and BCE favored by some religious scholars. I feel this will be more familiar and comfortable to most Western readers who come from the Jewish-Christian tradition. Much of the material itself is unfamiliar enough without adding to the confusion.

1

HINDUISM

✳ THAT OLD-TIME RELIGION

In any study of the religions of the world, India deserves special treatment. According to a recent Gallup survey, no country has a higher percentage of respondents who believe that religion is "very important" in their lives. (The United States ranks second.) Of India's approximately 850 million residents, 680 million, over 80 percent, are Hindus. Historians agree that the earliest known civilizations that left written records flourished at about the same time in Mesopotamia and the Indus Valley in northern India. But since we have no record of a mystical religion practiced in Sumer, as we do for the Indus region, the oldest recorded mystical teachings in the world belong to India.

One way in which India's religious tradition differentiates itself from the major faiths of the world is its vastness—the enormous expanse of time it covers and the bewildering array of distinct philosophies and beliefs that can still be called Hindu. Unlike Buddhism, Christianity, and Islam, Hinduism is not founded on the life and teachings of a single

1

charismatic figure such as Buddha, Jesus, or Muhammad. We can't name one or even several key individuals without whom the religion of India would not be recognizable, notwithstanding the fact that Indian history—as well as modern India—is replete with brilliant and saintly teachers, sages, philosophers, and reformers of all varieties.

In fact, variety may be the single most characteristic element of Indian religion. Hinduism admits as many different spiritual attitudes and approaches to salvation—or, more properly, "liberation"—as one could imagine. As the oldest extant recorded tradition on earth, it has roots planted firmly in the Neolithic Age while its branches have grown immeasurably in breadth and sophistication to the modern day.

But for all its diversity, Hinduism is a unique religious tradition. To begin with, it is more closely identified with the geographic location in which it originated and grew to its current state than any other major religion, with the possible exception of Taoism in China. The vast majority of Hindus still reside in India, with 20 to 30 million more—barely 5 percent—scattered about North America, Southeast Asia, Bali, Fiji, eastern and southern Africa, the Persian Gulf, Kuala Lumpur, Singapore, Hong Kong, Nepal, and Sri Lanka.

The words *Hindu* and *India* both come from the Sanskrit name of the Sindhu River (now the Indus), as pronounced by the Persians. Indians themselves refer to their religion, however, with the Sanskrit term **Sanatana dharma** ("eternal truth or religion"), implying a derivation directly from God rather than a human founder and seeking to connect the earliest Vedic Sanskritic tradition, the sectarian worship of Vishnu, Shiva, and Shakti, and the intellectual complexities of the philosophical system called Vedanta. (**Sanskrit,** the sacred and classical language of India, derives from the same Indo-European language group as most European languages, except that it preserves more of the mother tongue.) The very geography of India is considered holy, encompassing hundreds of sacred places, trees, shrines, and pilgrimage sites called **tirthas.** The **Ganges,** the sacred river of India, is said to wash away the sins of anyone who bathes in it, including sins accumulated in past lives.

The multiple gods and sects of Hinduism, its hundreds of local deities and many esoteric physical and spiritual practices, can give Westerners the impression that Hinduism is a confusing, polytheistic, even pantheistic religion. Add to this the regional folk nature of much of Hindu worship in India proper—a country in which not only certain towns, rivers, and trees are held sacred, but also cows, snakes, rats, and vultures—and the effect can completely overwhelm a Westerner's sense of propriety, of what religion *ought* to be.

Nonetheless, the underlying principles of Hinduism are specific enough to lend it cohesion and coherence wherever it may be practiced.

HINDUISM BY THE NUMBERS

Despite India's reputation for developing the most profoundly mystical practices, Hindus apparently enjoy classifying almost everything to do with life and religion into neatly numbered, logical systems or groupings. Here are a few of the major categorizations by which they live.

The four Vedas: The term *Veda* refers to the orthodox, revealed sacred scripture of India as a whole. It is divided into 4 Vedas: the *Rig Veda, Yajur Veda, Sama Veda,* and *Atharva Veda,* also called Samhitas ("collections") because they are gatherings of various hymns, prayers, and spiritual lore. Each Veda has its appended set of more recent scriptures, known as Brahmanas, Aranyakas, and Upanishads (see THE GOOD BOOK for more details). The Vedas are believed by Western scholars to have been composed and passed on orally between 1500 and 600 BC and put into writing sometime after 1000 BC. Yet most scholars acknowledge that the origins of the beliefs expressed in the Vedas (other than that they derived from common Aryan sources), and of the rishis who composed them, are shrouded in mystery, as are the precise dates of their initial composition. Some Indian historians date certain hymns as far back as 4000 BC or earlier. The lengthy Vedas were each the responsibility of various brahman families, who collected and passed them down among themselves. From many internal references to sections of the Vedas and Upanishads that no longer exist, scholars have deduced that much of the original scriptures have been lost.

The four castes: Also known as *varna* ("color"), caste traditionally divides Indians into four major social classes (with hundreds of subcastes in between):

brahman: priest-philosophers and scholars
kshatriya: warrior-rulers, politicians, civil authorities
vaishya: merchant-agriculturists, free peasants, artisans
shudra: workers, servants, unskilled laborers

It is essential to understand that these are societal rather than religious distinctions and were imposed by the invading Aryans on an indigenous population that was darker-skinned.

The four yogas: Sometimes called **margas** ("paths"), the yogas offer four distinctly different approaches to enlightenment, tailored to different temperaments and orientations. None is considered better than the others.

Jnana yoga is the path of knowledge, leading to God through intellectual analysis and discrimination.

Karma yoga is the path of selfless work or action. The aim is to get to God by acting without attachment to the fruits of one's work.

Bhakti yoga is the yoga of love and devotion, first voiced in the epic *Ramayana* but perhaps most famously in the great holy book, the *Bhagavad-Gita* (where the focus is on devotion to the God-man Krishna), as an addition to karma and jnana yogas.

Raja yoga is the "royal" yoga, which has been described as "the way to God through psychophysical experiments." One aspect of those experiments is a series of movements and postures known as *hatha yoga,* the most popular form of yoga in the West.

The four stages of life: Ashrama encompasses the four stages of life. Discussed in more detail later, they are, briefly, *brahmacharya* (student); *grihasthya* (householder); *vanaprasthya* (hermit); and *sannyasin* (wandering mendicant).

The four aims of life: Hindus subscribe to four ideal goals in life, known as **chaturvarga,** or the **purusharthas:**

Dharma ("duty"). Although *dharma* can be translated many ways, including "truth," "righteousness," and "religion," all of those are contained in the sense of dharma as one's moral and spiritual duty in life.

Artha ("material gain"). Contrary to popular opinion, the Hindu scheme of things does not look askance at success, wealth, or possessions but merely seeks to keep them in their proper place. One of the duties of a Hindu householder, according to the scriptures, is to begin each day pondering how to improve both dharma and artha.

Kama ("physical and sense pleasures"). The same holds true for the enjoyment of earthly pleasures, including but not limited to sexuality, when pursued during the appropriate stage of life.

Moksha ("release or salvation"). The fourth goal parallels the fourth stage of life, representing the ultimate direction in which all Hindu life is aimed.

The six darshanas: The **darshanas,** or philosophical systems, like the four yogas, are meant to be complementary rather than competitive. They incorporate not only philosophy and theology but also psychology, philology, physics, meditation, and other esoteric spiritual practices. Together they form the six schools of orthodox Hindu thought that had evolved by the end of the 4th century AD. Only a few of them are still active in modern Hinduism, since they developed out of each other and tended to make previous darshanas somewhat obsolete. They are generally arranged in pairs, and each is divided into various subschools.

Nyaya and **Vaisheshika** cover logic and physical principles.

Sankhya and **Yoga** deal with Hindu metaphysics and psychophysical exercises.

Purva-Mimamsa explores the theology of Vedic sacrificial ritual. **Vedanta** (originally referred to as **Uttara-Mimamsa**) is the complex system of philosophy that rules much of Hindu religious thought today, both within and outside of India.

The seven chakras: The **chakras** are the traditional energy centers of the astral body*, a subtle energy plane that is said to coexist with the physical body. The chakras are the areas of interconnection between body and spirit that, when purified or opened up through the process of raja yoga, lead the adept to enlightenment. They are often pictured as lotus blossoms or spinning wheels (in Sanskrit, *chakra* means "wheel" or "circle"), and each subtle chakra roughly corresponds to a location in the physical body. (A similar system, with different terminologies, is employed by some schools of Buddhism and Taoism.) The first, or **muladhara,** chakra lies at the point where the kundalini energy is pictured as a coiled serpent between the anus and the genitals. (*Kundalin* is Sanskrit for "she who lies coiled"; kundalini yoga is a process of raising the "serpent" by purifying all the chakras.) The second chakra is at the root of the genitals; the third corresponds to the solar plexus; the fourth is located near the heart (although usually placed either in the middle of the chest or closer to the right side); the fifth is in the throat region; the sixth is located slightly behind the space between the eyebrows, or cavernous plexus (the so-called **third eye**); the seventh is actually located just above the crown of the head, although it corresponds to the pineal gland. This last is called the **sahasrara** chakra, from the Sanskrit word for "thousand," referring to the "thousand-petaled lotus of enlightenment." It is considered higher than the others, which are sometimes referred to merely as the six chakras. In addition, there are six minor chakras, which are rarely mentioned.

The three gunas: Although the Sanskrit term **guna** means "fundamental quality," the gunas are thought of more as tendencies or forces that need to be balanced in order for harmony to prevail. All material objects and beings are composed of some mixture of the three, yet when they are in perfect balance, they disappear altogether. **Sattva,** usually associated with light, virtue, and goodness, is the force that tends to reveal the true nature of things. **Rajas,** associated with passion or restless action, reflects the projection onto reality of some illusion, typified by greed or ambition. **Tamas,** associated with darkness, heaviness, or inertia, is the force that tends to obscure reality, often expressed as laziness, immobility, dullness, or ignorance. One of the three gunas is usually dominant, lending its nature to a person's character and to his or her state in life. In general terms, sattva represents an ideal or goal to be obtained, tamas is the obstacle to be overcome, and rajas is the means to overcome it. Tamas holds us back by concealing reality and can be countered by the active quality of rajas, which in turn must be tamed and clarified by the wisdom of sattva, which reveals our true nature. If the job of the spiritual seeker is first to balance the three gunas, the ultimate goal is to become detached from all of them.

The five elements: All of creation is made up of earth, air, fire, water, and **akasha** ("ether" or "space"). In addition, prana ("energy") is the power that acts in akasha.

❋ WHOSE HINDUISM IS IT, ANYWAY?

> It is impossible to give a precise definition of Hinduism or to point out the
> exact place and time of its origin.
> —KLAUS KLOSTERMAIER, *A SURVEY OF HINDUISM*

Hinduism is an endlessly complex and varied collection of beliefs and belief systems, but they are all based on ideas and principles that can be
traced back to an extensive collection of scriptures called the Veda
("knowledge"), said to have been revealed to seers, or **rishis** (traditionally seven great rishis, but in reality many more), during states of deep
meditation or contemplation. The Vedas themselves are a welter of conflicting opinions and laws. For example, suicide is considered a crime
leading to a rebirth at much the same level in life; but when committed
by an advanced yogi, especially at a sacred pilgrimage site, it is said to
ensure liberation from the cycle of rebirths. The Hindu philosophical system is rife with differing darshanas, or "points of view," although of the
six orthodox darshanas, only Sankhya, Yoga, and Vedanta are considered to have lasting significance, and only the last two still hold prominent places in contemporary Hinduism. Yet all six have the same goal:
liberation from the endless cycle of death and rebirth and identification
of the individual soul (Atman) with the Absolute Godhead (Brahman). In
the Hindu system, liberation is the equivalent of Christian salvation.

As the Absolute Godhead, **Brahman**—unchanging, infinite, timeless—
is considered too abstract and impersonal for the human mind to relate
to directly. The first manifestation of Brahman in a personal deity is
called **Ishvara** ("Lord of the Universe," from Skt. *ish,* "to rule") and is
the highest conception of God that the mind can embrace. All the other
deities of Hinduism, such as Vishnu and Shiva, are aspects of Ishvara, the
personal God who is the actual creator of the universe.

Hindus view humanity's relationship to Brahman in two general ways.
Either God is a separate Being of whom the human soul is a mirror image and whom one worships with great devotion, calling his name,
singing his praises, entreating for help, and offering sacrifice. Or God is
identical with the Self or **Atman,** which dwells in each person and which
it is one's lifework to locate, identify, and ultimately realize as one's True

Being. The former, theistic approach is more commonly associated with the Indian people and their focus on devotion and image worship. The latter is the version most commonly sought out by Westerners, although it is also quite prevalent in India, from sages who wander the forests with only a staff and bowl to the most intellectually astute masters of mystical practice. On yet another level, the two approaches are seen as different ways of imaging the same reality, according to one's tendencies, and neither one is inherently superior to the other.

In theory, the darshanas themselves are considered not opposing but rather complementary systems, allowing the Hindu to choose one or more as paths to realization of Brahman. However, in practice, the doctrinal differences among the six "viewpoints" have been the subject of often fierce debate by theologians and believers. Because the darshanas evolved in sequence, each in turn clarifying certain "loopholes" left by the previous darshanas, some of the six may appear contradictory. The same principle holds true for the myriad minor laws, duties, and obligations surrounding everything from one's caste to one's specific sect, or **sampradaya** (of which there are over 300). This nitpicking between supporters of different darshanas and sects can inject an element of parochialism into the otherwise inclusive and tolerant atmosphere of Hinduism.

Yet the sense of plurality summed up in the famous line from India's oldest scripture, the *Rig Veda*—"Truth is One, but the wise have given it different names"—has imbued the Indian spirit with forbearance of differing beliefs and a respect for healthy skepticism. In one of the best-known hymns near the close of the *Rig Veda*, the so-called **nasadiya sukta,** a series of questions about the creation of the universe ends with a statement so brazenly skeptical that it almost seems strange appearing in the sacred text of a major religious tradition. (Seen from another perspective, however, the final line may not be an expression of skepticism but of the fact that the Absolute has no way of knowing Itself.)

There was neither being nor nonbeing then, neither atmosphere nor the sky above. What stirred? Where? Under whose protection?

There was neither death nor immortality then. Day was not separate

9

from night. Only the One breathed, without an alien breath, of Himself—and there was nothing other than He.

Was there below? Was there above?

Who really knows? Who will here proclaim it? Whence was it produced? Whence is this creation? The gods came afterwards with the creation of the universe. Who knows then whence it has arisen?

Whence has this creation arisen—perhaps it formed itself or perhaps it did not? He whose eye watches over it from the summit of heaven, He alone knows. Or perhaps even He doesn't know.

—*RIG VEDA*, 10.129

✳ DRAWING COLOR LINES

One of the dominant creation scenarios that the author of the preceding passage was questioning involves a cosmic egg, from which Brahma, the first god of the Hindu Trinity, emerged to carry out the creation of all the worlds. Later in the *Rig Veda*, a hymn called the **Purusha sukta** describes the creation arising from the sacrifice of the primal person (Purusha), from which the various entities of the world derived. Along with the sun, moon, earth, air, sky, and various gods, the **caste** system was also created.

The Sanskrit word for caste, **varna**, also means "color." Since this system was devised by the taller, lighter-skinned, fairer-haired (yet probably not blond), and possibly blue-eyed conquering Aryans and was imposed on the darker-skinned aboriginal inhabitants of northern India, the caste system had unmistakably racial underpinnings from the start. Typical of the hierarchic and patriarchal societies of the pastoral nomads who wreaked havoc on the more peaceful, agrarian cultures of Europe and the Middle East beginning in about the 5th millennium BC, the Aryan invaders had structured their society to preserve the power of the strongmen as ratified by the priestly class.

The laws regarding caste appear in greater detail in the *Ramayana* and the *Laws of Manu,* or *Manu Smriti* (see THE GOOD BOOK), but the basic divisions are simple enough. Starting at the top, the **brahman** caste embraces priest-philosophers, holy men, and scholars, whose duties include

10

teaching and studying the Vedas, conducting sacrifices, and giving and collecting alms. Originally warrior-rulers, the **kshatriya** evolved to include politicians and civil authorities, all the administrative people who make the country run. Below them are the **vaishya,** merchant-agriculturists, free peasants, and the skilled artisans who make up the majority of tradespeople. The lowest caste is the **shudra,** composed of servants and unskilled laborers of all sorts.

Below the shudra and effectively outside the caste system are the **outcastes,** or so-called untouchables—higher castes are not to make physical contact with them because they are considered "unclean"—who make up about 20 percent of the population and perform the most menial tasks. People become outcastes by violating caste laws, by breaking rules regulating marriage or occupation for their caste, or for other offenses. Although untouchability has been abolished in modern India, outcastes still live de facto miserable lives, similar to the plight of black sharecroppers in the post-Emancipation South.

More than 3,000 subdivisions of caste, called **jatis** ("births"), evolved over the centuries through intermarriage, and membership in these is determined by one's occupation. Only the male children of the three highest castes are allowed to become **dvija** ("twice-born"), initiated by a ceremony called **upanayana** at which they are invested with a sacred cord (**yajnopavita** or **janeu**) to be worn night and day until they enter the fourth and final stage of life. Their new status permits the twice-born to read and study the Vedas, traditionally forbidden to women, shudras, and outcastes, but increasingly available to the general public.

Various rationales have been extended for the caste system, including the necessity to prevent the spread of disease among groups that had different immune systems—namely the conquering Aryans, who occupied the three upper castes, and the aboriginal Indians, who fell into the lowest caste. Before corruptions and abuses set in, the caste system may have served several other useful purposes, including the protection of trade secrets among differing professional guilds. As a signal of how important religion was considered at this early stage of Indian culture, the class of priests and philosophers was placed above warriors, kings, and moneymakers. However, the brahmans (the word originally meant "sacrificer") were not paid as much as the next two castes, in keeping with their more spiritual mission. In all likelihood, the ruling kshatriyas may have used the brahmanic caste to validate their dominant role as well.

In the early centuries of caste, upward mobility was still possible through marriage or accomplishment, but as the system solidified to the point where it became purely hereditary and intermarriage or even dining together was anathema, improving one's station in life was increasingly difficult. Beginning in the 1st millennium BC, voices began to be raised in opposition, especially by religious reformers, including the Buddha (himself a kshatriya by birth), who is quoted as saying, "Not by birth does one become a brahman. By his actions alone one becomes a brahman." By the 19th century, political reformers were seeking to abolish the rigidity of the caste system, which still exists today, and, especially at the urging of Mohandas K. Gandhi, to eliminate the mistreatment of outcastes. But the most compelling arguments against the idea of caste have come from spiritual leaders such as the 19th-century Bengali saint Sri Ramakrishna, who said simply, "Those who love God belong to no caste."

Each caste has its own dharma, or set of moral and social obligations (sometimes called **swadharma**), a notion evolved from the earlier Vedic concept of **rita** ("cosmic order"); to go against swadharma is a grave sin. But as duties vary by caste, so do punishments and their relative severity. Killing was traditionally a much more serious crime for a brahman to commit than for a shudra. However, the killing of a shudra or outcaste by a member of a higher caste was often considered only a minor offense, less grievous than killing a cow—which, after all, could provide milk, plowing, and fertilizer for an entire family. And crimes committed by the lower castes against the higher were punished more severely.

✳ ARYAN NATION

Scholars don't agree on much about the historical time frame of developing Hinduism, largely because Indians have traditionally regarded the practice of keeping precise dates for historical events as relatively unimportant. Furthermore, Western scholars propose dates for many key events that are vastly different from those of Hindu scholars, who tend to date things much further back in time. Recent archaeological discoveries by Marija Gimbutas* and others in the Middle East and Europe, however, suggest that the Hindu scholars may be closer to the truth. Agriculture in South Asia was previously agreed to have begun by 5000 BC, and the Indus Valley to have been cultivated by 3000 BC, although recent dating techniques are now pushing those figures back closer to 8000–6000 BC. The two centers of Indus civilization that have been uncovered so far, at Harappa and Mohenjo-daro, previously believed to have crystallized by 2700 BC—probably by the Dravidian people, an ancient Australoid race—may well have been in place thousands of years earlier. Whoever inhabited the land, they appear to have worshiped both a male deity similar to the later Hindu god Shiva, associated with the lingam, or phallic stone, and a goddess, Shakti, somewhat akin to Mother Nature, associated with the yoni, or ring-shaped stone.

Somewhere between 4000 and 1200 BC, depending on whose figures we follow, the Indus was invaded in successive waves by **Aryans** ("noble ones"), a group of nomadic warrior clans who probably came from Iran or Baluchistan (now part of modern Pakistan) in southern Russia and who may have originated in the grassy steppes north of the Black Sea between the Carpathian and Caucasus mountains. The Aryans, purportedly bigger and fairer than the aboriginal inhabitants of the Indus, invaded with horses and chariots and overran the indigenous cultures (Gimbutas labels the invaders Kurgans* and places their incursions into Europe between 4300 and 2800, but nobody has done the kind of detailed archaeological work in India that has been done in Europe and the Middle East.)

Although the evidence is not decisive, certain elements of the native cultures were absorbed by the Aryans and became an integral part of the religion that has come to be known as Hinduism. Some of those elements almost certainly came from the Dravidians, who later fled the invading Aryans to Tamilnadu in the south. Since the indigenous people worshiped male and female counterparts, it seems likely that their beliefs derived from mystical insights regarding the nature of the universe based on complementary male and female principles (which in China would become known as yin-yang*). Some of the complexity within modern Hinduism stems from this early blending of the very different cultural and theological streams of the Aryans and the indigenous population.

Aryans did not hold cattle sacred as later Hindus did, but raised them for food, along with pigs and sheep, combining their nomadic pastoral economy with agricultural practices that they may have learned from the more stationary Neolithic cultures they conquered and absorbed. The Aryans brought with them their religion of Brahmanism and the *Rig Veda,* a system that stressed animal sacrifice and ritual purity through ablution with water. Using the caste system to maintain control, they assimilated the natives. But it is also likely that some aspects of the indigenous spiritual culture remained outside the pale of the Brahmanic or Vedic system, specifically the group of people known as **shramanas** ("strivers"). These were wandering ascetics who may have practiced the earliest forms of yoga, along with meditation and a nonviolent way of life, quite distinct from the ritualistic animal sacrifices that made up much of Brahmanic practice. (The term *shramanism* is sometimes applied to any nonbrahmanical sect or school, including Buddhism and Jainism, and is probably connected linguistically to the word *shaman*.)*

Eventually, a number of Dravidians migrated to the south with their Indus culture, to reinfluence the north at a later date. Scholars argue, for instance, that many of the great Indian epics incorporate non-Aryan deities belonging to the Indus culture with Sanskrit forms of their names substituted for the originals. Dravidians may have contributed animal deities such as the elephant-headed god of wisdom, **Ganesha,** and the superhuman monkey-king, **Hanuman,** along with the theory of transmigration of souls. (Modern representatives of Dravidian culture are the **Tamils** and **Telugus.**) In any event, the Aryan-dominated culture spread slowly from the Punjab in northwest India to the Gangetic Plain, an area reaching across central India to modern Benares.

Islamic incursions beginning in the 8th century AD in the north, along the Indus River in what is now Pakistan, diverted but did not overcome Hinduism. During the 10th to 12th centuries, Turkish Muslims invaded further, and in the 16th century, the **Moguls,** or **Mughals,** Mongolians who subdued most of northern India, created an empire that lasted until the beginning of the mid-19th century. By the end of that century, the British had taken over in Bengal. Nearly 200 million Muslims still live in India, but the Hindu religion and culture continue to dominate—except in the north, where Sikh separatists are battling for their own independent state.

The elephant-headed, pot-bellied Ganesha, son of Shiva and Parvati, is a familiar figure in Indian art and popular culture, usually depicted with four arms but only a single tusk. God of wisdom, lord of celestial armies, patron of businesspeople and scholars, he can remove all obstacles to material and spiritual success.

According to one of many legends, Ganesha's human head was burned to cinders when Parvati invited Shani, god of planets, to look at her son, forgetting in her pride the destructive power of Shani's gaze. Brahma counseled Parvati to replace Ganesha's head with the first head she came upon, which happened to belong to an elephant. Ganesha's popularity continues in modern India, as shown in this scene from the Ganapati Festival on Chowpatty Beach in Bombay. (Ganapati is another name for Ganesha.)
BERKSON/ART RESOURCE

✺ THE VEDIC WORLDVIEW

The period during which the sacrificial rituals of the brahmans, derived from the Vedas, dominated Indian religion is often referred to as **Brahmanism** or the **Vedic** era to differentiate it from the later development of

15

Hinduism with its philosophical schools such as Vedanta. However, we should keep in mind that brahmanic ritual and the Vedas are still very much in evidence in modern Hinduism. Although the sacrificial rituals of Brahmanism tended to become rigidified with age, they served (and, according to many practitioners, continue to serve) a valuable function, especially for householders who did not have as much time as the brahmans to devote to meditative practices.

More than anything else, the rituals of Brahmanism revolved around the **sacrifice.** The origin of the universe from the grand sacrifice of the gods in the Purusha sukta established sacrifice as essential to the smooth functioning of the Vedic world. It was a means not only of appeasing the gods but also of asking favors and ultimately ensuring the proper order (rita) of things. Furthermore, the sacrifice had to be performed with meticulous precision, determining the supreme importance of the brahman and ensuring his place at the top of the caste pole. At a certain point, the understanding arose that when a sacrifice was precisely carried out, the gods must automatically grant the wish asked of them. If the wish was not granted, the sacrifice must have been improperly performed.

Some evidence exists that human sacrifice (**purushamedha**) occasionally took place. The most important sacrifice, however, was the **ashvamedha,** the horse sacrifice, to be performed by kings—more precisely, clan leaders who ruled the many small kingdoms that made up India at the time. The horse sacrifice could last over a year and involved a prize stallion, a hundred other horses and young warriors, and considerable financial investment. At the end of the year, the stallion was slaughtered, the ceremonies culminating when the principal queen simulated copulation with the body of the sacrificed horse.

The ostensible purpose of these and countless other animal sacrifices was to store up merit for later use in heaven, a Vedic concept that was prevalent before belief in reincarnation entered the Hindu world during the 1st millennium BC. Merit could also be gained by repeating the names of a deity, by performing the ritual worship service known as **puja,** or through voluntary acts of asceticism or self-mortification (**tapas**).

16

SO OLD, IT'S NEW AGE

Seen through the rearview mirror of history, the Vedic approach to sacrifice presents a curious adumbration of the "positive affirmations"* made popular by Norman Vincent Peale* and taken up by many New Age proponents. Take, for example, the notion that if the wish for which one performed a sacrifice was not granted, the sacrifice must have been improperly carried out. This parallels the teachings of modern advocates of positive thinking who claim that the failure of positive affirmations or visualizations results from an imperfect mindset, from clinging to a belief that you are guilty of an unforgiven sin or are in some other way unworthy.

The Aryan religion was this-world oriented, and its heaven, the **World of the Fathers,** resembled the Norse Valhalla (a vast drinking hall where heroic warriors are served by beautiful Valkyries); their hell was called the **House of Clay.** But the tenth and last book of the *Rig Veda* begins a new phase of Indian religion, focused on a speculative search for first principles and on a sacrificial symbolism not found in earlier books. In that book, the search for a first cause leads to the creation of **Prajapati,** Lord of Progeny, father of the gods and everything else.

The earliest pantheons of Vedic Hinduism included several gods who declined in importance or virtually disappeared from later Hinduism. By far the most popular god of the Vedic period is **Indra,** a god of cosmic power (also associated with thunderstorms) who may have been based on a historical warrior-leader of the Aryans. **Agni** is the personification of fire, especially sacrificial fire. **Soma** is a plant, personified as a god, which was used in early religious rituals. (The plant was pressed and its juice mixed with milk, resulting in a hallucinogenic drink whose use was sanctioned only during brahmanic sacrifices; the psychoactive form of soma disappeared rather early from Vedic Hinduism, never to return.) In general, the Vedic gods represent heaven, light, and fire, opposed to the

The Vedic god of fire is shown with his two heads representing the fires of the hearth and the sacrifice. As the archetype of the household priest and sacrificer, a linchpin of Vedic Hinduism, Agni is addressed in the very first hymns of the Rig Veda. He is also linked to Soma in the concept of the fiery liquid, the prototype of the elixir of immortality, the original ambrosia of the gods. In another manifestation, he is the firebird who carries the sacred Soma down to humanity. However, the great historian of religion Mircea Eliade found a connection between Agni and deeper levels of Hindu spirituality: "By virtue of the rites and asceticisms that pursue the increase of 'inner heat,' Agni is . . . bound up, though sometimes indirectly, with the religious valorization of 'ascetic heat' (tapas) and some of the practices of Yoga."
GIRAUDON/ART RESOURCE

demons of darkness and chaos. This dualism was shared by Zarathustra, or Zoroaster, the prophet of the Iranians, who in all likelihood descended from the same nomadic peoples who invaded the Indus Valley. It is also consistent with the pattern of warlike gods of mountains, sky, storm, wind, and fire worshiped by pastoral invaders not only in India but also in southern Europe and the Middle East, supplanting the Goddess*, who had been universally worshiped in those cultures.

The Vedic gods followed and preserved rita, the cosmic order, just as they would later uphold the dharma. Other Vedic deities are **Vaya** (wind god), **Usha** (dawn goddess), **Surya** (sun god), and Vishnu, who appears as a minor god, an ally of Indra. Vishnu later developed into one of the three great gods of the Hindu Trinity. Earlier Aryan deities such as **Dyaus** (god of heaven) were already fading by the time of the *Rig Veda,* to be replaced by **Varuna** as chief god of the heavens and guardian of rita. Today, Varuna is only a minor god of oceans and rivers.

Of all the gods, **Trimurti,** or Trinity, evolved as the most important of the Hindu pantheon, often depicted as one figure with three heads facing in different directions:

Brahma, the creator, represents diversity in Unity; he is the primeval, uncreated cause of all worlds. His sign is the **lotus,** which is also the symbol of spiritual attainment through nonattachment. The lotus, a beautiful Indian water lily that floats above the muck of swamps, represents the ideal of living within the world without being corrupted by it. Brahma has virtually no following in India today and few temples.

Vishnu, the preserver, represents Divine Love. The most famous religious ceremonial procession in India is the annual procession of Vishnu as **Jagannatha** ("Lord of the World"), at **Puri,** a well-known pilgrimage site on the Bay of Bengal. There the faithful, either accidentally or purposefully as a **sacrificial act,** are crushed under the massive wheels of Vishnu's **ratha** ("procession carriage"), perhaps while trying to pull themselves into the carriage to ride along with the god. (From this phenomenon, the English word *juggernaut,* meaning an object or belief calling for blind devotion or ruthless sacrifice, is derived.) Vishnu's sign is the **discus.**

Shiva, the destroyer, devastates in order to re-create Unity. The **lingam** (phallus) symbolizes his male power; the **yoni** (womb), the symbol of the goddess Shakti, represents his female creative power. Since both aspects reside in the same deity, Shiva often appears in paintings and statues as half-male and half-female (**ardhanarishvara**). Shiva is not mentioned in the Vedas, where his place is taken by **Rudra,** but he appears as a personal divinity in the *Ramayana.*

Shakti is more than just a goddess in the Greek or Roman sense. As the personification of primal creative energy, the female principle through which the gods act, she is venerated across India in different

19

forms and under different names, including the counterpart to each of the three deities (often referred to as their shaktis). The shakti of Brahma is **Sarasvati;** Vishnu's is **Lakshmi,** the model wife; Shiva's is **Kali,** the Divine Mother. Kali is depicted as a many-armed figure wearing a garland of human skulls and carrying a severed head in one hand, a sword in another, and offering her gifts with yet another. She represents both destructive power and maternal tenderness. Of these deities, the most prevalent today are Vishnu, Shiva, and Shakti, especially in the image of Kali or some other form of the Divine Mother, such as Durga.

The Good Book I: The Veda

Most of Hindu scripture can be divided into two basic types, shruti and smriti.

Shruti ("that which is heard") consists of the Veda, which encompasses the four Samhitas ("collections") or Vedas—*Rig Veda, Yajur Veda, Sama Veda,* and *Atharva Veda*—plus the series of texts appended to each of the Vedas, called Brahmanas, Aranyakas, and Upanishads.

Smriti ("that which is remembered") is composed of traditional texts not as directly inspired as shruti, e.g., the Dharma Shastras (legal and ethical texts derived from the Dharma Kalpas), the Puranas, the *Mahabharata,* and *Ramayana.*

Somewhere between shruti and smriti are the sutras, which are derived from the Brahmanas but are composed of terse statements that are difficult to comprehend without an attached commentary. A prime example is the **Vedanta Sutra** of Badarayana, which is much less important than the commentaries on it by Shankara and Ramanuja, which defined the philosophical school known as Vedanta.

The four Vedas were handed down orally over thousands of years, and although the earliest hymns in the *Rig Veda* go back to at least before 1500 BC and possibly as far as 4000, the oldest written version in existence dates from only the 14th century AD. The Vedas were not popular texts but were reserved for the brahman caste and related largely to the various sacrificial rituals around which early Hindu practice revolved. The *Rig Veda,* for example, collects 1,028 hymns to various gods, to be chanted at sacrifices (mainly animal) where soma was drunk. It is composed of 10 sections or books called **mandalas** ("cycles"). Most of the hymns were addressed to Indra, Agni, and Soma and were transmitted orally by **pandits** ("scholars," from which we get the word *pundit)* who memorized long texts in Sanskrit. The meaning was less important than getting the sound exactly correct, based on the principle that certain combinations of sacred syllables, or **mantras,** could effect powerful changes in the sayer. So crucial was this fact that a series of supplementary texts called **Vedangas** was created to assist brahmans in the study and execution of the Vedas, including the precise pronunciation of the sacred syllables, the details of various rituals, grammar, etymology, and other matters.

The *Yajur Veda* contains mantras for use in sacrifices, some with explanations of their meaning and instructions for proper use in ceremonies. The *Sama Veda* is largely a revision of hymns and verse from the *Rig Veda* arranged for singing rather than merely chanting; it is generally of interest only to scholars. The *Atharva Veda* is a collection of spells, charms, curses, and incantations not related to the sacrifice, for purposes such as casting out demons of disease, creating love potions, or seeking success, sometimes using sympathetic magic. Having more of a literary than a religious significance, it was the latest Samhita to be redacted, but its contents are thought to be very ancient.

Brahmanas are prose addenda to the Vedas. As rituals became more complex, the Brahmanas were needed to explain mysteries and symbolism, often in the form of fanciful allegories. The word *brahman* once referred to the supernatural power inherent in incantations and by extension came to mean the impersonal Source of the universe. Later, the name Brahma was applied to one of the three chief gods (a role taken over from Prajapati), and *brahman(a)* indicated a priest (sometimes spelled *brahmin)* in charge of the incantations. The Brahmanas were composed beginning c. 900 BC. The most important one is the **Shatapatha Brahmana,** attributed to **Yajnavalkya.**

Aranyakas, supplements to Brahmanas, are mystical reflections and descriptions of significant rites detailed in the Vedas, which often treat sacrificial details as symbolic of esoteric truths. The term means "belonging to the woods," as Aranyakas were composed for the use of forest-dwelling ascetics and were taught only after proper instruction and authorization, perhaps signaling the beginning of secret knowledge.

The **Upanishads** take up where the Aranyakas leave off, forming the most mystical level of teaching in the Veda. There are 108 canonical Upanishads, of which 13 are of primary import as authentic additions to the Vedas and Brahmanas. Generally dated from c. 700–300 BC, they may actually have been composed during a much wider span of time, c. 1200 BC–AD 200, in approximately this order: **Brihadaranyaka, Chandogya, Isha, Kena, Aitareya, Taitiriya, Kaushitaki, Katha, Mundaka, Svetashvatara, Prashna, Maitri,** and **Mandukya.** Their common theme, according to one American commentator, is the "inner realization of the identity of Atman and Brahman."

Clearly, the Upanishads sought to move beyond the ritualistic, sacrificial religion of the early Vedic period to an emphasis on the kind of realization that could be gained only through intensive self-examination and meditation. These lines from the *Mundaka Upanishad* make the point:

Ignorant fools, regarding ritual offerings and humanitarian works as the highest, do not know any higher good. After enjoying their rewards in heaven acquired by good works, they enter into this world again. . . . But those wise men of tranquil minds, . . . contemplating that God who is the source of the universe, depart, freed from impurities, to the place where that immortal Self dwells whose nature is imperishable (1.2.10).

Like the Hebrew Bible (the Old Testament" in Christianity), the Vedas often aim to appease a righteous but irritable Deity with sacrifices and hymns of praise. The Upanishads and *Bhagavad-Gita,* in contrast, are closer in spirit to the New Testament*; in both cases a more mystical theology seeks to expand and supplant old ways of thinking and believing. And like the New Testament, the later Hindu writings also contain mundane expositions on personal ethics and conduct in light of the newer teachings, often in the form of short texts called sutras.

As a whole, the **sutras** form a kind of bridge between shruti and smriti. The word *sutra* means "thread," and the sutras generally consist of a series of short, aphoristic phrases or sentences strung together like beads on a string. Among other things, the sutras set down for the first time ordinances on the four stations of life. For instance, although traditional Hindu law permitted a man to marry as many as four wives, and in the *Mahabharata,* the central female figure, **Draupati,** is married to five brothers, monogamy is now the norm. The **Kalpa Sutras** are brief texts on ritual, ethics, and law, composed largely from c. 500 to 200 BC. The **Dharma Sutras** were later expanded in verse as **Dharma Shastras,** which were used in courts of law. The *Vedanta Sutra* (or *Brahma Sutra),* by Badarayana, sought to recapitulate and organize the essence of Upanishadic philosophy (based largely on the *Chandogya Upanishad)* in some 550 aphorisms.

The first and most important smriti is the **Manu Smriti** or **Manava Dharma Shastra** (also called *Laws of Manu* or *Manu Samhita*), composed between 200 BC and AD 100. Said to be ancient, it contains laws as promulgated by the mythical Manu (the progenitor of the human race) regarding caste, ashramas, civil and criminal law, sacrifice, and other subjects. Completely authoritative, it was used by the British after they took control of India to settle matters of law in the Indian courts. Along with the *Yajnavalkya Smriti* (1st to 2nd century AD), it details proper courses of conduct for Hindu men and women in any given situation. Other shastras, or law texts, include **Kautilya**'s prominent *Arthashastra* ("Treatise on Material Gain") about the proper principles of statecraft.

Of greatest importance in the daily lives of Hindus both past and present, however, are the **Puranas** ("ancient narratives"). These invaluable texts are collections of legends, myths, and moral precepts bearing on everyday life for the common Indian. They may be less sacred than the Vedas, but no less essential. Finalized between the 4th and 12th centuries AD, there are 18 principal or **Mahapuranas** of oft-redacted ancient lore and 18 secondary or **Upapuranas,** divided into those concerning worship of Brahma, Shiva, and Vishnu (**Brahmana-Puranas, Shaiva-Puranas, Vaishnava-Puranas**). The most famous and traditional are the *Vishnu* and *Bhagavata Purana.*

✵ IT'S MY KARMA, AND I'LL CRY IF I WANT TO

During the Upanishadic era, from about 500 BC to AD 500, Indian religion underwent a synthesis that brought about what is generally called *Hin-*

24

duism to distinguish it from the earlier Vedic or Brahmanic era. Most of the concepts developed then have carried over to the present day and constitute the basic web of Hindu life and belief, including the six darshanas, the four ashramas, and traditional law or dharma. But when Westerners think of Hinduism, they generally think of terms like *asceticism* and *yoga, karma* and *reincarnation.* The ascetical practices for which India is renowned, consisting of everything from existing for long periods without food to living naked in the forest, may have had their origins in shamanistic* ordeals performed to gain magical abilities. Near the beginning of the later Vedic period (c. 1000 BC), the belief developed that asceticism accumulated tapas ("heat"), which eventually developed into supernormal powers, called **siddhis.** Other reasons for practicing asceticism probably included guilt and a desire for security in the afterworld, but also the development of willpower and control of mental and physical sensations.

Some ascetics lived as hermits in huts or caves in the forest, some traveled as mendicants. Still others may have sought relief from society or tried to discover the deepest meaning of existence and the cosmos. This entailed finding the Great Unborn Self, or Atman, that dwells within each heart but has to be realized through meditation. The wise man trained until his soul realized "full identity with Brahman" and then would not have to be reborn.

According to some scholars, belief in **reincarnation** (or **transmigration of souls,** as it was also called until this century) may have evolved from general pessimism caused by the breakup of secure tribal society and, with it, the old belief in the World of the Fathers. Others assume that the notion of rebirth originated with the aboriginal inhabitants of India, perhaps the Dravidians, who passed it on to the Vedic Aryans. It then became intermingled with Hindu beliefs, emerging as a given in the Upanishads.

The first mention of reincarnation comes in the *Brihadaranyaka* and *Chandogya Upanishads* with the idea that as one uses up, after death, the merit earned from good deeds and bad deeds, one eventually must return to earth. According to the texts, those who understand this "mystery," by which souls descend from the gods through sacrifice and return to the heavens when the body dies, end up in the **World of Brahman** after death. "For them there is no return," say the Upanishads, voicing a perennial aim of Indian spirituality. For other believers, it was a matter of spending time in the World of the Fathers until they used up their merit, then going back to earth for another round. Those who pleased the gods were reborn in a higher caste. Those who didn't were reborn as outcastes or animals. But to understand fully how reincarnation fits into the Indian worldview, we have to keep in mind that souls can be reborn into any one of several different levels of reality other than the human, including the animal world, the world of spirits and demons, even the god realms. Life in the god realms may be delightful, but escape from samsara can result only from a human birth.

Karma ("deed, action"), refers to specific mental or physical acts but is also defined as the law of cause and effect whereby deeds done in this lifetime are like seeds planted. They inevitably ripen and bear fruit (for better or worse, depending on the nature of the deed) in future lives. The karma each individual is born with is created by his or her **samskaras,** the tendencies inherited from the accumulated karma of past lives. In a sense, the law of karma necessitates reincarnation, because as you accumulate karma throughout life, you then need further lives to pay off those karmic debts. This cycle of birth, karmic activity, death, and rebirth, is called **samsara.** The good news of this theory is that the soul cannot be destroyed; the bad news is that it may require countless rebirths to achieve liberation.

The doctrine of reincarnation probably began as a secret teaching of the elite that later spread to the masses, and may have developed from ideas that crystallized in similar ways in different sages. It appears in the *Brihadaranyaka Upanishad* around 650 BC, for instance, but it also appears in Greece with Pythagoras* around 550 BC, although no evidence exists of a direct link between the two cultures. In the 4th century BC, Plato also mentions it, notably in the "Myth of Er," about a soldier who was taken for dead in battle and apparently had what would today be termed a near-death experience* during which he was instructed to return and tell people what the afterlife is like. Although the theory of reincarnation is anathema to Western religions like Christianity and Islam, with their notions of a single life followed by an eternity in heaven or hell, a 1982 Gallup poll showed that nearly one-fourth of all Americans believe in reincarnation.

Karma may have evolved from Vedic notions of rita and the sacrifice, in which specific actions yield specific results. Cause-and-effect principles

26

already active in Indian thought developed to a finer point during the introspective, mystical revolution of the Upanishads. And what began as an inflexible law gradually moderated after the Upanishadic period in both Hindu and Buddhist traditions to the point where karma could be set aside—by any form of the Hindu God or by the heavenly Buddhas and bodhisattvas* of Mahayana Buddhism. The *Bhagavad-Gita,* for instance, says that an evil man who devotes himself to Krishna—especially at the hour of death—can go to his eternal rest. (This reflects the beliefs of Pure Land* Buddhism and is even echoed in the last line of the Christian prayer known as the Hail Mary*.)

If the theory of karma predates the Upanishads, it received its clearest statement there. "As is [one's] desire, such is his resolve; as is his resolve, such is the action he performs; what action [karma] he performs, that he procures for himself. . . . He who is without desire, who is freed from desire, whose desire is satisfied, whose desire is the Soul—his breaths do not depart. Being very Brahman he goes to Brahman" *(Brihadaranyaka Upanishad).* And "According unto his deeds [karma] the embodied one successively assumes forms in various conditions" *(Svetashvatara Upanishad).* Failure to recognize the true nature of the Self and its identity with Brahman leads to eternal rebirths (samsara), whereas realization of this truth leads to liberation (moksha).

Karma was often visualized as adhering to the **subtle body** (a kind of invisible sheath surrounding the Atman), so that it would accompany the Self after the physical body was shed in death. The Upanishads offered "secret knowledge" that would allow the follower to shed his or her karma completely, like an old skin. In the Hindu view, although good karma is better than bad karma, the best karma is no karma at all. Good works (pilgrimages, prayer, worship, almsgiving) allowed one to store up **punya** ("merit"), a kind of celestial bank account ensuring a long stay in heaven and a favorable rebirth. Less desirable than complete freedom from samsara, it was better than slipping down the transmigrational ladder. This notion has counterparts in the Christian concept of partial and plenary indulgences*. But the ideal, stated in the *Bhagavad-Gita,* is to act with no attachment to the fruits of one's actions, good or bad, and so not to accumulate any karma at all and to obviate the need for rebirth.

Although by the end of the 1st millennium BC, the vast majority of Indians subscribed to the concepts of karma and reincarnation, a few schools of skeptics refused to do so. One group of Indian materialists, sharing certain beliefs with the Greek Epicureans*, was led by **Ajita Kesakambalin** (whose last name means "hair blanket"). Ajita took an approach echoed by certain modern-day beer commercials, that "you only go around once in life." Another such school derived from **Charvaka**, an Indian philosopher who lived around 600 BC and believed in seeking happiness and fulfillment in the here and now. This school is sometimes referred to as **Lokayata** and by the 14th century had developed many followers who felt that wealth and pleasure are the main goals in life and who had no belief in gods or an eternal soul. Charvakas are still common in India. Hindus historically have looked askance at such belief systems; their contemptuous term for any person or school of thought that does not believe in the Vedic teachings, gods, or rituals, including Buddhism and Jainism, is **nastika** ("atheistic").

❊ TOUCHING ALL FOUR BASICS

One of the most appealing aspects of Hinduism is the way it integrates spiritual and metaphysical principles with the natural cycles of human life. In fact, the Indian system divides life into four distinct stages through which each twice-born Hindu male ideally passes.

Brahmacharya (student). After initiation, or upanayana (which takes place at age 8 for a brahman boy, 11 for a kshatriya, 12 for a vaishya), each twice-born is expected to spend a minimum of 12 years living in the home of his guru. His life during this time is austere and celibate, given to mastering yoga and other spiritual disciplines and reading and studying the Veda. In modern India, the boy usually stays at home but takes instruction in the dharma from the family's pandit, or Vedic scholar.

Grihasthya (householder). After completing brahmacharya, the next phase of life includes marriage, raising a family, and earning a living. It encompasses the enjoyment of earthly pleasures and recognition for success, along with the duty of carrying out one's responsibilities to the community.

Vanaprasthya (hermit). Having fulfilled his duties and, especially, having ensured the continuation of the family name (traditionally, after the birth of his first grandchild), the Hindu is free to enter the penultimate phase. Nearing his twilight years, he retires to the forest to meditate and seek spiritual wisdom. Living in a small hermitage with or without his wife (who is welcome to join him or not), he devotes his time to gaining a fuller understanding of his spiritual nature. He still performs the basic Hindu rituals.

Sannyasin (wandering mendicant). Leaving even the relative security of the hermitage and abandoning all possessions save his staff and begging bowl, he now seeks only the final goal of Hindu life: **mukti,** or liberation from the endless round of rebirths. Women whose children are fully grown may also enter this phase of life, and many women have become realized masters.

Although these are considered ideals, not necessarily followed by all or even most twice-borns, the fact that three of the four stages involve spiritual study and search underlines the role of religion in Indian life. The four stages are designed to help Hindus realize the four ideal aims in life, or chaturvarga: dharma (spiritual duty), artha (material gain), kama (physical and sense pleasures), and moksha (liberation). The first stage of life prepares one to achieve the first goal, the second stage in life is devoted to the second and third goals, and the last two stages seek to gain the fourth goal. Finally, loosely complementing the four stages and four aims of life are the four paths, or margas. Since the four margas are also known as the four yogas, this may be a good place to outline the complicated and generally misunderstood notion of yoga in the Hindu world.

✸ THE FLAVORS OF YOGA

When the five senses and the mind are still, and reason itself rests in silence, then begins the Path supreme. This calm steadiness of the senses is called Yoga. Then one should become watchful, because Yoga comes and goes.

—*KATHA UPANISHAD, 6.11–12*

The word *yoga* derives from the same root *[yuj]* as does the English word yoke, and yoke carries a double connotation: to unite (yoke together), and to place under disciplined training (to bring under the yoke, or "take my yoke upon you"). Both connotations are present in the Sanskrit word. Defined generally, then, *yoga* is a method of training designed to lead to integration or union.

—*HUSTON SMITH, THE WORLD'S RELIGIONS*

Although the word *yoga* appears for the first time in the *Katha Upanishad,* some archaeological evidence seems to indicate that yogic practices existed in the Indus Valley before the arrival of the Aryans and their Vedic culture in the 2nd millennium BC. The soapstone seal of **Pasupati,** or Lord of Animals, shows what appears to be a forerunner of the god Shiva seated in a classic hatha yoga posture. Sometime between 200 BC and AD 400, the basic principles of yoga were codified in a series of aphorisms by **Patanjali** in his *Yoga Sutra,* still the most authoritative text on yoga we have.

However, the yoga with which Westerners are most familiar is **hatha yoga,** a series of largely physical exercises and stretching postures originally developed as just one step along the way to liberation. According to this system, the spinal column supports 72,000 **nadis** ("tubes, vessels") or energy channels through which **prana,** the life energy force, flows to the rest of the body. The most important nadi is the **sushumna,** which reaches from the base of the spine to the brain; it is centered between the **pingala nadi** and the **ida nadi,** which curve around it. The pingala (symbolized by the masculine sun), the conductor of intellectual energy, begins on the right side of the spine and flows upward; the ida (symbolized by the feminine moon) conducts physical-emotional energy and flows downward, beginning on the left side of the spine.

From the Sanskrit *ha* ("sun") and *tha* ("moon"), hatha yoga involves the balancing or union of the pingala and the ida so that they merge back into the sushumna, internalizing and releasing the main flow of consciousness-energy. As popularly taught these days, hatha yoga has generally become detached from its spiritual culmination. For Patanjali, hatha yoga makes up only part of raja yoga, a way of purifying the body and preparing it for the rigors of intensive meditation. By combining pranayama (control of the prana or breath) and a series of **asanas** (postures) and **kriyas** (purifications), hatha yoga seeks to activate the chakras, or centers of psychic energy in the body, beginning the rise of the kundalini power from where it resides at the base of the spine. The actual postures, breathing, and cleansing techniques are described in many yoga texts such as the 15th-century *Hatha Yoga Pradipika* and the later *Geranda Samhita.* This knowledge was kept secret, even in India, passed among esoteric communities until a little

The **caduceus** is usually identified as the wand or staff of Hermes, the Greek messenger of the gods (represented in Roman myth as Mercury). But it has much earlier resonances with Indian theology, which sometimes depicts the ida and pingala rising in a crisscrossing pattern from left to right around the sushumna; this tripartite configuration shows up in the famous trident of Shiva, the god most closely associated with yoga and the control of the nadis. But Shiva in his earliest depictions is also associated with the erect phallus and is venerated in the form of the lingam, or phallic stone.

The name Hermes probably means "he of the stone heap"; his earliest cult among the pre-Homeric Greeks centered around magical practices connected with stone heaps erected on mountaintops, and the spirit residing in the stone heap was originally represented by a phallic stone. The staff of Hermes—magician, trickster, patron of travel and trade—may also reflect the staff of the wandering ascetic of early yogic tradition. The connection is deepened by the way in which the caduceus appears to replicate the image of the nadis, with twin serpents twining around the central staff, topped by two wings. This ancient symbol has been adopted by the healing profession, specifically as the insignia of the U.S. Army Medical Corps. In fact, two configurations of the caduceus exist, the second consisting of only one serpent wound around the rod. This form is usually associated with the Greek god of healing, Asclepius* (Roman Aesculapius), whose priests were associated with snakes. The patient visited the temple of Asclepius and usually spent the night sleeping there in a special room, hoping either for a cure or for a dream that would offer a clue to one. Some modern scholars believe that the connection goes back further, to the Neolithic Goddess* culture, an association that probably applied to both healing and prophecy. Curiously, the Indian symbol of medicine is the mythical bird, Garuda, half-human and half-eagle. Vishnu's steed, Garuda is the enemy of serpents and is often depicted with poisonous snakes hanging from his beak—a powerful symbol of the transmutation of disease.

COURTESY OF THE FREE MUSEUM OF PHILADELPHIA

31

over a century ago. The underpinnings of yoga traveled to China with the wandering ascetics and Buddhists who had absorbed its principles, and there it left its mark on the Taoists. Some yoga scholars speculate that it may have reached as far as Central and South America: the Mayan jaguar deity is often depicted in the locust posture (**salabhasana**) with his legs arched over his back, feet resting on his head—not a typical pose for the jaguar.

The yoga texts describe groups of 8, 24, 80, 84, 100, or more asanas, of which the best-known and most widely used is the lotus posture (**padmasana**). They are sometimes said to have derived from positions that the bodies of ancient practitioners naturally assumed during states of meditative ecstasy. The kriyas, rarely taught in hatha yoga classes in America, include purifying and energizing practices such as swallowing (and later retracting) a wet cloth to a length of 24 feet to cleanse the intestinal tract, and running a 10-inch thread up each nostril and out the mouth.

The goal of all this preparation and training is the achievement of various states of meditative absorption, or samadhi. **Meditation** is one of the key practices of Indian religion, although it is not performed by all or even most Hindus. The variety of meditation techniques is vast and highly detailed, but the general direction is the same: stilling the mind until the meditator realizes some glimpse of the Absolute, some sense of identification with It, and the spontaneous insights, bliss, perhaps even psychic abilities, and liberation that follow. The great yogis and rishis are the ones who perfected meditation to heights of ecstasy and union with the Absolute that the ordinary Hindu might never have the time or will to achieve. Theoretically, the rigors and rewards of meditation are available even to the lowliest outcaste, but because of the amount of dedication normally required to achieve samadhi and moksha, most yogis either live as wandering mendicants or are supported by their followers.

According to the Sankhya point of view, all reality is divided into two aspects: purusha and prakriti. **Purusha** is the transcendent Godhead, uncaused and unchanging pure consciousness. **Prakriti** is the manifestation of that consciousness, sometimes referred to as the phenomenal world, composed of varying combinations of the three gunas. This is the Hindu version of dualism, distinct from Western religion,

THE JOY OF MEDITATION

The numerous obstacles and distractions on the path of meditation have often been chronicled by teachers and yogis, who also describe the unexpected energies that intense meditation can unleash within the human body and mind. The following account comes from the spiritual autobiography of one of modern India's most renowned teachers. One day in the lengthy course of his meditations, he found himself "possessed by sexual desire." Despite his admitted lack of interest in sensual pleasure, the visions, particularly of "a beautiful naked girl" encased in a divine red light, came and refused to go away. These continued through several days of meditation, with accelerating force, until one day the woman appeared "beautifully adorned and extraordinarily attractive."

My mind became very restless. My sexual organ became agitated with great force. I opened my eyes. I still saw her outside. I closed my eyes and saw her inside. Tearing my loincloth, my generative organ dug forcibly into my navel, where it remained for some time. Who was raping me like this? I was completely conscious, and my meditation stopped. For meditation, I used to wear a muslin loincloth, leaving the rest of my body completely naked. When I saw that the loincloth was torn, I got very angry, so angry that my mind became clouded. It was 5:00 in the morning. I got up, put on a new loincloth, and went outside.

—SWAMI MUKTANANDA, *PLAY OF CONSCIOUSNESS*

which views spirit as good and matter as evil. Sankhya gives rise to the notion of the witnessing consciousness, the awareness that our thoughts and feelings are not who we are. It is as if we have two selves, one which *has* the thoughts and feelings and another which is *aware* that we are having them. The self that is capable of witnessing thoughts and feelings is our true Self and is connected to the Ground of all being, Brahman.

Purusha is the Godhead dwelling within the body, our True Nature, which we can't see because of the physical, mental, and emotional layers that conceal it from our awareness. This real Self, or Atman, remains unknown to us, causing us to mistake the ego—made up of the mind and senses—for who we actually are. And this is what causes all misery. By controlling the activities of the body and the thought patterns of the mind through various yogas, we can learn to recognize the Self and finally achieve complete union with it. That union is the aim of yoga.

While rivalry often exists among followers of the four major yogas, the paths are generally accepted as being equally valid—an attitude unique to Hinduism. One American swami likened them to the four lanes of a superhighway: practitioners may switch from one lane to another until they realize that all four lanes are part of the same highway and lead to the same destination.

Jnana yoga is the path of knowledge, leading to God through intellectual analysis and discrimination—especially the ability to discern the difference between the limited self of apparent thoughts and feelings and the infinite Self that resides in the background and witnesses the actions of the limited self. Jnana draws heavily on the mystical knowledge contained in the Upanishads. The image used in the sacred texts to describe jnana is an infinite sea of Being that underlies the waves of our finite self. Some feel that jnana is the most arduous route to realization, and although it is practiced by relatively few in India, it is of great interest to Western students of Hinduism.

Karma yoga is the path of selfless work or action. Selfless detachment in the act of doing is the karma yogi's ideal. This may apply to traditional acts such as ritual Vedic sacrifices or to the way the yogi performs the simplest daily actions. Karma and jnana are probably the oldest paths, somewhat similar to the medieval Christian division between the *via activa* and *via contemplativa*, although, like them, they overlap at times. The next two yogas may also overlap with karma and jnana, depending on the orientation of the practitioner.

Bhakti yoga is the yoga of love and devotion, crystallized in the *Bhagavad-Gita* (which focuses on devotion to Krishna) as an addition to karma and jnana yogas. Requiring less mental discipline but more devotional fervor, bhakti probably has more adherents than the other three yogas. A follower is called a **bhakta,** and one of the basic practices is **japam** or **japa** ("whisper, murmur"), the constant repetition of one of God's names. The name chosen depends on one's **ishta** or **ishtadeva** ("beloved or chosen deity"), a concrete image of the Divine, which may be one of many images of God, an avatar, or saint. For japa, bhaktas use a **mala** or **japamala,** a string of 108 prayer beads made of rudraksha or tulasi berries. Focusing on japa or mantra as the main tool of meditation is sometimes called japa yoga. Another popular bhakti practice is the **kirtan:** communal singing, chanting, or dancing to honor God. The most visible sect of bhakti yoga in the West is the **International Society of Krishna Consciousness,** better known as the **Hare Krishnas** because of their constant chanting of Lord Krishna's name. Transcendental Meditation (TM), popularized by Maharishi Mahesh Yogi, is actually a form of japa yoga, since it relies so heavily on the use of mantras.

Raja yoga is the "royal" yoga, which has been described as "the way to God through psychophysical experiments." This is the so-called eight-limbed or **ashtanga yoga** presented by Patanjali in the *Yoga Sutra* (the term *raja yoga* was created long after Patanjali). The thesis of raja yoga is that the human self is composed of body, conscious mind, the subconscious, and Being Itself and that by mastering certain techniques for mind and body control, the yogi can experience the bliss of Being Itself that already exists in each of us. There are eight sets of techniques in all, the first five governing external activities so as to pave the way for the last three, which concern the inner functions of the mind.

1. **yama** ("control"). The don'ts: moral restraints against harming, lying, stealing, sexual incontinence, and greed.
2. **niyama.** The dos: disciplines involving inner and outer purity, calmness or contentment, asceticism, study of sacred writings, and submission to God.
3. **asanas** ("easy"). Body positions for hatha yoga, the purpose of which is not so much physical development as transcendence of

bodily awareness. Of the 84 asanas recorded in most yoga texts, only a few are commonly used.

4. **pranayama** ("breath control"). Control of vital energy flow through regulation of the breath.

5. **pratyahara** ("sense control"). Withdrawal of the senses from their accustomed focus on external sense objects so that they may center on the inner plane.

6. **dharana** ("concentration"). Focusing the mind on one thing as a prelude to entering deeper states of meditation. It is achieved through practices such as **tratakum** ("steady gaze"), fixing the eyes on the tip of the nose, a spot between the eyebrows, or a candle flame, or concentrating the mind on the navel, the heart, or other areas of the body.

7. **dhyana** ("meditation"). Absorption of the mind in the object of concentration, leading to the final stage.

8. **samadhi** ("establish"). Total absorption in the object of concentration; if that object is God, then the state amounts to union with God. Some levels of samadhi are more nearly total than others: the deepest is **nirvikalpa** ("no thought") **samadhi,** the loss of awareness of any duality or subject-object relationship; below that is **savikalpa** ("one thought") **samadhi,** which retains an aspect of duality—equivalent in Christian mystical terms to seeing God rather than merging with God.

✳ WHAT ABOUT THOSE OTHER YOGAS?

In addition to the four main yogas, several others, such as **kriya, siddha,** and **tantra** or **kundalini yoga,** advance different techniques for achieving specific goals. The aim of kundalini yoga, for instance, is to awaken the psychospiritual energy (kundalini) that lies dormant at the base of the spinal column. This is accomplished by intense concentration on the kundalini, along with purification exercises, certain asanas and mudras (specific hand gestures), and practices common to other forms of yoga. Siddha and Kriya Yoga are specialized systems disseminated by Swami Muktananda and Paramahansa Yogananda, respectively, and are often capitalized. Kriya Yoga emphasizes the process of purifying the spine to prepare the way for the flow of kundalini energy and was also taught by Swami Kriyananda. The early-20th-century sage Sri Aurobindo named his version **Integral Yoga** because he claimed it incorporated all previous forms of yoga in preparation for an evolutionary advance in the spiritual nature of humanity. In 1966, Swami Satchidananda came to the U.S. and founded a second school of Integral Yoga based on the teachings of his guru, Swami Sivananda Saraswati of Rishikesh. **Yogi Amrit Desai** named his practice **Kripalu Yoga** after his guru, **Swami Kripalvanandiji.** Desai came to America in 1960 and now runs the Kripalu Center for Yoga and Health in Lenox, Massachusetts, where he stresses awareness of one's inner self while one is in the postures. An offshoot created by an American disciple of Yogi Desai, which uses the postures as a kind of therapeutic device, is called **Phoenix Rising Yoga Therapy. Bikram's Yoga,** a demanding series of postures created by **Bikram Choudhury,** is especially popular in Hollywood, despite the fact that it is more challenging than most of the hatha yoga taught in informal courses across America as a combination of aerobics, stretching, and relaxation therapy.

In a wider sense, yoga can refer to any spiritual system or path that aims to "yoke" the senses in the search for God, and any serious seeker can be called a yogi. When writers speak of Tibetan or Chinese yogis, they are referring to dedicated practitioners of Buddhism or Taoism. Those traditions have indigenous terms to describe their mystics, such as lamas* or tao-shih*, but the term yogi is a useful catchall which also hints at the implicit connection between ancient forms of Indian mystical practice and these other systems.

The Good Book II: The Epics and the *Kama Sutra*

Itihasa ("history") is a term referring to legends, heroic sagas, and myths, of which the best known are the *Mahabharata* and the *Ramayana*. Alongside the Puranas, these two epics are probably more influential on the mass of Hindus than any other scriptures. The collective term **Itihasa-Purana** ("ancient history") includes the *Mahabharata* and *Ramayana* plus the 18 Mahapuranas and is sometimes referred to collectively as the **Fifth Veda,** since it provides guidance for the masses the way the four Vedas did for the brahmans. Besides myth and legend, Itihasa-Purana offers valuable and accurate information on geography, politics, medicine, astrology, customs, and mores.

The *Mahabharata* contains material from as long ago as 600 BC, updated as late as AD 500, with revisions and insertions by many hands. At about 100,000 stanzas, it is four times the size of the Bible, or eight times the *Odyssey* and *Iliad* combined. According to tradition, it began as *Jaya,* a poem about the victory of the **Pandavas** over the **Kauravas,** composed by **Vyasa** (**Krishna Dvaipayana**) and dictated to Ganesha. The rishis who compiled the Vedas and Puranas are also called Vyasa; some sources contend they are the same Vyasa, but that can be true only in a traditional sense. The name Vyasa means "collector" and was often assumed by rishis who, like the anonymous Christian artists and architects of the Middle Ages, felt that their personal identity was of no importance. Over the centuries the long narrative of the *Mahabharata* was interlarded with many a didactic and religious aside as brahmans, who recited the epic poem at lengthy Vedic sacrifices, sought to mix religious edification with drama. The best-known and most significant of these interpolations is the

Bhagavad-Gita ("Song of the Lord"), which forms one chapter of the *Mahabharata.*

The most important gods in the *Mahabharata* are Brahma and Indra, and like the lesser gods and humans involved, they are controlled by karma and **daiva,** or **vidhi** ("fate"). **Krishna,** friend of the Pandavas in their war against the Kauravas for the kingdom of the Kurus (around 1000 BC, near what is now New Delhi), appears as a godlike figure who nonetheless shows a very human willingness to use trickery and deceit to help his side win. As the eighth and most important incarnation of Vishnu, Krishna serves as charioteer for the warrior hero **Arjuna,** one of the Pandava leaders and a prototype of the spiritual seeker. The *Mahabharata* is filled with local nature spirits (**yakshas** and **yakshis**) and magical serpents (**nagas** and **naginis**).

Overall, the epic is a sort of multivolume family feud, full of warring dynasties, wise and holy kings, saintly seers and forest sages, romantic assignations, and supernatural interventions. (A critical edition of the *Mahabharata* published in Poona, India, in 1966 filled 22 volumes. A greatly condensed stage version was mounted in the U.S. in the 1980s by British director Peter Brook. The play took three nights to perform and was later presented as a six-hour "miniseries" on public television.)

As an avatar or incarnation of Vishnu, Krishna had a history of human births, and so he was not wholly God but, like Jesus Christ, both man and God. His elevation to major deity status progressed gradually. Early in the *Mahabharata,* he appears as a hero with superhuman powers, yet by the time of the *Bhagavad-Gita,* he is addressed as the "Divine One," as Universal Consciousness itself. This deification is escalated in the Puranas. But legend also emphasizes the human side of Krishna, who plays his flute and frolics with **gopis,** or milkmaids, by the dozen. As described in the 12th-century Sanskrit poem **"Gita Govinda"** by **Jayadeva,** for instance, Krishna disports with these beautiful gopis while his mistress, **Radha,** waits patiently and passionately for his return. Whichever aspect is emphasized, his status as the greatest hero of Indian myth and India's most popular deity seems assured.

One memorable scene in the *Mahabharata* that is a key plot point occurs when Pandu, the head of the Pandava clan, slays a stag and its doe in the act of copulation. The dying stag reveals himself as a rishi who had taken the form of a deer. He puts a curse on Pandu, not for killing a brahman (which he couldn't have known), nor for hunting deer (which was allowed), but for killing animals in the act of love, considered a sacred act for all beings. According to the curse, if Pandu ever embraces his wife to make love, he will die instantly (which, after much beating about the bush, finally does happen). According to some knowledgeable sources, taking on animal form was one way that the rishis, with their vows of celibacy, could experience the joys of physical love.

The *Ramayana,* said by orthodox Hindu tradition to describe events of 870,000 years ago and composed shortly thereafter (hence its nickname, the **Adikavya,** or "primeval poem"), is even more popular than the *Mahabharata* and only about one-fourth as long. Traditionally attributed to the sage **Valmiki,** it was originally sung by itinerant balladeers and may actually be older than the *Mahabharata.* **Rama** is the seventh avatar of Vishnu, although he appears that way only in the first and seventh books. In the core of the poem, books 2–6, Rama is merely "a mighty hero favored by the gods" and the heir apparent to the kingdom of Ayodhya. To win the hand of the lovely **Sita** in marriage, for instance, he has to bend the intractable bow of Rudra, reminiscent of a similar feat in the *Odyssey.*

The epitome of virtue, honor, courage, and loyalty, Rama invariably does the right thing. Forced into forest exile with wife Sita and brother **Lakshmana,** he accepts his condition with no complaint. When Sita is kidnapped by the 10-headed demon king **Ravana** and taken to Sri Lanka, she is ultimately rescued by Rama with help from an army of monkeys ("shape-shifters" with human intelligence) led by General Hanuman. This monkey-king, gifted with supernatural powers and a working knowledge of miraculous healing herbs, became a popular Indian god. Sita later undergoes ordeal by fire to prove that she has remained faithful to Rama while in captivity and emerges unsinged. Even so, she is forced to d more time in forest exile before she finally disappears into the earth, calling on the Mother Earth Goddess to acknowledge her faithfulness.

On one level, the *Ramayana* can be taken as an allegorical account of the Aryan migration into India, highlighting the initial conflicts between the agrarian natives and the nomadic invaders. Members of one of the largest subsects of Vaishnavism, **Shrisampradaya,** worship Sita and Rama and have their main center in Ayodhya, Rama's hometown. (The destruction of a Muslim temple there, believed to have been built on the site of Rama's birth, led to bloody conflict between Muslims and Hindus in 1992.) Some of the sect's more fervent male members, who come from the uneducated classes, like to think of themselves as Sita and often wear women's clothing, makeup, and jewelry. In some areas they run **Goshalas,** which amount to retirement homes for aging cows.

The *Bhagavad-Gita,* inset into the *Mahabharata,* is the single most important and influential religious text of India, the first to be translated into European tongues (by Charles Wilkins in 1785). It culminates the Upanishadic tradition, having been composed probably by the 3rd century BC or later (based on the fact that it supports Hindu tenets that had come under attack by Buddhists and Jains). Its setting within the much longer epic is the field of the impending Battle of Kurukshetra, which would result in the triumph of the Pandavas over the Kauravas. Arjuna, the great warrior son of Indra, is experiencing misgivings as he faces the opposing forces made up of his own relatives. He questions the rightness of killing to his friend Krishna, saying he would rather give up all worldly claims and become an ascetic than slay his cousins and teachers. Krishna offers his response in 18 chapters of verse. As one scholar has pointed out, the *Gita* would have taken over two hours to recite just as the battle was about to start, creating one of the more wonderfully pregnant pauses in the history of mortal combat.

In essence, the *Gita* is a long tract on the joys of selfless action. Its chief moral argument is that bodies can be killed, but not souls. Since warfare is Arjuna's dharma, or class duty, as a kshatriya, it's all in a day's work. The key teaching of the *Gita* is the "doctrine of motiveless action," Krishna's admonition to focus "on action alone . . . never on its fruits." The text also introduces several tenets of later Hindu thought: the doctrine of the three gunas, the triangle of forces that make up all objects and beings; the basics of Yoga and Sankhya; and the mystical impersonal Absolute, Brahman. All of these are developed in more depth here than in the Upanishads.

For better or worse, the *Gita* also defends the caste system. Krishna says, "It is better to perform one's own duty, however badly, than to do another's well" and "It is better to die engaged in one's own duty; the duty of other men is dangerous" (3.35, 18.47).

Finally, the **Kama Sutra,** or **Aphorisms of Love,** by **Vatsyayana** (c. AD 300) has achieved fame not for its spiritual teachings but for its graphic descriptions of sexual techniques. Yet the Indian penchant for precise analysis and categorization, when applied to physical love, yields less of a simple sex manual than a cross between the medieval *Art of Courtly Love,* a Masters and Johnson text, and the *Playboy* advice column. And so the *Kama Sutra* includes tips on how to dress and how to be a successful man about town in addition to its notorious catalog of erotic positions and oral sex tips. The author admits that his text is based on earlier *Kama Sutra*s, and is in fact a condensation of what must have been a genuinely exhaustive encyclopedia of sexuality.

✳ THE WISDOM OF VEDANTA

> The Dualists are always at loggerheads with each other; the Advaitists
> have no quarrel with anyone.
>
> —*MANDUKYA UPANISHAD*

The philosophy of Vedanta grew out of the Upanishads and the *Bhagavad-Gita* to form the basis of modern Hindu spirituality. The name itself, which can be taken to mean literally "the end of the Vedas" or "the end of knowledge," implies a closure of the older Vedic system of Hinduism as well as the culmination of mystical wisdom. Vedanta emphasizes the individual's personal experience of enlightenment more than did the earlier teachings of Vedic Hinduism. The Vedic system that the Buddhists and other heterodox ascetics largely rejected midway through the 1st millennium BC—the rote rituals, priest class, and caste system—was precisely what the teachers of Vedanta sought to break down.

Three major schools of Vedanta developed over the centuries, espousing three ways of uniting with the One. In **dualism (dvaita)**, one relates to God as servant to master; in **qualified nondualism (vishishtadvaita)**, one feels a part of God; in **nondualism** or **unqualified monism (advaita)**, one feels union with God when conscious of Atman.

The 9th-century philosopher **Shankaracharya** (or simply **Shankara**) proposed advaita or nondualism. His key mantra, taken from the Upanishads, is *Tat tvam asi* ("Thou art That" or "You yourself are It"). In other words, God and the Self are one: Brahman is Atman. Another way of saying this is to realize that our True Nature is identical with the Ground of the universe, the Absolute. This is experienced as the realization of a truth that has always been there, expressed in the Sanskrit phrase *Aham brahmasmi* ("I am Brahman"). But what exactly is Brahman? The *Chandogya Upanishad* defines Brahman as "One without a second." Since this means that there is nothing outside of or opposed to Brahman—nothing It can be compared to because It encompasses everything—we find it impossible to say what Brahman is. And so the best definition comes by way of negating: Shankara says that

43

Brahman is the Nondual, the Not-two. The concept of nonduality*, which appears in all other expressions of the Perennial Philosophy* derived from the mystical experience of union with the Absolute, is a way of seeing the world that demands compassion. If there is only One, then I am identical with all other beings: why would I want to injure or kill or be cruel to or steal from myself?

Although Shankara taught the identification of God and Self, he did distinguish between that Self and the body-mind complex commonly known as the ego (or lowercase self). He wrote in his *Atma Bodhi* that one must "understand the Self (Atman) to be distinct from the body, sense-organs, mind, intellect and its tendencies, and always a witness of their functions, as a king." In other words, just as a king is aware of everything that goes on in his domain, one can learn by meditation to focus on the pure Awareness that "witnesses" all phenomena, an idea that also functions in jnana yoga. "The Self is the witness, beyond all attributes, beyond action," says the *Vivekachudamani* ("The Crown-Jewel of Discrimination"), attributed to Shankara. This concept of the Witness is the keystone of what has come to be known as **Shankara Vedanta:** "You are pure Consciousness, the Witness of all experiences. Your real nature is joy. Cease this very moment to identify yourself with the ego."

"One without a second" means more than simply One; it is entirely all-encompassing, and so embraces the Many which are part and parcel of the One. Some see the Many as merely a manifestation of the One, which brings us to the concept of **maya.** This term, which literally means "appearance," is often translated as "illusion," but that is too simplistic. In Vedanta, *maya* refers to the phenomenal world as an expression of Brahman. In the sense that material concerns can veil our true spiritual nature, they can be seen as illusory. But since maya proceeds from Brahman, it should not be looked at as somehow evil in the Western understanding of matter as intrinsically tainted (which would be dualistic), but merely as a source of confusion. "Brahman projects the universe through the power of His Maya," reads the *Svetashvatara Upanishad*. "Then He becomes entangled in that universe of Maya. Know, then, that the world is Maya, and that the great God is the Lord of Maya." Shankara's famous example of maya's work-

NARADA, KRISHNA, AND MAYA

The power of God to manifest is an integral part of the God-head, and thereby eternal; however, the particular manifestation in this world is finite and temporal. In the sense that the many forms of God's manifestation in the material universe are ephemeral, their appearance is certainly illusory. Not least of those appearances is time. The following story, retold by an American-born teacher of Vedanta, attempts to put the illusory nature of time in perspective.

Once, the legendary sage Narada was out walking with Krishna, who is representative, in literature, of God. In the course of their conversation, Narada asked God to explain to him the mystery of His Maya. And the Lord said, "All right—but before I do, since my throat is a little dry, please fetch me a drink of water."

So, Narada ran off to find some water for the Lord. Soon he came to a pleasant little hut, where he stopped to get directions to the nearest water, but when the door to the hut was opened, there stood the most beautiful young maiden, with whom Narada was smitten. As she invited him inside, Narada forgot all about his mission to fetch some water to his Lord; and, as the days passed very pleasantly, Narada fell more and more in love with his beautiful hostess, and soon they were wed.

The blissful couple soon had children, and Narada toiled in the field to grow food for his growing family. He was extremely happy . . . and thought himself to be the most fortunate of men to have such a beautiful wife and such fine children. But, one day a great monsoon rain fell. The river-banks overflowed, and the little hut was filled with water. . . . First one child, then another was swept away in the raging torrent; and finally Narada felt his darling wife slip away from his grasp. Then he too was swept away in the flood, crying out in the darkness for his wife and children.

At last, nearly unconscious and completely exhausted, Narada found himself washed up on a wreckage-strewn shore. And as he lay there lamenting the loss of his family, suddenly he looked up to see the feet of Krishna at his head. Quickly he struggled to his feet, and Krishna, with an ironic smile, asked, "Where have you been, Narada? I sent you for water nearly ten minutes ago!"

—SWAMI ABHAYANANDA, *THE WISDOM OF VEDANTA*

ings states that appearance may lead one to mistake a piece of rope lying on the ground for a snake and respond in fear. The same kind of confusion can cause us to think that the body or the ego is the real Self, a mistake that causes much of our fear and suffering. It is only ignorance, **avidya,** that makes us fail to see that everything is Brahman.

Ramanuja, who died in AD 1137 (at the age of 120, according to tradition), was the leading voice of Vishishtadvaita Vedanta, or qualified nondualism. He saw God and man as distinct entities. For him, reality is one, but made up of three basic components: the material world, individual beings, and Brahman (specifically, Vishnu). Salvation consists of communion of the soul with God rather than a complete identification of the two, as Shankara held. Since this view provided a metaphysical basis for the devotional path of bhakti, which had achieved great popularity by then, Ramanuja became probably a more pervasive influence on Hindu thought even than Shankara. His most famous text is the *Shribhashya,* his commentary on the *Vedanta Sutra.*

The underlying principle of Ramanuja's philosophy is the difficulty of conceptualizing the Absolute (Brahman), an impersonal, unlimited Being without qualities. Instead, one seeks It in a personal, local divinity—an ishta or ishtadeva. (In Christianity, for instance, God is conceived in similarly absolute and impersonal terms, whereas Jesus Christ is the personal form who can be visualized and worshiped.) This personalized devotion is the basis for the practice of bhakti. Each divinity can have several different names representing different aspects, often of different sexes.

THE THOMAS AQUINAS OF INDIA

The major doctrines of Vedanta, culled from teachings in the Upanishads about the relationship of Atman to Brahman, were gathered as aphorisms sometime after the 4th century BC by **Badarayana** in his work known as the *Brahma Sutra* or *Vedanta Sutra*. Modern Vedanta is based on commentaries on this work, the most famous of which was written by Shankaracharya in the 9th century. Born in 788, Shankara became a sannyasin at age 18, and by the time he died at 32 had written enough influential works to be considered the leading philosopher of Vedanta. The impact of his synthesis of Hindu theology is often compared with that of the Christian theologian Thomas Aquinas*, but Shankara's influence has probably been even more pervasive.

The version of Vedanta that Shankara promoted is known as advaita, or nondualistic, because he proposed that Atman and Brahman are one despite appearances to the contrary. Our perception of differences results only from relative states of "higher" and "lower" knowledge. When one achieves higher knowledge, all sense of plurality vanishes. Since Shankara believed that liberation could come only to sannyasins, he founded an orthodox brahmanic order to teach upper-class men this path. His interpretation of Advaita Vedanta has become so dominant as to be virtually synonymous with it and ultimately formed the source of the Vedanta Society of Vivekananda in the 19th century, and Maharishi Mahesh Yogi's Spiritual Regeneration Movement (better known as TM, or Transcendental Meditation) in the 20th century.

Finally, **Madhva** (1199–1278), also called **Madhvacharya** or **Ananda Tirtha,** was the voice of Dvaita Vedanta. He saw the world as consisting of three essentially separate entities: God, the human soul, and the material world. Madhva was a bit of a fanatic, however, so devoted to his particular system that he had a local king impale thousands of Jains who didn't subscribe to it; hence his nickname, "Hammer of the Jains."

OUTSIDE ORTHODOXY: BUDDHISM, JAINISM, AND THE AJIVIKAS

Sometime before the middle of the 1st millennium BC, wandering ascetics had begun to question the efficacy of the Vedas and the whole orthodox brahmanic priesthood. They sought to release themselves and others from the bonds of samsara by what seemed to them the most direct path: renouncing all worldly ties, owning nothing, perfecting ascetical acts. To these mendicants, or shramanas, the worst form of karma was violence. Hence they were devoted with varying degrees of intensity to the principle of **ahimsa** ("nonharming"). The reason was simple: according to the laws concerning reincarnation, that pig you just roasted and ate could have your grandmother's soul. Or your late husband's. Shared to differing degrees by all the Indian heterodoxies, ahimsa led to an eventual end to animal sacrifice and an emphasis on nonviolence that reached its culmination in the politics of passive resistance made famous by Mahatma Gandhi. As a result of the influence of the two major heterodoxies, Buddhism and Jainism, most Hindus practice some form of vegetarianism.

Buddhism, which went on to become one of the great spiritual traditions of the world, is covered in detail in the following chapter. The **Ajivikas** have disappeared along with their sacred texts, and all our information about them comes from undoubtedly self-serving accounts in the writings of their competitors. We know that they were founded by **Makkhali Gosala** during the same period that Jainism and Buddhism developed (6th–5th centuries BC) and that they were fatalists who believed they were at the mercy of a cosmic power they called **niyati.** Liberation came only after a preset number of reincarnations, the last of which was as a monk of their ascetical order. Perhaps because of this fatalistic philosophy, it has been suggested, the Ajivikas simply depressed themselves out of existence.

The most intriguing of the heterodoxies may be the **Jains,** or **Jainas.** **Jainism** began by rejecting the authority of the brahmans and the Vedas; Jains instead follow a **jina** ("conqueror") or **tirthankara** ("ford maker," one who provides a path across the sea of ignorance). There were 24 jinas stretching back thousands of years, the last of whom, **Mahavira,** was a contemporary of the Buddha and founded Jainism in the 6th and 5th centuries BC. However, he was preceded by **Parshva,** perhaps by as much as 250 years, and many modern Jains think of him as their true founder. Like the Buddha, Parshva was raised in a palace but set out on his own to pursue the ascetical life. None of the tirthankaras is considered supernatural, just, like the Hindu sages, extremely holy and fully realized. Jains don't believe in a Supreme Being but rather in achieving liberation of the soul, or **jiva,** by individual effort, mainly ascetical practices.

In the Jain cosmology, humans are not the only ones with jivas. As souls pass through the multitudinous stages of transmigration, they become trapped in plants, animals, insects, stones, earth, air, and fire. Since all matter possesses living souls, violence and killing of any sort—including animals and insects—is evil. Jains accept many other aspects of the Hindu worldview, such as reincarnation and samsara.

Karma exists for the Jains as karmic matter, the subtle matter making up the senses, mind, speech, and will. Karmic matter is everywhere in the form of tiny, invisible particles similar to atoms and can enter a human as a result especially of violent acts or emotions. In most other respects, Jains view the cause-and-effect nature of karma in much the same way as Hindus and Buddhists. But the fact that they see bad karma resulting even from unintentional acts of violence—accidentally harming insects or water bodies—can sometimes lead them to inaction. In fact, their strict observances and denial of sensuality under almost any circumstances may have contributed to their relatively small numbers in the world today. To achieve liberation from the bondage of karma, Jains take five great vows: not to hurt others, steal, lie, become attached to possessions, or practice sexual impurity. Their emphasis on asceticism has led some Jains to undertake a holy death fast—an extreme practice that distinguishes Jainism from the Middle Way of Buddhism.

Awakening (**kevala**) begins with a momentary vision of the true Self,

Images of the 24 tirthankaras or jinas, who embodied Jain beliefs over the centuries, tend to be more formal and sedate than most other Indian statuary. The posture and attitude are reminiscent of the Buddha, who, like the jinas, rejected brahmanic sacrificial rites and the authority of the Vedas. Jinas are usually shown as standing or seated ascetics wearing little or no clothing. The one in this 9th-century AD bronze figure is surrounded by saintly or celestial attendants and two small devotees kneeling below his throne.

achieved through study and faith in the teachings of the tirthankaras, with a strong emphasis on philosophy and reasoning and a rejection of ritual sacrifice. The perfected one, or **kevalin,** is akin to the Buddhist arhat*. The Jains' focus on salvation through proper ethical conduct and the practice of ahimsa have placed these virtues at a higher level of importance than in almost any other religion. Although most Buddhists and Hindus practice ahimsa, none do it with the thoroughness of the Jains, whose monastics are known to carry small brooms to sweep the path in front of them lest they unknowingly crush small insects, to wear face masks to avoid breathing in tiny insects, and to eschew swimming or bathing so as not to injure invisible water bodies.

A major schism occurred among the Jains around the time of Mahavira's death. One group became known as **Digambaras** ("air-clothed") because, like Mahavira, they practice total nudity to avoid all attachments. The **Shvetambaras** ("white-clothed") reject nudity as an exterior symbol having no significance to their inner spiritual development. Unlike the Digambaras, Shvetambaras also accepted women into the monastic community early on.

The chief sacred texts of the Jains are the 11 **Angas** ("limbs") compiled by **Indrabhuti,** plus the 12 **Upangas** ("secondary limbs") and the *Uttaradhyayana Sutra.* Jain scriptures are considered to be the teachings of enlightened men, not the revealed word of God.

Because of their extremely strict adherence to vows against lying and stealing, Jains are highly regarded in India as businesspeople of the utmost integrity. As a result, they have become very successful and influential in commerce. The roughly 2 million Jains in India today share a disproportionate amount of the country's wealth.

✿ GETTING PERSONAL: WORSHIP OF SHIVA, SHAKTI, AND VISHNU

At its core, the Hinduism of the Upanishads sought to discover an abstract Godhead through mystical practices such as extended meditation. But the almost primordial mass appeal of bhaktism—devotion to God, specifically a personal god or avatar, such as Krishna—eventually began to reassert the theistic element that had been present in Hinduism from the earliest days of the Vedic sacrifices. Around the time of the *Bhagavad-Gita,* which was probably composed between 300 BC and AD 100, interest in the worship of its key figure, Krishna, started expanding.

By the 7th century AD, a great revival of Shiva worship led to a lessening of Buddhist and Jain influence in India, a process that was aided by the poet-saints of the 7th to 11th centuries, traditionally 63 **nayanars** or singers of Shiva's praises. The southern Indian state of Tamilnadu became the stronghold of Shiva worship, or **Shaivism,** perhaps because of its strong Dravidian presence. Among the most famous nayanars are the 7th-century **Appar** and **Sambandar** (who is said to have written 10,000 hymns by his death at 16) and **Lalla Yogishwari,** a 14th-century Kashmiri Shaivite woman who also studied with a Sufi master. She wrote in the bhakti tradition about the kundalini experience, and her poems are still very popular in Kashmir.

51

Nataraja (Skt. "King of the Dance") is the most celebrated motif of Shiva, the great creator/destroyer, and one of the most famous images in all Hindu art. According to tradition, members of the Mimamsa school sent the evil dwarf to overthrow Shiva, who responded with his cosmic dance of wisdom that leads to liberation. With one leg, Shiva is crushing the dwarf demon Muyalahan or Mujalaka, symbolic of ignorance and evil; his other leg is raised to represent the supraconscious state of deliverance. In two of his four hands, Shiva holds a drum to beat the rhythm of life and a pot of flames with which to destroy it, and on his face he wears the imperturbable smile of transcendence. The animal-skin loincloth he wears and the snake ornaments on either side of his head represent untamed mind and egoism, respectively, which Nataraja has overcome. Shiva's two empty hands are extended in gestures of reassurance and liberation. The flame halo which surrounds the entire image symbolizes the forces of nature and emphasizes again the destruction of one period of time and the creation of a new cosmos.
GIRAUDON/ART RESOURCE

Shaivas view Shiva, whose roots go back to the pre-Aryan Indus culture, as Supreme Being, the creator, maintainer, and destroyer of the universe, and worship him alone. The abstract phallic lingam, usually in the form of a smooth oblong stone, has been a symbol of Shiva from the earliest days of pre-Aryan civilization, possibly derived from a more ancient fertility cult of the Dravidians; it is still the main object of Shiva worship today. The Dance of Shiva, portrayed in numerous artworks, represents his maintenance of cosmic order through energy and power.

Shiva is also commonly represented in the image of **Mahayogi,** the great yoga adept seated in the meditative lotus posture, cradling his trident, symbolic of his mastery of the three main channels of the central nervous system.

The main texts of the Shaivites, who often refer to Shiva as **Hara,** are the *Svetashvatara Upanishad* and the Shaiva-Puranas. Shiva's mount is **Nandi,** a bull that often appears in front of temples dedicated to Shiva. The most important Shaivite subsect, **Shaiva-Siddhanta,** founded in the 13th century, emphasizes divine grace and the conditional split between Brahman and Atman. Its main text is the *Shaiva-Siddhanta-Shastra.* **Kashmiri Shaivism** is another large subsect.

Alongside Shaivism, especially in the provinces of Bengal, Assam, and Orissa, developed the worship of **Shakti**—"power" or "energy" embodied in the female form. **Shaktism,** also called **Tantrism,** may extend back to the ancient worship of the Mother Goddess and was expounded in esoteric texts called **Tantras.**

Followers of Shaktism see Shakti as the force that maintains the universe and makes all life possible. Its primary expression is reproductive energy, but, in general, Shakti is energy as personified in the Divine Mother Goddess, **Devi,** who reappears in different forms throughout history, like the avatars of Shiva and Vishnu. Adherents, called **shaktas,** worship various manifestations of Shakti or Devi, who can be mild and beneficent—as in **Gauri** ("the brilliant"), **Uma** ("splendor"), and **Parvati** ("the mountaineer")—or malignant—as in **Durga** ("the inaccessible"), **Chandi** ("the fierce"), and **Kali** ("the black"), who drips blood and is adorned with snakes and human skulls.

In Shaktism or Tantrism, the dualistic nature of Indian religious culture is on display. Tantra ("continuum, system") is a fundamental spiritual practice of Hinduism, based on a group of texts in which the divine energy represented by the female aspect of a god is personified as a goddess. Some of these texts relate esoteric practices divided into **Vamachara,** or left-handed path, and **Dakshinachara,** or right-handed path. The latter is a relatively benign spiritual discipline requiring worship of

53

Devi as Divine Mother and Supreme Goddess. But to experience the Ultimate Reality by following the Vamachara practices, shaktas indulge in the Five M's: **madya** (alcohol), **mamsa** (meat), **matsya** (fish), **mudra** (parched grain and symbolic hand gestures), and **maithuna** (sexual intercourse either with one's spouse or promiscuously). Ascetic and esoteric Tantric sects sometimes combined with shaktas to form small worship groups in which brahmans and outcastes met for orthodox rites followed by the Five M's. Over time, the physical expressions gave way for the most part to psychic ones, such as kundalini yoga, but some Tantric groups still practice Vamachara in Bengal (although, of necessity, they remain secret).

Hindu Tantras may have been influenced by Mahayana Buddhist Tantras relating to Tara*, the female aspect of compassion who can manifest in either a peaceful or wrathful form. Entrance to Tantric cults requires diksha, or initiation. Tantrists (or **Tantrikas**) make use of **yantras,** geometric diagrams symbolic of the goddess, and rely on awakening the kundalini through yoga. The Tantric approach is more body-oriented than most orthodox Hindu teachings, and matter is not shunned as an illusion.

The primary text of Shaktism is the *Devi Bhagavata Purana.* The center of Shaktism today is Kamarupa in the province of Assam.

The largest modern Hindu sect, **Vaishnavism,** prevailed in the north of India (although today members of the three major sects mostly live side by side). **Vaishnavas** view Vishnu (or **Hari**) as the Supreme Being and worship him in his 10 incarnations, primarily Rama and Krishna. The focus of Vaishnavism is generally on image worship, and devout Vaisnava households keep an image of Vishnu or one of his avatars in the home. The sect spread to the south after the 11th century, its intellectual groundwork having been laid by Ramanuja, who favored worship of a personal deity as opposed to the abstract Absolute of Shankara.

The chief Vaishnavite scriptures are the Vaishnava-Puranas, *Bhagavad-Gita,* and *Ramayana.* Vishnu's divine body is depicted with four arms, resting on **Shesha,** the king of the serpents, or riding on the great bird **Garuda.** Hari resides in **Vaikuntha,** his paradise, located on **Mount Meru** or in the northern ocean.

Prominent Vaishnavites included **Chaitanya** (c. 1485–1533), an eminent scholar who abruptly renounced worldly pursuits to become a fervent devotee of Krishna, embracing outcastes, sinners, and Muslims, and **Ramananda** (early 15th century), who began the cult of Rama worship, which over the years spawned two movements. One of those was purely Hindu and included **Tulasidas** (c. 1532–1623), a mystic poet and one of the best-known proponents of bhakti yoga. The other movement mixed Hindu and Muslim beliefs and included figures such as **Kabir** (c. 1440–1518) and **Dadu** (1544–1603), whose book of poems *Bani* ("Inspired Speech") is still considered scriptural by some Indian followers. Kabir was the first great spokesman for a devotional faith that combined elements of Hinduism and Islam. The common bond was the Hindu notion of bhakti, which coincided with Islam's goal of salvation through the passionate love of God.

✳ THE SIKHS

Kabir was also a **Sant** ("holy person"), i.e., a member of a fellowship of like-minded seekers who believed in one supreme, formless God. With the Sants, the pendulum began to swing back somewhat from worship of a personal divinity that had come to prominence in the 7th to 15th centuries to belief in an abstract Absolute. Sants rejected image worship and caste and expressed their beliefs in vernacular songs accessible to the lower castes. More to the point, Kabir's synthesis of Hindu and Muslim beliefs in a devotional base had a profound influence on the founder of the next major sect to unfold in India.

One side effect of the Muslim incursions into India, particularly in the northwest, was the development of a new religion that came to be known as **Sikhism**. Today there are 12 million Sikhs in India, 1 million in the U.S. and Canada, 500,000 in Great Britain. The foremost advocate in the U.S. is **Yogi Bhajan** (**Harbhajan Singh Khalsa** or **Puri,** b. 1929) and his **Healthy, Happy, Holy Organization** (3HO).

As with Hinduism, where "Atman is Brahman," the goal of Sikhism is union with God, who is said to dwell in each human being. But although Sikhs accept the laws of karma and reincarnation, Sikhism rejects Hindu image worship, Vedic rituals, asceticism, yoga, and caste

"THE LORD IS ONE"

Many observers think of Hinduism as polytheistic; others insist that its many gods and goddesses are subsumed under the one Absolute, Brahman. Some schools of Indian philosophy are even atheistic, e.g., Sankhya, which is nonetheless regarded as Brahmanistic because it accepts the authority of the Vedas. But what do the common folk of India, who constitute the vast majority of Hindus, make of the tangled web of deities? A Western scholar who has traveled extensively in India gives this assessment:

Many Hindu homes are lavishly decorated with color prints of a great many Hindu gods and goddesses, often joined by the gods and goddesses of other religions and the pictures of contemporary heroes. Thus, side by side with Shiva, Vishnu, and Devi one can see Jesus and Zoroaster, Gautama Buddha and Jina Mahavira, Mahatma Gandhi and Jawaharlal Nehru, and many others. But if questioned about the many gods, even illiterate villagers will answer: *bhagvan ek hai*, the Lord is One. They may not be able to figure out in theological terms how the many gods and the One God hang together and they may not be sure about the hierarchy among the many manifestations, but they know that ultimately there is only One and that the many somehow merge into the One.

—KLAUS KLOSTERMAIER, *A SURVEY OF HINDUISM*

distinctions in favor of the simple love of God, who is seen as the Original Guru. Furthermore, Sikhs accept the equality not only of castes but also of women. The major difficulty for Westerners in understanding Sikhism is that what began as one man's devotionally inspired vision of transcending the conflict between Hindus and Muslims in the north of India became, in later generations, a militant religion that even today is involved in a war of territorial independence from Hindu India.

Sikhism (derived from a word meaning "disciple") developed from divine revelation bestowed on **Guru Nanak** (c. 1469–1539), a contemporary of Chaitanya. Born into a kshatriya family in an area of India that was heavily populated with Muslims, Nanak first abandoned the Hinduism of his family, then tried and rejected Islam. According to tradition, he disappeared for three days while bathing in a river and returned claiming to have been taken to God's court and given **amrita** ("nectar") to drink. He said he had been told to rejoice in the name of God and teach others to do the same. His first pronouncement upon returning reportedly concluded, "God is neither Hindu nor Muslim, and the path I follow is God's."

Through meditation and singing God's name, Nanak developed a theology that combined elements of Hinduism, Islam, and Christianity while seeking to transcend what he saw as the limitations of all of them. He accepted the Hindu concepts of karma and reincarnation along with belief in a formless God. That dovetailed nicely with an emphasis on surrender to a single imageless God characteristic of Islam—hence the symbol **Ek Oankar** ("There is One God") displayed on the canopy over the Sikh holy scripture. Separation from God results from self-centeredness, the major evil of Sikhism. Nanak's teachings, monotheistic and egalitarian, oppose idolatry and the oppression of women.

Nanak established a Sikh community based in northwestern India in a region known today as the Punjab. By naming **Guru Angrad** to succeed him, Nanak began a chain of Sikh gurus that continued unbroken until the tenth, **Guru Gobind (or Govind) Singh** (1666–1708), named the holy scripture—**Adi Granth** ("Original Collection")—as the only true guru. Begun by Guru Amar Das and added to by Guru Arjan in 1604, the Adi Granth was completed by Singh in 1705 and is now known as **Guru Granth Sahib**. It contains over 3,300 hymns written not only by Nanak and other gurus but also by non-Sikh authors considered to have spoken divine revelation, like Kabir. Meditation and **kirtan,** the devotional singing of God's name and praises, are an important part of Sikh spiritual life.

During the 17th and 18th centuries, historical events set Sikhs against Muslim rulers in the north. **Guru Hargobind** (1606–1645), the sixth guru, encouraged Sikhs to abandon vegetarianism and develop strong bodies, something still true of Sikhs today. He also began a Sikh army and assumed the title **Miri Piri Da Malik** ("Lord of the Secular and the Spiritual"), effectively uniting religion and politics in a blend that is an integral part of the modern Sikh community.

Guru Gobind later formed a brotherhood to fight against the Moghul invaders. His Pure Order, or **Khalsa,** forbade alcohol, tobacco, and sexual intercourse with Muslims. Members took on the marks of their faith, the Five K's: unshorn hair worn in a turban (**kes**), the comb (**kangha**), a dagger (**kirpan**), an iron bracelet or wrist guard (**kara**), and undershorts (**kach**). Male members of the Pure Order took the name **Singh** ("lion") as their second name, and women took **Kaur** ("princess"). Because of their self-defense orientation, Sikhs became known as great fighters, and their regiments in the Indian army were highly regarded by the British.

The center of Sikh activities is the **Golden Temple** complex in Amritsar (named for the nectar Nanak was given), which includes the **Akal Takht,** or "Timeless Throne," built by Guru Hargobind and dedicated to the merging of spiritual and secular spheres. The complex has been the site of bloody clashes with Indian troops beginning in 1984, when Indian forces stormed the holy shrine and killed hundreds of Sikhs demanding independence from India. After two Sikhs in Indira Gandhi's personal bodyguard assassinated the prime minister later that year, Hindus rioted and slaughtered hundreds of Sikhs in New Delhi. The continuing conflict claims thousands of Indian lives each year.

Concentrated in the Punjab, richest of India's provinces, the industrious and successful Sikhs are more determined than ever to become an independent nation called **Khalistan,** the state of the Khalsa. Some Sikh extremists imagine Khalistan extending to include most of present-day India, although Sikhs make up only about 2 percent of the entire population.

THE BRITISH INVASION

One sign of the inherent strength and resiliency of the Indian tradition has been its ability to absorb colonizing forces over the centuries. Beginning with the Dravidians of the Indus culture, who absorbed the brahmanic religion of the Aryans and eventually transformed it with yoga and the mystical teachings of the Upanishads, through the incursions of Muslim forces, and finally the struggle against colonization by European powers, Hindu spirituality has always managed to reassert itself. By the end of the 18th century, the British had won the battle of the foreign powers for colonizing India and had begun to put their stamp on the subcontinent. Their presence had complex and often contradictory effects on Indian religion: it caused certain Hindu leaders to band together against the Christian influence while at the same time leading some Hindu scholars to attempt to "explain" Hinduism in the context of Western religion; still others sought to cleanse Hinduism of the excesses and abuses that had set in over the centuries. A number of influential figures stand out during British colonization, summarized on the following timeline.

Ram Mohan Roy
1774–1833

Founded the religious and social reform movement known as **Brahmo Samaj** in 1828 in an attempt to purify Hinduism of various corruptions. Persuaded the Indian government to outlaw **sati,** the ancient practice of widows' throwing themselves on the funeral pyres of their husbands in the belief that they would meet in the afterlife. Proposed the doctrine of a single God who should be worshiped under no name or title. The Brahmo Samaj was open to all regardless of religion, race, caste, or nationality and rejected the use of idols and the traditional belief in transmigration of souls. It has been called Hindu Unitarianism because it lacks the richness and color of most Hindu culture. But Ram also attacked Westerners who reduced Hinduism to its most exotic elements.

Debendranath Tagore
1817–1905

The real organizer behind the Brahmo Samaj, father of the mystic and poet **Rabindranath Tagore.** His *Brahma Dharma* was the textbook of the movement.

Keshub Chandra Sen
1838–1884

Disciple of Tagore who became the leader of the Samaj in 1852 and strongly opposed caste and child marriage, substituting new rituals for traditional **samskaras,** or sacraments. Split with Debendranath, who renamed the society **Adi Samaj** as Keshub formed a new Brahmo Samaj. Attempted to combine Eastern and Western spiritual principles.

Mahadev Ranade
1842–1901

Member of the Marathas, a race of Govind Indians living in Maharasthra, a large state in western India of which Bombay is the major city. He also advocated an end to child marriage, to the seclusion of women, and to sati. Joined the **Prarthana Samaj,** who pushed for the reform of Indian social institutions with an aim to breaking free of British dominion.

Dayananda Saraswati
1824–1883

One of the leading figures behind the **"Hindu Renaissance,"** a trend that moved away from Ram Mohan Roy's assimilation of Western values to a revival of pure Hindu tradition. Founded the **Arya Samaj** in 1875. It was both anti-Christian and anti-Muslim, seeking a return to the Vedas and monotheism, rejecting both idol worship and reliance on the great epics and Puranas.

Bal Gangadhar Tilak
1856–1920

Took Dayananda's approach to a political level, opposing cooperation with the British. Bal rejected the view that scriptures advocated meditation and world negation, drawing on the *Bhagavad-Gita* to support political action and even violence against colonialists.

GREAT SAINTS AND SAGES OF RECENT YEARS

Sri Ramakrishna (1836–86), known as the "Madman of God," was the leading 19th-century Hindu sage. His radical openness to religious traditions other than Hinduism often scandalized brahmans and other visitors to Dakshineswar Temple in Bengal, where he served as a temple priest. A mystic and devotee of the Divine Mother Kali, Ramakrishna preached that "all religions have a valid claim to the truth." He experienced all three forms of Vedanta and was declared an Incarnation of God. Holy people from Calcutta and Bengal often sought him out for help on their path to enlightenment. The stories told about his powers of intuition and identification with others sometimes sound preternatural. In 1866, he was initiated into Islam, had a vision of the Prophet Muhammad, and began practicing Islam alongside his Hindu beliefs. In 1874, he heard the Bible and

RAMAKRISHNA, A MAN BEYOND REASON

Ramakrishna considered himself a child of Goddess Kali, the Divine Mother of the Universe. As a child who knew nothing and decided nothing, he would speak and act spontaneously as She spoke and acted through him. He did not even regard himself as a guru or teacher. When holy scholars proclaimed him to be an Avatar, or special emanation of the Divine, Ramakrishna sat among them unself-consciously, intoxicated by the bliss of Divine Presence, half-naked, chewing spices, and repeating, *If you say I am, you must be right, but I know nothing about it.* However, although *knowing nothing,* this child of the Divine Mother was intensely sensitive. He responded to subtle changes of psychic and spiritual energy as plants respond to their environment. Once, Ramakrishna was observing from the temple garden two boatmen exchanging blows far out on the river Ganges. Marks from these blows appeared immediately on his own body.

—LEX HIXON, *COMING HOME*

became interested in Christianity, after which he experienced a vision of Jesus and merged with him. Ramakrishna believed that Christ was a Divine Incarnation and that Christianity was a valid path to awareness of God. He later accepted the Buddha on much the same level. He is often called by the honorific **Paramahamsa,** which means literally the "greatest swan," one who has attained the most advanced level of the sannyasin state.

After Ramakrishna died of throat cancer, his favorite disciple, **Swami Vivekananda** (1863–1902), formed the Paramahamsa's iconoclastic beliefs into a movement, despite the fact that Ramakrishna never advocated such a thing. Continuing Ramakrishna's practice of devotion to the Divine Mother, Vivekananda once said, "Western women will be the salvation of the world," meaning that the feminine principle represented by Kali, in union with the growing spirit of liberation spearheaded by the women of America and Europe, would emerge to take a dominant role in world religion. In 1893, Vivekananda attended the World Parliament of Religions* in Chicago. There before an audience of international religious leaders and theologians, he gave a dramatic and influential address that sought to counter the stereotype of Hindus as superstitious and intolerant. In doing so, he probably also painted a rather idealized mural of Hinduism that was closer to the conception of the British Orientalists—scholars who studied the religion without participating—than to the swarming reality of Indian life. For better or worse, Vivekananda's intellectualized and spiritualized vision of Hinduism is the one that caught the modern Western imagination. Even today, the aspects of Hindu belief practiced by Americans bear only a nominal resemblance to the sectarian worship of the average Indian. The combination of metaphysical principles and yogic practices taught by the succeeding waves of Indian gurus to come West are all more or less descendants of the Vivekananda approach and in one form or another were appropriated by the Beat culture of the 1950s, the counterculture of the '60s, and the current New Age movement.

Thereafter, Vivekananda became the chief interpreter of Hinduism to the West. He established the **Vedanta Society** in the U.S. in 1894 and later in England. In India in 1897, he founded the **Ramakrishna Mission,** considered by some to be the most important modern organization of reformed Hinduism. It is unique in India in that it is involved in social welfare concerns such as building and running hospitals and orphanages, a result of cross-pollination by Western members. The order's motto reads, "For one's own liberation and the welfare of the world." There are currently 13 Ramakrishna and Vivekananda Vedanta Centers around the U.S. run by mostly American-born monks of the Ramakrishna Order of India.

Rabindranath Tagore (1861–1941), son of Devendranath, won the Nobel Prize for poetry in 1913. He favored freedom from the British but opposed Indian nationalism. His writings typified the humanistic approach to Indian religious thought.

Aurobindo Ghose (1872–1950) is usually referred to as Sri Aurobindo. Educated in England, Aurobindo joined the nationalist movement on his return to India in 1893, became politically radical, was jailed for a year for sedition, but was finally acquitted. While in prison, he deepened his practice of yoga and meditation and claimed that the voice of the recently departed Swami Vivekananda instructed him during meditation. In his later years, Aurobindo became an ascetic in the southern, French-controlled Pondicherry, where he founded a yoga ashram. He developed a complex doctrine of the evolution of the human soul from lower to higher levels of spiritual consciousness and the transformation of matter into spirit, not unlike that of the Jesuit paleontologist and philosopher Pierre Teilhard de Chardin. But his writings in books like *The Life Divine* always emphasize the effects of mystical thought on the social condition. In 1914, he met a French woman named **Mira Richards** (1878–1973), who became his spiritual companion and helped to spread his ideas and his Integral Yoga system. Known as **The Mother,** she took over the daily running of the ashram in 1926, after Aurobindo experienced what he called "the Day of Siddhi," as divine consciousness descended into his physical form and he began a period of silence and seclusion that lasted until his death. In 1968, The Mother founded a model global village called **Auroville,** based on principles espoused by Aurobindo, which is still in progress.

Ramana Maharshi (1879–1950) was an advocate of Advaita Vedanta who became realized by asking himself continuously, "Who am I?" He applied this form of self-inquiry, or **vichara,** to visitors, asking them, "Who are you?" until they were reduced to silence. He is remembered for his utter simplicity and humility, maintained despite his reputation as the greatest sage of his day. A man who never completed his formal education, Ramana wrote virtually nothing until asked to consign his teaching to paper, at which point he composed 30 short verses, first in Tamil and later in Sanskrit, called the *Upadesha Saram.* In it he says of his practice of vichara, "If the mind uninterruptedly investigates its own true nature, it discovers that there is no such thing as mind. Such constant investigation is the shortest path for all to attain true wisdom."

Mohandas Karamchand (**Mahatma,** or "great soul") **Gandhi** (1869–1948) represents one of the great fusions of spiritual thought with political action. Gandhi's activism was underlaid with the ethics of ahimsa not merely as a political tool but as a way of life. He embraced a tolerant and generous version of Hinduism, recognizing other religions and opposing the status of outcastes, or "untouchables," whom he called instead **harijan** ("children of God"), as they are known today. His movement of nonviolent resistance to social injustice and British colonial rule was called **Satyagraha** ("holding to truth").

Sarvepalli Radhakrishnan (1888–1975), was an academic and author who became president of India from 1962 to 1967. Intelligent, spiritual, and nonsectarian, he sought in his writings to place Hinduism in the context of evolutionary change and improvement.

Swami Sivananda Saraswati (1887–1963) was the founder of the **Divine Life Society** based in Rishikesh and combined interests in ayurvedic medicine and meditation. Although he never traveled to America, his disciples, especially Swami Satchidananda and **Swami Vishnu Devananda,** have been enormously influential in spreading hatha yoga in America.

Jiddu Krishnamurti (1895–1986) was chosen by C. W. Leadbeater* and Annie Besant* of the Theosophical Society* as the avatar of the 20th century. But despite gaining a worldwide following, in 1929 Krishnamurti rejected Besant and her attempt to found a church around him. He refused any formal following, speaking and writing for the general public and settling in Ojai, California.

Ma Anandamayi (1896–1982), whose name means "mother of bliss," was one of the leading female saints of India. She became enlightened without the usual practices of reading the sacred texts or studying with a guru.

Sai Baba of Shirdi (d. 1918), worshiped by Muslims and Hindus as a divine avatar, was reportedly able to appear in two or more places simultaneously (bi- and **multilocation)** and to effect miraculous healings.

Satya Sai Baba (b. 1926), whose portrait hangs in the Hard Rock Café in Manhattan, is easily recognizable by his bright red robe and Afro hairstyle. Claiming to be a reincarnation of Sai Baba of Shirdi, he is also said to practice healings and siddhis, chiefly the ability to manifest objects—gemstones, clocks, sacred ashes, and photographs of himself—from his mouth or his hands.

Paramahansa Yogananda (1893–1952) was sent by his guru, **Sri Yukteswar Giri,** to transmit yoga to the U.S. Arriving in 1922, he resided in California until his death. His body reportedly lay in state in an open coffin for 20 days without showing any signs of decay. Most famous as the author of *Autobiography of a Yogi* (1946), he also founded a Yoga

Institute in Los Angeles in 1925 and established the **Self-Realization Fellowship (SRF)**, to teach his path of Kriya Yoga. The SRF still serves to disseminate his Advaita Vedanta views worldwide.

Maharishi Mahesh Yogi (b. 1911) is renowned as the founder of Transcendental Meditation, or TM. After the Beatles "discovered" him lecturing in a London hotel in August 1967, he was catapulted to worldwide fame. Although the Beatles disowned Maharishi less than 6 months later, his influence continued to grow in America as Clint Eastwood, Mike Love of the Beach Boys, Mia Farrow, Merv Griffin, and other pop culture figures openly embraced TM. Transcendental Meditation, his copyrighted distillation of Hindu meditation techniques, verged on becoming a household word. Besides the fully accredited Maharishi International University in Fairfield, Iowa, he has opened Vedic universities in Washington, D.C., and Moscow. TM claims 3 million members worldwide, with close to a million in the U.S. Maharishi has also established medical clinics based on a "modified and simplified" form of traditional Indian medicine, **ayurveda,** which applies knowledge of the Vedas to restoring the body's balance through natural means. The outstanding modern practitioner of ayurveda in America is **Deepak Chopra.**

Swami Satchidananda (b. 1914), a disciple of Swami Sivananda, was initially popular with the counterculture movement of the 1960s, giving the invocation at the Woodstock Festival in 1969. Since then he has remained out of the spotlight but has quietly taken up residence at his ashram called Yogaville in Buckingham, Virginia, where he teaches and practices his own version of Integral Yoga.

Swami Muktananda (1908–83) was, like his teacher before him, **Bhagavan Nityananda,** a practitioner of siddha yoga, the way of the siddhas, or semidivine beings mentioned in the Puranas. His main emphasis was on awakening the kundalini, which he claimed could be accomplished by receiving initiation from one's guru, sometimes merely by a touch—a process referred to as **shaktipat.** In America, he created the **SYDA Foundation,** which still has its chief ashram in South Fallsburg, New York. Before his death, he named two co-successors: **Gurumayi Chidvilasananda** now runs the SYDA ashram and is perhaps the most prominent woman guru of the Hindu tradition to come to the West. **Swami Nityananda,** named for Muktananda's teacher, teaches siddha yoga at a number of locations across America.

Sri Chinmoy (**Chinmoy Kumar Ghose**, b. 1931) lived and studied at Sri Aurobindo's ashram at Pondicherry where, at 14, he experienced nirvikalpa samadhi. In 1964 he came to America to teach kundalini yoga. A musician himself, Chinmoy attracted a number of professional jazz and rock musicians, including Larry Coryell, John McLaughlin (Mahavishnu), and Carlos Santana. Some of his followers left, however, amid accusations that Chinmoy was making sexual advances toward the wives of his disciples. He has consistently applied his teachings to the realm of the arts (producing paintings, recordings, and books of poetry) as well as the athletic arena, sponsoring long-distance races and performing feats of weightlifting.

The Indian government has tried to regulate the multitudinous movements and subsects of Hinduism and even to register genuine holy persons. The few "government monks" who have registered are regarded sarcastically by most other holy people, or **sadhus.**

Vedanta has influenced many American spiritual teachers as well. The most widely known include self-improvement guru **Wayne Dyer** and the former Harvard professor and associate of Timothy Leary who changed his name from Richard Alpert to **Baba Ram Dass** after studying with a guru in India and is now known simply as Ram Dass. Master Charles*, who changed his Italian birth name to Charles Connor and was called Brother Charles before he assumed the title of Master, is a former disciple of Swami Muktananda based in the Blue Ridge Mountains of Virginia. He has developed a series of audiotapes to enhance meditation and accelerate enlightenment, combining recent brain-entrainment techniques with the chanting of ancient sacred texts.

The championship of name changes, however, is held by another one-time disciple of Muktananda who has evolved a distinctive teaching of his own. Born Franklin Jones in Jamaica, New York, in 1939, he changed his name during various stages of enlightenment to, among others, **Bubba Free John, Da Free John, Da Love-Ananda** (under which names many of his early books were published), **Da Kalki, Da Avabhasa,** and currently **Adi Da** (The Avatar). He now lives and teaches in Fiji, and his followers form the **Free Daist Avataric Communion** in the U.S. Although Adi Da's serious followers number only in the low thousands, his books have been widely read and circulated and have influenced many modern seekers.

TALES OF THE TAPE

Among the increasingly affluent middle and upper classes, especially in the urban centers, beliefs and practices may be trimmed to eliminate so-called superstitious or cult observances, focusing on the teachings of certain highly respected figures of Hindu theology, from Shankaracharya and Ramanuja to Vivekananda and Aurobindo, along with prominent swamis such as Muktananda or Ramana Maharshi. These more cosmopolitan city dwellers may be motivated by a desire to modernize Hindu practice, to universalize it in much the way it is viewed and admired by Westerners. The gradual wearing away of Brahmanic power and exclusive control of the Vedic rituals underlies the continuing evolution of Hinduism in India, as outlined by the following Western observer who has spent many years in the country.

One indicator of vitality and experimentation in Hinduism has been described by scholars as a process of Sanskritization, whereby Brahmanic faith and practice, and Sanskrit texts, become increasingly more significant to non-Brahmanic strata of society. This is, of course, a process already documented in early Vedic religion, and one that is apparent in every subsequent phase of the history of Hinduism. The Brahmans, once the educated and educating elite, protected the Sanskrit language, the Vedas, and the *shastras* and limited access to the law codes, great temples, *tirthas,* and monastic institutions. In modern India they have seen their priest power base eroded by the secular state, upwardly mobile caste groups, and political institutions. Education is open to all. Untouchables, tribal peoples, "backward classes," and "weaker sections" are given special catch-up privileges and positions in affirmative action programs. Temples may no longer exclude Hindu untouchables, some Vedic schools and even major temples are administered by state governments, and the Vedas and Sanskrit devotional *slokas* [scripture verses] can be heard by all at public bathing facilities, fairs, and festivals. Radio and TV broadcasts democratize the faith. *Mantras* are recited by women and recorded on cassettes, and the epic *Ramayana* has been serialized for Sunday morning television. A Brahman recitant is not required if the Sanskrit classics are available on a personal videocassette recorder.

—DAVID M. KNIPE, *HINDUISM*

✵ HINDUISM TODAY

If the Hinduism purveyed to Westerners by visiting gurus does not necessarily correspond to the religion as practiced in its homeland, how can we accurately characterize it as a living tradition? Based on the accounts of scholars and adherents of Hinduism familiar with India, Hinduism is observed there on several overlapping levels and dozens of sublevels. In the villages, devout masses of people, largely still uneducated and reflecting the harsh economic conditions of the country, practice a form of Hinduism that is based around temple and shrine worship and a succession of outdoor festivals and pilgrimages to sacred sites. Some common practices may not be sanctioned by sacred scriptures or the government, yet they occur, often with the support of sectarian leaders. One example is sati, the supposed self-immolation of widows, which is in fact often enforced by male in-laws for financial reasons. Another is the growing cult of the bachelor god Ayyappan, son of Shiva and **Mohini**, a female incarnation of Vishnu. Young men of various castes come together to perform an annual 41-day penance and 500-mile pilgrimage.

Family-oriented rituals with a Vedic base take place in the home, usually around a home altar or shrine, or in elaborate temples, all dedicated to the propagation of the dharma. Rooted in ancient tradition, these practices, like the village rituals, are largely devotional in nature. Particularly in urban areas, family practitioners may seem far removed from the shrine and temple worship of Shaivite or Vaishnavite villagers. But the more affluent city folk may also donate money to the shrines and temples or travel to pilgrimage or festival sites all the same.

Finally, there is the practice of the sannyasins, whose standard of living may range from the rather comfortable status of monks of the Ramakrishna Order living in their monasteries to the more arduous life of wandering sadhus, of whom a good number still remain.

THE MARK OF ZOROASTER

Around the time one group of Aryans was invading northern India, another group or groups of the same race, also called Indo-Iranians, made their way south into what is now Iran. There they developed a religion with many similarities to Vedic Hinduism, but with quite a few significant differences too. Their language, deriving from the same source, was similar, and much of the terminology of the ancient Iranian religion echoes the Sanskrit of the Vedas. The Iranians worshiped gods with similar names, like **Mithra,** equivalent to the Indian Mitra, a sun god and lord of the day. They divided the spirit world between **ahuras** and **daevas,** roughly equivalent to Hindu asuras and devas. *(Daeva* and *deva* are both related to the Latin *deus,* "god." The devas of the Vedic Indians became the "heavenly" or "true gods" while the asuras took on the role of darker, more occult spirits; just the opposite evolution took place in the Iranian religion.) And the sacred drink of the Iranians, which featured prominently in their early sacrificial liturgies, was called **haoma,** a clear relative of soma.

But other than this, little is known about the beliefs and practices that preceded the arrival of Zoroaster in the 1st millennium BC. No sacred texts equivalent to the Vedas remain; only some archaeological evidence exists and accounts in documents from the time of Zoroaster and later. **Zoroaster** is the Greco-Latinized version of the Iranian name **Zarathustra,** from an ancient root meaning "camel." All we can be certain about is that he was a prophet who lived sometime in or just before the 1st millennium BC and was credited by the Greeks and Romans with having founded the wisdom of the **Magi,** a mysterious class of sorcerers or priests skilled in dream interpretation, prophecy, and astrology. Some scholars, following tradition, place his life between 628 and 551 BC; if that is accurate, he was remarkably close in time to other great spiritual revolutionaries, including the Buddha; Mahavira (a founder of Jainism);

Lao-tzu* (fl. c. 600 BC), whose *Tao Te Ching** forms the basis of Taoism; and Pythagoras* (c. 570–490) in pre-Socratic Greece. Other scholars insist on a much earlier date, somewhere before 1200 BC, which would place him closer to Moses* and Ahkenaten*.

From tradition and internal evidence in the hymns attributed to him, Zoroaster was a sacrificing priest and chanter (or *zaotar*, similar to the Sanskrit *hotr*) and was probably poor. According to legend, at age 30 he had a heavenly vision in which an angel brought him to **Ahura Mazda** ("Lord of Wisdom"). Ahura Mazda (also **Ormazd** or **Ormuzd**) charged Zoroaster with the task of founding a new religion to supersede the cruder ethnic beliefs of the Iranians at that time. The visions continued over a 10-year period, but Zoroaster quickly met with stiff resistance to his attacks on the traditional priests. Like the Buddha in India, he rejected many of the ritual practices of the Aryan-derived religion that surrounded him, especially the sacrificial slaughter of cattle and the drinking of intoxicating haoma. (An aristocratic warrior class of Iranians participated in initiatory brotherhoods, working themselves into orgiastic states of violent frenzy after consuming haoma.) But unlike the Buddha, Zoroaster was forced to flee, seeking refuge at the court of King Vishtaspa of Bactria (north of the Hindu Kush Mountains, which separate India from Central Asia, corresponding with modern Balkh in Afghanistan). After first being imprisoned for teaching his radical new religion, Zoroaster converted the king and his family to his beliefs. According to tradition, Zoroaster was slain by unbelievers in his 77th year.

The basic element of Zoroaster's belief system is the duality between good and evil. This separation is the result of a choice initiated by Ahura Mazda, the world's creator; in the beginning, according to Zoroastrian cosmogony, one of the twin spirits engendered by Ahura Mazda, **Spenta Mainyu** ("Beneficent Spirit") chose good and life, while the other, **Angra Mainyu** ("Destroying Spirit," or **Ahriman,** as he is known in the later documents) chose evil and death. As a result, mortals must make the same choice, and they will be judged accordingly upon their death, the just rewarded with entrance into paradise, or the "House of Song," the wicked condemned to the "House of Evil." In an ancient hymn attributed to Zoroaster, he declares, "Truly, there are two primal Spirits, twins renowned to be in conflict. In thought and word, in act they are two: the better and the bad. And those who act well have chosen rightly between these two, not so the evildoers" (Yasna 30:3).

Zoroaster was not a strict monotheist. He posited a **Divine Heptad** consisting of Ahura Mazda and six lesser deities whom he created to help him, the **Amesha Spentas** ("Holy Immortals"). These subordinate divinities Zoroaster associated with the idealization of Right Law, Good Thought or Purpose, Noble Power or Government, Health, Devotion, and Immortality, all of which he saw as reifications of aspects of God's own nature.

The Zoroastrian duality between good and evil should not be confused with the opposition of matter and spirit that drives Christian theology and plays a role in the later stages of Hinduism as well. Nor is it the same duality as that of Manichaeism*, a Gnostic-influenced religion initiated in the 3rd century AD by the Persian prophet and ecstatic Mani*, who saw spirit as good and matter as evil. In Zoroastrianism, for instance, fasting and celibacy are forbidden (except during the rituals of purification that all young Zoroastrians must go through) and are actually condemned as evil.

Of the various Zoroastrian systems that developed since the founder's death, including Zurvanism, the only coherent one is called Mazdaism. According to its teachings, history, which consists of the ongoing struggle between good and evil in which overmatched evil is born to lose, is divided into four 3,000-year periods. The first was a period of creation; during the second and third, Mazda and Ahriman ruled in succession. During the final period, which was begun by Zoroaster's ministry and in which we still find ourselves, good and evil battle. With the help of the Messiah, or **Saoshyant** ("He who will save the world"), the God of Light will be victorious. History will end in AD 2401, and Ahura Mazda will reign in bliss forever.

Zoroaster's moral code, similar to the precepts of all the great religions, forswears robbery, plunder, and murder, "not even to avenge life or limb." His saying "I confess good thoughts, good words, good deeds" became the motto of his religion. Like other founders, Zoroaster left precepts and beliefs but no rites or rituals, which were created entirely by his followers after his death. The Avestan priests eventually reinstated the animal sacrifice and haoma orgies that Zoroaster had reformed and elevated the Amesha Spentas to gods on a level with Ahura Mazda.

The chief scripture of the Zoroastrians is the **Avesta,** composed of several sections which were not committed to writing until about the 4th or 5th century AD. The **Gathas,** or hymns, are the only scriptures attributed to Zoroaster, said to be authentic sayings that survived from sermons he gave in the court of King Vishtaspa. The Gathas occur in the part of the Avesta called the *Yasna,* recited during the sacrifice for which it is named (cf. Skt. *yajna,* "sacrifice"). Other sections include the *Vendidad* ("Against the Daevas," statutes regarding purity), *Siroza, Yashts* (hymns to each of 21 deities), and *Hadhoxt Nask* ("Section Containing Sayings"). The *Zand* (or *Zend) Avesta* ("Great Avesta") refers to a compilation of holy texts committed to writing primarily in the 9th century AD, plus the life and legends of the prophet, doctrine, law, science, and other writings. After successive waves of destruction by Arabs, Turks, and Mongols during the Islamic period, only about a quarter of its original material has survived. Zoroastrian sacred texts are written principally in **Avestan** and **Pahlavi,** two dead liturgical languages.

Although Zoroastrianism shares a linguistic and theological heritage with the founders of Vedic Hinduism, its link to the Jewish-Christian tradition may be more significant. Because it developed in the Middle East during the era when Judaism and Christianity were taking shape, it is not surprising that similarities abound, but the question of who influenced whom is difficult for scholars to answer. Depending on when Zoroaster actually lived, he could be seen as a forerunner of the monotheistic impulses of Akhenaten and Moses; at the very least, he contributed to the belief that each human being has the freedom to choose to live an actively virtuous life in the struggle of good against evil. Assorted Judaic and Christian beliefs—such as the appearance of a Savior or Messiah* who would signal the end of the world and the beginning of a new creation, the division of humanity into good and evil at the Last Judgment*, followed by the reunion of body and soul, with life everlasting for the righteous—have been attributed to the influence of Iranian religious thought, perhaps through the Parthians during the two centuries before Christ. The Jewish and Christian practice of keeping an eternal flame burning before the altar may be derived from a similar Zoroastrian practice. (Zoroastrians are still known for their worship of the sacred fire, symbol of illumination—fire being considered the Son of Ahura Mazda and the highest gift of the creator, since it allowed great advances in culture.) And the Christian concept of the Holy Spirit* as the executor of God's will on earth seems to come directly from the Spenta Mainyu of Zoroaster, although some observers identify the Spenta Mainyu instead with the Logos*, or creative agent, of Zeno*, Philo*, and the Gospel of John*, where it refers to Jesus Christ.

One of the oldest and least understood of the great traditions, Zoroastrianism faces extinction today, with barely 125,000 members left. Only small pockets of Zoroastrians remain in Iran, where it was the dominant religion until the coming of Islam in the 7th century. But the tradition is carried on elsewhere by the **Parsis** (or **Parsees,** "Persians"), descendants of Iranian refugees who brought Zoroastrianism to India beginning in the 10th century. The Parsis began in India as farmers but went on to become successful in business and industry. They got along well with the British during the colonial period and adopted many Western customs, to the extent that some observers feel their practice of the religion is only a dim shadow. North America has a small Zoroastrian community, numbering fewer than 10,000, of whom the famed orchestra leader Zubin Mehta is probably the most visible. The fact that it has evolved from a credal religion, preached to all who would listen, to an exclusively ethnic faith has not helped its chances of survival.

✳ INSIDE A HINDU TEMPLE

Just as all Christian churches are built along the basic outline of the cross, so the architectural design of Hindu temples, in India and elsewhere around the world, is based on the pattern of a human figure enclosed by a square (**Vastu-Purusha**). And if Catholics believe that the Blessed Sacrament residing in the tabernacle is the presence of God, then Hindus believe that the god to whom the temple is dedicated (usually either Vishnu, Shiva, or a Devi) is present in their sacred image or may be summoned by ringing a bell.

The overall square of the temple is subdivided into nine smaller squares, the central one belonging to Brahma, the God of Creation. Around it are ringed any number of pathways and circuit walls, often enclosed by an exterior terrace.

Services may take place at least three times a day, at varying hours, but attendance is never mandatory. At other times, templegoers perform whatever worship activity they choose, from praying or prostrating themselves before the main image to practicing yoga or reading sacred texts.

As for sacred feasts or public festivals, consonant with Hinduism's multifaceted approach to worship, there are over 1,000. The major ones (which cannot be assigned fixed dates in the Western mode since Hindus follow a lunar calendar) are **Krishnajayanti** (Krishna's birthday), **Ganesha chaturthi, Dassera** (a postmonsoon holiday season), **Divali** (the picturesque feast of the lamps), **Shivaratri** (the principal feast of Shaivites), and **Holi** (a carnivallike New Year's Day).

Coming to Terms

Most of these terms are taken from Sanskrit, the classical and sacred language of India and a variant of the Indo-European tongue believed to have been brought in by the conquering Aryans during the 4th–2nd millennia BC. Sanskrit is the language of most Hindu scriptures and prayers and of the Indian priest class, but not of the common people, having ceased to be a spoken language, by some estimates, as early as the 8th century BC. Many of the more common Sanskrit terms, however, have come to us with the contemporary pronunciation of South Asia, which tends to drop the final *a* or *n*. And so *ashrama, avatara, darshana, yuga,* and *karman* often become *ashram, avatar, darshan, yug,* and *karma.* For purists, an *h* following any aspirated consonant is pronounced separately, as in "hand-holding." And so *dharma* is properly said "duh-*harm*-uh," and the Buddha, "*bood*-huh," although few Westerners observe these rules. This glossary takes a more commonplace approach; standard Sanskrit diacritical marks have been dispensed with in favor of a phonetic pronunciation guide.

As a general rule, two-syllable words are accented on the first syllable, but multisyllable words are often accented in ways that sound odd to Western ears. Neither the *Ramayana* (ruh-*my*-uh-nuh) nor the *Mahabharata* (muh-*hah*-bah-ruh-tuh) are pronounced the way I'd always assumed. Since *maha,* Sanskrit for "great," is accented on the second syllable, all the compound words with which it begins sound awkward when properly pronounced, including *maharishi* (muh-*hah*-ri-shee) and *Mahavira* (muh-*hah-vee*-ruh). Vowels are also problematic since different Sanskrit characters are often represented by the same letter in English. An accented *a* is usually pronounced "ah," unaccented *a*, "uh"; accented *i* = "ee," unaccented *i* = "ih"; accented *u* is pronounced as in *boot*, unaccented *u* as in *full*; *e* is almost always said like the *a* in *way*, as in *Veda (vay*-duh) and *deva (day*-vuh); *ai* is said like the *y* in *my*: *advaita* (ad-*vye*-tuh), Vaishnava *(veyesh*-nuh-vuh); and *o* is pronounced long, as in *yoga* and *yoni*.

advaita (ad-*vye*-tuh)   Branch of Vedanta that teaches the doctrine of the One without a second; nondualism.

ashram(a) (ash-*rah*-mah)   Any one of the four stages of life for Hindus; the same word, which originally meant a training school for brahmans, now also refers to any place where people gather for spiritual instruction and meditation.

Atman (*aht*-mun)   The Self that exists as Brahman in each individual.

avatar (*av*-uh-tar, "descent")   A divine incarnation, particularly of the god Vishnu, but by extension of any Divine Presence in a human or animal body.

Bhagavad-Gita (*bug*-uh-vud *ghee*-tuh, "Song of the Lord or Blessed One")   The most important and influential religious text of India, probably composed during the 1st millennium BC and inserted into the *Mahabharata*. It contains invaluable teachings on the various yogas, the theory of the gunas, and the basics of Vedanta.

bhagavan (*bahg*-uh-van)   The exalted one; a personalized name for the Supreme Being, Brahman, although the title is more often applied to great saints and sages by their disciples.

bhakta (*bahk*-tuh)   A practitioner of bhakti yoga.

Brahma (brah-*mah*)   One of the gods in the Hindu Trinity, representing creation.

Brahman (*brah*-mun)   From *br*, "to breathe," and *brih*, "to expand infinitely." As originally used in the Vedas, *Brahman* meant "sacred utterance," then "ritual," and later was applied to those in charge of rituals. By the time of the Upanishads, it had come to mean the Absolute, Being without condition, or Godhead. Its chief attributes are sat ("being"), chit ("awareness"), and ananda ("bliss"). (See Swami Satchidananda.)

brahman   The highest caste in the system of varna; a Hindu priest.

Brahmana (*brah*-muh-nuh)   An addendum to the Vedas.

Brahmo Samaj   Reform movement founded in 1828 to return to the purity of the Vedas.

chaturvarnashramadharma (chah-tur-*vahr*-nash-**rah**-muh-*dar*-muh, "religion of four castes and stages of life") The compound Sanskrit term that incorporates the underpinnings of Hindu society, based on the four levels of caste (varna) and stages of life (ashrama).

chela (*chay*-luh) Student or disciple of a guru.

darshan(a) ("seeing") One of six orthodox variants of the Hindu philosophy. Also, a visit to a holy person or place.

deva (*day*-vuh, "shining one"), or **devata** (day-vuh-*tah*) Generally speaking, a divine being. It can be a god such as Indra or the manifestation of a transcendent power in a natural object such as fire (Agni), soma, storm winds (**Maruts**), or Mother Earth (**Aditi**). Distinguished from **asura**, which in the *Rig Veda* means "god" or "divine" but later came to refer to the dark, occult powers or beings who often oppose the gods. A similar dichotomy exists in Zoroastrianism between daevas and ahuras.

Devi (*day*-vih) The Mother Goddess in any form; any female divinity.

dharma From a root meaning "sustain" or "uphold," *dharma* has several meanings for Hindus, the most important being a combination of moral and ethical law, duties, and obligations that connect the individual to his or her social position. These include varnas, ashramas, sacrifices, rituals, and marriage laws. Dharma also includes specific laws against violence, theft, unlawful sexual practice, and greed; it requires practicing charity, aiding those in distress, reciting scripture, and, above all, upholding the dharma.

diksha Initiation by a guru into the secrets of a particular practice, usually accompanied by the giving of a mantra.

gunas (*goo*-nuhs) Three attributes or qualities that characterize the primordial substance, hence all objects and activities. More like a triangle of forces, sattva, rajas, and tamas represent peace, activity, and inertia, respectively. Another way of viewing them is as the forces that tend to reveal, project onto, or cover up reality.

guru From the Sanskrit *gu* ("darkness") plus *ru* ("remover"), the word means "teacher" and can refer to parents, educators, spiritual masters, or avatars—anyone who dispels ignorance; the third is the most common meaning.

ishta, ishtadeva (*eesh*-tuh-*day*-vuh) An image of a specific, personal deity or aspect of a divinity chosen as the object of one's adoration as a way of relating to the vast, impersonal Absolute or Brahman.

Ishvara (*eesh*-vuh-ruh, "Lord of the Universe") The superimposition of a personal identity on Brahman so the mind can conceptualize It. All Hindu deities are aspects of Ishvara, but especially Vishnu and Shiva.

jivanmukta One whose soul has been released from samsara but is still living in a body. The guru helps the chela to enjoy a state of **jivanmukti**, or liberated living.

jnana yoga (*gyah*-nuh)   The path of realization through intellectual knowledge of God.

Kali (kah-*lee*, "The Black One")   The name of Devi, the Goddess, in her terrible form. One of the feminine manifestations or shaktis of Shiva, often referred to as the Divine Mother. Although pictured with a belt of human arms and a necklace of skulls, symbolizing destruction, she is also experienced as the embodiment of bliss. Her best-known devotee was Ramakrishna, one of the saintliest men in Indian history.

Kali Yuga ("Age of Strife")   The last period in each world era, or **kalpa**, and the one in which we are at present. Traditionally said to have begun with the Great War between the Pandavas and Kauravas, or with the death of Krishna, it runs 360,000 years. Here *Kali* means "strife" or "fight" and does not refer to the Goddess Kali.

Kama   Indian god of love and sexual desire. Lowercase, *kama* is one of four ideals in Hindu life, relating to the earthly enjoyment of physical and sense pleasures.

karma   The law of cause and effect by which good or bad actions performed in the present yield good or bad fruits in the future.

kirtan   Communal singing, chanting, or dancing to honor God.

Krishna   Eighth and most important incarnation of the god Vishnu, he features prominently in the *Mahabharata* and *Bhagavad-Gita*. Since Krishna had had many previous human lives, he is considered to be both God and man, like Jesus in Christian belief.

kshatriya (k'*shah*-tree-yuh)   The caste of warrior-rulers, including politicians, civil authorities, and government administrators.

Kumbha Mela   Acclaimed by the *Guinness Book of World Records* as the largest gathering on earth, this great month-long spiritual assembly is held four times during the 12-year cycle of Jupiter, once each at Allahabad (Prayaga), Nassik, Ujjain, and Hardwar. The 1989 Kumbha Mela at Allahabad attracted 30 million pilgrims, including hundreds of thousands of sadhus and sadhvinis, yogis, and other ascetics who came out of caves and forests to attend.

Lalla   Fourteenth-century Kashmiri Shaivite and Sant who wrote many influential hymns.

Mahabharata (muh-*hah*-bah-ruh-tuh)   Long epic poem incorporating the *Bhagavad-Gita*.

mantra   Holy words or sounds repeated as prayer. Can be a single syllable *(Om)* or a succession such as *Om namo narayanaya* ("Om, honor to God within the heart of all beings").

math (mutt)   A monastery.

maya   The literal meaning is "deception" or "appearance" and comes from the same root as *magic* (a usual translation in the *Rig Veda* is "wily tricks"). But to define *maya* merely as "illusion" is insufficient. In

Vedanta, Maya is seen as "God's power of world-projection," the manifestation of the One or Absolute as the many, the phenomenal world; and so Maya is to Brahman as the Greek Logos* is to Theos. In the sense that the material world is only one insubstantial manifestation of Brahman and undue attachment to it can distract the soul from its primary goal of union with the Absolute, it can then be seen as illusionary or misleading, "the veil that conceals Absolute Reality."

mlecchas The Greeks called them barbarians, the Jews, goyim; to the Hindus, any non-Hindu is an "outsider."

mudra ("sign") Hand gesture intended to help focus the mind on God. Placing the palms together with the fingertips pointed upward, for example, is the Christian mudra of prayer.

munis ("silent sages") Shamans* associated with Rudra, a storm god and archer whose arrows felled the righteous and evil alike, but who also knew healing herbs (later taken up by the Jains). In the *Rig Veda,* munis knew healing arts and levitation; they are thought to be the non-Aryan forerunners of brahmanic ascetics.

murti ("embodiment") An image of a divinity used for worship.

nirvikalpa samadhi The highest level of samadhi; complete union with Brahman.

Nyaya The science of logical argument or rational proof; one of the six orthodox philosophical schools of Hinduism.

pandit A scholar, particularly one knowledgeable about sacred scriptures and techniques who studies them intellectually, but not with an eye to self-realization. Pandits sometimes practice techniques such as yoga or meditation but do not teach them as gurus do.

prana ("breath") Cosmic force or vitality that vivifies and regulates the human body. (Cf. ch'i in Taoism.)

pranayama (prah-nuh-*yah*-muh) Breath control; a stage in the practice of raja yoga.

puja (*poo*-jah) Ceremonial homage to a god, avatar, or saint in a Hindu temple or home, using at least five items, each pleasing to one of the five senses—e.g., Ganges water, food, flowers, bells, incense, or fire. A practitioner is a **pujari** or **pujaka.**

Purana ("ancient") Collection of legends, myths, royal genealogies, and moral precepts linked to sacred tradition.

Purva Mimamsa School of orthodox Vedic interpretation.

rakshasa (rahk-*shah*-suh) Evil spirit who inhabits the forests of Indian folklore, sometimes thought to be a stand-in for the dark-skinned aboriginal inhabitants subjugated by the Aryans.

Rig Veda The oldest of the four Vedas, composed mostly of creation hymns and hymns to Indra, Agni, Soma, and the various gods, to be chanted at sacrifices.

rishi   Great seer who received direct revelations of truth from God, which were then compiled in the Vedas. Classically there were seven rishis, all sprung from the mind of Brahma, but many more existed.

sadhana (*sah*-duh-nuh)   Derived from *sadh*, "to arrive at the goal, to accomplish," it is the pursuit of spiritual enlightenment through any of a number of disciplines. One who follows a sadhana is a **sadhaka;** one who has arrived is a **siddha.**

sadhu (*sahd*-hoo)   A holy man or saint; a just person. The feminine form is **sadhvi** (pl. **sadhvini**).

samadhi (sah-*mah*-dih)   Literally, "with the Lord," from *sam*, "with" plus *adhi*, "lord." (Cf. Hebrew *Adon, Adonai*, Lord.) A state of complete ecstatic absorption in the Absolute. Of the many levels of depth and duration, the highest is arguably nirvikalpa samadhi, although the three schools of Vedanta debate this point.

samhita   Collection of hymns that make up each of the four Vedas.

samsara (sahm-*sah*-ruh)   The continuous cycle of birth, death, and rebirth. By extension, the phenomenal world and its many attractions and distractions, perhaps the least of which is the trademarked perfume of the same name.

samskaras ("impressions, consequences")   Tendencies, potentialities, and latent states existing in the unconscious as a result of one's actions, including previous lives. Also, the generic name for Hindu sacraments, including marriage (**vivaha**), name-giving (**namakarana**), renunciation (sannyasa), initiation (upanayana), and funeral rites (**shraddha**).

sanatana dharma (suh-*nah*-tuh-nuh)   "Eternal Dharma," the name by which most Hindus refer to their own religion.

sannyasa   The final stage of life, in which one renounces all possessions, including a permanent home of any sort, in order to achieve the most profound spiritual realization. The term has undergone severe pejoration, especially in the West, where *sannyasin* now refers merely to the disciple of a particular guru or to anyone following a spiritual path.

sati ("true wife")   A widow who voluntarily throws herself on the funeral pyre of her husband, named for a consort of Shiva who started the practice. Hindu reformers from Ram Mohan Roy to Gandhi fought to abolish this odious practice, with only partial success. Often it is the male in-laws who enforce sati in order to obtain dowry. (It survives in spirit among some ethnic European wives in America for whom it is de rigueur to throw themselves onto the casket or even into the freshly dug grave of the departed spouse.)

Shakti   Any feminine manifestation of a male divinity, including Kali, Durga, or Uma.

Shiva   One of the three main gods of the Hindu Trinity, responsible for destruction or dissolution. However, he does not simply destroy but dissolves to re-create Unity and so is the quintessential recycler.

shramanas (*shruh*-muh-nuhz) Early ascetics of the pre-Aryan Indus culture who lived in the forests or as wandering mendicants, probably practicing yoga, meditation, and nonviolence. Jainism and Buddhism both derived in some measure from their practices.

shruti ("that which is heard") Specifically the four Vedas plus the Brahmanas, Aranyakas, and Upanishads, which are all considered to have been divinely revealed to the rishis while in meditative trance states. In orthodox Hinduism they may be commented on but never questioned. (Cf. smriti.)

siddhis Supernatural abilities that may be gained as a by-product of certain advanced yogic practices. Siddhis include telepathy, clairvoyance, clairaudience, materialization, levitation, invisibility, bilocation, and entering into other bodies.

smriti ("that which is recalled") Namely, holy scriptures which are based on tradition rather than direct revelation, including but not limited to the *Mahabharata* and *Ramayana*, the *Manu-Samhita*, the Puranas, and Vedangas. (Cf. shruti.)

soma Sacrificial drink personified in the Vedas as the god Soma. The soma plant was pressed and its juice mixed with milk, resulting in a highly hallucinogenic drink sanctioned only during brahmanic sacrifices. It was later identified with amrita, the "nectar of immortality," perhaps because it seemed to impart supernatural powers, at least temporarily, to the brahmans who drank it. In its powerful hallucinogenic form, soma disappeared rather early from Vedic practice, replaced by a fairly innocuous brew. No one today seems to know the precise identity of the plant involved, although the renowned mycologist R. Gordon Wasson has presented convincing evidence that it was the hallucinogenic fly-agaric mushroom, which has properties similar to LSD. Aldous Huxley, who was conversant with both Hindu lore and hallucinogens, gave the name *soma* to the dream-inducing drug in *Brave New World*.

Sri, Shri, Shree ("splendor; venerable one") A title of respect for a deity or a great saint or teacher, such as Sri Ramakrishna.

swadharma (or **svadharma**) The specific set of duties and obligations connected with one's caste and stage of life. The need to follow one's swadharma for the sake of the greater dharma is the key teaching of the *Bhagavad-Gita*.

swami ("sir," or "master" of one's senses) Respectful title used before the name of a monk or certain holy men or gurus.

Tantra The divine energy of the shakti, in the form of a goddess. Also a series of texts explaining potentially dangerous secret practices including the so-called Five M's: wine, meat, fish, mystical gestures, and sexual intercourse.

tirtha   A site for a pilgrimage, usually on a sacred riverbank. The premier river is the Ganges (or Ganga), whose water is often taken home in bottles for future use—like that of the Christian Lourdes*. The holy city of Benares is the goal of many pilgrims.

Trimurti   The Trinity of Hindu gods: Brahma, Vishnu, and Shiva.

Upanishads   Mystical and philosophical treatises appended to the Vedas and laying the foundation for much of Vedanta.

Vairagi (vye-*rah*-ghi)   A renunciate of the Vaishnava sect.

Valmiki ("Ant")   Traditional composer of at least part of the *Ramayana*. Having lived as a robber for many years, he repented by meditating for so long that a colony of ants built an anthill that covered him entirely.

Vedanta ("the end of the Vedas" or "the end of knowledge")   One of the six orthodox "viewpoints" or darshanas of Indian philosophy. Vedanta is the most popular of the six among modern Hindus and can be divided into at least three major schools or approaches.

Vedas (*vay*-duhz, "knowledge")   The earliest sacred scriptures of the Hindus, of which there are four principal types: Rig, Yajur, Sama, and Atharva. Their ritualistic, sacrificial approach defines the Vedic era of Hinduism.

vedi   The sacrificial altar of the brahmans.

Vishnu   One of three chief Hindu deities, associated with preservation and divine love. His shakti is Lakshmi.

vratyas   Itinerants who wandered India performing magic rituals. Including musicians and prostitutes who sometimes engaged in self-flagellation, they may have been forerunners of the Gypsies.

yajna (*yuhj*-nuh)   The Vedic sacrifice; an epithet for Vishnu.

Yama   God of death and the netherworlds.

Yoga   One of the six darshanas, it has many specialized varieties, including hatha, kundalini, and kriya, but its four general branches are jnana, bhakti, karma, and raja yoga. A practitioner is called a yogi or **yogin** (yo-*gheen*) or yogini (f., yo-*ghee*-nee).

2

BUDDHISM

✳ "STOP THE WHEEL, I WANT TO GET OFF"

Buddhism originated in the 6th century BC in India, spread south to Sri Lanka, Southeast Asia, Java, and Sumatra, north to China, Tibet, Korea, and Japan, and, beginning in the 19th century, to Europe and America. As one of the four largest active traditions, it inspires hundreds of millions of people around the world today. And yet, unlike Hinduism, Christianity, or Islam, Buddhism is not based on a conception of a Supreme Being or Godhead, notwithstanding the fact that many Buddhists venerate the historical Buddha, other buddhas, and realized beings called bodhisattvas in a manner that might appear similar to the way Westerners or Hindus worship God. For first and foremost, Buddhism is about the effort of a human being—without question an extraordinary, enlightened one, so far above the day-to-day thrum of humanity as to seem perhaps a different species, but human nonetheless. Buddhist teachings are based on his efforts to become enlightened and his compassionate teachings to others to do likewise; for this reason, Buddhism has been uncommonly congenial to other faiths.

And perhaps as a result, the religion based on the Buddha's teachings has been able to absorb and be absorbed peacefully by other cultures. No major war has ever been fought in the name of the Buddha, although tyrannical rulers have sometimes sought to impose their Buddhist faith on their citizens and to suppress other beliefs. But because there is no direct link to a deity but only to an enormous body of scripture, there is no central authority in Buddhism—even the Dalai Lama, for all the respect and veneration directed to him by people of many different faiths, serves as the spiritual leader for only a part of the international Buddhist community.

As a religion, Buddhism has sometimes been criticized as being unconcerned with the great social dilemmas of our time, but the Buddha's teaching of compassion and an increasing sense of activism in both Asian and American Buddhism renders that critique questionable. The terrible invasion of Tibet by the Communist Chinese over 30 years ago not only has caused the great teachings of the Tibetan lamas to be scattered like seeds across the globe but has also infused the teachers themselves with a profound personal awareness of social justice issues.

Like the other major religions, Buddhism did not spring fully formed from the mind and soul of one individual isolated in time. The Buddha is traditionally believed to have lived an innumerable number of previous lifetimes, both human and animal, and to be the fourth of five earthly buddhas. The number is less significant than the notion of one personage arriving at the right time and creating a sort of critical mass for the spiritual explorations and teachings of earlier masters.

Another interpretation of the same phenomenon might be found in the Hindu concept of the avatar*: a God-like figure who is reincarnated from time to time in human history, when he or she is most needed. The Buddha was human, but the key principle is similar: building on or reconfiguring existing laws, beliefs, and spiritual insights. Among the Western traditions, for instance, Jesus said that he built on the work of his biblical forerunners: "Think not that I have come to abolish the law and the prophets; I have come not to abolish them but to fulfill them" (Matt. 5:17). Muhammad later transmitted a teaching that built on elements of both Judaism and Christianity. In a similar way, the Buddha's experience grew out of the Vedic* philosophy prevalent in his day, which he radically reconfigured. (However, we should also note that both Hinduism and Judaism have continued to evolve in the two millennia since Buddha and Jesus and to deal in their own ways with the issues addressed by those two great teachers.)

Although the Buddha taught no reliance on a Supreme Being, he apparently accepted much of the existing worldview of ancient India, with its panoply of gods and demons. In Buddhist artwork and scriptures, Buddha is sometimes portrayed as preaching to or interacting with various deities. How is a Westerner to understand this apparent contradiction? Perhaps we can begin by noting that modern Buddhists practice their faith in different ways, just as Jews and Christians do. For many Asian Buddhists, elements of the supernatural surround and suffuse their religion, partly the result of Buddhism's having for so many centuries existed alongside the folk religions of India and China which are resplendent with gods and goddesses and demons and ghosts and all manner of supernatural happenings. Other Buddhists, particularly Western converts to Zen, choose to follow teachers who stress the nontheistic core of Buddhism, with its reliance on personal effort to achieve realization. Still others may interpret the teachings regarding celestial beings, demons, paradises, and hells as metaphors for various psychological and spiritual states, metaphors that help them in their practice but that they do not need to take literally.

In any event, the Buddha seemed to take as given the prevailing Indian beliefs in reincarnation* and karma* found in the Upanishads*, although he altered them as he incorporated them into his own philosophy. And so he didn't essentially question the Hindu vision of samsara*, the Wheel of Existences with its continuous cycle of rebirth over thousands of lifetimes. Instead, he was looking for a way to exit the wheel with some dispatch. In fact, according to some Buddhist commentators, the Buddha held a view of the gods similar to that of the Greeks, feeling that the gods suffered from the same frailties and failings as humanity. He saw Brahma*, one of the three great Hindu gods, being every bit as caught up in samsara as any mortal, so that even his status was not worthy of aspiration.

On the other hand, the Buddha rejected the Upanishadic concept of the Atman*, or individual soul, that seeks to realize its oneness with Brahman*, the Godhead. The Buddha conceived of individuals as dynamic aggregates of various states, or **skandas**—the constituents of personality, including the body-mind, feelings, ideas, subconscious predispositions, and conscious

85

awareness—which dissolve and are reconfigured constantly (much the way medical science now tells us that every cell of our body dies and is re-created about every three years). He believed that one has no permanent, identifiable soul, a doctrine known as **anatta** or **anatman**. All the while, he accepted the notion of karmic transfer from one form of existence to the next, but he saw each of these successive forms of existence more as a continuity of development toward completeness than as an individual "personality" or soul—today we might call this "conditioning." Different philosophical schools offer various explanations of how the law of karma functions while still maintaining the cardinal Buddhist position of no permanent, intrinsic identity. One way of stating Buddhist teaching might be to say that certain tendencies are created in the subtle structure of our being by all of our past actions, and those tendencies—as constantly changing and impermanent as the cells of our physical body—are what are transferred across limitless lifetimes.

But the Buddha found no useful purpose in such speculation since it would not lead to release from suffering. And since he didn't find theological disputation helpful in achieving liberation, the Buddha maintained a "noble silence" about metaphysical questions as to whether the universe is eternal or infinite, whether an enlightened being continues to exist in some form after death, and whether there is a Supreme Being on the order of the Hindu Brahman.

The Buddha was preoccupied with much more tangible problems, chief among them the suffering caused by the illusion of the separate ego and the rampant violence of the age into which he was born, violence that was a direct outgrowth of the illusory sense of separation between the individual and the rest of society. Ever since nomadic tribes had begun disrupting civilization sometime around the 5th millennium BC, spreading terror and destruction from Central Asia across northwestern India, Iran, the Middle East, and southern Europe, society had been extremely chaotic. The Buddha may not have been the first to propose the practice of ahimsa*, or nonviolence; it was also taught by Mahavira*, believed to be his direct contemporary and the founder of the Jain* religion, and was probably developed among the wandering ascetics of India who were in existence before the Buddha arrived. But in teaching that the conception of the "self" as an individual entity is an intellectual misapprehension requiring constant gratification and defense against other isolated selves, he burst the rationale behind violence as a way of life. Over the ensuing centuries, his teachings of nonviolence and compassion helped transform much of Asian society into a far more peaceful, refined, and spiritually liberated culture.

✸ THE STORY SO FAR

The tradition of Buddhism began in the 6th century BC with the historical personage born **Siddhartha Gautama,** but better known by a variety of titles including **Shakyamuni, Tathagata,** or just the **Buddha,** the Enlightened One. The legend of the Buddha's life has acquired plenty of variations and embellishments over the years, but the basic facts are accepted as traditional, including the dates of his birth and death (563–483 BC by Western reckoning, 624–544 according to Sri Lankan tradition).

The story of the Buddha's birth is as encrusted with myth and fable as that of any God-figure in human history. For instance, he is said to have issued from his mother's womb stating that his cycle of rebirths was about to end. Again, some Buddhists piously accept the fables as Christians accept the Christmas narratives, while others choose to focus on the truths beneath the myths. We do know with some certainty that the Buddha was born to a royal family in northern India, in the foothills of what is now Nepal. Siddhartha Gautama led a sheltered existence in the court of his father, **Shuddhodana,** the king of the **Shakya** clan, who shielded him from any encounter with aging, sickness, death, or the ascetical Hindu monks of the time.

According to the legends, Siddhartha bore the traditional 32 marks of an Enlightened One, and soon after his birth a soothsayer named **Asita** predicted that he would become, in the words of one commentator, "either a king whose chariot wheels would roll everywhere, or a preeminent sage who would set rolling the wheel of the good law throughout the world." Shuddhodana, a member of the warrior-ruler caste, preferred the royal vocation and provided his son with three palaces and anywhere from 10,000 to 40,000 dancing girls to keep his mind firmly rooted in the "real" world. But, as so often happens when manipulative fathers groom their sons to take over the family business, Siddhartha rebelled.

Legend states that at 16 he married a beautiful young princess named **Yasodhara,** by whom he fathered a son, **Rahula.** He is also said to have had several more "official" wives. Esoteric or Tantric accounts (see later in this section) insist that the dancing girls were in fact well-trained sexual partners who sometimes combined their talents to perform the so-called yogini chakra with Gautama, during which he made love simultaneously with as many as nine women.

But by the age of 29, Gautama had come across aging, sick, and dying men outside the palace. These encounters with mortality blew down his father's carefully constructed house of cards, horrifying the young Siddhartha with the realization he later verbalized as "every living thing must decay." How could he enjoy his life of pleasure once he knew it all must end eventually? Hedonism having lost its appeal, Gautama was struck one day by the self-possessed and tranquil figure of a passing monk. The ascetic seemed to have found an answer to the dilemma of human pain and mortality, and Gautama determined to become a monk himself. Leaving behind his wife and child, he renounced the riches and pleasures of the palace and went in search of deliverance from suffering.

According to traditional accounts, for a while the future Buddha practiced two yoga meditation traditions, which he then decided did not show him a way to permanent release from suffering. For the next six years he practiced the asceticism of the yogis of that time and place, nearly starving himself to death in the process. Finally he came to the conclusion that asceticism in and of itself was not the answer. No matter how much he fasted, he eventually had to replenish his body so that he could continue traveling and learning. Furthermore, the logical conclusion of denying the physical body is death. But the principles of reincarnation dictated that he would return in another body and be forced to repeat the process ad infinitum. During his last, life-threatening fast, he realized that enlightenment could be reached only through the vessel of the body, and there was a limit to how much deprivation his body could safely endure. And so Gautama abandoned the extreme asceticism he had been practicing in favor of what came to be called a **Middle Way** between devotion to pleasures of the senses and complete denial of them.

Accepting a bowl of rice and milk that was offered him, he ate, and his strength began to return. He then went and sat at evening under a nearby pipal or fig tree (now known as the **Bodhi**, or **Bo**, tree, or "Tree of Wisdom"), refusing to move until he had become "enlightened" and had discovered the

Images of the Buddha abound throughout Asia, from northern India to the ends of Indonesia, showing the Enlightened One in various stages of his life and in different postures indicating his roles as teacher, protector, contemplative, or compassionate one. This 2nd-century AD stone sculpture from Gandhara in northwestern India shows the Buddha at the height of his ascetical phase, an unusual subject for depiction and remarkably naturalistic compared to other, more ethereal Buddhas. Some art historians feel that later Greco-Roman depictions of Christ, particularly the Christ of the Passion, were influenced by Buddhist paintings and statues such as this.

SCALA/ART RESOURCE

secret of release from suffering. In the early morning hours he realized the nature and cause of suffering and the way of release from these causes that constituted his enlightenment. He came to understand that one could be freed from suffering in this life by moderating its real causes: passionate craving, hatred, and ignorance. Some Buddhists speak of completely removing **trishna** (Skt. "thirst," or "craving"), while others emphasize that ignorance—falsely conceiving a permanent, independent self—leads to craving and hatred, and hence to all suffering. According to legend, after sitting in meditation, the Buddha looked up at the morning star and said, "How wonderful. How wonderful. All things are enlightened exactly as they are!" He continued meditating for another 49 days.

All agree that he experienced **nirvana,** a Sanskrit word meaning "blown out," like a candle, representing the extinguishing of all craving. According to tradition, the Buddha was tempted by **Mara,** the Evil One, to keep this insight to himself and continue to realize the bliss of nirvana, shedding his body and forgoing a return to the physical world. (One myth has it that the gods themselves were so disturbed by this prospect that they sent Brahma to convince the Buddha to go forth and teach what he'd just learned.) The Buddha chose to wander the land for the next 45 years, begging food and shelter and teaching in the vernacular to men and women of all castes (a parallel with Moses*, who wandered in the desert with the Israelites for 40 years before he died and his people were allowed to enter the Promised Land).

That the Buddha taught all comers was in itself a radical departure from the religious conventions of India, which aimed to keep spiritual knowledge esoteric and to allow only members of the highest caste (brahmans*) to become priests. Further, the Buddha's Middle Way relied on ethical conduct and compassion for fellow humans rather than on the external ceremonies and costumes and philosophies of Brahmanic Hinduism. The establishment of monasteries and orders of monks replete with costumes, ceremonies, liturgies, and hierarchical ranks came later in the development of Buddhism. Although this ritualism may seem at odds with the Buddha's belief that rituals in and of themselves did not transform people, many Buddhists find value in ceremonies that have developed for taking various kinds of vows or for venerating the Buddha or other figures in the Buddhist iconography. Many modern Buddhist teachers, especially in America, view ritual as a way of transcending the ego and at least in part as an aid to meditation practice.

Buddha himself traveled with a small group of monks, known as **bhikshus** (Skt. "mendicants"), who begged for food and shelter as they went. (The Buddha's original **sangha,** or community, represents perhaps the first formally disciplined monastic order in the world.) The earliest Buddhist communities consisted of lay disciples and **renunciates**—those who renounced the world in its more material manifestations. Both groups included women, many of whom were considered to be enlightened, although the first formal order of female monks, or nuns (**bhikshunis**), was founded only after the Buddha's death by his stepmother.

THE NUNS' STORY

Historically, both women and men were achieving enlightenment from the earliest days of Buddhism to the present time. Early nunneries were well supported by Buddhist kings and wealthy communities, patronage falling off only later in the first millennium of Buddhism. But as in Christianity and Islam, the founder's acceptance of women was not always shared by his followers, as described here by an American convert to Buddhism who spent several years as a Buddhist nun in India.

There has been much discussion amongst Buddhist scholars as to which statements attributed to the Buddha were actually the words of the Buddha and which should be attributed to the monks (some of whom were obviously misogynists) who followed and wrote down what the Buddha is supposed to have said hundreds of years after his death. I. B. Horner in her scholarly book *Women Under Primitive Buddhism* makes an extensive study of the relationship between Buddhism and women. According to her research on the subject of women's acceptance into the monastic order, it seems that the Buddha was torn between his cultural conditioning and the Hindu social system, which clearly and unequivocally considered that women should be primarily child-bearers and servants to their family, and his conviction that women were as capable as men of attaining enlightenment. Although there was the precedence of Jain nuns, the idea of women living a religious life outside of the family was still thought to threaten social stability. The subordination of nuns to monks was most likely a compromise allowing women to pursue the spiritual path ascribed by the Buddha without completely disregarding the conventions of Hindu society of the day. . . .

Women were provided under Buddhism with an alternative to female servitude; although they were subject to males, they were no longer chattels of their fathers and husbands. The life of a Buddhist nun also provided a positive alternative for unmarried and widowed women, who were considered to have little status in Hindu society. . . .

The Buddha protected nuns from exploitation by monks by saying that the nuns should not be called upon to sew, dye, or weave for the monks. Neither could the monks take for themselves donations made to the nuns.

—TSULTRIM ALLIONE, *WOMEN OF WISDOM*

Some early bhikshus dwelt in the forest, moving from place to place, while others formed stable communities on the outskirts of various towns and villages. The latter eventually developed into monastic orders with monasteries and temples. By that time, negative attitudes toward women had developed among the orders—just as they would among Christian monastic orders hundreds of years after the death of Christ.

✳ ROLLING THE WHEEL

When the Buddha preached his first sermon, following his enlightenment, in the Deer Park at Sarnath, usually titled "Setting in Motion the Wheel of the Dharma," he put forth the **Four Noble Truths** that he experienced in the course of his enlightenment:

1. All existence involves suffering (**duhkha**).
2. The cause of suffering is craving (trishna).
3. Release from suffering (nirvana) comes through eradicating passionate craving for material or sensual satisfaction.
4. The way to achieve that release is the **Noble Eightfold Path.** These eight ways of right being encompass right understanding, thought, speech, action, livelihood, effort, mindfulness, and concentration.

Because of the way these four truths are formulated, some Westerners mistake Buddhism for a largely negating, pessimistic, and moralistic religion. But in keeping with his Middle Way, the Buddha spoke of different kinds of happiness—the happiness of sensory pleasures as well as of renunciation, of the family and of the monk. Scholars point out that his word *duhkha,* usually translated as "suffering," also has overtones of "impermanence," "insubstantiality," and "discontent," giving it less the sense of pain than of the fleeting and illusory nature of existence.

Furthermore, two of the Buddha's basic teachings are to do no violence to any sentient being and to strive for the liberation of all others. Perhaps for this reason, as much as for the Buddha's teaching of the irrelevance of worldly striving, Buddhism has proven to be the least warlike of the major religions.

After 45 years of preaching, at the age of 80, the Buddha died. Although he vowed never to take a life, he was not a strict vegetarian, since as a self-declared mendicant he was bound to eat whatever was offered him. The story goes that although he knew the pork given him by a smith named Chunda was tainted, he ate it anyway, so as not to hurt the feelings of his humble host. His last words are said to be "All composite things are decaying. Work out your salvation with diligence." (*Composite* refers to the belief that all objects and people are composed of various changing and changeable factors, both psychological and physical.)

The Buddha left no writings. All Buddhist scriptures are based on accounts of his life and teachings passed down orally by his disciples from generation to generation. Traditionally, the accounts were committed to writing—in Sanskrit and in **Pali,** a Sanskrit-derived Indian dialect that may have been close to that spoken by the Buddha—within 100 years of the Buddha's death, but modern scholarship places the dates closer to the 2nd or 1st century BC. The written records of his sermons and dialogues are known as **sutras,** similar in format to Hindu sutras*, but closer in spirit to the Christian Gospels*.

❋ THE THREE VEHICLES

The process of development of the Buddha's message probably began immediately following his death. After the conversion to Buddhism of the third emperor of India, **Ashoka** (c. 273–237 BC), who ruled all but the southernmost part of the Indian subcontinent, Buddhism spread across most of India. According to tradition, Ashoka was horrified at the human toll taken by his conquests in pursuit of a unified Indian empire, and he embraced the Buddha's teachings of nonviolence. His edicts in support of the Buddhist precepts against harming humans and animals and in favor of religious tolerance were engraved on large rocks and stone pillars for all the people to read. Vegetarianism became state policy.

Between 200 BC and AD 200, Buddhism gradually divided into a number of schools and subschools to which the pejorative term **Hinayana**

("Lesser Vehicle") was applied by members of the second major branch, who called their school **Mahayana** ("Great Vehicle"). Among the Hinayana, the only surviving school is the **Theravada** ("Teachings of the Elders"), which spread south and east from India into what is now Sri Lanka, Southeast Asia, and Bangladesh. The Mahayana probably developed between 100 BC and AD 100, traveled east and north in the 1st century to northwestern India and the Himalayas, Central Asia, and China, later to Korea and Japan, and in the 7th century to Tibet. The modern Theravada tradition does not accept the term *Hinayana* to describe its views, which in a number of points do differ from the scholastic traditions called Hinayana; however, the term is convenient if used without prejudice.

Both Hinayana and Mahayana accept the basic tenets of Buddhism, but Hinayana stresses the liberation of the individual from the cycle of existence. The Hinayana ideal is the **arhat,** or fully liberated being who experiences nirvana at the attainment of arhatship. Perhaps influenced by Hindu bhakti practices, Mahayana developed the ideal of everyone becoming a bodhisattva and then a buddha endowed with omniscience and compassion and the ability to help limitless beings through rebirth in samsara. This belief is predicated on an individual's limitless lifetimes and the development of limitless abilities with which to help others achieve enlightenment, including the miraculous power to read minds and know one's own and others' previous lives. A **bodhisattva** ("enlightenment hero") is a being who, out of compassion, has made a vow to reach enlightenment for the sake of others and who by definition is on the path to buddhahood. Bodhisattvas exist at various levels of development over many lifetimes; in the Mahayana tradition there are earthly and transcendent bodhisattvas. The former are still ordinary beings, male or female, who are developing their skills at helping others; the latter, who could also be called celestial or angelic bodhisattvas, are possessed of perfect wisdom and are no longer subject to samsara. Avalokiteshvara and Samantabhadra (discussed later in the chapter) are two of the most important. Transcendent bodhisattvas can also be female, and few celestial beings are more highly revered by Tibetan Buddhists than **Tara** ("Savior"). The embodiment of the feminine aspect of compassion, in one legend she is said to have sprung from the tears of Avalokiteshvara,

All bodhisattvas are devoted to compassion, so Avalokiteshvara, as the Bodhisattva of Compassion, occupies a special place in the hearts of all Mahayana Buddhists, especially in the Tibetan tradition, where he is considered the patron and guardian of the entire country and where the Dalai Lama is believed to be his manifestation. Avalokiteshvara, in turn, is a manifestation of the power of Buddha Amitabha, whose image is visible in his crown. The literal meaning of the name Avalokiteshvara is disputed: "The Lord Who Looks Down" and "One Who Hears the Sounds [i.e., Supplications] of the World" are two interpretations. Traditionally, he took vows to free all beings from suffering, and his help is sought in times of great danger. So intense was his compassion that he vowed that if he became discouraged in his efforts to liberate all living beings, his body should be ripped into 1,000 pieces and his head torn into 10; when this in fact happened, he called out to Amitabha for help. Amitabha, his spiritual father, caused the fragments to become 10 heads and 1,000 arms, each with an eye in the palm, the better to see where he was needed. In one hand he holds a mala or rosary for counting his special mantra, "Om mani padme hum." The two hands clasped in front of his chest in the prayer mudra also hold the wish-fulfilling jewel. Most images of Avalokiteshvara show him with 11 heads (counting one of Amitabha) and four, six, eight, or ten arms (rarely 18 as in this 18th-century Nepalese bronze), representing his 1,000 arms, which in turn are symbolic of his boundless compassion.

WERNER FORMAN/ART RESOURCE

95

who wept as he looked down from his celestial realm at the suffering beings who continued to grow in number despite his best efforts to save them. Tara has 21 forms, most notably **White Tara** and **Green Tara,** her peaceful and fierce manifestations, respectively.

Theravadins believe that both men and women can attain arhatship but that monastic vows are a prerequisite—the laity must first be reborn as monks. Mahayanists also have a strong monastic tradition, but they hold that the bodhisattva path to buddhahood can be practiced by both laity and monastics, male and female.

The understanding of nirvana itself in these two schools also differs substantially. For Theravadins, nirvana is the extinction of craving, a one-shot deal that accompanies complete liberation from the bonds of trishna. Mahayanists, on the other hand, believe that by the bodhisattva's very postponement of the bliss of nirvana, he or she has realized *true* nirvana—that is, a condition of total detachment from any selfish craving, including the craving for eternal bliss. However, the description of a bodhisattva as one who apparently postpones his or her enlightenment is taken by some Buddhists as a metaphor to describe the compassionate ardor with which a bodhisattva is motivated; of necessity, he or she would probably realize enlightenment before others because of their very aspiration to help them. Mahayanists avoid making any ultimate separation of nirvana from the world of sense experience, as indicated by the phrase "Nirvana is samsara and samsara is nirvana." This leads to many questions about the Buddha's relationship to nirvana, put succinctly by the 2nd-century Patriarch **Nagarjuna:** "What is the Buddha after his Nirvana? Does he exist or not exist, or both, or neither? We never will conceive it!"

In the mid-2nd century, Nagarjuna, a South Indian and one of the land's greatest intellects, founded what is considered the first Mahayana school, the **Madhyamika** ("Middle Way"), whose main premise is that no affirmation of the nature of things is possible, thus proving their illusory essence. This was summed up in the line from the *Prajnaparamita Sutra* that has become a commonplace Buddhist chant (recalling the biblical creation story in which God created the world from the formless void, or *tohu wa-bohu):* "Form is emptiness, and emptiness is form."

The second major Mahayana school was the **Yogachara** ("Application of

NAGARJUNA AND THE FERRYBOAT

The Sanskrit word *yana* means "vehicle" and refers specifically to the ferryboat so invaluable in carrying travelers across the often treacherous streams and rivers of tropical India. It is similar to the raft referred to by the Buddha as useful for crossing the river (representing samsara) to get to the other shore (enlightenment). Nagarjuna is known for his interpretations of the *Prajnaparamita Sutra* (literally "Sutra of the Wisdom That Reaches the Other Shore"), the basic scripture of all schools of Mahayana Buddhism. In his writings, he distinguished between what he considered the simpler vehicle of Hinayana and the more sophisticated vehicle of Mahayana, although both sets of teachings are attributed to the Buddha. The major difference is that, from the Mahayana viewpoint, once you've reached the other shore, concepts such as austerity, attachment, and enlightenment appear significant only to the beginner. And so it would be a mistake to talk about nirvana and samsara as different states, or even about enlightened versus unenlightened beings. This premise, paradoxical as it sounds, leads Mahayanists to accept that all beings are already buddhas but don't realize it, although they have the potential to realize that nature.

Yoga"), which opposed certain philosophical points of the Madhyamika but also emphasized the use of yogic practices, especially meditation. Yogachara set the stage for the development of the third major vehicle of Buddhism, **Vajrayana** ("Diamond Vehicle"), which evolved in northwestern and southern India starting in about AD 500 and worked its way east to China, Japan, and especially Tibet, where it played a prominent role in the development of Tibetan Buddhism. Vajrayana is actually the esoteric version of Mahayana and is sometimes called the Esoteric or Tantric Vehicle. Rather than wait the limitless lifetimes required by the Mahayana ideal of the bodhisattva, Vajrayana seeks to achieve buddhahood right now, in one lifetime. It works on a subtle level of reality, employing what in the West is often pejoratively called magic but which amounts to very advanced yogic techniques including visualizations of archetypal embodiments (e.g., of compassion, wisdom, or purification) or even of death, out-of-body states, and rebirth.

The spirits and subtle beings, including ghosts and demons, who populated indigenous Indian culture were absorbed and transformed into peaceful and fierce deities who are viewed by some practitioners as metaphors of various psychological states. The female principle began to receive its due as well. Female bodhisattvas such as Tara and Prajnaparamita were venerated. The **dakini,** or "skywalker," in Indian folk belief a flesh-eating demoness who fed on the remains of the dead, was transformed into a manifestation of the inspiring power of consciousness which can be called on by practitioners to help them both in their spiritual practice and in their everyday life.

Visions of celestial buddhas and bodhisattvas revealed in meditative trance were given names and iconographic representations, and these figures were venerated in the later Vajrayana tradition. Some practitioners view them as actual celestial beings, others as manifestations of their own internal energy or psychological states, but in both cases they are invested with an elaborate iconography, and their depiction in paintings, thangkas, and statuary makes up a vast and visually powerful body of Asian art.

The Buddhist Tantra on which much of the Vajrayana is based developed in northern India around the same time as Hindu Tantra, beginning in about the 6th century AD, and was influenced at least in part by Hindu esoteric yoga and Tantric practices, the use of mantras* and mandalas*, and the Hindu emphasis on the necessity for having a guru lead the student through complex practices and advanced realizations. Among the practices that Buddhist Tantra developed were some that were magical and sexual in nature. With its emphasis on moral precepts, early Buddhism had tended to undervalue the body in general and sex in particular. Mahayana Buddhism, however, had added to early Buddhism's teaching that all composite things are characterized by suffering, impermanence, and no-self (or anatman), the further condition of emptiness (**shunyata**). Contrary to appearances of substance, all things were said to be empty of any qualities; by extension, therefore, all things were also neither inherently pure nor impure, good nor evil. This understanding tended to remove much of the sense of taint that had adhered for Buddhists to commerce, art, science, women, and sexuality. If all things were essentially empty, then one could associate with them without becoming contaminated.

Ultimately the principle of emptiness cleared the way for working with previously taboo sense pleasures, much as Hindu practitioners of Vamachara*, or the left-hand path, worked in the dangerous realm of indulgence in meat, alcohol, and sexual intercourse. The aim of Tantric practice in general is to transform ordinarily dangerous or forbidden practices, as well as pain and suffering, into tools for enlightenment, and in the Vaj-rayana this approach was elaborated into a highly complex and sophisticated system. The Tantric masters wrote their discoveries down in ritual manuals called Tantras and passed them on in secret to their followers, often writing in code to shield their works from the uninitiated. Semen was called "camphor" or "elixir," for example, and the male and female genitals were referred to as "thunderbolt" and "lotus."

The idea behind Tantra was to undermine and finally eradicate the poisonous nature of the forbidden acts and the passions themselves by using the very things that are to be avoided by ordinary folk, much like becoming immune to poison by ingesting tiny amounts of it in a controlled fashion (the concept behind homeopathic* medicine). Such a course to enlightenment required great skill and experience, and so the guidance of a master was considered essential. By the 9th century, Tantra had become rather respectable and began to shift from actual physical practices involving sexual intercourse, alcohol, and other taboos to purely contemplative practices. These practices are still very much in evidence in the various Vajrayana schools that flourished in Tibet and have since been brought to the West. Images of bodhisattvas holding skullcups filled with blood or having intercourse with their consorts form a prominent part of the iconography of Tibetan Buddhism today, an iconography that seems to have an especially strong appeal for Western converts.

Some modern Buddhist teachers prefer to emphasize that the three vehicles of Buddhist dharma (Hinayana, Mahayana, and Vajrayana) should not be conceived as separate, opposed paths based on dogma and geographical location, but as three overlapping stages of development, both personal and historical, each with its own significance. And in fact, the

A LOVE SUPREME

Certain Tantric works contradict the view of the earliest schools of Buddhism that monastic celibacy is a requisite on the path to enlightenment. One of the most extraordinary is *The Pilgrimage of Sudhana*. In it, a young seeker named Sudhana encounters a number of spiritual guides from all walks of life, including three beautiful women. The first two are highly spiritualized, but the third, Vasumitra, is considerably earthier.

A worshiper of Agni, the God of Fire, Vasumitra had golden skin, black hair, and a well-proportioned body decorated with countless jeweled ornaments. Her practice was to appear to men in the most pleasing form they could imagine and then transmute their intense passion into spiritual bliss. Some men could be transformed just by seeing Vasumitra, but others needed to hold, kiss, or embrace her fully. Vasumitra likened her practice to "a womb that receives all sentient beings without rejection"; she used passion to lead men to the "ultimately dispassionate," urging them to enter her in order to go beyond the physical. Vasumitra instructed Sudhana in the skill of achieving dispassion by using all the senses.

—JOHN STEVENS, *LUST FOR ENLIGHTENMENT*

Tibetan orders of Buddhism in which Vajrayana is most prominent practice the teachings of all three vehicles simultaneously. The American Buddhist scholar Robert Thurman, a close associate of the Dalai Lama, refers to Hinayana as the Monastic or Individual Vehicle because it "provided institutional, doctrinal, and contemplative methods for individuals to liberate themselves from egocentric delusion." On an individual level, this vehicle corresponds to a personal focus on the external precepts against killing, lying, stealing, drinking, and sexual misconduct with the goal of achieving one's own liberation. The Universal Vehicle (Mahayana) developed "because it fostered the messianic resolve to liberate all beings by transforming the entire universe into a realm of peace, abundance, and happiness." As individuals refine themselves through monastic self-discipline, they begin to see that they are exactly the same as other beings: limited, confused, suffering. At this point, the Universal Vehicle is helpful in developing a willingness to work with oneself in order to help others more effectively. The Apocalyptic or Tantric Vehicle (Vajrayana) was created "for those whose messianic resolve becomes too intense for them to bear waiting for limitless eons before becoming able to free others from suffering." The Apocalyptic Vehicle makes use of esoteric practices (described later in the section on Tibetan Buddhism) to speed up the process of becoming a bodhisattva. It also teaches that buddhahood is not some special state but is who we are already, except that we don't believe it and don't express it. Through the practices of Vajrayana, a practitioner dares to believe that he or she is a buddha and to relate to himself or herself as a buddha.

At least among the lay population, Buddhism requires no special initiatory rites or ceremonies akin to the upanayana* of Hinduism, Christian baptism* and confirmation*, or the Jewish rites of circumcision* and bar/bat mitzvah*. Still, many lay Buddhists choose to take vows of various sorts, for which rituals do exist, or simply to acknowledge themselves publicly to be Buddhists by reciting the threefold refuge formula—announcing that, until enlightenment is realized, they are taking refuge in the Three Jewels (triratna) of Buddha, Dharma, and Sangha. The Jewels represent the Buddha as teacher, his teachings as "medicine," and the sangha or community of fellow Buddhists. Official acceptance into a sangha generally requires the recitation of the refuge formula under the guidance of a monk, whereupon the entrant may receive a "dharma name," Sanskrit words referring to some essential aspect of his or her nature or aspiration. Zen Buddhists, for instance, perform a ceremony called jukai (Jap. "receiving the precepts") at which they commit themselves to the Three Jewels and the ten main precepts and to do good, avoid evil, and work for the liberation of all beings.

The moral guidelines of Buddhism vary: Theravadins teach five precepts, requiring one not to destroy life (human, animal, or even insect), not to steal, commit adultery, lie, or drink intoxicants. Mahayana has ten main precepts, adding to those five gossiping about the faults of others, immoderate self-praise, giving spiritual or material aid reluctantly, aggression, and speaking ill of the Three Jewels. The precepts are generally followed by all Buddhists but are strictly binding on those who have taken monastic vows. Among American Buddhist converts, for instance, vegetarianism, chastity, and total abstinence do not appear to be mandatory. Buddhists who take the precepts more seriously still employ situational ethics in interpreting them. Drinking alcohol, but not to the point where it clouds the mind, or wiping out an infestation of rodents or insects that threaten health can be acceptable. Common sense and compassion are the final arbiters. From a Buddhist point of view, abortion is killing; but the Dalai Lama himself has said that an exception can be made "if the birth will create serious problems for the parent," adding that "abortion should be approved or disapproved according to each circumstance."

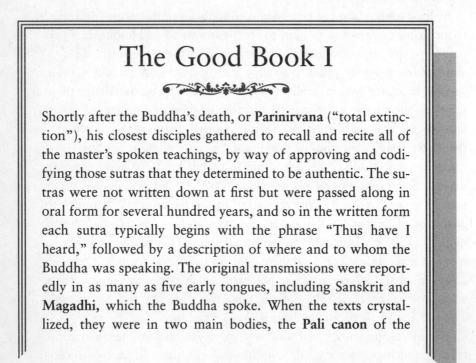

The Good Book I

Shortly after the Buddha's death, or **Parinirvana** ("total extinction"), his closest disciples gathered to recall and recite all of the master's spoken teachings, by way of approving and codifying those sutras that they determined to be authentic. The sutras were not written down at first but were passed along in oral form for several hundred years, and so in the written form each sutra typically begins with the phrase "Thus have I heard," followed by a description of where and to whom the Buddha was speaking. The original transmissions were reportedly in as many as five early tongues, including Sanskrit and **Magadhi,** which the Buddha spoke. When the texts crystallized, they were in two main bodies, the **Pali canon** of the

The sutras contain the words of the Buddha as recalled and passed on orally by his disciples and later written down. This paper scroll from the T'ang dynasty was found in the sealed library at the famous Caves of the Thousand Buddhas at Tun-Huang in central China, where over a thousand copies of the Lotus Sutra were discovered.
COURTESY OF THE LIBRARY OF CONGRESS

southern Theravada tradition and the Sanskrit of the northern Mahayana tradition.

The original sutras were divided into 5 collections known as **nikayas,** from the Pali word for "corpus." These 5 nikayas make up the **pitaka** ("basket") called the **Sutra-pitaka.** The fifth or **Khuddaka** nikaya, for instance, contains the famous *Dhammapada* (Virtue-path), 426 pithy verses of the basic Buddhist teachings, especially popular today in Theravadin countries. The same nikaya also collects the **Theri-gatha,** or songs of the female elders, some of the earliest enlightened women in Buddhism. The Buddha's most celebrated utterances are scattered throughout the sutras, such as his "Fire Sermon," which

T. S. Eliot used as a major source for Part III of *The Waste Land*.

Along with the Sutra-pitaka, the **Vinaya-pitaka** (accounts of the origins of the sangha and the rules for monks and nuns) and the **Abhidharma-pitaka** (Buddhist psychology and philosophy) make up the **Tripitaka** ("Three Baskets"). This is the Pali canon of southern Buddhist scriptures and is paralleled by the even more extensive northern Buddhist canon, which was probably written down later than the Pali canon but originated at about the same time.

Most of the scriptures have never been fully translated into English, which is understandable when we consider that no other tradition on earth has created a larger body of sacred texts. To take one example, the 40 sutras known collectively as the *Prajnaparamita Sutra* take up, in their Tibetan block print editions, 100 volumes of about 1,000 pages each. Set down in writing somewhat later than the Tripitaka, this sutra is believed by Western scholars to reflect elaborations on the words of the Buddha by Indian Buddhists beginning about 100 BC, and as late as Nagarjuna (2nd century AD). Mahayana Buddhist scholars, however, believe that the *Sutra* records the actual words of the Buddha but that the texts were removed from the human realm by gods and dragons for 400 years to allow time for the renunciative, monastic life to purify and prepare people for the messianic nature of its teachings. Over the centuries, abridged versions of this great sutra have appeared, from the extremely short *One Letter Sutra* (its text is the letter *A)* to versions of 8,000, 18,000, 20,000, and 25,000 lines. In its original form, called the *Great Mother,* it purports to be a complete record of Shakyamuni's audience on Vulture Peak Mountain, in which the Buddha states that he is only the latest of a line of avataric predecessors and constantly asserts that Prajnaparamita—the female embodiment of the *Sutra*—produced all the Buddhas and is their mother and instructor. It also gives us the classic

Buddhist mantra *Om mani padme hum* and predicts the coming of **Maitreya** ("Loving One"), the fifth and last earthly Buddha, who waits to emanate at some time in the future to help any who have not yet realized enlightenment. Besides the sutras, the Mahayana canon contains many **shastras,** treatises that interpret and comment on the philosophical statements contained in the sutras.

Most Buddhist sects are based on one or another sutra, e.g., Nichiren Buddhism, the Japanese sect whose followers chant their faith in the *Sutra of the Lotus of the Wonderful Law,* or *Lotus Sutra,* a key sutra of Mahayana Buddhism. The Chinese school of **T'ien-t'ai** ("School of the Celestial Platform") also bases its doctrine on the *Lotus Sutra.*

One of the most often quoted scriptures is a small section of the *Prajnaparamita* known popularly as the *Diamond Sutra*—somewhat easier to say than its Sanskrit name, the *Vajrachchedika-prajnaparamita Sutra.* The first part of that name actually means "diamond cutter," implying the penetration of the most impenetrable wisdom. Translated into Chinese in AD 401, the *Diamond Sutra* later became the first book ever printed (in 868), more than 5 centuries before the Gutenberg Bible.

Of all the Buddhist texts, the most popular in Europe and America, where it has sold millions of copies, does not directly present the teachings of the Buddha. Known in the West as *The Tibetan Book of the Dead,* a title coined by W. Y. Evans-Wentz, the American scholar who first translated it into English in 1927, the book's Tibetan name is **Bardo Thödol Chenmo** (The Great Liberation Through Hearing in the Between). It was originally committed to writing in the time of the 8th-century Buddhist master Padmasambhava, probably either written or collated by him. Subsequently hidden in caves, it was revealed in the 14th century by the Tibetan **Rigzin Karma Lingpa,** himself believed to be a reincarnation of Padmasambhava. The word *bardo* means, roughly, "suspended between" and refers to various states of consciousness experienced between death and re-birth. The *Bardo Thödol,* then, is nothing less than a guidebook to help dying and just-departed souls find their way through the potentially tortuous and confusing stages of the afterlife—or, more properly, between-lives. Reportedly based on the accounts of lamas who had total recall of their own between-lives expe-riences, the text is designed to be studied during one's life and to be read over the dying or newly dead. (Buddhism and Catholicism, with its last rites and funeral masses, are the only contemporary religions that feature services explicitly designed to help the souls of the dead make the transition from the bodily state.)

The *Bardo Thödol* gives very specific, detailed accounts of the journey from death to rebirth, dividing it into three distinct stages: the **Chikhai, Chonyid,** and **Sidpa Bardos.** Remarkable correlations between the first stage described in the text and modern accounts of near-death experiences* have been cata-loged in Raymond Moody's popular book *Life After Life.*

✳ ZEN: BUDDHISM MADE SIMPLE

One of the things that made the Buddha's teachings so radical, apart from his choice to preach to the masses irrespective of caste, is that he emphasized personal experience. In his sermons, he repeatedly urged the curious to "come and see," to investigate his teachings and techniques for themselves rather than to base their beliefs on faith. Since he did not teach belief in a Supreme Deity, he urged his followers to rely on them-selves for their salvation—in his words, to "be your own refuge."

Building on the meditation practices that he learned from the yogis and ascetics with whom he came in contact, the Buddha developed techniques that anyone with sufficient desire and commitment could learn. Without the intercession of priests, the average man or woman could achieve enlightenment by seeing through to the reality of their "true nature." Monks might assist the seeker, but priestly ritual was insignificant compared with the radical process of self-observation and ethical living.

Yet as time progressed, layers of commentary that accrued to his teachings and increasingly complex rituals were perceived by some as obscuring the power of Shakyamuni Buddha's original message. In response to that development, from time to time certain followers set out to clarify the religion and recover its essential energy and purity.

About a millennium after the Buddha's death, in the 6th century AD, **Bodhidharma** carried his teaching of Buddhism from India to China, where it became known as Ch'an—a shortened transliteration of the Sanskrit word *dyana*, meaning "meditation." This teaching is now known by its Japanese title, **Zen.** Over a century after Bodhidharma, the Chinese master **Hui-neng** (638–713) gave this new teaching a distinctly Chinese flavor, assimilating aspects of Taoism, and he is considered by some to be the real founder of Zen. (However, recent scholarship suggests that the legend of Hui-neng as an illiterate genius and Sixth Patriarch of Ch'an in China may be largely the construct of his disciple and promoter **Shenhui.**) But Buddhist monks had been infiltrating China via the trade route known as the Silk Road for hundreds of years before Bodhidharma or Hui-neng, subtly interacting with the philosophy of Taoism. Perhaps the fact that the Chinese mind was in many ways more practical and earth-centered than the Indian mind set the stage for the development and acceptance of Ch'an Buddhism. In any event, Zen is traditionally described in the classic saying of Bodhidharma "A special transmission outside the scriptures, not dependent on words and letters. Direct pointing to the mind of humanity lets one see one's own true nature." It is an attempt to bypass the centuries of priestly and scholarly accretions and return to the essence of the Buddha's approach: sitting meditation leading to enlightenment.

The 28th Patriarch in line of descent from the Buddha, and often referred to as the First Zen Patriarch, Bodhidharma was an extreme character. Some speculate that he was fed up with the calcification of Buddhist practice in India and left for China without naming a successor, effectively ending the Indian patriarchate. But after his new dharma met with a cool reception in the south of China, he set up shop at **Shaolin Monastery** in northern China. (In the same monastery, according to tradition, Buddhist monks developed **kung fu,** a form of Chinese ch'i-kung* exercises aimed at regulating body, mind, and breath. Although kung fu began as a system of spiritual exercises, it is now widely practiced as a martial art form. On the television series *Kung Fu,* David "Little Grasshopper" Carradine did his internship at Shaolin Temple.)

Once again, myth and legend are inextricably mingled with historical fact. At Shaolin, Bodhidharma began an extended period of sitting meditation. For nine years, according to legend, he sat facing a wall and refused to move, waiting for someone to take his new teachings to heart until finally his legs atrophied. (His austerity actually seems mild compared with that of the Christian saint Symeon Stylites*, who in the previous century in Syria sat atop a pillar 60 feet high and 6 feet wide for 37 years.) Bodhidharma was sitting **zazen,** a form of meditation done with the eyes half-closed and the attention focused on the breath, emptying the mind of all thoughts—or rather letting them float harmlessly by, like figures passing before a mirror.

After 9 years of this sitting, Bodhidharma was approached by a would-be disciple named **Hui-K'o** (487–593), who pestered him with a nagging problem. Hui-K'o had no peace of mind and desperately sought a way to achieve it. The Master kept putting him off, telling him that to achieve peace of mind required arduous discipline and work, probably more than the upstart was willing to do, and to go away. After standing in the snow and pleading for hours without getting a real answer, Hui-K'o in desperation hacked off his own hand and tossed it in front of Bodhidharma. This got the old guy's attention. "You're the one I've been waiting for," he said and agreed to take Hui-K'o as a disciple.

By 1100, Buddhism had largely disappeared from India proper, while Zen had spread through China to Korea and Japan. Beginning near the turn of this century, it was brought to America by Japanese Zen masters and has taken root here alongside the various Vajrayana schools known generically as Tibetan Buddhism. Along with daily sitting meditation, Zen emphasizes living in the present moment, without fear of the future or regret for the past. As the Buddha once said in explaining the manifest happiness and good health of his monks, "They do not repent the past, nor do they brood over the future. They live in the present. Therefore, they are radiant. By brooding over the future and repenting the past, fools dry up like green reeds cut down" *(Samyutta-nikaya).* This attitude, which in practice requires the most assiduous moment-to-moment awareness, has been oversimplified and distorted in popular American culture, especially during the 1960s and '70s with slogans like "Do It Now" and in pop songs like the Grass Roots' "Let's Live for Today." The real flavor of the Zen teaching lives in classic stories like those attributed to the Buddha himself.

One of the favorite teaching tools of Zen masters is the **koan,** a question or riddle that can't be solved by reason but that points to a deeper

THE ETERNAL NOW

One of the identifying characteristics of Zen is its emphasis on being alive in the present rather than dwelling in the past or fearing the future. But that requires full attention to the activity of the immediate present, or, in the words of the German Zen master Karlfried Graf Dürckheim, "to taste divine Being in the here-and-now." The following stories, three very ancient, one modern, attempt to convey this notion.

A man who was traveling across a field encountered a tiger. He fled, the tiger after him. Coming to a precipice, he caught hold of the root of a wild vine and swung himself down over the ledge. The tiger sniffed at him from above. Trembling, the man looked down to where, far below, another tiger was waiting to eat him. Only the vine sustained him.

Two mice, one white and one black, little by little started to gnaw away the vine. The man saw a luscious strawberry near him. Grasping the vine with one hand, he plucked the strawberry with the other. How sweet it tasted!

—PAUL REPS, *ZEN FLESH, ZEN BONES*

Two Buddhist monks, Tanzan and Ekido, were once traveling together down a muddy road. A heavy rain was still falling.

Coming around a bend they met a lovely girl in a silk kimono and sash, unable to cross the intersection.

"Come on, girl," said Tanzan at once. Lifting her in his arms, he carried her over the mud. Ekido did not speak again until that night when they reached a lodging temple. Then he no longer could restrain himself. "We monks don't go near females," he told Tanzan, "especially not young and lovely ones. It is dangerous. Why did you do that?"

"I left the girl there," said Tanzan. "Are you still carrying her?"

—PAUL REPS, *ZEN FLESH, ZEN BONES*

So what really matters is not just the practice of sitting but far more the state of mind you find yourself in after meditation. . . . I like the Zen story in which the disciple asked his master:

"Master, how do you put enlightenment into action? How do you practice it in everyday life?"

"By eating and by sleeping," replied the master.

"But Master, everybody sleeps and everybody eats."

"But not everybody eats when they eat, and not everybody sleeps when they sleep."

From this comes the famous Zen saying, "When I eat, I eat; when I sleep, I sleep."

—SOGYAL RINPOCHE, *THE TIBETAN BOOK OF LIVING AND DYING*

During a retreat open to the public at Zen Mountain Monastery in Mt. Tremper, New York, the conversation came around to sex. A visitor who had grown tired of the rather theoretical discussion of sex asked bluntly and with evident relish, "So, tell me, is there a Zen attitude toward fucking?"

Without pausing, the abbot of the monastery, John Daido Loori, Sensei, replied, "When fucking, just fuck."

(**Sensei** is the Japanese honorific for a Zen teacher who has received "dharma transmission" from a senior teacher. **Roshi** is another Zen honorific, the meaning of which varies by use but generally signifies a senior teacher with more experience or authority than a Sensei.)

truth. Perhaps the most familiar example, thanks to J. D. Salinger's use of it as an epigraph, asks, "What is the sound of one hand clapping?" Koans originated in China as questions between monks, often working side by side in the rice fields, and were later perfected as a teaching art by **Ta-hui Tsung-kao** (1089–1163). Their purpose is not so much to produce the right answer as to force the student to abandon the process of rational thought altogether, much like the goal of zazen. A variation on the koan is the **mondo** ("question and answer"), in which the student and master engage in a dialogue to the same end of eliciting the intuitive aspect of the student's mind.

The Zen that survives in Japan today is divided into two major schools, **Soto** and **Rinzai,** which developed between the 9th and 11th centuries in China as the **Tsao-tung** and **Lin-chi** schools, respectively. Lin-chi emphasized a rapid or short path to enlightenment that made use of koans, shouts, and compassionate whacks with a stick called a **kyosaku** ("wake-up stick") to startle the student into sudden awareness. Its founder was **Lin-chi I Hsuan** (d. 867), and, with him, the school of Ch'an that was to become Zen in Japan coalesced around the basic elements of training that would conclusively distinguish Zen from the other schools of Buddhism. Known for his straightforward language, Lin-chi derogated the practices that had developed of worshiping the Buddha and striving to become a bodhisattva. Speaking of the Buddha as just another bald-headed monk, he is reputed to have said, "If you meet Gautama, kill him," a classic restatement of the Buddha's teaching to work out one's own salvation. The Lin-chi school was introduced to Japan, where it was called Rinzai, by Eisai (1141–1215).

Tsao-tung, or Soto, was founded by **Tung-shan Liang-chieh** (807–69) and his disciple **Tsao-shan Pen-chi** and was transplanted to Japan by the great Zen master **Dogen Zenji** (1200–53) in the 13th century. Soto stresses silent practice (**mokusho**), the highest form of which Dogen called **shikantaza**—a state in which no aids to zazen, such as counting the breath or meditating on koans, are used, reverting to the way it was presumably practiced by the Buddha and his immediate disciples. Soto practitioners nonetheless are likely to use images of the Buddha and bodhisattvas in a worshipful way (as do Rinzai, for that matter, in the temple practices common among the Japanese masses). However, today koans

111

also play a role in Soto, just as silent meditation does in Rinzai; the difference is one of emphasis.

In Japan, Zen spread among the Samurai, where it led to the cult of **Bushido,** or the "Way of the Warrior," an association that one English Buddhist scholar has called "one of the more astonishing transformations of Buddhism." Zen was applied to the martial arts, especially archery (**kempo**) and swordsmanship (**kendo**), but also to the more domestic arts of calligraphy, flower arrangement (**ikebana**), and the tea ceremony (**cha no ya**). The goal of these practices is the same as that of zazen or koan study: an opening of the mind's eye, known as **kensho** ("seeing into one's own nature") or **satori.**

Technically, kensho and satori both mean enlightenment, but because

HIT ME WITH YOUR WAKE-UP STICK

The *Pi Yen Lu* (Blue-Green Cliff Record) is the oldest existing collection of Zen or Ch'an koans, redacted in the 12th century from earlier sources. It features about 100 examples, along with commentaries and explanations. A typical mondo involves the founder of Rinzai Zen and a dharma student and preserves an example of the sudden awakening that was the goal of Rinzai:

The head monk Ting asked Lin-chi, "What is the great meaning of Buddha's dharma?" Lin-chi came down from his seat, grabbed him, hit him with his hand, and pushed him away. Ting stood there stunned. The monk next to him said, "Head Monk Ting, why don't you prostrate yourself?"

As Ting proceeded to do so, he experienced profound enlightenment.

satori is the word traditionally used to describe the enlightenment of the Buddha and the early patriarchs, according to Buddhist scholars it implies a deeper experience of enlightenment. Does that mean there can be different *levels* of enlightenment? Why, yes, there can—just as there are said to be four stages in the development of nirvana.

The term **samadhi,** for instance, which in Hindu parlance means a blissful state of meditative union with the Absolute, in Zen refers to a state of intensely effortless concentration, but not necessarily of enlightenment, unless the person experiencing samadhi is *already* enlightened. And neither state should be confused with nirvana, the ultimate release from all craving realized by the Buddha.

The great Rinzai master **Soyen Shaku** (1859–1919) introduced Zen Buddhism to America in 1893 at the same World Parliament of Religions* in Chicago at which Swami Vivekananda* presented Vedanta*. Through the books of Shaku's student, the eminent Zen author **D. T. Suzuki,** Zen was popularized in the West. Today a half-dozen or more American-born Zen masters who are authentic lineage holders run Zen centers or teach. Among them are the following:

Philip Kapleau Roshi, founder of the Zen Center in Rochester, New York, and author of the extremely influential book *The Three Pillars of Zen,* now an independent teacher.

Bernard Glassman Sensei, a former aeronautical engineer who is currently abbot of the Zen Center New York in Yonkers. His unorthodox mingling of Zen with a profitable bakery and an ambitious housing project for the homeless, among other endeavors, has added further dimensions to the way Zen is practiced in the West.

Richard Baker Roshi, abbot of the San Francisco Zen Center from 1971 to 1983, at the time the largest and best-known Zen community in America, whose Tassajara Bread Bakery served as the initial model for Glassman's bakery. Baker resigned his post in 1983 under pressure from his own students after acknowledging affairs with women students, including his best friend's wife, and other inappropriate behavior. He now teaches in Colorado.

Jiyu Kennett Roshi, born in 1924 to Buddhist parents. In 1970 she founded the Zen Mission Society near the foot of Mount Shasta in northern California. She studied at Soto headquarters in Japan.

Charlotte Joko Beck, a former student of the Los Angeles–based Japanese master Maezumi Roshi, has become well known through her books *Everyday Zen* and *Nothing Special*. She teaches at the San Diego Zen Center.

Jakusho Bill Kwong, a Chinese American Soto priest and abbot of the Santa Rosa, California, community's Soto Zen Buddhist temple, Genjoji, or the Way of Everyday Life Temple. Kwong's teacher was the eminent **Shunryu Suzuki Roshi,** author of the classic guide to meditation *Zen Mind, Beginner's Mind*.

❋ ON THE ROAD TO TIBET

After America was opened to Buddhism at the end of the 19th century, only a handful of schools succeeded in spreading beyond the confines of small groups of Asian immigrants who carried their practices with them. Zen was the first to come over, seeded by Soyen Shaku and later popularized by American authors like **Alan Watts, Allen Ginsberg,** and **Peter Matthiessen.** The next to arrive were several orders of Tibetan Buddhism and to a lesser extent Nichiren Buddhism.

Tibetan Buddhism, sometimes referred to as **Tantric** or **Esoteric Buddhism,** took hold in Tibet in the 8th century. A century earlier, the first king of a united Tibet had introduced Buddhism into his country through marriages to Buddhist princesses from Nepal and China. He made Buddhism the state religion after converting from **Bon,** the Tibetan folk religion that combined shamanism, ritual divination, exorcism, and burial rites with belief in the doctrine of rebirth. However, Buddhism failed to catch on until a later king in 747 invited the Indian Buddhist sage **Padmasambhava** to oversee the completion of a royal monastery. Padma (popularly known as **Guru Rinpoche,** or "Precious Guru") also began the first community of Tibetan **lamas,** a word meaning "superior" and referring to a spiritual teacher who may be either lay person or monk.

To help popularize Buddhism with the Tibetan people, Padma incorporated certain superficial aspects of the Bon religion, adopting some local Tibetan deities as well. He may even have transformed some of the Bon deities and demons into **lokapalas** (Skt. "guardians of regions"), protective deities that embody the extreme forces of nature. They follow in the Tantric tradition of the "fierce deities" known as **dharmapala** (Skt.

WHAT IS THIS THING CALLED SATORI?

Although Buddhism is rife with major branches, schools, orders, sects, and subsects, the goal of most of them is pretty much the same, whether it's called kensho, satori, enlightenment, seeing one's true nature, Buddha nature, or the nature of mind. But describing that state has proven elusive for even the most gifted Buddhist adepts and scholars. The following explanation, from a living Tibetan master, is perhaps as simple and elegant as any.

It is said that when Buddha attained enlightenment, all he wanted to do was to show the rest of us the nature of mind and share completely what he had realized. But he also saw, with the sorrow of infinite compassion, how difficult it would be for us to understand.

For even though we have the same inner nature as Buddha, we have not recognized it because it is so enclosed and wrapped up in our individual ordinary minds. Imagine an empty vase. The space inside is exactly the same as the space outside.

Only the fragile walls of the vase separate one from the other. Our buddha mind is enclosed within the walls of our ordinary mind. But when we become enlightened, it is as if that vase shatters into pieces. The space "inside" merges instantly into the space "outside." They become one: There and then we realize they were never separate or different; they were always the same.

—SOGYAL RINPOCHE, *THE TIBETAN BOOK OF LIVING AND DYING*

"guardian of the teaching"). These are usually depicted as furious, frightening beings whose real purpose is to protect the dharma and its teachers from hostile forces and powers. (**Mahakala,** for instance, shown with a

*His name (sometimes written Padma Sambhava) means "Lotus-born," referring to the legend surrounding his birth in the country of Uddiyana in northwest Kashmir (modern Pakistan or Afghanistan). A direct emanation of Amitabha Buddha, who appeared as a radiant eight-year-old boy on a lotus petal in a lake in Uddiyana, Padmasambhava became a Buddha and an adept. He learned the power of longevity, and tradition holds that he was already a thousand years old when he was invited to Tibet by the 8th-century Buddhist King Trisong Detsen. The myths of Padma are clearly rife with magic and mystery, especially in Tibet and Bhutan where he is often revered as sangye nyipa, the "Second Buddha." He is said, for instance, to have arrived in Bhutan on the back of a flying tiger that landed near the top of a sheer, 3,000-foot cliff, marked today by the precariously placed Takstang ("Tiger's Nest") monastery. He is renowned for having spent years meditating in wildernesses and the great cremation grounds of India and the Himalayas, where, according to legend, flesh-eating demonesses called dakinis fed on the remains of the dead; he is also said to have attained his highest realization there and to have converted many of the dakinis. In Vajrayana practice, dakinis are female skywalkers, angelic or wrathful figures who help the practitioner integrate those powers released by visualization and other esoteric practices. As in so much of Padma's life story, reality and magic are more confoundingly intermarried than in a Latin American novel. His iconography combines elements of his many attainments, both as a Buddha and an adept, as in this 17th–18th-century gilt-bronze figure. In his right hand he holds the vajra (Tib. dorje), the double thunderbolt that represents the indestructible energy of enlightenment which can transmute anything, including suffering and evil. In his left hand he holds the skull-cup (symbolizing the death of the ego and the realization of shunyata), in which is a small vase holding the elixir of immortality. Cradled in his left arm is the **khatvanga**, an adept's staff on which are three heads (freshly severed, decomposing, and skull), symbolizing the conquest of the three poisons (desire, hate, and ignorance), and the trident (not clearly visible here), emblematic of his mastery of the three channels (ida*, pingala*, sushumna*) of the yogic nervous system. The trident may have served as a similar symbol in much earlier images of Shiva*, the pre-Aryan yogic deity. Despite the fabulous legends, Padmasambhava was undoubtedly a historical personage who changed the face of Tibet and added untold depths of richness to the practice of Buddhism.*

WERNER FORMAN/ART RESOURCE

black body and terrifying visage, is a guardian of the Kagyu schools and the Dalai Lama; he is believed to be a manifestation of Padma himself.)

Padmasambhava's system eventually became known as the **Nyingma** (Tib. "Ancient") school, the oldest of Tibet's four principal schools of Buddhism. The most advanced form of the Nyingma teaching is known as **Dzogchen** (Tib. "Great perfection"), which, vastly simplified, holds that the pure and perfect nature of mind already exists within each of us and needs only to be recognized.

The esoteric aspects of Tibetan Buddhism derive from Padmasambhava's origins as a professor of tantric yoga at the Buddhist monastic university in Nalanda, India, and his reputed skills in occultism*. (One example is the **yoga of the dream state,** a once-secret practice whereby initiates learn to become awake in the midst of their dreams and a forerunner of lucid dreaming* as fostered by Patricia Garfield, Stephen LaBerge, and others.) The story goes that Padmasambhava was originally invited to Tibet to exorcise demons that were causing earthquakes and stymieing the king's attempts to build a Buddhist monastery there. Padma expelled the demons, the earthquakes quit, the locals were suitably impressed, and he was given control over the monastery. He is also traditionally credited with having originated the *Bardo Thödol Chenmo* (popularly if inaccurately known in the West as the *Tibetan Book of the Dead),* a guidebook for passing through the afterlife experience, viewed as a series of varying states of consciousness between death and rebirth (see THE GOOD BOOK I).

There are four categories of Tantric practice:

Kriya ("action") **tantra** focuses on actions, thoughts, and words, and requires strict diet, meditation, and celibacy.

Charya ("performance") **tantra** is akin to the Hindu practice of Vamacharya* with its use of the five forbidden things (meat, mudra, fish, alcohol, and sexual intercourse).

Yoga tantra requires the use of yogic practices, visualizations, and initiation by a guru.

Anuttara-yoga ("unexcelled yoga") **tantra** takes yoga tantra to the extreme, seeking to develop psychic powers. The identification of the worshiper with the object of worship, akin to the union of lover with beloved, lends Tantra much of its sexual imagery, as seen in drawings of the **yab-yum** motif. In the Vajrayana tradition, yab-yum symbolizes the unity of the masculine principle, or skillful means (**upaya**), with the feminine principle, or wisdom (**prajna**). The anuttara-yoga tantra is the most sophisticated and involves very advanced, very precise visualizations of one's own death and reincarnation toward the end of developing greater wisdom and compassion.

The **Kagyu** (Tib. "Oral transmission") school has its roots in the Tantric systems transmitted by the 11th-century Indian master **Tilopa.** His teachings were passed in succession to **Naropa,** who for a time was abbot of Nalanda University. From Naropa they went to the Tibetan **Marpa** and then to **Milarepa,** the greatest of the Tibetan yogis, who is said to have put the *Bardo Thödol* into its current form and to have kept himself warm during the frigid Tibetan winters with the "fury-fire" yoga he had learned from Marpa. His many disciples dressed like him in only light cotton garments and sang the folk songs into which he put many of his teachings. As the first "ordinary" Tibetan believed to have achieved buddhahood in a single lifetime, Milarepa was a great inspiration to the common folk of that country.

The central teaching of the Kagyu school is the **Mahamudra** (Skt. "Great Seal"), revealed to Tilopa by the bodhisattva **Samantabhadra,** corresponding to the Dzogchen of the Nyingma. The best-known representative of the Kagyu school after Tibetan Buddhism was brought to America in the 20th century, and the first Tibetan to have a major personal impact here, was **Chögyam Trungpa Rinpoche** (1939–87). (As an honorific, **Rinpoche** signifies a senior abbot or lama believed to be a reincarnation of earlier lamas.) Besides his work as a teacher and author of numerous books, Trungpa established a Buddhist college and learning center in Boulder, Colorado, called **Naropa Institute** after the great Indian teacher. Unfortunately, Trungpa died of various maladies that probably resulted from his chronic alcoholism. The American regent he appointed as his successor, **Ösel Tendzin,** then died of AIDS after having passed the infection to one of his students. Despite the ensuing scandal, other leaders of the Kagyu school stepped in and began the process of reforming their **Karma Kagyu** subschool, which continues to flourish in the States. In Tibet, the Kagyu developed into at least four more major and eight minor schools, of which few still exist.

Meanwhile in America, the Nyingma order became established in

The term yab-yum, Tibetan for "father-mother," describes the union of masculine and feminine principles, usually depicted as a male and female deity in the act of coitus. In this conception, the masculine symbolizes upaya, the "skillful means" by which a bodhisattva leads other beings to liberation, including skill in expounding the teachings of Buddhism. The feminine principle is synonymous with prajna, an immediately experienced intuitive wisdom that goes beyond mere intellect and is emblematic of universal unity. The enlightenment that can result from the blending of these two different energies is likened in this image to the bliss of sexual union. Here Samantabhadra (Skt. "All Good"), one of the great bodhisattvas of the Mahayana, is shown as the primordial Buddha, whose dark blue body symbolizes shunyata, with his white consort. In Japanese tradition, where he is known as **Fugen**, Samantabhadra is prepared to assume any form to help liberate human beings; this includes becoming a courtesan to teach those who are unable to overcome their sexual desires.

SCALA/ART RESOURCE

San Francisco, and the **Geluk** order, to which the Panchen and Dalai Lamas belong, has gained a following as well. The Dalai Lama's cause has been championed by his best-known American student, the actor Richard Gere, which may or may not be a point in the order's favor. The fourth major school is the **Sakya,** perhaps the least known outside of Tibet.

The Tibetan schools placed a great deal of emphasis on teachings about reincarnation and the identification of certain individuals as the reincarnation of previous lamas. Known as **tulkus,** these reincarnated individuals are important in maintaining the lines of succession in the four major orders as well as a number of other, unrelated lineages. The best-known tulku is probably the Dalai Lama. Mongolia was converted from shamanism to Buddhism in the late 16th century by **Sonam Gyatso** (1543–88), who was given the title **Dalai Lama** ("Oceanic Wisdom Master") by the Mongol Altan Khan. The title was then applied retroactively to his two previous incarnations, back to **Gendun Drub** (1391–1475), now called the first Dalai Lama. (The fourth Dalai Lama was Mongolian, as is the word *Dalai.)* Each Dalai Lama is considered the reincarnation of the previous one, right up to the fourteenth and current lama, **Tenzin Gyatso** (b. 1935). Since the fifth, **Losang Gyatso** (1617–82), the Dalai Lama has also been considered the direct emanation in human form of **Avalokiteshvara,** the Bodhisattva of Compassion. Losang also bestowed the honorific title of **Panchen Lama** (Skt.-Tib. "Great Scholarly Master") on his master, whom he considered to be an incarnation of Amitabha Buddha. Until the 20th century, the Panchen Lama played a solely spiritual role in Tibetan Buddhism.

The reincarnational relationship holds true for the tulkus of the Karma Kagyu, the oldest such lineage, who are known as **karmapa.** The first karmapa, **Düsum Khyenpa,** died in 1193, and the sixteenth, **Rigpe Dorje,** in 1982. Mongolian Buddhism follows a similar scheme. Its spiritual leader or God-king is called the **Bogd Gedeen.** As with the Tibetans, the Mongolian monks were scattered or killed during the Communist Chinese invasion. The ninth and current Bogd Gedeen is a Tibetan living in India.

Tibet is extraordinary on a number of levels. By the 17th century, as the secularization of society was well under way in Europe, China, and Japan, Tibet was combining its secular government with a powerful and highly developed chain of Buddhist monastic orders. Meanwhile, all three major teachings of Buddhism—Hinayana, Mahayana, and Vajrayana—were being expounded pretty much simultaneously by these orders with varying points of emphasis and a minimum of sectarian conflict. And in the process, Tibet developed a rich array of spiritual teachings and practices, from the broadly devotional to the deeply esoteric, allowing the faithful to participate at highly nuanced, individualized levels of involvement and sophistication. Most of these teachings are available today in the West, offering advanced yogic techniques and meditation practices, multidimensional visualizations, the engagement of the senses with chanting, the use of brightly colored **mandalas** (circular designs used in meditation) and **thangkas** (iconographic scroll paintings), devotional prayer and services ranging from the simple to the elaborate, and especially helpful practices in the realm of death and dying. The increasing appeal of these teachings in America has been highlighted by the surprising success of *The Tibetan Book of Living and Dying* by a previously little known, Oxford-educated Tibetan lama named **Sogyal Rinpoche.**

Having been established for a longer time in America, Zen has produced more American dharma-successors with authentic ties to Asian Buddhist lineages. However, the Tibetan tradition has also begun to produce American dharma-successors, notably **Pema Chödrön,** an American Buddhist nun and one of the foremost students of Chögyam Trungpa. In 1986, he named her director of Gampo Abbey, a monastery for Western men and women in Cape Breton, Nova Scotia.

The apparent tragedy of the devastation of Tibet's people and rich spiritual and artistic treasures by the Communist invaders is seen by many Tibetans, including the Dalai Lama, as serving a necessary, if extremely painful, function. At the very least, it has forced many highly realized lamas to seek refuge in the West, spreading their teachings to a new audience at a time of rampant confusion.

❋ TURNING JAPANESE

Long before the reforms and innovations of Zen arrived in Japan in the 12th century, Mahayana Buddhism was officially introduced there from Korea in 552, as part of a gift offering from a Korean monarch looking for military assistance. Despite fierce initial resistance from native clergy and practitioners of Shinto, Japan's ancient folk religion, Buddhism was gradually accepted and established in the imperial court. By the **Nara** period (710–94), six schools had been brought over from China: **Sanron** and **Jojitsu** (both established in 625), **Hosso** (654), **Kusha** (658), **Kegon** (736), and **Ritsu** (754); Jojitsu, Kusha, and Ritsu were Hinayana, the other three Mahayana. Of the six, only Hosso, Kegon, and Ritsu have survived in modern Japan, and these have only historical significance and slight membership.

Confucian* ethics and Taoist yin-yang* philosophy had already penetrated these essentially Chinese schools along with belief in various deities. At the beginning of the 9th century and with the full patronage of the imperial court, Nara Buddhism had achieved such power and influence that it was rife with corruption and lavish expenditure, becoming an increasingly aristocratic religion. To counter that development, during the **Heian** period (794–1185) Emperor Kwammu sent two men named Saicho and Kukai to China to explore more viable forms of Buddhism.

Saicho (posthumously called **Dengyo Daishi,** 767–822) studied a form of Buddhism called T'ien-t'ai in China, where it had been realized by **Chih-i** (538–97) along with Ch'an and Tantric Buddhism. He combined them into a system that became known as **Tendai,** the Japanese pronunciation of its original name. Like its Chinese forerunner, which was built on Nagarjuna's Madhyamika doctrine, Tendai emphasized the value of a morally pure life and the universality of Buddhism. Salvation could be attained by even the lowliest lay person because everyone possesses or, more precisely, *is* **Buddha-nature** (**bussho**). This means that a substrate of perfection and complete awareness is already immanent in all beings, they just don't know it the way an awakened person does. Tendai also taught the doctrine of One Reality, positing a single, Absolute Reality behind the manifest multiplicity of the universe, a primordial, transcendent Buddha of which the historical Buddha is but a temporal embodiment. Unlike earlier schools of Buddhism, which saw earthly cravings as the cause of suffering and a stumbling block to enlightenment, the Tendai interpretation of the *Lotus Sutra* views earthly craving as not essentially different from enlightenment. In Tendai, enlightenment does not consist of extinguishing craving but is a state of mind that is experienced by transforming innate desires.

Saicho taught a meditation practice called **shikan,** which encompassed what is known as **vipassana** meditation, an analytical examination of and insight into the true nature of being. He founded his sect in 805 and established monasteries on Mount Hiei that became the starting points for most of the major Buddhist innovators to come. **Kukai** (later known as **Kobo Daishi,** 774–835) founded the **Shingon** school based on the esoteric teachings of **Hui-kuo** in China, where they were known as Chen-yen. From his monastery center on Mount Koya, he taught not only a universalized form of Buddhism open to all classes but also the arts and sciences, Confucianism, and Taoism. Shingon's Tantric or esoteric practices, which included mystic formulas, ritualistic hand gestures (mudras*), and the promise of wealth, appealed to the common folk.

The most popular school of Buddhism in China and Japan today is commonly known as **Pure Land.** The Indian cosmology amid which Buddhism grew already included many images of heavenly environments, viewed largely as pleasant resting places between reincarnations during the endless cycle of rebirths. As Mahayana Buddhism began to develop during the 2nd and 1st centuries BC, related visions of buddha-fields or buddha-paradises were conceived as existing in outer space, each ruled over by a particular buddha who provides individuals with the fulfillment of their needs. These include the **Tushita** (Skt. "Contented" or "Joyous") **Heaven,** where buddhas dwell who have only one more rebirth to go through, the most prominent being Maitreya, the last of the five earthly Buddhas, expected to appear in the distant future. But Tushita was later supplanted in China by **Sukhavati** (Skt. "Blissful"), also known as the Western Paradise, a kind of halfway house on the road to nirvana. This is the heavenly realm of **Amitabha** (Skt. "Infinite Light"), a Mahayana figure unknown in earlier Buddhism. He is imagined as 90 million miles tall, overseeing a vast land flooded by his incomparable radiance, located countless universes to the West. The faithful who are fortunate enough to be reborn in this realm of fragrant flowers and gem-bearing trees may each sit on an individual jewel lotus and study the dharma with Amitabha himself, free from all sadness, misfortune, or pain, progressing toward their inevitable buddhahood and nirvana.

The Pure Land school, based in part on the *Sukhavati-vyuha,* or *Sutra of the Land of Bliss,* which describes Amitabha's paradise in exquisite detail, was essentially founded in AD 402 by a Chinese monk named **Hui-**

yuan (336–416). More exclusively devotional than most previous forms of Buddhism, Pure Land emphasizes deep faith in the power and compassion of Amitabha, who achieved buddhahood conditioned on his vow to cause everyone who places trust and devotion in him to be reborn in Sukhavati, where there will be no painful or inferior modes of existence. There will also be no women, since all women are reborn there as men; hence, the pleasures of love will be absent. The doctrine of Pure Land is somewhat similar to the Protestant notion of justification* by faith (as opposed to good works), and Hui-yuan's aim was much the same as that of the Protestant reformers: to simplify devotion in an age of religious decadence and complexity. Pure Land devotion consists mainly of what the Japanese call **nembutsu,** recitation of the name of Amitabha (called **Amida** in Japan) and visualization of his paradisaical land, which is enough to guarantee rebirth there.

Other forms of Pure Land practice add devotion to **Kuan-yin** or Avalokiteshvara and **Ta-shih Chih** or **Mahasthama,** bodhisattvas representing the compassion and wisdom, respectively, of Amitabha; statues of all three show up in Chinese Buddhist temples. Pure Land Buddhism was part of the teachings brought over to Japan in the 9th century by Saicho and his disciple **Ennin (Jikaku Daishi,** 793–864), but it didn't take hold of the popular imagination until the 12th century, during the **Kamakura** period (1192–1335). Its simplicity and undemanding practice—no meditation required—made it a natural for the masses. The first Japanese sect was the **Yuzu Nembutsu,** but it was supplanted by the **Jodo** ("Pure Land") sect founded in 1175 by **Honen** (1133–1212), the first to institutionalize the practice of nembutsu as an independent school of Buddhism. Hoping to convey an "easy path" as an alternative to the time-consuming practices of asceticism, meditation, and sutra study that the common people had no time for, Honen required only recitation of the phrase *Namu Amida Butsu,* or "Veneration to Amida Buddha." Perhaps for the first time in Buddhism, a school placed more significance on the intervention of an outside force than on personal effort or the effects of karma, something that would appear to go against the Buddha's admonition to "be your own refuge." But Honen believed that traditional Buddhist disciplines were no longer effective in the decadent era in which he lived. In such a time, he held, one's own efforts—whether good works or religious exercises—are of no avail. One must rely on a higher power, in this case, Amitabha/Amida Buddha. Nonetheless, Honen admonished his followers to observe the monastic regulations and to respect the sutras.

Honen was followed by a disciple named **Shinran** (1173–1262), whose **Jodo Shin** ("True Pure Land") sect eschews monasticism, although its leadership is hereditary. He believed it unnecessary to call on Amida constantly; even once was enough to ensure rebirth in the Western Paradise and further repetitions were expressions of gratitude for Amida's assurance of salvation. Jodo Shin is the leading school of Buddhism in Japan today, with no religious rules whatever that distinguish its members from ordinary folk. Its two main subschools are **Otani** and **Honganji.**

The distinguishing practice of **Nichiren** and **Nichiren Shoshu** Buddhism, two similar devotional sects based on the teachings of the fiery Japanese reformer Nichiren (1222–82), is the continual chanting of the phrase *Namu myoho renge kyo:* "I trust in the *Sutra of the Lotus of the Wonderful Law*" (also called the *Lotus Sutra*). A fisherman's son who became a monk of the Tendai sect at age 15, Nichiren came to the conclusion that the only true Buddhism was that of the *Lotus Sutra,* which contains the words of the Buddha himself, as opposed to other schools supposedly based on the writings of Buddhist adepts or commentators. (For the Tendai sect, the *Lotus Sutra* is one of several key scriptures, whereas in Nichiren it is the only one.) But Nichiren went even further, attacking the doctrines of established Buddhism, including Shingon, Amidism, and Zen, and teaching that anyone who chanted *Namu myoho renge kyo* would achieve buddhahood and paradise on earth, for which he was ostracized and persecuted. Nichiren's beliefs had a strongly nationalistic aspect; he felt that Japan could prosper only through teaching the *Lotus Sutra* and that he was the nation's savior as well as an incarnation of two bodhisattvas. He demanded the dissolution of all sects but his. In fact, his intolerance and extreme nationalism seem to represent a departure from the essence of Buddhism. Followers of Nichiren today imagine Japan as the center of a buddha-world that will in time encompass the globe, a truly universal religion.

The Nichiren chant is often accompanied by drumming, something that may have helped attract a number of prominent American musicians to its practice, most notably jazz pianist Herbie Hancock and pop singer Tina Turner. Nichiren Shoshu developed in 20th-century Japan based on the teachings of a Nichiren disciple named **Nikko.** A modern lay organization of the Nichiren sect, called the **Soka Gakkai** ("Value Creation Society"), was founded in 1930 by **Tsunesaburo Makiguchi** (1871–1944), who died in prison because of his refusal to participate in state-sponsored Shinto rituals during the war. Its theology has been described as fundamentalist and intolerant Buddhism.

Under the shepherding of his principal disciple, **Toda Josei** (1900–58), Soka Gakkai grew exponentially and became involved in Japanese politics, in the process reviving what had been marginal interest in Nichiren. Today it claims 8 to 10 million adherents in Japan and another 2 million worldwide, mostly from the lower and lower-middle classes, appealing to them with the simple provision that they may chant for money, a new car, anything they want. Initially leftist, anticorruption, and pro-welfare, Soka Gakkai accumulated vast wealth and was recently exposed for corrupt financial practices of its own. In 1991, the main temple of Nichiren Shoshu in Japan excommunicated the entire membership of Soka Gakkai, forcing its members to choose between orthodox Nichiren and their disenfranchised sect. Most have stayed with the parent group, which is now known as Soka Gakkai International and has about 300,000 members in the U.S.

✳ TRANSMISSION SPECIALISTS

How do Buddhists explain all these variations on the original preachings of the Buddha, which were reportedly codified at the first Buddhist Council of 480 BC? One tradition holds that during his lifetime the Buddha transmitted certain secret doctrines to one of his disciples, **Mahakashyapa,** who alone was capable of understanding them. The transmission occurred while the Buddha was preaching on **Vulture Peak Mountain,** and it was not necessarily verbal but rather "from heart-mind to heart-mind," a passing along of the dharma on a level of subtlety not easily explained in words. Presented with a wreath of flowers by Brahma, who requested that he explain his teaching, the Buddha simply took one of the flowers and twirled it between his fingers while smiling. No one present understood the gesture except Mahakashyapa, who smiled back at the Buddha. The transmission acknowledged, Mahakashyapa after the Buddha's death became the First Patriarch of Buddhism in India.

The esoteric knowledge was then passed on from patriarch to patriarch, to surface when the faithful were ready to receive it—beginning in the case of Zen with the 28th patriarch, Bodhidharma. Similar principles can be applied to the emergence of tantric teachings in India or, at a later date, of new teachings or interpretations like the Tibetan and Pure Land schools. The 2nd-century Indian patriarch Nagarjuna, for instance, is said to have found teachings in the realm of the serpent spirits, or **nagas,** who protected them until the time was right for their transmission. In Tibet, the tradition of **termas,** or hidden sacred texts rediscovered by **tertons,** who propagated them at the appropriate time, is a reflection of the earlier Indian tradition. Not all Buddhists accept all the rediscovered teachings or grant them equal authenticity—Buddhist scholars aim to define those texts that are to be believed as the actual words of the Buddha and those that are to be interpreted—but most accept the principle of delayed transmission.

Because so many different traditions, cultures, and languages interact and coexist within Buddhism, no one simple explanation can be expected to cover every event or set of beliefs. Even the devotional practices of Pure Land, which appear to be at odds with the core teachings of the Buddha, can perhaps be traced back to the tradition of venerating the Buddha and the early Buddhist saints in small memorial monuments called **stupas.** Originally serving as royal funerary monuments, stupas came to represent the eternal Buddha presence. And so, although no concrete proof may exist in some cases, one can argue that lines of transmission of one sort or another do run from the later traditions back to the time of the Buddha.

Was the Buddha human or divine? Most Buddhist apologists refuse to view the historical Buddha as a Supreme Being or incarnation of the Deity, or even as a savior similar to Christ who suffered and died for the sins of humanity. In this, they hold, Buddhism is unlike most other major traditions, which insist that their founder is either God or an incarnation of God or was inspired directly by God. Instead, most Buddhists view the Buddha as he saw himself: a man fully awakened and complete just as he was, who became enlightened by his own efforts, not because of any divine nature. They stress the fundamental tenet of his teaching that all beings contain within themselves the ability to become enlightened, to realize their Buddha nature, and so to transcend suffering and death as he did.

A similar conception is common among many American converts to Buddhism, particularly Zen, who find the self-salvation ethos a happy antidote to the often dogmatic and devotional religions of their childhood, whether Christian or Jewish. By clearing the mind through meditation, they feel they can achieve enlightenment without what they consider to be the theistic mumbo jumbo of Western religion. As admirable as such a belief may be, it overlooks the rich tapestry of painted and sculpted images by the thousands, not only of Shakyamuni Buddha but of other, primordial and transcendent Buddhas, of numberless angelic bodhisattvas, male and female, of pure lands and buddha-paradises of all description which constitute the fabulous art and culture of much of Asia. For the majority of Buddhists today, especially in Asia, the Buddha has always been and will probably continue to be both a means of salvation and an object of great faith and devotion, as the prevalence of temples, stupas, home altars, and the many images of him clearly show. If he is not actually considered to be God in the Western understanding of an all-powerful Creator, he is nonetheless believed in as a refuge from the perils of earthly existence.

❊ SHINTO: THAT OTHER JAPANESE RELIGION

As in China, religion in Japan is an amalgam of three distinct yet interrelated traditions. Confucianism* entered Japan from the mainland in AD 405 through the Korean scholar Wani and served mainly as a guide to ethics and filial relationships; Buddhism came from China by way of Korea during the 6th century; and **Shinto,** the native folk religion of the islands, which dates from before the Christian era, still survives in a variety of forms. One reason Shinto has proved of so little interest to Westerners, as opposed to, say, Zen Buddhism, is that it is viewed as essentially a state religion based on ancestor worship, the ancestors in this case being the Japanese imperial family. Try to imagine a state religion in Great Britain based on ancient Celtic or Druidic rituals but serving as a

MAN OR SUPERMAN?

The understanding of who the Buddha was is far from easily summed up. At best, the complexities of belief can be laid out lucidly, as they are here by a prominent English author and teacher of world religions, who also points out that the "utilitarian agnostics" of the West who embraced Buddhism as a system of self-improvement and self-salvation "would have been shocked to see inside a Buddhist pagoda, with its idols and joss-sticks."

It is common nowadays for Buddhist apologists, in East and West, to claim that the Buddha was only a man, or a man like us, but no Buddhist thought this in the last two thousand years, since the Buddha was for him the object of faith and the means of salvation. Even the 13th century Japanese reformer Nichiren, who rejected many of the later developments and celestial beings of northern Buddhism in favor of a return to the Buddha, saw him on the Vulture Peak surrounded by thousands of gods and men as depicted in the Lotus scripture.

Buddhism has often been called agnostic or even atheistic, in modern times, and it did reject or ignore much Hindu theology. Hindu gods appear in the Theravada scriptures, Brahma, Indra and the like, but they are lay figures or attendants upon the Buddha who occupies the center of the stage. None of these gods is the Supreme Being, and the Buddha did not acknowledge them as such. He himself was not called a god, indeed that would be unworthy, since the gods are not yet fully enlightened but are caught up in the round of transmigration. But the Buddha is above all these beings and is called "Teacher of gods and men." Functionally he is the Supreme Being, and in a confession of faith that dates from early years men cried, "I go to the Buddha for refuge," as Hindus go to Krishna or Shiva for refuge.

—GEOFFREY PARRINDER, *THE WISDOM OF THE EARLY BUDDHISTS*

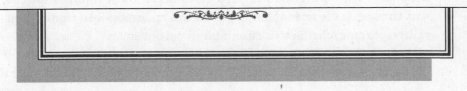

vehicle for the worship of Queen Elizabeth, Prince Charles, and Princess Diana. Then ask whether Japanese intellectuals would be interested in the study and practice of that religion.

But the image of Shinto as ceremonial state religion is inaccurate. Its name is actually derived from the Chinese terms *shen* and *tao,* meaning "Way of the Gods," and was coined retroactively in the 6th century to distinguish the native religion from the new import, Butsudo, or "Way of the Buddha." Yet the practices and beliefs of Shinto are ancient, combining nature-worship and animism* (the belief that personal, intelligent spirits inhabit almost all natural objects, from stones and rivers to animals, trees, and hills) with ancestor worship* (which, as in the Chinese and Aryan traditions, often included the glorification of tribal heroes) and a great emphasis on ritual cleanliness. All these features are still part of modern Shinto and of Japanese cultural life in general. Ritual ablution, for instance, is performed not only before worshiping at a shrine but also in purifying restaurants and other public places with cones of salt (reflecting the saltwater with which Japan is surrounded and which was used in the earliest purification rites).

Shinto was the national religion of Japan until about the 9th century, when it came to be subsumed by Buddhism for almost a millennium. But Shinto developed its own distinctive theology during the **Muromachi** period (1392–1568) and reemerged as the official state religion following the Imperial Restoration of 1868. That revolution ended the virtual usurpation of power by successive dynasties of **shoguns,** or military governors of Japan, abolished the shogunate, and ushered in the modern era. During the **Meiji** period (1868–1912), Shinto was elevated above all other religions, which were forced into virtual seclusion for a time, and was used as a tool of government to advance various Japanese war efforts. It might be more accurate to say that Shinto and the concept of the emperor's divinity became a kind of shield for the Japanese militarists, who had transformed Japan from an isolated society to a military and industrial power capable of defeating China and Russia. The militarists succeeded; until World War II, Japan had never lost a war. But the cost was terrible, not least for Shinto, which was transmogrified from a naturalistic peasant religion to a cult of blind patriotism.

Archaeological evidence indicates that the aboriginal inhabitants of the Japanese islands, the Stone Age **Ainu,** were gradually pushed out by waves of invasion from the mainland via Korea between about 300 BC and AD 300. The story of the Neolithic invaders is told in mythological form in the earliest written chronicles of Japan, the *Kojiki* (Ancient Records), completed in AD 712, and the *Nihongi* (Chronicles of Japan), compiled in 720. Although the works claim to cover Japanese history back to 660 BC, scholars now feel that their narratives begin just before the Christian era. Both books recount the legends of the divine founding of Japan and detail many of the deities of the **Yamato** people, who gradually occupied the islands, plus a number of historical figures through the 7th century.

Shinto boasts "eight hundred myriads of gods," only a fraction of whom are listed in the *Kojiki*, many with evocative compound names such as Princess Blossoming Brilliantly Like the Flowers of the Trees, the Heavenly Alarming Female, or Prince Wave Limit Brave Cormorant Thatch Meeting Incompletely. Shinto deities are generally called **kami,** a word of mysterious origin and meaning that can refer to any awe-inspiring spirit: the personification of natural forces (rain, wind, earthquakes), animate or inanimate objects (birds, animals, trees, mountains, food), deified souls of the dead (especially emperors, heroes, and sages), or the human qualities of mercy, courage, or fear. A better translation of *kami* might be "sacred," anything that appears strange, powerful, uncontrolled, or incomprehensible, whether advantageous or disruptive. (Older variants *kamu* or *kupu* are probably related to the Polynesian term *tabu*, sometimes spelled *kupu*, from which *taboo* comes, suggesting a link to the South Seas Islands.) The current pantheon incorporates ancient Yamato kami with the spirits worshiped by the Ainu before they were pushed out.

Shinto ideas of kami are free of the kind of transcendence found in Christian and Islamic conceptions. There is no sense of an Absolute, of an omnipotent and omniscient Supreme Being, predestination, or other Western notions. And yet the polytheism of Shinto, as one scholar has said, is the kind "where all the *kami* are thought of as working together harmoniously, so that in effect the universe is just as unified as in the religions claiming to be monotheistic." Also missing from the Shinto scheme is the standard religious concept of a creation divided into good and evil, or God versus Satan; kami may be helpful or troublesome, but these are not taken as moral characteristics.

Among the chief Shinto kami are **Amaterasu Omikami** ("Heaven Shining Great August Deity," or Sun Goddess), **Tsukiyomi** (Moon God), and **Susanu** ("Impetuous Male," or Storm Cloud God). All three were created by the Sky Father **Izanagi** ("Male Who Invites") after the death of his sister-wife, the Earth Mother **Izanami** ("Female Who Invites"). This primeval pair, still popular in modern Japan, with the help of certain phallic rites also begot the Japanese islands and the kami, until the fire kami burned his mother's birth canal, killing her. From earliest times, phallicism was even more prominent in Japan than in India, and stone and wooden phalli as tall as seven or eight feet were common sights in the countryside until 1868, when the Meiji government decided they were bad for tourism.

JAPANESE EXISTENTIALISM

Shinto is not without an ethical basis, although its ethics tend to be relative, calling on the Shintoist to search his or her heart and mind for the intention behind an act. Since Shinto offers no categorical code of right and wrong, just as it posits no one omniscient God, the course of right conduct can change from era to era and from situation to situation. Some sects do advocate codes of moral and ethical conduct absorbed from Confucian ethics or Buddhist precepts, but these vary so widely as to elude classification. And genuine Shinto ethics, as described in the following excerpt, have more in common with existentialist notions of "bad faith" and "situation ethics" than with most Eastern systems of thought.

There is no absolute word handed down from a transcendent source of authority. There is nothing resembling the Law of Moses or the Code of Manu. The word Shinto means "the way of the kami," but man is capable of walking that way. He is not called to an impossible task. The basic attitude toward life is expressed by the word *makoto*. *Makoto* is common both to kami and to men. The term is usually translated as honesty, conscientiousness, or truthfulness. However, if these are taken in a narrowly ethical sense, something of the essential Shinto flavor is lost. There is a dynamic, psychological dimension that is very important. He who practices *makoto* is "true" to the total situation. He is in harmony with kami and is doing his very best under the circumstances. "Truth" here is not an abstract something but a concrete living-out of the present situation. The search for Truth in the Western philosophical sense of an "Ultimate Truth" is foreign to the life of Shinto. Many Japanese call this attitude a purely Western one. Truth in the sense of *makoto* involves an inner searching of the heart which is just as important as the outer confronting of the situation.

When a man is "untrue" to the situation and does that which is harmful to himself or to others, it is not because there is some source of evil in himself. It is because of lack of proper awareness.

—FLOYD H. ROSS, *SHINTO: THE WAY OF JAPAN*

According to the *Kojiki*, Amaterasu magically produced a son, **Ho Mimi,** whose son **Ninigi no Mikoto** ("Prince Rice-ear Ruddy Plenty," or God of the Ripened Rice Plant) descended to Earth with a whole entourage of priests and nobility and founded the imperial dynasty. (In all likelihood, the heaven from which Ninigi and company descended referred to Korea to the north and west.) His great-grandson, **Jimmu Tenno,** became the first ruler of the Yamato, the powerful clan that dominated central and south Japan. Jimmu may have been a historical figure who lived c. 40 BC; Tenno ("Heavenly Sovereign") is the title attached to all subsequent Japanese emperors, who are more commonly referred to by Westerners as the **Mikado.** The Yamatos became both rulers and the chief priests of the nature religion, and legends about them formed the basis for popular belief in the divine origin and superiority of the Japanese race.

The emperors were endowed with the **Three Sacred Treasures,** symbols of power that were given to Ninigi when he descended to earth: a **mirror,** a **sword,** and the **jewels.** The mirror was a symbol of Amaterasu, the sword was won by her brother Susanu, and the jewels were said to number 500. The treasures were passed on from ruler to ruler, and without them the emperor or empress could not occupy the throne. (Several copies have been made, some of which were destroyed, and it is not clear if the originals still exist, although they are said to reside in the Inner Shrine of Amaterasu at Ise.) The same dynasty has ruled Japan continuously for 2,000 years, probably the oldest active dynasty in the world; their claim of descent from the Sun Goddess was a major part of the Japanese war effort in the 1930s and 1940s, right down to the image of the sun on the national flag. Implicit in this Japanese nationalism is the ancient belief that Japan is the center of the world and that it is the Japanese mandate to spread its religion to all humanity.

The Confucian doctrine that the Chinese emperor was the Son of Heaven may have influenced Japanese mythology and led to the Shinto cult of the emperor. But in the Confucian tradition the emperor was chosen because of his great virtue and was still considered a mortal. If he proved corrupt or inept, he could be removed through revolution, as Mencius* had stated. The Japanese, in contrast, saw their emperor as a direct physical descendant of the gods, divine by definition—the possessor, as one historian put it, of "a divinity and sacredness preserved in the germ plasm."

Shinto's detractors point to the disastrous role the state religion played in herding the Japanese people toward a blind allegiance to the emperor and the Japanese war machine, forgetting that Christianity and Islam have served much the same function in the past or that the divine right of kings was essentially a Christian notion. Meanwhile, Shinto's supporters claim that it is, in fact, "the natural religion of humanity," unencumbered by assertions of divine revelation or theologically convoluted concepts of the nature of God. They point with regret to the Meiji period, when Shinto was seized upon by government advisers as a device for promoting nationalist fervor, and disavow the excesses committed under that delusion.

Very early in the development of Shinto, before the name was even invented, four priestly classes developed: the Ritualists, the Abstainers, the Diviners, and the Musicians and Dancers. The latter were mainly women and may have evolved from temple prostitutes. The major place of Shinto worship, even more ancient, is the shrine, the **jinja** or **miya,** a simple, austere wooden structure. The most famous is probably the shrine of Amaterasu at Ise, built around the 3rd century AD and actually consisting of 16 shrines and other structures covering an expanse of land. Since most shrines are made of wood, they have to be rebuilt frequently. Government-approved shrines alone number about 100,000, divided into 12 categories. The kami are believed either to dwell there or to arrive when summoned by the proper rites. The shrine to the war god **Hachiman** in Kamakura, for instance, was a center of feverish worship in the late 13th century when Kublai Khan, the founder of the Mongol dynasty in China, twice attempted to invade Japan. After storms lashed his fleet and caused him to give up both times, the myth that Japan was protected by the gods was greatly enhanced. The unique Japanese form of drama called **Noh**, perfected by a Shinto priest and his son in the 14th and 15th centuries, developed out of religious dances performed in front of such shrines.

Buddhism, arriving in the 6th century with its doctrines about the after-death worlds, succeeded in absorbing much of the ancestor and hero worship of Shinto. Kukai, the founder of the Shingon sect of Buddhism in the 9th century, preached that the Buddha reincarnates when and wherever necessary to help humanity (a variation on the Hindu avatar) and that the national gods and goddesses of Shinto were actually ancient incarnations of various Buddhas and bodhisattvas. Beginning with the Buddha as the reincarnation of Amaterasu (the Sanskrit name of the transcendent Buddha of the Shingon system, **Vairochana,** means "He who is like the sun"), Kukai taught that there was essentially no difference between worshiping Buddhist or Shinto figures. This belief later came to be called **Ryobu** ("Two Faced") **Shinto** and allowed the common folk to consider themselves at once Buddhists and Shintoists. Combined with the One Reality of the Tendai school, Kukai's approach allowed for an endless absorption of kami by Buddhism and led to the temporary eclipse of Shinto.

But Buddhism also brought to Japan literature, medicine, the arts and sciences, and a deeper sense of compassion and tolerance along with improvements in skilled occupations from canal and bridge building to weaving and brewing. During the Dark Ages of Europe, Buddhist monks served much the same function as did Christian monks (with whom they were roughly contemporaneous), preserving learning while improving living conditions.

The principal configurations of Shinto in modern times are Koshitsu, or State Shinto; Jinja, or Shrine Shinto; Kyoba, or Sect Shinto; and Minkan, or Popular Shinto. Following the Imperial Restoration of 1868, Buddhism was denounced, Shinto was made the official state religion, and the emperor was worshiped as a god. This **State Shinto** had obvious consequences in building popular support for the Japanese war effort, first against China in 1931 and later against the Allies in World War II. After Japan surrendered in 1945, Shinto lost its role as state religion, and the emperor was forced to forgo (for a time, at least) any claim to personal divinity. However, **Shrine Shinto** continued to be practiced on a private level under the so-called Shinto Directive imposed by the victorious Allies, which returned freedom of religion to the Japanese people. Buddhism and Christianity could again be practiced openly, alongside Shinto, and that situation prevails today. Although Shrine Shinto did not exist as a religious organization until after 1868, it is associated with the ancient forms of nature worship that took shape around shrines devoted to particular kami, local or national. Following the war, shrines were removed from government control and became dependent on support by the people.

Sect Shinto consists of a wide range of sects with very different philosophies and practices. Thirteen are officially recognized, from the so-called pure sects of **Shinto Honkyoku, Shinri Kyo,** and **Taisha Kyo** to the overtly Confucian-influenced sects **Shusei Ha** and **Teisei Kyo.** Hundreds of subsects were either subsumed by these or continue to thrive quietly alongside them. Some sects focus on worship of mountains, which make up 80 percent of the landmass of Japan yet are almost uninhabited. Members of **Jikko Kyo** and **Fuso Kyo** worship **Mount Fuji** (synonymous with the ancient fire kami named Fuji); **Mitake Kyo** centers around the worship of **Mount Ontake.** The spiritual founder of Jikko Kyo was a 16th-century ascetic named **Hasegawa Kakugyo,** whose last name means "block austerities," reflecting the fact that he stood for as long as 2,000 consecutive days of penitence and prayer on a square block of wood, in the grand tradition of Bodhidharma and Symeon Stylites*. **Shinshu Kyo** and **Misogi Kyo** stress purification rites over everything else.

The remaining sects, only marginally Shinto, are dedicated mainly to faith healing and were founded within the last century and a half through the work of charismatic individuals. All three sects tend to extreme emotionalism and the use of magic in healing. **Konko Kyo,** whose founder claimed divine revelation, worships an invented deity, **Tenchi Kane no**

Kami ("The God Who Gives Unity to Heaven and Earth"). **Kurozumi Kyo** is based on the self-healing experiences of **Kurozumi Munetada** (1780–1850), who was taken ill with consumption after both his parents died within a week of each other. Nearing death himself two years later, Munetada had a spontaneous healing, followed by two experiences of inner rebirth connected to his worship of the sun. He saw in the Sun Goddess Amaterasu Omikami a kind of Absolute Divinity. His attitude toward illness was remarkably similar to that of the American founder of Christian Science*, Mary Baker Eddy*, who believed that evil and illness were illusions of the mind. "Of a truth, there is no such thing as sickness," Munetada wrote. Yet his outlook was unmistakably Eastern and nondualistic: "If you foster a spirit that regards both good and evil as blessings, then the body spontaneously becomes healthy."

But another faith-healing sect known as **Tenri Kyo,** founded by a woman, is the one sometimes referred to as the "Christian Science of Japan." **Miki Nakayama** (1798–1887) was a pious Buddhist whose plan to become a nun was thwarted when a marriage was arranged for her in traditional Japanese fashion at the age of 12. In her 28th year of marriage, Nakayama, her husband, and her son were all suffering from various ailments when she unexpectedly went into a trance. A voice apparently speaking through her declared, "I am the Commander of Heaven. I am the original and true God who has come down from heaven to save the whole world." Three days later, she emerged from the trance and all three family members were spontaneously healed.

Tenri Kyo is noteworthy in that it teaches belief in reincarnation and exalts service to one's neighbor. The sect supports active social service through clinics, a tuberculosis sanatorium and research institute, orphanages, and other social welfare organizations. Officially recognized in 1908, it separated from Shinto in 1970.

Ryobu Shinto shrines merging Buddhist and Shinto elements remain the site of hero worship, and various districts have their clan gods, or **Ujigami,** to whom infants are presented shortly after birth. The presentation may be accompanied by ceremonies intended to keep the newborn spirit from wandering, a concern based on historically high infant mortality rates. Modern Shinto marriages are frequently performed at the shrines, even with the fading of the old tradition of arranged marriages and go-betweens; the custom of taking nine sips of sake (a fermented rice

SCIENCE AND FAITH

Miki Nakayama was born 23 years before Mary Baker Eddy and, like her, suffered from delicate health yet lived to be nearly 90. But the similarities between the religious sects they founded run deeper than that. This comparison comes from a Western scholar of Shinto.

At heart both are faith-healing societies that profess to displace a negative evil, manifested in the form of the maladjustments of sickness and wrong, by establishing a normal relationship with the great health-giving stream that flows from the Great Source of all life. Each was founded by an extraordinary woman. During the creative periods of their lives, all unknown the one to the other, these two women were contemporaries. The churches which they established took form during the middle decades of the nineteenth century, the Japanese institution slightly antedating the American. The similarity extends even to names and their significations. Tenri Kyo means "The Teaching of Divine Reason." It claims to inculcate a reasonable or "scientific" attitude toward life's fundamental verities. It says that this is a reasonable universe. Final reality is a divine reason. He who lives according to reason shall prosper, he who violates reason shall perish. . . . The name Christian Science suggests practically the same thing. . . .

The chief teachings of Tenri Kyo are embodied in four texts [including] the *Mikagura Uta*, or Dancing Psalms, produced by the founder between the months of January and August, 1867, and added to between the years 1871 and 1875. It is worth noting that these dates coincide almost exactly with the discovery of the secret of the "Science of Christianity" by Mrs. Eddy in 1866 and her publication of the first edition of *Science and Health with a Key to the Scriptures* in 1875.

—D. C. HOLTOM, *THE NATIONAL FAITH OF JAPAN*

drink) remains as popular as ever. Buddhists still control most ceremonies connected with death, including funerals, memorial services, and cemeteries, and both religions share ancestor worship.

Festivals called **matsuri** form a large part of common Shinto practice today. Many of them have to do with food, although they also serve as vehicles for requests for anything from a successful crop to the birth of sons, for thanks, to pacify destructive kami, or for divination. The **kagura,** for instance, is a popular peace offering of food, music-making, and dancing that can be held at any time the worshipers request it of the temple attendants. The imperial household conducts 64 separate rituals in the course of a year, although the emperor participates in only a portion of them. The most important is the **Nii Name Sai** or **Festival of New Food,** during which the first fruits of the harvest are offered in thanksgiving. Celebrated by the emperor on November 23–24, it focuses on the all-important grain harvest and reaches back to the point of transition in Japanese culture from hunting and fishing to agriculture. The festival was then called the **Dai Jo Sai,** or **Great Food Festival,** a term that is now applied to the first Festival of New Food offered by a new emperor after his accession to the throne. The Dai Jo Sai was most recently performed by Emperor **Akihito** in 1990, after the death of his father the previous year. During the ceremony, the new emperor dished out food for visiting kami, then retreated behind a screen where Amaterasu invited him to enter her womb. When he emerged, he was no longer considered an ordinary human, but rather the living embodiment of Ninigi no Mikoto, the God of the Ripened Rice Plant. One of the reasons constantly cited by Japanese government officials for their resistance to lowering the extremely high import tariffs against American rice, in fact, has to do with its sacred function in rituals such as this one.

✴ INSIDE A SHRINE ROOM

Buddhist temples and monasteries range from the elaborate to the very simple. The **zendo,** or meditation hall, of a Zen monastery may be little more than a quiet room adorned with an image of the Buddha. Zendos may also vary depending on the particular order, and especially in China they may incorporate or share elements of Taoism. One increasingly pop-

The Good Book II: Shinto

Just as Shinto has no single founder akin to the Buddha, Jesus, or Muhammad, so it has no body of sacred scriptures on a parallel with the Tripitaka, Bible, or Quran. What it does have are historical accounts of the formation of the world and the coming of the kami to Japan, providing both an historical and spiritual basis for Shinto. The first and still the most important major accounts of Shinto cosmogony are the *Kojiki*, committed to writing in 712 AD, and the *Nihongi*, compiled in 720. The *Kojiki* provide the oldest written record of the Imperial Family and the clans that created the Japanese nation, constituting the basis on which Japanese society is built. The *Engi Shiki* (Ceremonial Law of the Engi Period), written in 927 AD, contains 27 Shinto rituals, laying down the ground rules for offerings. The absence of an elaborate Shinto canon of sacred writings is a direct reflection of the role of the shrine as the focal point of the religion, taking the place that written doctrine assumes in other traditions.

ular manifestation in homes of American Buddhists is the shrine room, an equally simple altar along the lines of those that appear in homes throughout Asia. Ideally an entire room is set aside for the purpose and used for nothing else, although where space is at a premium, a corner of a bedroom or other room may be used. The altar or table holds images or statues of the Buddha and various bodhisattvas or teachers, depending on the school or lineage of the householder. Followers of any of the Tibetan orders currently popular here, for example, might have images of Padmasambhava, who established Buddhism in Tibet, as well as the Dalai Lama or other Tibetan lamas under whom they have studied, along with their respective teachers. Especially in America, one is likely to find images from other traditions as well, including Jesus or Mary, Kuan-yin, Shiva, a Goddess figure, or personal teachers from other traditions.

thangkas, or iconographic scroll paintings, featuring one or another Buddha or celestial bodhisattva, mandalas, or other images are often hung on the walls behind or alongside the shrine itself.

Traditionally, 8 offering bowls are placed before the images, with offerings representing each of the 5 senses: food (rice or fruit), water, incense, candles, flowers, bells or finger cymbals, and so forth. Part of daily practice includes the care of the shrine room, replacement of flowers and food, lighting of candles, and other devotional duties. The shrine room is then used for sitting meditation, chanting, visualizations, prostrations, and other practices.

Coming to Terms

Because Buddhism has spread across different cultures with different languages, including Sanskrit, Pali, Chinese, Tibetan, and Japanese, much of the Sanskrit terminology of Indian Buddhism was translated into or intermingled with foreign words. As a result, several transliterations exist for most key terms. This glossary features the most common English spellings.

Avalokiteshvara (*uh*-vuh-*low*-key *taysh*-vuh-ruh)   One of the four chief bodhisattvas of Mahayana Buddhism, whose major attribute is compassion. He is a manifestation of the Buddha Amitabha. In China he is worshiped in female form as Kuan-yin, and in Tibet as Chenrezi, whose reincarnations include the Dalai Lama.

Bankei (*bahn*-k'eye)   Seventeenth-century Rinzai Zen priest generally considered to be one of Japan's three greatest Zen masters. His first enlightenment experience occurred when, after nearly dying of consumption brought on by two years of continuous zazen, he coughed up a blood clot.

Bodhidharma (boe-dee-*dar*-muh)   The man who established the Ch'an (Zen) tradition in China. Around 520, he traveled by boat from India to southern China before heading north to Shaolin Temple on Mount Sung-shan, where he performed his famous 9-year meditation, sometimes called "facing the wall." Drawings picture him as a fierce-looking character with a gnarled brow, doing his best to live up to his nickname, the Barbarian from the West.

bodhisattva (*boe*-dee-*saht*-vah)   In general terms, anyone who is on the path to buddhahood. Specifically, someone who is freed of the self, possesses perfect wisdom, and has escaped the pull of samsara, but who has put off the ultimate bliss of nirvana to turn back and free others from their suffering and lead them to enlightenment. In times of need, bodhisattvas may assume various forms to help others and stir them to the pursuit of liberation, often taking on others' suffering or transferring their own karmic credits. (Compare the concept of the saint* in Christianity or the lamedvovnik* in Judaism.) Some Buddhists consider the notion of a bodhisattva postponing his or her enlightenment as a metaphor to describe the depth of compassion with which he or she is motivated. A pop song of the same name was a minor hit for the band Steely Dan in the 1970s.

Bon   The indigenous, pre-Buddhist religion of Tibet, Bhutan, Sikkim, and western China, whose members are known as Bonpo. It derived from the work of local shamans* and involved blood sacrifices (human and animal) and the use of juniper berries to induce ecstatic trances. After the entry of Buddhism to Tibet in the 7th century, Bon was absorbed and transmuted, so that modern Bon closely resembles Buddhism, although primitive elements such as animal sacrifice still persist in isolated areas.

Buddha   (*bood*-huh, Skt. "Ultimate Truth," "One awakened to that Truth")   The historical Buddha, often called Shakyamuni, is generally considered to be one in a continuing chain of past and future buddhas, to culminate in Maitreya—sometimes numbered at 5 earthly Buddhas, sometimes at 1,000. In addition, 5 cosmic or transcendent Buddhas have become popular over the centuries, including Vairochana, the first of the transcendent Buddhas; Amitabha (Amida in Japan), who is prayed to by members of the Pure Land schools; **Akshobya,** whose help is sought in overcoming anger; **Ratnasambhava,** who is associated with transforming the addictions of pride and avarice; and **Amoghasiddhi,** who symbolizes the practical realization of the wisdom of the other four and is associated with the earthly Buddha Maitreya. The term *buddha* can also be applied to any being who has achieved enlightenment, even though he or she may appear as a bodhisattva, as if still on the path; buddhas may take on an earthly body in their extreme ardor to help save all other beings, while still in possession of their buddha powers such as omniscience. (*Also see* Siddhartha Gautama.)

butsudan   (*boot*-sue-*dahn,* Jap. "shrine of the Buddha")   A shrine in the form of an altar in Buddhist temples or households, often containing an image of the Buddha inside a small box or enclosure that can be shut when not in use. In the home, the names of the family dead may be included, and food, water, or flowers offered in their memory or to the Buddha are placed in front of the image.

Dalai Lama   Literally, "Ocean Teacher," or one whose wisdom is as great as the ocean. Beginning in 1391 in Tibet, 14 Dalai Lamas have served in an unbroken line of succession as heads of state with spiritual authority as well, although much of that spiritual role has traditionally been played by the Panchen Lama. Each Dalai Lama is considered to be the reincarnation of the previous one. The current Dalai Lama, Tenzin Gyatso (b. 1935), has been in exile from Tibet since 1959, when he was forced out by the Communist Chinese. He now tours the world enjoining political support for the liberation of Tibet and advocating nonviolence and compassion, for which he was awarded the Nobel Peace Prize in 1989.

dharma For Buddhists this term has several different meanings, some of which overlap its original sense in Hinduism of truth, order, and the basis of religion. The Dharma is one of the Three Jewels (along with Buddha and Sangha, or Buddhist community) in which the faithful take refuge, encompassing the law of karmically determined rebirth as well as the Buddha's teachings as a whole. In a larger sense, it denotes the collective doctrines of Buddhism, but it also has several narrower meanings in Buddhist terminology.

kami In Shinto, the many deities believed to be native to Japan as opposed to those imported from other countries and cultures.

karma Literally, "action." In Hindu terminology, karma refers to mental or physical actions, their consequences, the sum of all the consequences of those actions, and the continuing principle of cause and effect across numerous lifetimes. But in Buddhism, karma refers only to "volitional action," with the emphasis on intent. This law of action and reaction, with good actions producing good karma and bad actions producing bad karma, bears little relation to the Jewish-Christian scheme of reward and punishment. Actions simply leave traces in the psyche of the doer that shape his or her destiny, not only in this life but in future ones. In fact, the doing of either good or bad actions, charged with desire, hatred, or delusion, creates *more* karma and hence the need for more rebirths. Only enlightened buddhas or bodhisattvas act without desire, good or bad, without the "thirst" for continuing and becoming that arises from what Buddhists call "the false idea of self." And so only they can act without accumulating more karma and requiring rebirths.

kensho The Zen term for the enlightenment experience, from the Japanese for "seeing (one's true) nature." There are different levels of clarity and intensity to these experiences of "self-realization." Although often used interchangeably with *satori,* kensho traditionally implies an experience that needs to become deeper still.

Kuan-yin (gwahn-yin) The Chinese version of Avalokiteshvara, one of the four chief bodhisattvas and the embodiment of compassion, is said to manifest herself in any imaginable form when called on by anyone in desperate need or by childless women. Originally a male figure, Kuan-

143

yin has often been represented since the 10th century as a woman in a white robe, called the Goddess of Mercy.

Maitreya (my-*tray*-uh) The Buddha-to-come, last of the 5 earthly Buddhas (of which Shakyamuni was the fourth). Especially among Mahayana Buddhists, Maitreya is viewed as the embodiment of all-encompassing love who will deliver all those who have not yet reached enlightenment. According to some sources, he is to appear 5,000 years after the death of Gautama, or about 2,500 years from now; other sources expect him in anywhere from 30,000 to 100,000 years.

mandala A circular design, usually with one or more squares or other circles within it, containing images of various demons and deities, buddhas and bodhisattvas, used as a visual focal point or mnemonic device for meditation. Mandalas may be painted, drawn on the ground with colored sand, or pictured in the mind; in the 1960s they were often executed in fluorescent paint and sold in head shops. The term can also refer to an assemblage of elements or spheres of activity within a Buddhist community, such as spiritual study, livelihood, social action, and communications.

Nagarjuna (nuh-*gahr*-juh-nuh) Buddhist philosopher of the 2nd or 3rd century AD who is best known for his interpretations of (and perhaps additions to) the *Prajnaparamita Sutra* and for founding the Madhyamika ("Middle Way"), the first school of Mahayana Buddhism.

nembutsu The meditation of the Pure Land school, which consists of reciting *Namu Amida Butsu* ("Veneration to the Buddha Amitabha"). Combined with visualization, nembutsu yields the desired result—a vision of Amitabha and his paradise and rebirth there.

nirvana Not a state of being, not a condition, but rather the end of all states and conditions, the extinguishing of all craving, hatred, and delusion that accompanies enlightenment. It implies nonattachment rather than nonbeing. Books have been written about nirvana, and Buddhist scholars and teachers of various sects and schools differ as to how to conceive of it. But all agree that it is beyond the ability of words to describe or explain adequately.

parinirvana (Skt. "total extinction") Although this term can refer merely to the death of a Buddhist monk or nun or be used as a synonym for *nirvana,* it is most often applied to the Buddha's realization of complete nirvana at his death. Does this make it different from the nirvana he realized at the time of his enlightenment 45 years earlier? Good question. Some Theravadin scholars hold that the Parinirvana represents the total dissolution of the Buddha's being, as opposed to the earlier nirvana in which he remained in earthly existence but was no longer subject to its conditional nature—in Christian terms, "in the world but not of the world."

samsara (Skt. "journeying") The Wheel of Existences involving a succes-

144

At his enlightenment under the Bodhi Tree, the Buddha is said to have experienced nirvana, yet chose to return and teach. The term parinirvana is usually applied to his physical death, depicted here in an exquisite sculpture from Thailand.
SCALA/ART
RESOURCE

sion of rebirths based on karmic merit; by extension, the entire phenomenal world. One may be reborn into any of three higher and three lower modes of existence, or **gati.** The higher modes are humans, gods, and **asuras** (demigods); the lower are animals, hungry ghosts (**pretas**), and hell beings. The only way to exit the cycle is to become fully enlightened and liberated from the passionate craving, hatred, and ignorance that keeps one addicted. This can only occur during a human lifetime when one can recognize craving as the root of all suffering, karma, and rebirth. Since there is no suffering in the god realms and existence there is so pleasurable, no opportunity or motivation exists to get off the wheel; a being in the celestial or god realms who is not enlightened would first have to be reborn as a human to escape samsara. The Buddha, incidentally, never speculated when or how samsara began, because knowing that wouldn't help anyone achieve enlightenment. His attitude is roughly comparable to that of Sherlock Holmes, who, when he learned that the earth revolved around the sun, immediately put the knowledge out of his mind because it had nothing to do with solving crime. The Hindu understanding of samsara is somewhat but not entirely similar.

sangha (*sung*-guh)   The Buddhist community; along with Buddha and Dharma, one of the Three Jewels of Buddhism. Although in its narrow sense limited to monks, nuns, and novices, in modern usage the sangha generally includes lay people. In India, the word originally denoted a council of elders, such as the one that ruled the Shakyas among whom the Buddha grew up.

satori (suh-*tor*-ee)   The Zen term for inner awakening or enlightenment as applied to the Buddha and the Zen patriarchs.

Shakyamuni   The "Silent Sage of the Shakyas," the Buddha's birth clan. The title Shakyamuni Buddha generally distinguishes the historical Buddha from other earthly or transcendent Buddhas.

shunyata (shun-yuh-*tah,* Skt. "emptiness")   The concept developed by the Mahayana that objects and beings are not substantial, as they appear on the surface, but rather are lacking any independent reality—in a word, empty. One's essential nature is not an object, then, but a transparent interpenetration of all life, a void free of identification with any being, object, or event. Shunyata applies ultimately to all phenomena, so that, when seen from the far shore of enlightenment, samsara is ultimately no different from nirvana.

Siddhartha Gautama   The given and family names (in Sanskrit version) of the historical personage known as the Buddha, sometimes used to refer to him before his enlightenment and the beginning of his teaching. Curiously, the title character of Hermann Hesse's classic 1922 novel *Siddhartha* is not the Buddha himself, but a contemporary who follows a somewhat parallel path of enlightenment. In the novel, Hesse's Siddhartha at first rejects the Buddha before discovering a similar path of his own.

sutra (*soo*-truh)   The Sanskrit word means "a thread," as for stringing jewels, and is the root of the English words *sew* and *suture.* In Buddhism, the jewels are the words of the Buddha as contained in his various sermons and dialogues; only a small portion of the more than 10,000 sutras have been translated into English. For Hindus, *sutra* refers to an aphorism or rule or a collection of them.

Tathagata (tah-*tah*-guh-tuh)   The name the Buddha applied to himself in his own sermons. It translates as "thus-perfected," "thus-come," or "One Who has come to the Truth," i.e., has attained the highest enlightenment. The implication of "One who has come and gone like former buddhas" is also present. The name can refer to other fully realized beings, or buddhas.

Theravada (ter-uh-*vah*-duh, Skt. "Teachings of the Elders")   The oldest surviving school of Buddhism, and the only extant Hinayana school, Theravada is considered the most conservative on several counts. It focuses on the concept of the arhat, a holy person who overcomes passions and ego and liberates himself or herself, as opposed to the bodhisattva ideal of the Mahayana school.

vipassana (vih-*pahs*-uh-nuh, Pali "insight")   A Mahayana technique of meditation by analytical examination of the nature of all things that leads to seeing the universe as ultimately void (shunyata).

yab-yum (Tib. "father-mother")   The union of masculine and feminine principles, usually depicted as a male and female deity in the act of coitus.

3

TAOISM

❋ THE MOTHER OF THE WORLD

Although Taoism is traditionally said to have sprung from the writings
of the man called Lao-tzu (a name that simply means "Old Master"), it
is almost certainly older than the 6th century BC, when he is presumed
to have lived. As Taoism is practiced even today in China, where it has
survived both the Communist and cultural revolutions, it is connected to
the rhythms of nature and the earth in ways that are remarkable. In that
connection, it harks back to a much earlier time when the roles of men
and women are said to have been more equitably apportioned and when
spiritual practice, in the opinion of some scholars, centered around the
birth of all creation from the Divine Mother. Lao-tzu wrote of an ancient
time when the feminine principle was not yet dominated by the masculine:

147

There was something complete and nebulous
Which existed before Heaven and Earth,
Silent, invisible,
Unchanging, standing as One,
Unceasing, ever-revolving,
Able to be the Mother of the World.
I do not know its name and I call it *Tao*.

—*TAO TE CHING* 26

Perhaps more than any of the major religions, **Taoism** (pronounced *"dow-ism"*) is imbued with the cultural view that the cyclical changes in the human body and the changing seasons of nature are intimately related. Through careful observation of the natural world and insights gained in deep meditative trance, the early Chinese sages developed the concept of **yin-yang,** opposing forces that complement each other and, through interaction, give rise to the rest of the phenomenal world. According to this ancient polarity, the male generative principle of yang is represented by the sun (day) and the heavens, and the female life-bearing powers of yin by the moon (night) and the earth. Their interplay gives rise to the **Five Elements** (water, fire, wood, metal, earth), which are emblematic of the changing seasons, the four cardinal directions plus the center, the five senses, and much more. Likewise, Taoists relate the inner microcosm of the human body to the outer macrocosm of the world (earth, heavens, and underworld). Together, the opposing principles of yin-yang, the cyclical interplay of the Five Elements, and the mirroring of the cosmos in the body contain the essence of Chinese spirituality.

These basic principles, however, manifested in an often bewildering array of Taoist schools and practices that developed over centuries and were further modified by contact with Buddhist and Confucianist sages. As a practice, Taoism became organized in the 4th and 3rd centuries BC, based on the *Tao Te Ching* and the writings of **Chuang-tzu** (c. 369–286 BC). The *Tao Te Ching,* the great book of Taoist wisdom, is usually attributed to Lao-tzu, who is said to have been born around 600 BC but whose authorship of the book has been questioned. Taoists insist, furthermore, that Taoist principles derive from the oral teachings of sages as far back in history as 3000 BC, which would make it nearly as old as the Vedic era of Indian religion.

In this classic depiction, the Old Master rides off on a water buffalo from his life at court to a life of contemplation. In one version of his famous (and perhaps fictional) encounter with Confucius, Lao is supposed to have advised the younger man, "I have heard it said that a good merchant will conceal his wealth and act as if he were poor. A noble person with sufficient inner virtue may give the appearance of a fool. Therefore, give up your high-handed manner, your desires, your vanity, and your zealousness, for they are of no use at all."
FOTO MARBURG/ART RESOURCE

We have no direct evidence of a link between Hindu, Jain*, or Buddhist thought and the early Taoist mystics, some of whom may have come in contact with the wandering ascetics of India. But ascertaining whether the early Taoists were influenced by migrating Indian sages or discovered similar insights in their own pursuit of stillness during meditative states is less important than understanding that Taoism developed along different lines from the Indian traditions. It has certain aspects in common with those traditions, yet is distinctively Chinese; in turn it exerted a major influence on Buddhism as that Indian-born religion passed through China on its way east.

Two complementary, equal but opposite, forces: one passive, one active. All existence flows from the interaction of these two forces, which yields the Five Elements and ultimately the Ten Thousand Things that make up the manifest world. Yin and yang do not oppose each other as good and evil do in Christian thought or Ahura Mazda* and Ahriman* in Zoroastrianism*. Their complementary polarity is more akin to the Hindu system of three gunas*, in which the interaction of rajas* (mobility, lightness) and tamas* (immobility, heaviness) produces sattva* (purity, peace). As indicated by the symbol, each pole contains within it the seed of the other. The identification of yin with feminine, receptive, cool, and dark aspects, and of yang with masculine, creative, hot, and bright, dates back to the I Ching, *the ancient Chinese book of oracles. Its complex system of hexagrams interpreting all eventualities comprises only two symbols: unbroken (—) and broken (– –) lines, which are said to represent pictographically the male and female sexual organs.*

Prior to the development of specifically Taoist practices, popular folk religion in China embraced ancestor worship, animal sacrifice, exorcism, divination, and other practices associated with shamanism*, one of the oldest forms of spiritual practice on the globe. The Chinese traditionally conceived of heaven as a place where ancestors waited for those on earth to join them. In the meantime, their progeny made sacrifices to the ancestors, who responded by sending signs, or auguries, of impending good fortune or disaster, which had to be interpreted.

Although Taoism both influenced and was influenced by Buddhism as it worked its way across China from India to Korea and Japan, most Taoists did not and do not share the Hindu-Buddhist belief in reincarnation*. Many popular Western accounts of Taoism stress the Taoist concern, bordering on obsession, with attaining physical immortality. Yet observers who have spent considerable time in China report that the Chinese have long believed in an afterlife, complete with heaven, hell, and purgatory—concepts borrowed by the West.

But how else does Taoism differ from the other major Eastern traditions? Although it features fewer sects and subsects than the fascinating yet tangled profusion of Hinduism (a mere 86 or so to Hinduism's 300 plus), Taoism is still rife with the multiplicity of exotic beliefs that can be simultaneously dazzling and off-putting to the Western mind. Filled with fanciful images of wizards with long hair and longer fingernails who have a disconcerting habit of flying off to heaven on the backs of cranes or dragons, and of so-called immortals who achieve longevity through a mixture of formidable breathing techniques, diets of dew and herbs, alchemy, and demanding sexual practices, this quintessentially Chinese religion often appears to be only a step or two removed from the magical absurdities of a Bruce Lee movie.

And yet the system of Chinese medicine encompassing acupuncture, medicinal herbs, and sophisticated diagnostic techniques is being seen as increasingly valuable in treating a number of troublesome maladies in the West, from drug addiction to AIDS. Further, the core teachings of Taoism—the *Tao Te Ching* and the book of Chuang-tzu (usually referred to simply as the *Chuang-tzu*)—are among the most frequently translated and widely read books of Eastern religious thought. Deceptively simple and often the source of wildly divergent interpretations (including, in modern China, a Maoist reading), these teachings have nonetheless been accepted as offering something of value to the West and having deeply influenced the development of Zen Buddhism. How can we account for these seemingly incompatible versions of China's great contribution to world religion?

The simplest answer is that the term *Taoism* is a convenient conglomerate used by Westerners to encompass at least two disparate traditions of Chinese wisdom, embracing both a proto-Zen philosophy and a raft of esoteric practices such as alchemy and "inner hygiene." Despite their differences, these traditions and practices share several reference points: the *Tao Te Ching*, the search for immortality or at least great longevity, a varied pantheon of Taoist deities, and a certain rebelliousness against both the demands of society and the rigors of traditional Confucian morality and social codes.

The Chinese themselves use separate terms to distinguish between the two major currents within Taoism. The first, **Tao-chia,** is commonly translated as "Philosophical Taoism" and consists of mystical teachings about the Tao ("Way") and the art of **wu wei** ("nondoing," or letting things take their course) as defined by Lao-tzu and Chuang-tzu. Through

151

meditation, students of Tao-chia learn to "go with the flow," to let things proceed as they want to proceed, and not to "push the river." Because it is philosophically oriented, Tao-chia was never institutionalized, passing rather from teacher to student without benefit of an organized church structure or hierarchy.

The overarching principle of this stream of Taoism is to reduce the friction inherent in most of life's actions by way of conserving one's vital energy. If longevity is a by-product of such conservation, then so be it. But the notion of making strenuous efforts to achieve this goal is antithetical to the earliest Taoist teachings, as it would be to those later developed by Zen Buddhism. Also as with Zen, this philosophical version of Taoism is the one that has been taken to heart by Western intellectuals and seekers, producing a profusion of books and courses that attempt to view Western, action-oriented phenomena through the reductive lens of Taoism— e.g., *The Tao of Physics, The Tao of Golf, The Tao of Sexual Massage, The Tao of Balanced Diet, The Tao of Pooh, The Te of Piglet,* and *The Tao Jones Averages: A Guide to Whole Brained Investing.*

Besides Lao and Chuang, prominent early Taoist mystics include **Lieh-tzu** and **Yang Chu,** of whom very little is known; the authenticity of any of their extant writings is questionable.

THE TAO KNOWS, BUT ISN'T SAYING

The dualism inherent in the Western opposition of matter and spirit, or even the ancient Zoroastrian opposition of good and evil, is noticeably absent from Taoist thought. The apparent duality of yin and yang dissolves in any deep meditation on their genuinely complementary nature. They are not opposing forces at war with each other but more like opposite sides of the same coin, one arising out of the other before folding back into itself. The venerable religious scholar Huston Smith illustrates the nonduality with a classic Taoist tale.

In the Taoist perspective, even good and evil are not head-on opposites. The West has tended to dichotomize the two, but Taoists are less categorical. They buttress their reserve with the story of a farmer whose horse ran away. His neighbor commiserated, only to be told, "Who knows what's good or bad?" It was true, for the next day the horse returned, bringing with it a drove of wild horses it had befriended. The neighbor reappeared, this time with congratulations for the windfall. He received the same response: "Who knows what's good or bad?" Again this proved true, for the next day the farmer's son tried to mount one of the wild horses and fell, breaking his leg. More commiserations from the neighbor, which elicited the question, "Who knows what is good or bad?" And for a fourth time the farmer's point prevailed, for the following day soldiers came by commandeering for the army, and the son was exempted because of his injury.

—HUSTON SMITH, *THE WORLD'S RELIGIONS*

The second tradition is **Tao-chiao,** generally called "Religious Taoism" or "Church Taoism." This term refers to the institutional Taoist Church itself but can also encompass a collection of body-mind techniques. The church has its own line of succession beginning with **Chang Tao-ling,** a healer and official of the Han dynasty in the 2nd century AD, and reaching to the present day in Taiwan, a lineage that is sometimes compared to that of the Popes of the Roman Catholic Church. One of its functions has traditionally been to make the more obscure and difficult practices and rituals available to the masses on some level. Composed of many different schools, Tao-chiao focuses more pragmatically than Tao-chia on ways to achieve longevity or even immortality through the augmentation and preservation of one's essential vitality, or **ch'i.** These methods make up a kind of yoga related to the raja* yoga of India but with a Chinese twist. Taoist yoga includes elaborate sexual techniques known as dual cultivation (**huan-ching** and **huan-ching pu-nao,** or "returning the semen to strengthen the brain"), breath control (hsing-ch'i), the use of medicinal herbs, body movement (especially t'ai chi ch'uan, a combination of exercise and self-defense), and alchemy.

Although these practices are all lumped under Tao-chiao, many of them have traditionally been practiced by Taoists having no official connection with the Taoist Church. Unaffiliated shamans and alchemists, reclusive adepts and practitioners of Chinese yoga, and small sects of believers follow many of the same practices that the Taoist Church has made available to the masses. As with Hinduism, a lot of overlap occurs; the lines between different divisions or styles of practice were never as rigidly drawn as they have been in Western religions. Whereas Roman Catholics and fundamentalist Christians who believe in Jesus Christ and embrace of the same Bible may feel very uncomfortable in each other's presence, Taoists can and often do embrace elements of Religious and Philosophical Taoism while practicing one or more versions of inner hygiene. To make matters more confusing, at least until the cultural revolution drove most religions underground, individual Chinese often practiced not only differing versions of Taoism but also Buddhism and Confucianism without any noticeable discomfort.

✳ CONFUCIUS SAY WHAT?

Did somebody mention Confucius?

Before going further with Taoism, we'll need to say a few words about the one man more popularly associated in the West with Chinese philosophy and culture than any other. The name **Confucius** is a Latinization of **K'ung-tzu** or **K'ung Fu-tzu** ("Kung the Master or Ancestor"), who lived from 551 to 479 BC. Despite starting young in a life of study, Confucius failed at his avowed goal of becoming a public servant. He wound up instead teaching his revolutionary principles to a small but loyal band of followers outside the mainstream of Chinese political life. Not especially popular in his own day, K'ung's teachings began to exert a tremendous influence on the moral and philosophical thought of all China in the centuries after his death.

Concerned about the constant disorder and warfare among the clans during his lifetime, K'ung searched through the old rituals for ethical human guidelines and moral principles to help see people through that tur-

Like many other moral reformers of ancient history, Confucius did accept certain conventions of his time, such as the existence of slavery, the divine right of kings, and the secondary position of women in society. What is surprising in retrospect is the revolutionary nature of the changes he and other visionaries promoted at the time, however incomplete they may seem by today's standards. The Buddha's decision to teach all castes and women, Jesus's defense of the woman taken in adultery, and K'ung's demand that women be treated benevolently by their husbands can be seen in the context of their times as ground-breaking, antiauthoritarian acts.
GIRAUDON/ART RESOURCE

bulent era. In the process, he founded the first recorded Chinese wisdom tradition. (Although Taoism is said to be as old as Chinese culture itself, it did not begin to take on written form until after the time of Confucius, and Confucianism seems to have spread more quickly than Taoism.) Confucius systematized and taught much of the accumulated social wisdom and ideals of the ancients, referring to himself as a "transmitter" rather than a creator. "In me, knowledge is not innate," he said. "I am one who loves antiquity and is earnest in the study of it." Like the ancient philosophers who had come before him, Confucius realized that the only way to establish a harmonious society was to inculcate ethical conduct in individuals, and much of his philosophy was aimed at doing just that.

Social conditions continued to deteriorate after K'ung's death, culminating in the egregious era known as the **Period of the Warring States** (401–221 BC). The violent social upheaval that was ripping up Chinese society during that time may have created the fertile soil in which K'ung's teachings began to bear fruit. What had been a superficially heroic approach to warfare ruled by chivalric codes known as **li** ("rites") became much more vicious and atrocity-laden in those centuries, threatening the stability of the empire and the peace of mind of the populace.

Confucius taught the human Way as opposed to the cosmic or mystical Way of Lao-tzu, who was roughly his contemporary. (About 50 years his senior, Lao-tzu is said to have met Confucius once.) Proclaiming that one must follow the four cardinal virtues of love, righteousness, propriety, and wisdom in a social context of duties and obligations, K'ung voiced his highest principle in what is probably the earliest formulation of the Golden Rule: "Do not do unto others what you would not have them do unto you." For Confucius, this applied especially to what he termed the **Five Relationships** (**Wu-lun**): between ruler and subject, husband and wife, father and son, elder and younger brothers, and older and younger friends. The Confucian equation called for the respect and obedience of one group (subjects, wives, sons, and younger brothers) in return for the benevolence and support of the other group (rulers, husbands, fathers, and elders). Although the male-dominated language may offend modern readers, his formula was radical for its day in that it at least called for a reciprocal kindness and benevolence on the part of the more socially empowered group. Over time, however, Confucianism became mired in an artificial construct of rituals, standards of conduct, and hierarchies of precedence.

Confucius has been credited with editing or writing parts of several classics of Chinese history and culture, but his essential teachings are contained in *The Analects (Lun-yu),* a compendium of his sayings and dialogues compiled by his disciples, and *The Doctrine of the Mean (Chung Yung),* a collection of Confucian tenets authored by his grandson **K'ung Chi.** Those tenets include the **Wu-ch'ang** ("Five Constants"), the cardinal virtues of Confucianism, among them **jen,** or love of fellow humans, a sense of compassion based on the dignity of human life and great self-respect, and li, an evolution of the older sense of li as chivalric codes governing warfare and rituals of ancestor worship. As Confucius used the term, *li* meant a reverence and loyalty for others that includes knowing the right thing to do and doing it appropriately under any and all circumstances; this is the primary way of expressing jen. Li encompasses both ritual manners and respect for the Five Constant Re-

lationships. The rest of the Wu-ch'ang are i ("transformation"), a sense
of moral uprightness that evokes the right response from selfless motives; **chih** (wisdom); and **hsin** (trust). The Confucian ideal is the **chun-
tzu** ("superior person"), the noble-minded or princely man who embodies jen and practices li.

Confucius had about 3,000 pupils, educated, compassionate people of
the sort who would make good government officials. He saw himself as
a reformer of a corrupt, nepotistic class system but did not openly attack
traditional religious beliefs like ancestor worship. He also accepted the
conventional Chinese deities and expressed his faith in heaven that
he was on a mission, but he did not believe in asking the deities for
help through prayer and thought that the divination and shamanism
common to Chinese folk religion of his day were practices unworthy of
a chun-tzu. And so his paradigm was not individual mystical experience
but compassionate and honorable conduct in a social context. Still, his
understanding of the individual was much more communal, less ego-
identified than the Western ideal, and closer to the Eastern mystical notion of union with the One. This sense is captured in the title of a book
by the modern philosopher Herbert Fingarette, *Confucius: The Secular as
Sacred.*

During the Han dynasty, Emperor Wu-ti (156–87 BC) proclaimed Confucianism the state religion. In 130 BC, the works of Confucius became
required reading for anyone wishing to be a public official and remained
so with a few interruptions until 1911, ultimately forming the basis of
civil service exams. In a country that modeled its heavenly hierarchy after the structure of government bureaucracy, this may have been the ultimate tribute. It's difficult to think of Confucianism as a complete spiritual tradition, however, since it has so little involvement with either
deities or transcendent states, concentrating only on codes of humane,
moral behavior. Perhaps for this reason, Confucianism, unlike Buddhism
or Taoism, has been of little interest to Western spiritual seekers and
shows up mainly in the garbled form of condescending fortune cookie
maxims uttered by pseudo-Oriental Charlie Chan characters, invariably
beginning with "Confucius say. . . ." Yet a careful reading of the man's
teachings reveals not the pious maunderings of a sententious moralist but
rather a keen sense of justice and wisdom tempered with compassion.
And despite the fact that few Asians would be likely to define themselves

FIVE THINGS CONFUCIUS REALLY DID SAY

The failure to cultivate virtue, the failure to examine and analyze what I have learned, the inability to move toward righteousness after being shown the way, the inability to correct my faults—these are the causes of my grief.

When you see a good man, think of emulating him; when you see a bad man, examine your own heart.

When a man is generally detested, or when he is generally beloved, closer examination is necessary.

Chi Wen Tzu used to reflect three times before he acted. When told of this, the Master said: "Twice would do."

Your goody-good people are the thieves of virtue.

—*THE ANALECTS*

principally as Confucianists, K'ung's influence on China, Korea, and Japan has been incomparable.

✳ TAO THEN

According to the eminent Chinese historian Ssu-ma Ch'ien, the meeting of Lao-tzu and Confucius in the year 517 BC was a comedy of diverging views. Lao-tzu, some 50 years older than Confucius, advised the younger sage to abandon his arrogant ways, suave demeanor, and unbridled ambition. K'ung, perhaps overawed, later admitted to his students, "Roaming animals may be caught in a pit or cage, fish with a net or rod, and birds can be shot down with an arrow. The dragon, however, cannot be caught by such cleverness. It soars toward heaven riding upon the wind and clouds. Today I have seen Lao-tzu, and he is like a dragon."

Apocryphal or not, the essence of the exchange rings true in that, although Confucius may have elevated ethical conduct and mores to an almost spiritual level, for Lao-tzu the entire universe was imbued with a mystical presence, an overarching eternal principle he referred to only as the **Tao**. The original pictogram for Tao may be translated as "Way" or "Path" but can also mean "Teaching." The term was apparently already in use before the time of Lao and Confucius; K'ung used it in the context of human activity or mores, whereas Lao-tzu may have been the first to give the word a purely mystical connotation. For Lao (or whoever composed the *Tao Te Ching*), the Tao is a mystery whose essence is unnameable. In the sense that it is also the primordial source of the universe, it resembles the Hindu Brahman*, the impersonal Absolute, rather than any personal deity. And like Brahman, the Tao is knowable only in the depths of the heart in silent meditations not unlike the trances of the rishis* and Upanishadic seers.

Now generally thought to have been finalized between the 4th and 3rd centuries BC, with the earliest existing copy dated at around 200 BC, the *Tao Te Ching* may be the work of one or more anonymous Taoists seeking to offset Confucianism and **Legalism** (or the **School of Force**, a pessimistic power-oriented sect that flourished in the 3rd century BC). The historicity of Lao-tzu is unprovable; some place him in the 6th century BC, casting further doubt on his connection with the book. He is said to have lived 160 years and to have been the curator of the Imperial Library at K'au, leaving in his later years when he found the triviality of court and city life unnecessary to his inner existence. The story goes that as he was exiting the empire on a buffalo, he was stopped at the frontier by the Keeper of the Pass and asked to record his wisdom for posterity. Lao then wrote out the 5,000 characters that became the *Tao Te Ching,* or "Book of the Way and Its Manifestation."

Composed of 81 very brief chapters, the *Tao Te Ching* is a short book that can easily be read in one sitting. Although much of it sounds vague and theoretical, it also conveys specific, practical advice on the ruling of nations:

When a country is governed with tolerance,
The people are genuine and honest.
When a country is governed with repression,
The people are more deceitful and dishonest. (60)

Despite the minimalist feel of these instructions, history does record the results of the reign of one Taoist ruler who actively followed Lao-tzu's formulas for governing. Among other accomplishments, **Emperor Han Wen Ti** (179–157 BC) did away with punishment by mutilation and with laws requiring the execution of an entire family because one member had committed a capital crime. Instead of warring on the northern barbarians, he approached them with presents and an exchange of trade. And he did all this while lowering taxes and cutting waste and corruption in the royal court. Chinese historians praised him because "the Empress's skirt did not touch the ground"—cut short as an austerity measure. According to another account, Wen abandoned the building of the projected Dew Tower because it would cost a hundred ingots of gold. "I will not spend on this building what will furnish ten households with a fortune," he said. The upshot of Wen Ti's policies was that the Chinese empire flourished under his rule as it had not done for centuries.

For all that, the basic thrust of the *Tao Te Ching* is away from activity of any sort, and in this sense it is related to the goal of nonattachment to the fruits of one's actions espoused in the *Bhagavad-Gita**. Lao-tzu's response to the chaos of his times can also be seen as an alternative to that developed by Confucius and his followers: if civilization is so unpredictably violent, venal, and cruel, why have anything to do with it at all? The question of whether Ch'an Buddhism, which became known as Zen in Japan, influenced more than it was influenced by Taoism may be unresolvable. For example, "returning to the root" is a Taoist practice accomplished by emptying the mind of desire (cf. the Buddhist trishna*), subtracting and decreasing until "he finally reaches a non-action which only the Tao can fill." In addition, Taoist terms such as wu wei ("non-doing"), "sitting in forgetfulness," practicing "a fast of the mind," and becoming an "empty vessel" receptive to everything and anything resonate with the principles of Zen meditation. Much of the *Tao Te Ching* objects to the foolishness of purposeful action in a way that is clearly coherent with Zen:

The more prohibitions you have,
the less virtuous people will be.
The more weapons you have,
the less secure people will be.
The more subsidies you have,
the less self-reliant people will be. (57)

Chuang-tzu, who lived c. 389–286 BC and grew up in the same part of China as Lao-tzu knowing the *Tao Te Ching,* expanded on its short, pithy maxims in the *Chuang-tzu* (sometimes called *The Divine Classic of Nan-hua*). Although it is 33 chapters long, only the first 7, or Inner Chapters, are considered to be indisputably the work of the master, the rest presumably coming from his disciples and later commentators. Chuang's most famous story concerns his dream of being a butterfly. The dream felt so real, he said, that when he awoke, he couldn't be sure whether he was Chuang-tzu who had dreamed that he was a butterfly or a butterfly dreaming that he was Chuang-tzu. The authors of the Upa-

THE BALLAD OF NO-TOES
AND CONFUCIUS

Many of Chuang-tzu's stories and comments were directed against the teachings of Confucius, which from his Taoist point of view seemed to support the status quo. In a witty and biting style, Chuang-tzu lampooned the Confucian ideals of jen and li as superficial and superfluous, further examples of interfering with the natural order of things. Recognizing or discovering that natural order in oneself and in the outer world was one of the chief virtues proposed by both Chuang and Lao. In this story believed to come directly from Chuang-tzu, Confucius is shown as a judgmental moralizer rather than one who intuits the natural way.

There was a cripple in Lu named Shu Shan No-Toes. He came walking on his heels to see Confucius. Confucius said, "You did not take care. You committed a crime and brought this trouble upon yourself. What is the use of coming to me now?"

No-Toes said, "I didn't know how to behave properly, and took my body lightly, so I lost my toes. I have come here with something more precious than toes, and it is this which I seek to preserve. There is nothing that heaven does not cover. There is nothing that earth does not sustain. I thought that you, Master, were like heaven and earth. How was I to know that you would receive me this way?"

Confucius said, "It was stupid of me. Why don't you come in! Let us talk."

But No-Toes walked out.

Confucius said, "This is a good lesson, disciples! A toeless cripple is still willing to atone for his past misdeeds. How much more can be done by those who haven't had such bad luck."

No-Toes went to see Lao Tsu and said, "Is Confucius yet a perfect man? Why does he keep imitating you? He is trying to gain a reputation by pretending to know strange and extraordinary things. He does not know that real sages look upon these as cuffs and fetters."

Lao Tsu said, "Why don't you simply make him see that life and death are one thread, the same line viewed from different sides—and thus free him from his cuffs and fetters? Is that possible?"

No-Toes said, "If heaven wants to punish him, who can free him?"

—*CHUANG-TZU: INNER CHAPTERS*, TRANSLATED BY
GIA-FU FENG AND JANE ENGLISH

nishads* could hardly have stated the illusoriness of the phenomenal world any more deftly.

Lieh-tzu, whose authorship of a book named after him is disputed, and **Yang Chu,** of whom no writings remain, come to us with no biographical details. But they are said to have pursued themes common to Philosophical Taoism, such as the direct experience of the Tao and the point-lessness of personal striving or intervention in human affairs.

Toward the end of the Han dynasties (AD 220) Taoism began to out-strip Confucianism as the philosophy of choice of the intellectual elite, es-pecially as Confucianism became reduced to little more than ritualized codes of conduct and a kind of handbook for civil servants. Confronted with the same disordered society, in which the race was so clearly not al-ways to the swift, Taoists chose to base their behavior on inclinations that came to them in their meditative trances, preferring to be true to their own natures rather than to established conventions.

Over time, Taoists began to combine yogic and mystical practices with self-hypnosis, restrictive diets, and drugs, not only to induce transcendent states but also in the hope of achieving greater longevity. More and more, Taoism came to be associated with ways of prolonging life; fantastic sto-ries about masters who lived very long lives, exercised magical powers, and ascended into heaven in broad daylight became commonplace. Again, some observers claim that the import of these elements has been

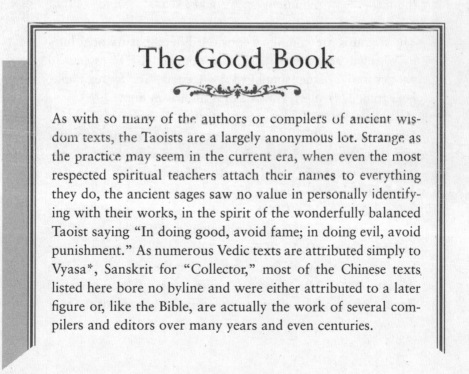

The Good Book

As with so many of the authors or compilers of ancient wis-dom texts, the Taoists are a largely anonymous lot. Strange as the practice may seem in the current era, when even the most respected spiritual teachers attach their names to everything they do, the ancient sages saw no value in personally identify-ing with their works, in the spirit of the wonderfully balanced Taoist saying "In doing good, avoid fame; in doing evil, avoid punishment." As numerous Vedic texts are attributed simply to Vyasa*, Sanskrit for "Collector," most of the Chinese texts listed here bore no byline and were either attributed to a later figure or, like the Bible, are actually the work of several com-pilers and editors over many years and even centuries.

I Ching ("Book of Change")

The oldest and best-known book of Chinese wisdom was composed primarily during the late 2nd–early 1st millennium bc, with later additions of mostly Confucian but some Taoist ideas. Primarily used for casting oracles, the I Ching is believed by many Taoist adepts to be a guide to the secrets of the "celestial mechanism," a tool for understanding and living in harmony with the flow of events in the universe. It is based on the opposing principles of light and dark, later referred to as yin and yang, whose interaction yields change. The Ching is made up of different arrangements of broken (– –) and unbroken (—) lines which represent yin and yang, respectively. The lines are arranged in 8 groups of 3 lines, called **trigrams**, each of which has specific associations:

heaven ☰ earth ☷ fire ☲ water ☵
thunder ☳ mountain ☶ lake ☱ wind ☴

The trigrams are combined into 64 different pairs of 6 lines each called **hexagrams**, originally obtained by throwing 50 yarrow stalks, later simplified to 3 coins. So, for example, hexagram 1, *Heaven,* consists of 6 unbroken lines: ䷀
Hexagram 2, *Earth,* consists of 6 broken lines: ䷁
Hexagram 3, *Difficulty,* is made up of the trigrams for water and thunder: ䷂ Hexagram 4, *Darkness,* consists of the trigrams for mountain and water: ䷃ Hexagram 64, *Unsettled,* combines fire and water: ䷿

Traditionally, the *Ching* was composed by four different men—**Fu Hsi** (c. 2850 BC), Chou dynasty founder **Wen Wang** and his son the **Duke of Chou** (12th–11th century BC), and Confucius—taking its final form during the rest of the Chou dynasty (1150–249 BC) and remaining essentially unchanged since. However, no convincing proof exists that any of the four men was involved at all. The two traditional ways of arranging the 64 hexagrams are known as the **Fu Hsi Sequence** and the **King Wen Sequence,** after two of its purported developers. The Fu Hsi, composed in the 11th century, looks somewhat different from the King Wen as in the examples just shown. For instance, the first 8 hexagrams in the Fu Hsi Sequence look like this:

The Fu Hsi is said to have led the 17th-century scientist-philosopher **Gottfried Leibnitz,** credited with fathering calculus, to the discovery of a functioning binary system, as described by the modern translator R. L. Wing in *The Illustrated I Ching:*

A Jesuit priest in China at the time, Father Joachim Bouvet, showed this sequence to Leibnitz, who was astonished to discover that if you substitute 0 for each solid line and 1 for each broken line—and then take the hexagrams in order, reading upward on each—you get the sequences 000000, 000001, 0000010, 000011, and so forth. This is none other than the binary notation for numbers 0 through 63! The uncovering of such a binary code allowed Leibnitz to change the path of mathematics for all time.

This is the same mathematical system that is the basis of all computer languages. Furthermore, since the powers of 2 seem to manifest in all physical and natural structures, it is not surprising that Chinese scholars have been able to apply the 64 hexagrams to nearly everything—from crystalline structures, to DNA, to the movements of the galaxies.

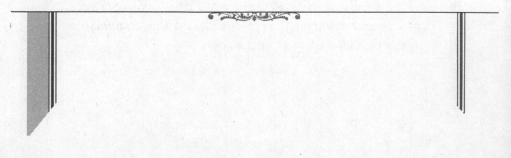

Tao Te Ching ("Book of the Way and Its Manifestation")

Despite its seminal importance to Taoism and its influence on Zen Buddhism, this work is often mystifying, perhaps the inevitable result of trying to describe in words what the author insists is ineffable, unnameable, and unknowable. In the notes to his clear, eminently readable modern translation, Stephen Mitchell quotes the modern Chinese poet **Po Chu-:**

"He who talks doesn't know,
and he who knows doesn't talk":
that is what Lao-tzu told us,
in a book of five thousand words.
If he was the one who knew,
how could he have been such a blabbermouth?

Although it was traditionally attributed to Lao-tzu, many scholars now believe that the work was composed centuries after his death.

Chuang-Tzu

Only the first seven of this work's 33 chapters are accepted as the genuine work of the master, yet they contain more elaboration and detail than the 81 wispy chapters of the *Tao Te Ching*. The extent to which Chuang expanded on that book has led one commentator to remark that he was to Lao-tzu what St. Paul was to Jesus Christ and Plato was to Socrates, exploring and developing the other's ideas with a combination of rigorous logic and sheer imagination.

Lu Shih Ch'un Ch'iu ("Spring and Autumn of Master Lu")

Compiled, according to tradition, by **Lu Pu-wei** in the 3rd century BC from the teachings of upwards of 10,000 scholars in the Taoist, Confucianist, Legalist, and Mohist traditions.

Huai Nan Tzu

A 2nd-century BC compilation of contemporary teachings, with an emphasis on the developing systems of Taoism, including the Five Elements and yin-yang.

Hua Hu Ching ("Classic on Converting the Barbarians")

An account of Lao-tzu's missionary travels, created c. 300 AD, to back up the theory that when Lao left China he headed west to India where he converted the Buddha! This supposedly proved that Buddhism was an imperfectly understood spin-off of Taoism. Another version of the same concept was that Lao-tzu had somehow *become* the Buddha. The Buddhists countered by revising history to claim that the Buddha was actually born in the 11th century BC, thus obviating the possibility that Lao-tzu could have had any impact on him whatsoever.

Tao Tsang

A large body of writings, much of it esoteric, makes up the basis of Taoist doctrine. Encompassing almost 1,500 works, undated and anonymous, in nearly 5,500 volumes, including material as old as the 5th century AD, the *Tao Tsang* began to be compiled during the 8th century, was catalogued during the 10th, and first printed in 1019. After further work, it was completed during the Ming dynasty in essentially the same form in which it exists today.

T'ai Shang Kan Ying P'ien ("Tractate on Actions and Retributions")

This Sung dynasty text outlines the reporting of an individual's good and evil deeds by the Three Worms (San Ch'ung) and the God of the Stove, Tsao-chun (or Lord of Destiny, Ssu-ming), and the lengthening or shortening of his or her life accordingly. The penalties range from 100 days lopped off for a minor offense to 12 years for serious evil—whereas 300 good deeds will make a person a terrestrial immortal, capable of healing and helping others, and 1,300 ensures celestial immortality. Good deeds can be as simple as printing and distributing free copies of the *Tractate* itself or other **shan-shu** (folk manuals of religious ritual and devotion) or as elaborate as building hospitals and orphanages or doing other charitable works. Another popular practice described in the *Tractate* is the burning of paper money, created expressly for this purpose, in furnaces located just outside a temple. Following the Chinese metaphor of heavenly and underworld bureaucracy, the paper money is thought to be deposited in the underworld bank, where its interest can bribe corrupt officials and pay for atonement of wrongs in hell.

The punishable offenses are less Taoist than Confucian and Buddhist, including disobedience or contradiction of one's elders or superiors, boastfulness, bribery and fraud, stealing, lying, adultery, and the killing of animals. The faithful are also advised against urinating in a northerly direction (the realm of the spirits) or spitting at a falling star. Probably because of its mundane nature, the *Tractate* is the most influential religious book among the Chinese masses to this day, whether in mainland or maritime China or the large overseas Chinese community.

T'ai I Chin Hua Tsung Chih ("The Secret of the Golden Flower")

Showing the influence of Taoist schools of alchemy and inner hygiene, as well as Ch'an (Zen) Buddhism, this text expounds the method for creating a sacred embryo within the adept's body as a way of achieving immortality. Attributed to **Lu Tung-pin** of the T'ang dynasty (618–907), it is now believed to have been composed in the 17th or 18th century. Carl Jung*, who wrote a lengthy commentary to the 1929 German translation, is responsible for introducing this work to the West.

The Four Books and the Five Classics

Together, the Four Books and Five Classics make up the basic texts of Confucianism. By no means were they all written by Confucius, although he did have a hand at least in editing a number of them. The Five Classics were written by the 2nd century BC: the *I Ching,* the *Shih Ching* ("Book of Odes"), the *Shu Ching* ("Book of History"), the *Ch'un Ch'iu* ("Spring and Autumn Annals"), and the *Book of Rites.* Sometime in the 12th century AD, two chapters were removed from the *Book of Rites* and made into two of the Four Books: *Great Learning* and *Doctrine of the Mean.* The *Analects* of Confucius and the *Book of Mencius,* by the great Confucian idealist, are the other two of the Four Books.

exaggerated by Western popularizers and that they do not make up a significant portion of current Taoist beliefs.

❋ IN THE BEGINNING: TRADITIONAL CHINESE RELIGION

The standard start-up dates for Taoism—somewhere between Lao-tzu in the 6th century BC and Chuang-tzu and others in the 4th and 3rd—may give a mistaken impression that Chinese religion is merely a contemporary of Buddhism and not as ancient as Hinduism or Judaism. But the underlying principles around which Taoism developed and which still inform much of Chinese ritual life—yin-yang and the Five Elements—were already present much earlier. The root text of the *I Ching,* which is based on the yin-yang system, dates from at least the 12th and 11th centuries BC. Its symbolism revolves around cycles of insemination and maturation, indicating that it probably reaches back to a much earlier time when worship of the Goddess* may have been tied to all human, animal, and agricultural gestation.

These principles form an integral part of Chinese folk religion. And like Confucianism, both branches of Taoism developed and continue to exist alongside folk religion, sometimes influencing, sometimes borrowing from it. To understand Taoism, we need at least a passing acquaintance with the basics of China's traditional religious beliefs.

The first conceptions of deity in Chinese religion were personifications of natural forces (thunder, lightning, mountains, rivers, bodies of water, flora and fauna) or metaphysical notions. From the earliest days of shamanism, for example, the concept of a **Supreme One** (sometimes called the **Pole Star Deity** after its identification with the North Star) or **T'ai I** ("Grand Unity") was accepted. Early texts like the *Chiu-ko* ("Nine Songs") already speak of making sacrifices to T'ai I, perhaps in a similar spirit to the earliest Vedic sacrifices of India. References to the One appear in Lao-tzu, Chuang-tzu, and Confucius, and the ancient concepts of yin and yang were later said to have developed from their original united form in T'ai I. Later still, T'ai I was worshiped as ruler of the **Three Ones,** or **San I,** the other two being the Celestial One (**T'ien I**) and the Earthly One (**Ti I**).

Somewhat synonymous with T'ai I is the concept of **T'ai Chi** ("ridge beam," i.e., "Ultimate Cause"), which appears in the *I Ching* and which indicates a primordial essence out of which everything else develops. According to the *Ching,* the complementary energies of yin and yang grew out of T'ai Chi, and the rest of the universe, called the **Ten Thousand Things,** arose from the mingling of yin and yang. (T'ai Chi should not be confused with **t'ai chi ch'uan,** the art that combines movement and breathing for use as physical exercise, meditation, and self-defense, dating from early in the 2nd millennium.) T'ai I and T'ai Chi both are thought to have arisen out of **T'ai Hsu** ("Great Void").

One of the earliest personified deities in the folk religion is **Ssu-ming**

("Lord of Fate"), who later became popular as **Tsao-chun** ("Stove or Kitchen God") and is still the most significant Chinese folk deity today. Said to have originated as early as 800 BC, Ssu-ming keeps a record of each individual's sins and failings, which he presents to T'ai I each New Year's Day, along with his recommendation for extending or shortening that person's life. The goal of one school of Taoism was to remove one's name from Ssu-ming's *Book of Death* and have it written in his *Book of Life,* which contains the names of the immortals.

Already in these early times, the Chinese imagined heaven as a vast bureaucracy overseen by the **Jade Emperor (Yu Huang)**, who appoints spirits of the virtuous deceased as administrative gods to hold heavenly offices and respond to earthly requests. Following the age-old spiritual principle of "as above, so below," these gods were assigned specific tasks and areas of responsibility. If they did not perform well, they could be demoted, removed, and replaced by other gods; if they succeeded, they were promoted. In this heavenly mirroring of the way the earthly empire was run, we see how highly the Chinese regarded the orderliness of bureaucratic government. So essential was it that the celestial bureaucracy was later internalized by an important sect, the Inner Gods Hygiene School, for whom each significant figure among the gods had a counterpart in the running of the human body and spirit.

The celestial bureaucracy is arrayed against the forces of evil and disorder, especially demons called **kuei** ("ghosts") who cause pain, illness, natural calamities, and death. And so the minor gods are not worshiped so much as petitioned for aid in specific situations, much the way pious Christians call on St. Anthony to help them find a lost object.

Probably influenced by Buddhist notions of hell realms with different levels of punishments, the Chinese believe in a period of processing and purification in hell after death, whereupon the soul, after leaving the yin underworld, ascends into the pure yang of heaven. Unlike the Western version of hell, though, it is not a place of eternal damnation, except perhaps for certain demons and politicians; for everyone else it is a purgatory where the alchemical fires of the cosmos purify the spirit. To help speed up this process of refinement and assist the souls of the dead on their journey from hell to heaven, the Chinese employ Taoist and Buddhist funeral ceremonies and memorial services; in recent years, Christian funeral rites have been added and are often performed in tandem

171

with Buddhist services. According to this scheme of things, Taoist sages who practice the various alchemies or refinements of ch'i and ching and live to 120 years or so do not need further purification and may fly off to heaven in broad daylight.

Along with deity worship, the popular faith also incorporated elements of shamanism, sacrifice, divination, sorcery, and alchemy, in no particular order of significance.

Shamans*, a difficult group to characterize, may be among the most ancient spiritual practitioners. Usually associated with tribal societies of north and central Asia, North America, and the Arctic, shamans are spiritually gifted people who through a variety of means have acquired the ability to help others with psychic powers, trance, and dream journeying. They played a key role in developing the early concepts of deity.

Besides being directed to deities like T'ai I, sacrifices* were offered to departed ancestors, who were believed to play a crucial role in people's lives. The spirits of the dead could be benevolent and helpful by sending signs from the beyond. Or they could be dangerous and malevolent, in which case they were known as kuei (pronounced "gway"). Kuei were not one's ancestors but the souls of those who suffered bad or unjust deaths (drowning and hanging were two of the worst) or whose bodies were not interred according to proper custom. They could be expected to avenge any wrongs done to them on earth and were to be fought off with the aid of spirit mediums or Taoist priests.

Signs transmitted from the beyond by ancestors were difficult to read. Any event that could not be otherwise explained—a vase or fan falling off a table, a sudden fit of coughing or sneezing—could be a signal from the beyond, which then needed to be interpreted. **Divination** or **augury** developed to help predict future events by reading these signs, as well as through other means such as by tossing yarrow sticks or coins and consulting the *I Ching*.

Alchemy is the attempt both to transmute base metals like lead or iron to gold and to find the elixir of life, a potion that when drunk bestows immortality. (Since gold is an incorruptible metal, some alchemists believed that by ingesting small portions of it they could assume its incorruptible qualities.) Sometimes credited to the 1st-century Egyptians, alchemy is now believed to have originated in China and is usually traced to **Tsou Yen,** who flourished early in the 3rd century BC (although the first recorded experiments didn't take place until the next century). After his era, magicians supposedly began spreading his prescriptions for immortality even as they sought new ways to concoct an elixir. Known as **fang shih** ("masters of prescriptions" or "recipe gentlemen"), these early magicians and shamans from the northeast coast were masters of the secrets of vitality, sexual practice (fang-chung shu), and geomancy (**feng shui**), the science of choosing auspicious sites and layouts for buildings, graves, or the furniture in one's home. The fang shih claimed to have learned the secret of immortality from immortals (**hsien**) who dwelt on distant mountain peaks and insisted it all had to do with safeguarding one's ch'i.

Techniques for preserving ch'i include a form of breath control and energy recirculation called **hsing-ch'i** ("the microcosmic orbit" or "inner alchemy"), the use of medicinal herbs, alchemy, and **tao-yin** (breathing and stretching exercises based on the movements of cranes and tortoises, which were believed to lead long lives). Fang shih created and imbibed concoctions of potentially deadly metals like gold, lead, and mercury, which were said to have been transmuted into elixirs of immortality. The first elixir was thought to be cinnabar, or mercuric sulfide (the only important ore of mercury), which can be synthesized and is now used mainly as the pigment vermilion.

Historically, alchemy has usually had an esoteric, mystical dimension in which the transmutation of base metals into gold or some elixir of life serves as a metaphor for transforming the individual's preoccupations from the material to the spiritual—a search for celestial rather than physical immortality. But the fact remains that many alchemists and those who sought their services were after more material benefits. Sad to relate, the thirst for immortality among the ancient Chinese was apparently such that even the deaths of many prominent figures, including several emperors, did not deter others from ingesting what can only be described as poisonous metallic substances. Before we dismiss the experiments of the Taoist alchemists too lightly, though, we should note that the by-products of these experiments included the discovery of new metallic alloys, porcelains and dyes, medicinal herbs and compounds, the compass, and gunpowder.

The quest for immortality also led, beginning in the reign of Duke Wei

MAJOR CHINESE DYNASTIES
AT A GLANCE

Hsia →	c. 2000–1523 BC
Shang and Yin →	c. 1523–1027 BC
Chou →	1111–255 BC
Ch'in →	221–206 BC
Hsi (Western) Han →	206 BC–25 AD
Tung (Eastern) Han →	AD 25–220
T'ang →	618–907
Sung →	960–1279
Yuan (Mongol) →	1260–1368
Ming →	1368–1644
Ch'ing →	1644–1911

of Ch'i (357–320 BC), to mariners' searching for the **isles of the immortals.** These islands, called **P'eng-lai, Fang-chang,** and **Ying-chou,** were thought to lie somewhere off the eastern coast of China, where the mushroom of immortality (ling-chih) was said to grow.

Between 220 and 120 BC, fang shih began to influence emperors, the first of whom, Shih Huang Ti, united China in 221 BC and started the **Ch'in dynasty,** which gave China its name. One of the most influential fang shih was **Li Shao-chun,** who specialized in alchemy as a path to immortality and contributed two important firsts to Chinese and world history. In 133 BC he convinced Emperor Han Wu Ti to permit experiments seeking to transmute cinnabar into gold, the first recorded alchemical efforts in history, predating those of the Egyptians by about 200 years. (The cinnabar wasn't eaten, as it was later in China, but was made into bowls for food. The desired result of eating from these bowls was longevity rather than immortality.) Li also persuaded the emperor to support the worship of Tsao-chun, whose popularity has since increased to the point at which, as the Kitchen God, his image hangs in innumerable

174

TAO BY THE NUMBERS

As with the other major Eastern religions—and most Western ones for that matter—many of Taoism's important principles come in numbered groups. Why spiritual traditions have a predilection for numbering is unclear, except that it may make complex subjects easier to remember—like the Ten Commandments.

The Three Treasures To preserve and extend life, the adept must learn to achieve the appropriate balance of 3 essential factors.

Ching ("essence") refers to the male and female sexual fluids (semen and menstrual flow). But it usually connotes the subtle essence of those fluids, which can be increased by mingling with the ching of the opposite sex, as long as the coarse male ching is retained as much as possible. This explains the significance of the Ho Ch'i festivities, which offered ample opportunity for multiple ching-mingling. (The same word, written as a different Chinese character, refers to a classic work, as in *I Ching* or *Tao Te Ching*.)

Ch'i means "breath, energy, or vitality" and can refer to either the human breath or a kind of cosmic vitality or life force, the manifestation (**te**) of the Tao. Ch'i collects near the navel and, like ching, must be conserved; the loss of either spells illness or death. There are many different designations of ch'i, such as **nei-ch'i** ("inner breath"), **wai-ch'i** ("outer breath"), **yuan-ch'i** ("primordial breath," or cosmic energy), **yin ch'i** ("earth vitality") and **yang ch'i** ("cosmic vitality").

Shen refers to mind, or the personal spirit, which arises from the union of ching and ch'i and which can be either pure (**yuan-shen**, "spiritual consciousness") or impure (**shih-shen**, "ordinary consciousness"). In its pure form, shen may be akin to the Holy Spirit* of Christianity or the ishtadeva* of

Vedanta. (The same term can also refer to deities that dwell in either the universe or the individual body.)

All humans are endowed with the Three Treasures, but material desires coarsen them, and they must be refined through various kinds of alchemy, meditation, physical exercise, and breathing techniques.

The Five Elements Collectively known as **wu hsing,** the Five Elements are, in order of importance, water, fire, wood, metal, and earth, although they are thought of as more than material elements. The Chinese term means "five movers," emblematic of the qualities and proclivities of those elements. The theory of wu hsing was probably first propounded in the 4th or 3rd century BC by the alchemist Tsou Yen and may have been responsible for starting the search for an elixir of life. The **Five Elements School,** which Tsou Yen represents, is now considered part of the **Yin-Yang School** that flourished during the 3rd century BC; they are currently referred to collectively as the Yin-Yang Five Elements School. According to the general theory, the Five Elements create each other in seasonal, cyclical fashion: wood/spring gives birth to fire/summer (wood creates fire by burning), fire to the cyclical pattern of earth, earth to metal/autumn (metals come from the earth), metal to water/winter. But they also destroy or conquer each other in a specific sequence: wood grows from earth, metal chops wood, fire melts metal, water extinguishes fire, earth clogs waterways with mud. The elements reflect not only the seasons but also characteristics such as color, flavor, compass directions, and internal organs and bodily components including the liver, pancreas, blood, bones, kidneys, muscles, and heart and, by extension, all created things, including successive dynasties and human growth.

The Eight Immortals

The Eight Immortals, or **Pa-hsien,** developed between the T'ang and Ming dynasties and symbolize good fortune. They inhabit **Mount K'un-lun** and are ruled by **Hsi Wang Mu,** the ancient goddess of the plague who became known as the **Queen Mother of the West** and who grows the **Peaches of Immortality** (eating one of them bestows perpetual life). More folkloric than strictly religious, these 8 figures and their symbols turn up in popular crafts and artworks, on utensils, fans, and clothing, as well as in literature and are said to represent 8 different states in life: youth and age, poverty and wealth, aristocracy and the masses, feminine and masculine. Some are based on historic personages whose actual biographies have since faded into the mists of legend; others are figures of myth. Their precise identities and depic-tions vary from era to era, but certain aspects remain constant.

Chang Kuo Lao (d. c. AD 745)   Symbol: fish-drum consisting of a section of bamboo and two sticks. A T'ang Taoist, he owned a magic white donkey that could be folded and carried in his pocket and brought back to life size by sprinkling it with water.

Chung Li-ch'uan (Han Chung-li)   Symbol: palm-leaf fan. A Han dynasty bald man with a big stomach and a long beard, Chung was a former general who lost a war with Tibetan rebels, retreated to the forests, and there learned the secret of immortality from Taoist sages.

Ts'ao Kuo-chiu (d. AD 1097)   Symbol: a pair of wooden castanets. A bearded man with a winged hat. The most famous story about Ts'ao has two other immortals asking him where the Tao is located. When he points to heaven, they then ask where heaven is. He points to his heart, and they acknowledge him as a master of the Way.

Lu Tung-pin (c. AD 800)   Symbol: his sword. He used his sword not for combat but to render himself invisible and to "lop off passions and desires."

Ho Hsien-ku Symbol: a lotus leaf. The only female immortal, Ho was a T'ang dynasty hermit vowed to chastity. When pressured to marry, she disappeared, leaving behind her slippers, a Chinese symbol of having achieved immortality.

Li Hsuan (Li T'ieh-kuai) Symbol: an iron staff or crutch and a hollow gourd containing magic potions. Various legends attribute his bad leg to an incident that occurred after his spirit left his sleeping body to go by astral travel* to a sacred mountain. When the person Li had assigned to guard his body was called away to attend his dying mother, he either abandoned Li's body to be devoured by animals or mistakenly burned it. In any case, when Li's spirit returned, it was forced to inhabit instead the deformed, lame body of a beggar who had recently died.

Han Hsiang-tzu Symbol: a flute. A young T'ang dynasty scholar who wrote poetry and loved music.

Lan Ts'ai-ho Symbol: a basket of flowers. Tradition says he wandered the streets dressed like a beggar with one foot bare, singing songs for money. He wore heavy clothes in summer, light things in winter, and stayed drunk most of the time. He is said to have flown off to heaven on a crane while still alive.

The Three Teachings From at least the 1st century AD, Confucianism, Taoism, and Buddhism have each been considered sacred, and by the 11th century, Chinese religious culture was thoroughly steeped in a synthesis of the three. It wasn't just that believers of one tradition accepted the others as valid but that they actually practiced elements of all three. Referred to as **San-chiao kuei-i,** or "Three religions, one culture," this openness reflects the sharing of the basics of yin-yang cosmology in popular religion. Despite the occasional attempts by certain emperors to counteract, persecute, or stamp out one or another of these traditions, most Chinese assimilated the Three Teachings in different proportions in their own belief systems, so that in general a Taoist could feel comfortable worshiping in a Buddhist temple and vice versa; a Buddhist might have an image of the Kitchen God or K'ung-tzu alongside images of Buddhas and bodhisattvas in the home. One saying goes, "Confucian head, Buddhist heart, Taoist belly," implying that even today, at least among those Chinese who are not doctrinaire Marxists, elements of Confucian ethics and morality, Buddhist funeral rituals and prayers for the dead, and Taoist philosophical attitudes toward nature all form a part of their lives. Along with that, they are likely to incorporate elements of folk religion and the ancient cult of ancestor worship, making the Chinese perhaps the most religiously pluralistic people on earth.

The Three Pure Ones Presumably because of growing competition from elaborate Buddhist temples, with their imposing statues of the Buddha, Taoist temples began to exhibit statues of the Taoist Trinity, who came to be known as San Ch'ing. Odd as it may seem to Western minds, not all temples agree on the identity of the Three Pure Ones, even though they have gone on to become the highest deities of Religious Taoism. Four or five figures share these high positions.

Yuan-shih t'ien-tsun ("Celestial Venerable of the Primordial Beginning") resides in the Heaven of Jade Purity, the first and highest heaven. He is considered to have created heaven and earth, and is responsible for transmitting the Scriptures of the Magic Jewel to lower gods.

Ling Pao, or T'ai-shang tao-chun ("Celestial Venerable of the Magic Jewel") is the embodiment of yin and yang and past time. He lives in the second heaven, the Heaven of High Purity.

Lao Chun ("Master Lao"), the deified form of Lao-tzu, is

the embodiment of Taoism and of the future; he lives in the third heaven, the Heaven of Highest Purity. He is also known as **Tao-te t'ien-tsun** ("Celestial Venerable of the Tao and Its Power").

Yu Huang (the **Jade Emperor**) embodies the Primal Cause and the present and is responsible for all events on earth and in heaven. The Jade Emperor began as the assistant of Yuan-shih t'ien-tsun, and despite the fact that he later supplanted Yuan-shih, in some temples the latter appears instead of the former.

Another figure who sometimes appears among the Three Pure Ones is **Chin-ch'ueh yu-ch'en t'ien-tsun** ("Celestial Venerable of Jade Dawn and the Golden Gate").

the point at which, as the Kitchen God, his image hangs in innumerable Chinese homes today.

Among other things, Li Shao-chun claimed to have visited one of the isles of the immortals and to have become immortal himself. When he died, the emperor, to whom he had promised immortality, decided that Li hadn't actually died but had merely been "liberated from the corpse" (**shih-chieh**) and departed to the land of the immortals.

❋ INTO THE MYSTIC

Philosophical Taoism continued to evolve after Religious Taoism became prominent, proceeding in a more mystical and less pragmatic or superstitious mode than Tao-chiao. One development was a 3rd-to-4th-century AD movement known as **hsuan-hsuch** ("dark and mystical teaching" or "secret of secrets"), commonly called Neo-Taoism. **Neo-Taoism** combined Philosophical Taoist theory with Confucian principles, but leaned toward Confucius.

The adherents of this school developed a way of discussing the works of Lao-tzu and Chuang-tzu known as Ch'ing-t'an ("pure conversation"), or philosophy for its own sake. **Ch'ing-t'an** involved reinterpreting Taoist and Confucian writings in a Neo-Taoist way and was later applied to a school that emphasized this practice. Members of the school argued that Confucius was more of a Taoist than Lao-tzu because, unlike Lao, who spoke of vanquishing desire, K'ung had entirely given up the urge to try (inferred from the fact that he never mentioned it in his writings). By this curious logic, they found it acceptable to seek political office as Confucius had, and in fact they sought to make Taoism compatible with public life. The school's most prominent members were **Wang-pi** (226–249), who wrote major commentaries on the *Tao Te Ching* and *I Ching* and is considered a founder of the Ch'ing-t'an school; **Hsiang-hsiu** (c. 221–300), who wrote a famous commentary on the *Chuang-tzu;* and **Kuo Hsiang** (d. c. 312), who wrote one on Lao-tzu.

Perhaps the most fascinating pure conversationalists were the **Seven Sages of the Bamboo Grove (Chu-lin ch'i-hsien)**. Made up of 3rd-century Neo-Taoist artists and scholars, the Seven Sages led a carefree life, reading poetry, drinking wine, playing the lute, and practicing **feng liu** ("wandering from conversation"). This latter practice entailed having pure conversation until they reached a point at which they stopped talking, which led, according to **Fung Yu-lan**, one of the Seven, to "silently understanding each other with a smile"—a phrase that recalls the secret transmission of knowledge from the Buddha to Mahakashyapa*. The Sages invariably wound up at a local tavern to complete the day's carouse and practiced giving in to every impulse, whether socially acceptable or not.

The group's name came from a bamboo grove near the home of their leader, **Hsi K'ang;** other notable members were **Juan Chi** (210–263), **Juan Hsien,** and the biggest winebibber of them all, **Liu Ling** (221–300). Liu reportedly was followed closely by a servant with a wine bottle in one hand and a spade in the other, in the event that Liu either sobered up too much or drank himself to death. Famous for walking around his house in the nude, Liu was once questioned by a Confucian visitor who was shocked that he wasn't wearing trousers. "The whole universe is my house and this room is my trousers," Liu Ling responded. "What are you doing here inside my trousers?"

Perhaps because of such hijinks, the early Neo-Taoists fell into disfavor with the likes of **Ko Hung** (284–364), an influential but eclectic alchemist and author, who found them lacking in strong religious values. Called **Pao P'u-tzu** after his encyclopedia of practices for becoming immortal, Ko used Taoism as a basis for alchemy and combined various Taoist beliefs with Confucian morality. He preferred Confucius to Lao and Chuang because the latter two opposed the notion of physical immortality as one more earthly vanity. Confucius, once again, had nothing to say on the matter and so left the door open to dabblers like Ko. An early version of today's smart-drug users, Ko claimed recipes for magic pills that would allow users to walk on water, raise the newly dead, avoid contracting contagious diseases, achieve any civil service position, enormously enhance memory, and even waterproof their clothing.

SCHOOLS ARE IN

Church Taoism can be divided into two main branches. The first, the **Way of Right Unity (Cheng-i tao)**, encompasses those schools that use magical practices such as amulets, talismans (**fu-lu**), and exorcisms. This branch was begun by **Chang Tao-ling** (or Chang Ling, AD 34–156), who worked as a healer in Szechuan province, employing magical cures. The price for a cure was five pecks of rice, the same name applied to the very important school he founded. **The Five Pecks of Rice School (Wu-tou-mi tao)**, based on teachings found in the *Tao Te Ching* and aimed at healing maladies caused by evil deeds, remained active through the 15th century. Members indulged in mass confessions, fasts, and orgiastic feasts. It was also known as the **School of the Celestial Masters (T'ien-shih tao)**, since Chang Ling was venerated as a Celestial Master, or **t'ien-shih**, a title that was inherited by each of his successors down to the present day. (When this lineage of "Taoist popes," as they are sometimes called, was kicked off the mainland by the Communists in 1949, it continued on Taiwan.) In AD 190, the Celestial Masters sect set up its own political state, ruled along military lines by Chang Ling's grandson **Chang-lu** (2nd century AD), assisted by priestly officials called **libationers (chi-chiu)**.

T'ien-shih should not be confused with the **tao-shih,** a scholar or priest who headed the hierarchy of a Taoist Church congregation and whose office was also hereditary. Tao-shih often wore long robes with wide sleeves and were trained in the use of talismans and ritual spells to ward off evil demons. Even if the tao-shih lived in a monastery, he was allowed to have a wife and family and was supported by an annual banquet at which parishioners gave him certain gifts and by the celestial rice tax, an annual donation of five pecks of rice from each family—obviously descended from Chang Ling's Five Pecks School.

During the 2nd century AD, famine and plagues caused great turmoil and led hundreds of thousands of Chinese to embrace Taoism, which offered a more personal and emotionally appealing form of religion than state Confucianism. The Han dynasty's oppressive rule added to the peasants' suffering and helped to accelerate the swing. One sect that especially profited from this development was the **Way of Supreme Peace (T'ai-p'ing tao)**, founded by **Chang Chueh** (a follower of **Huang-Lao Chun**), who pursued conversion through the use of missionaries. Like the Five Pecks School, Chang believed that public confession of one's sins was an important step toward healing illness and encouraged fasting rituals called **chai.**

In 184, the government took steps to stem the flood of conversions, which led to a reaction among the Taoists. Some 360,000 of them put yellow cloth on their heads on the same day as a show of solidarity (and in honor of the **Yellow Emperor, Huang-ti,** a legendary ruler of the 3rd millennium BC). The rebellion, which became known as the **Rising of the Yellow Turbans (Huang-chin)**, was suppressed and Chang Chueh executed, but the Taoist Church had been established; it continued to function alongside the other currents of Philosophical Taoism and individual Taoist magicians and sorcerers. Although it made ample use of magical elements, including talismans, amulets, holy water, and magic spells, the focus of the early church was more on healing, especially faith healing, than on the elusive search for physical immortality. In this sense, it laid the groundwork for what is today one of the major contributions of Chinese medicine—healing through a variety of methods previously unknown in the West, from herbal remedies to acupuncture* and ch'i-kung.

Buddhist teachers had already begun to trickle into China as early as the 1st century AD (although Bodhidharma would not arrive until about AD 500). They were successful in passing on the dharma for much the same reason that Christianity finally erased paganism in Europe: Mahayana Buddhism offered a plan of general salvation and protection for the masses while the complex Buddhist metaphysical system and scriptures appealed to the intellectual elite. Meanwhile, Buddhist monasteries and rituals for the dead provided physical and spiritual solace in times of stress.

The monks not only taught Buddhist practices and doctrines but also translated Buddhist texts into Chinese. Several of these, especially the *Sukhavati-vyuha* and the *Amitabha-sutra,* put forth the ideas of Pure Land* Buddhism. With its relatively simple requirements of devotion to the Buddha Amitabha* and the recitation of his name, resulting in a ticket to paradise, the Pure Land school grew quickly among the Chinese masses. By the 11th century, Taoist and Buddhist ideas had merged with folk practices to create a popular religion that survives to this day.

Some Buddhist teachings—abstention from stealing, lying, adultery, and alcohol—and practices such as performing good works, building roadside rest stations, and the use of incense, were absorbed by Taoism with the support of the emperors, who found all of the above conducive to order, productivity, and prosperity. But the Taoist Church added a few wrinkles of its own, most notably large public confessions, smaller ritual fasts, and lunar festivities. The festival called the **Union of Breaths (Ho Ch'i)** consisted of a series of sexual orgies held on the first day of the full or new moon from the Han to the Sung dynasties. The union involved was that between yin and yang, female and male vitality, said to enable participants to achieve immortality (or at least feel as if they had): the

184

format was ritual dance and copulation with as many partners as possible.

Ho Ch'i employed a special technique based on the principle that the male sexual fluid, or ching, the essence of yang, is nourished by the yin of the female orgasm. Therefore, the more orgasms the male can induce in his various partners during the festivities without having an ejaculation, the greater his vitality will become. To prevent ejaculation, the adept has to squeeze the urethra near the base of the scrotum with his index and middle fingers. The idea is then to draw the semen, or at least the sexual essence, up through the spinal column to the head. (Medically speaking, the semen itself enters the bladder and is later excreted.) The adept is finally allowed to have an orgasm at the end of the ritual to avoid getting "stoppage sickness." This practice may be the basis of the legend that the Yellow Emperor could have intercourse with 1,200 concubines at a stretch without draining himself.

In alchemical terms, the mingling of mercury (the male essence) with cinnabar (the female essence) reflects the union of heaven and hell in the cauldron of the human body. More orthodox teachers such as Ko Hung insisted on practicing this dual cultivation without the interference of lust and did not allow the male to ejaculate at any time, viewing this as a waste of valuable ching. Other Taoists considered this sexual yoga potentially dangerous in much the same way that most Hindus viewed the Tantric yoga of the Vamachara*, or left-hand path. The danger, though, is not based on any perception that sexuality is gross or immoral but rather that indulgence in the passions can overpower one's spiritual pursuits. These practices, known collectively as **fang-chung shu,** were followed openly until about the 7th century when they were driven underground by Confucian morality.

In modern Taoism, as taught in the West by masters such as **T. K. Shih** and **Mantak Chia,** the emphasis remains on the male's avoiding ejaculation while the female is encouraged to have as many orgasms as she wants but to restrict her menstrual flow, which is where her ching resides.

HYGIENE: WITHIN YOU, WITHOUT YOU

Between the 2nd and 6th centuries AD, alongside Neo-Taoist and Confucianist developments, a movement arose within Religious Taoism of the

THE TENTH CIRCLE

Buddhist ideas of hell were absorbed into the folk religion of China over a long period of time and are reflected in current Chinese folk art. One example is a folk manual called the *Yu-li Pao-ch'ao,* which can be found today in Hong Kong, Taiwan, and Southeast Asia. In a series of drawings it illustrates the levels of punishments lavished on those who commit offenses against their neighbors, as described here by an American scholar who has spent many years in China.

A variety of scrolls depicting hell's punishments are used to decorate the walls of the room where funeral rites are being held, temple halls dedicated to freeing souls from hell, and shan-shu [folk manuals], distributed freely to win merit. Wood block prints depict the ten stages of hell, where every possible offense is punished in gory detail. Thieves' arms are cut off, liars' tongues impaled, male chauvinists sodomized by the saw-like beaks of giant swordfish, gossiping women boiled in a bloody pool, and (in modern versions) bad drivers eternally run over by Taipei taxicabs.

—MICHAEL SASO, *BLUE DRAGON, WHITE TIGER*

Cheng-i Tao branch that came to be known as the Inner Gods **Hygiene School.** According to the Inner Gods school, the body is a microcosm of the universe, with three energy centers called **Fields of Cinnabar (tan t'ien),** and is inhabited by 36,000 gods. These gods correspond to the 36,000 in the outer pantheon (or t'ien), where they serve as heavenly bureaucrats running the physical universe. Hell also has a bureaucratic structure and, greatly influenced by Buddhist notions, was divided into 10 sections dedicated to punishing different kinds of sins, similar to the 9 circles of Dante's *Inferno.*

The most significant inner deities, the San I (Three Ones), live in a compartment in the head and are presided over by T'ai I. The Kitchen God, Tsao-chun, also lives there, keeping his records: the *Book of Death,* which lists the names of mortals, and the *Book of Life,* which lists the immortals. The main goal of the Interior Gods school is to shift one's name from the *Book of Death* to the *Book of Life.*

Alongside the 36,000 gods live the **Three Worms (San-ch'ung),** which also dwell in the Cinnabar Fields and cause illness, aging, and death. They report on the sins of their host in an effort to shorten his or her life and so set themselves free. Since the Three Worms live on the five grains (wheat, barley, millet, rice, and beans), true adepts must avoid grains (a practice called **pi-ku**), reducing their diets until they have eliminated all solid foods, not unlike certain raw juice advocates today. Under no circumstances are they ever to partake of meat or wine, because the inner gods dislike their smell. Adepts must regularly cleanse their colons (as advocated by modern Western naturopaths like Bernard Jensen* and Robert Gray*) and perform gymnastic exercises based on animal movements to prepare their inner bodies for **Embryonic Respiration (T'ai-hsi).** This requires lying down in quiet, holding one's breath for anywhere from 12 to 1,000 heartbeats, and learning to circulate it throughout the body (hsing ch'i), moving through all the internal organs as a way of stimulating and healing them. The adept then swallows the saliva that has accumulated in the mouth. Considering that the faithful were expected to sustain themselves on breath and saliva rather than meat, grains, and alcohol, it's impressive how far and fast the school spread.

The Inner Gods school also required charitable works, such as building roads and bridges and contributing to orphanages, not for any moral or ethical reasons but because good deeds helped accumulate credits toward personal immortality. The main texts of the school are *Jade Classic of the Yellow Chamber (Huang T'ing Yu Ching,* c. AD 200) and *True Classic of the Great Mystery (Ta Tung Chen Ching).*

During the 6th century, the **School of the Magic Jewel (Ling-pao p'ai),** which had begun to develop during the two previous centuries, displaced the Inner Gods Hygiene School. The Magic Jewel sect taught that individual liberation was dependent on outside help from the **T'ien-tsun** ("Celestial Honored Beings or Venerables"), the highest gods of the Taoist Church. Their title came into use during the 3rd century AD, just as Buddhism was gaining a foothold in China. They were led by Yuan-shih t'ien-tsun, pictured as the preexisting Creator and Ruler of heaven and earth, who spontaneously sprang into existence before the rest of the world. Others leaders included the equally important **Tao-te t'ien-tsun** and the Jade Emperor (Yu Huang).

After the 3rd century, the T'ien-tsun gradually became identified with the Buddhist concept of the bodhisattva* in the sense that they were said to descend from heaven to instruct humanity. The scriptures that Yuan-shih dictates to the lesser gods at the start of each new aeon are the **Ling-pao Ching.** The gods then pass the scriptures along to the immortals, who in turn teach humankind. In China, Gautama Buddha was referred to at first as a T'ien-tsun, but his title was later changed to **Shih-tsun** ("Earthly Venerable") so as not to confuse him with the gods.

By the middle of the 1st millennium, Taoist priests who lived in monasteries began to practice celibacy, and Taoist women entered convents. Both developments reflected the influence of Buddhism and were popularized by the 6th-century author and reformer **Sung Wen-ming,** who also promoted the Ling-pao gods. The Five Pecks of Rice tradition and the Union of Breaths both began to fade from common practice (although the latter merely went underground in many regions, just as the Five M's* had become secret in India). And as had happened at times with Hinduism and Buddhism, many churches and monasteries began to become corrupted and in some cases luxuriant.

✳ GOING WITHIN

The other principal branch of Religious Taoism, at least since the religious reformation of the Sung dynasty, is the **School of Perfect Realization (Ch'uan-chen tao)**, sometimes called **Chung-yang** ("Pure Yang") or **Chin-lien** ("Golden Lotus"). Founded by **Wang Ch'un-yang** (or Wang Che, 1112–1170), who reputedly received a secret transmission from a passing hermit, the aim of the school was total asceticism. Reflecting the influences of both Buddhism and Confucianism, with their emphasis on strong codes of personal ethics and moral living, members of Perfect Realization abstained from alcohol, sex, and other pleasures of the senses, refused sleep whenever possible, and practiced Zen-style meditation. One story goes that Wang had himself buried under 10 feet of earth and remained there for 2 years, emerging unscathed. Perfect Realization was dualistic in its attempt to place yang (heaven or spirit) over yin (earth or matter). The focus was on inner alchemy (hygiene and meditation) and did not require monastic life, although the tao-shih were supposed to be celibate.

The Perfect Realization school quickly generated branch sects, starting with those created by 7 of Wang's own disciples. The most significant, though, came to be identified as the Northern and Southern Schools. The **Northern School,** also known as **Lung-men** ("Dragon Gate"), was led by Wang and his successor, **Ch'ang Ch'un,** who used the **White Cloud Monastery** in Beijing as his base beginning in 1224. The **Southern School** was founded earlier than the Northern by **Liu Hai-ch'an,** who claimed spiritual transmission from Hui Neng*, the Ch'an (Zen) Buddhist master known as the Sixth Patriarch in China.

Over the centuries, the Inner Gods Hygiene School's practice of exterior breath circulation fell out of favor and was replaced during the T'ang dynasty by the practice of circulating the "interior breath" (nei-ch'i). This procedure didn't require holding one's breath for dangerously long periods of time (although that technique did have the added advantage of hallucinations induced by carbon dioxide intoxication). Similarly, the alchemy of creating an elixir of immortality from lead or mercury was gradually replaced by the search for an inner elixir (**nei-tan**), beginning during the Sung dynasty, especially in the sects of the Ch'uan-chen tao, and came to be known as the **Inner Elixir School.** The aim of nei-tan was to create within the adept a new being called the **sacred embryo** (**sheng t'ai**), which would depart the body at the instant of death and ascend to heaven, much like the concept of the immortal soul in Western religion. The embryo was sometimes called the golden flower, lending its name to one of the school's key texts, *The Secret of the Golden Flower.* The best-known proponents of the Inner Elixir School were **Chen T'uan** (906–989) and **Chang Po-tuan** (984–1082).

The Inner Elixir was one manifestation of a religious reformation that swept China during the Sung dynasty. Somewhat paralleling events surrounding the Protestant Reformation in Europe, the Chinese laity began to assume for itself the expression of religious fervor without the intervention of priests and monks, whether Taoist or Buddhist. The clergy re-

189

tained their function during funeral services, but the people took over officiating at birth, marriage, and healing rituals, among others.

Through yogas pertaining to the inner alchemy, some adepts claimed to be able to use the sacred embryo as an **astral body,** a subtle configuration that contains the soul but is usually invisible. This allowed them to leave the physical body while alive and travel on the astral plane*, a phenomenon referred to as astral travel. This sometimes had unforeseen consequences, as with Li Hsuan, one of the Eight Immortals.

✺ CAN WE ALL GET ALONG HERE?

For centuries, Buddhism coexisted in China with Taoism and Confucianism as one of the Three Teachings. Nevertheless, the Taoist Church was also responsible for occasional persecutions of Buddhists during the 1st millennium, when the Taoists feared that their hierarchical power was being threatened. Major persecutions resulting in many deaths took place in AD 446 and again in 845, when a Taoist emperor moved to counter Buddhism's growing popularity by closing thousands of Buddhist monasteries and defrocking their monks and nuns, leading to the eventual decline, but not disappearance, of Buddhism in China.

Today there are at least 86 sects of Taoism, including many lay societies that, apart from their religious beliefs, have a history of opposing autocratic or tyrannical rule. One prominent non-Taoist sect is the **I Kuan Tao (Way of Pervading Unity).** Like the Vedanta Society of Vivekananda*, it embraces all major traditions, including the Confucian, Taoist, Buddhist, Christian, Muslim, and Hindu, along with their gods and prophets. Its main deity is the **Mother of No-Birth,** the creator of the world. Members abstain from meat, alcohol, and tobacco and focus on controlling the mind by lessening desire. The Communist government of China has sought to suppress this and other antiauthoritarian sects, for obvious reasons.

ANOTHER NEO WORTH KNOWING

Neo-Confucianism (c. 1100–1912), often called **Tao-hsueh,** combined Taoist and Buddhist concepts in a Confucianist setting. Since Confucius had never created a metaphysical basis for his ethical principles, and since Taoism was beginning to lose its appeal to the intelligentsia and the upper classes, the new synthesis was welcome. For example, Neo-Confucianism borrowed the Taoist notion of the underlying unity of all things and called it T'ai Chi ("Ultimate Cause"). Neo-Confucians worked to lessen desires and discover their True Natures à la Buddhism, practiced Neo-Taoist feng liu ("wandering from conversation"), and expanded the Confucian notion of li from human laws to natural ones.

The most famous Neo-Confucianist and its greatest theoretician was **Chu Hsi** (1130–1200), who taught that the world was composed of vital essence, ch'i, configured according to the ordering principle of li. Most people's ch'i, he said, gets in the way of their li, i.e., their material urges (both physical and psychological) obscure their spiritual and intellectual goals. Meditation on the li is required to achieve maturity and vision, which in Confucian terms translates to good family values and strong, honest government. By 1237, Neo-Confucianism had become state orthodoxy, and Chu Hsi's commentaries on Taoist and Confucian texts were de rigueur when preparing for civil service examinations. Neo-Confucianism kept its privileged status until early in the 20th century, when it began to be persecuted by the Chinese Communists. It now continues in Hong Kong, Taiwan, and the American Chinese community.

TAO NOW

Neo-Confucianism lost its state sponsorship around the time the ancient system of empire was discarded in favor of a republican form of government modeled on Western systems, about 1912. But the status of the Three Teachings did not change substantially until the People's Republic of China was established along Communist lines in 1949. The Marxist government discouraged religion but did not ban it outright; that prohibition occurred during the disastrous period of the Great Cultural Revolution, 1966–78. Then, many Buddhist and Taoist temples and shrines were closed or destroyed and the clergy forced into labor. The same thing happened to the Catholic, Protestant, and Islamic clergy and places of worship that had been established in China.

But since the reforms begun by Deng Xiaoping in 1979, religions of all varieties have been allowed to return to active participation in public life. Temples, mosques, and churches have been rebuilt, sometimes with government funds. The current government no longer holds the old Marxist view of religion as the opiate of the oppressed people, since China, as a classless socialist society, by definition has no oppressed people. In fact, scientific surveys conducted by state organizations discovered that production output among believers was the same as among nonbelievers but that the crime rate was lower among believers and that family values and cooperation improved. So, just as the earlier emperors endorsed the arrival of Buddhism as a force for peace and prosperity, the state now sanctions Taoism and Buddhism, along with Western religions. The latter account for only a small percentage of the population, and official statistics say that 6 percent practice Taoism openly—a figure challenged by many outside observers, who feel the number should be much higher. Inner alchemy, feng shui, augury, tao-yin, and ancestor worship (although not specifically Taoist) still flourish among the populace, as does belief in the traditional deities such as San I, Tsao-chun (the Kitchen God), the Queen Mother of the West, and the Pole Star Deity.

As a spiritual practice, Taoism has made fewer inroads in the West than its sister traditions of Buddhism and Hinduism. Despite the popularity of its great classics the *I Ching* and the *Tao Te Ching*, the specific practices of Taoism have not been promulgated in America with much success. For one thing, Taoism has lacked the articulate and captivating spokesperson that Indian religion found in Swami Vivekananda* or that Buddhism had in D. T. Suzuki*, Chögyam Trungpa*, and the Dalai Lama*, all capable of translating a foreign theology and practice into language that Western minds could both grasp and be enthralled by. But toward the end of the 20th century, the West has begun to take a serious and growing interest in Chinese medical wisdom, from acupuncture to herbs, as discussed in the chapter on the New Age. Serious study of the ageless underlying principles of yin-yang and the Five Elements may not be far behind. Given the earthy, skeptical nature that has always been the essence of the Chinese spirit, it is hardly surprising that the practical application of Taoist metaphysics is what the West finds most persuasive. In the end, that spirit, which resonates with the practical, scientific bent of the Western mind, may serve as the conduit to deeper exploration of the whole rich world of Taoism.

✳ INSIDE A TAOIST TEMPLE

Modern-day Chinese temples have assumed a somewhat generic quality, although they are usually overseen by either Buddhist or Taoist clergy, and popular gods are responsible for practical needs, from healing and childbirth to protection and prosperity. Nonetheless, a specifically Taoist village temple is organized on a directional basis, although the ritual north wall does not necessarily face north. The figures of the Three Pure Ones are arrayed against that wall, and entry is from the ritual south wall. In the center of the temple is an incense burner, which represents the alchemical fire in which the elixir of immortality and various precious metals are continually being refined—emblematic of personal inner refinement. On the ceiling above the burner are depictions of the 8 trigrams from the *I Ching*.

Outside on either the west or east side is a container for burning the ceremonial paper money that is offered to kuei to appease the hungry spirits or to help liberate the souls of departed relatives or loved ones from hell. Buddhist images are as likely to appear in the temple as Taoist figures, as long as they are properly positioned. An image of Kuan-yin*, the Buddhist Bodhisattva of Compassion, is stationed at the entrance to many Chinese shrines, whether Buddhist or Taoist.

As for the Taoist monastery, like the Buddhist, it is more than just a place of worship. It also serves as a retreat center or wayside resting place (including overnight stays), a place to get away from city life and anxieties. The priests and monks who ran and run the monasteries focus more on magical than moral advice and assistance.

The most important annual religious festival is **New Year's**, which lasts more than a month. The **Pure and Bright Festival** in early April and the **Cold Food Festival**, during which all fires are extinguished for three days and the people eat prepared cold foods, are the major spring celebrations.

Midsummer Festival (the fifth day of the fifth lunar month, at the summer solstice) and the **Feast of All Souls** (fifteenth day of the seventh lunar month) are other high points. One of the most important regional festivals is the communal **Chiao,** a three-day festival of renewal that takes place each year at the winter solstice. It celebrates renewal of the Five Elements, crops, and offspring by the transcendent inseminating power of the Tao.

Coming to Terms

The old-fashioned style of transliterating Chinese characters into English, known as Wade-Giles romanization, has officially been replaced by the pinyin system adopted by the People's Republic of China in 1979. Mao Tse-tung, Lao-tzu, *I Ching,* and ch'i are Wade-Giles; Mao Zedong, Lao-zi, *Yi-jing,* and qi are pinyin. Clearly, Wade-Giles is still the most familiar form in most cases; it is also the one most commonly used in books on Chinese religion, except for the most recent names and terms. The advantage of pinyin is that it's more phonetically self-explanatory, but a brief chart should help with the traditional spellings used here.

Vowels are generally pronounced as in German or Italian:

a = ah, e = eh, i = ee, etc.　　ao = ow as in *how*

ai = eye　　final u = ee

Initial consonants are pronounced as they would be in English only when followed by an apostrophe:

ch' = ch

k' = k, etc.

Otherwise, the following pronunciations apply:

ch = j　　　　　　　　　　e = u as in *gut*

j = r　　　　　　　　　　k = g

p = b　　　　　　　　　　t = d

ts = dz　　　　　　　　　hs = sh

So *ching* is pronounced "jing," while *ch'i* is "chee"; *t'ai* is said like "tie," *tai* like "dye." More or less, of course. Since Chinese characters can be pronounced as many as four different ways, these pronunciations are at best approximate.

chai (jeye)   Ritual fasting, generally in a monastic setting, an important aspect of Religious Taoism from its earliest days. Various sects perform different kinds of fasts, some of which include confession of sins and blackening oneself with charcoal and culminate in physical frenzies of repentance.

ch'i (chee)   The Chinese equivalent of Hindu prana*, *ch'i* refers literally to the air we breathe, and on a deeper level to our vital essence, the life force. In medical terms, *ch'i* is the energy that circulates along the invisible meridians of the body, its flow being facilitated when necessary by acupuncture* or acupressure*.

ch'i-kung (chee-*goong*, "energy work")   A system of exercises including body work, breathing, and massage for the purpose of healing and strengthening the individual.

ching (jing)   Classic book; sexual fluids.

Complete Reality School   Developed during the Sung dynasty (960–1279), it sought to restore the Taoist teachings regarding the elevation of consciousness by integrating physical, social, and spiritual aspects of life. It has been credited with devising the form of exercise-cum-self-defense known as t'ai chi ch'uan.

feng shui (fung-shway, "wind and water")   Geomancy, the Taoist science of selecting the most auspicious site for, or interior design of, a building, residence, or grave, based on finding the correct balance of yin and yang (two-fifths yin and three-fifths yang being the ideal). The founder of this science is said to be **Kuo P'o** (d. c. AD 324). Its basic premise is that ch'i flows along invisible lines in the earth (called **dragon paths**) similar to the meridians of the body, and manmade structures must be properly placed to maximize its power and promote health. Tall objects, for instance, can be disruptive; one of the causes of the Boxer Rebellion of 1900 was the placement of telegraph poles in the countryside.

hsien (shyen)   One who has achieved physical immortality. The term is also used by Taoists to distinguish their perfected sages from those of the Confucians. Hsien eventually became instructors who helped others on their own path to immortality—the Taoist equivalents of Buddhist bodhisattvas.

Hsi Wang-mu ("Queen Mother of the West")   A powerful goddess who presides over a Western paradise of the immortals in the K'un-lun Mountains, riding on geese and dragons. Her male consort is **Tung Wang-kung,** who represents creative yang to her receptive yin. Her symbol is the Peach of Immortality, which she grows in her garden.

Hsun-tzu (shun-*tsee*, d. 215 BC)   A Confucianist who, unlike Mencius, believed that humanity was not inherently good but had to have goodness inculcated into it. He taught that t'ien (heaven) was really just the laws of nature, a vision of order without purpose similar to the Western

Deist* view of a clockmaker God. More skeptical about religion than Confucius, he scoffed at ritual, propitiatory prayer, and other conventional practices.

Huang Lao Taoism   Sometime in the 3rd century BC, Huang-ti (the Yellow Emperor) and Lao-tzu began to be worshiped as the cofounders of Religious Taoism. Over time they evolved into Huang-lao-chun. Huang-ti was one of the five emperor-sages from China's Golden Age (c. 2850–2250 BC), a time when humans supposedly lived in communion with nature and understood the secrets of healing and living to a very old age. To say something dates to the time of the Yellow Emperor means that nobody knows how *old* it is. The Yellow Emperor was said to be a shaman capable of entering trance states during which he visited the spirit realms.

Huang-lao-chun ("Ancient Yellow Lord")   The chief deity of the Way of Supreme Peace (T'ai-p'ing tao), commonly seen as the ruler of the universe, evolved from Huang-ti and Lao-tzu.

Ko Hung   Taoist alchemist who incorporated Confucian ideas. A great systematizer, Ko collected and codified the previous writings and teachings on immortality in his encyclopedia, the *Pao-p'u-tzu.*

Kuan Ti, Kuan Kung   Some gods in the Chinese pantheon are heroic historical figures who were deified after their death. Kuan Yu was a 3rd-century Chinese general, famous for his loyalty, who was strangled to death. Between the 7th and 19th centuries AD, he was venerated first as a guardian of Buddhist temples and later as the Taoist war god, Kuan Ti or Kuan Kung, patron of martial arts and merchants. His iconography is rich with military attire, including armor and a halberd.

K'un-lun   Mythical mountain range located somewhere in Western China, similar to the Western paradise of Pure Land Buddhism. Hsi Wang-mu, the Queen Mother of the West, dwells there along with the many immortals. Like the isles of the immortals, which lie in the opposite direction off the east coast, the K'un-lun mountains were the subject of numerous quixotic expeditions.

Legalists   A sect flourishing in the 3rd century BC; the leading philosopher was **Han Fei** (d. 233 BC). Unlike Confucius and Mencius, who believed that humanity was basically good, the Legalists believed human nature to be essentially evil. For them, strict enforcement of law was the sole means of creating efficient government and an orderly society. Power could be maintained through Machiavellian and even fascistic methods, including violence and murder, whenever necessary. Legalists had no use for philosophy, literature, the arts, compassion, or gratitude.

Li Shao-chun (d. c. 133 BC)   A Taoist fang shih who pursued immortality through alchemy. Despite his assertion that he was himself immortal, had visited Ying-chou where the mushroom of immortality grew, and

The influence of Taoist folk religious ideas on Buddhism is apparent in the feminine features of Kuan-yin, the Bodhisattva of Compassion who in Indian Buddhism is the male Avalokiteshvara and in Tibet, Chenrezi. But in China, especially since the 10th century, he was gradually transformed into a woman known as the Goddess of Mercy, although the name Kuan-yin (or Kuan-shi-yin) means "One Who Hears the Sounds [or Outcries] of the World," one possible translation of the Sanskrit Avalokiteshvara. The influence of Tantrism, in which buddhas and bodhisattvas are associated with female counterparts, may also account for the transformation. This lovely gilt bronze shows a figure reclining at royal ease in a typical pose.

GIRAUDON/ART RESOURCE

was well versed in techniques for attaining longevity, he died of an ailment before he had lived out his natural life span.

Mao Meng (3rd century BC)   One of the earliest Taoists to pursue physical immortality. His means, like those of other Taoist masters who followed him, including avoiding grains (a method called **ku tao**), bathing only at certain times and according to precise rituals, performing yogic exercises and breathing techniques, engaging in meditation, and using mantras.

Ma-tzu, T'ien Hou ("Grandmother")   A popular deity who died in her twenties and now serves as goddess of fishermen and sailors.

Mencius (Meng-tzu, also **Meng K'o,** 372–289 BC)   A Confucianist who

197

espoused Taoist sentiments, Mencius was later considered the legitimate inheritor of the Confucian mantle over the more pessimistic Hsun-tzu. Mencius believed in the innate goodness of human nature, which could be perfected to a saintly state. He also posited the principle that rulers must be of high moral caliber and that if they weren't, the people had the right to overthrow them. In *The Real Man,* he wrote: "The people are the most important element in a State; the ruler is the least. The empire is not given by one man to another. The choice of Heaven is shown in the conduct of men. It is an old rule that the oppressor may be put to death without warning." The Chinese people, of whom it has been said that they can't go 50 years without a rebellion, may have taken this teaching to heart.

Miu Chi   Second century BC Taoist magician who introduced the concept of T'ai I to the Han dynasty.

Mohists   Followers of **Mo Ti** (**Mo-tzu** or "Master Mo," 5th–4th centuries BC), who opposed the teachings of Confucius. Discounting K'ung's emphasis on filial love as too selfish and limiting, Mo proposed, as a solution to social unrest, universal love (**chien ai**), mutual regard, and nonmilitarism. He taught that **Shang-ti** (the Supreme Ancestor, a personal god known as the Sovereign on High) created the world and wanted only its happiness. Shang-ti puts kings and rulers in place to help people improve their material well-being and dispatches spirits and demons to reward the good and punish the wicked. Not quite pacifists, the Mohists believed in self-defense, and since many of them were engineers, they excelled in creating defenses and defensive weapons for cities under siege. By the 4th century BC, Mo-tzu's system was rivaling Confucianism, but it died out around the 1st century AD.

precious square inch   Taoist term for the third eye, the sixth chakra* of the Hindu system, located just back of the forehead between the eyes.

p'u ("uncarved block," originally the lumber that came from trees before it was dressed)   Lao-tzu used p'u to describe the original innocence of humanity. It is reminiscent of Buddha-nature* and can be realized in like fashion, by abandoning attachment and desire. Other symbols of the same concept are **nu,** or undyed raw silk, and **ying erh** ("the Unborn Child"), the individual before being shaped by society.

shih-chieh ("corpse separation")   The process by which a Taoist immortal appears to die, when in fact the transition from a live body to a corpse is merely an intermediate stage before ascending into heaven.

Tao   Commonly translated as the "Way" or "Path," the word can also mean "Teachings." The sense of the Tao as an all-pervading, impersonal Absolute is roughly equivalent to the Brahman of Hinduism. But only roughly. When a prominent Taoist scholar was asked about alternative translations of the term, his reply was a terse "Tao means Tao."

198

T'ao Hung-ching (AD 456–536)   A follower of Ko Hung who became a noted Taoist scholar and physician, seeking connections among Taoism, Confucianism, and Buddhism.

te   Power, efficacy, vital force; the manifestation of the Tao.

t'ien ming   The will of heaven.

wan-wu ("the Ten Thousand Things")   The Chinese version of Maya*, or the great multiplicity of the phenomenal universe. Wan-wu results from the mingling of yin and yang, which in turn exist as One in T'ai I.

wen   The arts: painting, music, poetry.

world of dust   Earth, the material world.

wu   Nothingness.

wu wei   Letting things be as they are; nondoing, nonintervention. It does not preclude all action, only hostile or aggressive action. However, even aggression can sometimes be performed in keeping with wu wei (e.g., violence used as a last resort, without hate or malice), and nonaggression can violate it (e.g., making others feel inferior by a holier-than-thou attitude).

Yen Lo Wang   Chinese Buddhist ruler of the underworld who judges sinners (similar to the Indian Yama*), sending them to a hell of fire or ice. But unlike in Western religions, eternal damnation is almost never assigned. The evil serve their time and then are released.

Yu-Chi (Kan Chi, d. AD 197)   Taoist savant and miracle healer who cured with incense and holy water. Writing magical sayings on pieces of paper, he burned them and mixed the ashes in water that he gave to his patients to drink.

4

JUDAISM

❋ THE ONE AND ONLY

If any single concept characterizes all religion in the West, it is **monotheism,** the belief in one God, omnipotent, omniscient, and omnipresent. The Brahman* of the Hindus essentially fits that description, of course—an all-pervading Absolute, the Infinite Source of all being. But in practical terms, few Westerners think of Hinduism as monotheistic. Its adherents worship too many forms or manifestations of that Absolute. Buddhism, strictly speaking, is nontheistic, despite the fact that its followers venerate numerous celestial beings. And Taoism offers a blend of the cosmic (yin-yang*, the Tao*) with the down-to-earth (the Kitchen God*, the Yellow Emperor*). Besides, an integral component of Western monotheism is its absolute refusal to acknowledge any god other than the One. Christianity may have its Holy Trinity*, but it has shed blood insisting that the Three Persons of that Trinity (Father, Son, and Holy Spirit) are really only one God. Judaism and Islam are even less ambigu-

201

ous about this subject, at least in their orthodox manifestations: "The Lord is one," says a part of the Hebrew Bible that reaches back over 3,000 years. And nearly 14 centuries ago, the Islamic Quran declared, "There is no god but God."

Monotheism had made other appearances before Moses codified it, most notably in Egypt, but the Jewish tradition is the one responsible for establishing the concept firmly and irrevocably in Western culture. Further, the God of Israel is a personal God, and an ethically demanding one, and this combination of characteristics—one, moral, personal—is clearly unique. Unlike most other personal deities of comparable antiquity, the God of Judaism is never described or given any visual image, nor, in the strict sense, is God's name even to be spoken aloud by the faithful. Yet this God interacts directly and decisively with humanity. God is also, for better or worse, now referred to as male, notwithstanding the fact that, as a pure, transcendent spirit, God can have no physical attributes and no sexual identity. The male identity of the Jewish God was passed on to Christianity and Islam, separating these three traditions from the rest of the world's conception of the Absolute in a significant way. Indeed, as modern scholars have shown, the idolatry that the three monotheistic traditions of the West so assiduously and often violently opposed was in large part based on the much older, female-centered worship of the Goddess* in one form or another.

Although the Jewish people have historically been dispersed over the face of the globe, and their numbers are relatively small today—only about 15 million—the Hebrew conception of God is at the core of Christianity and Islam, indelibly coloring the two most populous religions on earth, with close to 2.5 billion believers between them. And along with the concept of ethical monotheism, over the centuries a whole collection of phrases, metaphors, characters, and familiar stories derived from Judaism have become fixtures in the Western cultural landscape—witness the Garden of Eden, the Promised Land, David and Goliath, and the patience of Job.

The argument that, in the modern world, the Jewish faith has been subsumed by Jewish culture or that Judaism has lost much of its relevance as a religion overlooks not only the enormous influence which the Judaic view of God has had on Western religious life and thought, but also the renewed vitality and interest among modern Jews in Judaism as a living religion. Certainly the ability of the Jewish people not merely to survive impossible hardships but to continue to influence modern culture, from Hollywood films and stand-up comedy to science and fine arts, is itself the stuff of myth.

Judaism may have evolved significantly from the early era of animal sacrifices, but there are ways in which it hasn't changed from its earliest roots. Every week in synagogues around the world, observant Jews still proclaim one of the oldest passages in the Bible, "Hear, O Israel: The Lord our God, the Lord is one" (Deut. 6:4).

❋ PERSONALLY SPEAKING

From the beginning, the Israelites believed they were selected by God for a specific function: to spread knowledge of Him and of the moral nature of His laws. They believed in the uncompromising superiority of those laws not only to the idol worship they saw flourishing around them but also, later, to the secular laws of nations. Out of this sense of mission, the Jews developed a long and powerful tradition of the oral and written recording of their history down to the most minutely observed detail, all of which was meticulously copied and preserved over many centuries. Perhaps also related to the notion of chosenness and mission is the underlying reality that, above all, Judaism is a religion of community—a truth that will have a bearing on its development of an unprecedented sense of responsibility for one's fellow human being.

It's possible to see the notion of a "chosen people" as self-serving or elitist, but that doesn't explain the relentlessly self-critical tone of the early books of the Bible. God often calls the Israelites "a stiff-necked people" and finds them wanting in many ways. By their own admission, they are constantly being caught in the most blatant acts of backsliding into idolatry (which some feminist scholars see as references to the continued popularity of Goddess worship among the Jewish commonfolk). This tone continues through the last works of the prophets, who seem to spend less time critiquing the "idolatrous" ways around them than berating the failings and moral wanderings of their own kind. Of the concept of being chosen, the great 12th-century Jewish philosopher Maimonides wrote, "The selection was not due to our inherent worth.

Indeed, we have been distinctly told so in the Scriptures." Taken as a whole, the Hebrew Bible is the "warts and all" autobiography par excellence of an entire race of people.

If the early Hebrew patriarchs Abraham and Moses believed that they were instructed directly by God, the later prophets of the Israelites spoke in trance, their words resembling superficially the revelations received by ancient Indian and Chinese sages in their meditative trance states. But there were significant differences between the earliest Hebrew cosmology and those of the Eastern traditions. The Hebrews may have conceived of God as absolute, omnipotent, and omnipresent, but He was also extremely personal, capable of forming a direct relationship with selected individuals to change the course of history. Accounts of Brahman or the Tao speaking directly to specific human beings with words that can be quoted simply do not exist.

More significantly, the earliest passages of the creation scenario in Genesis, the first book of the Bible, make clear that God approved of the physical or material world. After each act of creation, beginning with the separation of the waters and the dry land into earth and seas on the third of the six days of creation, the passage appears: "And God saw that it was good." Unlike the Hindus, whose concept of Maya* views the phenomenal world as a manifestation that veils Absolute Reality, the Hebrews accepted the essential goodness of material things and saw a holy life as indivisible from a life of enjoyment of God's bounty—as long as certain inviolable moral laws were obeyed. But unlike the polytheistic and nature-worshiping cultures of the Mesopotamian and Egyptian lands surrounding them, the Israelites believed that God exists *apart from the material world* and has the power to affect and change it through His interactions with humanity. The Israelite sense of enjoying the world was predicated on following God's law, not on appeasing a slew of arbitrary gods connected with unpredictable forces of nature while enjoying a life devoid of consideration for one's neighbors.

Judaic lore is distinct from the early history of Indian or Chinese religion in the relative precision with which early biblical figures can be dated and aligned with verifiable personages and events. Archaeologists and scholars tell us with some certainty that key features of the biblical accounts of Noah and the Flood, Abraham, the Hebrew patriarchs, and the Israelites themselves have historical parallels and that specific events and persons can be assigned dates within a reliably narrow span. **Abraham,** the patriarch of the Jewish people, for example, can be placed near the beginning of the 2nd millennium before the Christian era. Comparisons of the king lists in the early books of the Bible with nonbiblical Egyptian and Assyrian lists even make it possible to date within a few years the deaths of the earliest kings of the Israelites—Saul, David, Solomon—near the beginning of the 1st millennium BC. The fall of Jerusalem can be placed exactly at March 16, 597 BC. And the pharaoh from whom the Jews escaped under the leadership of Moses was almost certainly **Rameses II** (1304–1237 BC).

❋ THE BIBLE TELLS ME SO

The creation account in the opening chapter of **Genesis,** the first book of the Hebrew Bible, is familiar throughout the entire Western world. It has even been said that this scenario, in which God brings forth the earth and everything on it in a burst of creation, fits with modern scientific theories about the origin of the universe, specifically the Big Bang. The fact that Genesis reflects elements of earlier accounts from Sumerian and Babylonian literature or that its narrative actually incorporates two distinctly different stories of creation has done little to efface its popularity. In the account, God creates the world in six days and rests on the seventh, a justification for the idea of the **Sabbath,** which in Judaism and certain strictly Bible-observing Christian sects takes place from sundown Friday to dusk Saturday.

In a curiously phrased verse, on the sixth day God says, "Let us make man in our image, after our likeness" (1:26), indicating either that at this early stage the Hebrews still conceived of God as simply the chief god among several others or that He spoke in a kind of royal plural like the one He later used in the Quran. Confusing matters further is the fact that Judaism has almost from the first sternly forbidden the creation of physical images of God. The contradiction between this seminal law and the clear biblical statement that God created "man" in His image and likeness has created some misunderstanding, although Jewish teaching generally agrees that the "image" referred to here reflects the human ability to exercise free will in making moral choices. But the notion of human-

BLOOD COMPLEX

The sanctity of human life affirmed in the Bible has important consequences in the evolution of Jewish and Western law and morality, from prohibitions against murder to a disapproval of slavery. The Israelites were probably the first ancient people to abolish human sacrifice, for instance, and much of the Mosaic code was aimed at eliminating the conflicts that so often led to blood feuds. Not that the Israelites didn't shed plenty of Canaanite blood in occupying the Promised Land, and the blood of many more in defending it, nor that Judaism today doesn't accept the principle of capital punishment. But the idea of murder for its own sake, or merely to placate the Divinity, became anathema. Religious scholars believe that even the strict laws requiring the draining of all blood from slaughtered animals before they could be eaten springs from this principle.

ity mirroring God did help to underline a crucial contribution of Judaic theology—the belief that human life itself is sacred because it is modeled after the Supreme Being.

In a sequence immediately following the familiar creation scenario, beginning with Genesis 2:4, we have what amounts to a flashback to the middle of creation: "In the day that the Lord God made the earth and the heavens, when no plant of the field was yet in the earth and no herb of the field had yet sprung up . . . then the Lord God formed man of dust from the ground, and breathed into his nostrils the breath of life; and man became a living being." (Biblical scholars now agree that this account actually stems from an earlier text than Genesis 1 and that the two were brought together in consecutive chapters by an editor in the 7th century BC.)

What follows is the famous account of the temptation by the serpent, who "beguiled" Eve into eating the fruit of the tree of the knowledge of good and evil (no mention of an "apple," by the way), which she passed on to Adam. God then observes, "Behold, the man has become like one of us, knowing good and evil; and now, lest he put forth his hand and take also of the tree of life, and eat, and live for ever," God casts them out of the garden of Eden.

The early chapters of Genesis also narrate the familiar stories of Cain slaying his brother Abel, the general decline in humanity following the fall of Adam, and the Flood sent by God to punish the wicked ways into which men and women had descended. This latter story, in which God selects the one righteous man left on earth, **Noah,** and commands him to build an ark to preserve human and animal life, has unmistakable parallels in preexisting literature of the region. Archaeologists have for some time agreed that a real flood or floods of astonishing proportions did take place in the region of Babylonia and Sumeria sometime during the 4th and 3rd millennia BC. An ancient Babylonian account written in the 17th century BC describes a flood sent by a god who regrets having created humanity. In this story, another god intervenes to warn a priest-king named Ziusudra, who survives by building a large boat. An early Sumerian king list identifies Ziusudra as a historic personage, king of the city of Shuruppak in Babylonia c. 2900 BC. Whether the biblical authors were relating a story that had been handed down to them or reinterpreting an old narrative in a moralistic, monotheistic context is hard to say.

Abram, a descendant of Noah whose name God later changes to Abraham, is said to have come from Ur, a historical Sumerian city of the 4th and 3rd millennia, not far from Shuruppak. God directs Abram to leave his father's house in "Ur of the Chaldees" and go "to the land that I will show you." God promises to make of Abram's descendants "a great nation" and makes a covenant with him, saying: "To your descendants I will give this land." Historically, the **Hebrews** probably began as one of a group of wandering tribes known as Habiru, neither Bedouins, nomads, nor regularly migrating tribes but a hard-to-classify group of herders, often warlike and predatory, who roamed the regions of Mesopotamia, Syria, Palestine, and Egypt in search of water and pastures. They tended to settle near established kingdoms until their numbers grew too great and the local powers urged them to move on. According to the accounts in Genesis, Abram moved around quite a bit, seeking greener pastures in Egypt during a famine, then heading back to the Negev and Bethel, just north of modern Jerusalem. The image of the

Jewish people as "strangers and sojourners" occurs repeatedly in the Bible and in retrospect appears to have had prophetic overtones.

The fact that Abram came from a highly civilized city such as Ur explains his sophistication in dealing with various local kings and finally in executing the covenant with God, accepting obedience to a higher moral law in exchange for land for him and his descendants. That **covenant,** originally offered to Noah after the Flood, is a continuing theme throughout the first five books of the Hebrew Bible, as it passes from Abraham to **Isaac** to **Jacob** (whose name is changed by the Lord to **Israel**). The covenant is not merely inherited, however; it is renewed personally by God with each patriarch, as when God appears to Jacob and says, "I am God Almighty: be fruitful and multiply; a nation and a company of nations shall be of thee, and kings shall come out of thy loins. And the land which I gave to Abraham and Isaac, to thee I will give it, and to thy seed after thee will I give the land" (Gen. 35:11–12).

The same covenant is later renewed with **Moses,** who in some ways played a more decisive role in the evolution of Judaism than Abraham did. Abraham was the founding father of the Hebrew people, but Moses was the one whose leadership and shaping of the laws formulated the essential Jewish contribution to world religious thought. The **Promised Land** of the covenant took on greater significance as the Israelites sojourned in Egypt as a slave people and dreamed of returning. It was generally referred to as the land of Canaan, roughly corresponding to later Palestine and modern-day Syria, Lebanon, Jordan, and Israel. Although the Hebrews inhabited Canaan in small numbers before the Egyptian captivity and many never left to go to Egypt, it was not made into an Israelite nation until the return of Moses and Joshua from Egypt.

✳ THE GOD OF ABRAHAM

Abraham was not so much a monotheist as a **henotheist**—a believer in one God, though not to the exclusion of belief in others. The noted Indologist Max Müller introduced the term to describe Brahmanism*, whose followers worshiped one God as Supreme, but often changed loyalties over time. The term can also refer to belief in one God as Supreme among others. Abraham most likely believed in a single God for his peo-

*Even before the reign of **Akhenaten** (or Amen-
hotep IV), a pharaoh of Egypt's 18th Dynasty
who ruled c. 1353–1336 BC, Egypt had begun
consolidating its many gods into a few principal
ones. **Amon** (or Amen) of Thebes, probably a
god of reproductive forces, and **Re** (or Ra), the
sun god of Heliopolis, had become **Amon-Re**, a
creator god and "father of the gods." While
quite young, possibly during a contemplative
state or vision, Akhenaten (also spelled Ahkna-
ton or Ikhnaton) evolved the idea, radical for
the time, of a single controlling intelligence behind and above all sentient beings, including the
gods. This intelligence, whom he later called Aten, was supreme and enforced his will
by means of his "Word," a notion that anticipated not only the monotheism of
Moses but also the Logos of Philo Judaeus (a Jewish theologian who lived in Egypt
around the time of Christ). After Akhenaten became high priest of Egypt, he had the
names of all the other gods erased from the monuments, although he may have
couched his worship of a single god in the image of the solar disc, familiar to Egyptians from their worship of Re/Ra, to make it more palatable.
Accompanying his changes in worship, Akhenaten encouraged a new sense of
heightened realism in art that shook up the conventions of the previous millennium.
The king with his attenuated chin, epicene features, pot belly, and thick thighs was
depicted naturalistically in countless statues and reliefs, along with his wife **Nefertiti**,
sometimes rendered beautiful, sometimes misshapen, in what amount to some of the
least flattering royal portraits of all time. The contention has been made that Akhenaten culminated an Egyptian tradition of monotheism dating back as far as 3500
BC. Yet there is strong evidence of an entrenched predisposition toward polytheism,
and Akhenaten's plan to abolish all other Egyptian cults did not endear him to his
people or to the priests of the god Amon. He was forced to move his capital from
Thebes and build a new city some 200 miles away, which he called Akhetaten. After
his death, his cult of Aten soon died out, but in all likelihood it was absorbed by
various mystery schools which carried on his tradition in relative secrecy.
A controversial theory, posited by Sigmund Freud in* Moses and Monotheism, *holds
that Moses was himself an Egyptian. By psychoanalyzing the curious birth story in*
Exodus, *Freud deduced that Moses was a nobleman who adhered to Akhenaten's
teaching of monotheism and passed it on to the Jews. Imaginative and highly speculative, Freud's theory has never been definitively proved or disproved. Interestingly,
Akhenaten's "Hymn to Aten," voicing his gratitude to God for the gift of life, is
said to have influenced Psalm 104. The point is somewhat moot, because Akhenaten's religion focused on worship of the sun and did not embody an ethical code
with exacting demands like the codes Moses and the Hebrews developed.*

ple but also allowed for other tribes or races to worship a God of their own. The belief in strict monotheism, a universal God, appears to have evolved gradually in the Bible. Even during the centuries following the revelation of the one God to Moses, many Israelites continued to worship other gods or goddesses and were constantly having to be called back to the monotheistic path by various prophets. The book of Samuel, for instance, chides the Israelites to "put away the foreign gods and the Ashtaroth from among you, and direct your heart to the Lord, and serve him only." And so "Israel put away the Baals and the Ashtaroth and they served the Lord only" (1 Sam. 7:3–4). **Ashtoreth** (pl. **Ashtaroth**), was the Hebrew name for the Canaanite goddess Astarte, and Baal was a generic name for local gods in ancient Syria and Palestine.

The Israelite religion of a single God differs from the earlier worship of Brahman in many ways, but the most notable and characteristic difference is the injunction against worshiping an *image* of God or any other manifestation. After the time of Abraham, the Israelites were sworn to destroy the images of any other gods they might come across in other lands or among other peoples (Exod. 34:13). A century or so before Moses presented his visions to the Israelites, the Egyptian pharaoh Akhenaten espoused a kind of monotheism in his worship of **Aten** (or **Aton**), the solar disc emblematic of One Universal God.

✳ THE GREAT ESCAPE

One aspect of the biblical narratives that distinguishes them from much of the fabulist literature of equivalent antiquity is their grounding in specific detail and the down-to-earth portrayals of characters that lend the accounts an undeniable air of realism. This is significant because Judaism is so closely tied to the history of the Jews and to the notion of the direct intervention of God throughout that history. If we take the stories of the early Hebrews as having some basis in historical fact, which many scholars argue is likely, we can follow the course of that intervention. Nowhere is the importance of such interconnection more apparent than in the stories recounted in the book of Exodus about the Israelites' escape from the powerful Egyptian empire to which they had become slaves and their eventual deliverance into the Promised Land of Canaan.

The narrative begins in Genesis when **Joseph,** one of the twelve sons of Jacob, is sold into slavery by his brothers (more accurately, his half brothers). In one of the great success stories of all time, Joseph works his way up from servant in the house of Potiphar, an officer of Pharaoh (perhaps Rameses I), to virtual co-ruler of Egypt under Pharaoh, largely as a result of his ability to interpret Pharaoh's dreams. Those dreams predict seven years of plenty followed by seven years of famine; based on Joseph's dream interpretation, Egypt is flush with warehoused food stocks when the famine comes. Joseph's brothers, his father Jacob, and ultimately the rest of the Hebrew tribes come to Egypt for food during the famine (a classic reunion scene ensues when Joseph reveals himself to his father and brothers), and remain and prosper under the amicable rule of Joseph and Pharaoh.

As the book of **Exodus** begins, however, sometime after the death of both Joseph and Pharaoh, a new Egyptian ruler has become concerned about the growing presence of the Hebrews in his land and downgrades them to the status of slaves. The new pharaoh, who has been identified historically as Rameses II, puts the Hebrews to work in his massive building program and generally makes "their lives bitter with hard service, in mortar and brick, and in all kinds of work in the field."

Moses is born to Hebrew parents during the stage of Egyptian captivity when all male children of the Hebrews were to be put to death at birth. He escapes this fate when his mother leaves him at the riverbank in a basket made of bulrushes and Pharaoh's daughter discovers him there. Growing up in Pharaoh's household, Moses doesn't forget his roots; when he sees an Egyptian beating a fellow Hebrew, he kills the man and hides his body in the sand. Found out, he flees from Egypt to the land of Midian, where God appears to him "in a flame of fire out of the midst of a bush." Identifying Himself as the God of Abraham, Isaac, and Jacob, He promises to deliver Moses' people "out of the hand of the Egyptians, and to bring them up out of that land to a good and broad land, a land flowing with milk and honey."

Exodus then recounts the stunning escape of the Israelites from Pharaoh around 1260 BC, the role of Moses in leading his people out of Egypt, through the desert, and up to the Promised Land of Canaan. In the process, Moses receives for transmission to the Israelites the **Ten Commandments** (or **Decalogue**) plus a long list of other laws, known as **mitzvot,** most of which have to do with making restitution for various accidental or intentional injuries to the person or livestock of one's neighbors. (Later tradition gave the number of these laws as 613, which does not correspond to the number of laws actually stated in the relevant books of the Bible. Rabbinic teaching combined the figures 248, for the different parts of the body, and 365, for the days of the year, to arrive at 613—the meaning behind the figure possibly deriving from the basic commandment to love God with all of one's being and at all times.) The ostensible intention of these laws is to prevent bloodshed. The text says little about the basic ethical or moral underpinnings for the laws, as in the Eastern religions' precepts against lying, stealing, or sexual misconduct. Instead, Moses presents an extremely detailed prescription for ascertaining guilt and reparation so as to prevent the kinds of massive vendettas that often strained the social fabric of the time.

When Moses first encounters God in the burning bush in Exodus 3, and God tells Moses that He has "come down to deliver" the Israelites from the Egyptians, Moses asks by what name he should refer to God when he reports his vision to the people. God answers, *"Eheish Asher*

THE NAME OF THE LORD

The Jews may have been the first monotheists, but the concept took a while to evolve. Early in the Bible, God is referred to as *El* (a common Semitic name for God) and the plural *Elohim,* which has never been fully explained. Elsewhere the curious *El Elion* ("Most High God") seems to imply a pantheon of lesser gods. But by far the most common name used is **Yahveh,** a simplified pronunciation of the Hebrew consonants YHVH, or *Yod Hay Vav Hay,* which (except in the sanctuary) are not to be spoken by pious Jews, who may substitute *Adonai* ("My Lord") or *Elohim.* The four consonants are also known by the Greek term **Tetragrammaton** and the Hebrew **Shem ha-Meforash** (shortened to *Hashem,* "The Name," and said in lieu of YHVH). A modern scholar, Merlin Stone, has pointed out the close relation of the name to the Sanskrit word *yahveh* ("everflowing") which seems like a fair description of the fire and smoke that continually emit from Mount Sinai when the Lord is present there. During the 16th century, the name Yahveh was distorted by Christian readers of the Bible into **Jehovah.** But even Yahveh is just an approximation of how the four sacred syllables are to be pronounced, which is the subject of much esoteric study and speculation.

Eheieh" ("I Am Who I Am" or "I Am What I Am") and goes on, "Say this to the people of Israel, 'I AM has sent me to you.' "

The Israelites, either clinging to their old animistic roots or easily influenced by the Goddess-worshiping tribes who surround them, are constantly falling back into idol worship accompanied by drunken revelry and orgiastic activity. Their creation and worship of a golden calf is so repugnant to Moses that, upon his return from the mountain, he smashes the tablets of the law which had been written by the very finger of God. Later, he goes back for a rewrite and then spends the better part of 40 years leading the Israelites through the desert. At one point, God Himself speaks to the 600,000 Israelites assembled at Mount Sinai and presents them with

ARK OF THE

COVENANT

As depicted by the 19th-century English artist James Tissot.
JEWISH MUSEUM/
ART RESOURCE

His new covenant: the Promised Land in exchange for keeping His moral code.

The rest of Exodus is taken up with meticulously detailed instructions delivered by God to Moses for the construction of the **Ark of the Covenant** (also called the "tent of meeting"), an altar for performing animal sacrifice, precise designs for clothing to be worn by the priests, and other minutiae of ritual sacrifice. The Ark (a wooden structure 4 by 2½ feet) was created as a repository for the stone tablets on which God had written the Decalogue and, according to some theorists, as a material object for the Israelites to venerate as an alternative to the Goddess worship that surrounded them and that probably lay in their ancestral past, so ready were they to take it up at the drop of a golden ingot. One exception to the taboo against image worship appears to have been the **cherubim,** winged guardians or intermediaries between God and humanity,

HEBREWS, ISRAELITES, AND JEWS

The father of the Jewish people is Abraham, but he and his immediate offspring are more properly referred to as Hebrews. Their name changed as the result of a famous and mysterious incident in Genesis whereby Jacob was renamed Israel after he spent the night struggling with an unidentified angel in the form of a man. *Israel* may mean "he who strives with God" or "God strives" or "the upright one of God" or several other variants. The incident is not clearly explained in the Bible, but it does mark the beginning of the use of the terms *Israel* and *Israelites,* as in the **Twelve Tribes** of Israel, named for the 12 sons of Jacob. As scholars have pointed out, the notion of struggling or arguing with God implied by the name Israel fairly describes the Jewish relationship with the Creator.

After the 10th century BC, the land of the Israelites was divided into two kingdoms, Israel and **Judah;** from the latter come the terms *Judaism* and *Jew,* which are generally applied to the time after the loss of the physical home of Israel, when the Jews shared only the common bond of exile. Like the outmoded term *Negro, Hebrew* applied to Jewish people or institutions can sometimes be inappropriate, but nevertheless it appears in the names of some prestigious and venerable Jewish institutions, such as Hebrew Union College of Cincinnati (the first American rabbinical seminary), the Hebrew Immigrant Aid Society, and, of course, Hebrew National, makers of kosher hot dogs.

who were depicted covering the Ark with their wings, both in the desert and later in the Temple of Solomon, by which time they were said to symbolize the male and female aspects of Yahveh.

The books of **Leviticus, Numbers,** and **Deuteronomy** are largely filled with the completion of the Israelites' journey to the Promised Land as well as lengthy catalogs of dietary laws and restrictions, among other things.

The books of **Joshua, Judges, Samuel,** and **Kings** relate the slow process of infiltration, conquest, and consolidation of the land. Joshua's military leadership (following a command given to him by Moses) helped conquer the city of Jericho and defeat the Amorites in two famous biblical battles that probably took place around the 13th–12th century BC. The entry of Moses' people into the Promised Land may have been a dramatic spectacle worthy of Cecil B. DeMille, but the actual conquest and settlement of Canaan, or Palestine, was accomplished over several hundred years by disparate groups of Israelites. A large number of Israelites had almost certainly remained in Canaan during the Egyptian captivity, making its conquest after the exodus a less implausible feat. The conquered Canaanites were usually slaughtered and their sacred idols and images, such as Baal and Ashtoreth, were smashed by the Israelites as God had instructed them in Exodus: "You shall tear down their altars, and break their pillars, and cut down their Asherim," which were groves sacred to **Asherah,** the Canaanite goddess, mother of Ashtoreth.

According to the theories of some modern scholars and archaeologists, the Israelite assault on the "idolatry" of the Canaanites derived from a previous shift from a peaceful, matrilineal, agrarian society that worshiped various images of the Goddess to one dominated by warlike, nomadic men worshiping mainly warlike male gods. The nomadic culture to which the Hebrews belonged was characterized by a powerful father figure, the head of the clan, reflected in the powerful and often wrathful-seeming figure of Yahveh, and one of the purposes of the mitzvot, according to these theories, was to shift power and value away from women and onto men. The laws of the Israelites were designed not only to focus the people's attention on the Father God and away from the goddesses of the Canaanites, but also to eradicate their cult practices, including sexual intercourse with the temple priestesses and the raising of children born of those couplings. On a theological level, the whole thrust of the Israelite religion was away from worship of the images and sacred groves themselves so as to center awareness on the deeper dimension beyond the surface. And although this may have had valuable spiritual benefits, it has contributed to the modern Western attitude shared by Christianity of dominion over nature rather than participation in it, with possibly dire consequences for the future of the earth. In other words, to progress from "nature worship" (the trees and animals of the Goddess) to a more inward sense of spirituality, it was deemed necessary to eradicate all the emblems of Mother Nature; the dangerous corollary is the potential death of nature itself.

✳ KINGDOM COME

By the beginning of the 1st millennium BC, the kingdom of Israel was largely unified, although still composed of many small tribal groups under separate leaders. These tribes often fought against each other, until the threatening presence on the coastal plain of the **Philistines** (Palestine is named for them) more or less forced them to unite against a common enemy. Until this time, the Israelites had ruled themselves by **theocracy**, a term created by the 1st-century Jewish historian **Josephus** to denote democratic rule in which God has the final say. Civil complaints and criminal charges were settled at first by Moses himself, later by a tribunal trained by Moses to handle disputes, based on the law handed down by God. This system was as much a part of Moses' contribution to Jewish religion as any of his theological pronouncements, since Judaism is a religion of the law and its proper observance, rather than of dogmatic belief.

But having accomplished their objective of conquering Canaan and now obliged to hold it against organized tribal aggressors from outside, the Israelites settled into a period of kingship during which theocracy was often at odds with the evolving military and legal rulers. Incursions by the Philistines with their iron weapons increasingly created the need for a centralized military government to defend the newly conquered country from other would-be conquerors. The first king was **Saul** (d. c. 1005 BC), who was anointed by the early judge and prophet **Samuel** after the Jews insisted on having a king (but not before Samuel warned them repeatedly of the dangers of kingship and laid out its various rights and duties at some length). Saul was chosen by lot, effectively leaving the decision to the Lord, and his kingship was not to be hereditary. When Saul failed to follow God's orders, Samuel denounced him; again with God's help after Saul's death, Samuel replaced him with **David** (d. c. 966 BC), who is described as being ruddy and handsome, with "beautiful eyes."

David's 40-year reign is considered the most successful in Jewish history, a combination of military security and theocratic openness. A poet and musician as well as a great leader, David is remembered for composing a number of the Psalms and slaying the great Philistine "champion" **Goliath** with a stone from a sling. He went on to defeat the Philistines and to conquer the city of Jerusalem, which was then still held by the Jebusites. But David also was a great, if repentant, sinner. His worst excess was perhaps lusting after **Bathsheba**, the lovely wife of one of his generals, **Uriah.** Arranging to have Uriah "set up" by his own men during a battle in which he was easily slain, David then married his widow.

Solomon (d. 925 BC), a son of David, proved to be a pragmatic and sometimes ruthless king, with several foreign wives, including the daughter of the Egyptian pharaoh. He built a famed **Temple,** which contained a completely dark inner sanctum known as the **Holy of Holies,** in which the Ark of the Covenant resided. Believed to have been 180 feet by 90 feet and 50 feet high, it was destroyed by the Babylonian invaders nearly 400 years later. Solomon's "Song of Songs," a love poem often rational-

The Temple as it appeared in a drawing from a 1729 Moravian haggada, containing the text that is read at a Passover seder.
SCALA/ART RESOURCE

ized as a metaphor of humanity's love for God, is as sensual and worldly-wise as David's Psalms are spiritual and metaphysical.

Some time after the death of Solomon, the Israelites, living in two small kingdoms in the area of Palestine—the more populous and prosperous Israel in the north and the more religiously purist Judah in the south—split apart and were destroyed separately by outside forces. The Assyrians invaded the kingdom of Israel in 722 BC, removing the elite and skilled laborers back to Assyria and resettling the region with their own people, eradicating 10 of Israel's 12 tribes in the process. The kingdom of Judah lasted some time longer but finally fell to the Babylonians under **Nebuchadnezzar,** who conquered the city of Jerusalem and destroyed the Temple of Solomon in 587 BC.

✺ PROPHETS OF DOOM

From the beginning, the Israelites established the primacy of the prophet
in their spiritual and political life, and the tension between a righteous
moral voice and sheer survival has remained entwined in an often uncomfortable alliance, right down to modern Israel. Abraham was a
prophet, and Moses was considered the greatest. At some point the term
for prophet evolved from the old word *roeh* ("seer"), a kind of prognos-
ticator, to *nabhi* ("one who is called"). In a state of trance or frenzy,
sometimes abetted by music, chanting, narcotics, or strong drink, the earliest prophets relayed their visions in "a singsong voice." On one level
these prophets parallel the Eastern masters whose meditative trances produced insights and holy books (sometimes with the aid of hallucinogens
like soma*). However, they were probably closer in spirit to shamans* of
many ancient cultures who performed their trances in public rather than
in solitary meditation. There is even some reason to believe that the role
was frequently abused and reduced to that of modern fortune tellers who
"see all, know all."

Later, the art of prophecy evolved to a much higher and more significant pitch. Prophets began to confront the powerful for their religious
and social failings, as **Elijah of Tishbi** did to the infamous **Ahab** and
Jezebel in the 9th century BC. Elijah was the first recorded prophet to support the individual conscience, and although he did not have a book of
the Bible devoted to his preachings, his story is told in 1 Kings. The Lord
spoke to him in a "still, small voice," a phrase that has come to mean the
inner urgings of spiritual conscience. His preaching that even kings had
to answer to inner principles was not popular, and he spent most of his
life as a fugitive. In the end, he was swept up to heaven in a whirlwind
preceded by a fiery chariot. Like most of the prophets and other heroes
of Israel, he came from extremely poor, humble origins.

Hosea, a prophet at the time of the breakup of the northern kingdom
of the Israelites, predicted the kingdom's downfall. He traced the causes
to the moral failings of the chosen people, their violence and political
purges, institutionalized priesthood, and backsliding into pagan activities,
saying, "They have sown the wind, and they shall reap the whirlwind."

Isaiah was a prophet of the 8th century BC, although the second half of

219

the book attributed to him in the Hebrew Bible was composed a century or two later by an unknown prophet referred to as **Deutero-Isaiah.** The early Isaiah raised the ante with a call to social justice, including a cessation of warlike activities: "And they shall beat their swords into ploughshares, and their spears into pruning hooks; nation shall not lift up sword against nation, neither shall they learn war any more" (Isa. 2:4). He also predicted the coming of a **Messiah** (**Ma-shi-akh**), a savior who would lead the people out of darkness, a "Prince of Peace." These prophecies were later quoted in the Christian New Testament* as proof that Christ's coming had been predicted by the prophets. However, the Jewish Messiah was supposed to gather the Jews to Israel from all over the world and usher in an era of universal peace, events which appear not to have happened yet.

Finally, **Jeremiah,** who lived around 600 BC, railed against the impending collapse of the southern kingdom, Judah, in fatalistic fashion—a long, virulent tirade that has given us the word *jeremiad.* Toward the end, the prophets looked on the impending doom as part of God's will, saying in an almost Eastern sense that whatever happens is meant to be and should be accepted, including the destruction of the Israelite kingdom. Once Jerusalem was conquered by the Babylonian leader Nebuchadnezzar, the **Diaspora,** or dispersal, of the Israelites began in earnest. By 587 BC, Jerusalem and the Temple of Solomon were destroyed. The Babylonian Exile was under way. (The Temple was rebuilt 70 years later—called the Second Temple—only to be destroyed again, for good, by the Romans in AD 70.)

Just as the shramanic* yogis of India and the heterodox ascetics of early Jainism* and Buddhism rejected Brahmanism*, the later prophets of the 9th to 6th centuries BC, especially Hosea and Isaiah, opposed the institutionalized priestly religion of ritual and sacrifice. But their emphasis on righteousness and the need for social justice and their courageous, relentless attacks on elements of the political and social status quo that they believed fell short of God's will mark them apart from early Indian reformers who were more concerned with a belief system than with political and social realities. The forcible admonitions of the prophets laid the groundwork for a tradition of social justice and change that is deeply ingrained in Western thought and is readily apparent in the disproportionate number of Jewish Americans who have traditionally been involved in social justice causes.

✻ BY THE RIVERS OF BABYLON

During the 50-year period of exile, also known as the **Babylonian Captivity,** the Jews began the strict observance of religious laws and rituals necessitated by the fact that they had no common land or nation to hold

EZEKIEL SEES THE WHEEL

The tradition of the prophets continued well after Jeremiah. One of the most exceptional prophets was **Ezekiel,** who lived and wrote during the Babylonian Exile. His vision of fiery wheels in the sky is so vivid and inexplicable that commentators have ascribed it to everything from a full-blown mystical experience to a literal if uncomprehending description of the landing of UFOs, and it became the basis for at least one memorable Negro spiritual. Unlike other prophets describing their visions in the Bible, Ezekiel does not try to explain the significance of what he has experienced, even in metaphorical terms. Here is a brief excerpt from the book of Ezekiel, taken from the Revised Standard Version of the Bible:

As I looked, behold, a stormy wind came out of the north, and a great cloud, with brightness round about it, and fire flashing forth continually, and in the midst of the fire, as it were gleaming bronze. And from the midst of it came the likeness of four living creatures. And this was their appearance: they had the form of men, but each had four faces, and each of them had four wings. . . . And their wings were spread out above; each creature had two wings, each of which touched the wing of another, while two covered their bodies. And each went straight forward; wherever the spirit would go, they went, without turning as they went. In the midst of the living creatures there was something that looked like burning coals of fire, like torches moving to and fro among the living creatures; and the fire was bright, and out of the fire went forth lightning. And the living creatures darted to and fro, like a flash of lightning.

Now as I looked at the living creatures, I saw a wheel upon the earth beside the living creatures. . . . Their appearance was like the gleaming of a chrysolite; and the four had the same likeness, their construction being as it were a wheel within a wheel. . . . The four wheels had rims and they had spokes; and their rims were full of eyes round about. . . . And when they went, I heard the sound of their wings like the sound of many waters, like the thunder of the Almighty, a sound of tumult like the sound of a host; when they stood still, they let down their wings.

—EZEK. 1:4–6, 11–16, 18, 24

them together. The identification of Judaism with an ethnic and cultural bond as much as a set of religious principles probably had its beginnings in this period of dispersion. **Circumcision,** the Sabbath, and the feasts of Passover (commemorating the escape from Egypt and the founding of Israel), Shavuot or Pentecost (the giving of the law to Moses), Tabernacles (wandering in the desert), Yom Kippur (the Day of Atonement), and Rosh Hashanah (the New Year) became part of every Jew's life and were passed along with the laws and scriptures from generation to generation.

The Jews dispersed not only to Babylon (modern Iraq) but also to Samaria, Edom, and Moab in the north and to Egypt. But within less than a century, under the benevolent rule of the Persian king **Cyrus the Great** (whose alliance with the Medes had superseded the Babylonian Empire) and his son **Darius,** the Jews were allowed for the most part not only to worship as they wished but also to return to Judah, which more than 50,000 did. According to historians, the returning Jews then imposed on all Jews the rather rigorist version of religious law developed in exile.

Sometime between 450 and 200 BC, the Hebrew Bible was assembled in nearly its current configuration, and the Jews who had returned to Jerusalem all gathered to sign a new covenant to agree to follow its teachings, marking the official inauguration of the religion of **Judaism** as based on the biblical texts.

The earliest five books of the Hebrew Bible, known as the Torah and later by the Greek term Pentateuch ("five books"), were probably canonized late in the 7th century BC. **Canon,** from the Sumerian word for "reed" and the Greek for "rule" or "straight line," refers to writings whose authenticity as inspired holy scriptures has been accepted by religious authorities. In Judaism, the canon originally referred to the Torah and by the 3rd century BC was expanded to include the books of the prophets and others.

Officially sealed early in the Christian era, with no more additions or changes to be allowed, the Bible was taught in specially designed centers called **synagogues.** Following the destruction of the Second Temple in Jerusalem in AD 70 and the codification of the Bible, the roles of the priest and scribe were greatly reduced. As worship by blood sacrifice faded from Judaism, it was gradually supplanted by prayer and Torah study; the priest and scribe were replaced by the **rabbi,** a man specially trained to teach the law and the scriptures. The synagogue was the popular teaching place; the academy where scholars deliberated on and taught the law was called a **yeshivah** (pl. **yeshivot**). In medieval and modern times, the yeshivah became the center of training for rabbis and religious scholars.

18TH-CENTURY POLISH

TORAH SCROLL

—————

JEWISH MUSEUM/
ART RESOURCE

223

The Good Book I: Tanakh and Torah

In the Quran*, the holy book of Islam, the Jews are referred to as "the People of the Book," connoting that the Bible has served them, through all their centuries of wandering and oppression, as what another observer called "the portable fatherland of the Jews." The **Hebrew Bible,** or **Tanakh,** contains all the revealed sacred texts of Judaism and corresponds to the Old Testament* of the Christian Bible (although the books are organized differently and some are in variant forms). The word *Bible* itself, from the Latin for "little books," ultimately comes from the Greek name of the Phoenician city Byblos, which produced the papyrus on which the Bible and most other works of the day were written. *Tanakh* is an acronymic abbreviation of the Hebrew for the law, prophets, and writings.

The 39 books of the Hebrew Bible (which we will refer to now as the Bible) can be categorized in three ways. The first 5 books, collectively called the **Torah** or **Chumash** in Hebrew and the **Pentateuch** in Greek, are, in English, Genesis, Exodus, Leviticus, Numbers, and Deuteronomy. Their Hebrew names, respectively, are **Breisheet** ("In the Beginning"), **Shmot** ("Names"), **Va-Yikra, Ba-Midbar,** and **Devarim.** Genesis tells the stories of creation, the Flood, and God's selection of Abraham as the patriarch of the Jewish people and ends with Joseph's rise to power in Egypt. Exodus recounts the Egyptian captivity, Moses' birth and selection by God to lead the Israelites out of Egypt to the Promised Land, and the giving of the law to Moses on Mount Sinai. The last three books of the Torah intermittently continue the saga of the 40 years of wandering in the desert, ending with Moses' farewell address and death and the entry into the Promised Land. More significantly, they contain the ordinances covering the entire range of civil and criminal law, ritual and sacrificial rules, and moral and ethical commandments.

Although tradition insists that Moses authored the Torah, modern scholarship has shown the books to be the work of at least four main sources and probably many other writers and editors over a long period of time. Different scriptural documents, the oldest of which date to the 9th and 8th centuries BC, were cobbled together, traditionally by **Ezra the Scribe** in the mid-5th century BC, although the redacting process began before then and continued even after the destruction of the Second Temple. This much is self-evident in any careful reading of the text, which not only repeats unnecessarily but also contradicts itself. To mention two obvious examples: the Ten Commandments are actually listed twice, for no particular reason, in Exodus 20:1–14 and Deuteronomy 5:6–18, with somewhat different wording; and two markedly different stories of the creation of man and woman (Gen. 1:26–28 and 2:7–25) reflect contrasting sources. A controversial recent book makes the case, based on internal evidence, that the author of a large portion of the original material was a woman. A number of other recent books by feminist scholars argue convincingly that when the Hebrew Bible was given its final major redaction in the 5th century BC, the priestly scribes went out of their way to discredit the Goddess worship that had not been totally eradicated from the land they had occupied.

The two other groupings of books are the Prophets, or **Neviim** (major and minor), and the Holy or Wisdom Writings, or **Ketubim,** which include the Psalms and Proverbs, Job, Ecclesiastes, and the "Song of Songs." All of these were canonized under **Rabbi Johanen ben Zakkai** between AD 70 and 132. The Greek translation of the Hebrew Bible, or **Septuagint,** reputedly begun by 72 Jewish scholars brought from Jerusalem to Alexandria during the reign of Ptolemy II (c. 270 BC), was probably completed by the time of Christ and varies slightly from the Hebrew original, which is known as the **Masoretic** text.

Hebrew remains the sacred language of Judaism, much as Sanskrit* is in Hinduism. As a spoken language, Hebrew had been supplanted by **Aramaic** sometime around the 5th or 6th century BC—Jesus spoke Aramaic, as did most Jews of his day in Judea. During the centuries of the Diaspora, Aramaic was replaced by Greek and later by many locally derived languages, especially **Yiddish,** as the common spoken language of Jews. Hebrew was reserved for liturgical purposes and for sacred writings, and so remained virtually unchanged for thousands of years. With the founding of the modern state of Israel, however, Hebrew once more became a spoken language, the national tongue of Israel, and the process of linguistic evolution has recommenced.

PHARISEES AND SADDUCEES

Even before the fall of Jerusalem, Judaism was influenced by the rise of the Greek city-state and its penetration into parts of Asia and the Near East. After about 330 BC, the Jews in Palestine and elsewhere began to come under the rule of various Greek empires, beginning with Alexander of Macedon, the successive dynasties of Egyptian Ptolemys and Syrian Seleucids. Some Jews retreated into desert communities like those of the **Essenes,** some of whom preached a nonviolent asceticism while others, like the Essene sect at **Qumran**, prepared for a militant overthrow of the colonizing Greeks. Still other Jews embraced the Hellenizing process, learned Greek, and became assimilated into Hellenic culture and commerce.

But many pious Jews, known as **hasidim,** resisted Hellenization because it also sought to mix Greek and Jewish concepts of God and places of worship. In refusing to go along with the new demands of the Seleucid rulers and the Jewish high priests controlled by them in the 2nd century BC, these Jews became the first religious martyrs, hundreds of years before the early Christians. Their persecution led to a guerrilla-style fight against the Seleucids and their Jewish collaborators by **Judah Maccabee** ("Hammer"), who in 166–165 BC rid Jerusalem and its environs of all Greeks and cleansed the Temple of their sacrilegious innovations. In December 164, the Temple returned to its original state of ritual purity and was rededicated to Yahveh in a ceremony still celebrated by modern Jews as the feast of Hanukkah ("Dedication").

For a time the Jews ruled themselves and developed the synagogue and a system of schools for teaching the Torah to Jewish boys. The **Sadducees,** descendants of the Davidic high priest Zadoc (from whom their name probably derives), held unwaveringly to the written law. Aristocratic and conservative, the Sadducees rejected apocalyptic piety and supported the Roman occupation; their *Book of Decrees* codified punishments for moral miscreants, including stoning and beheading. Under the Sadducees, a hereditary high priest combined religious and secular power, executed by a council of elders called the **Sanhedrin,** located in every city (the Great Sanhedrin, the highest court in the land, sat on the Temple Mount).

The Sadducees were opposed by the **Pharisees** ("Separatists"), a populist, antiestablishment religious party that began to teach an oral law for adapting the original Mosaic laws to contemporary situations. The Pharisees revolutionized some aspects of the Mosaic code, such as the famous "eye for an eye" law, allowing the offending party to pay the victim the equivalent value of the lost eye (or tooth or limb) rather than exact physical retribution. The Pharisees were separatists in the sense that they set themselves off from the run-of-the-mill Jews, or **am ha'aretz** ("people of the land"), by rigorously observing the age-old ritual purity laws that formerly applied only to priests or only to believers in the Temple. Unlike the Sadducees, with whom they shared power on the Sanhedrin, they opposed the Romans.

Living constantly on the brink of civil war, the Jews elected to make a deal with Rome, which had begun to supplant Greece as the new power in the region, to administer law in Judea. Under the reign of **Herod the**

Great, a Jew with strong ties to Greece and Rome, the **Second Temple** was enlarged in 20 BC, and animal sacrifices—reportedly two lambs every morning and evening—continued under the supervision of the Temple priests. Expanded at great expense, the Second Temple became a tourist spot for Jews and Gentiles alike. At this time the known world contained about 8 million Jews, including 2½ million in Palestine.

Ten years after the death of Herod in 4 BC, the Romans took over direct rulership of Palestine, something the Jews did not recover until the creation of the state of Israel in 1948. From AD 6 until the Great Revolt of 66–73, the Jews resisted the Roman occupation in a variety of ways.

✳ THE EMERGENCE OF JESUS

Among other things, the Pharisees promoted the idea of a final judgment at death and an afterlife, which were not mentioned in the Torah. The idea of judgment appears in Egyptian writings such as the *Book of the Dead,* from the 2nd millennium BC, and in the teachings of Zoroaster* in Iran; an afterlife—or at least a between-life—was a persistent element of Eastern religions even before that, but it was relatively new to Jewish thought. The Pharisees, and perhaps the Essenes as well, took their ideas from the book of Daniel, set in the 6th century BC and probably written in the 2nd or 3rd. Daniel is an example of apocalyptic literature, a word meaning "revelation" but used to refer specifically to predictions about the end of the world. (The last book of the New Testament, Apocalypse or Revelation, is probably the best-known example.)

Apocalypticism developed in Judaism mainly as a response to intolerable conditions of Greek and Roman imperialism. Daniel, for instance, predicts the fall of a political empire (specifically, that of the Greeks in the time it was written) and the potential coming of a "Son of Man"— the Messiah ("anointed one"), first mentioned by Isaiah—who will initiate God's kingdom on earth: "His dominion is an everlasting dominion, which shall not pass away, and his kingdom one that shall not be destroyed." Although the Jewish book was aimed at the Greeks, its themes were picked up by the earliest Christians, who were mostly Jewish anyway, and have reappeared in Christian millenarian groups from the Mid-

228

dle Ages to the 19th and 20th centuries, most notably Jehovah's Witnesses*. Apocalypticism in general offers an oppressed people the promise of imminent transformation of life on earth, brought about by supernatural powers and shared collectively by the group.

The notion of a Messiah who would help the Jews establish the Kingdom of God *on earth* was an appealing one to a people whose former homeland was under Roman occupation. As intermeshed as Jewish religious and political life was, the hope for a spiritual Messiah dovetailed with the expectation of a military leader to overthrow the oppressors. Apocalyptic ideas also appeared in certain **pseudepigrapha,** books purporting to have come from biblical figures like Moses or Abraham but not accepted as canonical and so not included in the Bible. The most notable is the 1st-century **Book of Enoch,** which contains visions of heaven and hell, the fall of the angels, and two historical apocalypses.

The **Zealots,** a splinter group of Pharisees, believed in using violence against the Romans and their Jewish collaborators, of whom there were plenty in Palestine. Believing in the imminent arrival of the Messiah, the Zealots organized numerous uprisings against the Romans; when the Zealots were defeated, the Romans crucified them, sometimes by the thousands. They were associated with rural groups of bandits or brigands made up largely of peasants who had been forced off their lands by the Romans. Another violence-oriented resistance group, the **Sicarii,** could probably be called the world's first urban terrorists. Named for the short daggers they concealed beneath their cloaks, they mingled in festival crowds and assassinated Jews they considered guilty of collaborating with the Romans. They were immensely successful at escaping undetected.

Less violent but still virulently anti-Roman were the various desert sects known loosely as the Essenes. They were generally apocalyptic and promoted asceticism as one sure way to purify and prepare oneself for the coming of the Messiah and the final judgment. In the case of the Qumran monks, they could be paranoid of the Romans, as shown by their text *The War of the Children of Light Against the Children of Darkness.* The Qumran community, located on the northwest shore of the Dead Sea, made a practice of concealing leather and papyrus manuscripts in large earthen jars for safekeeping in nearby caves. The **Dead**

Sea Scrolls, discovered in 1947, were their work, consisting of copies of biblical texts as well as their own writings.

The Essenes were among the first monastics of the Jewish-Christian tradition, and they practiced the kinds of asceticism, fasting, prayer, and meditation we associate with the early Buddhist monastics, eschewing violence and cruelty and professing communal love and strict celibacy. A similar order located near Alexandria, Egypt, known as the **Therapeutae** ("healers"), practiced austerity and meditation as a way to heal themselves of the ills of worldliness. However, the Therapeutae were formed from the educated upper-class Egyptian Jews and admitted women to their congregation, although they also took vows of celibacy. Since they existed long before the birth of Jesus, they must be considered one of the principal models of early Christian monasticism.

In all, as many as 24 sects have been identified in this period of Palestine Judaism. Among them were the Morning Bathers or **Baptists,** whose most notable member, John the Baptist*, preached the coming of the Messiah while he ritually cleansed Jews of their errors with water in the Jordan River. **Jesus of Nazareth** arrived on the scene in the midst of all this political upheaval, which probably accounts for the wild expectations among some Jews that he could be the longed-for Messiah. Jesus' disparagement of the primacy of the Temple religion, with its ritualized worship and burnt sacrifices, did not endear him to the entrenched religious powers, either the fundamentalist Sadducees or the more liberal Pharisees. Like the Buddha, he taught all comers—clean and unclean, poor and rich, man and woman, Jew and Gentile—an approach as radical as it was unwelcome. The expectation that he might be a political messiah was also troubling to the Romans, who had experienced the uprisings and turmoil these claimants could cause.

The theories about Christ's true identity are difficult to unravel. Since the only prominent sect *not* mentioned in the Gospel accounts written by his followers is the Essenes, it has been hypothesized that Jesus and his followers must have been members. Certainly his ascetical habits, including long periods of prayer, fasting, and meditation in the desert, reflect their influence. But since the next chapter of this book is dedicated to Christ's teachings and the spread of Christianity, we will leave his story here for the moment.

WHAT NEXT?

Given the large role that the rewards of heaven, or Paradise, and the pains of hell play in Christianity and Islam, it's surprising to learn what scant attention Judaism has paid to the afterlife (**olam ba-ba**). Although Jews believe in the next world, the Torah is silent on the subject. Later Kabbalistic teachings introduced the Eastern concept of reincarnation*, but that belief remains outside the Jewish mainstream. Here a modern rabbi contemplates the question of life after death and its curiously small role in Judaic teaching.

I suspect that there is a correlation between [the Torah's] nondiscussion of afterlife and the fact that the Torah was revealed just after the long Jewish sojourn in Egypt. The Egyptian society from which the Hebrew slaves emerged was obsessed with death and afterlife. . . . In contrast, the Torah is obsessed with this world, so much so that it even forbids its priests from coming into contact with dead bodies (Leviticus 21:2). . . .

In Judaism the belief in afterlife is less a leap of faith than a logical outgrowth of other Jewish beliefs. If one believes in a God who is all-powerful and all-just, one cannot believe that this world, in which evil far too often triumphs, is the only arena in which human life exists. For if this existence is the final word, and God permits evil to win, then it cannot be that God is good. . . .

According to Judaism, what happens in the next world? As noted, on this subject there is little material. Some of the suggestions about afterlife in Jewish writing are even humorous. In heaven, one story teaches, Moses sits and teaches Torah all day long. For the righteous people . . . this is heaven; for the evil people, it is hell. Another folktale teaches that in both heaven and hell, human beings cannot bend their elbows. In hell people are perpetually starved; in heaven each person feeds his neighbor.

—RABBI JOSEPH TELUSHKIN, *JEWISH LITERACY*

❋ RISE OF THE RABBI

In AD 66, the Roman garrison in Jerusalem was massacred by a Jewish population outraged at Roman mistreatment, the beginning of the **Great Revolt.** When Roman reinforcements arrived from Syria, they too were routed by the Jews who had taken over the city. Over the next three years, four Roman legions systematically advanced on the city, laying siege to it in AD 70. Aided by conflict among the various Jewish factions within, the Romans succeeded in taking the city and decimating the Jewish inhabitants and their sacred buildings. The Second Temple was burned and razed. One of the last strongholds of Jewish resistance was the mountain fortress of **Masada,** once a resort built by Herod the Great. A group of Sicarii held out there as long as they could against a full Roman legion and, when defeat and capture seemed inevitable, 960 of them committed mass suicide rather than surrender in AD 73.

Resistance continued for some years throughout Palestine, most notably under the leadership of **Simon bar Kochba** or **Koseva,** but by AD 135, all the rebels were destroyed and Jerusalem was leveled and rebuilt by the emperor Hadrian. (A remnant of the foundation of the Second Temple remains, though, and is known today as the **Western Wall.**) The Jewish state was effectively dead and would remain that way until the mid-20th century.

If the teachings of Jesus regarding Temple rituals and other mainstays of Jewish practice were hard for many Jews to accept, the belief of his followers, led by the converted Jew Saul of Tarsus (Paul)*, that he was divine—both God and man—was anathema. This difference of belief led to a split between the redispersed Jews and the emerging followers of Christ that was marked by polemical attacks and mounting viciousness on both sides. Anti-Semitism had already been growing among Greeks and Egyptians who viewed the Jews as separatists. They were offended by the Jews' refusal to acknowledge the right of others to believe in gods other than Yahveh and by Jewish laws of diet and ritual cleanness that prevented not only intermarriage but in many cases even socializing. Now these feelings began to take on a doctrinal slant, as both Gentiles and Jews joined the forces of Christianity and began to blame the Jews for Christ's crucifixion.

Deprived of a homeland, Judaism began to grow away from its priestly and sacrificial focus and into the study of the Torah—a term that broadened to include not just the first five books of the Bible but all of scripture, plus the laws and customs and observances that make up Judaism. The synagogue replaced the Temple; the rabbi, a teacher rather than a priestly or political leader, became the central religious figure. At the same time, the books of the Bible were canonized, and no new material was to be introduced. As a result, Jews stopped writing history and revelation and began to study and comment on it. Increasingly, Hebrew ceased to be a spoken language, replaced either by Aramaic among the populace or Greek among learned and successful Jews, and became the language of scripture.

Around this time, work also commenced on the Mishnah, the writing down of the oral law, which had been growing for hundreds of years and was completed by the end of the 2nd century AD. No sooner was that accomplished than the large body of commentaries on it known as the **Talmud** began to be added to it. The term *Talmud* then came to mean the entire corpus of Jewish law and learning exclusive of the Bible and was assembled by thousands of scholars and holy men over at least 5 or 6 centuries.

The Good Book II: Navigating the Sea of the Talmud

Next to the Bible, the Talmud is the most important source of Jewish spiritual teaching. However, it is much larger and more complex than the Bible and consists of many volumes containing many different layers and kinds of material. Its contents fall roughly into three groups: Mishnah, Gemara, and Midrash.

Mishnah ("Repetition")

is the code of oral law elaborated largely by the Pharisees in the 2 or 3 centuries before the Great Revolt. Despite the reputation that the Pharisees have acquired because of Christ's pungent rebukes of them in the Gospels, they were the liberal Jews of their day—responsible for doing away with slavery, for instance, well before other ancient societies did. The Pharisees were willing to interpret the written law and scriptures to fit changes in the social and political situation under Greek and Roman rule. The written Mishnah code, begun early in the 2nd century AD by **Rabbi Akiva ben Josef** and his disciple **Meir,** was edited into final form around 200 by **Judah Ha-Nasi (Judah the Patriarch**) and his followers. Rather than a strict code of laws, it is a compilation of the opinions and rulings of previous rabbinical sages and scholars on a wide variety of situations—giving the majority and dissenting opinions in many cases—and is used as a guideline. These sages were known as **Tannaim** ("teachers"); the two most prominent were **Hillel the Elder** and **Shammai.**

For many years the authority of the Mishnah was heightened by attributing it to Moses, who was said to have received it from God on Mount Sinai along with the written law and to have passed it on orally to Joshua; from Joshua it passed to the elders and prophets and so on. As the Talmudic saying goes, "Whatsoever any earnest scholar will innovate in the future, lo this was already spoken at Sinai." This line of oral transmission outside the written law sounds very much like the retrospective claims of Zen Buddhists that Zen practice was transmitted silently by the Buddha to his disciple Mahakashyapa* on Vulture Peak Mountain, to be revealed to the world at the appropriate time.

The Mishnah is made up of 63 treatises or tractates, divided into six orders:

1. **Zeraim** ("Seeds") covers agricultural produce and ritual offerings.
2. **Moed** ("Festivals") deals with the laws of the Sabbath, feasts, and fast days.
3. **Nashim** ("Women"): betrothal, marriage, and divorce.
4. **Nezikin** ("Damages"): civil and criminal laws and accompanying punishments.
5. **Kodashim** ("Sacred Things"): sacrifices, sacrileges, and offerings.
6. **Toharot** ("Purification"): cleanliness and uncleanliness in the ritual sense.

Gemara ("Completion" Or "Tradition")

is the commentary on the Mishnah compiled by the **Amoraim** ("Expounders"), successors to the Tannaim, whose opinions made up the Mishnah. Gemara is technically what is meant by the term *Talmud* and is often referred to as the Talmud proper. Two sets of Gemara were created, one in Babylonia completed by the 4th or 5th century, and one in Palestine, known as the Jerusalem Talmud, completed about a century earlier. Both are incomplete, commenting on a little more than half the treatises in the Mishnah, yet they comprise numerous volumes representing the work of hundreds of scholars over several centuries.

Midrash ("Interpretation")

is an assessment of the Bible, but especially the Pentateuch, aimed at clarifying various points of law. Compiled over a thousand-year period ending in 1040, it consists mainly of various forms of anecdotal and allegorical material that often began as sermons or homilies based on a passage of scripture—a method that later became popular with Christians.

At the same time, the Talmud as a whole is formed of two kinds of material: halakhah and aggadah. The **halakhah** includes all the legal decisions in the Mishnah and the two Gemaras; the **aggadah** comprises a wide range of legends, myths, anecdotes, parables, and aphorisms aimed at explaining the laws, beliefs, and rituals of the Mishnah to the common folk. This collection expands as it expounds, in the process creating a colorful body of folk material.

The whole massive, often confusing corpus of laws, commentaries, and anecdotal accompaniments is referred to popularly by Jews as the "Sea of the Talmud."

✳ LIVING IN THE MATERIAL WORLD

Judaism was now characterized by the expanded role of the rabbi as scholar and teacher rather than ritual priest, but this **rabbinic Judaism** retained its this-world orientation. Unlike Christianity and some Eastern religions, Judaism does not teach the duality of soul and body, spirit and matter. Although Jews began the monastic tradition in the West, and the Essene and Qumran monks among others practiced celibacy and vegetarianism, rabbinic Judaism ultimately declared such private practices of asceticism—including even abstention from wine—to be sinful. And so Judaism has always fostered an appreciation for the good things in life, and an inclination to take satisfaction and joy in the present moment. Judaism also was the first great religion to require all the faithful, not just clergy, to look after their neighbors. That included such previously unheard of concerns as visiting the sick, feeding the poor, and ensuring the welfare of widows and orphans. Jews were instructed, in the words of

Leviticus 19:18, later quoted by Jesus, to "love your neighbor as yourself."

Lamentably, following the destruction of Jerusalem in 135, Jewish fortunes in this world began to decline. The Greek ideal of universal humanity had begun to spread, and Jewish separateness was seen as antithetical, especially their maintenance of ancient dietary and ritual cleanliness laws. As Christianity expanded and was made the state religion under the emperor Constantine, who became a Christian in 313, what had been a growing stream of anti-Semitism since the Second Temple days expanded to a torrent of Christian attacks on Jews and their property. Blaming the Jews for Christ's death, notwithstanding the obvious fact that Jesus was a Jew and one imbued with the most compassionate teachings of Judaism, Christians persecuted the Jews with the same kind of ferocity with which they themselves had only recently been persecuted by the Romans. In many cases, the attacks had an economic subtext, forcing Jews either to pay outlandishly high taxes or outright ransom for their lives or confiscating land, property, and wealth that the Jews had accumulated through their industry.

Furthermore, since Christians were forbidden by their own doctrines from lending money at interest, this role was gladly given to Jewish merchants and in some cases was the only occupation they were allowed to perform in the Christian world. Many Christians used this involvement with moneylending and later banking as yet another pretext to excoriate and attack the Jews in their midst, conveniently overlooking the fact that Jewish loans financed the building of many of the great churches and cathedrals of Europe.

JEWISH MYSTICISM: THE KABBALAH

Medieval Judaism was up against increasingly severe attempts to destroy it, especially from Christian and Muslim fundamentalists, and sought to keep its far-flung communities together by any means necessary. On a personal level, Jews took up occupations that were valuable to the non-Jewish community and that left them mobile, e.g., trading in precious stones, which were readily portable, or practicing medicine—the preponderance of Jewish doctors in modern society is no accident.

For similar reasons, Judaism accepted and incorporated seemingly heterodox belief systems rather than place yet another strain on the community. And so the mystical practice and study known as **Kabbalah** (or Cabala) was allowed to grow within or at least alongside mainstream Judaism. (The rabbis thought it potentially dangerous, though; in the 17th century, they ruled that it should be studied only by married men over 40 who were also adept in Talmud and Torah.) In return, Kabbalah offered Jews a mystical approach to religion within the context of the accepted beliefs and practices of Judaism. By modern times, Kabbalistic themes had entered the Jewish mainstream, influencing certain prayers and liturgies and contributing its own set of customs and folk beliefs, notably belief in reincarnation. Some scholars even argue that the Kabbalah succeeded because it has roots in Judaic tradition reaching back to the Talmud and possibly earlier.

Originally, the word *Kabbalah,* from a root meaning "to receive," referred to the received tradition of the Bible. But it later came to signify **esoteric** knowledge, i.e., mysteries known only to a select few who are usually either forbidden or unwilling to reveal them. This secret knowledge tended to be pantheistic, giving detailed descriptions of God's body parts along with secret names and numerical interpretations of scriptural texts, seeing creation as a manifestation of the Divine Word. Kabbalists believe that the letters of the Torah, along with the numbers they symbolize, provide a direct knowledge of God in the classic mystical sense; the combination of these letters is one of the major techniques of Jewish mysticism. The magical or occult elements of Kabbalah for the most part developed separately from this mystical theology, and from about the 15th century the two sets of teachings became known respectively as Practical Kabbalah and Speculative Kabbalah. The aim of the latter was to give the Kabbalist inner spiritual guidance; the former delved into the more questionable realms of white (helpful) and black (harmful) magic.

The Kabbalah dates back probably as far as the literature of the **Hekhalot** ("divine palaces"), which has been dated as early as the 2nd century AD. Between those early writings—which describe a mystical journey past gates guarded by seraphim, culminating in the contemplation of God on His throne—and the reemergence of Kabbalah in the 12th century, not much is known for certain. **Gaon** (pl. **Geonim**) was an honorific title given to rabbinic rectors of the academies of Sura and Pumbeditha in Babylonia. During the long **Geonic** period (589–1038), the Jews who had settled there dominated Jewish thought, and Judaism was influenced by many of the mystical and magical concepts derived from Egyptian, Hellenistic, and Persian sources. These found their way into the underground stream of Kabbalism, which surfaced during the early Middle Ages in Europe, incorporating the Hindu concept of reincarnation with Babylonian astrology* and the numerology of 6th-century BC Greek philosopher and mystic Pythagoras* (of "music of the Spheres" fame). **Numerology,** the study of the occult significance of numbers, became an especially significant part of Kabbalah.

The blend of disparate sources matured in Provence in the late 12th century from the work of **Judah Halevi** (c. 1075–1142), the great Jewish poet of the Middle Ages, and later in Catalonia and Castile in Spain and favored direct experience of God over the prevalent intellectual, rationalist approach. Drawing on earlier Kabbalistic texts like the *Sefir Yetzirah* ("Book of Creation," c. 100–500), attributed to Rabbi Akiva ben Josef. Kabbalists believed that each of the 22 letters of the Hebrew alphabet had a specific meaning and a numerical counterpart. When properly combined and added, these values would release great creative powers inherent in the "Word," a concept similar to the Logos* of Philo Judaeus. Kabbalists taught that the first five chapters of Genesis in particular were written in a kind of code that could be correctly interpreted only by knowing the specific values of each Hebrew letter.

Obscurantist as that may sound, some Kabbalists argued that the original Hebrew of the Bible was purposely altered to hide certain secret knowledge when it was translated into Greek for the Septuagint and later into Latin by St. Jerome (a version known as the Vulgate*, on which the famous King James Version* was based). Only by learning the Kabbalistic values of the Hebrew letters was it possible to unravel the deeper, esoteric meaning of the Torah.

The Provençal Kabbalist **Isaac the Blind** (d. c. 1235), who was the first to refer to God as **En Sof** ("Without End," or "Infinite"), and **Rabbi Moses ben Nahman** (known as **Nahmanides** or by the acronym **Ramban,** 1194–1270), who supported Kabbalistic mysticism and brought it into the mainstream in Spain, were among those most responsible for the development and spread of Kabbalistic mysticism in Europe. The concept of En Sof as the undifferentiated Absolute beyond comprehension is key to the identity of the Kabbalah as an esoteric study, since it implies that even biblical conceptions of God do not reveal the true nature of the infinite Source of the universe. But despite attempts to keep Kabbalistic teachings limited to an inner circle, the ideas and practices began to filter into Jewish society on both a folk magic and a theological level.

Abraham Abulafia (c. 1240–1292) developed a so-called Prophetic Kabbalah based on his own ecstatic approach. An illuminated sage who may have been influenced by the Sufis*, Abulafia promoted a mystical technique, based on meditations on the sacred names of God and the Hebrew letters, which he claimed could bestow the ability to prophesy. He wrote 26 prophetic books and a number of manuals explaining his technique, most of which were considered highly controversial by the rabbinic authorities of his day.

Around 1286 in Guadalajara, **Moses ben Shem Tov de Leon** (1230–1305) produced a work called the *Sefer ha-Zohar,* commonly called the **Zohar** ("Splendor"), the best-known Kabbalistic text to this day. De Leon presented the Zohar as being, in fact, a more ancient work by the 2nd-century **Rabbi Simeon ben Yochai,** written while he hid from the occupying Romans in a cave. Some scholars have insisted that he made this claim merely to bolster the book's believability, since it has been proven that the Aramaic of the book could not have come from the 2nd century. But others now suggest that de Leon may have received the work through the process of automatic writing* and may have believed that it was being channeled* from Rabbi Simeon. In an age when it was common for even the most pious and orthodox rabbis to consult with an angel or discarnate spirit called a **maggid** over important decisions regarding Jewish law, such an interpretation is not out of the question. In any case, the Zohar, written in the form of a mystical commentary on the Torah, the "Song of Songs," and the book of Ruth, is widely considered to be the most profound expression of Jewish mysticism in existence.

Building on the work of Isaac the Blind, de Leon propounded a Kabbalistic theory of creation that attempts to describe the creation of the Godhead from within Itself. At the root of the theory is the concept of divine **"emanations"** that take the form of the 10 **sephirot** (sing. **sephiraph**). These are manifestations or attributes of En Sof which in turn contain the archetypes of the rest of creation, implying that all material objects have some divine aspect. A whole literature grew up describing the sephirot and their complex relationships with each other and with other matter and beings that come into existence from them. The *Encyclopaedia Judaica* describes this process as "the emergence of God from the depths of Himself into creation." This notion of the One manifesting Itself as the particular or the many raises echoes of the similar Hindu concepts of Prakriti* and Purusha*, or Brahman* and Maya*, and the Theos and Logos of Neoplatonism*, which directly influenced Kabbalistic thought. But if the notion that all matter is good because it is of God is fully coherent with Jewish tradition, the concept that God exists *within* all matter clearly goes counter to Judaic monotheism and is close to pantheism. Later Kabbalists argued that the sephirot were not the substance of God but merely His power or manifestation.

The Zohar contains material on astrology, demonology, numerology, and transmigration of souls which many conservative Jewish authorities found threatening and potentially heretical. But because the Kabbalah was also supported by renowned rabbinic scholars and holy men, it avoided direct attacks and charges of heresy and was absorbed into the mainstream, especially through the Hasidic traditions that developed later.

The ultimate goal of Kabbalistic thought, if it may be said to have one, is devekut, or cleaving to God. And yet as explained by Gershom Scholem (1897–1983), the undisputed father of modern Kabbalistic research, the absorption of the mystic into the Godhead that is the goal of classic mysticism is absent from Jewish mysticism. "It is not union," Scholem wrote, "because union with God is denied to men even in that mystical upsurge of the soul according to Kabbalistic theology. But it comes as near to union as a mystical interpretation would allow." Again, other Kabbalists disagree; in either case, devekut is achieved through observation of the commandments, mystical prayer, and meditations that may involve combinations of Hebrew letters, the Tetragrammaton, and sacred names of God, in some cases used almost as mantras*. Some Kabbalists employ breathing techniques and specific meditation exercises reminiscent of yoga and Sufism, showing some of the cross-pollination peculiar to all mystical traditions.

Because it is considered a bona fide system of mystical practice, the Kabbalah has been picked up by non-Jews interested in mysticism, just as yoga has been appropriated by non-Hindus, Zen by non-Buddhists, and Sufism by non-Muslims. As in these other cases, it can be argued that true Kabbalah can be practiced only within the context of the belief system from which it grew, specifically the Torah. But this hasn't kept thousands of Christians and unaffiliated seekers from borrowing its teachings, practices, and terminology.

✳ IN THE GHETTO

The confinement of Jews in a **ghetto,** or segregated area of a city, began in 1515 in Venice and carried across Italy with the enthusiastic support of the Vatican under Pope Paul IV. In short order, Jews were literally walled off from the rest of society in major European cities such as Frankfurt, Prague, and Warsaw. Although they could enter and leave for business purposes during the day, their freedom of movement was severely restricted, with ghetto gates closed at night and on Christian holidays. The Jews had always held themselves apart from Gentile society, but now the Gentiles were taking revenge in a peculiarly vicious way: the segregation of Jews made them easier to attack whenever an outburst of anti-Semitism led to persecutions or outright massacres. In 18th- and 19th-century Russia, Jews were confined in the **Pale of Settlement,** a stretch of Western provinces outside of which Jews could not travel without authorization, which again led to a series of massacres known as **pogroms.** At the same time, the ghetto helped reinforce in Jews their reliance on each other and on their unique mixture of religion, social life, and commerce.

During this period, the Kabbalah became increasingly significant in the life of popular Jewry, incorporating apocalyptic and messianistic material with its mystical teachings. A school of Kabbalah studies grew in Palestine at Safed, spearheaded by **Isaac ben Solomon Luria** (c. 1534–72), who divided his time between mystical studies and his import-export business and is considered the most important Kabbalist of post-15th-century Judaism. Luria believed that the long suffering of the Jews—which had been brought into stark relief by their expulsion from Spain and Portugal in the 1490s—reflected a dissolution of the cosmos. The dissolution resembled a mirror shattered into countless fragments, each of which contains a spark of divine light. It is the job of the Jews to reassemble or restore the

THE NAME GAME

In Kabbalah study, Judaism comes closest to the systems of the Eastern religions, particularly in its teachings on emanation and the male and female principles. The Kabbalistic **Tree of Life** containing the 10 sephirot and their many interconnecting paths is formed into three columns, one feminine, one masculine, and one middle column mediating the other two. This is comparable to the ida* and pingala* surrounding the central sushumna* nadi of kundalini* yoga, the yin-yang* of Taoism, the Shiva* and Shakti* of Hinduism, and the yab-yum* of Tantric Buddhism. Many Kabbalists conceive of God as embodying both male and female energies, which were divided during creation as part of the process of emanation. They speak of the **shekhinah**, which in traditional Judaism means the divine presence on earth, as the feminine aspect or mystical bride of God. And they often use language as a means to analyze such mysteries, as in this excerpt from a contemporary non-Jewish Kabbalist which offers an explanation for the mysterious use of the plural form for God early in the Bible:

The Hebrew word used to denominate God in Genesis is Elohim. This word is a plural formed from the feminine singular ALH (Eloh) by adding IM to it. Since IM is the termination of the masculine plural, added to a feminine noun it makes ELOHIM a female potency united to a male principle, and thus capable of having an offspring. The same intended misconception is given in the Christian idea of the Holy Trinity: Father, Son, and the Holy Ghost. In the Kabbalah the Deity manifests simultaneously as Mother and Father and thus begets the Son. We are told that the Holy Spirit is essentially masculine, but the Hebrew word used in the Scriptures to denote spirit is Ruach, a feminine noun. The Holy Spirit is really the Mother, and thus the Christian Trinity properly translated should be Father, Son and Mother.

—MIGENE GONZÁLEZ-WIPPLER, *A KABBALAH FOR THE MODERN WORLD*

The sense of the Holy Spirit as a feminine essence appears memorably in the closing image of "God's Grandeur" by the great Jesuit poet Gerard Manley Hopkins:

Because the Holy Ghost over the bent
World broods with warm breast and with ah! bright wings.

fragmented cosmos by strict observance of the law with correct intention and concentration, culminating in the coming of the Messiah. This restoration or redemption of the cosmic order he called **tikkun.** Luria practiced and taught meditation and other methods of inducing ecstatic experience, but the outer-directed spiritual activism of tikkun differentiates this Kabbalistic system, with its roots in the work of Nahmanides, from the more individualistic mysticism of Abraham Abulafia.

Despite its esoteric nature, Kabbalah had a major influence on Judaism. Especially through the popularity of Practical Kabbalah among the Hasidim, it reached the Jewish masses and became intertwined with folk legends and customs.

❋ JEWISH RATIONALISM: MAIMONIDES AND SPINOZA

While Isaac the Blind and other mystics were working out the ramifications of the Kabbalah, **Maimonides** (**Rabbi Moses ben Maimon,** or **Rambam** for short, 1135–1204) was developing a strain of Jewish rationalism that was to become even more influential in the long run. A Spanish-born scholar, philosopher, and physician and a prolific writer, Maimonides fled to Egypt to avoid persecution and there became personal physician to the Sultan. He was the first to write a complete code of Jewish law, the highly respected **Mishneh Torah,** which was intended as a simple, rational guide to Jewish behavior based only on the Torah, allowing Jews to avoid sinking in the Sea of the Talmud. It is still studied in yeshivot around the world. Maimonides's best-known work, *Guide of the Perplexed*, explains the basics of Jewish theology and philosophy, especially the "Thirteen Articles" of faith, which he felt defined Jewish belief. The *Guide* was particularly useful in Rambam's day, when Jews were under enormous pressure to convert to Christianity or Islam, either to advance their fortunes or to escape murderous persecutions. His rejection of literal readings of the Bible and his generally logical approach to religion impressed Christians like Thomas Aquinas* as well as Muslim theologians. Arguably the single most influential Jew of the medieval period, Maimonides left his imprint on all subsequent Jewish thought.

A scholar and lens grinder in Amsterdam at the height of its intellectual influence, **Baruch de Spinoza** (1632–77) was the son of Jewish émigrés from Spain and Portugal. He followed the rationalizing tradition of Maimonides, but took it a step further, stating that the Bible should be treated critically and scientifically. Spinoza more or less began the modern approach to biblical scholarship, insisting on a complete knowledge of the authors of the various books, their social and historical contexts, and the long process of editing, revision, and redaction by which the books reached their present form.

But many of Spinoza's contemporaries thought he went too far, arguing against the existence of angels, biblical miracles, and the immortality of the soul. Even before he published his theories in his 1670 *Tractatus Theologico-Politicus*—which amounted to denying the divinely inspired, literal truth of the Bible—he had been excommunicated from the Jewish community at the age of 24, kicked out of his home by his father, and banished from Amsterdam. He lived a frugal and almost ascetical life, ate little, never married, and died of tuberculosis at age 44. Spinoza's system of ethics was based on reason rather than biblical commandments, and he was often accused of being an atheist or at best a pantheist. He believed that there was only one completely independent substance or being, which he called God but identified with Nature ("He did not *create* Nature but is Nature"). But in this sense his writings reflect an almost Eastern detachment: "The intellectual love of the mind toward God is part of the infinite love with which God loves himself." To an orthodox Jew or Christian, that sort of talk sounds pantheistic and dangerous. And yet the

THE FALSE MESSIAH

In 1665 **Shabbetai Zevi** (1626–76), a Turkish Jew, was proclaimed the Messiah by a cunning and brilliant Kabbalist known as **Nathan of Gaza** (1643–80), a student of Luria's techniques for inducing visions and ecstasies. Although Nathan orchestrated the whole affair for self-serving purposes, most rabbis and at least half of all Jews—predisposed by yet another wave of anti-Jewish atrocities to hope for the arrival of the Messiah—were convinced that Zevi was the real thing. Zevi even set a date, June 18, 1666, for the Redemption to take place. But he was imprisoned by the Turks, the date passed eventlessly, and he was denounced as a fraud. To save his life, he agreed to convert to Islam, sparking one of the greatest historical and spiritual crises in Jewish history. Even after Zevi's death in 1676 and Nathan's in 1680, the **Shabbatean** movement continued to flourish and evolved into a new religion under a supposed reincarnation of Zevi, **Jacob Frank** (1726–91). Frank later converted to Islam, then Roman Catholicism, then Russian Orthodoxy. Some scholars, most notably Gershom Scholem, believe that the birth of Hasidism was a direct response to Shabbateanism.

18th-century romantic German poet and novelist Baron Friedrich von Hardenberg (Novalis) referred to Spinoza as "the God-intoxicated man."

DANCE OF THE HASIDIM

Just as Eastern religions developed on two different levels—one for the monastic elite and another for the plain working folk—so Judaism's rabbinic leaders, with their emphasis on study and discipline, had begun to

Drawing of a member of the Hasidim by the American artist Abraham Walkowitz, c. 1910.
JEWISH MUSEUM/
ART RESOURCE

lose touch with the Jewish masses, especially in Eastern Europe. Even the Kabbalists were preaching asceticism, advocating that Jews fast twice a week despite their long tradition of savoring God's largesse. Throughout the 18th century, various pietistic movements developed that appealed to the needs of the masses for a more devotional and joyous approach to their religion, along the lines of the bhakti* movement in India. The most successful of these was **Hasidism** (or Chasidism), derived from the same word for "the pious" (*hasid,* pl. hasidim) that had been applied to the early group of martyrs who resisted Hellenization.

Hasidism may have developed partly in reaction to the scientific rationalism of the day—influenced not only by Spinoza but also by Sir Isaac Newton and his mechanical model of the universe—and partly as a way of moderating and rechanneling the messianic impulses set aflame by the Shabbateans. The new Hasidic movement was pioneered in 1735 by **Israel ben Eliezer,** known familiarly as the **Ba'al Shem Tov** ("Master

247

of the Good Name," c. 1700–60) or by the acronym **Besht.** Not strictly rabbinic, he was more in the tradition of the **ba'al shem,** a kind of wandering holy man who worked outside the mainstream, like the Hindu sadhu* or Taoist fang shih*, and who sometimes employed white magic, made charms and amulets, and exorcised evil spirits from the possessed. The Ba'al Shem Tov was an ecstatic mystic whose devotional approach fed the people's need for an emotional, love-based religion. But his teaching that love and doing good works were more important than following the letter of the law offended many orthodox Talmudists, known as **Mitnagdim,** Hebrew for "Opponents." (It is an indication of Hasidism's success that to this day the term *Mitnagdim* is applied to all non-Hasidic rabbis.) In particular, Rabbi Elijah of Vilna, better known as the **Vilna Gaon** ("Genius of Vilna," 1720–97), the undisputed, if unofficial, spiritual leader of Lithuanian and Russian Jewry, opposed the movement and had Hasidism banned. Still it continued to spread rapidly all over Poland and Lithuania, across Eastern Europe and around the world, until almost half of all Jewry was Hasidic. But as the liberalization of Jewish law toward the end of the 18th century was perceived as a threat by both the Hasidim and Mitnagdim, the two groups closed ranks. Hasidism merged with the rabbinic mainstream and stands today as a bastion of Orthodox Judaism, a somewhat closed society similar to the Amish*, right down to their 18th- and 19th-century black garb and strict mores.

Then as now, however, Hasidic communities employed music and dance, often leading to ecstatic states similar to those sought by Sufi dervishes* or modern Pentecostalists*. The Ba'al Shem also developed a kind of spontaneous prayer based on divine possession, akin to speaking in tongues*. Much like leaders of the Protestant Reformation* and the born-again* movement in modern Christianity, he promoted a direct communion between the faithful and God, sidestepping the priestly or rabbinic class. In its place he restored and transformed the ancient concept of the **zaddik** (pl. **zaddikim,** "righteous")—a superior man or saint, not necessarily a rabbi, who could intercede for the people with God. This charismatic figure, sometimes called a **rebbe,** dispensed wisdom and, like the ba'al shems of old, created amulets and talismans to ward off evil spirits and grant wishes. Under his successor, **Dov Baer** of Mezrich (1710–72), the zaddik became central to Hasidism.

YES, BUT WAS IT KOSHER?

Because of the conservative dress of most modern Hasidim, it's easy to forget that the movement was once considered liberal to the point of radicalism. Their ecstatic dancing and spontaneous prayer, as evidenced by this Hasidic legend, did not so much go against the grain of rabbinic Judaism as seek to transcend it.

At the festival of Simhat Torah, the day of rejoicing in the law, the Ba'al Shem's disciples made merry in his house. They danced and drank and had more and more wine brought up from the cellar. After some hours, the Ba'al Shem's wife went to his room and said: "If they don't stop drinking, we soon won't have any wine left for the rites of the Sabbath. . . ."

He laughed and replied: "You are right. So go and tell them to stop."

When she opened the door to the big room, this is what she saw: The disciples were dancing around in a circle, and around the dancing circle twined a blazing ring of blue fire. Then she herself took a jug in her right hand and a jug in her left and—motioning the servant away—went into the cellar. Soon after, she returned with the vessels full to the brim.

—MARTIN BUBER, *TALES OF THE HASIDIM: THE EARLY MASTERS*

Like many great mystics before them, the Hasidim found God in the most mundane activities and practiced "physical worship," praising God not, like many religious Jews of the time including the Kabbalists, through prayer and asceticism but in presumably profane activities such as eating, sleeping, and making love. The goal was the same as it was for the Kabbalists: devekut, or mystical union, and the Besht taught that any act performed with devekut in mind would lead to ecstasy.

After the Ba'al Shem's death, the rebbes inevitably began to acquire more power, often along with sizable incomes. The position became hereditary, and localized dynasties of rebbes developed: the familiar cycle of reform, decay, and institutionalization was at work. Dozens of these dynastic lines of leadership survive today, e.g., the **Satmar,** the **Bobov,** the **Telem,** and, most visibly, the **Lubavitcher,** who are active in American Hasidism. Despite the apparent conservatism of the Hasidic movement today, it is one of the great repositories of Jewish mystical thought and practice, couched in an unlikely amalgam of profound study, populist devotionalism, and religious fundamentalism.

Unlike other modern Hasidic sects, the Lubavitchers spend much of their time in the larger society, seeking to attract nonobservant or Reform Jews to their rigorous Orthodox practice. For instance, the Lubavitcher Mitzvah Tank (actually a large van) roams the streets of New York bringing their message to other Jews. The most recent leader of the Lubavitcher community, **Rabbi Menachem M. Schneerson,** was the seventh in a dynastic lineage stretching back to Lubavitch, Russia, in the 18th century. Until Schneerson's recent death in June 1994, Jews of all stripes, from the Israeli ambassador to Bob Dylan, queued up to seek the rebbe's advice and blessing every Sunday at Lubavitcher headquarters in Brooklyn, New York, in a Hasidic equivalent of the Hindu darshan*. With a worldwide following of about 200,000, the rebbe commanded the respect and donations of millions of secular Jews as well, many of whom believe he might well be the long-awaited Ma-shi-akh, the Messiah. Among the Brooklyn community of 30,000, the men invariably wear dark suits and overcoats, black hats, and full beards, and the women dress very modestly by current standards.

✸ HASKALAH, THE JEWISH ENLIGHTENMENT

As part of the wave of Enlightenment that led to the American and French Revolutions near the end of the 18th century, legal and social restrictions against Jews began to come down all across Europe, along with

THE GOOD THIEF
IN HASIDIC LORE

A thief in his old age was unable to ply his "trade" and was starving. A wealthy man, hearing of his distress, sent him food. Both the rich man and the thief died on the same day. The trial of the magnate occurred first in the Heavenly Court; he was found wanting and sentenced to Purgatory. As he approached the entrance to Purgatory, however, an Angel came hurrying to recall him. He was brought back to the Court, where he learned that his sentence had been reversed. The thief whom he had aided on earth had stolen the list of his iniquities.

—THE YEHUDI (HASIDIC RABBI, D. 1815)

the physical walls of the ghettos that had separated them from Gentile society for almost 300 years. New, revolutionary governments in France and England, for example, found it increasingly hard to talk about the "Rights of Man" while trying to exclude the Jews living among them, and some began to champion Jewish freedoms. Ironically, in the anticlerical atmosphere of the Enlightenment, supposed iconoclasts such as Voltaire and Diderot now attacked the religiosity and "superstition" of the Jews, just as Christian fundamentalists had previously assaulted them as a threat to Christianity.

During the Jewish **emancipation,** as this social development came to be known, Jews began to seek ways to integrate themselves into society without losing their ethnic and religious identity. But years of isolation in the ghettos of Europe had cut off the Jewish population from the cultural mainstream. **Moses Mendelssohn** (1729–86), the prototype of the **maskil,** or enlightened Jew, spearheaded a movement known as **Haskalah** ("Enlightenment") that sought to counter that isolation. He opposed the concept of the chosen people and translated the Bible into German to encourage German Jews to become fluent in that language (rather than Yiddish). Predictably perhaps, Mendelssohn's attempts to mix secular and Jewish values were resisted less by Gentiles than by Orthodox Jews seeking to keep their separate identity. As proof of the dangers inherent in his approach, his coreligionists pointed to the fact that four of his six children converted to Christianity.

But the call for a modernization of Jewish laws and customs spread among European Jewry, and by 1820 in Germany the Reform movement was under way. Modeled on the Protestant Reformation, Reform Judaism, under leaders like **Rabbi Abraham Geiger** (1810–74), introduced new elements such as the sermon, organ and choral music, and a new prayerbook, and urged Jews to abandon the concepts of the Messiah and the return to Zion.

❋ THE FOUR BRANCHES OF MODERN JUDAISM

For a religious tradition that has been active over more than three millennia, Judaism has surprisingly few sects and only four major divisions, which can be rather easily distinguished.

The **Reform** movement arose in Germany in the early 19th century as a response to the gradual dropping of legal and political barriers against European Jews, accompanied by a weakening of the prevailing antipathy toward them. Denying the eternal validity of any one formulation of Judaic law or beliefs, the Reform movement sought to integrate Jews into a mainstream society that was increasingly available to them politically and socially. It abbreviated the liturgy, introduced prayers and sermons in the vernacular and singing with organ accompaniment, and rendered dietary and Sabbath restrictions optional and inessential. Rabbi Abraham Geiger opposed the traditional beliefs that the Jews are a people rather than simply adherents of a religious tradition and that kinship with others of Jewish birth is an integral part of the religion (although Reform Jews later reversed his position). Faced with the opportunity to be accepted into German society without having to convert, many German Jews felt compelled to eliminate anything that might be seen as incompatible with German citizenship, which meant all tribal and ethnic aspects of their Jewish identity, including beliefs that might be construed as superstitious by 19th-century rationalist standards. They went all out, as one modern American rabbi put it, "to try to be as Protestant as possible," even to moving their Sabbath, for a time, from Saturday to Sunday. In America, the Reform movement became known for its relaxation of ritual overall, preferring to stress the Torah's teachings on ethics.

Orthodox Jews insist on retaining traditional Jewish laws and customs, as they relate not only to liturgy but also to diet and dress. They demand full submission to the authority of halakhah, the massive accretion of written and oral laws of Judaism, feeling that the revealed will of God, not the value system of a particular age, is the ultimate standard of conduct. Those laws include separation of the sexes during worship and other roles for women that are at odds with social changes sought by the modern women's movement. The various Hasidic sects constitute a significant segment of Orthodox Judaism—all Hasidim are Orthodox, but not all Orthodox are by any means Hasidic.

Conservative Judaism, originally known as "Historical Judaism," began in the mid-19th century as something of a counterreformation in response to the perceived excesses of the Reform movement. Conservative Jews hailed the westernization of Judaism in the areas of education and culture (embracing modern dress, for instance) but kept the use of Hebrew in the liturgy, the observance of dietary laws and the Sabbath, and almost all Torah rituals. In the 1980s the Conservatives decided to admit women as rabbis. The center of the movement is the **Jewish Theological Seminary** of New York; more American Jews are affiliated with Conservative synagogues than with Reform or Orthodox.

Reconstructionist Judaism was founded in 1922 in the U.S. by **Rabbi Mordecai M. Kaplan** (1881–1983) in an effort to adapt classical Judaism to the modern intellectual emphasis on science, art, and reason. Reconstructionists see Judaism as an evolving civilization rather than a religion and reject the notion of a personal Deity, miracles like the parting of the Red Sea, and the whole concept of the chosen people. With only about 60,000 members, it is a minor branch, headquartered in Philadelphia, but it has strongly influenced Reform Judaism in particular. Rabbi Kaplan performed the first bat mitzvah, allowing young women to celebrate a religious rite of passage previously celebrated only by Jewish males, but now commonplace for females among all but Orthodox congregations. He also began the **havurah** movement, in which Jews meet in small groups to study and observe Jewish rituals. Recently, Reconstructionism has restored references in its prayerbooks to supernatural events that it had earlier excised as being unbelievable. They are now accepted on the level of "myth."

❊ REMEMBERING ZION

The hill in Jerusalem on which David placed the Ark of the Covenant, where Solomon built the First Temple and Herod the Second, is **Mount Zion.** The name Zion came to be used as a synonym for the land of Is rael (or **Erez Israel**), and by extension for the Kingdom of God; over cen-

LEAVING THE FOLD

Some Jews responded to Haskalah by leaving Judaism altogether. They chose either to be baptized in the Christian faith or at least to have their children baptized. Among those of Jewish parentage who were raised as Christians were Benjamin Disraeli, Karl Marx, Felix Mendelssohn, and Heinrich Heine. Heine (1797–1856), one of Germany's most beloved poets, formally abandoned Judaism in the hopes of getting his doctorate, saying that baptism was "the admission ticket to European culture." He didn't get the doctorate anyway and by the end of his life was rereading the Bible and books on Jewish history, although he never explicitly reembraced Judaism. For all that, his work influenced Richard Wagner's *Flying Dutchman* and *Tannhäuser*. And the Nazis, who once used a statue of Heine for target practice, included his poem "Lorelei" in numerous anthologies, presenting it as an anonymous "folksong."

turies it also became the focal point of the desire of many Jews to return to their homeland. The continual onslaught of persecutions, pogroms, and massacres wherever in the world Jews congregated lent momentum to the logic of such a return. During World War II, the massive, systematic slaughter of the **Holocaust,** virtually eradicating the Jewish population of Germany, Eastern Europe, and western Russia (a third of all Jews overall), added a premise of urgency and inescapability.

The movement to reestablish the Jewish homeland, which became known as **Zionism,** gathered official status in the 19th century. Through the intercession of Great Britain, Jews from all over the world began settling in Palestine, and in 1948 the **state of Israel** was officially declared. The Jews had the distinction of being the first people in history to reclaim their homeland after having been exiled from it. Unfortunately, the achievement has been an uneasy one. Conflicts ensued, not only between Jews and Palestinians and neighboring Arab states, but also among differing factions within Israel and the larger Jewish community worldwide over how best to handle the dilemma. The complicated moral issues and complex political (and military) maneuverings involved in this process have continued right up to the present day.

The Middle East seems to have been fated almost from the beginning of civilization to be a locus of strife and contention. The land alternately known as Palestine or Israel has been involved in a kind of cyclical drama for over 3,000 years, amid shifting levels of irony. The Israelites, under direct command from God, took the land from the Goddess-worshiping Canaanites, only to have it taken from them by the Babylonians; they were allowed to return briefly by the Persians, before being overrun by succeeding waves of Romans and Greeks. By the time the horrors of the Holocaust made it imperative for the Jews to reclaim a homeland, it was occupied mainly by Palestinian Arabs. Under pressure from Arab and Communist nations a UN resolution was passed in 1975 denouncing Zionism as "a form of racism" but was later rescinded. In 1993, Israel and the Palestine Liberation Organization (PLO) under Yasir Arafat signed an agreement on self-rule for nearly 2 million Palestinian Arabs in the Israeli-occupied West Bank and Gaza Strip. Still shared uncomfortably by Jews and Palestinians, the state of Israel remains a focal point of struggle and suffering, of great religious fervor and political unrest, recalling the old Yiddish saying "God is not an uncle; he is an earthquake."

✳ EMANCIPATION RECLAMATION

The social changes that swept Europe and allowed Jews to integrate more freely with European society and later to find unprecedented freedom in the New World were not without an impact on the historical development of Judaism, which was never quite the same after the 18th century. What happens when a traditional tribal culture encounters the secular modern era? The effects on Judaism of the emancipation have been compared to what occurred in the 1st century AD after the Second Temple was destroyed. Then, Jews began a long, slow process of replacing ritual sacrifice with prayer, Torah study, and deeds of loving kindness. A similar massive shift occurred in the 19th and 20th centuries. As modern nation-states formed which accepted Jews as citizens, the Jewish community began to be more fully assimilated, although the events of the Holocaust show how superficial that assimilation was.

Although the United States still has "restricted" country clubs and other social organizations from which Jews are excluded, not to mention occasional incidents of anti-Semitism, it has proven to be more open to Jews than any European nation. In America, as far back as the 17th and 18th centuries, assimilation of Jews into mainstream society became a genuine option for the first time in modern history. The only choices available to Jews in Europe and Russia had been to convert to Christianity or to retain their Jewish religion and cultural identity in exchange for surrendering certain legal and political freedoms and at the risk of property confiscation and death.

The question of whether and to what extent assimilation threatens the Jews with the loss of their identity as a people remains problematic. Assimilated Jews often change their names to make them less Jewish-sounding, stop observing religious laws and customs, and marry non-Jews, all tending to dilute the strength of the Jewish community, and this is viewed with alarm by many modern Jewish leaders. But given the freedom to assimilate without coercion, many Jews have opted instead to rediscover and reassert their religion and culture. The movement of secularized or assimilated Jews back to the synagogue and to a fuller observance of their religious traditions is one of the more noticeable recent trends among American Jewry. Whether this movement is enough to offset the rate of assimilation is not entirely clear, but the odds have to favor continuation of one of the most resilient traditions in history.

JEWISH HUMOR: FROM YAHVEH TO OI VEY

One of the great cultural contributions of the Jewish people, apart from their enormous intellectual, artistic, and scientific achievements, has been the gift of a unique sense of humor that stems from a combination of folk wisdom and irony developed over thousands of years. Brilliant Jewish comics from Lenny Bruce to Jackie Mason have made Jewish humor the benchmark of 20th-century American wit and have inspired non-Jewish comics as diverse as Richard Pryor and George Carlin. The roots of that humor as a response to continual oppression, and its genius for self-deprecation and verbal aggressiveness, have been documented and examined at great length by sociologists. Here are two examples that happen to have a religious texture, one given by a modern rabbi, the other from one of the renowned Jewish novelists of the 20th century.

How do we know Jesus was Jewish? Four reasons:
1. He was thirty, unmarried, and still living with his mother.
2. He went into his father's business.
3. He thought his mother was a virgin.
4. And his mother thought he was God.
—RABBI JOSEPH TELUSHKIN, *JEWISH HUMOR*

The radio was playing "Easter Parade" and I thought, But this is Jewish genius on a par with the Ten Commandments. God gave Moses the Ten Commandments and then He gave to Irving Berlin "Easter Parade" and "White Christmas." The two holidays that celebrate the divinity of Christ—the divinity that's the very heart of the Jewish rejection of Christianity—and what does Irving Berlin brilliantly do? He de-Christs them both! Easter he turns into a fashion show and Christmas into a holiday about snow. Gone is the gore and the murder of Christ—down with the crucifix and up with the bonnet! *He turns their religion into schlock.* But nicely! Nicely! So nicely the goyim don't even know what hit 'em. They love it. *Everybody* loves it. The Jews especially. Jews loathe Jesus. People always tell me Jesus is Jewish. I never believe them. It's like when people used to tell me Cary Grant was Jewish. . . . So—Bing Crosby replaces Jesus as the beloved Son of God, and the Jews, the *Jews,* go around whistling about Easter! And is that so disgraceful a means of defusing the enmity of centuries? Is anyone really dishonored by this? If schlockified Christianity is Christianity cleansed of Jew hatred, then three cheers for schlock. If supplanting Jesus Christ with snow can enable my people to cozy up to Christmas, then let it snow, let it snow, let it snow! Do you see my point?

—PHILIP ROTH, *OPERATION SHYLOCK: A CONFESSION*

❋ INSIDE A SYNAGOGUE

A synagogue, from the Greek for a "bringing together" or "assembly" (the Yiddish term is **shul**), can be any room or building reserved for prayer but also serving as a place of religious study. In fact, many of the elements of synagogue services evolved from and incorporate elements of Talmudic study. But although a rabbi is usually retained to serve the community, his or her presence is not necessarily required at services, which can be conducted by the laity. Membership in a specific synagogue customarily requires annual dues, but attendance at services is open to nonmembers and non-Jews, and provision is always made for the indigent. Since money may not be handled on the Sabbath or religious festivals, there is no collection as at Christian services. A **minyan,** or minimum of ten members, is required for reading the Torah and certain prayers.

The focal point and the one element that all synagogues have in common is a copy of the Torah, the first five books of the Bible, in scroll form. It may be draped in robes and should be housed in a cabinet (**Aron Kodesh,** "Holy Ark") recalling the original Ark and facing east, toward Jerusalem. The scroll itself is made by stitching parchment sheets together and rolling them around twin wooden poles so the scroll can be read and displayed to the congregation. Since the scroll must be written by hand with a quill pen, and the writer, or **sofer,** must take a ritual bath before writing the name of God, a scroll can take as much as a year and cost upwards of $50,000 to complete.

Also required is a lectern from which to read the Torah and a lamp that is kept burning as in the Temple of Jerusalem. A **menorah,** a holy candelabrum with seven candlesticks, isn't requisite but is fairly common. (The seven-branched menorah mentioned in Exodus is one of the symbols of Israel. The candelabrum with nine candlesticks used to celebrate the eight days of Hanukkah—one of the candles is used to light the other eight—is technically referred to as a **hanukkiyah,** although most people call it a menorah anyway.) As with the Islamic mosque, no representations of human or divine figures are allowed, even in the stained-glass windows or other artwork. Orthodox synagogues almost always have separate seating for women, usually in a balcony or a section aside or behind the men's area.

Synagogue prayer (**siddur**) includes morning (**shakharit**), afternoon (**minkha**), and evening (**ma'ariv**) services, which are largely elaborated on for Sabbath (**Shabbat**) or the High Holy Days. Traditionally, Sabbath (the period from twilight on Friday to Saturday evening) is observed by resting from all physical labor, including the cooking of food. Eating, however, is not restricted, and the Sabbath meal on Friday at sundown is a focal point of many Jewish homes. The Orthodox and other observant Jews do not drive cars, use the telephone, or handle money during this time. On a more metaphysical level, Sabbath represents a time of vacating the mind and body from any thought or activity to do with business, a kind of extended meditation. The great modern Jewish activist and scholar **Rabbi Abraham Heschel** (1907–72) used to tell the story of a renowned rabbi who, while strolling in his garden one Sabbath, noticed that the branches of his apple tree needed pruning. Although he took no action, he did make a mental note to do so after the Sabbath. But when he returned to the garden, he found the tree withered. God had apparently destroyed it to teach the rabbi that even to think about doing work during the Sabbath goes against the spirit of the law.

Jewish holidays are numerous and are often of interest to non-Jews, particularly in New York City, where they can result in the suspension of alternate side of the street parking regulations. As in most religions, the major holidays are seasonal. The Jewish calendar is lunisolar. Its months follow the lunar cycle of 29½ days, adding up to only 354 days a year. If this calendar were followed absolutely, as it is in Islam, all the holidays would move back 11 days each year and would end up shifting from season to season over the years. To avoid this and to keep their holidays connected to their original agriculture-based cycle, Jews add a leap month seven times during a 19-year cycle. Holidays still move as much as several weeks from year to year, but they remain relatively fixed within their seasons. In this fashion, the Jewish calendar continues to reflect the cyclical nature of the Jewish religion, based on agricultural feasts which in some cases predate Judaism (and can be traced to the Canaanites) but which have been given new interpretations and meanings, much the way Christian holy days later subsumed and transformed preexisting pagan festivals.

Rosh Hashanah, Hebrew for "New Year," occurs in the fall and ushers in a 10-day period of recollection and repentance popularly known as the **High Holy Days** (although many Jews now prefer the Hebrew name, **yamim noraim,** or "Days of Awe"). This period culminates in **Yom Kippur,** the **Day of Atonement** that traditionally consists of fasting and prayer and is the most solemn day of the Jewish calendar. **Sukkot (Tabernacles)** follows closely with a 7-day festival which initially celebrated the harvest with a ceremony of gratitude to God. But with its use of a temporary outdoor structure called a **sukkah** ("hut" or "booth"), it was transformed into a celebration of the Exodus and the wandering of the Israelites in the desert. **Simhat Torah,** a one-day celebration, follows the last day of Sukkot, when the yearly cycle of reading the Torah scroll is completed and begun anew.

The major festival of winter is the eight-day **Hanukkah,** or **Festival of Lights,** which celebrates the victory of the Hasmonean Jews under Judah Maccabee over their Greek-Syrian occupiers in 165 BC. The light referred to is that of the menorah in the Temple which, following the victory, was miraculously kept burning for eight days with only a single day's supply of olive oil.

Purim ("Lots") begins the spring holidays by celebrating the triumph of Mordechai and Esther over the cruel and cunning Haman, who had set out to exterminate all the Jews in the Persian Empire during the 6th century BC. The story is recounted in the biblical book of Esther, which is read from a **megillah,** or scroll, during the celebration. The major spring holiday, **Pesah (Passover),** celebrates the Exodus of the Israelites from Egypt and continues for seven days. It centers around the **seder,** a meal featuring kosher wine and unleavened bread called **matzoh,** which recalls the fact that there was no time to wait for bread dough to rise while fleeing the Egyptians. **Shavuot (Pentecost)** is a two-day festival that celebrates the gift of the Torah at Mount Sinai. The only major summer holiday is **Tisha B'Av,** a fast day that falls between late July and mid-August and that commemorates the many historical tragedies the Jewish people have suffered; it is celebrated on the anniversary of the destruction of the Second Temple in AD 70.

Coming to Terms

Pronunciation and transliterated spelling for Hebrew terms and names varies between that favored by the Sephardim, who tend to accent the last syllable of words like *Torah* and *mitzvah,* and the Ashkenazim, who accent the first. The former approach is prevalent in Israel, and will be familiar to those who have studied modern Hebrew. It is more or less the "official" pronunciation. The latter approach, informed in part by Yiddish, is more common in many Jewish communities in the U.S., especially among the Hasidim. Likewise, the final *tay* ("t") of many words is transliterated and pronounced "s" in Ashkenazic Hebrew. Hence, *Shabbat* may be pronounced shah-*baht* or *sha*-bis (in which case it may be transliterated "Shabes" or "Shabbes"). In reality, American Jews often combine the two approaches.

abracadabra The sense in Aramaic is "it is created as I speak," i.e., the magic word used in incantations for folk medicine. But it also derived from an ancient demon name, sometimes attributed to the devil himself.

Adam Kadmon ("Primordial Man") In Kabbalistic lore, he is the primordial man formed by the 10 sephirot and from whom both light and the written word emerged.

Ashkenazim   Jewry from Eastern Europe, especially Germany, the largest of the two major divisions of the Jewish community, the other being Sephardim. Many of them spoke Yiddish.

B'nai B'rith   Founded in 1843 by German Jewish immigrants to the U.S., it is a kind of fraternal organization for Jews, with lodges around the world. A spin-off group, the Anti-Defamation League, is widely noted today as a major fighter against anti-Semitism and other forms of racism.

circumcision   The oldest ritual in Judaism, reaching back to Abraham who, at the age of 99, was told by God to have himself circumcised and to have all his descendants circumcised 8 days after birth as part of the original covenant. No rationale is ever given for removing the foreskin of the penis, although theories abound, from reducing the risk of infection to a symbolic submission to God. The practice originally differentiated Jews from non-Jews, but circumcision is now prevalent among non-Jews in America and is also practiced by Muslims as a nonbinding custom. The decision of Paul not to make circumcision mandatory for Christians (especially adult converts) is considered to have been a deciding factor in the wider spread of Christianity than of Judaism in the Greco-Roman world.

Diaspora (dye-*as*-poor-uh, Gr. "dispersion, scattering")   The term applies to the act of scattering the Jews from their homeland, beginning with the fall of the northern kingdom of Israel in 721 BC, through the fall of Judah in the south and the destruction of Solomon's Temple by Nebuchadnezzar in 586 BC, and culminating in the destruction of Jerusalem and the Second Temple by the Romans in AD 70. But it also signifies the series of geographic locations to which the Jews fled, from Babylonia and Egypt to Spain, Eastern Europe, Russia, and America. Since in the 8 centuries between the beginning and completion of the Diaspora (721 BC–70 AD), many Jews returned to live in Palestine for long periods of time, the term Diaspora Jews is used to distinguish those who remained outside of Palestine or Judea during that span.

dybbuk   In the Polish ghettos of the Ashkenazim, this term was applied to devils capable of entering and possessing a person.

Essenes   An apocalyptic sect devoted to an extremely strict and ascetic way of life, who probably produced such apocalyptic works as the books of Enoch, from c. 250 BC. About 4,000 members lived in Palestine during the time of Christ, whom they may have influenced. They were the only celibate group in early Judaism, and this practice probably explains their short life as a sect.

Falasha   Sect of Ethiopian Jews, Hamite by race but Jewish by religion, although with a different canonical scripture from the rest of Judaism.

Falasha is a somewhat derogatory name, meaning "exiled," given them by other Ethiopians. They are now known by the name they call themselves: **Beta Esrael** ("House of Israel").

genizah (geh-*nee*-zah)   The storeroom of a synagogue where old papers and books are kept that cannot be destroyed because they bear the name of God. The most famous was at the Ezra Synagogue of Fostat (Old Cairo), where Maimonides had taught and where many valuable documents were discovered, giving clues to how life was lived over a period of time from the 8th to the 15th centuries.

golem   An artificial man created from a homunculus or a lump of clay by a person of great holiness and esoteric knowledge, who then breathes life into it by pronouncing the Tetragrammaton. The golem became a figure of Jewish folklore during the Diaspora and was capable of performing helpful or hurtful deeds.

Hillel the Elder (c. 60 BC–10 AD)   The most revered of all the rabbinic sages and a liberal Pharisee, Hillel is believed to have begun the process of gathering and codifying all the unwritten laws for the purpose of memorizing and passing them on orally, leading eventually to the written Mishnah. When asked by a pagan to explain the complex system of Jewish law succinctly enough that he could stand on one leg throughout it, Hillel replied famously: "That which is hurtful to you, do not to your neighbor. This is the whole doctrine. The rest is commentary—go and study it."

Josephus (juh-*see*-fuss, c. AD 37–100)   Jewish historian during the Roman occupation of Judea in the 1st century. He was involved in the Great Revolt of 66–73, was imprisoned by the Romans, but later was released when his prophecy was fulfilled that the Roman general who assigned him to record the war, Vespasian, would become emperor. Despite his opposition and incarceration, some Jews feel he was too sympathetic to the Romans. His major works were *The Jewish Wars* and *The Antiquities*.

kosher   The word means "proper" or "in accordance with the religious law" and is applied to any food that satisfies the requirements of Jewish law (as well as to any item that is prepared in accordance with the law, including the Torah scroll, mezuzah, and tefillin). Dietary laws revealed by God to Moses in the Torah were later elaborated in the Talmud, not for health reasons, as is commonly believed, but for the sake of spiritual discipline. Pigs and shellfish are forbidden, but so are the horse, the camel, and the hare—animals that are no dirtier than cows and goats, which are allowed. Underlying the prohibition against consuming certain animals may be the notion that if you're going to be nourished not only by the vegetation of the earth but also by eating flesh, then you should eat only animals that are nourished by the earth—in other words, those that don't eat humans or other animals, as carnivores and scavengers do. Laws of **kashrut** regulated not only which species could be eaten, but how they were to be slaughtered, examined for signs of disease, and how soon after consumed. Only animals with cloven hooves that regurgitate their food may be eaten, and they have to be slaughtered in the most humane way. Only fish with fins and scales are acceptable— no shellfish. Poultry (chicken, duck, turkey) is acceptable, but not birds of prey or meat-eating animals. Passages in Exodus and Deuteronomy forbade boiling "a kid in its mother's milk," and this led to a prohibition against eating meat and milk products together, and so to the use of two separate sets of dishes and cutlery, a practice still followed in observant Jewish homes.

masoretes Biblical scholars who specialized in the proper writing and spelling of the sacred Hebrew texts as handed down by the scribes. The canonical version they produced is called the Masoretic text.

mezuzah ("doorpost") A piece of parchment containing two passages from Deuteronomy, including the Shema, rolled into a small wooden, metal, or glass tube and attached to the doorpost of one's home (and, ideally, to every room in the home except the bathroom). The passages themselves (6:4–9 and 11:13–21) require this to be done.

mitzvah (pl. **mitzvot**) A commandment of biblical or rabbinic law. The word has taken on the meaning of a good deed, although even in earlier times it had the sense of a meritorious act rather than a positive commandment.

Nazarite ("dedicated") Among the early Hebrews, a consecrated person who did not drink wine, wore few clothes, and had long, unkempt hair. King Samuel and Samson were Nazarites.

Pharisees Sect that created the oral law to apply Mosaic law to contemporary situations. Modern Jews are descended from the Pharisees in the sense that the other sects died out after the destruction of the Second Temple.

Philo Judaeus (*fye*-low joo-*day*-us) Rabbi, Platonist, and mystic scholar who lived in Alexandria, Egypt, c. 20 BC–50 AD.

Pirkei Avot (*peer-kay* ah-*vote*, "Sayings of the Fathers") A collection of popular aphorisms from the rabbinic sages.

pogrom (puh-g*rahm*) Although taken from the Russian word for "devastation," pogroms against the Jews did not originate there. These fierce attacks involving massacres and confiscation of property began in the Near East after the Jews were swept out of Palestine in the 2nd century, and chased to Moorish Spain. Similar massacres forced them out of Spain in 1492, and they congregated in Eastern Europe, especially the Rhineland, Poland, and western Russia. Hundreds of thousands of Ukrainian Jews were slaughtered in a revolt against Polish rule in the Ukraine in 1648, and more large-scale pogroms took place in Russia in

1871 and 1881. These are only the largest recorded pogroms; smaller-scale attacks and confiscations were a part of everyday life for European Jewry from their arrival on the continent until the Holocaust.

pseudepigrapha Sacred writings purporting to have been written by biblical figures, e.g., the book of Enoch, the Testament of Moses, or the Ascension of Isaiah.

Qlipot (Kelippot) The powers of evil or forces of darkness that emerged when the vessels intended to hold the light of the sephirot could not contain it all and shattered. The purpose of tikkun ("restoration") is to reintegrate these fragments and thus heal creation.

Rechabites Extremely austere, strictly monotheist fundamentalist sect of early Israelites who came together in reaction to the corrupt practices of the big landowners, merchants, and city officials. They retreated to the desert and often massacred those who didn't share their views. The prophet Elijah came from their ranks.

Sadducees Sect that was at odds with the Pharisees because they supported only the written law, strictly interpreted. They centered around Temple life, and after the destruction of the Second Temple in AD 70, they soon faded away.

scribes Originally secretaries who wrote down the preachings of the prophets, the scribes evolved into a priestly class charged with writing down, interpreting, and maintaining the laws and records, copying previous scrolls and committing oral traditions to paper.

Sephardim Jews of Spanish or Arabic descent, making up roughly 20 percent of modern Jewry. They often spoke **Ladino,** a Jewish form of Spanish that is to Sephardim what Yiddish is to Ashkenazim.

shekhinah (sheh-*key*-nuh) In traditional Jewish writings, shekhinah is defined as the female aspect of God or the divine presence on earth. Specifically, it referred to the radiance and glory of God manifested in the cloud and fire over and in the tabernacle, the burning bush, the cloud above Mount Sinai, or even a potent divine radiation from the Holy of Holies, capable of killing any unauthorized person who came near. As the feminine aspect, the shekhinah is said to attend the beds of sick people and to greet the dying as they leave the physical plane.

Shema (shmah, "hear") The most often said prayer of Judaism, taken from Deuteronomy 6:4–9, to be repeated twice daily: "Hear, O Israel: the Lord our God, the Lord is One.'. . . ."

Tannaim (tah-nah-*eem*) Teachers of the oral law during the first 2 centuries AD. The most prominent were Hillel the Elder and Shammai.

tefillin (t'fill-*een*) Two small black boxes with straps attached, to be worn by men each weekday morning, one on the head and one on the arm. They contain scrolls with four sets of verses from the Torah, to remind Jews of their relationship with the Lord.

Torah   Specifically, the Torah refers to the first five books of the Bible, especially as enshrined in every synagogue on handwritten parchment rolls. Traditionally, however, the Torah includes all the teachings of the Hebrew Bible as well as the Talmudic commentaries that were written from the 3rd century BC to the 5th century AD. Derived from the Hebrew verb meaning "to guide or teach," in its broadest sense Torah means the entire doctrine of Judaism, the law, much like the Hindu term dharma*.

yarmulka   The Yiddish form of the Hebrew **kippah,** a small skullcap customarily worn by Orthodox males almost all the time, and by Conservative and some Reform males in the synagogue and at meals. Some Conservative women may wear them at times. Nothing about the head covering is mandated by Jewish law; Orthodox men often wear hats instead. In all cases it is a sign of respect for and submission to the Lord above, possibly based on an ancient Roman custom of having servants wear a head covering.

Yiddish (from the German *jüdisch,* "Jewish")   Vernacular language used by Jews in the Rhineland as early as the 11th century, brought about by the Jewish habit of transliterating non-Hebraic languages with Hebrew letters, effectively altering spelling and pronunciation. This vernacular was then spread to other European Jews, with swatches of Slavonic languages added and with terms borrowed from Hebrew, Aramaic, and Arabic; it became the dominant nonsacred tongue. Once the language reached America, Yiddishisms were brought into the national slang by popular Jewish comedians, among others, adding words like *schmaltz, schmuck,* and *schlemiel* to mainstream American English. A whole Yiddish literature also developed in the years since the Emancipation of the late 18th century, led by popular favorites such as Sholom Aleichem, Y. L. Peretz, and Sholem Asch.

Zealots   Sect founded in AD 6 by Judah the Galilean protesting Roman rule and taxes. The Zealots believed in violence as a legitimate tool against the occupying Romans and their Jewish collaborators. The terrorist fringe of Zealots, who carried concealed daggers and committed political assassinations, were called Sicarii by the Romans.

Zionism   A movement that officially began in 1895, led by Jewish journalist **Theodor Herzl** (1860–1904), and that sought to create a homeland for the Jews where they could avoid the endless rounds of persecution, pogroms, and anti-Semitism they had suffered for centuries.

5

CHRISTIANITY

✳ ON THE FAITH OF IT

Probably the most telling distinction between Eastern and Western spirituality—after allowing for the West's insistence on belief in one God conceptualized as male—is that the East relies more extensively on direct experience of the Absolute, whereas the West depends on faith in God. That's not an unequivocal rule, since practitioners of popular religion in the East do rely on faith in certain personal deities or earthly and celestial Buddhas and bodhisattvas* for protection, productivity, and prosperity. Even in more elitist, monastic versions of those religions, a practitioner may require deep faith that a teacher's spiritual techniques will actually lead to enlightenment after as many as 20 or 30 years of practice (although presumably he or she will receive intimations along the way and may experience other benefits as well).

Moreover, the Western traditions do offer guides to direct experience of God through meditation. But **mysticism,** a catchall term for various

267

approaches to such direct knowledge of or union with God, is not a prominent part of Western worship and in effect is often discouraged. By and large, Jews must believe that God intervened in human history to lead the Israelites out of Egypt and select them to deliver his law to humanity. Muslims must believe that the Quran represents the divine word of Allah as revealed to his Messenger, the Prophet Muhammad. Likewise, Christians must take it on faith that Jesus Christ is God, that he was begotten of God the Father and not of human seed, that he nevertheless lived as a man, was crucified, died, and rose from the dead, proclaiming everlasting life of the spirit for those who believe in him.

"Believe in him" is the key phrase. Christians take it on faith that their belief will save them, that after death, presuming they have lived a righteous life (or at least repented of their unrighteous ways), they will be let into heaven to spend eternity in blissful direct knowledge of God—sometimes referred to as the **Beatific Vision.** But that direct knowledge of the Divine is expected in the next world, not in this one. And so the identity of the Christ in whom Christians have faith is crucial, and the hundreds of Christian sects worldwide—more than any of the other major religions, including over 200 denominations in the U.S. alone—are some indication of the vast diapason of understandings of Jesus and his teachings. To begin to comprehend the many faces of Christianity, we first have to try to come to grips with who Jesus was.

❋ WHO IS THE REAL JESUS OF NAZARETH?

Since indeed many people have tried to draw up an account of the things fulfilled in our midst as transmitted to us by those who were eyewitnesses from the beginning and became servants of the word, I thought that I also, having followed it all from the first, would write it down for you correctly. . . .

—LUKE 1:1–3

The opening of the Gospel according to Luke lays out two of the major problems confronting anyone who wants to approach the teachings of Jesus directly through scripture rather than through the filters of Christian theology. For openers, Luke tells us that "many people" have written their accounts of the Jesus teachings. Yet not one of them contains all the relevant information—as evidenced by the fact that four separate Gospel accounts are included in the New Testament, selected from the "many" that were circulating among Christians in Luke's day. And more to the point, the accounts were based on data "transmitted . . . by those who were eyewitnesses," meaning that we are dealing with thirdhand information at best. The idea that the Gospel accounts were themselves written by eyewitnesses was disproven authoritatively by 19th-century biblical scholars. So what's a poor Bible reader to do?

The first move might be to examine the current state of a branch of biblical scholarship that endeavors to find out precisely which of the sayings and deeds attributed to Jesus in the Gospels he actually said or did. This search for the **historical Jesus** has challenged some of Christianity's most cherished traditions. Yet the challengers, for the most part, have not been atheists eager to disprove Christ's existence but active Christian believers including clergy, theologians, and highly respected biblical scholars. The welter of new speculations about the historical Jesus is enough to confuse anyone raised on traditional Christian teachings and may give the interested non-Christian pause over whom to believe.

Within the past three decades, Jesus has been cast by various scholars as everything from a social revolutionary, magician, or Essene* ascetic to an apocalyptic prophet or a disciple of Rabbi Hillel*. Some of the theorizing may seem farfetched, but based on the evidence presented, the underlying argument—that much of the language of the Gospels is the creative invention of their authors and assorted intrusive scribes rather than the actual words and deeds of Jesus—is often difficult to dispute. The early Christian church that took shape after the death of Jesus developed theological agendas of its own that at times went contrary to or were not supported by the existing Gospel texts, so words and deeds were inserted or deleted to fit those agendas. The changes often created other problems of continuity or contradiction, either between different authors writing without knowledge of each other or in the same author trying to juggle too many nonhistorical assertions.

Biblical scholars start with the contradictions and improbabilities and work backward to deduce what the original sources, now missing, may have said concerning Jesus. Their deductions have led them to question the beloved Christmas stories (which appear in only two of the four

Gospels, in contradictory accounts) and much of the passion drama, and in the process to cast doubt on some of the time-honored traditions of Christianity. Most historical Jesus scholars insist that their work does not contradict basic Christian belief but only clarifies certain elements of that belief. Even in the midst of the wide-ranging disagreement over the Gospel narratives, most Christians continue to accept the divine nature of Jesus and the ultimate truth of the Gospels. But in order to understand the radical nature of the new scholarship, we should know the story of Jesus as it is presented in the four Gospels, which make up just under half of the New Testament on which the Christian tradition is based.

✳ THE OFFICIAL STORY

The four Gospels differ from each other in time frame and some important details, but the basic narrative goes like this. During the Roman occupation of Judea, **Mary,** a virgin betrothed to the carpenter **Joseph** (both living in **Nazareth,** a town of about 1,600 in the northern province of **Galilee**), is "found to be pregnant" before "knowing" Joseph. Joseph is understandably upset at this development, but angels appear separately to Mary and to Joseph explaining the situation. The child that has been mysteriously conceived is "of the Holy Spirit" and will "save the people from their sins." Joseph agrees to take Mary into his household and not to sleep with her until the child, to be named Jesus, is born.

The modern name Jesus is derived from the Greek version (Iesous) of the Aramaic name Yeshua or Yeshu, shortened forms of the Hebrew Yehoshua (Joshua). The name was then so common that the appellations Jesus of Nazareth and later Jesus the Christ—from the Greek Christos ("Anointed One")—were necessary to distinguish him from other 1st-century Jesuses. However, nowhere in the Gospels does Jesus refer to himself as the Christ.

After Jesus is born in **Bethlehem,** almost nothing is heard of him until he is baptized in the river Jordan by **John the Baptist** some 30 years later. (Speculation is rife about where Jesus may have gone and what teachings other than traditional Judaism he may have studied during this unrecorded period of his life. For more details, see "Jesus: The Early Years" on p. 293.) Little is known about John except that he came from a sect of **Morning Bathers** or Baptists, one of several Jewish communities that offered baptism as a form of forgiveness for sins prior to an expected end to historic time. "Repent for the kingdom of heaven is at hand," he preached. John's apocalypticism* and his focus on purification by water may reflect an Essene past. He was later executed by Herod Antipas. On being baptized by John, Jesus sees "the Spirit descending on him like a dove" and hears a heavenly voice proclaiming, "This is my beloved Son."

Immediately after this experience, Jesus goes alone into the desert for 40 days, where he fasts and is "tempted by the devil." The cumulative effect of his spiritual experience in the Jordan River and his time meditating in the wilderness propels him back into Galilee to begin his ministry. Calling four local fishermen (among the lowest occupations of the day), he goes to the town of **Capernaum** by the **Sea of Galilee**, where he starts healing and teaching. Two things immediately set him apart from other teachers in the minds of the people there. He teaches "as one who [has] authority, and not as the scribes" (i.e., speaking from his own spiritual experience, not merely interpreting canon law), and he heals people of maladies ranging from demonic possession to blindness and paralysis.

Jesus' authoritative teachings and healings make him the talk of Palestine, and he is mobbed by poor, afflicted peasants seeking cures. At the same time, he begins to attract the attention of the authorities, including the Jewish scribes, or canon lawyers, who find his inner-centered spirituality threatening to the outward power of their rituals and religious hierarchy. They accuse him of consorting with "tax collectors and sinners." Tax collectors, Jews who collaborated with the Romans and paid a fee for the right to extort as much tax money as they could from fellow Jews, were viewed as vile traitors by their Jewish contemporaries. For Jesus to teach and eat with them, along with women, especially prostitutes, was a sign of how radical and potentially dangerous to the Jewish establishment his ministry was. To the Romans, who held the ultimate power as the occupying force in the region, he presented the more immediate threat of fomenting rebellion among the peasantry, a common occurrence in that day.

Jesus takes on more followers, 12 men and a number of "women who had been healed of demons and infirmities." The most prominent of these is **Mary Magdalene**, "from whom seven demons had gone out." Jesus teaches in **parables**, metaphorical stories couched in immediate terms familiar to the rural peasants, farmers, and artisans who make up much of his following, sometimes explaining their meaning in private to his disciples. These common folk, known as am ha'aretz* ("people of the land") have been referred to by one scholar as "a kingdom of nobodies" and by another as "outcasts and sinners for whom the law was too much." Their eager response to Jesus may have given the religious establishment concern that he was leading away their flocks.

Jesus' teaching in the Gospels draws heavily on existing Judaic precepts, although his emphases are unique. Concern for one's neighbor, or fellow human being, was already an essential aspect of Judaism, extending even to strangers. Leviticus 19:34 has it, "The stranger who sojourns

THE GOLDEN RULE THROUGHOUT HISTORY

Asked to name the most important commandment, Jesus combined one from Deuteronomy (6:4–5) and one from Leviticus (19:18): "The first is, 'Hear, O Israel: the Lord our God is one; and you shall love the Lord your God with all your heart, and with all your soul, and with all your mind, and with all your strength.' And a second is like it: 'You shall love your neighbor as yourself.' On these two commandments depend all the law and the prophets" (Matt. 22:37–40; Mark 12:29–31). Earlier in the Gospels, he had issued a variant of the latter which, in slightly different wording, has come to be known as the Golden Rule: Do unto others as you would have them do unto you. However, as Jesus himself noted, his statement was hardly original. The Golden Rule attributed to him has appeared in other times and places in almost identical form, including the teachings of his contemporary Rabbi Hillel, with whom some scholars believe Jesus may have studied. However, it has been pointed out that the positive form in which Jesus couches his version is even more demanding.

272

What you do not wish done to yourself, do not do to others.

—CONFUCIUS, *THE ANALECTS* (5TH CENTURY B C)

What you yourself hate, don't do to your neighbor. This is the whole Law; the rest is commentary. Go and study.

—RABBI HILLEL (40 B C-10 A D)

So whatever you want people to do for you, you do the same for them; for this is the law and the prophets.

—JESUS OF NAZARETH (MATT. 7:12, C. 30 A D)

According to Anas, the Prophet [Muhammad] said, "None of you really has faith un less he desires for his neighbor what he desires for himself."

—HADITH (7TH CENTURY A D)

with you shall be to you as the native among you, and you shall love him as yourself; for you were strangers in the Land of Egypt." But Jesus stretches the definition further, telling one of his most famous parables about a Samaritan—one of a mixed race living between Galilee and Judea who were especially loathed by the Jews after some Samaritans had desecrated the Temple* early in the life of Jesus. The **Good Samaritan** helps a stranger who has been robbed, beaten, and left for dead, after a priest and a **Levite** (a member of a dynastic priestly family) each avoided the bloodied stranger rather than risk becoming ritually unclean.

Forgiveness also plays a large part in the teachings—not forgiveness of sins by God so much as forgiveness of oneself and others. When the disciple **Peter** asks if he should forgive his brother for sinning against him, "as many as seven times," Jesus answers, "Not seven times, but seventy times seven" (Matt. 18:21–22). He also advises that if you are about to make an offering in the Temple, "and you remember that your brother has something against you, leave your gift on the floor and go; first make up with your brother, then go make your offering" (Matt. 5:23–24).

Jesus often speaks about the **Kingdom of God,** a phrase that appears to indicate a state of inner being rather than either a heavenly afterlife or earthly freedom from Roman rule. He likens the kingdom to a mustard seed, "which is smaller than any other seed; but when it is sown, it grows up and becomes the largest of shrubs," and to a merchant looking for pearls who found a "pearl of great price, and he went and sold everything he had and bought it." The last image seems obvious, yet it leaves the listener wondering what the merchant is supposed to do with his expensive pearl. If he keeps it, he's out of business. In this sense, the Kingdom of God transcends rationality.

Similarly, Jesus says that "unless you return and become like children, you cannot enter the kingdom of God" (Matt. 18:3), implying a simplicity and spontaneity at odds with the blind following of religious ritual or, for that matter, devotion to worldly possessions.

It is clear from the questions and statements of some of his followers that they expect the Kingdom of God to be an apocalyptic kingdom, one that will come with great tribulation and result in the destruction of the world ruled by Romans and the simultaneous creation of a new one ruled by God. Yet any hope that Jesus will lead a political or military rebellion would be at odds with his attitude of nonresistance: "Do not resist one who is evil," he says. "But if anyone strikes you on the right cheek, turn to him the other also; and if anyone would sue you and take your coat, let him have your cloak as well" (Matt. 5:39–40).

Jesus apparently accepts the then current Judaic worldview that a Messiah will appear to lead Jews in the approaching apocalypse, and he may have been for a time a disciple of John the Baptist, preaching, like John, "The kingdom of God is at hand; repent and believe in the good news." But after his baptism and meditative withdrawal to the desert, Jesus appears to shift his emphasis from a distant, vengeful Lord who would destroy the wicked to a fatherly God willing to forgive any who ask Him. (At one point, in Mark 14:36, he calls God "Abba," an intimate local term equivalent to "Papa," later picked up by St. Paul in Romans 8:15 and Galatians 4:6.) Furthermore, Jesus often describes the immediacy of a kingdom that is already available to anyone on earth, man or woman, Jew or Gentile, slave or free, as long as they make themselves "like little children" and learn to recognize its presence within them. This should not be construed to mean that Jesus shows contempt for the religion of Judaism. Despite the fact that he sometimes questions those who observe the letter of the law but not its spirit (contrary to strict Jewish law, for example, he heals on the Sabbath*), for the most part he observes the law and rituals.

However, he is clearly expanding the written law, building on what is already there. "My purpose is not to destroy the law and the prophets, but to fulfill them," he says.

> You have heard that it was said to our forefathers, "You shall not kill; and whoever kills is liable to judgment." But I tell you that anyone who hates his brother is liable to judgment. . . . You have heard that it was said, "You shall not commit adultery." But I say to you that everyone that looks at a woman lustfully has already committed adultery with her in his heart. . . . You have heard that it was said, "You shall love your neighbor and hate your enemy." But I tell you, Love your enemies and pray for those who persecute you, so that you may be sons of your Father in heaven; for he makes the sun to rise on the evil and the good, and sends rain on the just and the unjust. (Matt. 5:21ff)

This may be the essence of Jesus' development of Mosaic law: taking an already revolutionary concept of ethical concern for one's fellow beings and the sanctity of human life and extending it to an internal ethics beyond the simple rationality of the law. Moses forbade unjustified physical and civil violence; Jesus says that we must not be violent even in thought or feelings toward others. "As far as we now know," writes one contemporary scholar, "no other Jew, or Jewish group, drew that extreme inference from the relevant ethical passages in the Old Testament."

Jesus sends his disciples out in pairs, at one point as many as 72 individuals, to heal and teach, advising them to depend on the hospitality of those they heal. "Carry no purse, no bag, no sandals, nor two tunics," he tells them. "Whatever house you enter, eat what is set before you; heal the sick in it and say to them, 'The kingdom of God has come upon you' " (Mark 6:8–10). This teaching of what one scholar has called "open commensality," sharing meals and lodging with strangers of any race, religion, or gender in an egalitarian fashion, goes against the grain of Jewish ritual purity and dietary restrictions. Likewise, Jesus scolds his disciples for telling someone to stop healing in his name because the man is not an authorized disciple. "Don't stop him," Jesus says. "Whoever isn't against us is for us."

In the course of his itinerant teaching, Jesus heals lepers, paralytics, demoniacs, the blind, deaf, dumb, and otherwise infirm, raises some from the dead, and on two occasions miraculously feeds four or five thousand by multiplying a few loaves and fishes. He also calms a storm on the Sea of Galilee and walks on the water. But what seems to threaten the reli-

ECHOES

Although most Christians recognize only the Old Testament as the scriptural basis for Christ's teachings, echoes of earlier Eastern teachings can be found in some of his utterances. Scholars suggest that the different contexts of these sayings lend them different nuances of meaning, and yet the similarities of phrasing and sentiment are sometimes remarkable, as in these comparisons of a classic Gospel passage with the teachings of Lao-tzu and the Buddha, both of whom preceded Jesus by at least 500 years.

You have heard that it was said, "You shall love your neighbor and hate your enemy." But I say to you, Love your enemies and pray for those who persecute you, so that you may be sons of your Father who is in heaven; for he makes his sun rise on the evil and on the good, and sends rain on the just and on the unjust. For if you love those who love you, what reward have you? Do not even the tax collectors do the same? And if you salute only your brethren, what more are you doing than others? Do not even the Gentiles do the same? You, therefore, must be perfect, as your heavenly Father is perfect.

—MATTHEW, 4:43-48

To those who are good to me, I am good; and to those who are not good to me, I am also good, and thus all get to be good. To those who are sincere with me, I am sincere; and to those who are not sincere with me, I am also sincere, and thus all get to be sincere. The sage does not accumulate for himself. The more that he expends for others, the more does he possess of his own; the more that he gives to others, the more does he have himself.

—TAO TE CHING, 49

Hatred is never appeased by hatred in this world; it is appeased by love. This is an eternal Law.

— DHAMMAPADA, 5

The Tathagata [Buddha] is equal and not unequal towards all beings, when it is the question to convert them: "He is . . . as the rays of the sun and moon, which shine alike upon the virtuous and the wicked, the high and the low; on those who have a good odor, and those who have a bad; on all these the rays fall equally and not unequally at one and the same time."

—LOTUS SUTRA (TRANSLATED BY HENRY DAVID THOREAU
FROM THE FRENCH TRANSLATION
OF EUGÈNE BURNOUF)

gious establishment more than his works is his open questioning of certain rigorist aspects of the law. He is constantly being challenged by the religious lawyers known as scribes* (whose job was to interpret and clarify the tangled web of Jewish law) and by the sect of Pharisees*, who try to find ways to trap Jesus into committing some offense that will allow them to eliminate him legally. Jesus in turn shows up the flaws inherent in observing the letter of the law and openly chides the wealthy, more conservative Sadducees*.

As it turns out, Jesus gives both the religious establishment and the Roman occupying force more than enough cause to do him in. He arrives in

Jerusalem near the long religious festival of Passover*, when the population of the great city normally swelled from around 20,000 to as many as 180,000 because of the great influx of Jews from all over the kingdom to present their sacrifices at the Temple. Because they all used different currencies, they had to exchange their money for Temple money with which to buy sacrificial birds and animals. Apparently outraged by the commerce going on in the Temple area, Jesus "cleanses" the Temple, overturning the tables of the money changers and chasing out the men who sell pigeons for sacrifice, saying, "It is written, 'My house shall be called a house of prayer,' but you have made it a den of thieves" (Matt. 21:13).

His actions not only disturb the Temple priests but also alarm the Roman authorities, constantly on the alert for charismatic leaders capable of inciting the peasants to revolt against Roman rule. Jesus holds a Passover seder* with his disciples, following which one of them, **Judas Iscariot,** betrays him to the Jewish authorities, who arrest him and bring him before their tribunal (probably the Sanhedrin*, although not mentioned by name). They in turn hand him over to the Roman procurator, **Pontius Pilate,** who, despite saying that he finds nothing dangerous or illegal in Jesus' words or actions, accedes to the demands of the crowd to have him executed and sentences Jesus to crucifixion. Jesus dies on the cross; although crucifixion often lasts several days, he is pronounced dead after only a few hours. He is taken down because, with the Sabbath approaching, Jewish law requires that his body be laid in a tomb.

When some of his women followers, including his mother and Mary Magdalene, arrive at the tomb two days later, they are informed by a "young man in a white robe" that Jesus has "risen." Known as the **Resurrection,** this event becomes the cornerstone of Christian dogma, proving the divinity of Jesus. In some Gospel accounts, Jesus later appears to his disciples in human form, preaches briefly, and after 40 days on earth ascends bodily into heaven.

✳ THE HISTORICAL JESUS

Christians have traditionally accepted the Gospel accounts just summarized with varying degrees of latitude. Fundamentalist Christians generally believe in biblical inerrancy, meaning that every word of the Bible is literally true: the world was created in 6 days, Methusaleh lived for 969 years, and Jesus was born in Bethlehem, where Mary laid him in a manger (a feed trough for livestock) because there was no room at the inn. Unfortunately for this approach, the Gospel accounts disagree on a number of details, such as those surrounding the birth of Jesus, and at times present information that contradicts historical fact.

We now know with some certainty that much of the Gospel language was created by the four Evangelists, or authors of the Gospels, in the course of stringing together the sayings of Jesus; their accounts were sometimes changed or embroidered by early Christian scribes who copied the manuscripts. These additions and deletions usually served the purposes of the Evangelists or scribes. For instance, the accounts of the passion and death of Jesus are relatively sympathetic to the Roman authorities while painting the Jewish religious establishment as primarily responsible for the crucifixion. History reveals that the Christians during the time the Gospels were composed (c. 70 to 120; see THE GOOD BOOK) were at odds with the Jewish community. The break between church and synagogue was probably official by 85 or so, and the early church was persecuted by the Jewish establishment. But Romans held the real power in both the Near East and Rome, where large Christian communities had formed, and Christians who were already under attack by Romans were not eager to alienate them further. So the Jewish scribes, Sadducees, and Pharisees were depicted as blundering hypocrites, clinging to the letter of the law when they weren't viciously plotting ways to have Jesus prosecuted. Pilate, by contrast, comes off as a just and sagacious Roman whose hands are tied by the demands of the Jewish authorities. However, St. Paul himself was a Pharisee, and Jesus embraced many of their liberal attitudes, whereas history shows Pilate to have been anything but wise and good. The Gospel story that Pilate offered to release to the crowd either Jesus or a criminal named **Barabbas** and that the crowd, stirred up by the "chief priests," asked for Barabbas, is most likely a pious fable meant to incriminate the Jews even further. "His blood be on us and on our children!" Matthew has the mob scream, a line that would be used to justify the ruthless slaughter of Jews for the next two millennia.

Jesus' teachings were probably closer to the Pharisees' than to those of any other Jewish sect of his day; when he said "The Sabbath is made for

279

SOME GOSPEL VERSES THAT HAVE NOT BEEN ADEQUATELY EXPLAINED

Mark 14:50–52

After Jesus is betrayed by Judas and taken away to be tried, Mark inserts this odd observation: "And [the disciples] left him behind and turned and ran. And one young man was following him, wrapped in a sheet and nothing else. And they seized him, but he jumped out of the sheet and ran off naked."

Matthew 6:22–23

The following verses have been interpreted in a mystical sense as referring to the third eye. Conventional theologians often try to give them a metaphorical meaning, as if a reference by Jesus to a mystical inner sense would be inconceivable: "The eye is the lamp of the body. So, if your eye is sound, your whole body will be full of light; but if your eye is not sound, your whole body will be full of darkness. If then the light in you is darkness, how great is the darkness!"

Mark 3:21

The following lines may refer to Jesus at the start of his ministry having a nervous breakdown, or appearing to go into a psychotic state that has often been observed in other mystics: "And when his friends heard it, they went out to seize him, for they said, 'He's gone mad.' And the scribes who came down from Jerusalem said, 'He is possessed by Beelzebub.' "

man, and not man for the Sabbath," he was referring to a Pharisaic template for adjusting the law to modern times. Still, he couldn't be identified completely with any sect, which led to problems for those trying to pigeonhole him even in his own day. "For John [the Baptist] was an as-

The feast of Pentecost, from the Greek for "fiftieth," was a Jewish feast that took place 50 days after Passover. According to Christian tradition, Christ ascended into heaven 40 days after he and his disciples celebrated the Passover seder that became known as the Last Supper. Ten days later, the Holy Spirit descended on the disciples and inspired them with the ability to preach the Gospel so that they could be understood even by those who did not speak their language. The event is traditionally represented by the appearance of tongues of fire above the disciples' heads, as described in Acts 2:3 and pictured in this painting by El Greco that hangs in the Prado in Madrid. Glossolalia, or speaking in tongues, is derived from the same tradition, although the words spoken in "tongues" are generally not understood even by those speaking them.
SCALA/ART RESOURCE

cetic," Jesus says wryly in Matthew 11, "and they said, 'He has a demon'; the son of Man [i.e., Jesus] came eating and drinking and they say, 'Look at this wine-drinking glutton who's friendly with tax-collectors and godless people.' "

In some cases, details may have been added to the narrative to fulfill certain Old Testament prophecies, often leading to inconsistencies or worse. For instance, Matthew's account of Jesus' triumphant entry into

Jerusalem prior to his arrest quotes the book of Zechariah (9:9): "Behold, your king is coming to you, humble and mounted on an ass, and on a colt, the foal of an ass." So Matthew has the disciples bring a colt and an ass to Jesus, and he apparently rides on both of them simultaneously, quite a dexterous feat for a carpenter's son.

One unquestionable asset of the new research has been to illuminate the social context in which Jesus appeared, which helps in grasping the full impact of his teachings at the time. His extension, or "fulfillment," of the law often had radical implications that are not always clear today. For instance, his teaching against divorce (except possibly on grounds of adultery) contravened the customs of the day, which allowed men to sue for divorce for any reason at all. Rabbi Hillel, for example, whom some historians credit with having influenced Jesus' compassion teachings, held that a man could divorce a woman just for burning his dinner. And with the exception of the Qumran* sect, husbands would not be violating their own marriage by sleeping with another woman, whereas a wife who slept with any other man was liable to death by stoning. Women were not permitted to sue for divorce, and when they were divorced by their husbands, they were often left destitute. To insist that divorce was against the law of God was a compassionate service to women and a threat to the male-dominated social structure. (Jewish law allowing the divorce of a woman against her will was changed in the 10th century by Rabbi Gershom of Germany.)

As much as Jesus' worldview and teachings reflect the Jewish tradition of his time, we have to acknowledge the points where his ideas were virtually unprecedented—and this was especially the case regarding women, marriage, and adultery. One of the times when Jesus most memorably contradicted the law is his defense of the woman caught in adultery. Although the earliest Gospel manuscripts do not have this story, and its authenticity is doubtful enough to be relegated to a footnote in the Revised Standard Edition of the Bible, it catches the resonance of Jesus' teaching so completely that it is hard to overlook and may reflect an oral tradition dating back to the time of Jesus. Jewish law called for both man and woman caught in adultery to be stoned to death (Deut. 22:22), but since biblical times the law had been changed so that men escaped punishment. When the scribes bring the adulterous woman before Jesus and ask his opinion on the law, he challenges them with a line that leaves them

BIRTH PAINS

The Jesus scholars are careful to emphasize that much of their work remains a matter of interpretation. And certainly most of the major religions have had to wrestle with mythologized additions to their historical cores. In Buddhism, for instance, fabulous myths about the birth of the Buddha abound, and to accept them one would have to believe that the Buddha was a supernatural being—a belief outside the core teachings of Buddhism. According to tradition, the newborn Buddha took seven steps in each direction and, with one arm raised to heaven and the other pointing to the earth, proclaimed, "I am the greatest in the world. This is my last birth. I will put an end to the suffering of birth, old age, and death." As he took his first steps, lotus flowers blossomed in his footprints. One renowned Buddhist master, to show his contempt for such supernatural legends, is said to have remarked that if he had been present and heard the Buddha speak in this fashion, he would have smacked him in the head.

speechless and has become a paradigm of compassionate fairness even among nonbelievers: "Let him who is without sin among you be the first to throw a stone at her." After her accusers leave, he asks the woman, "Has no one condemned you?" When she answers no, he adds, "Neither do I condemn you."

Although institutional Christianity later succeeded in returning women to inferior status, there is no evidence that Jesus was anything but comfortable with them. As with the Buddha, Jesus' most radical teachings were often misinterpreted or simply overlooked by some of those who came after him. Women did enjoy a relative equality of status and generosity of treatment in the early Christian church compared with their position in Judaism, but that was short-lived. Once the male clergy began to dominate church affairs by the middle of the 1st millennium, women were once again relegated to the level of subservient or even dangerous creatures, to be controlled at all costs. By the 13th century, cloistered life had become the norm for women's religious orders, and even today, the Roman Catholic Church does not allow women to be ordained as priests.

The Good Book

Without argument, the most significant text for almost all branches of Christianity is the Bible, specifically the **New Testament,** although the Old Testament, which is essentially identical to the Hebrew Bible*, carries equal authority, if somewhat less immediate relevance. (Marcion of Sinope was denounced as a heretic in the 2nd century partly for rejecting the Old Testament, which Martin Luther also questioned in the 16th century.) The word *testament* refers, in the Old Testament, to the covenant between God and the people of Israel and, in the New Testament, to the new covenant based on Christ's teachings and death on the cross. The Bible as a whole is considered to be the revealed word of God, written down and assembled by various human agents.

Biblical scholars continue to argue over and refine the dating and attribution of the New Testament, but the current consensus is that the four canonical Gospels, although attributed to two apostles (**Matthew** and **John**) and two followers of apostles (**Mark** and **Luke**), known collectively as the four **Evangelists,** were not eyewitness accounts written by people who knew Jesus personally. Composed in Greek from 40 to 70 years after the death of Jesus, they were based to some extent on an older written Greek source referred to by scholars as **Q,** from the German *Quelle* ("source"). This source was probably based on an earlier Aramaic text, perhaps by the apostle Matthew, or on collections of sayings, miracles, and passion narratives believed to have been written down by AD 50. The earlier source texts have not yet been discovered and may well have been destroyed in the process of standardizing the surviving Gospels. The four Gospels themselves are divided into three **Synoptic Gospels** (because their accounts and language are similar) and the Gospel of John. Of these, Mark is believed to be the earliest (c. AD 70), followed by Matthew (c. 80–90), Luke (c. 85), and John (early 2nd century). The authors of the Synoptic (Gr. "viewed together") Gospels also appear to have been familiar with different versions of each other's gospels as they went through various stages of revision, accounting for both their similarities and significant differences of emphasis. But the fact that the Evangelists did not actually write down the gospels attributed to them does not necessarily deny the possibility that those gospels derive from an oral or written tradition originating with the Evangelists. For Christian believers, in any event, the authoritativeness of the gospels as inspired by the Holy Spirit does not rest on the specific identity of their human authors.

Scholars have pointed out that much of the narrative that holds together the assorted sayings and miracles of Jesus was supplied by the four Evangelists at a historical remove. The words and the stories about certain miracles of Christ, taken from since-lost sources known to the Evangelists, were threaded into a narrative that may have been fabricated to some extent as a teaching device to help early Christians remember them. Many narrative details no longer hold up to historical scrutiny. According to Luke, for instance, Mary and Joseph went to Bethlehem to be registered in a worldwide census under Caesar Augustus, yet historians have shown that there never was a census under Augustus and that such a census would have required registration in the place where one lived and worked, not the place of one's ancestry. Nor is it likely that the disciples, who fled in fear of their lives when Jesus was arrested and brought to trial, could have retained any detailed knowledge of the events of his passion and death.

As with the Hebrew scriptures, the Gospels underwent considerable redaction over the years, and several versions of each probably existed before the manuscripts that we now have, which date no earlier than c. 200, and as late as c. 350. In other words, the Greek manuscripts on which all our translations are based are more than a century older than the first Greek versions, themselves translations of Aramaic source material either oral or written—making Christianity the only major religion that does not possess the words of its founder in something approximating his native tongue. But translation aside, it is unknown how much editing, scribal corruption, or just plain censorship occurred in those hundred years.

The earliest authentic New Testament works are the **Epistles** of Paul to the **Thessalonians, Galatians, Corinthians,** and **Romans,** which were written c. 50–55. Although Paul was not an immediate disciple, he claimed to have been spoken to by Jesus in a vision and in trance, and he did have contact with some of the original disciples. The two other major New Testament books are the **Acts of the Apostles** (c. 150), written by Luke and probably intended as the second book of his Gospel, and **Revelation,** or **Apocalypse** (c. 95), describing a vision of the Second Coming of Jesus Christ, written by a churchman named John in exile on the isle of Patmos. (Sometimes called **John the Divine,** he should not be confused with the apostle John, whose name is traditionally attached to the last of the four canonical Gospels.)

Certain other New Testament books are not included in all Christian versions of the Bible and are labeled differently by various branches of the church. Generally known as the **apocrypha** (Gr. "hidden or spurious things"), these books are printed in some Bibles between the Old and New Testaments. They derive from the Greek Septuagint*, although the apocrypha were, for various reasons, not included in the Hebrew canon. Roman Catholics refer to these writings as **deuterocanonical**, reserving the term *apocrypha* for those books that are considered completely outside the canon—books that Protestants call pseudepigrapha*. Included in the apocrypha/deuterocanonical works are **Esdras, Tobit, Judith, the Wisdom of Solomon, Ecclesiasticus,** and several books of **Maccabees,** among others, most of which date from about 200 BC to the closing of the Hebrew canon in the 2nd century AD. The books are sometimes called Old Testament apocrypha to distinguish them from the so-called New Testament apocrypha, which present divergent stories and views of Christ and the apostles but are not considered canonical.

The Christian Bible existed in Latin, the clerical and liturgical language of the Church from about the 4th century until the mid-16th century, when the Protestant reformers began translating the Bible into vernacular English and German. The commonly accepted English translation, the **King James (or Authorized) Version,** was prepared in England under James I and published in 1611. It is noted for its literary value, and many of its phrasings have entered into everyday language. The King James Bible is still placed in hotel rooms across the country by the **Gideon Society,** an interdenominational group organized in 1899 for that very purpose. A modernized edition called the **Revised Standard Version** is in common use among Christians today. The **Douay** or **Douay-Rheims Bible** remains the standard Catholic version, translated into English from the Latin Vulgate of St. Jerome by Roman Catholic scholars and published at Rheims, France (New Testament), in 1582 and at

Douay (Old Testament) in 1610. More scholarly, and more accurate, translations have appeared recently, such as the **Jerusalem Bible.** (The quotations from the Gospels that appear in this chapter are taken from various sources, including the King James and Revised Standard Versions and occasionally very recent translations by biblical scholars such as John D. Crossan. A few brief extracts come from *The Unvarnished Gospels* by Andy Gaus, an unusually faithful translation into modern American English from the original Greek, reflecting its colloquialisms and grammatical inconsistencies. Although traditionalists may find it jarring, Gaus's approach often shows familiar sayings in a refreshing light.)

HISTORICAL JESUS RESEARCH AT WORK

Perhaps the most controversial theories to come out of Jesus research have been several relating to Christ's parentage and the so-called **virginal conception,** a long-standing Christian tenet saying that Jesus was sired by divine intervention and had no human father. The Gospel accounts of Matthew and Luke include lengthy genealogies to prove that Joseph is descended from King David, in accordance with the prophecy that the Messiah will come from the house of David. But this apparently contradicts the claim that Joseph was not the biological father (no such genealogy is given for Mary). Several scholars have made the further point that Joseph never appears again in those Gospels. Stephen Mitchell notes that in Mark, Jesus is referred to as "Yeshu ben Miriam," rather than "ben Joseph," which in the male-dominated honor code of the Mediterranean would have been considered a gross insult. If Jesus was in fact illegitimate, the notion of divine intervention in his birth could be a convenient pious fiction to cover the harsh truth. Morton Smith suggests that the fiction may have been invented to fulfill the prophecy in Isaiah that, in its

Greek translation, read, "Behold, a virgin shall conceive and bear a son." But he notes that the original Hebrew reads "young woman" instead of "virgin."

A number of scholars point to the poor reception Jesus received in his hometown of Nazareth when he came to heal and teach there (Mark 6:1–7), ascribing this to the supposition that he was known to have been born out of wedlock.

Jane Schaberg, in her feminist interpretation *The Illegitimacy of Jesus*, argues that "the New Testament Infancy Narratives incorporate the tradition of Jesus' illegitimate conception . . . that is most likely historical." But, she adds, the "process of gradual Christian erasure of the tradition" began in the Gospels in an "attempt to minimize the potential damage of the tradition," because within the patriarchal structure of Christianity "the illegitimate conception of Jesus was a scandal so deep, an origin so 'unfitting,' that it simply had to be repressed." More radical feminist scholars such as Mary Daly see Mary "portrayed/betrayed as Total Rape Victim—a pale derivative symbol disguising the conquered Goddess."

Episcopal Bishop John Shelby Spong, in *Born of a Woman: A Bishop Rethinks the Birth of Jesus*, postulates that Mary was "a sexually violated teen-age girl" and that the birth of Jesus was freighted with a "significant sense of scandal."

John P. Meier, a respected biblical scholar who is also a Roman Catholic priest, attacks these theories, saying that "son of Mary" refers merely to the fact that Joseph had died by the time Jesus began his ministry. Meier's approach to this and other questions about the virginal conception seems to be that if such claims cannot be proven, they cannot be authoritatively disproven, either. For instance, Meier downplays Jesus' unfavorable reception in Nazareth as the result of "small-town resentment and envy," adding, "there is no indication that this information conveys moral stain or scandal—just ordinariness." That is plausible; but if Joseph was not Jesus' biological father, the Nazarenes would have had no way of knowing that Jesus was actually the result of divine insemination and might have considered him illegitimate anyway.

Curiously, the Catholic feminist theologian Uta Ranke-Heinemann cites the biological fatherhood of Joseph to counter what she considers

CHRIST'S FAMILY VALUES

Like most arguments about the historical Jesus, the theories regarding his illegitimacy are fascinating but rarely incontrovertible. Of more interest are the sayings of Jesus which present convincing evidence that, at the very least, he held a dimmer view of traditional family values than most Christian apologists would care to admit. Sometimes the actual Gospel texts are so discomfiting that believers choose to ignore them completely. The following verses (with the exception of one from the Gospel of Thomas, a noncanonical text believed by some scholars to represent authentic early source material) appear in all accepted editions of the New Testament. Some biblical scholars use them to argue that Jesus was illegitimate and experienced resentment toward his own family. Yet even without having such a controversial interpretation placed on them, they are difficult to explain. Incidentally, in the hierarchy of Jesus' authentic sayings established by biblical scholars, these rank very high because of what is known as the "embarrassment factor": potentially embarrassing or inexplicable sayings are likely to have been preserved only because of a very strong tradition that they were actually spoken by Jesus.

Do you think that I have come to bring peace on earth? No, I didn't come to bring peace but to wield a sword. For I have come to set a man against his father, and a daughter against her mother, and a mother-in-law against her daughter-in-law; and a man's foes will be those of his own household. (Matt. 10:34–36)

And [Jesus'] mother and his brothers and sisters came; and standing outside they sent to him and called him. And a crowd was sitting about him; and they said to him, "Your mother and your brothers and your sisters are outside, asking for you." And he replied, "Who are my mother and my brothers and sisters?" And looking around at those who sat about him, he said, "Here are my mother and my brothers and sisters. Whoever does the will of God is my brother, and sister, and mother." (Mark 3:31–35)

If anyone comes to me and cares about his father or his mother or his wife or his children or his brother or his sisters or even his own soul, he can't be my student. (Luke 14:26)

Whoever does not hate mother and father as I do cannot be my disciple, and whoever does not love father and mother as I do cannot be my disciple. (Gospel of Thomas, 101)

To another he said, "Follow me." But he said, "Lord, let me first go and bury my father." But [Jesus] said to him, "Leave the dead to bury their own dead." Another said, "I will follow you, Lord; but first let me say farewell to those at my home." Jesus said to him, "No one who puts his hand to the plow and looks back is fit for the kingdom of God." (Luke 9:59–62)

And call no man your father on earth, for you have one Father, who is in heaven. (Matt. 23:9)

And Jesus said to them, "A prophet is never dishonored if not in his home town, among his relatives, and in his own house." (Mark 6:4)

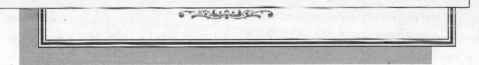

the more injurious myth of Mary's virginal conception. She argues that the insistence on Mary's total virginity—both before and after the birth of Jesus—led the church to denigrate sexuality in general and the status of women in particular.

✺ GONNA TAKE A MIRACLE

Despite all the controversy over what exactly Jesus said and didn't say, some facts *are* generally agreed upon. Both the Jewish author Josephus and the Roman Tacitus wrote that Jesus lived when the Gospels say he did and was crucified by Pilate. And we know from other sources about the major Jewish sects of the day, the Pharisees*, Sadducees*, Essenes*, and Zealots* (discussed in Chapter 4).

The miracles are more problematic. The context in which Jesus' miraculous cures took place is as significant as the cures themselves. The Jews of Palestine had been under Roman occupation for a century. The Jewish peasantry was dirt poor, with barely enough to eat, virtually no health care facilities, hospitals, asylums, doctors, or medicines. "When a healer appeared," writes the venerable Bible scholar Morton Smith, "a man who could perform miraculous cures and did so for nothing!—he was sure to be mobbed. In the crowds that swarmed around him desperate for cures, cures were sure to occur." Furthermore, healers were not uncommon in that time and place, and at least one, **Rabbi Hanina ben Dosa,** is considered to have been in the same class as Jesus. However, he cannot claim a billion and a half followers today.

Some scholars have made the further point that the numerous cases of demonic possession in Palestine may have resulted from years of colonial occupation, during which the spiritual and physical possession of their bodies by an all-powerful demon mirrored the possession of their land and lives by a stronger outside force. (These cases and those of the many paralytics brought before Jesus are reminiscent of the paralysis that afflicted Sigmund Freud's sexually abused or repressed clients in early-20th-century Vienna.) Jesus offered the possessed and otherwise afflicted a release from an overwhelming sense of colonial oppression by showing them the existence of a "kingdom of God" within themselves, more powerful than any exterior force.

While accepting the validity of the healing miracles, some biblical analysts question the so-called natural miracles: walking on water, calming the storm, feeding thousands with a few loaves and fishes. One theory is that these accounts were originally part of Jesus' post-resurrection miracles, invented and placed late in the original texts to show his supernatural abilities, and for a variety of complicated reasons were moved to earlier positions in the Gospel narratives.

One part of the Gospel stories that is almost certainly based on historical fact is the general course Jesus followed through Palestine. Beginning his healings and teachings in the province of Galilee, a poor and partly Jewish region north of Judea, he worked in towns such as Cana, Capernaum (or Capharnaum), and others around the Sea of Galilee, swung farther north to Tyre and Sidon on the Mediterranean coast of Phoenicia, inland to Caesarea Philippi, and down through the Decapolis region between Galilee and Judea. As long as he stayed in the provinces, he was relatively safe from close scrutiny by the Roman authorities. Not until he chose to bring his ministry south to Jericho, Bethany, and Jerusalem, the capital of Judea, did he run afoul of the law.

JESUS: THE EARLY YEARS

A number of unsubstantiated stories have been circulated that during the middle years of Jesus' life—between the time he "amazed" the teachers in the Temple of Jerusalem at the age of 12 and the time he began his ministry at about age 30—he underwent some kind of esoteric training and initiation. This purportedly happened either at one of the Essene communities in the desert around the Dead Sea or during travels to Egypt, India, or Tibet. Perhaps we shouldn't be surprised at the prevalence of tales like these, since the incisive nature of the most authentic sayings of Jesus have the ability to stop the mind dead in its tracks in the manner of the pithiest wisdom of the Upanishads* or of Zen Buddhism. For instance: "The disciples said to Jesus: 'Tell us how our end will be.' Jesus said, 'Have you already discovered the beginning, that now you seek the end?' " (Gospel of Thomas, 18). "The kingdom of God will not come with watching out for it; nor will they say, 'Here it

293

is!' or 'There it is!' because the kingdom of God is within you" (Luke 17:20–21). "Whoever tries to keep his life safe will lose it, and whoever loses his life will preserve it" (Luke 17:33).

No convincing proof exists of Jesus' having traveled to the East, although the Russian historian and itinerant scholar Nicolai Notovitch claimed that, during a stay at a monastery in Ladakh, in northeast India near Tibet, he was shown manuscripts which detailed the arrival of an Israeli youth named Isa (Arabic for Jesus). True to form, Isa irritated the brahmans by instructing the lower castes with his great knowledge and openly opposing the caste system as cheating the poor of their human rights, claiming, "God the Father makes no difference between any of His children, all of whom He loves equally." (The manuscripts have since disappeared.) Even apart from this story, however, Jesus could have encountered esoteric Essene spirituality along with the other teachings of Judaism prevalent at the time. Hindu yogic practices are known to have reached Egypt well before the time of Christ, so meditative techniques were available. In fact, the early Gnostic Christian sects, later repudiated by the church, combined Eastern philosophy and meditation with the teachings of Jesus.

Christ's life and teachings show many parallels to those of the Buddha, but they have many differences too, not least of which is the generally peaceful way the Buddha was received and was allowed to live out the full term of his natural life. One wonders how much of the church's embattled, aggressive, and violent history stems from the fact that its leader was cut down in the prime of life, in an act of casually ruthless violence.

Whereas Christians believe that Jesus is the incarnation of God and the Second Person of the Holy Trinity, and some non-Christians accept him as merely a reincarnation of the Buddha, Krishna, Lao-Tzu, or some other avatar or teacher, still others accept Jesus on a much simpler level. According to the universal precepts of the mystical process, through the meditation and fasting that Jesus practiced following his baptism in the river Jordan, he could have attained insights similar to those of the greatest Eastern sages. In Mark 1:35, Jesus slips off by himself to pray and meditate, causing his puzzled disciples to go looking for him. The famous accounts in Matthew and Luke of his temptation by the devil may be based on metaphorical accounts Jesus gave of the snares endemic to the enlightenment process, much as they are presented by Eastern masters. As a newly enlightened soul, he may have been tempted to use his spiritual powers for his own selfish purposes—in his case, to turn stones into bread to feed himself or to assume earthly power and glory.

✸ THE DEAD SEA SCROLLS

Discovered in Palestine in 1947 by three Bedouin cousins, the **Dead Sea Scrolls** had been stored in caves near the site of a monastery of exiled Essenes at Qumran, on the northeast coast of the Dead Sea, since at least AD 68, when Roman forces sacked and burned the town. Beginning in the mid-2nd century BC, Qumran had been occupied by a group of priests who left Jerusalem for the desert, led by someone referred to as the Teacher of Righteousness, apparently exiled from the Temple priesthood by one known only as the Wicked Priest. The scrolls themselves included, among other things, the teachings of the Qumran community and copies of several books of the Hebrew Bible, most notably a leather scroll of Isaiah at least a thousand years older than the oldest Hebrew manuscript of that book. Their main value, however, is the light they may shed on the origins of Jesus' beliefs and his possible connection with the Essenes. Because access to the scrolls themselves, not all of which have been translated, was restricted until recently to a select group of scholars, they have been surrounded by controversy. Scholars still debate the exact identity of the authors of the scrolls: one authority feels they were not Essenes but Sadducees, another claims they are related to the teachings of James, the brother of Jesus, who led the Jerusalem Jesus Movement. No fully satisfactory answers have yet emerged.

SPREADING THE GOOD NEWS

By all accounts, the early years of the Christian movement were extremely chaotic, marked by internal contention and rivalries. There were disputes between the followers of Jesus in Jerusalem, who tended to focus on Temple worship and appeared very much like a Jewish sect that emphasized charity and venerated Jesus of Nazareth as a martyred leader, and the Diaspora* Jewish Christians, who were wealthier, more cosmopolitan, and Greek-speaking. Further, the Jerusalem church was scattered with the destruction of Jerusalem in the 1st and 2nd centuries.

If the earliest followers of Christ, whom one historian refers to as members of the Palestinian Jesus Movement, were predominantly from the countryside, they quickly took their message to Mediterranean urban centers like Damascus, where they attracted the attention of **Saul of Tarsus.** Originally a Pharisaic Jew of the Diaspora, Saul was aghast at the Christian challenge to Judaic teaching and participated in the Jewish persecution of the earliest Christians, even joining in the stoning of **St. Stephen,** the first martyr, in AD 36. But as he rode to Damascus to search for Christians there, Saul was knocked from his horse in one of the most famous conversion experiences in history, as recounted in Acts 9: ". . . suddenly a light from heaven flashed about him. And he fell to the ground and heard a voice saying to him, 'Saul, Saul, why do you persecute me?' " The voice belonged to Jesus, and Saul was temporarily blinded. By the time he recovered his sight, he had embraced Jesus and begun to proclaim him in the synagogues as the Son of God. At some point, Saul became known as **Paul** and had an overwhelming impact on the shaping of Christianity.

Paul's conversion was not only sudden but total: a Pharisee who had followed the law strictly, he became a universalist who sought to do away with the Jewish law and separative rituals such as circumcision*. In this sense, he is often considered (favorably by some, pejoratively by others) the first Christian. He writes of the new church in his Epistle to the Colossians (3:11): "Here there cannot be Greek and Jew, circumcised and uncircumcised, barbarian, Scythian, slave, free man, but Christ is all, and in all."

Pauline Christianity spread rapidly through urban households, units that included family, slaves, freedmen, tenants, and others associated with the head of the family. These **household churches,** many of which were the homes of women who figured prominently in early Christianity, probably had their inspiration in the Jewish practice of adapting private dwellings into synagogues. The house meetings apparently also involved spontaneous prophecy, the reading of epistles, or letters, from Paul or other Christian leaders, and **glossolalia,** or speaking in tongues—a form of spirit possession in which people speak spontaneously in a language known only to them. (Glossolalia is still practiced in some modern Pentecostal Christian sects.)

Paul discouraged the ecstatic practice of tongues because he found it divisive; he also opposed circumcision and other rituals (sabbath observance, *kashrut**) because they set Jews off from Gentiles. At the Council of Jerusalem in 49, various apostles and elders including Paul and his traveling companion Barnabas, Peter, and James the brother of Jesus met to debate the question of circumcision for Gentile Christians. After much argument, the council agreed not to enforce circumcision but to demand compliance with certain Jewish laws about diet and sexual conduct. Paul, however, continued to press for a universal religion that would not exclude any potential converts on the basis of either circumcision or diet. The resulting inclusiveness may be one of the main reasons Christianity was able to convert the Roman Empire and Judaism was not. The ethical underpinnings of both religions are essentially similar; even though Jesus shifted the emphasis to a more mystical, present-oriented spirituality with his teaching of the Kingdom of God, the Pauline church had already somewhat lost touch with that teaching, substituting the belief that Jesus was God Incarnate, who died to redeem humanity from its sins. But Judaism was inextricably tied to its homeland and its Temple, its tribal past of ritual animal sacrifice, its separative dietary restrictions, and circumcision.

The earliest Christian communities shared the sense of communal living preached by Jesus; they also shared rituals of nude baptism. **Baptism,** which predated Christianity, was applied by Paul as the unifying and leveling ritual par excellence, leading to his metaphor of the "mystical body of Christ," which became embedded in later Christian, especially Catholic, theology. "For just as the body is one and has many members, and all the members of the body, though many, are one body, so it is with Christ. For by one spirit we were all baptized into one body—Jews or Greeks, slaves or free—and all were made to drink of one Spirit" (1 Cor. 12:12–13).

By now *Christ* has replaced *Jesus:* the Greek word *christos,* which usually meant "ointment," was the literal translation of the Hebrew word for "Messiah." Jesus Christ, the Anointed, the Savior who was crucified and died for the forgiveness of sins and who was resurrected from the dead so all might have eternal life, replaced in large measure the teacher of the Kingdom of God and of the immediacy of living in the moment of consciousness. As English scholar John Bowden put it in *Jesus: the Unanswered Questions,* "The center of Jesus' preaching is the kingdom of God; the center of Paul's preaching is Christ crucified and risen. . . . In other words, the Jesus who *has* the message changes into the Christ who *is* the message." Similarly, the early Christians, who at one point saw themselves as Jews who believed that Jesus was the Messiah, began to develop their own unique language and rituals and later to differentiate themselves from all other Jews.

Christians retained Jewish monotheism but soon divided the Deity into a **Trinity** composed of **Three Persons:** God the Father (**First Person**), Jesus the Son (**Second Person**), and the Holy Spirit (**Third Person**). Likewise, the open communalism of Jesus, sharing meals with whoever invited him and eating whatever was offered, was transmuted among the early Christians into the **Eucharist,** or **Holy Communion,** the sharing of bread and wine as symbols of the Body and Blood Christ. And they shared equally with women, which, as modern scholars have suggested, was threatening to both the Roman and Jewish establishments because it questioned their family structures, both of which subordinated women to their fathers and husbands.

The spread of Christianity was facilitated by the ease of travel in the Mediterranean of that era—aided ironically by the strong Roman military presence and the Romans' well-maintained system of roads. Paul made countless proselytizing journeys around the Mediterranean rim, establishing and overseeing communities of Christians. The Jerusalem Jesus Movement headed by James thrived for a time alongside Pauline Christianity. But it faded out shortly and was subsumed by the followers of Paul, whose more Hellenized and universalist version of Christianity is the one that converted Rome and prevailed in the West.

NO SEX PLEASE, WE'RE CHRISTIAN

Although Jesus made no statements either against sexual activity or directly in favor of celibacy, Christians from the church's earliest days showed a strong antisexual bias. Scholars disagree whether Christ, influenced by the celibate Essenes, remained unmarried or, as would be expected of any Jewish male of his time, married in his teens. But the first generations of Christians practiced celibacy to purify themselves for the **parousia, or Second Coming of Christ** which would announce the end of history. As their apocalyptic hopes faded over the ensuing years, and procreation became a necessity, an ambivalent attitude about sex became ingrained in the Christian mindset that survives in the doctrine of the Catholic church to this day. Here an English historian puts the Christian ambivalence about sex into perspective.

Justin [Martyr] in 150 presented his fellow-believers as heroes of restraint, rejecting remarriage after divorce, even discouraging second marriages for the widowed. Tertullian wished well-to-do Christians to take widows into their houses as "spiritual spouses." . . .

Attached to many early Christian communities were groups of ascetics, both men and women, some of whom demonstrated the supernatural character of their chastity by the sexes cohabiting, yet without sexual contact. . . . Writing to the Corinthians who thought sex in marriage incompatible with the spiritual life, [Paul] had insisted that marriage and procreation are no sin, while conceding to his opponents that, though good, marriage is not as good as celibacy. St. Peter was certainly married and on apostolic journeys took his wife with him. Philip the evangelist begat four daughters. But . . . Jerome was confident that even married apostles lived in mutual continence, after the example of their unmarried Lord and his ever virgin mother. For bishops, then for presbyters, finally for deacons, Western churches came to expect and ultimately to require celibacy (though the canonical compulsion was not enforced until medieval times, and even thereafter in parts of Europe, like Southern Germany and Wales, it was common for village priests to have a consort and a family, with the support of their flock and the connivance of their bishop who derived income from the annual fee or tax to allow the arrangement).

—HENRY CHADWICK, *THE OXFORD ILLUSTRATED HISTORY OF CHRISTIANITY*

✳ NO MORE GNOSIS

Discovered in an earthenware jar in December 1945 near Nag Hammadi in Upper Egypt, the **Nag Hammadi Codices** consist of papyrus manuscripts written in Coptic (Egyptian). The codices, 13 leather-bound books, contain 53 texts in all, most previously unknown. There are a number of alternative gospels, perhaps most notably the **Gospel of Thomas,** written early in the 2nd century in a form similar to the lost Q, or "source," manuscripts that the Evangelists drew upon. Some scholars believe that many of these sacred Nag Hammadi writings are older than the canonical Gospels and may date from as early as 50 BC. Among the manuscripts are fascinating titles such as the **Secret Book of John,** the **Gospel of Truth,** and **Thunder, Perfect Mind.** Many of the works express Gnostic beliefs.

Gnosticism is hard to define because so many different versions of it existed, and it is not even clear if it developed from Christianity or if the early Christians absorbed Gnostic tenets from the spiritual gene pool of their day. Gnostics embraced two basic concepts: they divided the world into opposing forces of good and evil (perhaps influenced by Zoroastrianism*), and they believed that they had access to secret wisdom (*gnosis* is Greek for "knowledge"). Gnostic teachings were held so secretly that many of them were never committed to writing; those that survive indicate that the Gnostics combined Oriental mysticism, magic, astrology*, and incipient Jewish Kabbalah* in a base of Christian belief. Among other things, Gnostics believed several variants of the widespread myth of the **Trickster,** sometimes a human or animal who, like the serpent in Genesis, tricks humanity out of its rightful enjoyment of the world. Sometimes the Trickster is a **demiurge,** a secondary, somewhat bumbling god who creates the world, identified by some Gnostics with the Old Testament God. The demiurge is inferior to the supreme God, but the created world of matter, corrupted by the devil, bears his mark. Consequently, many Gnostics saw matter as evil and spirit as good and so held that sex and marriage were potential evils to be avoided. Despite the orthodox church's disavowal and persecution of Gnostics, this attitude has seeped into the church's bias in favor of celibacy and virginity.

Most Gnostic beliefs and practices appalled the orthodox elements of the nascent church even more: Eastern-style meditation, secret rituals akin to the mystery schools of Greece, and belief in reincarnation and equality for women. One group of Gnostic Christians chose their priests by lot each week, so women often enjoyed priestly duties. Although Jesus himself appeared to have endorsed such egalitarianism in the strongest fashion, it was too much for the then male-dominated church. In the Gospel of Mary, one of the few Gnostic texts found before Nag Hammadi, Mary Magdalene recounts seeing Jesus in a vision after his death. The disciples whom she informs of this, including Peter and Andrew, immediately begin to ridicule her, no doubt indicative of the orthodox position toward both Gnostics and "uppity" women claiming spiritual authority. In the 2nd century, the church's attack on Gnosticism was already in full swing; by the 6th century, church councils had denounced all forms of Gnosticism as heresy, including reincarnation (Second Council of Constantinople, 553), and most Gnostic writings disappeared until the Nag Hammadi discoveries in 1945.

Not strictly a Gnostic but sharing much of their pessimistic attitude toward the body and the physical world, **Marcion** of Sinope (c. 80–155) believed that Jesus was radically different from the Jewish tradition that preceded him and that the Gospels had been altered to conceal this. He rejected those Gospels along with the entire Old Testament and reedited the Epistles of Paul and the Gospel of Luke to prove that Jesus taught a God of love rather than fear, quite distinct from the Old Testament God, whom Marcion considered an inferior being. Marcion was denounced as a heretic, but the rapid growth of the **Marcionites** led the church to establish a canonical set of New Testament texts, consisting of four Gospels, 21 Epistles, the Acts of the Apostles, and Revelation.

Montanus and two women named **Prisca** and **Maximilla** led a movement of charismatic prophecy in 2nd-century Phrygia in Asia Minor, claiming they were directly inspired by the Holy Spirit, or **Paraclete.** Many of Montanus's followers were women, who were allowed to teach, heal, and exorcise demons. Their most famous adherent was **Tertullian** of Carthage (c. 203), the great early Christian theologian, who first attacked the charismatic movement and then joined it. Nonetheless, the orthodox church, led by **Irenaeus,** the Greek bishop of Lyons, attacked **Montanism,** along with all other Gnostic manifestations, as heresy. The evidence indicates that these and other Gnostic sects thrived alongside orthodox Christianity throughout the Mediterranean rim and that in the early centuries the Gnostics may have outnumbered the orthodox.

✳ THE NEW ORDER

In a growing struggle to survive at all cost, the open and democratic nature of the early Christians gradually gave way to orthodoxy and hierarchy. By 200, what the pagan commentator **Celsus** called the "great church" had coalesced into a three-tiered hierarchy of **bishops, presbyters (priests),** and **deacons,** in descending order of authority (later followed by **sub-deacons, exorcists,** and **acolytes**). In part, the structure became necessary when the expected apocalypse failed to materialize and church leaders realized they were in for the long haul. But as conflicting beliefs, practices, and Gospel accounts mushroomed in the burgeoning Christian community, order was also required to prevent believers from flying off into innumerable warring splinter factions.

The roles and robes of bishops and presbyters were informal at first. Today's ecclesiastical vestments derive from the best formal wear of Roman aristocrats, much the way nuns' habits developed from the clothing of medieval ladies, simplified into black (for penitence) and white (for purity). The first bishops were selected by the original apostles of Christ, along with Paul; they had power over specific rural localities, as the bishop of Rome, say, or the bishop of Carthage. Later episcopal elections often became contentious affairs, with powerful families or social groups backing one or another candidate. Bishops were important because key doctrinal issues in dispute could be resolved only through **synods** (meetings of bishops similar to one held by the apostles in Acts), which later gave way to church **councils**. And as power coalesced into a hierarchy, geographical power came to focus in Rome, the center of paganism, where both Peter and Paul had been martyred.

PAGANS: UP CLOSE AND PERSONAL

Historiography's most glaring error has been its assertion that Judeo-Christianity defeated paganism. Paganism has survived in the thousand forms of sex, art, and now the modern media.

—CAMILLE PAGLIA, *SEXUAL PERSONAE*

To begin with, the term **pagan** was a Christian coinage, deriving from the Latin *paganus* ("country peasant" or "civilian") and implying anyone who wasn't a soldier in Christ's army against idolatry. The term was not applied to Jews, who at least worshiped Yahveh* (God the Father) but after the rise of Muhammad* in the 7th century, it was laid on Muslims for a time despite their unswerving monotheism. Paganism was Christianity's name for the official religion of the Roman Empire, which involved worshiping an array of gods and occasionally participating in orgiastic festivals. In an attempt to give Christians an alternative to those festivals (and to take their minds off the revelry they were missing out on), the church sometimes created holidays to coincide with the pagan calendar.

And so, beginning in the 4th century, the feast of the birth of Jesus, called **Christmas** ("mass of Christ"), played opposite a festival celebrating the birth of the sun at the winter solstice, which followed the orgiastic Saturnalia running from December 17 to 24. Saturnalia involved gift giving, feasting, the lighting of candles, and assorted forms of merrymaking, which were appropriated by the church. (The actual date of Christ's birth was unknown in any case and is now said by scholars to have probably occurred in the fall.) Other Christmas customs, including carols, the tree, the crèche, and Christmas cards, were added between the 13th and 19th centuries.

Pagans did not, however, spend all their time worshiping idols, chugging wine, and copulating in the streets. They were often astute intellectuals capable of engaging in learned exchanges with or attacks on Christian bishops. In their zeal, the triumphant Christians destroyed most pagan writings, so the arguments of prominent thinkers like Celsus are now known only through their quotation (and refutation) in the works of the Christian **apologists** Tertullian, Origen, and Augustine, who specialized in reasoned defenses of Christianity.

✳ BE AWARE OF THE GREEKS

One of the most influential early Christian communities grew up in Rome, in the teeth of its pagan persecutors, and it soon dominated other communities, such as those in Jerusalem and North Africa. Following the Jewish tradition of caring for the poor, orphans, and widows, emphasized by Jesus in his **Sermon on the Mount** ("Blessed are the poor, for theirs is the kingdom of God . . ."), the early church in Rome and elsewhere provided not only food and money for the poor and destitute, but also care centers for abandoned babies and the sick, all of which were foreign to the Roman way of life. Just as the Israelites cared even for strangers in their land, the Christians originally made no distinction as to whether those they supported were Christian or not. However, early Christians, much like the Jains* of India, were discouraged by their leaders from holding certain jobs that went contrary to their beliefs. Chief among these were any positions requiring the acceptance of idolatry or the execution of criminals, since the early church was strongly opposed to capital punishment.

The Roman religion was a state religion, ancient but lacking in profound spiritual content. It revolved around civic virtue and displays of loyalty to the emperor and household gods (**lares** and **penates**) and was administered by government workers. It was, in effect, a kind of official secularism that left citizens free to follow other creeds as long as they didn't interfere with the smooth functioning of government. Those other creeds included various moral schools, largely influenced by Greek philosophy, which reflected on vice and virtue and the ethics of familial and interpersonal duties—rather like Confucianism*, for centuries the state religion of China.

Cynicism, for example, as founded by the Greek **Antisthenes** and exemplified by **Diogenes of Sinope** (of lantern fame, c. 412–323 BC), derived from the Socratic notion that virtue is the only good and the chief means to happiness. By virtue, Cynics meant the knowledge of what is good, apart from the opinions of polite society. In principle, they believed in independence and a kind of asceticism that was indifferent to poverty or wealth, pleasure or pain. But in practice this often translated into calculatedly outrageous behavior and nose-thumbing, from which the modern use of the term *cynic* derives.

Stoicism, which was founded at Athens c. 300 BC by **Zeno,** borrowed most of its moral philosophy from the Cynics. Through Plato's influence, it was introduced to Rome, where its most famous adherents included **Seneca** and **Marcus Aurelius.** Underlaid with a generally fatalistic attitude, Stoicism placed great emphasis on logical thinking and a knowledge of physics, which amounted to a kind of pantheism that saw God (sometimes referred to as the Logos, or "Word") as indistinguishable from the world of matter. The Stoics' goal was to "lead a life according to nature" and, like Cynics, their highest good was virtue, which was in harmony with humanity's true nature. The greatest virtues were self-control (their indifference to pain or pleasure was quintessentially "stoical") and resignation to the way of things—including suicide as a viable form of expressing one's total independence from the world. Although Stoics placed little value on nationalism, they believed in justice and fellowship, in some ways looking back to the Buddhist ideal of freedom from desire and forward to Christian "brotherhood."

Epicureanism developed around the same time, in a school founded at Athens by **Epicurus** in 306 BC, but with an opposite spin. Epicurus taught that the object of morality is pleasure, but that happiness requires prudence and honor. Even if pleasure is the only good and pain the only evil, one must distinguish between the pleasures of the moment and those that endure. It might be necessary to accept present pain to ensure future pleasure or to avoid a momentary pleasure that might result in suffering. Since Epicurus did not believe in an afterlife (although he accepted the existence of various gods who kept their noses out of earthly affairs), for him and his followers the greatest good was to be free of fear and live as happily as possible. But in finding pleasure by having as few needs and desires as possible, stressing moderation, self-control, and independence, his teachings appear to share the goals of Stoicism. All three schools were commonly adopted and practiced by the Romans until Christianity became predominant in the 3rd or 4th century and stamped them out as formal schools.

Neoplatonism was the closest the Greek world came to a mystical belief system. **Plotinus** (AD 205–70), a Greek-speaking Egyptian, developed his philosophy in Alexandria, which supplanted Athens as the cultural nexus of the world, before founding his own school in Rome. Influenced by the teachings (since lost) of **Ammonius Saccas** (c. 174–242), Plotinus focused on the **One,** a single ultimate Being of pure Unity, or Godhead. His aim, as with all genuine mystics, was union of the individual soul with the One, for which he developed forms of meditation that he practiced constantly. Although Plotinus's teachings bore some relation to Plato's philosophy, the term Neoplatonism is more convenient than accurate in describing the school, which had no structured religious practices. Plotinus referred to the active principle of the One as Mind and to thought produced by that divine Mind as the Logos ("Word"). This philosophy influenced the Gospel of St. John (with its famous opening, "In the beginning was the Word and the Word was with God"), as well as Augustine and the Jewish philosopher Philo Judaeus*. Prominent Neo-platonists included Plotinus's student and biographer **Porphyry, Boethius,** and **Dionysius the Pseudo-Areopagite.**

Pre-Socratic Greek beliefs also influenced Christianity in several ways. The so-called tripartite anthropology that occurs in the writings of Homer, Hesiod, and others sees human nature in terms of three major components: **soma** (body), **psyche** (soul), and **pneuma** (spirit), where psyche has connotations of mind and personality. According to the ancient Greeks, at death psyche and pneuma separated from the body and traveled to the underworld, where the goddess Persephone judged them, sending them either to the heavenly **Elysian Fields** or the hellish **Tartarus,** where the wicked suffered punishment according to their crimes. The Christian concept of judgment at death, followed by the rewards of heaven or the pains of hell, was largely shaped by these Greek teachings, which may in turn be derived from Egyptian, Buddhist, Hindu, and Zoroastrian cultures.

Mithraism was a mystery religion that probably came into existence in the Greco-Roman world, perhaps from Asia Minor, sometime during the 2nd or 1st century BC. Some scholars believe that its origin goes back to much earlier Zoroastrian beliefs, since the cult's name derives from Mithra*, an ancient Iranian god of heavenly light (cognate with the Aryan* deity Mitra, the Greek form being **Mithras**), but this theory has been seriously questioned. The Greeks called this and other such cults—like those of Eleusis, Dionysus, and Isis—**mysteria,** from a root meaning literally "to keep one's mouth shut," and from which the English words *mystery* and *mysticism* are derived. The term *mystery* applies to a sect capable of conferring initiation on its members. But as with the Gnostics, we know so little about the Mithraic mysteries partly because they were open only to initiates who were forbidden to write down or speak to outsiders about the cult's mysteries and partly because almost all memory of them was eradicated by the Christians.

Images of Mithras survive, however, in paintings and sculptures found in hundreds of underground temples, from England to Asia Minor, that the Christians overlooked. He was usually represented as a handsome youth kneeling on a bull while stabbing the bull with his knife. One group of scholars has associated this figure with that of Perseus—who represents the northern constellation named for him—and hypothesize that the cult arose in response to newly developed information that the reign of Taurus as the constellation of the spring equinox had been replaced by that of Pisces. (In our own day, the news that Pisces itself was soon to be replaced in the spring equinox by Aquarius was enough to give rise to a hit Broadway musical centered around the so-called Age of Aquarius*.)

The Mithraic cult was introduced into Rome near the beginning of the 2nd century AD and proved especially popular among state bureaucrats, Roman legionnaires, and slaves, who celebrated it in grottoes and underground chapels. As paganism waned, Mithraism became Christianity's strongest competitor. The church formally suppressed it in the 4th century, but not before seeming to appropriate certain of its observances and symbols. According to refutations of Mithraism by Christian apologists, its members celebrated sacraments very similar to those of Christianity, including baptism and the eucharist, marked their foreheads with a cross, and believed in Mithras as their savior, redeemer, and final judge. Sunday had always been the holy day of the Mithraists, who also celebrated December 25 as the birthday of the sun, in reassurance that the days began to grow longer following the winter solstice.

Pythagoreanism probably had little direct impact on Rome, but its very existence hints at a mystical substratum that may have survived into the Christian era. **Pythagoras** (c. 570–490? BC) was born on the Greek island of Samos, which had close commercial links to an Indian community in Memphis, Egypt, that would have given Pythagoras access to Hindu and Egyptian knowledge. He later moved to Crotona in the Greek-controlled part of southern Italy, where he founded a religious order based on ascetic discipline and probably secret initiations. Pythagoras may well be considered the first great mystic of the West; unfortunately, none of his writings remain, and, as in the cases of many other non-Christian mystics, we have only the refutation of his beliefes in the works of early Church Fathers. He taught reincarnation and claimed knowledge of some of his past lives. Because of his concomitant belief that all living beings have souls, he stressed the sanctity of all life and practiced vegetarianism. He appears to have explored many connections between mathematics (the Pythagorean theorem named for him probably did not originate with him, however) and music—he was said to be able to hear the music of the celestial spheres, which may simply have been a reference to his mystical abilities. He also appears to have taught that an original Monad, or One, gave birth to various duads, and the related Pythagorean "table of opposites" (light and dark, male and female) seems to resonate with concepts from Taoist and Zoroastrian thought. Without doubt, Pythagoras was an exceptional individual, a rough contemporary of the Buddha and Lao-tzu who may have been the first to believe in the spherical shape of the earth and is said to have been the only Greek scholar who understood Egyptian hieroglyphics. But the order he founded probably came to an end by the middle of the 4th century BC, and as with the Mithraic cults, we don't have enough hard information to estimate his real significance on Western spiritual thought.

✳ COMPLEX PERSECUTION

Starting with the Emperor Nero in 64, the Romans persecuted Christians simply for professing their Christianity, a crime they could be forgiven if they acknowledged the Roman gods. But Christians considered such an acknowledgment a sin of **apostasy,** and when they refused they were tortured to death, fed to wild animals, or forced to fight gladiators in Roman arenas like the Colosseum. (Christians who could claim Roman citizenship, as St. Paul did, were allowed the honorable option of beheading.) Dying for their faith earned them the title of **martyr** (Gr. "witness"), a word borrowed from the Greek but a concept borrowed from the Jews of two or three centuries before. As with most religious persecutions, the Roman effort served only to strengthen the resolve of the persecuted while piquing the curiosity of citizens about a faith that people willingly died for. And willing they were. Death by martyrdom was quickly accepted by the ancient church as ensuring immediate entry into heaven—a teaching that was to appear later in Islam.

To follow the movement of the church during its early period, we have to outline the division of the Roman Empire itself. First brought under imperial rule in 27 BC, the empire was divided into west and east under Diocletian in AD 284, each with a Caesar and an Augustus sharing rule. In 395 the Western Roman Empire formally separated from the Eastern (or Byzantine or Greek) Roman Empire. The city of Rome fell to "barbarians" in 410 and the Western Roman Empire collapsed by 476; the East held on until 1453. The **Holy Roman Empire,** inaugurated under Charlemagne in 800, continued for over a thousand years, until 1806. Successive waves of invaders were ultimately absorbed by Roman and Christian culture, coming to speak the local languages and to accept the orthodox version of church theology.

Constantine the Great (280–337), whose mother (**St. Helena**) was Christian, became, on his father's death in 306, one of several men vying for rule of the western empire. Tradition holds that before a crucial battle with one of his competitors in 312, Constantine had a vision of a flaming cross inscribed with either Latin or Greek words meaning "In this sign you will conquer." After winning the battle, he converted to Christianity, although he continued to worship the sun god and was baptized only on his deathbed, 25 years later. He assumed the symbol of the **chi-rho**—the first two Greek letters in the name of Christ, drawn as a P (rho) surmounted on an X (chi)—a symbol that still appears on ecclesiastical vestments of the Catholic church. The year after his decisive battle, 313, Constantine and his co-emperor revoked the long-standing persecution of Christians in a series of letters that came to be known as the **Edict of Milan.**

By 325, Constantine had consolidated his position as sole emperor of the eastern and western empire. That same year he called the **First Council of Nicaea,** the first **ecumenical council** of the church, to try to get all Christians—mainly the two major sects, Arianism in the east and **Athanasianism** in the west—to agree on a single creed. The resulting **Nicene Creed** became the standard statement of Christian belief, although disputes over its wording about the Trinity contributed to the later split between the Western church and the Eastern Orthodox Church.

Constantine later moved the center of the Roman Empire from Rome to a new capital on the former site of **Byzantium,** and the rebuilt city was named **Constantinople.** The move represented a major shift from the persecution of Christians to the support of Christianity by the full power of the empire, gradually supplanting paganism and other cults like that of Mithras, to which Constantine himself probably belonged. In a matter of years, Christianity went from being a threat to the believer's life to a

THE NAME GAME

Catholic is a relatively modern term. Until the 16th century, it was simply "the church," or perhaps the "church catholic," in the sense of universal. Not until some years after the Protestant Reformation did the Rome-based church begin using the title Catholic to distinguish itself from Protestants. The church based at the Vatican with its apostolic succession of popes became the Roman Catholic Church to differentiate it from the various national branches of the Eastern Orthodox Church, which resemble the Catholic church in almost all major doctrinal elements with the notable exception of loyalty to the pope and the freedom of its priests to marry.

major career asset. By the 5th century, no particular advantage attached to being Christian, because almost everyone else in the empire was too. In fact, by the late 4th century, nonmembership in the Church was synonymous with disloyalty to the emperor and could be punished by exile. Christians trashed pagan temples with impunity, and purges were commonplace. From pagan bashing, it was a short step to synagogue burning and assaults on the Jewish population, which culminated in the expulsion of Jews from Spain in the late 15th century and the massive Russian pogroms of the late 19th.

These developments were all the more regrettable since Christians had once been marveled at among the Romans for their kindness and compassion, summed up in the classic observation reported by Tertullian "How these Christians love one another!" By the 3rd century, the clerical class with its hierarchical structure had taken control of the church, aided by its newly claimed power to remit sins as severe as adultery and apostasy. Christianity began to be firmly divided between clergy and laity, a division which sowed the seeds that sprouted much later in the Protestant Reformation.

WHY DO YOU THINK THEY CALL IT THE JUDEO-CHRISTIAN TRADITION?

Since the early church was made up largely of Jews, it's not surprising that many of its rites and customs were borrowed directly from Judaism. What is a little more surprising is how much the modern churches (Protestant, Catholic, and Orthodox) still owe to Jewish tradition. The Jews not only had the first martyrs but also the first monastics. The Christian Old Testament is essentially the Hebrew Bible; many of the prominent translations of the Bible are based on the Greek Septuagint*, the work of over 70 Jewish scholars translating from the original Hebrew. The Sabbath and feast days, the singing of psalms and hymns, choral music, the Catholic church's continuing use of candles and incense, an altar with a tabernacle and an altar lamp, the very concept of the "sacrifice" of the mass and the Eucharist, are all rooted in Judaic practices going back to the Temple days, as are the role of the priest and of special vestments to be worn during services. In fact, the earliest Christian churches were amalgams of the synagogue* (a teaching and worship place that could be located anywhere) and the Essenes' concept of a portable temple, not dependent on the Temple of Jerusalem. (The transformation of a single, centralized Temple to a mobile, universalized one is evident in Paul's notion that a Christian's body is "a temple of the Holy Spirit.") The structure of Jewish clerical authority headed by the high priest became the basis for the Christian hierarchy of priests, bishops, and cardinals, headed by the pope. Even the word *Amen,* a staple of Christian culture, is Hebrew, usually translated as "let it be" or "so be it," although it means "truly." And, as we know, the pope still wears a yarmulka—although he calls it a *zucchetto.*

Possibly as a reaction to the new Christian success, a movement toward asceticism began to spread among many believers. Another way to recapture that underdog community feeling of the early church was to honor those who had died for their faith. The **cult of martyrs** took many forms, from the veneration of **relics** (fragments of bone, clothing, or possessions of a martyr) to the insertion of martyrs' **feast days** into the liturgical calendar. Relics became requisite items placed beneath the altar of new churches (so decreed by the Second Council of Nicaea in 767), and pilgrimages to the sites of martyrs' burials or relics were de rigueur as expressions of Christian devotion. The setting for Chaucer's 14th-century *Canterbury Tales* was just such a journey, embarked on by a disparate group of believers, "The holy blisful martir for to seeke / that hem hath holpen whan that they were seeke." (The martyr was the famous **Thomas à Becket,** c. 1118–70, whose life and martyrdom are the subject of plays by T. S. Eliot and Jean Anouilh, the latter made into a successful film.) Veneration of relics was often drenched in superstition, a way of counteracting evil spirits by appealing to the supernatural power and energy of the saints, reminiscent of the Taoist use of talismans.

But relics could be faked and often were, so that a famous catalog of a 12th century relic collection of Reading Abbey in England claimed to possess, according to one historian, "Our Lord's shoe, his swaddling clothes, blood and water from his side, bread from the Feeding of the Five Thousand and the Last Supper, Veronica's veil and shroud, Our Lady's hair, bed, and belt, the rods of Moses and Aaron, and various relics of St. John the Baptist." The same author notes that the cathedral church of St. John Lateran in 13th-century Rome claimed the heads of Sts. Peter and Paul, the Ark of the Covenant, an urn of manna, John the Baptist's hair shirt, the ubiquitous five loaves and two fishes miraculously intact, the dining table from the Last Supper, and, in the nearby chapel of St. Lawrence, "the foreskin and umbilical cord of Christ, preserved in a gold and jeweled crucifix filled with oil."

FAVORITE MARTYRS AND
HOW THEY DIED

St. Stephen:
The first martyr, Stephen was stoned to death around AD 34.
He was most likely a Diaspora Jewish convert. The account
of his death in Acts 6–7 is rife with anti-Semitism and is
probably unreliable, although it also names Saul (later
Paul) among Stephen's accusers. The discovery of his relics in
the time of St. Augustine (5th century) led to a rage of veneration.

St. Sebastian:
The gap between fact and legend is nowhere more apparent
than in the iconography that has attached to the martyrdom of
Sebastian in the 3rd century. The story goes that as a captain
of the Praetorian Guard in Rome, he was able to help Christian martyrs without coming under suspicion. When he was
discovered, Emperor Diocletian ordered him to be shot to
death by archers. But he was found alive by a Christian
woman, who removed the arrows and nursed him back to
health. Undaunted, Sebastian returned to confront Diocletian
on his cruelty, and for his trouble was beaten to death and his
body tossed in the sewer.

St. Isaac Jogues:
The best known of the North American martyrs of the 17th
century, Jogues had his fingernails ripped out, several fingers
cut, chewed, or burnt off, and red-hot coals stuffed in his
mouth by the Iroquois. He escaped and returned to his native
France, but, eager for "the fulfillment of his dreams," he returned to America. Promptly captured by a Mohawk war

party, Jogues was tomahawked and beheaded, his severed trunk finally thrown into the Mohawk River.

St. Polycarp:

Bishop of Smyrna in the 2nd century, he was burned at the stake at age 86. When he was pierced by a sword, his blood flowed so profusely it put out the fire. Nonetheless, he soon died.

THE MARTYRDOM OF

ST. LAWRENCE

The church built over the tomb of this Roman deacon of the 3rd century is one of the seven principal churches of Rome. While being roasted alive on a gridiron, Lawrence allegedly told his tormentors: "You can turn me over now—I'm done on this side."
St. Lawrence became a popular image in Christian art, as shown in this page from a 14th–15th-century Bible.
GIRAUDON/ART RESOURCE

TWO CHURCH FATHERS: AUGUSTINE OF HIPPO AND THOMAS AQUINAS

Despite being based on the fact of Christ's incarnation and resurrection, the institution of Christianity was shaped to a huge extent by men who interpreted not only Christ's teachings but a vast range of Church **dogma** (fixed tenets with the weight of law) and **doctrine** (teachings). Two of the most influential such men lived almost a thousand years apart, and although their influence is more apparent in Roman Catholicism, their attitudes and values remain entrenched in the Protestant conception of Christianity as well.

Born to a pagan father and Christian mother, **Augustine** (354–430) was educated at a pagan school and lived with and had a son by his mistress in Carthage. He studied Manichaeism, Skepticism, and Neoplatonism before being baptized a Christian in 387 and ordained a priest four years later. After becoming auxiliary bishop of Hippo in North Africa, he began writing his many books, of which the most popular are *The City of God* and the *Confessions* (still famous for its accounts of his efforts to overcome his strong sexual proclivities, which some feel were overstated). Next to St. Paul, Augustine probably did more than anyone to frame Christianity. Unfortunately, his nine years of Manichaean training left their mark in his intolerant and antisexual orientation and dualistic approach to the problem of evil, which filtered into church thinking. He was the first to articulate the notion that infants are born with **original sin**—an inheritance of the first transgression of Adam and Eve—and said that the sin was passed on through the genitals, like a kind of social disease. Among other unmistakable signs of humankind's fall from grace, Augustine included involuntary bodily functions such as flatulence; once we ceased to obey God, we became unable to obey even ourselves and lost control over the body. Augustine's pessimism about the evil nature of humanity and his belief in the individual's absolute dependence on God led him to encourage the church in its persecution of heretics and nonbelievers and the pursuit of Christian conformity. He supplied the theoretical and scriptural underpinnings for the censoring and persecution of any who disagreed with orthodox church teachings, and many of his arguments were later used to justify the savage acts of the Inquisition.

Almost 900 years later, **Thomas Aquinas** (1224–74) was the leading theologian and philosopher of medieval Christianity. An ordained priest, Thomas was nicknamed the "Dumb Ox" because he was fat, slow, and serious. None of this deterred him from becoming a brilliant debater and prolific writer (all in Latin). Building on Augustine, he applied Aristotelian logic to Christian teaching and used reason to try to prove the existence of God; his famous **Five Ways** attempt to answer how God can be known from the physical world, including the need for a first cause or "prime mover." His most renowned and widely taught work, *Summa Theologiae,* was never finished, some say because of illness, others because of a mystical vision he experienced three months before his death which showed him the futility of all logical attempts to apprehend God. Many other churchmen of his day apparently agreed. Some of his teachings were condemned after he died (although this was later reversed), and other prominent scholastics attacked his inability to reconcile the logic of reason and the illogic of divine revelation. Over the centuries, **Thomism** has continued to enjoy resurgences, especially in Catholic teaching, up to the present day.

✳ HER NAME WAS MARY

Mary is the unrecognized Mother Goddess of the Christian tradition.
—ANNE BARING AND JULES CASHFORD,
THE MYTH OF THE GODDESS

Partly to counter vestigial Goddess worship in parts of Europe, the church in the 4th century began to emphasize the cult of Mary, sometimes referred to disparagingly as **Mariolatry.** Apart from her role as the mother of Christ, very little is said about Mary in the Gospels, and so an entire mythology had to be constructed around her. Chief among these beliefs was the **Immaculate Conception,** the notion that Mary was conceived without original sin (although this was not made into church dogma until 1854). The Immaculate Conception should not be confused with the **Virgin Birth,** the doctrine that Jesus was fathered by the Holy Spirit and that Mary remained a virgin even while giving birth to him.

317

Sometime after Christ's Ascension, Mary was assumed, body and soul, into heaven as well (the **Assumption** was defined as an article of faith in the Roman Catholic Church in 1950). Of these beliefs, only the Virgin Birth is accepted by Protestants.

Visions of Mary have been reported over 21,000 times in the last thousand years, often to young children. At **Lourdes** (1858), **Fatima** (1917), and **Medjugorje** (1981), Mary was the subject of prolonged visions, each time asking prayers for world peace. In America, she has been sighted in a backyard in Queens, New York, annually for over 25 years. The authenticity of these visions has often been challenged but has never been authoritatively proved or disproved. However, during her apparitions at Lourdes, Mary instructed **Bernadette Subirous** (played by Jennifer Jones in the movie *Song of Bernadette*) to dig for an underground spring. The spring did appear after she dug, and it now produces over 30,000 gallons a day; its waters are reputed to have healing properties. Also strongly associated with healing are the many statues of Mary as the **Black Madonna,** especially in France, Spain, Switzerland, and Poland (many on the sites of ancient goddesses) and in the United States.

Mary's astonishing popularity among common folk is sometimes attributed to her representation of the Mother Goddess who was suppressed after the Aryan and Semitic invasions of Neolithic Goddess* cultures in Europe and The Middle East. Even the widespread image of **Madonna and Child** has been traced to similar statues of the Egyptian goddess Isis nursing her son Horus.

❋ ONWARD CHRISTIAN SOLDIERS

As mass Christian conversions spread across Europe in the early centuries to the kingdoms of the Franks, Burgundians, Angles, and Saxons, among others, the local practice of the religion was influenced by the warlike orientation of many of the converts. Christ was now pictured as a Germanic warrior-hero toting battle-ax and lance, sometimes with the apostles following him into battle. Toward the end of the 1st millennium, particularly under the reign of Charlemagne, Christianity had already be-

MADONNA AND CHILD

ISIS AND HORUS

Isis, the goddess whose cult began in Egypt and spread to Asia Minor, Cyprus, Crete, Greece, Rome, and Britain, is the Great Sorceress Who Heals, Mother of Heaven, Queen of the Cosmos, Lady of Wisdom, the personification of the life force itself, especially as healer and protector. When her brother and husband Osiris was drowned by his loutish brother Set, Isis recovered the body, elicited his sexual essence from it, and conceived a child, Horus. When Set later discovered and dismembered Osiris's body, scattering the parts across Egypt, Isis and her sister Nephthys collected them and reassembled the body of Osiris. Many art historians, along with mythologist Joseph Campbell, believe that Isis and Horus became the model for countless Christian depictions of the Madonna and Child, just as Mary took on the titles once applied to Isis, such as Regina Coeli ("Queen of Heaven") and Stella Maris ("Star of the Sea"). The obvious similarity between this exquisite Egyptian statue of Isis suckling Horus and the 15th-century painting by the Master of Flemalle speaks for itself.

LONDON NATIONAL GALLERY   SCALA/ART RESOURCE gun to influence the way kings acted. The ideal ruler was seen as an ethical and prayerful man who spent a good portion of his kingdom's wealth supporting churches and monasteries.

This world in which church ritual was able to influence temporal behavior and even kingly power became known as **Christendom**. To its members—virtually all of Western Europe, Greece, and Asia Minor—it was synonymous with the civilized world. After the rise of Islam in the 7th century, Arabia, North Africa, and parts of Spain where the Muslims held sway were specifically excluded. By the time of the anointing of Charlemagne as Holy Roman Emperor in 800, the Christian domination of Western society, temporal and spiritual, was a fact of life, and Church laws ruled all conduct—economic, familial, and sexual. This virtual Christian theocracy paralleled the earlier Jewish theocracy, but it lasted longer and was more widespread.

The countryside was divided into **bishoprics** or **sees** ruled by local bishops. The development of **parishes** took place over centuries, beginning with communities of monks or priests that covered a wide expanse of territory around their churches and were later moved to the estates of the nobles. The parish church, usually with its appended graveyard, was supported by its parishioners, who were expected to contribute a **tithe,** or one-tenth of their earnings and produce. Christian burial was extremely important for believers, because resting in consecrated ground signified that one had died in a state of grace, allowing entrance into heaven. The excommunicated and suicides were not allowed this privilege.

Eventually, **canon law** developed apart from secular law and began to engulf the life of the church and its faithful, leading to a legalistic emphasis in the religion. The Jewish canon lawyers so despised by Jesus in the Gospels reemerged with a vengeance in Christianity. Usually minor clerics rather than priests who had taken vows, they adjudicated the growing moral and legal ramifications of church dogma. At the Lateran Council of 1216, Pope Leo III instituted compulsory private confession to a priest. Previously, public confession was the only way to ensure God's forgiveness, except for those who would risk their lives by confessing openly, such as adulteresses and murderers.

HOW THE LATIN MASS
DEVELOPED

Pope Damasus I (366–84) was instrumental in integrating Christianity with the imperial culture of the Roman world. He built huge churches and began the system of papal patronage that later fueled the Renaissance, completely Latinizing the church in the West, which had been Greek-speaking. The only bits of Greek that still remain are the prayer known as the *kyrie* in the Catholic mass and a number of theological terms. Under Damasus, St. Jerome created his Latin translation of the Bible called the **Vulgate**, which became the obligatory version. The **mass**, the centerpiece of Christian (now only of Catholic and Orthodox) ritual, was Latinized and expanded from its basic 2nd-century framework. Originally, writes one historian,

It consisted of readings from the memoirs of the apostles and the Old Testament; a sermon; a prayer followed by the kiss of peace, and the distribution of the blessed bread and water. This Sunday eucharist had become an absolute obligation by [about 150] and the words of the central prayer became formalized in the next generation or two. . . . The effect of the process of change introduced by Damasus was to change an essentially simple ceremony into a much lengthier and more formal one, involving an element of grandeur. The scriptural extracts were made longer and standardized, and prayers inserted at fixed intervals. This was how the West acquired the kyrie, the sanctus, the gloria and the creed, most of which were translated into Latin. Some of the ceremonial aspects were taken over from pagan rites, others from court practice. . . . The impetus in making the liturgy longer, more impressive, less spontaneous and so more hieratic was essentially Greek, but was seized on eagerly by Rome from the time of Damasus on ward. The object was partly to replace the magnificence of pagan ritual in the public mind, partly also to win the struggle against Arianism . . . by emphasizing the awe of Catholic sacrifice. Thus from the late fourth century there was a spectacular explosion of color in the vestments and hangings, the use of gold and silver vessels and elaborate marble piscinae [basins], silver canopies over the altar, a multitude of wax candles (a mark of respect in Roman domestic practice), and elaborate censering with incense.

—PAUL JOHNSON, *A HISTORY OF CHRISTIANITY*

✳ MEANWHILE, BACK IN THE EAST

From 330 to 1453, Constantinople served as capital of the Eastern Roman Empire. During the early ecumenical councils, debates flared over the nature of the Holy Trinity, how God can exist in the persons of the Father, the Son, and the Holy Spirit and still be one, and about the divine yet human nature of Jesus Christ. Beginning with the Council of Nicaea in 325, through the second ecumenical council at Constantinople in 381 and the third at **Ephesus** in 431, the question of whether Christ was one in essence with God the Father, whether the Holy Spirit was the equal of the two other persons of the Trinity, and Mary's role as Mother of God were debated in details too complex to explain briefly.

The fourth ecumenical council, at **Chalcedon** (451), reasserted the existence in Christ of two natures, Godhead and humanity, combined in one person. This theological viewpoint alienated a number of Egyptian and Syrian Christians who felt it implied a division between the human and divine in Jesus. The split deepened over the next two ecumenical councils, and these "non-Chalcedonian" Christians separated into other churches known as **Monophysite** for their belief that Christ has only one, divine nature (yet they did accept his humanity—once again, the details of the debate can be confusing). The Monophysite churches include the following:

Coptic Orthodox Church, non-Chalcedonian Egyptians. The Copts (derived from the Greek word for Egyptian) are considered a link with Egypt's pharaonic past, direct descendants of the original Egyptians. In the 1990s they increasingly came under attack from Egypt's militant Muslim fundamentalists.

Syrian Orthodox Church, sometimes called **Jacobite,** for the 6th-century bishop **Jacob Baradaeus.**

Ethiopian Orthodox Church, linked until 1959 with the Copts.

Syrian Orthodox Church of the Malabar (southern India), also known as the **St. Thomas Christians,** or **Mar Thoma,** for the apostle Thomas, whom they claimed as their founder and who supposedly suffered martyrdom near Madras.

Between the 8th and 11th centuries, a schism developed between the Eastern and Roman branches of the church; although the traditional date of the **Eastern Schism** is given as 1054, it was apparently a long, drawn-out process. Once again the theological differences seem minor: mainly whether the Holy Spirit, the Third Person of the Trinity, proceeds from the Father alone or from the Father and the Son. The Roman Church insisted on the Father *and the Son*—*filioque* in Latin, a term inserted into many church prayers and statements, to the dismay of the Easterners. But the Byzantine-Greek church in the East had other cultural and theological differences with the Roman-Latin church in the West. After the break, the Byzantine church developed into Eastern Orthodoxy, while the church in the West went on to become the Roman Catholic Church.

Orthodox belief emphasizes the Incarnation of God in the person of Jesus Christ. Since God is viewed as the Cosmic Creator, His taking on human form is a great inconceivable mystery. And so the Orthodox use of icons—representations of the Incarnated God, along with Mary and the saints—is their way of celebrating that mystery and not mere "idol worship" as Western Christians believed. The iconoclastic movement begun by Pope Leo III in 725 was intended to counter the Eastern belief in the legitimacy of icons (and perhaps was an acknowledgment of the growing popularity of Islam, which forbade all use of images). However, Leo's precepts were eventually rejected by the Church, and now both Roman and Eastern Christians are free to venerate statues, icons, and other images of Jesus, Mary, and the saints.

In addition to stressing the mystery of the Incarnation, Eastern Orthodoxy places greater emphasis on the role of monasticism and on the concomitant pursuit of mystical union with God than either Roman Catholicism or Protestant Christianity. However, with about 50 million practitioners worldwide, including about 3 million in the U.S., the Orthodox make up only a small fraction of the Christian population.

The **Eastern Orthodox Church** based in Constantinople later became identified as **Greek Orthodox** and then as **Serbian** or **Russian Orthodox** as conversion spread northward. After the conquest of Constantinople by the Muslim Turks in 1453, the Russian church assumed leadership of the Orthodox world. Modern branches include the **Romanian, Bulgarian, Albanian, Ukrainian,** and **Carpatho-Russian Orthodox,** all with churches in the U.S. The Orthodox profess most of the same beliefs as the Roman Catholic Church, with a few notable exceptions: they do not recognize the leadership and infallibility of the pope, preferring to follow their own local bishops, often called **metropolitans.** (Senior bishops are **patriarchs;** senior monastics are often given the honorific title **archimandrite.**) Eastern Orthodox priests are allowed to marry and have families, tending to create less separation between clergy and laity. Bishops, however, were required to be celibate from about the 7th century, and today they must be monks as well.

The Russian, Ukrainian, and other Orthodox churches in Eastern Europe went into virtual seclusion during the more than 70 years of Communist rule, when religious worship was considered antithetical to Marxist dogma. With the lifting of Communist domination beginning in the late 1980s, however, the Orthodox church has once again asserted itself as a spiritual force in these countries. Millions of Russians, for instance, have been baptized in recent years, including many former members of the Communist party. Over 6,000 churches and monasteries have been reopened and rebuilt in the former Soviet Union, and Russian leaders have begun attending services on major church holidays like Easter and Christmas as part of their civic duties.

❋ HERESY!

Like so many Christian concepts, the notion of heresy derives from Judaism. Early Christian heretics were punished by banishment from the church and its sacraments, but as the spiritual authority of the church merged with the power of the state, beginning with Constantine, heresy became a crime punishable by imprisonment, torture, and death. Heretical sects were usually named after their founders, but around the 12th century heretics began to have generic names such as **Cathars** ("the Pure"), **Publicans,** or **Bulgars.** Their argument was often as much with the corrupt state of the clergy as with points of doctrine, and they often set up separate religious societies. Influenced by Eastern Manichaeism, a form of Gnosticism that divided the world into good and evil, spirit and matter, some heretics developed ascetic codes of their own, forbidding sexual indulgence even in marriage, for instance, or requiring a strict vegetarian diet (except for fish, presumably because Christ ate it). A few even adopted the practice of fasting to death, reminiscent of the Jains* of India.

Although the heresies were generally crushed with great violence, they continued to pop up hundreds of years later in different parts of the world, and many still have strongholds throughout Europe. Here are a few of the major ones.

Montanism. As noted in the section on Gnosticism, Montanus, a 2nd-century Phrygian enthusiast, claimed direct inspiration by the Holy Spirit. Practicing charismatic prophecy, many of Montanus's followers were women, who were allowed to teach, heal, and exorcise demons.

Arianism. Arius (c. 256–366), an Alexandrian priest, rejected the concept implicit in the Trinity that God the Father and God the Son are identical in essence. To Arius, the Son was somehow less than the Father, the result of an act of the Father's will and so part of His creation. Arius was first banished for his anti-Trinitarianism and later taken back by Constantine, but his heresy continued through the centuries. The main difference between the Trinitarian Catholics and the "barbarians" who took over the Roman Empire in the 5th century appears to be that the barbarians (Vandals in North Africa, Visigoths in Spain and lower Gaul, Ostrogoths in Italy) were Arians.

Manichaeism or **Manichaeanism. Mani** (or **Manes,** 216–76), a Mesopotamian ecstatic, taught a dualistic philosophy with signs of an Iranian Gnostic influence and elements of Jewish and Buddhist belief. He divided all life into a kingdom of light overseen by a spirit of goodness and a kingdom of darkness or matter emanating from Satan and his an-

325

gels and taught that each human incorporates these kingdoms in varying degree. Manichaeans saw matter as evil and spirit as good, and their leaders, called the "elect," condemned marriage, sex, and animal food. Mani called himself "the apostle of Jesus Christ" and the sect had a Christian-styled clergy, baptism with oil, and a eucharistic meal, yet they were not specifically Christian heretics. They were, however, loathed and feared by most religions and governments throughout their zone of influence, which stretched from Western Asia to Eastern Europe.

Pelagianism. Pelagius, a British monk of the 4th and 5th centuries, taught that humanity was originally perfect and not tainted by original sin as a result of Adam's fall. Therefore, while baptism makes Christians of infants and entitles them to the kingdom of heaven, it isn't required in order to wipe away original sin. Pelagius was opposed by Augustine, his contemporary, who, in his inimitable pessimistic fashion, believed in original sin and in death as the penalty for sin.

The Bogomils. Named either after the Slavic for "beloved of God" or after a heretic named **Bogomile,** this Balkan sect c. 1000–1400 denied that Christ had founded an organized church. Adherents thus had no use for churches or ordained priests; they also rejected most of the Old Testament and church doctrine on saints, the virgin birth, all images, and infant baptism, among other things. Originally centered in Bulgaria, the Bogomil sect believed that God the Father had two sons: first came **Satanael** (Satan), who was thrown out of heaven for his sin of pride, and then Jesus Christ (the Logos). Satanael created humanity, but God gave them their souls; He then created Jesus, who overcame his evil brother, Satanael.

Waldensianism. Around 1175, a wealthy former merchant in Lyons named **Peter Waldo,** transformed by the sudden death of a friend, gave all his possessions to the poor. He went on to teach a literal application of the communal poverty practiced by the apostles and early Christians; like the Bogomils, he rejected most church doctrine not specifically spelled out in the New Testament. Some Waldensians opposed bloodshed in any form, including so-called just wars and capital punishment.

Albigensianism. Named for the town of Albi in southern France where it originated in the 11th century, this sect held doctrine that was basically Manichaean; as in many other heretical sects, its members railed against the vices and worldliness of the clergy. The church's organized persecutions of them in the 13th century are legendary for their mercenary cruelty. Crusaders were offered the confiscated lands of the heretics, whom they mutilated, tortured, and slaughtered by the thousands.

Jansenism. Cornelius Jansen, the Catholic bishop of Ypres, published his *Augustinus* in 1640, which propounded a doctrine of justification by faith and predestination, based on the writings of Augustine, much as Martin Luther's doctrines were. Jansenism was progressively condemned from 1653 to 1713, but Jansen's deeply pessimistic view of life, particularly of sexuality, continued to pervade French Catholicism for centuries. Many Irish clergy who were trained in France (after England had become predominantly Protestant) absorbed the Jansenist viewpoint and transmitted it to America during the great Irish emigrations, after which the Irish dominated the Catholic church in America.

✳ THE MONASTIC LIFE

The Western monastic tradition was clearly influenced by pre-Christian Jewish monastics like the Essenes of Judea and the Therapeutae* of Alexandria. However, Christian monasticism didn't get started until the 3rd century in the Egyptian desert, where hermits went to escape pagan persecution, taxes, military conscription, slavery, or the law. And yet by the 4th century in the East, they may have been seeking escape from a church that under the aegis of Constantine was growing more privileged, powerful, and materialistic than it had ever been. In either case, they are known today as the **Desert Fathers.**

The prototype of all Christian monks may have been the Desert Father known as **Anthony the Great,** a Coptic layman who is said to have heard the Gospel teaching "Go, sell all you have and give to the poor and you will have treasure in heaven, and come follow me," and did just that around 270. Living as an illiterate desert hermit (an **anchorite** or **eremite**) followed by an informal group of disciples, Anthony never washed or changed his clothes and died at the age of 105. During the 4th century, **Pachomius** developed a more organized form of monasticism in Upper Egypt known as **cenobitism,** or monastic community. In other parts of Egypt, groups of ascetics formed around an **abba,** or "father" (the source of **abbot,** a term later applied to the head of a monastery).

327

From Egypt to Syria, Palestine, and Arabia, various forms of monastic life were tried. In Syria, monks went around naked and in chains, coming close to the lives of Indian ascetics. One unusual group were the **Stylites,** hermits who lived on tall pillars. **St. Symeon Stylites** (c. 390–459) in 5th-century Antioch, for instance, sat atop a pillar 60 feet high and 6 feet wide for 37 years and spent much of his time prostrating himself. Other ascetics known as **Dendrites** nested in the branches of trees, while **Graziers** foraged in the woods like wild animals.

In Cappadocia in Asia Minor, monks such as **St. Basil the Great** (c. 330–79) were literate and upper-class theologians rather than simple ascetics and lived under a set of rules; Basil's are the first written rules we have.

But it was the Rule of **St. Benedict of Nursia** (c. 480–547), written in the early 6th century in Monte Cassino, Italy, that became the model for future orders in the West. Benedict based his Rule on collective, communal activity rather than isolation; the ideal monastery was a self-sufficient, self-governing unit under the direction of its abbot. His order of **Benedictines** combined manual labor and moderate asceticism guided by common sense rather than eccentric deprivation. The Rule, for instance, allowed each monk a daily pound of bread and pint of wine, along with healthy nonmeat dishes. Benedict's sister **Scholastica** founded a convent near Monte Cassino and presided over it. **St. Gregory the Great** (540–604), who helped to promulgate Benedict's Rule, began as an abbot and became pope—the first pope to call himself "the servant of the servants of God." Many descendants of the Benedictines, basing their communities on the Rule of Benedict, which had become fairly universal by the 10th century, are active today, including the Carthusians, Cistercians, and Trappists.

Carthusians, founded in 1084 by **St. Bruno** at Chartreuse, France, were extremely austere, living in separate cottages, taking meals alone just once a day, and coming together only to chant the daily office. They are supported financially by a community of lay brothers.

The **Cistercians** were founded in 1098 by **Robert de Molesme,** but their most renowned monk was **St. Bernard of Clairvaux** (1090–1153), who inspired the **Order of Knights Templar.** The Cistercians were noted for their devotion to a life of poverty, long fasts, and arduous labor. The inevitable loosening of austere restrictions beginning in the 13th century sparked a reform movement led by **Armand de Rancé,** abbot of La Trappe, a Cistercian monastery in Normandy. In 1664, he founded the **Trappists,** an order even more severe than the Cistercians, allowing no form of recreation while imposing strict silence and a vegetarian diet. Booted out of France during the Revolution, they established bases in Europe, China, and the U.S., where they produce a line of jams and preserves that has made their name something of a household word.

Dominic Guzman of Castile (c. 1170–1221) founded the **Order of Friars Preachers,** or **Dominicans,** as a traveling order bent on converting the Albigensian heretics. They were the first order of **friars,** or mendicant monks, soon followed by the **Franciscans, Carmelites,** and **Augustinians.** Whereas the Dominicans were middle or upper class and literate, the Franciscans were the only order that recruited mainly from the lower classes and illiterates. Both **Albertus Magnus** and Thomas Aquinas, the great scholastic philosopher, were Dominicans, as was the brilliant mystic Meister Eckhart, but so, unfortunately, was the infamous Tomás de Torquemada, the Grand Inquisitor. Famous Franciscans include **Duns Scotus** and **William of Ockham.** A reformed order of Franciscans called **Capuchins** was established in 1526 by **Matteo di Bassi** (capuchin monkeys were named after them because they appeared to be wearing similar hoods).

A DAY AT THE OFFICE

The schedule of prayers said by priests and monks of the Roman church and monks of the Orthodox church is known as the **Daily Office.** Built around a cycle of the Psalms and other prayers, the material was not gathered together until the late 11th century, but the notion of a series of prayers said at specific times of the day goes back to the early centuries of Christianity. As later codified and practiced today, the system of 7 daytime hours and a night office (collected in a book known in the Roman Catholic Church as the **breviary**) is based on an artificial 12-hour day stretching from 6 A.M. to 6 P.M. The names given to the hours by the Roman church are also the names of the prayers meant to be said or sung at that time.

Matins, begun before sunrise.
Prime, the first hour, 6 A.M.
Tierce, the third hour, 9 A.M.
Sext, the sixth hour, noon.
Nones, the ninth hour, 3 p.m.
Vespers, at sunset, ends the old canonical day and begins the
   new day.
Compline, said just before retiring.
Lauds, a midnight prayer that is combined with matins and
   said before dawn.

Prime may also be said together with matins and lauds in a long session that may stretch from 3 A.M. to after 6 A.M. Likewise, tierce and sext are often combined, as are nones and vespers. The hours are not meant to be strictly adhered to, but all the prayers should be said in the course of the day. For instance, matins can be said in anticipation in the afternoon or evening before. The **canonical hours,** as they are also known, bear a clear resemblance to the salat*, or five-times-daily prayer of Islam, except that the salat is said by all Muslims, who have no priest class or monastic orders.

In the 1530s at the height of the Protestant Reformation, **St. Ignatius Loyola** created the **Society of Jesus,** or **Jesuits.** An ascetic reformer who had served as a professional soldier until an injury cut short his career, Ignatius stressed absolute obedience to the church, although this did not keep the Inquisition from twice jailing him under suspicion of heresy. Loyola's *Spiritual Exercises* are still used by clergy and lay Catholics during religious retreats. Drawing his members from upper-class men of high education, he created perhaps the most effective teaching order of the Catholic church, famous for the saying "Give me a child until he is seven, and he will stay a Catholic the rest of his life." (In recent times this hasn't always proved out; a former Jesuit student, Abimael Guzmán, later became the leader of the Shining Path guerrillas of Peru, among the most ruthless Communist insurgents in the world.)

The order was famous for its discipline and worldly knowledge and its support of theater and the arts. But as they gained power, the Jesuits also sanctioned war and outright murder in the cause of fighting Protestantism, something they justified by a convoluted process of rationalization that came to be known as **casuistry** or **Jesuitry.** The Jesuits developed a near-fascistic insistence on conformity and obedience to the pope.

"Too often, in ancient as in modern times," writes the modern Eastern Orthodox bishop Kallistos Ware, "monastic history has been written exclusively from a masculine point of view." For this reason, the names of few monastic women have survived, yet their presence was significant. In Egypt, communities of nuns were in operation well before St. Anthony went into the desert. In Asia Minor, **St. Macrina** preceded her brother St. Basil into monastic life and may have been responsible for his vocation. **Melania,** the abbess of Mount of Olives in Jerusalem, led the great Greek mystic and writer **Evagrius of Pontus** to the monastic life.

For a time, double monasteries developed in which nuns and monks were housed in separate wings, in some cases both ruled by an **abbess,** such as **St. Hilda** at the 7th-century English abbey of Whitby. But this tradition began to be phased out in the 10th century. Among the most prominent religious women was **St. Hildegarde of Bingen** (1098–1179), a German Benedictine mystic whose writings— poetry, a medical book, plays, hymns, theological works, and an illustrated book of her mystical visions with commentaries *(Scivias)*—are notable for their concern for what we now call ecology. "The earth is mother of all that is natural, all that is human," she wrote. Hildegarde also created a language of her own, with a 900-word vocabulary and a 23-letter alphabet. Another mystic, **St. Bridget of Sweden,** was a mother of eight who founded a Cistercian abbey after her husband died. It housed 60 nuns and 25 monks in separate quarters with a common church.

Monks aided in copying manuscripts, mainly sacred ones, in rooms called **scriptoria** (sing. **scriptorium**), ensuring the preservation and dissemination of ancient and current knowledge, although without adding much to it except an occasional error in copying. On the material side, the monasteries, with their discipline, work ethic, and continuity, helped to systematize and stabilize the farming and land management process across Europe over a period of almost 1,000 years. Clearing forests and draining swamps, they laid the foundation for the Europe of today with its profitable farms and vineyards—wine being essential to the celebration of mass. Along the way, the monasteries often gained royal or aristocratic patrons and began to amass property and wealth, leading to laxity and corruption in monastic life and in turn to reform—a microcosm of institutional religion itself. One aspect of these reforms was the gradual imposition of celibacy on the monks, who during the 1st millennium were often married. Monastic celibacy was then extended to priests and deacons.

✳ THE INQUISITION

It is rating our conjectures highly to roast people alive for them.

—MONTAIGNE

One of the salient characteristics of Christianity at the start of the 2nd millennium was the way in which it suffused social and cultural life in the West, creating what one modern historian has termed the "Total Society." Everyone had a place and played a role upon which all agreed, just as they agreed on the underlying principles of Christianity, starting with baptism. Those who were not baptized—Jews or Muslims—were allowed to live and function within Christian society but had virtually no rights. And any Christians who challenged or turned away from the authority of the church were liable to be imprisoned, tortured, or killed as heretics. An unbeliever or agnostic was by definition a heretic, subject to persecution. Christian society was so total and authoritarian that the process of seeking out infidels and heretics inevitably led to abuses of power.

The creation of a permanent tribunal by **Pope Gregory IX** early in the

WORKING ORDERS

One ostensible difference between the monks of India and China and those of the West may be that, with the exception of the friars, Christian monks don't beg for money—although many of the great monasteries of Europe and Asia Minor were built by wealthy patrons or royalty. As a rule, monks support themselves by farming or cottage industry, making items they can sell to the public and using excess funds to help the local poor. Some of the items made and sold by monasteries have become famous:

Chartreuse. Carthusians make the potent liqueur, whose name derives from La Grand Chartreuse, the central house of their order near Grenoble, France.

Benedictine. Another popular liqueur, sometimes combined with brandy and sold as B&B.

Trappist Preserves. The Trappists, who have monasteries in Kentucky and elsewhere, market a line of jams and preserves.

St. Bernard. A large dog bred for the past thousand years at the hospice of St. Bernard in the Swiss Alps and reputed for rescuing travelers lost in Alpine snowdrifts.

Frangelico. A liqueur that seems not to have been named for the Dominican monk and painter (Giovanni de Fiesole) but for a hermit who lived in the 17th century near the river Po. According to legend he created unique liqueurs from his solitary studies of nature. The liqueur named after him is made from "wild hazelnuts with infusions of berries and flowers."

13th century, manned by Dominican friars, was intended to control these abuses. Instead, it made a bad situation worse, as the **Inquisition** allowed church courts ferreting out heretics to scuttle almost every principle of trial law as we now know it. One could be accused of moral or theological crimes by anonymous informers, including one's personal enemies, and then denied the right to defense. The mere accusation of religious wrongdoing was tantamount to proof of guilt; the burden to disprove lay with the accused, who could be tortured as part of the questioning process or jailed until either admitting guilt or denouncing others. (This tactic would reappear during the Salem witch trials of the 17th century and again in secular form during the "witch-hunt" led by Senator Joseph McCarthy in the 1950s, with the invitation to "name names" and root out "Godless" Communists.) Favorable witnesses or other advocates for the accused were certain to share in their guilt, and few people chose to take the risk. As a result, almost every person accused by the Inquisition suffered some form of punishment, the least of which was being forced to wear foot-long yellow Crosses of Infamy, which made getting a good job difficult. Although only a small percentage of those tried were actually put to death, a large number were imprisoned and all of them were forced to give up money and possessions to the tribunal—in itself a fair inducement to accuse the well-to-do.

The setting for such an egregious presupposition of guilt was the orthodox belief, accumulated over centuries, that most of humanity was going to hell. Hell itself was conceived of as a place of unthinkably painful torment that continued for eternity. The Christian apologist **Origen** (c. 184–254) had taught that all could be saved from hell, but in the 6th century his teaching was condemned by a church council. Thomas Aquinas reversed the odds to "few" saved and the "multitude" damned, and it was commonly believed that only one in a thousand would be saved. With so many potential damned running around, it only made sense that most people were already guilty as charged.

In Spain, **Tomás de Torquemada** (c. 1420–98) was named Grand Inquisitor in 1483, and the pace of persecution picked up. The Catholic monarchs Ferdinand and Isabella made the **Spanish Inquisition** an independent operation, not answerable to the papal Inquisition, and so Torquemada had a free hand to torture his victims with impunity. Since the church could not shed blood, the secular authorities were in charge of actual executions, of which Torquemada ordered more than 2,000. The Inquisition also became a convenient excuse for the continued hounding of the Jews, who were later blamed for the Protestant Reformation and expelled from Spain in 1492 (in the same month that Columbus was given the go-ahead to sail for the Indies), as well as of Muslim converts, called **Moriscos.** Famous for its brutality, the Spanish Inquisition continued to operate in one form or another into the 19th century, running out of steam only after the once abundant number of rich targets of confiscation began to dwindle.

✸ THE POPES AND THE CRUSADES

Jesus may well have chosen 12 apostles with the idea of creating a new 12 tribes of Israel; it's less clear that he intended Peter to be their hierarchical leader. The line "Thou art Peter and upon this rock I will build my church" (Matt. 16:18) was probably added by a church eager to authenticate its divine mandate. But after the death of Christ, Peter became the bishop of Rome and is considered the first **pope** in a line of succession by which the bishops of Rome became the papal rulers of the church. Early on, the pope was called the **Vicar** ("deputy, substitute") **of St. Peter**; by the 13th century the popes had elevated their title to **Vicar of Christ.**

During the 1st millennium, the power of the church appeared to reside in numerous local bishops, who struck alliances with temporal leaders rather than with the pope in Rome. With the election to the papacy of **Gregory VII** in 1073, that began to change. At the same time, the Papal Reform Movement, spearheaded earlier by **Pope Leo IX** (1049–54), sought to reform the priesthood, which meant eliminating the accepted practices of paying fees for ecclesiastical services and marriage for priests.

The beginning of the 2nd millennium also brought with it the onset of the **Crusades** (from the Spanish *crusada,* "marked with the cross"), a massive exercise of increasing papal power to shape temporal history. The **Holy Land** of Jerusalem, still a major pilgrimage spot for Christians wishing to view the land of their Savior's life, the site of the Temple, **Golgotha** where Christ was crucified, and his birthplace in nearby Bethlehem, had been taken over by Muslims in 637. Christians were given free access at first, but by 1073 conditions had become intolerable. The concept of the "just war" had been introduced into Christian theology by St. Augustine, reversing the attitudes not only of Jesus, who spoke of turning the other cheek, but also of St. Paul and the early Christians, who accepted death rather than violently resisting their persecutors. Once this theory, which held that war was justifiable if it was waged at the implicit command of God, was incorporated into Christianity, it made possible everything from holy wars to the jailing of conscientious objectors. Later popes developed the notion that death in battle for the sake of the church would result in heavenly rewards similar to those for martyrdom—a concept shared by Muslims to this day.

The Crusades sprang from a combination of conditions, including the tradition of defending the Holy Land developed by the monarchs who succeeded Charlemagne, and a population explosion in the 11th and 12th centuries, which necessitated more land and occupations. The custom of sending large armed escorts to accompany pilgrims to the Holy Land, with the approval of the Muslims, developed into mass journeys of armed conflict. With a partial aim of settlement in the areas around the Holy Land and elsewhere in Arabia and North Africa, the escorting armies also murdered Muslims, Jews, and even other Christians and engaged in looting and gratuitous destruction. Participation was stimulated by a papal promise not only of eternal salvation to any who fell in battle, but also of the remission of any penance and possibly of any temporal punishment due to sins and the right to keep as their own any lands the Crusaders might conquer.

The First Crusade was set in motion by **Pope Urban II** in 1095, reportedly after having the idea proposed to him by **Peter the Hermit**, whose pilgrimage to Palestine in 1093 was thwarted by the Muslims. Peter was active for a hermit; he rode about the French countryside on a mule whose face was said to resemble his, stirring up enthusiasm for the Crusade. To chants of *Deus vult!* ("God wishes it!"), the Crusaders took Jerusalem in 1099. The Second Crusade, instigated by the preaching of Bernard of Clairvaux in 1147 and led by King Louis VII of France and Holy Roman Emperor Conrad III, flopped in its effort to recapture Edessa, on the edge of the Syrian desert, from the Saracens. In 1187, Saladin retook Jerusalem from the Christians, sparking the Third Crusade by the three principal monarchs of Europe, including Richard the Lionhearted. They failed to capture Jerusalem but worked out a truce with Saladin allowing passage to the Holy Land. The Fourth Crusade was carried out not against Muslims but against the Eastern Orthodox of Constantinople in 1204. It succeeded in completely alienating the Greek and other Orthodox from the Roman church.

The multiple failures of the Crusades led many Christians to think not that violence in the service of God was a bad idea, but that the Crusaders were not innocent enough. So in 1212, when a French peasant boy preached a **Children's Crusade,** 50,000 French and German youths set out on one of the great follies of the Middle Ages. Most of them either perished while crossing the Alps or were sold into slavery in Marseilles. There were between seven and nine major Crusades in all, according to various accounts, most of them failures except for the stimulus they provided to European commerce and the arts as a result of extended interaction with the East.

The historical Christian attitude toward Islam was much the same as its approach to Judaism: it sought to exploit both groups by exacting taxes and tributes and by drawing on their skills where they were needed. Jews, for instance, were allowed to lend money at interest and the early Christians were not. Oftentimes, though, Christians tried to rescind debts by expelling or massacring the Jews to whom they owed large sums. Similarly, skilled Muslim artisans were preserved in conquered Muslim lands mainly because of their economic value.

✸ CHRISTIAN MYSTICISM

From the earliest days of Christianity, mystics have played a part in the church, but mysticism itself has had at best a tangential role. Many of the Desert Fathers were genuine mystics; **St. Francis of Assisi** certainly was, and Thomas Aquinas reportedly had a mystical experience the year before he died, saying, "Compared with what has been revealed in me, all my writings are as mere straw." The church has never been especially comfortable with mysticism or with the practices associated with it—a simple emptying of the mind akin to Eastern meditation—preferring the mental dialogue with God or Christ in prayers of petition, thanksgiving, praise, or atonement, or in the rituals of the mass or benediction.

Some meditation techniques are described in the writings of the Christian mystics and the anonymous 14th-century book *The Cloud of Unknowing.* The church may have found such practices threatening because they required no mediation by a trained clergy, although most forms of meditation require skilled instruction and supervision. A more likely reason is the reluctance of church leaders to trust individuals not to lose their way in the powerful realms of inner practice, just as the church often discouraged reading and personal interpretation of the Bible.

One of the most renowned Christian mystics was Johanne Eckhart (1260–1328), a German-born Dominican monk who earned a master of theology degree in Paris and thereafter was known as **Meister Eckhart.** Eckhart's teachings today are ranked with those of the great mystics of the world, but in his own time, despite his having presided over 50 monasteries and 9 convents in northern Europe, his mystical sermons got him in trouble with the church. He used the term **Godhead** to mean the kind of impersonal, transcendent Absolute the Hindus call Brahman*, as distinguished from God as the personal Creator of the universe. This kind of thinking disturbed the church, and Eckhart was tried several times for heresy. He was finally found guilty, and a papal **bull,** or edict, was issued against him, but he was never actually punished, having died shortly before the bull was published.

Nicholas of Cusa (1400–64) took an opposite tack, and his career of seeking reform within the church generally met with support, including papal appointments, despite the fact that, like all true mystics, he accepted the equal validity of all religions. Besides being a mystic and reformer, Nicholas was a gifted mathematician, scientist, and linguist, a sort of Renaissance man at the dawn of the Renaissance.

The Spanish mystic **John of the Cross** (or Juan de la Cruz, 1542–91) became a monk in the contemplative order of Carmelites at age 21. John was associated with **Teresa of Avila** (1515–82), who founded a reformed order called the **Discalced** ("Barefoot") **Carmelites,** stressing strict poverty, cloister, and fasting. Their asceticism and independence angered religious authorities to such an extent that John was tortured, found guilty of disobedience, imprisoned, and humiliated. During his imprisonment, he wrote his famous mystical poem **"The Dark Night of the Soul,"** a term that has since entered the mystical lexicon to indicate that point at which the soul has begun to break away from the separative ego and

"An angel in bodily form, such as I am not in the habit of seeing except very rarely" appeared to St. Teresa in one of her mystical ecstasies, as described in her Autobiography. "In his hands I saw a great golden spear, and at the iron tip there appeared to be a point of fire. This he plunged into my heart several times so that it penetrated to my entrails. When he pulled it out, I felt that he took them with it, and left me utterly consumed by the great love of God. The pain was so severe that it made me utter several moans. The sweetness caused by this intense pain is so extreme that one cannot possibly wish it to cease, nor is one's soul content with anything but God." This detail from the famous 17th-century sculpture by Bernini in a chapel of the church of Santa Maria della Vittoria in Rome reflects the erotically tinged rapture which Teresa herself claimed was "more beneficial than union." In The Interior Castle, she further likens the experience to marital union, writing that "in genuine raptures . . . God ravishes the soul wholly to himself, as being his very own and his bride, and shows her some small part of the kingdom she has thus won."

ALINARI/ART RESOURCE

its material consolations but has not yet achieved the higher consolations of union or mystical marriage with God.

In *Revelations of Divine Love*, **Julian of Norwich** (c. 1342–1416) recounts a series of 16 visions she experienced on a single day as she suffered from a near-fatal illness that she had asked God to send her; she adds her meditations on them over a period of 20 years. Julian lived in almost total isolation in a cell attached to the wall of the Norman church of St. Julian and St. Edward, although she occasionally served as a spiritual counselor to others.

The universality of mysticism, a phenomenon that the German philosopher Leibnitz called the Perennial Philosophy*, is sometimes evident in the language of mystics. Julian, for instance, writes that in one of her mystical visions the Lord showed her "a little thing, the size of a hazelnut, on the palm of my hand, round like a ball. I looked at it thoughtfully and wondered, 'What is this?' And the answer came, 'It is all that is made.' " This experience of God or creation as being infinitely small (or infinitely large) is also part of Hindu mystical thought and was succinctly expressed by the visionary poet **William Blake** (1757–1827) in "Auguries of Innocence":

To see the world in a grain of sand,
   And heaven in a wild flower;
Hold infinity in the palm of your hand,
   And Eternity in an hour.

❈ THE PROTESTANT REFORMATION

Beginning in the 14th and 15th centuries, a movement called **Devotio Moderna** ("Modern Devotion") spread mystical lay piety across northern Europe outside the official church. It was spearheaded by **Gerhard (Geert) Groote** (1340–84), who taught the value of a simple ascetic life of piety in the service of God and neighbor. Groote preached and wrote against the clerical abuses of his day, such as **simony** (the purchase of ecclesiastical office, ordination, or indulgences), and focused on the inner life of the soul, love of neighbor, and the imitation of Christ. These ideas were so radical for their time that the church revoked his preaching license (he was a deacon, but not a priest). Returning to his hometown of Deventer in Holland, Groote created a community of pious lay people who shared his vision and came to be known as the **Brethren of the Common Life.** They took informal versions of the traditional clerical **vows** of **poverty, chastity, and obedience,** lived communally, and devoted themselves to helping the poor, but were not a religious order. He gave his own house to a community of devout women, for whom he wrote a Rule. Groote's associates included the mystic **Jan van Roeysbroeck** (1293–1381), a major influence, and **Florens Radewijns** (c. 1350–1400). Radewijns organized subsequent communities and a monastery at Windesheim in Holland.

Groote conceived of his informal brotherhoods and sisterhoods as a crucial link between laity and monastics. The movement spread rapidly, its members supporting themselves by copying books and running an influential series of schools. The schools produced the great humanist **Erasmus** (who foreshadowed the Reformation, although he never joined it), along with Nicholas of Cusa and **Thomas à Kempis** (1380–1471), the German mystic who is generally credited with authorship of the popular devotional work *The Imitation of Christ* (although some scholars believe the real author to be Florens Radewijns). But the Brethren, their schools, and ideas were never embraced by the larger church, which missed a chance to purge itself of its own abuses and perhaps avoid the coming Reformation.

Prior to the 16th century, a number of other Christians attempted to initiate reforms in the church, but they met with little success. The famed Italian preacher **Savonarola** (1452–98) cleansed Florence of some of its worst abuses of church and state power for a time. But after running afoul of **Pope Alexander VI** (Rodrigo Borgia), perhaps the most corrupt of all the popes, he was hanged and burned by the citizens of Florence. In England, **John Wyclif** (c. 1329–84) supported the government's right to seize the property of corrupt clergy and questioned the faithful's need for a clerical class to mediate with God. His followers, called **Lollards**, believed that the Bible should be translated into the vernacular—something Wyclif began in his Wyclif Bible—and made generally available.

The medieval Roman church, meaning the clergy, had gradually assumed for itself the right to read and interpret the Bible. Until the printing press produced the first **Gutenberg Bible,** around 1455, Bibles were very costly and were forbidden to be translated into the vernacular, effectively enabling the clergy to keep the words of Jesus from the very peasant class to whom he had originally preached them. Instead, the church offered dogma based on interpretations of the New Testament by the early Church Fathers, further clarified by papal and conciliar pronouncements.

Martin Luther (1483–1546) had been an Augustinian monk, an ordained priest, and a doctor of theology at the University of Wittenberg in Germany when a passage in Paul's Epistle to the Romans convinced him that forgiveness of sins could come only from the **grace** of God, and **salvation,** or justification, from faith in God rather than from works or indulgences (by "works," Luther meant the workings of the Catholic Church and its sacramental system, which sought to "mount an assault on heaven," an approach he considered nonbiblical). This idea became one of the cornerstones of the Protestant Reformation, which Luther set in motion when he nailed his famous **95 Theses** ("On the Power of Indulgences") to the door of Castle Church in Wittenberg in 1517. Reformers like Luther and John Calvin in France developed the concept of

YOUR INDULGENCE, PLEASE

To understand the rationale behind the sale of indulgences, we have to enter the complicated theological mindset of the medieval Christian (largely retained by modern-day Catholics). Dying in a state of **mortal sin** (serious sin such as murder, adultery, or missing Sunday mass) puts one on the fast track to hell. Dying with unconfessed **venial sins** (lying, petty theft, unkind words) means doing time in **purgatory** before going on to an eternal reward in heaven. But all sins, even after being confessed and forgiven, incur a debt of **temporal punishment,** a finite amount of time spent in purgatory. The amount of temporal punishment due can, however, be reduced or eradicated completely through the application of **indulgences.** Christ, the Blessed Mother, and the saints were said to have earned more merit by their holy lives than they needed, and that excess merit is available to ordinary sinners by saying certain prayers, venerating relics, using religious articles such as rosaries, medals, and crucifixes, or, during the Middle Ages, paying money.

Penances back then could be very elaborate and time-consuming and sometimes involved public forms of self-abasement. So the idea of relaxing the severity of penitential duties in exchange for making contributions to the church became increasingly attractive. By the 7th century, canon lawyers allowed sinners to pay other people to perform the penances levied on them. This led by steps to paying money directly to the church (e.g., by endowing a monastery) to fulfill part of a penance obligation and finally to the outright selling of **plenary indulgences** directly for money. During the Crusades, the remission of penance and ultimately plenary indulgences were offered to those who went to the Holy Land or supported the Crusades financially.

Many of the reformers sought to return to the simplicity of the earliest Christians, basing their beliefs strictly on the New Testament rather than on the interpretations and elaborations of those texts by Church Fathers like Augustine and Aquinas or by the decrees of the various popes and councils. Some reformers wrote hymns in the vernacular, replacing the lovely but strictly Latin liturgical music called **Gregorian chant**— which dates from the time of Pope Gregory the Great (590–604) but actually derived from Hebrew psalmody and was not compiled and systematized until the 9th century. Luther, **Isaac Watts,** and John and Charles Wesley wrote memorable hymns for choir or congregation that are still sung by Protestants of all denominations. One of the most popular Protestant hymns, "Amazing Grace," was written in 1779 by converted former slave trader **John Newton.**

justification by faith alone; good works were okay, but you couldn't *earn* your way into heaven.

Luther intended only to open debate on the subject of indulgences, but when he was smacked down by the pope and summoned to Rome to defend himself against charges of heresy, he responded by staying in Germany and issuing a call for a general reform of the church. He advocated the abolition of priestly celibacy, monastic vows, fasting, masses and religious holidays, and abuses in the sale of indulgences. The pope officially excommunicated Luther in 1521, setting in motion a chain of events that led to the separation of the Catholic church from a mushrooming agglomeration of Protestant sects. Before Luther, Christianity had been divided into two main groups, the Roman Catholic Church in Rome and the Eastern Orthodox Church in Constantinople. Now were added not simply Protestant Christians but all manner of Protestant sects and subdivisions, which continued to multiply.

Following Luther's break with Rome, various sects took shape around leaders who differed in the extent of their disapproval of the Roman church, often disagreeing on how radically they wished to reconfigure Christian practice. Many of the major Protestant branches formed within a few decades after Luther, whereas others continued to sprout up over the centuries as sects divided and subdivided. Here are a few of the main ones.

Lutherans. Although Luther wanted to create a theologically democratic "priesthood of all believers" (much the way Judaism had been "a nation of priests"), Luther's version of Christianity was closely tied to the German state, which had served as his protector from the papacy. But he preferred the name **Evangelical** to Lutheran, believing that he was not founding a new religion but restoring the original church of Christ as contained in the Gospels of the four Evangelists. For example, Lutherans recognize only baptism and communion of the seven sacraments, because only these are mentioned in the Gospels. The originator of the Reformation, however, embodied much of the same intolerance that characterized the Roman church; he ended by banning Catholicism and seeking to extirpate fellow Protestants who disagreed with his vision, and he engaged in witch-hunts and the burning of supposed witches. And although Luther began by blaming the church for alienating the Jews, when the Jews didn't jump to convert he became a fierce

MARTIN
LUTHER

According to Erik Erikson's classic psychological study Young Man Luther, the German reformer was "a second generation ex-peasant," his father having left the farm to become a miner. This created in Luther "that split about ancestral images which is apt to occur in the second generation of migrating families." Although Luther may have felt a certain empathy and nostalgia for the hard simplicity of village life, writes Erikson, "in his later years, with increasing frequency and vehemence, he divorced himself from the German peasant whom he condemned for being vulgar, violent, and animal-like. During the great Peasants' War, he used his efficient propaganda machine to suggest the ruthless extermination of all rebellious peasants—those same peasants who, at the beginning, had looked to him as one of their natural leaders. Yet toward the end of his life he accused himself of having the blood of these peasants on his head—the brow of which had never known a peasant's sweat." In this etching by Hans Brosauer, it's not hard to see someone of peasant stock who had hardened into the kind of man who might feel very comfortable sitting on a barstool next to Archie Bunker.

FOTO MARBURG/ART RESOURCE

anti-Semite, calling for the destruction of all Jewish homes and synagogues, the confiscation of their property, and a ban on teaching and traveling. By placing the ultimate power in the hands of the state and demanding absolute obedience to the existing order of society, Luther in one sense laid the groundwork for the absolutist abuses of Bismarck and Hitler. (Indeed, Hitler often quoted Luther's anti-Semitic rantings. The Kristallnacht pogrom* of 1938 that began the Holocaust in earnest was scheduled by the Nazis to honor Luther's birthday.) Luther also had little use for rebellious Christian peasants who attacked the feudal status quo. "A rebel is not worth answering with arguments," he wrote, "for he does not accept them. The answer for such mouths is a fist that brings blood from the nose."

Anabaptists. Their collective name means "rebaptizer," although they rejected the title since they disavowed infant baptism and didn't consider their own early baptisms effectual at all. They believed instead in voluntary adult baptism by their peers, as well as a return to certain basic teachings of Jesus: love, commensality (sharing and redistribution of wealth), pacifism, and complete separation of church and state. The movement rose in Zurich in the 1520s and spread across German-speaking Europe before splitting into opposing factions. The Anabaptists were persecuted and many thousands slain not only by Rome but also by fellow Protestants who found their reductive radicalism threatening. A Moravian subsect called the **Bruderhof** ("Brotherhood"), an outgrowth of the evangelical movement led by Bohemian reformer **John Hus** (d. 1415), modeled itself on the earliest Christian communities. Some members, under the leadership of **Jacob Hutter** (d. 1536), became known as **Hutterites;** they produced a rich devotional literature and established a small community in America in 1870.

Reformed, Presbyterians, Calvinists. Known in continental Europe as Reformed churches and under **John Knox** in Scotland as Presbyterianism, the movement was sparked by **John Calvin** (1509–64) in France. In a restricted sense, **Calvinism** was based on Calvin's extreme form of **predestination** (an idea Luther had already picked up from Augustine), which held that individuals were destined by God, even before the Creation, to be saved or damned according to His plan. The surest way to determine if you were one of the elect was to be a member of the Calvinist communion, preferably through an individual experience of

346

regeneration, which in modern born-again Christian terminology is equated with "taking Jesus as one's personal savior." The congregation, in turn, had to inspect its members continually to be certain they were living up to the high moral standards required of them. In France, they set up what amounted to a theocracy, and Calvin used excommunication and execution to silence his opponents. Like Luther, he recognized only the sacraments of baptism and communion. His important work, *Institutes of Christian Religion* (1536), helped Protestants interpret the Bible for themselves without splintering into countless sects early on. By stressing that ordinary, everyday work, as opposed to clerical occupations, was a valid way of glorifying God, he laid the groundwork for the **Protestant work ethic.** Protestants who opposed Calvin and believed in **universal salvation** are sometimes called **Arminians** for Dutch theologian **Jacobus Arminius** (1560–1609). The Reformed church in France was known as **Huguenot;** Presbyterians arrived in America in the mid-17th century as the **Dutch Reformed Church.** In 1972 in Great Britain, Presbyterians joined Congregationalists to form the **United Reformed Church,** later joined by the **Churches of Christ.**

Anglicans (Church of England). As a result of Henry VIII's dispute with Rome over his right to divorce the first of his six wives, he separated from the Roman Catholic Church in 1533 and established the Church of England. Although he abrogated the power of the pope and dismantled monasticism in his *Six Articles,* issued in 1539, he also reaffirmed traditional Catholic Christianity. Mary Tudor in the 1550s reestablished the authority of the pope, but elements surfaced seeking a more purified form of worship, and they came to be called Puritans. Today, Anglicanism and its American counterpart, **Episcopalianism,** are the Protestant sects closest in spirit and practice to Roman Catholicism.

Puritans. Some members of the Church of England felt the English Reformation didn't go far enough toward purging the ceremonies of the Roman Catholic Church, such as kneeling at the altar for communion, using the cross in baptism, and wearing clerical vestments. Later called Puritans, they were also notable for their commitment to personal regeneration, household prayers, and strict morality. Under Elizabeth, James I, and Charles I, the Puritans suffered persecution but refused to stop agitating for a more Calvinistic church. A small group of radical Puritans insisted on disassociating themselves from the Church of England altogether. Few in number, these **Separatists** were punished by the Crown and even criticized by some Puritan preachers. In 1620, a group of 102 Separatists known as the **Pilgrim Fathers** left for America to create a new England and settled in Plymouth, Massachusetts. They were later joined by less radical Puritans who nonetheless adopted their **Congregationalist** form of church government, which vested all ecclesiastical power in the assembled members of each local church. The best-known English Puritan was **John Bunyan** (1628–88), who composed his classic *Pilgrim's Progress* during a 12-year stretch in Bedford jail for refusing to stop his preachings under the Stuarts.

Mennonites. Menno Simons (1496–1561) was an itinerant Anabaptist preacher who stressed nonviolence during the initial persecution of the sect. Menno didn't found the Mennonites, but they adopted his less fanatical version of Anabaptism. Because of persecution, the Mennonites migrated from the Netherlands and northern Germany to Russia and, in the 1640s, the United States. They were pacifists and protested the use of slaves in America as early as 1688. One of their best-known sects is the **Amish,** who separated from the mainstream in Switzerland around 1690 under **Jacob Ammon,** who insisted on a stricter observance of rules. The strictest branch of Amish, the **Old Order Amish Mennonite Church,** insists on plainness of dress, furnishings, and meals, as depicted in the 1985 film *Witness*. The Mennonites who were banished from Russia in the 18th century by Czar Peter came to America, bringing with them a hardy strain of red wheat that became the mainstay of the American grain belt and that the czar's descendants have been forced to buy back from the U.S. ever since.

Baptists. In the early 17th century in England, several movements evolved among the Separatists seeking a connection to the simplicity of the early apostolic church. Insisting on the separate autonomy of each church and the equal voice of each believer, they used the New Testament as their only guide and denounced the practice of infant baptism as developed by the Catholic Church, insisting instead on believers' baptism. Baptists today continue to deny any human founder or creed. The first Baptists were led in exile in Holland by **John Smyth** (c. 1570–1612). When Smyth discovered the Dutch Mennonites and, determining that they were an authentic church, recommended joining with them, he was opposed by **Thomas Helwys** (c. 1560–1616). Helwys's followers returned to England and became known as **General** (or **Arminian**) **Baptists**, as opposed to others known as **Particular** (or **Calvinist**) **Baptists**. In the U.S., the Baptists' emphasis on autonomy played a role in ensuring religious freedom through separation of church and state in the Constitution and the First Amendment. Today the Baptists make up the largest single Protestant denomination in America (over 35 million adults), second only to Roman Catholics overall. Their largest subsect is the **Southern Baptist Convention.**

Methodists. A movement focusing on personal experience and social consciousness was begun by **John Wesley** (1703–91) and his brother **Charles** (1707–88), both Anglican priests. The name derived from their methodical observance of fasting and prayer time (they began amid a small group of like-minded students at Oxford University dubbed the "Bible Bigots"), although they also spent time visiting the sick, poor, and imprisoned and doing other charitable work. Influenced by the simplicity of Moravian Christians, John had a spiritual experience during a reading of one of Martin Luther's tracts, feeling his "heart strangely warmed." He set out with Charles, a gifted hymnist, to preach salvation to the working classes in churches and open fields. Charles's hymns— over 7,000 songs and poems—had as great an effect as John's preaching. In the words of one scholar, "Methodism began on a campus and reached for the masses." Although John envisioned his movement as a society within the fold of the Anglican church, shortly after his death the Methodists separated and formed their own church. In the U.S., the driving force of the **United Methodist Church** (the country's largest Methodist denomination, with nearly 10 million members) is the notion that Christian duty lies in taking a direct, active interest in the lives of the less fortunate, an attitude that has shaped the agenda of First Lady Hillary Rodham Clinton.

✳ THE COUNTER-REFORMATION

The Catholic church of Rome responded to all the reforms sweeping the land in contradictory ways: by seeking to reform itself while counterattacking (sometimes militarily) the new Protestants. A papal commission was created in 1536 to reform the abuses of the papacy, from simony and the sale of indulgences to countenancing Roman prostitution rings. The church convened the **Council of Trent** in three separate sessions over 18 years (1545–63) to answer the theological attacks of the Protestant reformers and to correct the abuses that the reformers had rightly pointed out. The council settled many of the doctrinal and dogmatic points on which modern, sometimes called **Post-Tridentine** (post–Council of Trent) Catholicism rests. It defined the church's right to interpret scripture, confirmed the doctrine of original sin, reaffirmed the church's right to administer the five sacraments not recognized by the reformers (confirmation, penance, extreme unction, matrimony, holy orders), and defined church laws regarding clerical celibacy, the sacrifice of the mass, justification by faith and works, and transubstantiation.

At the same time, the church formalized the Index of Prohibited Books, reinvigorated the Inquisition, and set out to reclaim certain lands lost to Protestantism. Through the Jesuit, Dominican, Franciscan, and Augustinian orders, Rome began sending out missionaries to the newly discovered world of the Americas, eventually converting much of Central and South America, the Philippines, and parts of Africa and Asia to the Roman Catholic religion before the Protestants could get to them.

But the struggle to preserve Christianity as the universal religion of Europe, uniting political with ecclesiastical power, was beginning to unravel. With Protestantism and Catholicism vying for dominance and so many sects now demanding recognition and autonomy, it was no longer possible or even desirable to burn all the heretics. Over the 17th and 18th centuries, religious toleration of a sort began to spread across England and the Continent and had already been firmly established in the American colonies. If no one religious viewpoint was any longer recognized as absolutely supreme and incontrovertible, the door was open for a more reasoned approach to worship and to life in general.

This new reasonableness, corresponding with the historical period known as the Enlightenment in Europe, helped to end the constant religious warfare and fanaticism that had wracked the Continent. But as the fears of hellfire and damnation abated among the populace, the ruling class began to worry that crime would rise and thus increased the penalties for most criminal acts. Rational Christianity was better suited to the new economic forces of capitalism that were developing. Ironically, however, it soon declined into a version of the old "mechanical Christianity" of the Catholic church—with its pragmatic balance sheets of rewards and punishments, sins and indulgences—against which the Protestant reformers had rebelled in the first place.

The potential of Christianity to be the universal religion not merely of Europe and America but of the world finally failed because of its inability or unwillingness to adapt itself to the culture and customs of peoples that its European progenitors found unacceptably strange—often but not exclusively on the basis of racial prejudice. And so if Catholic missionaries were able to convert much of Central and South America and the Philippines (at the cost of destroying the indigenous cultures they found there), they were unable significantly to penetrate the more formidable political, cultural, and religious traditions of India, China, and Japan.

✳ CHRISTIANITY'S NEW FRONTIER

Since the American colonies were settled mainly by Protestant reformers seeking religious freedom in the New World, Catholic missionaries had no place there (although Catholics themselves were welcome). Almost from the beginning, the colonies and later the United States were conceived as a secular state where nobody could be compelled to practice a particular form of Christianity—or any at all. This made the U.S. the first nation since the Dark Ages where Christianity could be practiced in a condition of genuine religious pluralism. Not only did Protestant sects of all description worship alongside Catholics, but Jews and later Muslims were also subsumed into the melting pot, according to the assumption that what really mattered was not the particularities of one's beliefs but merely that they were based on a substratum of Judeo-Christian ethics and morals.

Christianity in America at first followed the European divisions, except that for the most part people of all faiths were able to worship freely alongside one another. Over time, however, specifically American denominations took shape. Although they have since spread their versions of the Gospel abroad, these Christian sects, like jazz and the motion picture, remain distinctively American.

The Mennonites (including the subsect of the Amish), the Quakers, and the Shakers are better known in their American incarnations. The **Quak-**

ers (also **Society of Friends** or just **Friends,** shortened from Friends of Truth) developed from radical English Puritans in the mid-17th century,

MASS TRANSITION

Since the 2nd or 3rd century, the mass had been conceptualized as a form of divine sacrifice, either in commemoration of Christ's passion or as an offering in reparation for sins. But the 16th-century Council of Trent confirmed its nature as a conscious transmutation of the ancient concept of the blood sacrifice. According to the council, "Christ is contained in a bloodless sacrifice who on the altar of the cross once offered himself with the shedding of his blood: the holy Synod teaches that this sacrifice is truly propitiatory." In 1215, the church had officially declared that during the mass the bread and wine were transformed into the Body and Blood of Christ (**transubstantiation**); the consumption of the bread completed the parallel to blood sacrifices, in which the participants ate some part of the sacrificial animal. At Trent, the mass achieved much of the form it was to retain until the mid-20th century and became a distinguishing characteristic of the Catholic and Orthodox churches. Protestants have Sunday services, and some continue the practice of holy communion, but they do not celebrate the mass.

Latin had been the clerical and liturgical language of the Roman Catholic Church since the 4th century. It stopped being a spoken vernacular by the 8th century and ceased to be the sacred language of all Christianity in the mid-16th century, when the Protestant reformers began translating the Bible into English and German. But Latin remained one of the uniquely unifying features of Roman Catholicism until the **Second Vatican Council** of 1962–65 mandated that the mass be said in the vernacular (the language of a particular place, as English is the vernacular of the U.S.). The priest, who had previously said mass with his back to the congregation, now turned around to face the people; members of the faithful were invited to read portions of the service previously reserved only for the priest. The Orthodox church has always said mass in the vernacular, whether Greek, Russian, or other Slavic languages.

and the name implied trembling with awe before the word of God. Their leader was **George Fox** (1624–91) who, probably as a result of spending six years in squalid prisons for his opposition to established Christianity, moved the Quakers early on to pursue social justice causes. A mystic, Fox stressed the importance of seeking the "inner light" of the living Christ that he said exists equally in every human being. To escape persecution, they moved to America, where one of the their leaders, **William Penn,** established the colony of Pennsylvania. Quakers were among the first to oppose slavery in America, have always been antiwar, and run some of the most prestigious schools in the country, including Sidwell Friends School in Washington, D.C. Theologically, they reject the sacraments entirely, dress and speak simply, and practice a form of meditation.

The **Brethren** trace their roots back to the Brethren of the Common Life and early German **Pietists,** who cultivated an inner spiritual life through prayer, scripture study, and fellowship, rather than institutionalized dogma. More radical and less creedal or dogmatic than many Protestant sects, the Brethren also tended to be separatist, and many of them were forced to migrate to America to avoid persecution. The name Brethren exists in a number of related churches, all of which stress the warmth and kinship of the earliest Christians that the name implies. Spinoffs include the **Brethren in Christ** and the **River Brethren** (a Lancaster County, Pennsylvania, subsect). The **Dunkers,** also called **Tunkers** (from the German *tunken,* "to immerse"), **Täufers,** or **Dompelaars,** believe in baptism by triple immersion, once for each Person of the Trinity. They favor early Christian practices such as the **agape** ("love feast"), ceremonial foot washing, and the Lord's Supper. Like certain other radical sects, including Jehovah's Witnesses, most Brethren and Dunkers refuse to engage in warfare, lawsuits, or oath taking. Other sects are the **Brethren Church, Old German Baptist Brethren,** and **United Brethren.**

The **Shakers** (United Society of Believers in Christ's Second Appearing, also known as the Shaking Quakers) are an offshoot of the Quakers, having come to America in 1774 by way of England, led by **Mother Ann Lee** (d. 1784). They live in utopian congregations, practice celibacy even among married couples who join them (there is no marriage for Shakers), abstain from meat, fish, alcohol, and tobacco, and, perhaps not surprisingly, live unusually long and healthy lives. They traditionally engage in communal séances and wildly ecstatic, shaking dances, accompanied by laughing and barking. They practice an extremely simple way of life, and their furniture, known for its unadorned esthetic appeal, is still sought after by collectors. Mother Lee believed that God contains both male and female principles, as does Christ, who manifested as the male principle in Jesus and as the female principle in Mother Lee. Because of her concomitant belief that sexual intercourse is always sinful and her insistence on total celibacy, the sect is slowly dying out; a mere handful of Shakers remains. The Shakers weren't alone in being named for their heights of religious frenzy. Besides the Holy Rollers, there was also a sect of Welsh Methodists known as **Jumpers.**

Belief in the imminence of the Second Coming dates back to the earliest Christians, who expected Jesus to return during their lifetime. Since then, millennial or **millenarian** groups have been a part of the Christian spectrum, although many of the smaller ones have come and gone rather quickly when their predictions failed to materialize. The term **millennial** derives from the general belief that a 1,000-year period will follow the present age; different groups hold that Christ will reign over a perfected world either during or after this millennium. **Premillennialists** believe that Christ will return at the start of the millennium, when the dead will rise and the living faithful will be "raptured up" to join in his 1,000-year rule. **Postmillennialists** believe that Christ will not actually appear until after a millennium of peace and the triumph of Christianity. One millennial denomination that remains active after several transitions is the **Adventists,** founded by **William Miller,** a Baptist who began preaching around 1831 that Christ would return in 1843 and 1844. When Jesus didn't show, his prediction was labeled the "Great Disappointment," and Miller quit preaching. However, **Ellen G. Wright,** the main founder of **Seventh-day Adventism,** formed a new church from the disappointed followers of Miller. (For an intriguing connection to a Middle Eastern offshoot of Islam, see Bahai in Chapter 7.)

The preeminent millenarian group of modern times, however, is **Jehovah's Witnesses,** who continue to thrive despite the fact that their numerous predictions of the end of the world, which they first prophesied for 1914, then 1918, 1920, 1925, 1941, and 1975, have not come to pass. As conceived under the original name **Zion's Watch Tower Tract Society** by a Pittsburgh haberdasher named **Charles Taze Russell,** the group holds a distinctive belief not merely in the destruction of the damned (unbelievers) in Armageddon but also in the elevation to heaven of the 144,000 elect as predicted in the book of Revelation, to rule over the remaining faithful who will live eternally on a perfected earth. Theologically, the Witnesses are only marginally Christian, since they do not believe in the divinity of Christ, or in the existence of the soul separate from the body. They have virtually no devotional life but spend most of their energy proclaiming their message door to door. Within recent years, the Witnesses have ceased predicting the Second Coming at a specific date. Other failed predictions of note include that of the Pasadena-based **Worldwide Church of God,** which foretold that Christ would return to earth in 1975 after a nuclear holocaust.

A number of modern sects worldwide trace their origins to a break with the Roman Catholic Church following Vatican Council I of 1870, which proclaimed the doctrine of papal infallibility. Known collectively as the **Old Catholic Church,** they hold most of the beliefs, customs, and rituals of the Roman church but reject papal rule, priestly celibacy, and the doctrine of the Immaculate Conception, claiming that these and other papal teachings have created a "new" Catholic church. Some sects in America still say the mass in Latin at times. The **Liberal Catholic Church** grew out of a merger of Old Catholics and Theosophists* in England and California (1916–18) and incorporates elements of Eastern mysticism with a nondogmatic approach to Catholic theology—a mix that seems close to the early Gnostic sects.

The first Negro churches in America were branches of the Baptist church in the 18th and early 19th centuries, but the first to carry a reference to their racial origins were the **African Methodist Episcopal Church** in Philadelphia and the **African Methodist Episcopal Zion Church** in New York, known nowadays as the **A.M.E.** and **A.M.E. Zion** churches. But the largest black denominations in the country today are the **National Baptist Convention, U.S.A.** and the **National Baptist Convention of America.**

Rastafarianism, originating in Jamaica in the 1930s and popular among Jamaican immigrants in the U.S., has a very small membership among African Americans. But the popularity of reggae, the music that is as much a part of Rastafarian culture as the smoking of ganja (Jamaican marijuana, which they claim was used by Solomon*), has made

ST. JOHN'S AFRICAN ORTHODOX CHURCH: GOD IS A LOVE SUPREME

In 1919, an African American Episcopalian rector named **George Alexander McGuire** separated from the Episcopal church in the belief that black Episcopalians in North America should have their own church. Originally called Independent Episcopal, the church changed its name to the **African Orthodox Church** two years later. The AOC incorporates elements of Western and Eastern Orthodox liturgies and creeds, with the emphasis on Roman Catholic, Anglican, and Greek symbols and practices, including the seven sacraments and some remarriage after divorce. Membership, which now extends to Latin America and South Africa, is relatively small, measured in the U.S. only in the thousands. Yet the church traces its lineage to the Syrian Church of Antioch, where the term *Christian* was reportedly first used, and claims direct apostolic succession from St. Peter.

One branch church located in San Francisco, **St. John's**

African Orthodox Church, is uniquely African American in that it is named not for John the apostle or Evangelist but for **John Coltrane,** the great jazz saxophonist and composer who died in 1967. By his own admission, Coltrane underwent a spiritual awakening in 1957, after which he began to pursue the spiritual dimensions of his music in albums such as *Meditations, Om,* and *A Love Supreme,* embracing Eastern religious thought as well as Christian concepts. The church, which is known to its parishioners as the Church of St. John Coltrane, often includes the music and musings of Coltrane in its liturgy, offers programs of food, clothing, and shelter for the homeless (administered by the **Sisters of Compassion**), and free classes in music theory and instruction on reed instruments. **Bishop Franzo King,** a former hairdresser who founded the small storefront church two blocks from historic Haight Street, refers to Coltrane as the "Divine Sound Baptist." The church boasts a multiracial congregation and sponsors a radio show devoted to the compositions of St. John Coltrane.

Rastas seem more prominent than their numbers suggest. Reading deeper meaning into a verse of Psalm 68 ("Let Ethiopia hasten to stretch out her hands to God"), Jamaicans saw Ethiopia as the Promised Land; after Ethiopian prince (Ras) Tafari was crowned **Emperor Haile Selassie** (1892–1975) of Abyssinia in 1930, they developed a political agenda with millenarian overtones, aligning with the African nationalism of **Marcus Garvey** (1887–1940). Viewing Selassie as God incarnate, they are actually anti-Christian because of that religion's identification with the white man. But their songs often quote Old Testament texts and they identify especially with the Israelites of the Babylonian captivity. "The Rivers of Babylon" and "The Israelites" were both big reggae hits.

✷ THE AFRICAN DIASPORA

Several religions practiced primarily in Latin America and the Caribbean, but increasingly in the U.S., are syncretistic mergings of African religion and certain elements of Christianity. These syncretistic faiths have a number of aspects in common, but each is considered distinctive by its practitioners and should not be confused with the others. The one aspect they all share is that they embody the ancestral beliefs of African slaves who were brought to the New World against their will. Those beliefs were not acceptable to the European slave traders and owners, who often forced their own Christian beliefs on the slaves. Mainly Protestant beliefs were imposed on Africans who were taken to what became the United States and who evolved a version of Christianity that was similar in substance, if not in style, to the beliefs of their owners. But in the Caribbean and South America, where slave owners were mainly Catholic, the religion of the slaves retained much more of their African ancestral beliefs, concealed by or integrated with those of the slavemasters. The most widespread and influential of these religions—sometimes called diasporan in reference to the forced Diaspora* of the Jews from their homeland—are Vodou in Haiti, Candomblé in Brazil, and Santería in Cuba.

The integration of Catholic and African beliefs was not as unlikely as it might seem. Most of the slaves who were taken to Portuguese colonies in Brazil or to French or Spanish colonies in the West Indies such as Haiti and Cuba came from an area of West Africa that slave traders called the Mina or Slave Coast (modern Togo, Benin, Ghana, and part of Nigeria). A preponderance of them, especially in Brazil and Cuba, were members of the **Yoruba** (or **Nago**) people, who practiced a religion that made extensive use of animal sacrifice in which some portion of the sacrificial animal was consumed. It was not such a great leap, then, for the slaves to embrace elements of the Catholic religion, with its mass serving as a ritual commemoration of the blood sacrifice of Christ on the cross, during which his Body and Blood, in the form of bread and wine, are consumed by the faithful. The ancestral gods and goddesses of the Africans were identified with certain Catholic saints, a practice that continues today. Although religions such as Candomblé have risen from outlawed cult to officially recognized religion and concealment is no longer an issue, some elements of Catholicism remain embedded in them. Mainly, however, all these religions center on dances of spirit possession leading to trance states.

The best-known and the oldest of the diasporan religions is the Haitian tradition called **Vodou** (originally *Vaudoux* and later many different spellings of which the most familiar is *Voodoo).* The term *Vaudoux* was first applied in the late 18th century to a serpent god with oracular powers celebrated in a vigorous communal dance by slaves from Arada (a town in modern Benin). The word *vodou* is roughly analogous to "spirit" in the African language from which it derived. (Most terms in Vodou are Creole, the language of Haiti that combines a variation of French with some West African and Spanish terms and is related to but not the same as the patois spoken by the Creoles of New Orleans.)

In Vodou and other African-derived religions in the New World, the spirits are not conceived as single entities but as combinations of personalities with several related identities. Some Vodou services are held to honor a spirit called a **lwa** or **loa** (called an *orisha* in Santería or *orixá* in Candomblé) on the feast day of the equivalent Catholic saint. The senior loa is Danballa, a form of the West African snake god who is identified with St. Patrick, traditionally said to have driven the snakes out of Ireland. **Ogou,** the Yoruban god of hunting, became in Haiti **Ogoun** or **Ogun,** the loa of iron and war, and is identified with the apostle James the Greater or Elder. **Xangô** or **Shango,** the Yoruban god of fire and thunder, transmogrified to St. Barbara, the Catholic martyr.

There are some 400 or so lesser spirits or loas, but one major spirit. The Yoruban religion on which many of the diasporan rites are based centers on what scholars call a **deus otiosus** (Lat. "inactive deity"), who is not involved in the day-to-day workings of creation. This deity the Yorubans call **Olorun** or **Olodumare,** the ruler of the universe; West Indians refer to him as the **Gran Met,** derived from the French for "great master." The lesser spirits partake of the abstract Godhead as various concrete manifestations. In addition, individual practitioners may have a **met tet** (Cr. "master of the head") who functions something like a patron saint.

Most Vodou rites still begin with a series of Catholic prayers including the Our Father, Hail Mary, and some variation of the Nicene Creed, recited in French by the **presavann** (Cr. "bush priest"), who is in charge of Catholic liturgical elements. But after this rather formal beginning, the language changes to Creole and the African elements come to the fore, including ecstatic dancing and drumming. As much as anything, Vodou is an ancestral religion meant to evoke the African homeland. Many of the rites are long and arduous, lasting several days and involving great personal privations aimed at opening the heart and mind of the initiate to the spirits. In that regard, Vodou is not so different from many Eastern religions that may require fasting, ascetical practices, and long bouts of chanting, meditation, and other practices designed to short-circuit the rational faculties and prepare the heart for enlightenment.

As practiced today, Vodou bears no resemblance to the religion of zombies, curses, voodoo dolls, and other fanciful, racist hokum cooked up by Hollywood movies and third-rate thrillers. It is, however, intimately tied up with the Haitian struggle against slavery, something which the colonial powers doubtless found as horrifying as any night of the living dead. As far back as 1791, slaves gathered in the north of Haiti where they sacrificed a wild boar to their ancestral gods and swore to overthrow the French slaveowners. Two years later, slavery was abolished in what was then called Saint Domingue, and in 1804 the republic of Haiti was formed, the first of the colonized lands of the New World to recognize the right of all to equality without distinction of color or creed, almost 60 years before the U.S. Emancipation Proclamation.

Candomblé is the generic name for a number of African religious traditions established by the slaves in 19th-century Brazil, specifically in the region of Bahia. (In the southeast it is called **Macumba;** Rio de Janeiro's sect is known as **Umbanda.**) The term *candomblé* refers to the community of devotees, the consecrated area where their rites take place, and to the dances that make up a large part of the religion. In some cases, freed slaves who returned to their African homeland and became initiated as priestesses or priests in their religion brought back to Brazil the spiritual powers they had acquired. The leading figures in Candomblé are women, especially senior women who direct the practice and pass it on to new initiates.

Spirits are called **orixás,** the equivalent of the orishas of Santería and the loas of Vodou. The spirits may become incorporated in human mediums who, in language similar not only to Christianity but to all the great traditions, must die to ordinary life and be reborn in a new life of the spirit. The Candomblé priesthood provides a wide range of counseling and therapeutic services to the community—of great value in many parts of Brazil where no conventional medical or psychological services are available.

The center of Candomblé is the city of Salvador da Bahia, also known for its great percussionists, who have played a major role in the development of Brazilian musical forms known as samba, Tropicalia, and axé, a mixture of samba and reggae whose name is taken from a Candomblé term for divine power or the objects channeling that power. Unlike the Haitians, the Africans of Bahia remained enslaved until their emancipation in 1888. Nonetheless, Candomblé has recently achieved the status of an official religion; priestesses and priests no longer need a police permit to perform ceremonies, and demands by the priesthood to remove images of the orixás from the annual Bahian Carnaval were upheld by the government.

Santería (Sp. "way of the saints") is the name given to the complex intermixture of Yoruban and Catholic beliefs and practices in Cuba, blending prayer, mysticism, and ritual animal sacrifice. Santería developed over the past 200 years in Cuba, but with the exodus of over a million Cubans following the Cuban revolution of 1959, it has spread to Canada and the United States. There it has been embraced by several hundred thousand Cuban emigrants and other members of the Caribbean American community and is spreading to other African American and Hispanic communities as well. Priestesses and priests are known respectively as **santeras** and **santeros** (the Spanish form of their Lucumi, or Cuban Yoruba, names, *iyalorisha* and *babalorisha*).

In the words of the scholar Joseph M. Murphy, "Santería is a way of interaction with the *orishas,* the elemental powers of life. By speaking, feasting, and dancing with the *orishas,* human beings are brought to worldly success and heavenly wisdom. Santería is the spiritual road the Yoruba developed in Cuba. It sustained them through slavery and freedom and continues to sustain them in the harsh world of urban America." But Santería is probably best known in America not for its elaborate spiritual disciplines or its interaction with the spirits but for its celebration of birth, marriage, and death by rites that include the ritual sacrifice (by decapitation) of goats, chickens, doves, and turtles, often more than a dozen of each at a given ceremony. Once their blood has been drained into clay pots (reminiscent of ancient Israelite practices), the animals are either cooked and eaten or buried in the earth. The religion was forced underground in Castro's Cuba and was practiced secretly for many years in America, mainly by Cuban exiles settled in Florida, before going public some years ago. However, the right of Santería believers to ritually slaughter animals has been attacked in the courts, despite the fact that one can freely boil lobsters for dinner, kill animals for food or sport, and destroy unwanted pets with impunity. The right of Santería's faithful to sacrifice animals was upheld in 1993 by the U.S. Supreme Court, which voided a Hialeah, Florida, city council law forbidding the practice.

Some African Americans who have been seeking out what is specifically African about their heritage have begun to look more closely at Santería and the other diasporan religions (Vodou and Candomblé being much less prevalent in the U.S.). Exploring beneath the surfaces presented by the mass media and the entertainment industries, they are beginning to find a rich trove not only of ancestral material but also of valid and useful spiritual guidelines.

✳ HOME GROWN RELIGIONS: MORMONISM AND CHRISTIAN SCIENCE

With between 3 and 4 million faithful, Mormons make up one of the larger American denominations, just ahead of Episcopalians and Pentecostals. They have aroused controversy because of charges that they keep secret dossiers on members who criticize church policies and discriminate financially against those who leave or denounce the church. Based in Utah, Mormonism has used its army of young missionaries to spread the faith across the country and around the world.

In 1830 **Joseph Smith** of New York published the **Book of Mormon,** claiming he had translated the text from a set of golden plates given to him by the angel **Moroni,** son of **Mormon.** The book is a Bible-flavored account of God's intervention in the history of America's ancient inhabitants, said to be descended from the Israelites and other biblical tribes who crossed the sea from the Tower of Babel in barges to become the ancestors of the American Indians. Christ figures in the 500-page text

(Smith also claimed visions of Jesus and God the Father), which enraged the local Christians enough that Smith and his followers were forced to flee to Ohio, Missouri, and then Illinois, where Smith was lynched by a mob in 1844. **Brigham Young** (1801–77) succeeded him as the group's leader and in 1847 led most of the sect to the Salt Lake basin in Utah, where the **Church of Jesus Christ of Latter-day Saints** (so called by Smith because he claimed to be returning Christianity to its original state) found a permanent home. The Mormon practice of polygamy (or, more accurately, polygyny) so incensed other Christians that they were forced to abandon it in 1890 to win statehood for Utah, a decision known as the **Great Accommodation.** However, in 1985 Michael Quinn, a Yale-educated Mormon scholar, discovered evidence that Mormon leaders continued the practice secretly for another 14 years. (The **Reorganized Church of Latter Day Saints,** a splinter group of Mormons centered around a descendant of Joseph Smith in Independence, Missouri, rejected polygyny early on. They boast about a quarter of a million members today.)

Mormons believe in the doctrine of **continuous revelation,** meaning that the Book of Mormon and two other works, *Doctrine and Covenants* and *The Pearl of Great Price,* are legitimate additions to the Bible, which they also accept. Apart from the early flirtation with polygyny, Mormons embrace a moral code similar to that of the most conservative Christian sects (tobacco, alcohol, and gambling are strictly forbidden), but some of their dogma is unique and places them well outside the Christian mainstream. For instance, they believe that God the Father is a male being of flesh and bones, that Jesus Christ is God but that men may become gods and many in fact have done so, existing in a complex level of spiritual worlds. Marriages that have been "sealed" continue to exist after death, when families are reunited in the afterworld. The church expects two years of missionary service from male members when they turn 19. Women are allowed but not encouraged to be missionaries. And as in the Roman Catholic Church, Mormon women have begun agitating for the right to become bishops—the Mormon equivalent of priests or ministers—an office that is currently closed to them, as it was to black men until a 1978 revelation. Paradoxically, a long-established Mormon doctrine holds that the spiritual parents of humanity included a female as well as a male Deity, a belief that is emphasized by a still-popular hymn written in 1843 by **Eliza Snow,** a major church figure who supported equal rights for women. The hymn, "Oh, My Father," includes the lines

In the Heavens are parents single?
No . . .
Truth eternal
Tells me I've a Mother there.

In recent years, amid the growing cry for equal treatment of women within Mormonism, the church has severely disciplined or excommunicated several Mormon scholars and feminists. Nonetheless, the Mormon church continues to be one of the fastest growing in the world, and the Book of Mormon is among the ten most popular books in America. (Like the Gideon Bible, it is now carried in the Marriott hotel chain.)

One American-born religion of note that shows no ostensible discrimination against women is **Christian Science,** the only major religion in the U.S. founded by a woman. Although its membership is small, well under a million, its highly respected media arms (the *Christian Science Monitor* newspaper and Monitor Radio) and its radical teachings regarding healing have kept its name in the public eye. Yet its precise origins remain somewhat mysterious.

Born into a staunchly Calvinist New England family, **Mary Baker Eddy** (1821–1910) rejected the notion of predestination embraced by her father, although she remained a member of the Congregational Church until she founded her own church. Mrs. Eddy suffered early on from convulsive fits (possibly from an inflamed gallbladder); in midlife her fits, combined with a series of personal losses (her brother, husband, and mother died and her young son was put into foster care within the same decade), left her near death, almost a total invalid. Suspecting a mental rather than physical element to sickness, she explored alternative healing practices like homeopathy* and hypnotic suggestion. A hypnotist and healer from Maine named Phineas Quimby* (1802–66), who believed that the mind could both cause and cure disease, helped to relieve her pain for a time. But shortly after he died, Mrs. Eddy became deathly ill following a nasty fall. After reading and meditating on a Bible account of Christ's miraculous healing, Mrs. Eddy was healed, and she "gained the scientific certainty that all causation was Mind, and every effect a mental phenomenon." She expounded that essential inference in all her later works, as in her assertion that "the only logical conclusion is that all is Mind and its manifestation, from the rolling of worlds, in the most subtle ether, to a potato-patch."

Over the next several years, Mrs. Eddy wrote her interpretation of the Bible, entitled *Science and Health with Key to the Scriptures* (1875), explaining that Jesus taught "our dominion over matter" and that spirit was the sole reality of existence. She claimed that her work was directly inspired by God, but reportedly asked a clergyman to help with the grammar. In 1879, she organized the **First Church of Christ, Scientist** in Boston; the Mother Church was built there in 1894 and later expanded.

Because Christian Scientists believe that evil and illness exist only in the mind, they rely on specially trained members called **practitioners,** who help other members heal injuries or disease through prayer, thought, and reading. The prayers are tailored to each situation and are based on the King James Bible, *Science and Health,* and other writings by Mary Baker Eddy, and the practitioner does not need to deliver them face to face. The practitioner is not believed to have healing powers, but rather helps the patient turn to God as the source of healing. Medical intervention is not necessarily forbidden, but is not encouraged, since it is said to interfere with spiritual healing.

Because of their controversial beliefs about healing, in recent years a number of Christian Scientists have been brought up on criminal charges, and several convicted, when their children died after receiving treatment through prayer rather than through conventional medical care. One Boston couple, for example, was convicted in 1990 of manslaughter in the death of their two-year-old son who became ill in 1986 because of a bowel obstruction and died five days later. However, all guilty verdicts have been overturned on appeal. In another case, the Delaware Supreme Court ruled that a Christian Scientist couple had the right to reject chemotherapy to treat cancer in their three-year-old son. Furthermore, spiritual healing is recognized by law. Christian Science practitioners' charges are paid by many large private insurance companies, and some Christian Science sanatoriums are providers of care under Medicare. The fees charged by practitioners, nurses, and sanatoriums are deductible as medical expenses from federal income taxes.

Some Christian theologians contend that Christian Science does not represent orthodox Christianity because it does not believe in the divinity of the man Jesus. However, Christian Scientists do understand Jesus Christ to be the Son of God, the Redeemer, and they accept the Gospel accounts that he was born of a virgin, was crucified, rose from the grave, and then ascended. In *Science and Health,* Mrs. Eddy writes, "The Divinity of the Christ was made manifest in the humanity of Jesus," implying some separation between the human and divine natures of Jesus Christ, whereas most Christians insist that both natures are united—that Jesus was "true God and true man." Christian Scientists see the Christ as an eternal principle, which sounds a little like the concept of the Indian avatar*. At other times Christian Science bears a resemblance to the Eastern philosophy of relative and absolute truth, as when it says that (on the level of absolute truth) there is no reality except Mind or Spirit and everything material—sickness, death, sin—is unreality, and yet (on a relative level) because humanity has not fully grasped or accepted that God or Mind is All, people do appear to become sick and die, and they rely on marriage, food, money, and other material necessities. But since Christian Scientists believe that Jesus Christ is the Redeemer, that the cross is the central element in human history, and that humanity's spiritual, God-given identity is indestructible and eternal, it would be difficult to exclude them from the Christian tradition.

Christian Scientists accept the word of Mrs. Eddy as final; no new teachings can enter the church. And so there is no preaching or sermonizing in the traditional sense. Each church has a First and Second Reader elected by the congregation who read selections of Scripture accompanied by selections from *Science and Health* without commentary or explanation. Members can and do share testimonies of healings that have taken place in their lives and sing hymns, some of them written by Mrs. Eddy.

❋ BORN-AGAIN IN THE U.S.A.

The differences between the designations of fundamentalist and born-again Christians are often blurred. **Born-again Christians,** who now number somewhere between 30 and 50 million Americans, have gone through an adult conversion experience in which they took Jesus Christ as their personal savior. The born-again experience is typically, although not always, preceded by a period of living by less than exemplary moral standards, after which the believer is "rescued" by the Lord and is called to regenerate his or her life. However, not all born-again Christians can be defined as fundamentalists.

When empirical philosophy was applied to biblical criticism during the 19th century, one result was to split Christians between those who could accept the Bible, especially the New Testament, as essentially metaphorical and those who clung to the old ways of thinking and insisted that every word of the Bible was literally true. Around the turn of the 20th century, the latter group came together at a nationwide series of revival meetings that culminated in the formulation of certain "fundamentals" of Christian belief, including biblical **inerrancy**, (literal interpretation of the Bible), belief in the Virgin Birth and the Second Coming of Christ, the notion that Jesus died to redeem humankind, and **apocalypticism**, the belief that the end of the world and the Second Coming of Christ are imminent. By definition, fundamentalists believe in some form of **creationism,** the doctrine that the universe was created a few thousand years ago, based on the biblical account, rather than the billions of years claimed by modern science, and that God created man and woman and all the species outright rather than by a process of evolution. (Creationists differ over how to explain fossil records that "appear" to be millions of years old. Some believe that God created them that way on purpose.)

Fundamentalism, the adherence to these fundamentals of Christianity, grew at least in part out of a desire to return to the days of a less ethnically and religiously diverse America, a less troubled time that predated not only the empirical approach to biblical criticism but also the influx of large numbers of immigrants from Southern Europe and the Mediterranean rim, mainly Roman Catholics and Jews. For these reasons, some fundamentalists tend to be intolerant of those who practice "modernized" or less rigorous forms of the same religion (something that is true to some extent of *all* religious fundamentalists, including Muslims, Sikhs, and Jews) and lobby to have their beliefs, including creationism, taught in public schools. They may also be rigidly conservative in their politics and unemotional in their practice. **Jerry Falwell,** who rose to fame as founder of the since disbanded Moral Majority, is a quintessentially Fundamentalist Baptist minister. However, it's important to note that national polls have indicated that as few as one-third of Americans who identify themselves as born-again Christians align themselves with the so-called Religious Right, which is dominated by politically active fundamentalists.

The term evangelist originally referred to the proclaimers of the "good news" (Gr. *evangel*) of Christ's teaching, mainly the apostles. But by the end of the 2nd century the term was applied to the four authors of the Gospels (Anglo-Saxon for "good tidings"), and **evangelism** to any form of conversion-oriented preaching. During the Protestant Reformation, the title Evangelical reflected Luther's emphasis on returning to the Gospel message itself, unencumbered by church doctrine. Today, the Lutheran church in Germany and several Lutheran sects in the U.S. have the word *Evangelical* in their names. But the most common application of *Evangelical* developed around the turn of the twentieth century in the U.S. among conservative fundamentalists within the Methodist, Baptist, Congregational, and Presbyterian churches and Pentecostal and Holiness sects. They emphasized preaching, reading the Bible, and personal spiritual experience, rather than the mediation of an organized clerical class or sacramental grace.

Evangelicals, as they call themselves, tend to favor warmth and emotionalism over formality, and despite their earlier association with fundamentalism, the latter's approach is subscribed to by only a minority fringe of Evangelicals today (specifically associated with **Bob Jones University** and the **American Council of Christian Churches**). Evangelicals may oppose worldliness, but not necessarily with the political narrowness and intolerance of fundamentalists in general. In a modern context, it's safe to say that the term *Evangelical* refers to Protestant religions that conform to the earliest teachings of the New Testament, apart from their interpretation by the Church Fathers and the apostolic succession of popes and bishops. Evangelicals do accept historic **Trinitarianism,** the belief in the three Persons of the Trinity (Father, Son, and Holy Spirit), differentiating the group from Christian Scientists, Mormons, and Jehovah's Witnesses. A number of Evangelical churches practice an emotional religion; many former Catholics have become Evangelicals, attracted by their more ecstatic approach to worship. But at least 14 kinds of Evangelicalism have been identified in the U.S., from conservative (including perennial evangelist **Billy Graham**) to charismatic (typified by **Oral Roberts**). Some confusion may stem from the fact that *Evangelical* is often used as a label rather than the name of a denomination. The word appears in the names of some conservative, mainline Protestant churches such as Episcopalian, Lutheran, and Presbyterian, whereas many other churches that consider themselves Evangelical do not use the word at all.

Pentecostalists or **Pentecostals** are fundamentalist Protestants who emphasize being born again in the (Holy) Spirit, often accompanied by speaking in tongues (**glossolalia**) and **faith healing** (or healing by laying on of hands). The Pentecostal movement began in the U.S. around 1900, taking its name from the descent of the Holy Spirit upon the apostles at Pentecost, enabling them to speak in foreign tongues. The largest Pentecostal churches are the **Assemblies of God**, the **Church of God**, the **Church of God in Christ** (the largest black Pentecostal sect), and the **International Church of the Foursquare Gospel**, founded by famed faith healer **Aimee Semple McPherson** (1890–1944), who is generally considered the first radio evangelist.

Most Pentecostals would probably consider themselves Evangelical, whereas not all Evangelicals are Pentecostal. Pentecostal and some Evangelical prayer meetings are likely to include hand-clapping, spontaneous prayer and testimony, glossolalia, faith healing, and upraised arms accompanied by shouts of "Praise the Lord!" When Jerry Falwell took control of the Evangelical sect **PTL** (for "Praise the Lord") during the much-publicized scandal in which **Jim Bakker** was convicted of pocketing millions of dollars in contributions, Bakker's followers objected. Falwell's dour fundamentalist style did not jibe with Bakker's more emotional, Evangelical one. In its extreme form, a small sect of Evangelicals became known as **Holy Rollers** because of their custom of thrashing about on the floor during their services, although the term has been applied generically and pejoratively to other demonstrative sects.

The widespread success of the Pentecostal and Evangelical sects has led Roman Catholic and mainline Protestant churches to accept within their own denominations **charismatic** movements that foster an emotionally charged atmosphere in the context of otherwise orthodox worship services.

Televangelists, who preach over the airwaves or cable TV and survive on mail-in contributions, don't belong to a specific sect, but are almost always born again. Some of them, like **Pat Robertson,** use their electronic pulpits to attempt to influence political events (or meteorological ones— Robertson once asked viewers to pray for the diversion of a hurricane that was bearing down on his Virginia headquarters and then thanked

SNAKE HIGHS

Extreme forms of Pentecostal fervor have sprung up from time to time in the U.S., in some cases adding the handling of poisonous snakes (usually various kinds of rattlesnakes) to the standard repertoire of speaking in tongues and laying on of hands. A cult of snake handlers founded in 1909 in Tennessee by G. W. Hensley spread across the Southeast through the 1940s, capturing national attention in 1948 when an interstate conference of snake handlers was held in Durham, N.C., to the obvious chagrin of local police. The snake handlers based their practices on the lines attributed to Jesus in the disputed final verses of the Gospel of Mark (16:17–18): "And these signs will accompany those who believe: they will speak in new tongues; they will pick up serpents, and if they drink any deadly thing, it will not hurt them; they will lay their hands on the sick, and they will recover." (The verses do not appear in all surviving manuscripts; the King James Version uses them, but the Revised Standard Version adds them as a footnote.)

One anthropologist described a typical snake-handling church as an independent fundamentalist sect that

. . . forbids theater-going, dancing, smoking, drinking, immodest dress, and the cutting of women's hair. . . . The men call each other "saints," hug and kiss each other with the greeting, "How are you, Honey?" [At a church meeting,] cymbals, tambourines, foot-stamping, and hand-clapping provided the rhythm for the worshipers who, men and women both, passed serpents from hand to hand while jerking violently all over their bodies. One man thrust a snake before a seated woman holding a baby; the woman smiled and the baby gravely reached forward and touched the snake. . . . Fire-handling by male saints was also performed: their hands, held in the flames of a kerosene torch and a miner's acetylene lamp, were blackened by smoke but otherwise appeared unhurt.

—WESTON LA BARRE, *THEY SHALL TAKE UP SERPENTS*

God when it did its damage on another part of the coastline). Others, like Oral Roberts, merely raise large sums of money and endow colleges and universities named after them. **Robert Tilton,** whose Dallas-based television ministry has been the subject of media exposés and an IRS investigation for fraud, talks in tongues and practices faith healing over the tube.

Most of those televangelists preach a traditional gospel of sin and repentance, which makes them all the more susceptible to charges of personal immorality. **Jimmy Swaggart** lost much of his following when it was discovered that he had used the services of a Florida prostitute. But the most successful electronic evangelist in America, at least from a ratings point of view, is **Robert Schuller,** whose "Hour of Power" is ranked first among religious broadcasts by both Nielsen and Arbitron, with about 1½ million viewers and listeners in 50 nations. Schuller preaches a sunny gospel from his Crystal Cathedral in southern California, borrowing from Norman Vincent Peale's* "Power of Positive Thinking" approach to religion with something he calls "possibility thinking." Schuller's sayings, such as "Dream Your Way to Unending Success," and his characterization of the resurrection as Jesus' "comeback" and of salvation as the ultimate "success" place him firmly in the school of modern preachers who see Christianity as a vehicle to personal prosperity. Since Jesus taught the inner joy of finding the Kingdom of God without respect to one's material well-being, many observers question whether what Schuller is preaching has any relationship to Christ at all.

371

AND MUCH, MUCH MORE

According to a 1993 Gallup poll, only 4 percent of Americans describe themselves as atheists or agnostics. Of the remaining 96 percent, an overwhelming 82 percent said they are Christians: Protestant, Roman Catholic, Eastern Orthodox, or unaffiliated. But whereas the Catholic and Orthodox churches have remained relatively monolithic, Protestants have splintered into countless denominations and individual churches. The seven traditionally liberal denominations that make up most of so-called **mainline Protestantism** are the Episcopal Church, the Presbyterian Church (U.S.A.), the United Methodist Church, the American Baptist Churches, the United Church of Christ, the Christian Church (Disciples of Christ), and the Evangelical Lutheran Church in America. But even those represent only a fraction of all Protestant sects, and their membership has declined sharply over the last 25 years, siphoned off into newer, often Pentecostal sects. What follows is an alphabetical listing of most of the denominations currently active in this country. Those in boldface caps are generic denominations, followed by their branches.

ADVENTIST
- Advent Christian Church
- Church of God General Conference
- Seventh-day Adventist

African Orthodox Church
Amana Church Society
American Ethical Union
American Evangelical Christian Churches
American Rescue Workers
Anglican Orthodox Church
Apostolic Christian Church (Nazarene)
Apostolic Christian Church of America
Apostolic Faith
Apostolic Overcoming Holy Church of God
Armenian Church
BAPTIST
- American Baptist Association
- American Baptist Churches in the U.S.A.
- Baptist Bible Fellowship, International
- Baptist General Conference
- Baptist Missionary Association of America

Bethel Ministerial Association
Black Baptist
Central Baptist Association
Conservative Baptist Association of America
Duck River (and Kindred) Associations of Baptists
Free Will Baptist
General Association of Regular Baptist Churches
General Baptist
General Conference of the Evangelical Baptist Church
Landmark Baptist
National Primitive Baptist Convention of the U.S.A.
North American Baptist Conference
Primitive Baptist
Reformed Baptist
Separate Baptists in Christ
Seventh Day Baptist General Conference
Southern Baptist Convention
Two-Seed-in-the-Spirit Predestinarian Baptist
United Baptist
United Free Will Baptist Church
Berean Fundamental Church
Bible Fellowship Church
Bible Protestant Church
Bible Way Church, Worldwide
BRETHREN
   DUNKERS
      Brethren Church, Ashland
      Church of the Brethren
      Fellowship of Grace Brethren Churches
      Old German Baptist Brethren (Old Order Dunkers)
   RIVER BRETHREN
      Brethren in Christ Church
      United Zion Church
   UNITED BRETHREN
      Church of the United Brethren in Christ
Christadelphian
The Christian and Missionary Alliance
Christian Catholic Church
Christian Church (Disciples of Christ)
Christian Church of North America, General Council
Christian Churches and Churches of Christ
Christian Congregation
Christian Union

Church of Christ (Holiness) U.S.A.
Church of Christ, Scientist
CHURCH OF GOD
   The Church of God (Huntsville, Alabama)
   The (Original) Church of God
   The Church of God (Seventh Day)
   Church of God and Saints of Christ
   Church of God by Faith, Inc.
   Church of God in Christ
   Church of God of Prophesy
Church of Illumination
Church of Jesus Christ
Church of Our Lord Jesus Christ of the Apostolic Faith
Church of the Nazarene
Churches of Christ
Churches of Christ in Christian Union
Churches of God, General Conference
Churches of God, Holiness
Churches of the Living God
International Council of Community Churches
Congregational Bible Churches
Congregational Christian Churches
Congregational Holiness Church
Conservative Congregational Christian Conference
EPISCOPAL
   Episcopal Church
   Reformed Episcopal Church
Evangelical Church
Evangelical Congregational Church
Evangelical Covenant Church
Evangelical Free Church of America
Fire-Baptized Holiness Church
International Church of the Foursquare Gospel
Free Christian Zion Church of Christ
FRIENDS (Quakers)
   Friends General Conference
   Friends United Meeting (Five Years Meeting)
   Religious Society of Friends (Conservative)
Grace Gospel Fellowship
Independent Fundamental Churches of America
Jehovah's Witnesses
Kodesh Church of Immanuel
LATTER-DAY SAINTS (Mormon)

Church of Christ (Temple Lot)
Church of Jesus Christ (Bickertonites)
Church of Jesus Christ of Latter-day Saints
Church of Jesus Christ of Latter Day Saints (Strangite)
Reorganized Church of Jesus Christ of Latter Day Saints
Liberal Catholic Church

LUTHERAN

Apostolic Lutheran Church of America
The Association of Free Lutheran Congregations
Church of the Lutheran Brethren
Church of the Lutheran Confession
Evangelical Lutheran Church in America
Evangelical Lutheran Synod
Lutheran Church—Misouri Synod
Protestant Conference (Lutheran)
Wisconsin Evangelical Lutheran Synod

MENNONITE

Beachy Amish Mennonite Churches
Church of God in Christ, Mennonite
Conservative Mennonite Conference
Evangelical Mennonite Church
Fellowship of Evangelical Bible Churches
General Conference Mennonite Church
Hutterian Brethren
Mennonite Brethren Church of North America
Mennonite Church
Old Order Amish Church
Old Order (Wisler) Mennonite Church
Reformed Mennonite Church
Unaffiliated Mennonite

METHODIST

African Methodist Episcopal Church (A.M.E.)
African Methodist Episcopal Zion Church (A.M.E. Zion)
Christian Methodist Episcopal Church
Congregational Methodist Church
Evangelical Methodist Church
First Congregational Methodist Church of the U.S.A.
Free Methodist Church of North America
Primitive Methodist Church, U.S.A.
Reformed Methodist Union Episcopal Church
Reformed Zion Union Apostolic Church
Southern Methodist Church
Union American Methodist Episcopal Church

United Methodist Church
Universal Fellowship of Metropolitan Community Churches
Missionary Church
MORAVIAN
Moravian Church *(Unitas Fratrum)*
Unity of the Brethren
New Apostolic Church of North America
OLD CATHOLIC
American Independent Old Catholic Church
Mariavite Old Catholic Church
North American Old Roman Catholic Churches
Old Roman Catholic Church (English Rite)
Open Bible Standard Churches
ORTHODOX (EASTERN)
Albanian Orthodox Archdiocese in America
American Carpatho-Russian Orthodox Greek Catholic Church
American Holy Orthodox Catholic Eastern Church
Antiochian Orthodox Christian Archdiocese of North America
Bulgarian Eastern Orthodox Church
Greek Orthodox Archdiocese of North and South America
Romanian Orthodox Episcopate of America
Russian Orthodox Church
Serbian Eastern Orthodox Church in the U.S.A. and Canada
Syrian Orthodox Church of Antioch
Ukrainian Orthodox Churches
PENTECOSTAL
General Council of Assemblies of God
Elim Fellowship
Emmanuel Holiness Church
International Independent Assemblies of God
International Pentecostal Church of Christ
Pentecostal Assemblies of the World
Pentecostal Church of God
Pentecostal Free-Will Baptist Church
Pentecostal Holiness Church, International
United Pentecostal Church International
Pillar of Fire
Plymouth Brethren
Polish National Catholic Church of America
PRESBYTERIAN
Associate Reformed Presbyterian Church
Bible Presbyterian Church
Cumberland Presbyterian Church

Orthodox Presbyterian Church
The Presbyterian Church in America
Presbyterian Church (U.S.A.)
Reformed Presbyterian Church of North America
Second Cumberland Presbyterian Church in the United States

REFORMED

Christian Reformed Church in North America
Hungarian Reformed Church in America
Netherlands Reformed Congregations
Protestant Reformed Churches in America
Reformed Church in America
Reformed Church in the United States

Roman Catholic Church
Salvation Army
Schwenkfelder Church
Social Brethren
Triumph the Church and Kingdom of God in Christ
Unitarian Universalist Association

UNITED CHURCH OF CHRIST

Congregational Church
Christian Churches
Evangelical Church
The Reformed Church in the U.S.

United Holy Church of America
Unity School of Christianity
Volunteers of America
The Wesleyan Church
Worldwide Church of God

—FROM FRANK S. MEAD (REV. BY SAMUEL S. HILL), *HANDBOOK OF DENOMINATIONS IN THE UNITED STATES*

INSIDE A CATHOLIC CHURCH

In reacting to the corruption and abuses of power within the Roman church, the Protestant Reformation managed to strip the church of many of its most appealing artistic, architectural, and ritualistic accretions. Many interesting examples of Protestant architecture do exist (for example, St. Thomas Episcopal Church in New York City, just a few blocks up Fifth Avenue from St. Patrick's). But for the most part, Protestant churches are, by definition, simplified and generally devoid of statuary;

most of the great cathedrals and churches were built either before the Reformation or by the Catholic and Orthodox churches afterward. One sure way to distinguish a Catholic from a Protestant church is that Catholics feature the **crucifix** (Christ on the cross), and Protestants use a bare cross.

All churches are supposed to be **cruciform,** i.e., built in the approximate shape of a cross. The focus of attention is the **altar,** where the main ritual of the mass takes place (in most Protestant churches, the focus is the **pulpit,** from which the minister gives a sermon). After the Second Vatican Council (1962–65), the altar was turned around to face the congregation, as it had been in the earliest churches. The longitudinal area, or **nave,** reaching from the front door to the **chancel** or **sacristy** behind the altar, consists of a center aisle flanked by rows of **pews** and is crossed by a **transept.** A choir loft and pipe organ in the rear of the nave is a common feature of larger churches, as is a steeple with one or more bells. Stained-glass windows with images of the saints and the Blessed Mother are common, along with the **Stations of the Cross,** a series of 14 statues or bas reliefs lining the walls on either side of the nave, each depicting an event in the passion and death of Jesus: e.g., station number 6, Veronica wipes Christ's bloody face with her veil (and, according to legend, comes away with a visible imprint of his features). Confessional booths are generally located in the back of the nave, with a poor box and holy water font in the vestibule.

Christian holy days are not celebrated in the U.S. with the same level of festivity as they are in Europe or other parts of the world, nor do most of them carry the familial and cultural significance for Christians that Jewish holidays have for observant Jews. Moreover, the Christian holidays that are celebrated in a big way—Christmas and Easter—have been absorbed into the secular mainstream to the point where their religious significance sometimes seems overwhelmed by rampant commercialism. Devout Christians sometimes complain about this secularization, with slogans like "Keep Christ in Christmas." But this is somewhat ironic, since it is fairly well known that the Christian holidays were designed by the early church to supplant non-Christian celebrations occurring at the same spot in the calendar.

As described earlier, Christmas, also called the feast of the **Nativity,** substituted the birth of Christ for the birth of the Sun at the winter solstice combined with the Roman Saturnalia. Easter was celebrated probably as early as the 1st century in commemoration of the Resurrection of Christ, probably in a conscious effort to create a parallel to the Jewish Passover, which coincided with the Crucifixion and Resurrection. But Easter also coincides generally with the beginning of spring and may have been intended to replace a very ancient pagan ritual celebrating the death and resurrection of Attis, a Phrygian god of vegetation and young life. During the pagan festival, an effigy of Attis was impaled on a pine tree, his death was mourned, and his body removed from the tree and laid in a tomb. At dawn on the fourth day, the tomb was opened and

BC, AD, CE, AND PC

The terms BC ("Before Christ") and AD ("anno domini," Latin for "in the year of the Lord") are, of course, Christian contrivances, reflecting the power of the church and the Holy Roman Empire to impose their calendrical computations on the rest of the world. (Because of early miscalculations, Christ is now believed to have actually been born between 7 and 4 BC.) Both terms are said to derive from the work of the late-5th-century Roman monk **Dionysius Exiguus.**

Archbishop Ussher of Armagh, Ireland, in 1650 calculated (by totting up the ages of the various patriarchs, counting backward from the birth of Christ to Adam) that the creation of the world took place on Saturday, October 22, 4004 BC, at 8 AM. This calculation, which appeared in his *Annales Veteris et Novi Testamenti,* was accepted for a time by Protestants, and still is by many fundamentalists. By contrast, Muslims begin their calendar at the year AD 622, when Muhammad made his journey from Mecca to Medina. Thus, 1994 corresponds to the Muslim year 1414/1415 (the Muslim lunar year is 11 days shorter than the solar year). Jews figure their calender from the creation of the world, calculated somewhat differently from

Archbishop Ussher, at 3760 BC; 1994 corresponds to the Jewish year 5754. Modern Jews follow a lunisolar calendar in which months are reckoned by the moon and years according to the sun. Its lunar months are, like the Muslims', about 29½ days each; but to keep Jewish festivals, which are connected to specific seasons, from wandering, the Jewish calendar adds an extra month in 7 of every 19 years.

As a move in the direction of nonsectarianism, religious scholars, including some Christians, have begun substituting the abbreviations CE ("common era") and BCE ("before the common era") for AD and BC, respectively. This is clumsy not only because it adds an extra letter but also because it appears to whitewash the fact that the dates themselves are still calculated from the birth of Christ, a convention we might as well acknowledge as long as we use it. (And who wants to relearn the dates of the Battle of Hastings or the Woodstock Festival this late in life?) At least in the West, the advent of Christianity so completely and irreversibly changed the course of history and culture, for better and worse, that you needn't be Christian to acknowledge its impact. Some argue that using a Christian frame of reference is offensive to other religions, but by the same token, our very use of terms like the West, the Orient, or the Middle East can be said to display a locational bias. Furthermore, it's hard to imagine what other forms of calculation all the world's religious cultures might agree on. It's not even clear what the phrase "common era" means. It's certainly not common to Muslims or Jews, let alone to the Indians or the Chinese. Presumably it means "commonly accepted," but then why erase the historical basis of this acceptance?

found empty, eliciting great shouts of joy from the worshipers at the god's resurrection from the grave into eternal life, symbolic of the return of vegetation in spring.

Both Christmas and Easter are preceded by periods of preparation marked by prayer and fasting, known as **Advent** and **Lent,** respectively. Other holy days, such as **Ascension Thursday,** celebrating the ascension of Christ into heaven 40 days after the Resurrection, and the feast of the **Assumption,** commemorating the bodily assumption of Mary into heaven, are celebrated primarily by Catholic Christians. In the Roman church, the feast of **Epiphany** (Gr. "manifestation") on January 6 celebrates the visit of the **Magi** (Gr. "wise men" or "magicians") to the Christ Child, but in the Eastern Orthodox church it commemorates the baptism of Christ in the Jordan. In the East, Epiphany is almost on a par with the Nativity in terms of popular fervor in its celebration, and both are exceeded only by Easter, which is the leading popular holiday among Orthodox Christians. During the celebration of Epiphany, baptismal water is blessed and so are many bodies of water, including the Jordan River.

✳ THE SAINTS GO MARCHING ON

Saints, men and women of exceptional holiness now believed to be in heaven and capable of interceding with God for the faithful on earth and for those souls still suffering in purgatory, have long been a part of Christian tradition. At first, saints were designated by local cults that grew up around martyrs, Christians who had died for their faith—a natural outgrowth of Christianity's central figure having himself died as a martyr on the cross. The cult of martyrs and saints also helped the church ease the transition from paganism to Christianity among the populace. Spirit-shrines were converted to shrines in honor of the Blessed Mother or of saints; pagan festivals became holy days or saints' days. For example, Asclepius*, the Greek god of medicine and healing, was subsumed by the martyr **Panteleimon** (or **Pantalein**) who, before his death in 305, had been physician to the Emperor Galerius Maximian at Nicomedia and is now the patron saint of doctors and the medical profession.

Some early Christians singled out for torture and imprisonment for having made a public confession of their faith did not actually die as a result. They were given privileged status in the church and often venerated after death as **confessors.** Once the success of Christianity made imprisonment or martyrdom much less likely, the focus shifted to men and women who, like the Desert Fathers, lived lives of exceptional self-abnegation and holiness—dying to the self and the pleasures of the world. Since one of the criteria of sainthood was a life of self-denial, especially denial of the pleasures of sex and marital companionship, most women saints were designated as virgins or widows, often in combinations such as "virgin and martyr."

The making of saints was originally an informal process that followed the formation of a popular cult around a deceased figure, whose remains, or relics, were often collected and venerated. But their veneration and worship frequently led to misgivings, and in the 3rd and 4th centuries the Church Fathers began to make clear distinctions between **latria,** worship due to Christ, and **doulia,** devotion due to saints.

Formal **canonization**—the process that results in the placing of a name in the list or canon of recognized saints—did not occur until 993, when **Ulrich,** bishop of Augsberg, became the first saint decreed by a pope. Canonization brings with it the honor of possibly being mentioned during the mass or having a feast day in the church's liturgical calendar, although with all the days given over to veneration of Jesus and Mary there are too few feast days left to accommodate all the canonized saints. Local churches kept their own canons until the 17th century, when a universal canon was established for the Roman church; the Orthodox church still relies on local calendars. From the earliest days, saints were believed to be responsible for miracles, especially miraculous healings, granted posthumously through their shrines or relics or to those who prayed devotedly to them. A candidate for sainthood today who is acknowledged to be responsible for at least two miracles qualifies for the lesser process of **beatification** (granting the rank of **Blessed**). Two more miracles after beatification are generally required for canonization, provided the candidate is also proven to have had an extremely holy character. As part of the research process, a church official called the "promoter of the faith" but commonly known as the **devil's advocate** once sought to disprove the evidence or find fault with the character of the candidate for either beatification or canonization. But in 1983

CHRISTIAN PATRONAGE UPDATED

Saint	Patron of
Bona	stewardesses
Our Lady of the Thorns	blood donors
Basilissa	breast-feeding, chilblain
Vitus	comedians
Ubald	dog bites
Martin of Tours	geese
Joseph	house hunting
Madonna of Castaliazzo	motorcyclists
Francis Xavier	Argentinian pelota players
Cassian of Imola	stenographers
Abbot Benedict	spelunkers
Vincent of Saragossa	wine makers
Archangel Gabriel	television

—BUTLER'S PATRON SAINTS

the role of devil's advocate was officially terminated by Pope John Paul II and his duties spread among a wide range of clerics. The Eastern Orthodox Church has no such formal criteria for canonization; after candidates are singled out for informal veneration on the local level, they may be designated saints by any of several patriarchates, or regional churches.

Only some 400 saints have been canonized by the popes, and the process itself is now governed by canon law. But saints have been designated unofficially throughout the church's history; over 10,000 saints are listed in the *Bibliotheco Sanctorum,* considered the most comprehensive work on saints, naming all those who have been venerated at one time or another. The list includes some pre-Christians, such as John the Baptist, and even some who, like the **Archangel Michael,** are not human. Saints are recognized today only by the Roman Catholic and Orthodox churches, sainthood having been one of the areas of contention by

Protestants during and since the Reformation. However, Pope Paul VI removed a number of early saints from the liturgical calendar for various reasons. The most surprising was St. Christopher, long venerated as the patron saint of travelers, who is believed to have been a mythical invention of early Christians.

The concept of the **patron saint,** who serves as protector and intercessor for a particular region, church, society, or occupation, probably derived from a well-established tradition of patronage in Rome: rich Romans often provided assistance and protection for poorer ones in exchange for services and political support. It was probably only natural that the early Christians transferred their dependence from secular to spiritual patrons. The earliest patron saints were, of course, martyrs; their feast days were the days on which they had died. Sometimes the identity of a patron saint rested on his or her occupation or life condition: St. Giles, said to have been a cripple, is the patron saint of cripples and, because begging was a necessity for most cripples in his time, of beggars as well. Other saints were merely attached by crafts guilds who shared in their local veneration or were made patrons based on an association of images. St. Lucy, a 4th-century martyr, is the patron saint of sufferers from eye diseases and of glaziers, possibly because her name suggests light or because legend holds that she plucked out her eyes to discourage a suitor. The Archangel Gabriel, who gave Mary the news of her divine insemination, is the patron of postal employees, telephone operators, and the radio and television industry. The process of designating saints as patrons is far less formal than that of canonization and has continued into the present day, with some unexpected new developments.

Coming to Terms

Abecedarians   A defunct German Anabaptist sect led by **Nicholas Storch,** who despised learning, even of the ABCs, because he believed it interfered with sanctity and direct experience of God through ecstasies and visions. The group believed that the illiterate could nonetheless interpret scripture.

Abelites   A 4th-century African sect mentioned by Augustine. Members married but did not have sex (something they claimed was true of Abel), believing that procreation led only to the perpetuation of sin. Not surprisingly, they are extinct.

Adamites A recurring sect reaching back to the 2nd century who believed that they could achieve the primal purity of Adam and Eve. They dispensed with marriage (in favor of promiscuous sex) and clothing (at least at their communal meetings, or "paradises"). They reappeared as late as the 19th century but haven't been heard from lately.

Adventists Any Christians who believe in the imminent Second Coming (Advent) of Christ, sometimes called *apocalypticists* or millenarians. Adventism has occurred in all periods of church history, from the Montanists to the Mormons.

Apocalypse The last book of the New Testament in the Catholic Bible, called Revelation (a translation of the Greek title) in Protestant versions. It depicts in allegorical form the end of time on earth, accompanied by **Armageddon,** the final battle between the forces of good and evil, and the Second Coming of Christ, followed by a millennium of peace.

apostles From the numerous disciples who aided Jesus in his ministry—at one point in the Gospel he sends out 72 to heal and preach—he chose 12 to be his apostles (from a Greek word meaning "one sent out") to act specifically in his name. The Synoptic Gospels and the Acts of the Apostles list 12 apostles' names, of which only 10 match up, and John gives only 6 names.

Aquarians Early Christian sects that used water instead of wine in observing the Eucharist, mainly as an ascetical measure.

Carpocratians Followers of 2nd-century Alexandrian Gnostic Carpocrates, who taught that ordinary humans can achieve a higher realization than Jesus himself, who was a mere man. They also practiced nude baptisms with possible homosexual overtones.

catechism A compendium of the tenets of the Christian religion, originally developed as a concise oral summary to be studied by new Christians or potential converts before baptism. Once infant baptism became universal in the 6th century, the catechism was used after baptism. After the Reformation, many sects developed distinctive versions. The Church of England Catechism became embedded in the Anglican **Book of Common Prayer;** perhaps the most famous catechism is the Presbyterian church's Westminster **Larger Catechism** of 1647. The Roman Catholic Church responded to the Reformation with a universal catechism at the Council of Trent (1566), but the Catholic version most familiar to generations of American Catholics is the **Baltimore Catechism,** which was taught in parochial schools as a series of questions and answers to be memorized: "Who made us? God made us. Why did God make us? God made us to know, love and serve Him in this life

385

and be happy with Him in the next." In 1992, the church issued a revised universal catechism, no longer in Q&A format, updated to include references to new sins such as tax evasion, drug abuse, mistreatment of immigrants, abuse of the environment, artificial insemination, and genetic engineering.

catechumen   A convert receiving rudimentary instruction in doctrine and morals preparatory to baptism, distinguishable in the early church from a member of the faithful. In early centuries, catechumens also prayed and fasted before their Easter baptism, a custom that developed into Lent.

Congregationalists   An Evangelical sect popular in the northeastern U.S. that views each individual congregation as an independent body, with all rights to elect clergy and settle matters of doctrinal belief and discipline without any outside interference. However, a loose fellowship with other like-minded congregations is an accepted part of the pattern.

Deists   Those who believe in God, or at least a divine principle, but follow few if any of the other tenets and practices of Christianity (compare with **Theists**, who believe in a personal God). Developed in the 17th and 18th centuries, Deism envisions a kind of clock-maker God who set the universe in motion but then let it run on its own, calling into question the Jewish and Christian notion of God's intervention in history. A number of prominent early Americans, including Ben Franklin, were Deists, along with French Enlightenment figures Voltaire and Rousseau.

Dionysius the Areopagite (dye-a-*nish*-yus ari-**op**-a-jite)   A Greek converted by Paul on a visit to Athens (Acts 17:34), later credited with having written certain Greek texts on mysticism. These writings are now generally attributed to a 5th-century author referred to as **Pseudo-Dionysius,** possibly a Syrian monk familiar with the Neoplatonists. The writings were translated into Latin and became part of the basis of medieval European mysticism. They describe, among other things, hierarchies of angels leading from God to humans and the stages proceeding to mystical union with God.

Docetism (from Gr. "to seem")   The belief among some early Christians, with Gnostic overtones, that Jesus was not actually human but only seemed to be.

Donatists   North African separatists of the 4th–5th century, followers of **Donatus,** who disavowed those bishops known as **traditors** ("betrayers") accused of collaborating with the Romans during their persecution of the early Christians. The Donatists formed their own church, replete with martyrs killed by the Roman church. Their main "heresy" was their belief that the validity of the sacraments and episcopal power was predicated on personal sinlessness, so that a traditor did not qualify to be a bishop.

Ebionites ("Poor Ones")   Jews who believed that Jesus was the Messiah but kept many of their Jewish practices and split with Paul over his dismissal of Mosaic law or Torah*. They believed that Jesus was human but not divine, accepted only the Gospel of Matthew, and disappeared after the 5th century. A similar group called the **Nazarenes** considered themselves Jews and believed in Jesus as Messiah, but they differed from the Ebionites in accepting Christ's divinity and supernatural birth.

ecclesia ("called out")   Originally a Greek term for a political assembly of citizens, it came to be applied by early Christians to their church assemblies, usually in someone's household.

Erasmus (c. 1467–1536)   The leading classical scholar of his day and the bastard son of a priest and a washerwoman, Erasmus was a humanist rather than a scholastic. In fact, he wrote a number of satirical attacks on scholasticism and (although he was an ordained priest) on monastic life and the corruption of Rome, most famously in his *In Praise of Folly*. He also published the first edition of the Greek New Testament in 1516, one year before Luther's 95 Theses. Erasmus pleaded the case for liberalism and tolerance so convincingly that before the Reformation he was the best-selling author in Europe (with the help of the printing press), and not long afterward his books were banned by the church. He remained a Catholic, even writing attacks on Luther's theology, but his respect for reason and opposition to clerical corruption gave him more in common with the Reformation and the later Enlightenment.

eschatology   Thought that is focused on the idea that the present time is the end of this age (the "end time" or "last days") and the dawn of a new era, one marked by the Second Coming of Jesus, the resurrection of the dead, the final judgment, and, according to some believers, a millennium or new age of Christ's rule on earth, along with the binding of Satan and the raising of the saints.

Eusebius (c. 265–341)   Bishop of Caesarea who wrote extensively about early Christianity, earning the sobriquet "Father of Church History."

Flagellants   During the Middle Ages in Europe, these fanatical Christians practiced self-abuse of the most flagrant sort, whipping themselves bloody in public, usually across their own bare shoulders. Their appearance often coincided with great strife or calamity, most notably the Black Death, and the self-torture was meant to appease an angry God. After first approving, the church condemned the Flagellants. In parts of Mexico and the American Southwest, modern flagellants known as **penitentes** practice similar austerities with a macho edge, as if competing to see who can bear the most suffering. And in the Philippines, numbers of people allow themselves literally to be nailed to a cross on Good Friday in a reenactment of the passion of Christ. Counterparts exist among certain modern sects of the Hindu and Muslim religions.

hesychia Inner stillness or silence of the heart that results, especially in Eastern Christianity, from repetition of some variant of the **Jesus prayer**: "Lord Jesus Christ, have mercy on me, a sinner." **Hesychasm** became a movement in the 14th century, centered around the famed ascetic monks of **Mount Athos**.

icon A visual representation of Christ, the Blessed Mother, an angel, or a saint. Icons were often painted on wood panels or displayed as mosaics and frescoes in the Eastern Orthodox churches as far back as the 5th century.

iconoclasts ("image breakers") People who believed that the worship of icons was equivalent to idolatry. By contrast, **iconodules** believed that Christ was truly human and that his image should be portrayed (cf. Hindu ishtadeva*) and argued that they didn't worship the icons but the God represented there. Major outbreaks of iconoclasm occurred between 725 and 780 and again between 815 and 843, and the effects can still be seen in ancient statuary and altarpieces from which the faces have been smashed.

Index of Prohibited Books Although the concept of books considered dangerous and heretical for the faithful to read had been around since the Middle Ages, the first official Index was published by Pope Paul IV in 1559, at which time it supposedly listed 75 percent of all books currently in print in Europe. The Index was not officially discontinued until 1966.

Justin Martyr (c. 100–65) One of the first Christian apologists and a convert from the mystical Greek schools, Justin argued in favor of Christianity against paganism, Judaism, and Gnosticism.

Logos ("Word") This Greek term has been employed with different shades of meaning by different authors and interpreted in a variety of ways. As used in the Gospel of John, it appears to refer to the creative power of God that was manifest in, or as, His Son, Jesus Christ ("and the Word was made flesh and dwelt among us"). This interpretation has parallels with *sophia* (Gr. "wisdom"), used in the Old Testament to express a similar concept. The use of *Logos* by Zeno and other Stoics to mean the rational principle inhabiting and governing the universe, by Philo Judaeus* to mean an intermediary agent between the transcendent God and the created world, and by the Neoplatonists add other flavors that are not specifically Christian. In the *Confessions,* for instance, St. Augustine says of John's use of the term, "This I never read of the Logos in the Neoplatonists." The root concept is common to many mystical traditions: in Hindu thought, Maya* is the manifestation of Brahman*; in China, the Te* represents the power of the Tao*, and so forth.

Mandaeans This 2nd-century Gnostic Christian sect, with Judaic and

Persian elements, still survives today around the Tigris River in Iraq. Known as Disciples of St. John the Baptist, or St. John's Christians because of their preservation of legends about John, members call themselves **Sabians** ("Baptists"), perhaps because a sect of Sabaeans is tolerated in the Quran.

Monophysites (Gr. "only one nature")   Based in North Africa in the early Christian era, they accepted the divine but not the human nature of Christ, a belief perhaps arising from the struggles of the early Desert Fathers to overcome their human appetites. In the 5th century, the church tried to suppress the movement, setting the stage for the loss of much North African territory to the simpler monotheism of Islam.

Origen (c. 184–254)   The most important theologian of the early Greek church, he abstained from meat and wine and reportedly castrated himself so as to instruct women without scandal (a practice also common among Chinese Buddhists). Although Origen created the first entirely Christian philosophy and was among the first biblical text critics and commentators, some of his teachings were later condemned by the church, such as his belief in the "preexistence of souls," or reincarnation*. "Each soul," he wrote, "comes to this world reinforced by the victories or enfeebled by the defeats of its previous lives."

original sin   The concept that Adam's sin in disobeying God in the Garden of Eden (Gen. 3:6–19) is passed on to all humanity. Paul was the first to point this out (Rom., 5:12ff), underlining Christ's role as a "type" of Adam who redeemed humanity as Adam had condemned them. Early theologians such as Tertullian, who invented the term concupiscence for humanity's ardent desires (akin to the Buddha's trishna*, or thirst), did not believe that children were born with original sin. It was Augustine who insisted on that notion, largely as a rationale for infant baptism.

papal infallibility   The Roman Catholic concept that the pope and ecumenical councils of bishops are free from error whenever they speak *ex cathedra* on matters of faith and morals. The concept was made dogma in 1870.

Pentecost (Gr. "fiftieth")   Originally a Jewish feast of the harvest that took place 50 days after Passover. On this day 10 days after the Ascension of Christ (which traditionally occurred 40 days after the resurrection), the Holy Spirit descended on the disciples and inspired them with the ability to preach the Gospel so that they could be understood even by those who did not speak their language.

Philokalia ("Love of Beauty")   Edited in the 18th century by St. Macarius of Corinth and St. Nicodemus of Athos, it collects spiritual texts on asceticism, mysticism, and the Jesus prayer developed during the centuries when the Greek Orthodox church was under Turkish rule.

Pietism   Although not widely known today because it was more of a movement than an established church, Pietism had a continuing influence on Christian spirituality. In the 17th and 18th centuries, Pietists, led by **Philipp Jakob Spener** (1635–1705), reacted against the growing rigidity and systematization of the Reformation, emphasizing good works and knowledge of the Bible.

presbyter (Gr. "elder")   An elder of the early Christian church, similar in function to a bishop. The Protestant Reform movement in 16th-century Europe focused on a return to the earliest church practices, giving rise to the term Presbyterianism, especially among followers of John Calvin.

Revivalism   Sporadic, spontaneous outbursts of religious awakening among Christians, often outside the context of established churches, resulting in increased piety, evangelism, missionary activity, and social reforms. In the broadest sense, revivals have taken place throughout Christian history, beginning with the Puritans and Anabaptists, and it's possible to view the entire Reformation as revivalism on a grand scale. In 19th-century America, the term took on a specific reference to camp meetings, vast open-air assemblies addressed by teams of evangelists, often with a fundamentalist and temperance-oriented bias (these later spread to the British Isles, too). The most famous revivalists of modern times are **"Billy" Sunday** (1862–1935), a former baseball player, and **Billy Graham**.

sacraments   Once as many as 30, they were whittled down to 7 by the 12th-century theologian **Peter Lombard** and proclaimed authentic at the Fourth Lateran Council in 1215, later elaborated by Aquinas in his *Summa Theologiae*. They are baptism, confirmation, eucharist (communion), penance, extreme unction (last rites), matrimony, and holy orders (ordination). Protestant reformers reduced the list to baptism and eucharist, both practiced by Christ in the Gospels, but the Catholic and Orthodox churches retain all 7. According to the Augustinian formula, they are outward and temporal signs of an inner, lasting grace that descends on the recipient simply by virtue of receiving the sacrament. They are distinct from **sacramentals,** such as holy water or rosary beads, which were instituted by the Catholic church rather than by Christ.

Salvation Army   A religious sect organized in England in the 1860s (originally as the Christian Mission) by **William Booth,** a Methodist who grafted evangelical practices and principles onto a military-type structure, complete with articles of war (declaration of faith), ranks of officers (Booth was made general), uniforms, and brass bands, to spur religious revival in the masses. Group members quickly became involved in social action, working for released prisoners, unmarried mothers, the unemployed, missing persons, lepers, and the homeless, and they still collect money and food and provide shelters and hospitals for the needy.

Their main publications are *The War Cry* and *The Young Soldier*. Volunteers of America, a splinter group, was founded in New York by Booth's son Ballington and his wife, Maud, in 1896.

Satan According to the Talmud*, Satan (Hebrew for "adversary") was an archangel who was expelled from heaven with his followers for his pride. They became the "fallen angels" of Christian theology (and Milton's *Paradise Lost*). The personification of evil in the world, Satan was translated in the Greek Septuagint as *diabolos* ("slanderer"), the devil, and was accepted as such by Christians. The horns and forked tail came later, in the Middle Ages.

Savonarola (1452–98) Dominican preacher who attacked the corruption of church and state in Italy and supported the poor and oppressed. Around 1497 in Florence he organized the original "bonfire of the vanities," urging the faithful to collect and burn their wigs, cosmetics, pornographic books, and artworks. By 1498, the Florentines had tired of his puritanical ways and, longing to return to their bad habits, had him hanged and burned in a public plaza.

scholasticism Deriving from the medieval monastery and cathedral schools of the 9th to 14th centuries, this approach to theology and philosophy emphasized logic and rationality, analyzing all possible questions on a specific topic, categorizing Christian beliefs with Aristotelian methods. Its greatest proponents, called **scholastics** or schoolmen, were Thomas Aquinas, Duns Scotus, Albertus Magnus, Anselm, Peter Abelard, and William of Ockham.

Seventh-day Adventists A spin-off of the original Adventists, this sect was founded by **Ellen G. Wright** after the "Great Disappointment" of 1844. Members now practice a strictly biblical form of Christianity with some elements similar to Judaism. For instance, they observe the Sabbath from sundown Friday to sundown Saturday (the seventh day) and many of the same dietary restrictions as Orthodox Jews, eating no pork or shellfish, only fish with fins and scales. They also avoid worldly pleasures such as dancing, movies, television, card playing, and gambling. A prominent member, **John Harvey Kellogg** (1852–1943) opened a sanitarium in Battle Creek, Michigan, in 1875 that advocated a vegetarian diet. An offshoot known as the **Davidians** began in 1930 as a reform movement led by **Victor T. Houteff,** a Bulgarian immigrant and Maytag salesman. Davidians espouse apocalyptic beliefs by which only 144,000 elect (a number taken from the book of Revelation) will survive the Second Coming and begin a new Kingdom of God. A renegade subsect calling themselves the **Branch Davidians** commanded national attention in 1993 when they engaged in a deadly shootout with federal and local law officers at their compound near Waco, Texas. Other Davidian sects quickly disavowed them, and most of the cult perished with their leader, **David Koresh**, in a fire that followed an FBI assault on their compound.

simony   The monetary purchase of ecclesiastical office, ordination to the priesthood, or indulgences. It was named for **Simon Magus**, a Samaritan sorcerer upbraided by St. Peter for trying to buy from the apostles the power of conferring the Holy Spirit (by laying on of hands).

stigmata (Gr. "marks of a pointed instrument")   Bodily wounds that appear in the hands, feet, side, shoulder, chest, or back as a visible sign of sharing the suffering of Christ's passion. Classically, they appear only in the hands and feet (where nails were thought to be driven) and side (where a Roman lance pierced Christ's heart during the crucifixion) and have occasionally been reported as appearing on holy paintings and statues. St. Francis of Assisi was the first person on whom they appeared, followed by many others, including Teresa of Avila, Julian of Norwich, Catherine of Siena—over 300 documented cases in all, most of them women. Catholic theologians look on the stigmata as a kind of psychophysical side effect of the mystical experience, and the church has played down its significance in modern times. Because the phenomenon may also be diabolically or psychologically induced, it is not considered in and of itself a sign of sanctity and is never used as a basis for canonization. The most famous stigmatist of the modern era is undoubtedly **Padre Pio (Francesco Forgione**, d. 1968), an Italian Capuchin friar who endured the wounds for 50 years. Some Muslim mystics have also manifested on their backs wounds like those suffered by the Prophet Muhammad in battle.

Swedenborg, Emanuel (1688–1772)   Swedish scientist and mystic who described elaborate experiences in the spiritual worlds among the angelic and hellish spirits. He also talked about the return of the Messiah and the creation of a New Jerusalem. After his death, his followers created the Church of New Jerusalem in 1787.

Tertullian (c. 160–220)   A Carthaginian Christian convert and polemicist, the first to write in Latin, famous for several classic statements of early Christianity, e.g., "Outside the church there is no salvation," "The blood of martyrs is the seed of the church," and "I believe because it is absurd." He also came up with the Latin word for the Trinity and wrote perhaps the first Latin *apologia,* or reasoned defense of Christian theology against various disbelievers.

ultramontanist   A believer in and vigorous supporter of papal supremacy, especially reasserted after the French Revolution.

Unitarianism   A marginally Christian denomination that denies the individuality of persons in the Holy Trinity and the divinity of Christ, stresses the inherent goodness of humanity, and opposes notions of original sin and eternal damnation. Unitarianism originated among various anti-Trinitarian proponents of the 16th century, although its modern members often claim that their ideas predated the Reformation. In America, Unitarianism arose independently as the liberal wing of the Congregational church and is often known for its extreme liberalism verging on secularism, a kind of "Ethical Culture" approach that is hardly Christian at all. (But they should not be confused with the **Ethical Culture Society** itself, a completely nonsectarian group first formed in 1876 by **Felix Adler** as an alternative to religions that rely on revelation and authoritarian structures. Ethical Culture teaches "the supreme importance of the ethical factor in all the relations of life—personal, social, national, and international, apart from theological considerations.") In 1961, the Unitarian church merged with the **Universalists**, an American amalgam of Gnosticism, Anabaptism, and mysticism, to form the **Unitarian Universalist Association**.

6

ISLAM

Despite all the centuries of seething animosity and open warfare among Muslims, Christians, and Jews in the Middle East, the history, scriptures, and rituals of Islam are intimately intertwined with those of its two sister traditions. In historical terms, Islam can be seen as its followers themselves view it: the third and final revelation in Western religion that began with Judaism and Christianity. In fact, Muslims do not regard these as three separate religions but as one continuously unfolding historical tradition. The birthplace of Islam in what is now Saudi Arabia is less than 1,000 miles from the lands where the Israelites took root and where Jesus taught his Gospel. The One God in Islam, called **Allah,** is absolutely identical with the God of Abraham, and in fact announces Himself as the same God who sent His message to the world through Abraham, Moses, and Jesus.

Much like the Israelites, the Muslims established a monotheistic, theocratic state in a land steeped in polytheism and tribal plurality. **Muhammad,** the great Prophet of Islam who received the Islamic holy book, the

Quran, as revelation from God, saw himself in the tradition of the Hebrew prophets. And like Jesus (whom he believed to be a great prophet, although not divine), Muhammad spent a period of time fasting and meditating in the desert before he embarked on his ministry. He taught a religion that focused on the Last Day, the resurrection of the dead, final judgment, the rewards of paradise and the punishments of hell. Muhammad proclaimed that the Virgin Mary, the mother of Jesus, is "the highest of the women of the people of Paradise," and the Quran states that the angels said to Mary, "God has chosen you. He has made you pure and exalted you above all womankind." The Quran itself affirms the doctrine of the Virgin Birth* of Jesus.

Besides the Quran, Muslims recognize several other books as holy scripture revealed by God, including the Torah* and Psalms of the Hebrew Bible and the Gospels* of the New Testament. Muslims believe that God revealed the same message anew to successive prophets with the aim of reforming a stumbling humanity but that each message was gradually distorted by the people who received it. The Quran frequently repeats (with God speaking in the royal plural) the concept of a continuum of revelation: "We have sent our apostles with veritable signs, and through them have brought down scriptures and scales of justice, so that men might conduct themselves with fairness. . . . We sent forth Noah and Abraham, and bestowed on their offspring prophethood and the Scriptures. Some were rightly guided, but many were evil-doers. After them We sent other apostles, and after those Jesus the Son of Mary. We gave him the Gospel, and put compassion and mercy in the hearts of his followers" (57:25–26).

Like Christians, Muslims have millenarian* movements, based on the expectation of the coming of the **Mahdi,** or ideal leader, prophesied to emerge at the close of history. The hidden Mahdi ("rightly guided one"), who in some ways also resembles the Jewish Messiah* and the Buddhist figure of Maitreya*, is tied in Muslim belief to the Second Coming* of Christ and the battle with the Antichrist. And like most other religions, Islam has a fundamentalist minority that insists on a narrow-minded interpretation of scripture and a rigid moral code. But as with other religions, Islam also embraces the full range of interpretations, from conservative to liberal, supporting differing levels of application of Muslim law, beliefs, and customs.

Islam

There are over a billion Muslims in the world today, including 3 to 5 million in the U.S., making it the second most populous religion on earth after Christianity. According to some estimates, Islam is the fastest-growing religion in the world. It encompasses most of the Middle East and North Africa but also exists in significant numbers throughout Africa and western Asia, especially Pakistan and parts of India, as well as Malaysia and Indonesia (except for the islands of Bali and Lompok, which are largely Hindu). Because it is common for Muslims to name their children after prominent figures in their history, at any given time there are more people on earth with the name Muhammad than any other. But because of political antagonisms between Islamic culture and the West (the U.S. in particular), the considerable accomplishments of Islam's founder and the 14 centuries of rich Islamic civilization, including the profundity of the religion itself, have often been obscured. Islam still bears the stigma in the West of a religion of violent fanatics, bent on conversion at all costs.

Yet the Arabic word *Islam* means "submission" or "surrender," as in surrender to God; it also derives from *salam,* the Arabic word for "peace." Both meanings are present in the actual experience of Islam. And a Muslim (the spelling preferred to *Moslem*) is "one who submits" or surrenders to the will of God, thereby attaining peace of mind and soul. However such a wide discrepancy in understanding came about, one thing is clear: the essence of this venerable religious tradition is very different from the images that have dominated the world's media in recent years.

Through a combination of divine revelation and great personal character, Muhammad brought humanity a religion that offered alternatives not only to the idolatry and bigotry of the desert Arabs but also to the Judaism and Christianity that were operating in and around the Arab world. In the Quran, Islam had its equivalent of the Torah and the Gospels; its Sabbath fell on Friday rather than Saturday or Sunday; and in place of the synagogue and church, Islam offered the mosque, combining the teaching and praying functions of both.

❋ CALL HIM ISMAIL

According to the Quran, the Israelites and the Arabs both descended from the same father, Abraham (Ar. Ibrahim). **Ishmael** (Ar. Ismail) was born to Abraham and **Hagar,** the Egyptian handmaid of his wife, Sarah. When Isaac was born to Abraham by Sarah, she insisted that Hagar and Ishmael be banished. They settled in the Becca Valley, along the "incense road," an ancient trade route. (According to Genesis 25:9, Ishmael later returned to the land of Canaan to help Isaac bury their father at Hebron.) When Hagar and her young child first arrived in this barren valley, Ishmael was taken ill and badly needed water. Hagar ran back and forth seven times between two nearby promontories desperately seeking help. She was searching for water for the stricken Ishmael when a spring named **Zamzam** miraculously appeared, sent by God when Ishmael's heel struck the ground there.

Abraham later visited his son, and, according to the Quran, God showed Abraham where he and Ishmael should build a sanctuary, called the **Kaaba** ("cube"), a square edifice whose four corners faced the four compass points. A cubical black structure that still stands in the open, the Kaaba was rebuilt several times (the modern Kaaba in present-day Saudi Arabia is a direct descendent of the original). A celestial **Black Stone,** brought to Abraham by an angel and now thought to be a meteorite, is built into the southeast corner of the Kaaba; Muslims today kiss the stone as the Prophet used to do. The current structure is roughly 40 by 33 feet by 50 feet high, with a marble floor and marble-lined interior walls. According to Muslim tradition, God told Abraham to begin the rite of pilgrimage to Becca (now **Mecca**). In a rite called **tawaf,** Arab pilgrims from time immemorial circled the stone counterclockwise seven times and ran seven times between the two promontories in memory of Hagar's seven passages.

The historicity of this Abrahamic tradition is difficult to confirm; the first verifiable reference to the Arab people occurs in an inscription of Shalmanezer III dated 853 BC. What is generally agreed is that over the centuries, the worship of the God of Abraham at the Kaaba was corrupted by the importation of idols. Abraham's descendants stopped coming, and the location of the well of Zamzam was lost. Before Muhammad appeared, the Kaaba was surrounded by 360 idols, and every Arab house had its god. Arabs also believed in **jinn** (subtle beings), and some vague divinity with many offspring. Among the major deities of the pre-Islamic era were **al-Lat** ("the Goddess"), worshiped in the shape of a square stone; **al-Uzzah** ("the Mighty"), a goddess identified with the morning star and worshiped as a thigh-bone-shaped slab of granite between al-Taif and Mecca; **Manat,** the goddess of destiny, worshiped as a black stone on the road between Mecca and Medina; and the moon god, **Hubal,** whose worship was connected with the Black Stone of the Kaaba.

The stones were said to have fallen from the sun, moon, stars, and planets and to represent cosmic forces. The so-called Black Stone (actually the color of burnt umber) that Muslims revere today is the same one that their forebears had worshiped well before Muhammad and that they believed had come from the moon. (No scientific investigation has ever been performed on the stone. In 930, the stone was removed and shattered by an Iraqi sect of Qarmatians, but the pieces were later returned. The pieces, sealed in pitch and held in place by silver wire, measure about 10 inches in diameter altogether and several feet high; they are venerated today in patched-together form.)

✿ THE PROPHET: VISIONS AND REVELATIONS

At the time of Muhammad's birth, the area around Mecca was occupied by the **Quraysh,** a powerful tribe of Arab clans descended from Ishmael. Muhammad's grandfather, **Abd al-Muttalib** of the Quraysh clan of **Hashim,** had rediscovered the well of Zamzam, earning for his family the lucrative honor of distributing water from the sacred well. The Kaaba itself was a popular pilgrimage site, a source of both great prestige and considerable commerce from the large numbers of pilgrims who came each year. Around the year 571, **Abrahah the Abyssinian,** the Christian viceroy of Yemen, sought to divert pilgrimages from the Kaaba for religious and commercial reasons to a church he had built in Sana in Yemen. But as his army approached the Kaaba, according to tradition, they were attacked by a swarm of birds armed with pea-sized pellets, which decimated the army. (Scholars speculate that an epidemic, possibly of small-pox, may have actually ravaged the Christian forces.) The army retreated in disarray to Sana, where Abrahah died shortly afterward.

Around that time **Abdallah,** the son of Abd al-Muttalib, conceived a child by his wife **Amina,** but he died before the child was born. According to tradition, as the time of Amina's delivery drew near, she was conscious of a light inside her and heard a voice saying, "You carry in your womb the lord of this people. When he is born, say: 'I place him underneath the protection of the One, from the evil of every envier'; then name him Muhammad." Some believe that Muhammad ("the Praised One") is an honorific that was applied later. In any event, he belonged to the Quraysh clan known as **Bani Hashim** ("Sons of Hashim"); his full name, in the traditional nomenclature of his day, was Muhammad ibn Abdallah.

Like many of the details of Muhammad's early life, the exact date of his birth is not known for certain. It may have occurred shortly after the miracle of the birds, in the Year of the Elephant (so named because Abrahah's army was preceded by a great pachyderm that refused to lead the charge against the Kaaba, kneeling instead every time it faced Mecca). That year is thought to be 571, the date often given for the Prophet's birth. In the tradition of the noble Arab city families, his mother gave him to a Bedouin wet nurse named **Halima.** This custom allowed the child to imbibe the strength and vitality of the desert nomads and created valuable connections for the nomads among the better-off townspeople. The tradition goes that at about the age of 5, Muhammad received a vision while walking in the fields and reported that two men clothed in white opened his breast, temporarily took out his heart, and removed a black clot from it. The incident, witnessed by his foster brother, has never been fully explained, although theories range from the devout observation of parallels to experiences of the prophets of Israel all the way to speculation about its resemblance to recent accounts of UFO abductions.

Amina died when Muhammad was only 6, and he was taken into the family of his grandfather Abd al-Muttalib and his wife **Fatima** for two years, after which time his uncle **Abu Talib** became his guardian. Muhammad spent much of his youth working the caravans as far north as Syria, talking along the way with the hermits, monks, and Jewish mystics who lived in desert caves and remote communities. Although Muhammad disapproved in principle of monastic asceticism and celibacy, he admired the humility of the Nestorian monks and Christian anchorites* he met in the desert. Unlettered but gifted with a retentive memory, he absorbed vast chunks of Jewish and Christian scripture and lore.

At age 25, Muhammad was managing the caravans of a wealthy female merchant named **Khadija.** Although she was 15 years his senior, she admired his character and truthfulness and offered herself to him in marriage. He accepted, and they produced four daughters and two sons, both of whom died in infancy. For the next 15 years he managed her estate and lived what was apparently a normal if suddenly prosperous Arab life, surrounded by family and friends. By all accounts, Muhammad was an upright and moral person in the eyes of his countrymen before he began his mission to the world. Because of his integrity, he was entrusted with storing the possessions of other Meccans, earning him the nickname **al-Amin** ("the Trustworthy").

In Muhammad's day, desert-dwelling contemplatives, or **hanifs,** already worshiped the One Creator God exclusively, his name Allah meaning in Arabic "the God." Although neither Christians nor Jews, the hanifs *were* monotheists profoundly influenced by Judaism and Christianity, and in his early days Muhammad could have been considered one of them. But then Muhammad began to have visions in his sleep, "like the breaking of the light of dawn." As a result, he sought solitude in a cave in **Mount Hira.** When he was about 40, an angel appeared to him in human form in the cave and commanded, "Recite!" Muhammad replied, "I am not a reciter," perhaps meaning that he could not read, but the angel embraced him and repeated the command three times until he recited as told. (Some commentators translate the Arabic word for recite, *iqra,* as "preach" or "proclaim," in keeping with the Prophet's mission.) As he fled the cave in awe, Muhammad heard a voice telling him, "You are the Messenger of Allah, and I am Gabriel."

The revelations continued, sometimes in the form of the reverberations of a bell, sometimes as a man speaking to him. **Gabriel** (Ar. Jibril) showed Muhammad the ritual ablution with water before worship and the prayer postures that are now part of Muslim practice: standing, inclining, prostrating, sitting. Ramadan was already the traditional Arabic month of retreat, but Muhammad instituted the practice of fasting from before sunrise to sunset. Two major divine names were revealed early on: **ar-Rahman** ("Infinitely Good") and **ar-Rahim** ("All-Merciful"). **Arqam** the Makhzumite, one of the earliest converts to Islam, first pronounced the two testifications that are now the core of Islamic truth: **la ilaha il-lallah** ("There is no god but God") and **Muhammadun rasulullah** ("Muhammad is the Messenger of God").

At the prompting of an early revelation, Muhammad had begun to pass on the practices of ritual ablution and prayer and other teachings that were being revealed, at first to his wife Khadija and her cousin **Waraqa,** a learned convert to Christianity who was also conversant with Judaism and had translated sections of the Torah and Gospels into Arabic. Soon they were joined by Waraqa's good friend **Abu Bakr** and Muhammad's slave and eventual adopted son **Zayd ibn Haritha.** The Prophet gradually expanded his teaching to take in other members of his clan, other clans, and any others who would hear him. The Christians of that area, perhaps from their reading of Christ's promise to send the "Spirit of truth" to his followers (John 16:12–15), believed in the coming of a prophet, just as the Jews still looked for the Messiah. Predisposed to see Muhammad as the expected one, many of them embraced Islam, although not at first.

Most of Muhammad's contemporaries and fellow Quraysh opposed his new teaching, fearing it would discourage other Arabs from visiting the Kaaba, a great source of commerce and repute. Some Meccans came secretly to Islam, not wanting to arouse the anger of parents or clan members, as Nicodemus the Pharisee came to Jesus at night (John 3:1). The socially unprotected followers were often ridiculed, threatened, and tortured by politically powerful polytheists. A few families emigrated to the more tolerant Christian Abyssinia (Ethiopia), where they set up a sort of Islam-in-exile. Elders of the Quraysh who were disturbed by the emergence of Muhammad and his following sent envoys to consult with Jewish rabbis living nearby for help in determining if he was a true prophet or simply a self-appointed impostor. As the "people of the first scripture," Jews were in a position to evaluate such things. But because Muhammad was not Jewish, the rabbis were reluctant to endorse him. Finally the Quraysh forced Muhammad to seek refuge in the mountain fortress of his uncle and protector, Abu Talib, where he became a virtual prisoner because of threats against his life. While he was sequestered there, the two clans closest to him by blood, Hashim and Muttalib, were singled out for a ban against intermarriage or commerce with the other clans of Quraysh for their support of the Prophet, but after two years, in

619, the ban was annulled and Muhammad returned to Mecca. That year, however, came to be known as the Year of Sadness, because of the deaths only a few days apart of Abu Talib and Khadija.

Then age 50, Muhammad married again, this time exercising the Arab option of taking several wives, which he had not done while married to Khadija. In Mecca he wed the widow **Sawda** and was engaged to **Aisha,** the 6-year-old daughter of Abu Bakr. He later married her in Medina at age 9, although the marriage was not consummated until she reached the age of womanhood in Arabic culture. Next he married **Hafsa,** the daughter of Umar, a notable **Companion,** as the circle of Muslims closest to Muhammad came to be called. Muhammad's marriage to **Zaynab,** the wife of his adopted son Zayd required some thought and several revelations. Zayd assured the Prophet that his marriage to Zaynab was not a happy one, and though Islamic law permitted yet disapproved of divorce as well as marriage to one's son's relations, Zayd and Zaynab were divorced and Muhammad married her. As the Prophet's revelations granted permission for his marriages, the outspoken Aisha remarked (according to oral tradition), "It seems that God is hastening to satisfy your desires"—demonstrating Aisha's remarkable freedom as a woman. Muhammad then married **Umm Salama** and two Jewish women, **Raihana** and **Safiya,** followed by **Umm Habiba,** a daughter of **Abu Sufyan,**

MUHAMMAD'S HAREM

The number and varying ages of Muhammad's wives have often been discussed inside and outside of Islam, usually in the context of the current status of Muslim women. However, in the context of the Arab world of the time, Muhammad was a radical, compassionate reformer who did much to liberate and protect women. Here is an objective viewpoint from the pen of a Western scholar.

Certainly the attitude of the Prophet as regards women has weighed heavily on Muslim civilization, for [his] examples and principles were forcibly warped by the natural tendency of men to seek their own advantage. He certainly improved woman's lot in the Arabia of his day. He prohibited infanticide and the prostitution of slave-women. He established the rights of women to inherit (a half-share). He proclaimed that . . . married couples have reciprocal duties and rights, and that women ought to be educated. He limited the number of wives a man may lawfully have to four. He did not set himself up as a model. As it was, he hardly surprised his contemporaries; on the contrary they were inclined to admire his amatory prowess, and were accustomed, like the contemporaries of Solomon, to measure the power of a ruler by the number of his wives. Polygamy was only permitted if one was capable of being perfectly fair to all. Concubines could only be obtained from the holy war, not from the purchase of slaves. Daughters could not be married without their own consent, and this ought to have done away with the right of *jabr* (arranging marriages for minors). As for unilateral divorce which, more than the now rapidly disappearing polygamy, is the curse of Muslim family life, it is condemned in the famous but little observed hadith, "There is nothing created that God likes better than the freeing of slaves, and nothing that He hates more than divorce."

—EMILE DERMENGHEM, *MUHAMMAD AND THE ISLAMIC TRADITION*

a famously idolatrous opponent of Islam, and **Maimuna,** sister-in-law of his uncle and the aunt of **Khalid,** the great Quraysh military leader. Besides these 9 official wives, Muhammad took as concubine—over the objections of Aisha and his other wives—**Mariya,** a Coptic Christian slave girl who was a gift from the ruler of Egypt.

Muhammad did not work miracles like previous prophets, something that was held against him by his Arab detractors. The Quran emphasizes Muhammad's fully human nature, and neither he nor his followers claimed that he was anything but the Messenger of God. (This is why the term *Mohammedanism* is inaccurate, since it implies the worship of Muhammad rather than of Allah.) The Muslim tradition does include accounts of Muhammad multiplying food to feed the faithful much as Jesus was said to have done with the loaves and fishes. To some observers, these stories suggest the pious imagination at work and run counter to the Quran's image of the Prophet as totally human; to others, they are but the epiphenomena that sometimes occur in the presence of amazing individuals.

And on a human level, Muhammad was genuinely amazing. Like other spiritually enlightened leaders, he clearly possessed a great intellect and acute powers of intuition. In battle, he had a talent for knowing when to follow the advice of his companions and when to go with his instinct. When Muhammad was born, Arab society lacked a recourse to justice without blood feuds, something the Jews and Romans and Abyssinians

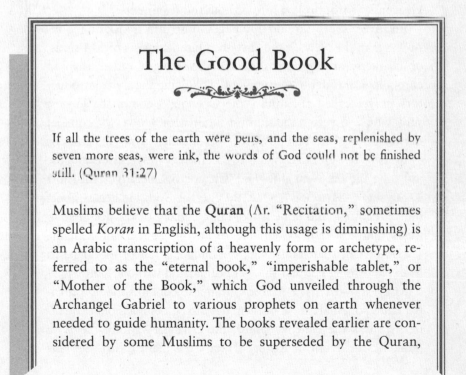

The Good Book

If all the trees of the earth were pens, and the seas, replenished by seven more seas, were ink, the words of God could not be finished still. (Quran 31:27)

Muslims believe that the **Quran** (Ar. "Recitation," sometimes spelled *Koran* in English, although this usage is diminishing) is an Arabic transcription of a heavenly form or archetype, referred to as the "eternal book," "imperishable tablet," or "Mother of the Book," which God unveiled through the Archangel Gabriel to various prophets on earth whenever needed to guide humanity. The books revealed earlier are considered by some Muslims to be superseded by the Quran, whose purpose is to correct the human imperfections that crept into the previous books. All Muslims respect those other revealed books as legitimate but believe that the Quran is the final, perfect transmission of the one heavenly book. Unlike Jewish and Christian scriptures, which are largely narrative or doctrinal with only occasional quotations from Yahveh or Jesus, the Quran presents itself entirely as the direct words of God, who sometimes speaks in the first person (both singular and plural), sometimes in the third, and occasionally changes from one to the other in midsentence. As one prominent Muslim scholar has noted, the fact that the Quran represents the direct communication of God may help to explain its difficult, seemingly jumbled text, almost impenetrable at times, as if "the language of mortal man were, under the formidable pressure of the Heavenly Word, broken into a thousand fragments."

Relatively short (around 400 pages in English translation, a little less than the New Testament), the Quran consists of 114 **suras,** or chapters, arranged in order of their length rather than in chronological order of transmission. Following the short introductory prayer called **al-Fatiha** ("the Opening") comes the longest sura, with 285 verses; the shortest suras, with 3–6 verses, come at the end. Suras are composed of verses called **ayats** ("signs" or "proofs"). The Quran contains two of the key prayers of Islam, the al-Fatiha and the **Surat al-Ikhlas** ("Chapter of Sincerity"), the short 113th sura: "Say: God is One, the Eternal God. He begets none, nor is begotten, and none is like Him." Many of the accounts in this scripture should be familiar to anyone conversant with the Jewish or Christian Bible, e.g., the annunciation of the angel to Mary, informing her that she will bear a child without "knowing" a man (19:16–21). The Arabic Quran also contains the 99 principal names of Allah, most of them describing compassionate qualities, such as the Patient (**Sabur**), the Loving (**Wadud**), the Wise (**Hakim**), the Truth or Reality (**Haqq**), the Light (**Nur**), the Forgiver (**Ghaffar**), and, most frequently, the Compassionate (**Rahman**) and the Merciful (**Rahim**).

Over a period of about 22 years, beginning in approximately 610, the Quran was revealed to Muhammad by the angel Gabriel (although Arabic has no separate word to distinguish angels from archangels, some are clearly more important than others, with Michael heading the list). The earlier revelations were received in trance states that caused the Prophet to groan, cry out, and shiver so intensely that he often covered himself with a cloak, and they were frequently accompanied by headaches and severe muscular tension. Later he became more accustomed to these states of deep absorption. His Companions committed all of the revelations to memory, and they were eventually written down on whatever was available, including leaves, shards of pottery, and, according to tradition, the shoulder blades of camels. By the time the Prophet had moved from Mecca to Medina, he was dictating to secretaries, the most prominent of whom was **Zayd ibn Tabit**.

After Muhammad's death, his successor, Abu Bakr, put Zayd in charge of collating the written suras with versions that had been memorized by several of his followers, but his compilation often ignored the order in which they were received. The Caliph Uthman (644–55), a direct Companion of the Prophet and his third successor, had a definitive text compiled from copies left with one of Muhammad's widows, Hafsa, and destroyed all the rest. The span of decades and centuries between the revelations of many previous religious founders and their committal to writing was thereby largely avoided in Islam, although some scholars think that certain suras were deleted or altered to serve the purposes of the early caliphs. For example, the Quran's most critical attacks on the Umayyad clans may have been expunged on orders from Uthman, himself an Umayyad. By having all variant copies of the text destroyed, he ensured that only his version remains today, although we have no reason to believe that anything essential was left out.

THE SATANIC CONTROVERSY

Among the controversies over changes in the original text, one tradition reverberates to this day. Early in his struggles with his own tribe, the Quraysh, and under pressure to avoid or moderate their wrath, Muhammad supposedly received a Quranic revelation that aimed to accommodate the idolatrous ways of his Arab neighbors. This revelation, which permitted some veneration or respect toward three daughters of Allah—al-Lat, al-Uzza, and Manat—came to be known as **The Satanic Verses.** According to tradition, Muhammad later said that he had been misled by a wily Satan, and those particular verses were expunged from the Quran, replaced by verses 19–23 of the 53rd sura. Orthodox Muslim scholarship now holds that the hadiths, or non-Quranic oral traditions, that form the basis for this story are later forgeries and that this transmission never took place. However, the mere existence of the legend has sometimes been seized upon in attempts to discredit the validity of Islam. By naming his 1988 novel after these infamous verses, author **Salman Rushdie** (b. 1947) signaled his intention to debunk Islam, spurring the Ayatollah Khomeini to declare the novel blasphemous and issue a **fatwa,** or formal legal judgment, calling for the death of Rushdie, who remains in hiding as of this writing. His marriage shattered, his literary life reduced to furtive, unscheduled appearances in England and the United States, Rushdie announced his conversion to Islam, but the fatwa has remained in effect.

already had. Muhammad established a more humane legal structure while abolishing usury, instituting systematic charity, fixing the lunar calendar, and, on a larger scale, bringing together a far-flung group of nomadic clans into a unified Arab people with one God, one book, one Prophet, and one form of worship.

Passages in the Quran appear to reflect aspects of Arabic tradition, along with elements of the Bible, the Talmud*, and the apocrypha*, with which Muhammad was surely familiar from his close contacts with Christians and Jews. The text acknowledges as much: "This Quran could not have been devised by any but God. It confirms what was revealed before it, and fully explains the Scriptures" (10:38). However, any notion that the Quran itself was "influenced" by the monks and rabbis whom the Messenger encountered in the desert, or by their scriptures, would be unacceptable to Muslims. Islam holds the Quran to be the direct revelation of God, not the work of any human; it is meant not only to confirm previous revelations but also to correct certain misconceptions that developed among the followers of Abraham, Moses, and Jesus. As the Messenger, Muhammad was not in a position to alter or influence the revelation as it came to him. Nonetheless, many of Muhammad's personal utterances, conveyed by oral tradition distinct from the Quran, resonate with aspects of the Judeo-Christian tradition. For instance, Muhammad's request that when fighting the jihad, or holy war, Muslim warriors should "avoid striking the face" of the enemy "for God created Adam in His image" reflects the rationale behind the Jewish law against shedding the blood of another.

Each sura but one opens with the Names of Mercy: *Bismillah ir-Rahman ir-Rahim,* "In the name of God, the Compassionate, the Merciful." (The exception, called the Sura of Repentance, deals with the harsh treatment of the idolators who continued in their ways after the Muslim occupation of the Kaaba in Mecca.) Many of the Quranic revelations are specific responses to historical events as they were happening to Muhammad and his followers, including updates or additions to the sacred laws of Islam as they had previously been revealed.

Of the 28 prophets mentioned in the Quran, 18 are from the Hebrew Bible and 3 from the New Testament, including Adam, Noah, Abraham, Ishmael, Moses, Elijah, Solomon, Job, John the Baptist, and Jesus Christ; the other 7 are for the most part obscure figures from Arabian tradition. Although the Quran venerates Jesus, it does not recognize his divinity, holding instead that "God . . . begot none, nor was He begotten."

Although Muslims do not question the authenticity of the Quran, they do disagree about whether every letter is the literal word of God or whether the message should be understood as a whole. Since the Quran was revealed in Arabic, many Muslims consider only the Arabic Quran, with its unique linguistic resonance, to represent the true word of God, and translations to be mere approximations, notwithstanding the fact that orthodox Muslims both translate the Quran and read it in translation. Only about one Muslim in five is Arabic-speaking, yet during the five-times-daily prayers they recite the Quran almost universally in Arabic.

Muslims accept four other books of revelation preceding the Quran, and these are fully regarded as holy scripture:

1. The Scrolls (**Suhuf**), 10 scriptures given to the Hebrew patriarch Abraham and since lost.
2. The Torah (**Taurat**) revealed to Moses on Mount Sinai.
3. The Psalms (**Zabur**) revealed to David.
4. The Gospels (**Injil**) revealed to Jesus.

The other major source of Islamic teaching, **hadith** ("narrative" or "report") consists of the sayings of Muhammad and his Companions passed down and collected in the centuries immediately following his death. It began as an oral tradition that the Prophet during his lifetime was careful to distinguish from the revealed teachings of the Quran. (An interesting parallel exists in Hinduism between shruti*, "that which is revealed," and smriti*, "that which is heard.") Six major collections of hadith were eventually compiled by a number of hands during the first 300 years after Muhammad's death, and not all of the sayings are considered to be of equal authenticity. Since considerable time elapsed before they were written down, there was room for invention and distortion, a problem recognized by early Muslim scholars. And so no absolutely canonical edition exists, although there is significant agreement about the major collections of hadith. The most important collection is by **Muhammad ibn Ismail al-Bukhari** (810–70), which is divided by topic into 97 volumes containing 7,300 individual items. Later collections also exist, especially those created by Shiite Muslims tracing hadith derived from the Prophet's son-in-law and third caliph, Ali, and his supporters. **Hadith qudsi** are those oral sayings that are manifested directly through the voice of Allah, i.e., they are believed to have been spoken by God but are not included in the Quran. To differentiate, the other kind are sometimes called **hadith nabawi,** or "prophetic tradition."

The hadith are based on **isnads,** or chains of authorities; each hadith generally begins with an attestation as to who heard it from whom, e.g., "Abdallah ibn Jafar records that he heard Ali ibn Abi Talib say that he heard the Prophet remark, 'The best of women [in the world] was Mary. The best of women [of this people] was Khadija.' " Some isnads are considerably longer, linking eight or ten names. In this fashion, not only were many details of the Prophet's life filled in, but further interpretations were also made of the law as stated in the Quran. Their application to the problems of everyday life gives hadith the same practical orientation that the Talmud bears in relation to the Hebrew Bible. For instance, one hadith has Muhammad telling the story of a woman who was cruel to a cat, shutting it in so that it died of hunger, and who was subsequently sent to hell. In another, he tells of a man who saw a dog panting with thirst near a well from which he himself had just drunk. The man climbed down the well and filled his shoe with water, "and taking it in his teeth, he climbed out of the well and gave the water to the dog. God was pleased with this act and granted him pardon [for his sins]." These hadiths are used to support kindness to animals, although there are no specific revelations in the Quran concerning this question. Hadith is not necessarily binding; despite the fact that one hadith has the Prophet saying, "The virgin cannot be given in marriage until her consent has been asked," the right of **jabr,** or the arranged marriage of minors without their consent, has long been practiced among certain Muslims. Taken as a group, however, hadith along with the Quran form the basis of the **sunna**—the way of life of the Prophet that Muslims take as their model or code of Muslim orthodoxy.

The third source of spiritual guidance for Muslims is **sira,** biography of Muhammad in chronological form. Siras are only somewhat reliable because of a large gap between the death of Muhammad and their composition. The earliest extant and the best is the **Sirat-ar-Rasul** ("Life of the Prophet") by **Ibn Hisham** (d. 834), which summarizes an earlier lost work by **Ibn Ishaq.**

❋ THE PROPHET AS MYSTIC

A good barometer of Muhammad's radicalness is the extent to which his teachings outraged the religious and social establishment. To begin with, the Prophet was declaring a casteless religion in which women, Bedouins, and members of foreign clans were to be treated with the respect normally reserved for the men of one's own clan. Besides calling for an end to promiscuous sex, alcohol consumption, and the common Arab practice of female infanticide, he was exceptional for his emphasis on compassion (one of his great personal traits) in a culture largely based on ego-driven codes of honor and shame.

Like Jesus, toward whom he felt great respect and kinship, Muhammad experienced certain events that fit the profile of classic mystical encounters. One in particular is still the source of dispute among Islamic scholars. Around the year 619 or 620, according to tradition, Muhammad had either an extraordinary vision or a miraculous journey. Awakened one night by the Archangel Gabriel, he was taken on a heavenly tour mounted on **Buraq,** a white, winged beast "between a mule and an ass," from Mecca to Jerusalem, with stops at Mount Sinai and Bethlehem. At the Temple in Jerusalem, he prayed with Abraham, Moses, and Jesus before ascending a celestial ladder of seven planes of being to the **seventh heaven** and beyond, where he communed with the formless God, utterly dazzled by this direct merging. Allah commanded Muhammad to have his people vow to pray 50 times a day. Moses, stationed a level or two below, buttonholed the Prophet as he descended and, when he heard what had transpired, urged him to go back and talk to God about a more reasonable deal. Muhammad returned, and God agreed to cut the number of prayers to 40. This still wasn't enough for Moses, who, in the great Abrahamic tradition of haggling with God for the sake of humanity, insisted that Muhammad return. After a few more intercessions, God finally reduced the number of daily prayers to 5. Although Moses advised Muhammad to negotiate a still better deal, Muhammad was loath to ask again, and Muslim law was set for all time.

This voyage is known as the Night Journey (**al-Isra**) and the Ascension (**al-Miraj**), and Muslim scholars still debate whether it occurred miraculously in bodily form or took place on the astral* or spirit plane. Aisha later claimed that Muhammad was sleeping beside her all night, and both versions have their supporters. The astral theory has marked parallels to mystical and out-of-body* experiences in other traditions, as well as to the ascension* in Christian and Gnostic* literature. Some scholars have remarked that the account of the Prophet's journey through the seven heavens may have influenced the medieval Christian poet Dante's *Divine Comedy.*

Beyond that account, many of the sayings of Muhammad recounted as hadiths or the wisdom transmitted through him in the Quran have the same sense of "living in the moment" urgency that we find at the heart of all the great traditions: "Do for this world as if you were to live a thousand years, and for the next as if you were to die tomorrow." "At evening, do not expect to be alive by morning. In the morning, do not assume that you will survive till evening." Since readiness to depart implies a spirit of detachment from ego, he could also say, "Live every moment in this world as if you were a traveler in a strange land." The Prophet's compassion clearly flows from his mystical experience of Divine Unity, or seeing all of life as the expression of One Reality. "A faithful person is brother to all," he said. "He never oppresses his spiritual brothers, never fails them, never deceives them, never regards them as inferior." And so it follows, as the Prophet said, "Among you there should be neither harming nor reciprocating harm," and "Never turn away from one another or undercut one another, even to the slightest degree." The realization of Divine Unity evidently stimulates the sense of human affinity, as it did for Jesus and the Buddha.

NIGHT FLIGHT

All attempts by the Quraysh to suppress the growing community of Islam having failed, the clans planned to assassinate the Prophet. In 622, fearing for his life in Mecca, Muhammad and his closest Companion, Abu Bakr, escaped in the dead of night and journeyed north by camel (named **Qaswa**) to the oasis of **Yathrib**, specifically to a place the Prophet had dreamed of, "the well-watered land between two tracts of black stones." The most heavily populated part of the oasis was known as "the city"—in Arabic *al-Madinah,* or **Medina**—and according to tradition he arrived there on September 27, 622. The journey of emigration was

Like the great cathedrals of Europe, the mosques of the Islamic world reflect sacred beauty in art and architecture. Every square foot of this minaret from the Masjid-el-Chan, or Mosque of the King, in Isfahan, Iran, is covered with different abstract, floral, or calligraphic designs. The circular rampart from which the muezzin traditionally calls the faithful to prayer has been augmented by a loudspeaker, a concession to modern necessity.
ART RESOURCE

called the **Hijra** ("breaking bonds," anglicized as **Hegira**). A number of Muhammad's followers had preceded him to Yathrib beginning on July 16 of that year, which later under the Caliph Umar became day 1 of the Muslim calendar. The year 622 became known as AH 1, for *Anno Hegirae,* or Year of the Hegira. The Meccans who accompanied or followed Muhammad were known as Emigrants (**Muhajirun**), and sympathetic Medinans as Helpers (**Ansar**).

In Medina, Muhammad was able openly to invite people to Islam and establish a fairly safe base of operations. He made compacts with the Jewish tribes living there and asked his followers to adopt the Jewish practice of circumcision, still today a mandatory part of Islamic custom even if not mentioned in the Quran. He continued to receive Quranic revelations, which prescribed regular almsgiving and fasting during the lunar month of Ramadan, from before sunrise to sunset each day, among other duties. During his time in Medina, the Prophet determined the manner of calling the faithful to prayer (originally from the highest house in the area of the humble mosque his followers were building with mud walls and palm leaf roof) and the form of the calling prayer, which was

414

revealed to one of the faithful in a dream. For the first **muezzin** to call the prayer, he chose his black African servant **Bilal** because of his stentorian voice. Following a divine command, Muhammad initiated the practice of turning to face the Kaaba in Mecca during ritual prayer and other rites; previously in Mecca, the faithful had faced Jerusalem as the sacred center of the prophetic tradition.

On the more mundane side, Muhammad was especially sensitive to odor and on at least one occasion refused to eat food that was cooked with an abundance of garlic. He also insisted on the practice of cleaning the teeth with a tooth stick. It was perhaps the last action he performed for himself before dying and has become a popular practice among Muslims. As happened with Moses, Muhammad began to spend much of his time in Medina adjudicating legal and familial disputes. He arranged numerous marriages among his followers, some of which were politically valuable.

Short of money and supplies after their emigration, the Medinan Muslims took to raiding caravans of the Quraysh bound for Mecca, which Muslim scholars argue was legitimate because Muhammad was in a state of war with the Meccans. After half a dozen unsuccessful attempts, his men finally captured a caravan, but through a misunderstanding they murdered an escort during the sacred months when combat was traditionally forbidden among all Arabs. This prompted a new revelation that concluded, "Idolatry is worse than killing," providing the rationale for future battles on behalf of Islam. In March 624 (AH 3), while setting out to intercept a large caravan from Syria, a few more than 300 Muslims met at **Badr** with a force of 1,000 Quraysh from Mecca that had come to protect the caravan. Miraculously, the Muslims carried the day, leading combatants on both sides to speculate that the Prophet's forces had been joined by heavenly hosts on horseback, reminiscent of God's intervention on behalf of the Israelites. In fact, the whole concept of waging war to gain control of the land and evict or destroy idol worshipers seems like a throwback to the biblical days of Exodus*, Judges*, and Kings*— with the difference that the Muslims had been driven from their own city by its power-conscious rulers.

Based on revelations he received, Muhammad promised entry into Paradise to any Muslim killed in fighting the holy war, or **jihad;** those who died came to be called martyrs. In the broader sense, though, *jihad* refers to striving against evil spiritually and physically. According to hadith, on returning to Medina from successful battles in Mecca and Hunayn, Muhammad exclaimed, "We return from the lesser holy war *(jihad)* to wage the greater holy war *(mujahada),*" which he explained as "the war against the soul," the struggle against the limited self or separative ego. In fact, many modern Islamic scholars of jurisprudence think that the only true jihads were those engaged in by the Prophet and his Companions; and all Muslims admit that compulsion in religion goes against the Quran (2:257). Beginning with Muhammad, Islam accepted Christians and Jews because they were "people of the book," possessing an authentic holy scripture—and, no doubt, because they also believed in one God. Later Muslims accepted religions as seemingly polytheistic as Zoroastrianism* and Hinduism for the same reason. Despite Islam's reputation as an intolerant religion, the teachings of the Quran are very clear on the subject of other religions (as opposed to idolatry): "We make no distinction between any of his Messengers" (2:285).

In 625, a force of 3,000 Quraysh, bent on exterminating the Muslims, attacked Medina at the foot of **Mount Uhud** and in the ensuing skirmishes badly routed the outnumbered Muslims, wounding Muhammad. The defeat seemed to strengthen Muhammad's resolve to fight to defend his community and to check his compassion toward any he suspected of being against him. He began by chasing one of the Jewish tribes out of Yathrib and raiding the Bedouins to the south of Medina, both for their support of the Meccans. The Meccan forces returned, 10,000 strong, to finish off the Muslims, but with the aid of **Salmon the Persian** (al-Farisi), who suggested an old Persian stratagem of encircling the stronghold with a wide trench, and a sustained storm, the Muslims once again held off the Quraysh. Muhammad then set about slaughtering a Jewish tribe of Yathrib who had collaborated with the Meccans.

❈ THE DOUBLE-EDGED SWORD OF ISLAM

Having decisively defeated the main Meccan force, Muhammad entered Mecca and took it almost without resistance and with few deaths. Another important victory followed at Hudayn, and Islam was on its way to becoming the religion of all Arabia. Contrary to the traditions of Arabian warfare, the Prophet did not take murderous revenge on his former enemies, and his compassion moved many of them to come to Islam voluntarily. Even discounting the supernatural abilities attributed to Muhammad in various biographies, he was an extremely gifted leader with an intuitive grasp of personality and human psychology. Full of spiritual charisma, he was also imbued with the compassion and common sense to offer reconciliation to idolators when they finally did embrace Islam, even as his Muslim forces were calling for retribution.

Because of its history of military conquests and of offering the conquered the choice of conversion to Islam or death, Islam has unfairly gained the reputation of being the religion of the sword. In this context it may help to recall that the Middle Eastern custom of warfare generally offered no choice at all—the vanquished were either killed outright, enslaved, or at best held for ransom. Triumphant Islamic generals offered the further choice to the conquered of paying a tribute rather than converting. Christian rulers, in contrast, frequently offered the limited options of death or conversion to Jews and Muslims already living peaceably within their own boundaries. Jesus himself said in a startling Gospel passage, "Do not think that I have come to bring peace on earth; I have come not to bring peace, but a sword" (Matt. 10:34). That Islam should be perceived as violent when the Quran speaks ceaselessly of God as "the Compassionate, the Merciful" may seem like a contradiction. Muslim scholars point to Muhammad's 13 years of nonviolent struggle in Mecca—where he "turned the other cheek," as it were—and the defensive nature of most of his battles as proof that he was a reluctant warrior. Ultimately, they argue, Muhammad was a pragmatist in his spirituality; his compassion and sense of justice by all reports far outweighed his fierceness as fighter and moral reformer.

❊ DEATH AND SUCCESSION

In 632, Muhammad died in Medina, in the hut of Aisha, his favorite wife. He had made no formal nomination of a successor, but he had appointed Abu Bakr to lead the prayers in the mosque and, by implication, to become the next leader of Islam. However, the actual selection of Abu Bakr was made by a consultation of elders and Companions, establishing that succession was not hereditary. Bakr's original title was **Khalifat Rasul Allah** ("Successor of the Messenger of God"), later shortened to Khalifa, or **caliph,** and he and succeeding caliphs were deemed the rightful successors of Muhammad and true guides of Islam.

The selection of Muhammad's successor led Muslims to divide into what are now Islam's two largest sects, Sunnis and Shiites. Shiites were supporters of **Ali ibn Abi Talib,** Muhammad's son-in-law (the word *Shia* means "partisans"). The Shiites contended that Ali should have been chosen to succeed Muhammad immediately, arguing that Muhammad had implied in various hadiths, accepted even by Sunni scholars, that Ali was to succeed him. They point additionally to the fact that Ali was the second person, after Khadija, to accept Muhammad's teachings, that he was the Prophet's cousin and son-in-law, and that his sons Hasan and Hussein were the only grandchildren of the Prophet to survive into adulthood. And yet, in the communal negotiations following the death of the Prophet, Ali was passed over. Shiites and Sunnis propose various reasons for this: some Shiites suggest that Ali was unwilling to encourage sedition by advancing an alternative claim to the caliphates of Abu Bakr and his successors Umar and Uthman. In any case, Ali held off recognizing Abu Bakr's authority at first, but after the death of his wife Fatima six months later, he gave in. His followers, the Shiites, never did give in, however, forging the earliest and most significant rift in Islam.

Abu Bakr's first utterance after Muhammad's death, in keeping with Islam's teaching about the humanity of the Prophet, was "If you worship Muhammad, know that he is dead; but if you worship God, know that God is living." The Quran made it clear that Muhammad was the last of the prophets—124,000 in all, according to tradition—and that his leadership would not be passed on by heredity. Abu Bakr died two years later, naming as the next caliph **Umar,** who ruled for ten years while extending the Muslim sphere of influence. Islam was thus a theocratic state from the beginning, and even converts like the great Quraysh general **Khalid ibn al-Walid,** victor over the Muslims at Uhud, were enlisted in fighting for the faith. Yet, as great a warrior as Khalid was also subject to standards set by the Prophet; when his extravagant, ostentatious style infuriated Umar, he was relieved of his command.

Umar himself was killed by a Persian Christian in 644 and was succeeded by **Uthman,** another of the original Companions, who was in turn assassinated in 656 by fellow Muslims disgruntled at what clearly appeared to be a greedy and nepotistic rule. Ali, the last of the Companions (and the last Arab) to be caliph, was elected and served for five years, during which he held his political adversary Aisha under house arrest for some time before finally letting her go. During this time he was opposed by **Muawiya,** a member of the Umayyad family of Uthman and governor of Syria, who refused to accept Ali's caliphate.

MUSLIM DYNASTIES AT A GLANCE

Dynasty	Dates	First Caliph
Umayyad (Syria)	(661–750)	Muawiyah
(Spain)	(756–1031)	Abd ar-Rahman I
Abbasid (Persia)	(750–1258)	Abul Abbas Abdallah (nicknamed as-Saffah, "Shedder of Blood")
(Cairo)	(1261–1517)	
Fatimid	(910–1171)	Ubaydallah al Mahdi
Safavid (Persia)	(1501–1732)	Ismail I
Mughal (India)	(1526–1858)	Babar
Qajar (Persia)	(1779–1925)	Agha Muhammad
Ottoman (Turkey)	(1281–1924)	Osman (Uthman) I

Following the assassination of Ali in 661 and the accession of Muawiya, the caliphate became hereditary, beginning with the **Umayyad dynasty,** which ruled until 750, when it was supplanted by the Hashimite **Abbasids** of Baghdad. They ruled until 1258, when the Mongols sacked Baghdad, the Abbasid capital. During the reign of the Umayyad caliph **Abd al-Malik** (685–705), the **Dome of the Rock** was built in Jerusalem on the former site of the Temple* of Solomon in 691. In modern Jerusalem, Muslims still worship at the Dome, which rises above the Western Wall*, the only remaining piece of the ancient Temple and a site sacred to Jews.

419

Meanwhile, the Muslim forces continued to absorb the Persian, Byzantine, and Visigoth empires with a powerful combination of military strength and religious worldview. At the fullest extent of Muslim military and cultural power (in 632, when Charles Martel contained their advance into Europe at Tours, near Poitiers), Islam was the religion of Arabia, Persia (Iran), and Syria; parts of the Caucasus (southern Russia), Afghanistan, and India; all of Spain; and almost all of North Africa, including Morocco, Algeria, Tunisia, Tripoli (modern Libya), and Egypt.

The Zoroastrian heritage of the Persian Abbasids, their mystical religion of light and dark, good and evil, and their great love of art and luxury colored the original moralistic nature of Islam. The Abbasids built the magnificent city of Baghdad in the 760s and made it the cultural and artistic center of the Middle East. Persian became the dominant language of Muslim poetry. Throughout the Umayyad and both Abbasid dynasties, the caliphs were increasingly obsessed with amassing and flaunting wealth and proved themselves capable of the kind of immense cruelty to their opponents (mutilation and agonizingly slow deaths were a favorite pastime) that would have filled the Prophet with righteous indignation. More often than not they ruled with complete indifference to the moral principles of the religion they imposed on those they conquered; they gloried in explosive paroxysms of military conquest followed by prolonged refreshment with an endless stream of courtesans, feasts, and revelry. The tenuousness of their grasp on leadership is probably best exemplified by the extraordinarily high percentage of caliphs who died by assassination.

The peculiar irony of Islam during this period is that the very unity and strength that Muhammad's religious reforms imposed on previously splintered and fractious Arab clans, his irresistible call to worship one God and follow one holy way of life, at the same time made it possible to direct that new cohesiveness to destructive and amoral ends. Much the same thing, of course, had happened during the furious spread of Christianity across Europe centuries before, and perhaps to a lesser extent during the consolidation of power by the Israelites in previous eras. What began as an idealistic impulse to expand a revolutionary mystical vision soon proved too much for the more conventional, less visionary, and far more self-absorbed leaders who followed Moses, Jesus, and Muhammad.

THE SLIPPERY SLOPE

As with other great religions, a period of distortion of Islam began soon after the death of its founder. Hardly was Muhammad buried under the floor of Aisha's hut in Medina than the forces which succeeded him, controlled to some degree by the first four "rightly guided" caliphs (whose terms added up to less than 30 years), had begun to undercut the Prophet's vision. A modern Muslim scholar evaluates it this way:

Many of the so-called cultural and ethnic habits that we see in Muslims today are not derived from the original teachings of Islam, but trace their origins back to that period of the corrupt Ummayad dynasty. Indeed dynastic rule itself was forbidden by Muhammad. The separation of men and women within the same house began in Damascus. There were men who wanted to have dancing girls in their palaces and so they created for the women of the household ladies' quarters, which had not existed in houses before. The mosque, which had been the center of the community where the general public met, and which was the center of economic, social, and political exchange as well as a place of worship, ceased to be so. The mosque became a place of ritualistic worship and lost its pivotal position in the life of the community. The caliph grew fat, often drank and did not want to leave his palace. Accordingly the palace became the center of power and governmental activities. In order not to have his debauchery openly exposed, the caliph separated the women and the children from himself, and thus the home was divided and fragmented.

—SHAYKH FADHLALLA HAERI, *THE ELEMENTS OF SUFIS*

Despite the decline in caliber of the leaders, a genuine spiritual experience endured and grew steadily among the faithful. At least a few of the early caliphs actually attended to spiritual matters. The Caliph **al-Mamun,** who ruled in the 9th century, presented a liberal interpretation of Muslim sacred law strongly influenced by Greek thought. He implied that the Quran was not immutable and that free will was not an evil that opened the door to sin but a blessing that promised freedom and joy. He was opposed in this by fundamentalists led by Ahmad ibn Hanbal. But Mamun was the exception that proved the rule, at least until the 14th century. An important spiritual impetus for Islam during much of this time was provided by less prominent Muslims with an ascetic and mystical bent, who came to be known as **Sufis.** Sufism is a significant and profound development within Islam and should never be considered separately from the main tradition. But before examining Sufism, it is essential first to look at the basic tenets of Islam and at some of its major divisions.

I SURRENDER, GOD: THE FIVE PILLARS OF ISLAM

As already mentioned, Islam shares many of its major tenets with Christianity and Judaism, including the expectation of an end of time followed by a final judgment. According to the Quran, "To Moses [God] gave the Scriptures, a perfect code for the righteous with precepts about all things, a guide and a mercy" (6:154). The Quran has praise for the Christians, especially their monks and priests (5:85), but it reveals that God is neither begotten nor begets (13:17), rejecting Christian teaching that Jesus is the divine Son of God. Muhammad had great reverence for the figure of Jesus, and although he believed that a crucifixion had taken place, he felt that another body had been substituted for Christ's. The Quran reads, "They did not slay Jesus, nor crucify him, only a likeness of it appeared to them" (4:156).

Many verses of the Quran speak of a broad religious tolerance not generally associated with Western stereotypes of Islam, e.g., "Believers, Jews, Sabaeans and Christians—whoever believes in God and the Last Day and does what is right—shall have nothing to fear or to regret" (5:69). (The

Sabaeans were an ancient people who flourished in southwestern Arabia around the middle of the 1st millennium BC, in the kingdom of Saba, called Sheba in the Bible.) However, the Quran admonishes that the Jews "have tampered with words out of their context" and that both Christians and Jews "have forgotten much of what they were enjoined."

YOU SAY POTATO: WHERE ISLAM PARTS COMPANY WITH CHRISTIANITY

Christians and Jews, labeled "disbelievers" (as opposed to infidels or *mushrikun* polytheists), were at least considered preferable to the "idolators" who acknowledged no God but worshiped idols of stone and metal. In fact, Islam shares a surprising number of Christian tenets while rejecting some crucial ones, including the belief in the Trinity*, the doctrine that there are three Persons in one Godhead: Father, Son, and Holy Spirit. Here are some other points of comparison:

A CHRISTIAN	A MUSLIM
Worships Christ as God.	Reveres Jesus as a great prophet.
Believes in the crucifixion, resurrection, and ascension of Jesus.	Believes that Jesus ascended into Paradise, but that he did not die on the cross.
Believes that all humanity (except the Blessed Mother) inherited Adam's original sin.	Accepts the original sin of Adam and Eve, but not the notion of inherited sin.
Believes in the Virgin Birth and the Second Coming of Jesus.	Believes in the Virgin Birth and the Second Coming of Jesus.
Confesses sins to a priest.	Asks forgiveness of sins directly from Allah.

One important belief that Muslims do share in large part with Christians is the vivid expectation of the **Last Day.** Just as described in the book of Revelation* in the New Testament, the Quranic Last Day will occur suddenly and with great cosmic upheaval: "When the sun ceases to shine; when the stars fall down and the mountains are blown away; when camels big with young are left untended, and the wild beasts are brought together; when the seas are set alight and men's souls are reunited; . . . when Hell burns fiercely and Paradise is brought near. . . . When the sky is rent asunder; when the stars scatter and the oceans roll together; when the graves are hurled about; each soul shall know what it has done and what it has failed to do" (81, 82).

At this time, Muslims believe, the Mahdi will appear, a Messianic figure interpreted differently by the various sects as either Jesus, Ismail son of the sixth Imam, or the hidden twelfth Imam. Most Muslims accept the coming of both Jesus and the Mahdi, who is his forerunner. As with the Jews, there have been instances of false Messiahs—misleading or deluded Muslims deceived into thinking of themselves as the Mahdi, the Guided One. The silence of the Quran on this subject allows for a wide range of traditional beliefs. But the Quran does describe a kind of final judgment in which a book containing an account of each person's actions will be placed either in the right hand (meaning entry into Paradise) or in the left (meaning condemnation to hell).

In the Islamic hierarchy of belief, the lowest degree is submission without faith, such as was practiced by the so-called **Hypocrites** of Medina, who joined Islam out of sheer expediency. Four higher degrees of faith, or enlightenment (in the Quran, *light* means "faith"), are specifically enumerated in the Quranic image of a niche in a wall containing a lighted lamp. The lowest of the four levels corresponds to the niche, illuminated but not luminous; next is the glass in which the lamp is placed; then the oil that "blazes in splendor even though earthly fire has not touched it"; and finally the flame itself, pure illumination.

Likewise, the Quran divides humanity into four groups: **those of the left,** who are condemned; **those of the right,** who are saved; the **righteous,** whose belief rises above the perfunctory minimum required to be saved; and the **foremost** or **slaves of God,** who are closest of all to God—theirs are "the souls which are at peace." Each group except those of the left will be rewarded in Paradise, but the degree will differ.

Paradise itself appears to be divided into two levels. One is the simple Paradise composed of earthly delights: "gardens that are watered by flowing rivers where they shall dwell immortal" and **houris,** the divinely chaste maidens who satisfy the desires of the saved, which are not considered physical desires except to the least mature Muslim understanding. The Supreme Paradise, **Ridwan,** adds to all that what Muhammad called "the meeting with my Lord," which would seem to parallel the Christian notion of the Beatific Vision*, the blissful and unmediated merging with God. For Sufis, Ridwan carries the further connotation of reabsorption by God, or eternal companionship with Him.

All these beliefs, important as they are, rest on what are called the **Five Pillars (Arkan),** or obligations, which uphold the very structure of Islam. Their practice is essential.

1. tashahhud, the profession of unity (**tauhid**): "There is no god but God, and Muhammad is the Messenger of God" (the **shahada,** "witnessing"). This is the keystone of Islamic belief, and it is sometimes said that the earnest profession of this spiritual commitment is enough to make one a Muslim. However, unless one follows the other four pillars, especially the daily prayers, one may be considered to have forsaken Islam.

2. salat: the five-times-daily prayer, performed just before dawn, just after noon, in midafternoon, just after sunset, and after nightfall. Ritual ablutions with water take place before the prayers, which consist of a strictly prescribed series of postures. The **raka,** or cycle of prayer, which has not changed since the dawn of Islam, begins with the phrase *Allahu Akbar* ("God is greater"—than human conception) followed by a short prayer of praise, followed by the Fatihah and the word **Amin** ("so be it," equivalent to the Hebrew Amen*). While reciting other prayers, worshipers lower their palms to their knees and bow the head, straighten up again, prostrate themselves on toes, knees, palms, and forehead, and return to a sitting position, hands on knees, for the final prayer. The number of requisite rakas varies from two to four depending on the time of day.

3. zakat: the compulsory annual charity, traditionally one-fortieth of a person's income, is distinct from the duty of giving alms (**sadaqa**) on a spot basis to those in need (Muslim tradition insists that one should never refuse a beggar). The zakat is spent to help needy members of the Muslim community, for debtors and travelers, and to win converts to Is-

SALAT

A Western Muslim describes the mystical background of the prayers of Islam:

The sublime Oral Tradition, or *hadith,* reports that Prophet Muhammad, upon him be peace, received *salat,* the five times daily prayer of Islam, during his mystical ascension through the heavens and beyond Paradise into the glorious Garden of Essence. During this journey, the Messenger of Allah was able to contemplate angels performing each of the various movements of *salat.* Some stood in rapture before the Divine Majesty, others bowed continuously in astonishment and awe, still others remained lost in full prostration—all of them merged consciously in Divine Unity. Therefore, *salat* is a gift from Allah, displayed first through angelic beings, rather than a ceremonial form springing from human intellect, will, or initiative. The Prophet of Islam proclaimed, *"Salat* is the ascension of the faithful," thereby indicating that his own mystical experience of ascending through the heavens to the Divine Throne and beyond can be replicated in the life of the humble practitioner of daily prayer.

—LEX HIXON NUR AL JERRAHI,
ATOM FROM THE SUN OF KNOWLEDGE

lam, which may include preparing for jihad. In the early days of Islam, since the zakat was not applied to the poor it amounted to a progressive tax, not merely on income (like the Jewish and Christian tithe) but on all assets. However, the zakat as a civil code is now virtually extinct, having been replaced by modern tax codes. It is a voluntary yet highly respected form of offering, often to the local mosque.

4. sawm: the fast from before sunrise to sunset each day for the full lunar month of **Ramadan,** the ninth month of the Muslim calendar. Ramadan may last 29 or 30 days depending on the cycle of the moon, and shifts earlier each year by 11 days, so that over 33 years it traverses all the different seasons. This time shift makes the fast of longer or shorter duration depending on the season and affects the hardship connected with it; during long, hot summer days, to go without food or water is no easy matter. The fast covers food, drink, medicine, tobacco, and sexual intercourse; believers should hear or recite the entire Quran at least once during the course of Ramadan. The proscriptions are lifted from sundown to dawn, and the breaking of the fast each evening during the month should be a joyous occasion. A three-day festival takes place at the end of Ramadan, as at the end of the month for pilgrimage. These are the two major holy festivals of Islam, and because of the Muslim lunar calendar they are not associated with a particular season, as with, say, Christmas or Passover. Children, pregnant or nursing mothers, the ill, travelers, and those involved in warfare are not obliged to fast.

5. hajj: the pilgrimage to the Kaaba in Mecca is expected of every healthy and solvent adult at least once in a lifetime. Compassionate and practical, Islam does not require the hajj of those who cannot afford the expense of the trip or of supporting their families while away. They may contribute what they can to the expenses of a substitute who represents a number of would-be pilgrims. Aside from its devotional aspects, one subsidiary function of the hajj is to cause Muslims of all races, colors, and economic brackets to meet on an equal basis, stripped of the accoutrements of class and status. One of the most famous examples of the inner transformation brought about by this experience is the effect of the hajj on Malcolm X, who became Malik Shabaz, and on his beliefs about race (see pp. 437–38).

If the Five Pillars are the absolute essentials of Islamic practice, the **sharia** is the entire spiritual law of Islam, encompassing both the sayings and practices of Muhammad as contained in the most authoritative hadiths (sunna, "well-trodden path" or "custom") and the revealed word of the Quran.

Other, less formal, but nonetheless commonly observed rules regarding diet clearly have a biblical basis. The eating of pork or the blood of slaughtered animals is forbidden; animals must be slaughtered by cutting

THE HAJJ

The pilgrimage to Mecca, or hajj, which ought to be made at least once in the life of any devout Muslim, was defined by Muhammad during his last triumphant pilgrimage there, based on the ancient rituals which are said to go back to the days of Abraham, Hagar, and Ishmael. It takes place annually at the time of the new moon following the summer solstice, between the 8th and the 12th or 13th days of the 12th and final month of the lunar year. Pilgrims put on simple attire, entering into a taboo state of **ihram** ("mortification"), or ritual consecration. The ritual dress for men consists of two white garments, one around the waist and the other across the shoulder and back, leaving the right arm free; women are expected to cover their entire bodies, although veiling of the face is actually forbidden while circumambulating the Kaaba.

Once at the Kaaba, pilgrims make 7 circumambulations (**tawaf**) of the monument at two different paces, the first three circuits quickly, the last four at a more stately pace, pausing only to kiss or at least to touch the Black Stone. Hundreds of thousands of pilgrims, men and women together, make this tawaf at one time. Next they drink the warm, salty water of the nearby well of Zamzam. Then they run between the two hills of **al-Safa** and **al-Marwa.** This celebrates the tradition of Hagar's search for help for Ishmael; but originally these hills, about 1,200 feet apart near the center of Mecca, were stones sacred to ancient Arab divinities. All of this is considered the **Lesser Pilgrimage.**

The **Greater Pilgrimage** begins with a journey of some 15 miles to the plain of **Arafat,** where pilgrims make a solemn standing (**wuquf**) and listen to a sermon. According to tradition, Arafat ("recognize") is the spot where Adam and Eve reunited after their expulsion from Paradise. The pilgrims then descend to the nearby town of **Muzdalifa** at dusk, pick up 21 small stones or pebbles off the ground, and stop at the plain of **Mina** to sacrifice sheep and camels. (Tradition holds that this small town about three miles from Mecca is where Abraham sacrificed a ram in place of his son Ishmael—Isaac in the Hebrew Bible). They next proceed to throw 7 pebbles at each of three pillars representing Satan (**Iblis**) who, according to Islamic traditions, tried to tempt Abraham, Ishmael, and Hagar to disobey God's command for Abraham to sacrifice his son. The pilgrims break the state of ritual consecration by cutting their hair and nails, and men and women who have faithfully completed every requisite element of the pilgrimage are allowed to call themselves **hajjis** or **hajjas**.

The hajj today is a huge affair; in recent years as many as 3 million pilgrims have come to the shrine annually. An optional addition to the pilgrimage which is deeply cherished by all Muslims is a visit to the tomb of Muhammad in Medina.

their throats while saying a blessing, as in Jewish law. The prohibition against alcohol is more strictly enforced in fundamentalist countries like Saudi Arabia than elsewhere in the Muslim world, but it is generally respected by serious Muslims. Circumcision is widely practiced, although it is not mentioned in the Quran, only in hadith, and is considered a sunna, or custom.

Growing out of Islam's struggles against idolators is the prohibition against the use of pictorial images of God, Muhammad, the caliphs, or anyone at all; the ban is strictly enforced only in mosques. Islamic art does occasionally portray the Prophet and other Muslim notables, but by European and Asian standards their appearance is relatively rare. Instead, Muslims have developed to a high art calligraphy, arabesque, and decorative abstracts using floral designs. Calligraphic icons of Quranic verses and the names of Muhammad and the caliphs are commonly found in both homes and mosques.

The counterpart of the external law comprising the sharia is the inner,

A door frame from
15th-century central
Asia.
FOTO MARBURG/ART
RESOURCE

spiritual reality, or **haqiqa.** The esoteric path of the mystics is known as
the **tariqa;** by extension, tariqa can refer to a Sufi or Dervish order.

❋ DEGREES OF SEPARATION

> Have nothing to do with those who have split up their religion into sects.
> God will call them to account and declare to them what they have done.
> — QURAN 6:160

The major division within Islam devolved from disagreements over the
succession in leadership after the death of the Prophet, between those
who felt that Ali, as the husband of Muhammad's only surviving daughter, Fatima, should follow Muhammad and those who did not. Ali was
passed over three times for other caliphs, and even after he was chosen
as the fourth caliph a schism developed that has lasted over 1,300 years.

Muslims who believe in the legitimacy of the first three caliphs are
Sunnis, meaning that they follow the sunna: the behavior, observances,
sayings, and values of Muhammad and, according to some sources, also
of his Companions and the first four "rightly guided" caliphs, Abu Bakr,
Umar, Uthman, and Ali. Roughly 85 percent of the 1 billion Muslims in
the world today are Sunni, although there are dozens of non-Sunni sects.

For Sunnis, the Quran and sunna determine the law, along with **ijma,** the consensus of Muslim scholars, and **ray,** or individual scholarly interpretation of the law. Sunnis are distinct from Shiites and other smaller sects who claim hereditary descent from the Prophet Muhammad, principally through Ali. Although the Sunnis began with great hostility toward Shiites and other sects, they developed tolerance and liberality over the centuries and today are generally more friendly and open to non-Muslims than are Shiites.

Aside from the early disputes over succession, the main factor dividing Sunnis and other sects of Islam is the principle of community consensus: how the majority interprets the example set by the Prophet. Even the four major schools of law (**madhhab,** pl. **madhahib**) of Sunni Islam are distinguished by how much weight they give to ijma, ray, and other elements.

Among Sunnis, the **Hanbalites** (named for juror-theologian **Ahmad ibn Hanbal**) make up one of the strictest schools, which developed in Iraq and Syria and is now located in Saudi Arabia. **Malikhites** (named for **Malik ibn Anas**) are also rigorous but they recognize supplementary principles of Islamic law such as **istislah,** which takes into account the public welfare. Malikhites are most powerful in North Africa and Sudan. **Hanafites** (named for **Abu Hanifa**) extend throughout Turkey, India, and into China. **Shafiites** cover the southern tip of the Arabian peninsula, Indonesia, and Egypt. But the four schools are all considered orthodox, and members sometimes change from one to the other.

Among the heterodox, the **Kharijites** ("seceders") are reputedly the oldest religious sect of Islam. Originally followers of Ali, they seceded in protest because Ali accepted an arbitrated decision to make him caliph rather than seizing the title they felt was legitimately his. They engaged in fierce terrorist attacks on those Muslims who did not agree with them, including Ali, who was assassinated by a Kharijite in 661. The Kharijites abhorred the notion that the succession of the Prophet was open only to select clans, as the Sunnis and Shiites hold, and felt that any true believing and righteous Muslim could be elected to the caliphate—and could also be removed if he strayed from pure Islam. They were and are strict fundamentalists and Quranic literalists, but were so prone to suicidal violence that their numbers soon dwindled. Their only remaining subsect, the **Ibadites,** live in Oman and northeast Africa.

Shiites or Shia insist on the importance of descent from Muhammad's family and feel that the role of the Prophet's successor ought to have gone to Ali. The key figures in their theology are the Prophet, Fatima, Ali, and their sons, **Hasan** and **Hussein.** Since the last three were all assassinated, Shiism carries a strong subtext of sacrifice, suffering, and martyrdom. It is the dominant religious community in modern Iran, Lebanon, and Bahrain but accounts for less than 15 percent of all Muslims. Although relegated to the southern part of Iraq and often persecuted by the government under Saddam Hussein, Shiites constitute roughly half the population of Iraq.

Shiites hold the same basic theological convictions as the Sunnis apart from slight variations in ritual and doctrine. For instance, Shiites do not accept the concept of ijma (consensus) but favor **ijtihad,** or individual interpretation of the law by scholars. They reject the hadiths that came through Aisha because of her adversarial position toward Ali, and add to the shahada, or declaration of Muslim faith, "And Ali is the Friend of God." They don't consider public worship mandatory and may substitute a pilgrimage to the sacred shrine of Ali in Najaf or to that of Hussein in Karbala for the traditional hajj. Of much greater importance, though, is their disagreement over the succession of the caliphs, whom they prefer to call **Imams.** This dispute more than any other has fueled the modern antagonism between Iraq, controlled by the Sunnis, and Iran, where Shiite beliefs have formed the official religion since the 16th century. To the Shiites, the Imam is a spiritual leader directly descended from Ali and a completely holy figure, infallible and without sin, who plays a more powerful spiritual role than the Sunni caliph. His decree, or fatwa, takes on the import of a divine command. (The Shiite use of the title Imam should not be confused with the more common **imam,** a spiritual guide who, among other things, leads the regular prayers at a mosque and delivers the Friday sermon.) Sunnis also honor Ali but do not venerate their imams as divine intercessors.

A major difference in custom is the Shia practice of **muta,** or temporary marriage. An ingenious expedient created by Shiites to resolve the tension of momentary lust without resorting to either dishonor or sexual repression, muta may last only a few hours, but it legitimizes any offspring of the union. Sunnis disavow such a concept, even though their treatment of women is considerably less generous than that of the Shiites

432

when it comes to family inheritance and participation in religious ritual. Because Shiites' minority status leaves them open to frequent persecution, they are allowed to feign belief in Sunnism when necessary, a practice called **taqiyya** ("dissimulation"). Shia hierarchy includes the **mullah** (preacher), **mujtahid** (one allowed to render independent legal and theological opinions), **Ayatollah** or **Ayatullah** ("Sign of God"), and **Ayatollah al-Uzma,** or Supreme Ayatollah—the rank held by **Ruhollah Khomeini** (1902–89). The last two are somewhat questionable 20th-century titles accorded by a combination of popular sentiment and the approval of high-ranking Iranian theologians and legists. In fact, there may be more than one Ayatollah al-Uzma at a given time, but generally only one is considered the spiritual leader of Iran. Khomeini assumed this role following the Iranian revolution of 1979, which overthrew the Shah and drew Khomeini from relative obscurity in France to *Time*'s "Man of the Year" within a span of 12 months.

In 765, the Shiites split into two sects, the **Seveners** and the **Twelvers** (**Ithna Asharis** or **Imami**). The moderate Twelvers supported Ali and his 11 directly hereditary successors, imputing to them doctrinal infallibility and freedom from sin. Today they embrace the concept of the 12th Imam, based on the historical figure known as **Muhammad al-Muntazar** ("the Expected"). He disappeared as a boy, and Twelvers believe he remains hidden somewhere, ready to return amid the evils of the world at the Last Day as the Mahdi. According to this eschatology, the Mahdi will reign for 7 years and return the earth to a state of right and justice, followed by the appearance of the **Antichrist**. The Antichrist will lead the forces of corruption but will be opposed by **Jesus the Son of Mary**, who will wage war on the Antichrist and will die again. His body will be buried in a tomb that is kept empty beside that of the Prophet in Medina before rising to conquer in God's name and rule the earth for 1,000 years. According to one hadith, Muhammad said, "There is no Mahdi save Jesus son of Mary." The Prophet also proclaimed that one sign of this impending end of days is the excessive height of buildings that humanity would construct, as in the biblical story of the Tower of Babel.

By the 16th century, Twelver doctrine became the state religion of Persia, and under the **Safavids** (1502–1736), two horses were kept saddled and ready at all times, pending the return of the Mahdi and Jesus. Until the revolution in 1979 which deposed the secular monarchy of **Shah**

Reza Pahlavi (who had himself ousted the Qajar dynasty by military coup and had become Shah in 1925) and his son **Muhammad Reza,** replacing it with an authoritarian Islamic government ruled by the Ayatollah Khomeini, the Shah had ruled in the name of the hidden Imam. In Syria and Lebanon, Twelvers are called **Matawila** ("friends of Ali"), and in Yemen, **Zaydites** (after a great-grandson of Ali).

The Seveners, also called **Ismailis,** recognize only 6 of the 12 Imams of the Shiites, the 7th being **Ismail ibn Jafar** (d. 760), who is not recognized by the Twelvers. Ismail's son **Muhammad** is said to have disappeared, and his return is awaited by many Ismailis just as the return of the Mahdi is awaited by the Twelvers. Ismail and his son Muhammad claimed descent from Ali and held many secret doctrines influenced by Hinduism and Neoplatonism*. The Ismailis are still an influential force, especially in India, led by Imam **Prince Karim.** But because they hold that Muhammad was *not* the last prophet but was actually followed by a number of others, they are considered wildly heterodox not only by Sunnis but also by other Shiites. The Persian poet Omar Khayyam is thought to have been an Ismaili.

A related sect called **Qarmatians** developed in the late 9th century in Iraq. Named either for **Hamdan Qarmat** (d. c. 899) or from the Aramaic for "peasants" (according to different sources), they worshiped the "Supreme Light" and venerated the 7th Imam, taking their membership from both the aristocracy and the peasant class. By the early 10th century, the Qarmatians dominated the entire Arabian peninsula; in 930 they occupied Mecca, filled the well of Zamzam with dead bodies, and smashed the Black Stone, removing the fragments to their capital at al-Ahsa and not returning them until 951.

The Qarmatians gave rise to the **Fatimid** caliphs, who claimed descent from Fatima and Ali. They flourished in the 10th century in North Africa and later in Egypt, basing authority not on authentic succession but on the inner enlightenment of an individual who proclaims himself a divinely appointed leader. In 1021, for example, the Fatimid caliph **al-Hakim** declared that he was God incarnate. Upon his mysterious disappearance shortly afterward, his followers created a closed community in Syria called the **Druzes,** who even today wait for his return. Numbering about 200,000, they have a powerful militia that figured prominently in the fighting in Lebanon in the 1980s. The Druzes take their name from

SECTS AND DRUGS

A minor offshoot of the Ismailis, known as **Neo-Ismailites** or **Nizaris,** created a legendary sect known in the West as the **Assassins,** derived from the Arabic *hashishiyyin* ("hashish users"). Founded around 1090 in the mountain fortress of Alamut, Persia, by **Hasan ibn al-Sabbah** (d. 1124), they soon garnered a reputation as the most feared killers in the Middle East, preying on local political and religious leaders, particularly Sunnis. During the Crusades, many Frankish leaders were done in by members of an independent Syrian branch of hashishiyyin, and the word *assassin* entered several European languages. The method reportedly used by Hasan (who came to be known in the West as the **Old Man of the Mountain**) to initiate his followers and future assassins sounds ingenious. After inviting them to his mountain fortress, Hasan had the initiates drugged and then brought to a secret inner chamber. In this seraglio they were given copious amounts of hashish to smoke as they enjoyed fresh fruit, rich clothing, and an abundant supply of lovely women. After a time, they were again drugged and taken outside, where Hasan made clear to them that the dreamlike world they had just inhabited could be theirs in the future if they would do his bidding in the real world. Thoroughly convinced of the efficacy of the bargain, they were then released into society where they worked their way into the service of public figures. When Hasan wanted to do away with one of these leaders, he called in his marker. The assassins believed that even if they died in the process, they would awaken in the glorious world of sex and drugs into which Hasan had initiated them. Clearly deluded and alienated from Islamic values, the sect was never endorsed by the Muslim community.

The Mongols destroyed the mountain strongholds of the Persian branch of the sect, and the Egyptian Mamelukes took care of the Syrian chapter, but in 1834 the Shah of Persia gave their Imam, who was by then a conventional Islamic ruler, the title of **Agha Khan.** He later fled to Bombay, India, where his hereditary descendant is considered the 48th Imam by his followers in India, East Asia, and Zanzibar.

Muhammad ibn Ismail al-Darazi, a Persian missionary who preached the doctrine of al-Hakim's divinity. The majority of Muslims consider the Druzes as well as the Qarmatians and Ismailites highly heterodox. The Druzes live mainly in Lebanon, Syria, and Israel.

The most reactionary of all major Muslim sects, the **Wahhabis** refuse any innovation in Quranic law. The movement was begun in 18th-century Arabia by **Muhammad ibn Abd al-Wahhab** (1703–92), a Hanbalite who recognized only the Quran and sunna as authoritative in determining Muslim law. Like the Protestant Reformers, he favored predestination over the concept of earning salvation by good works and abolished reliance on the insights of medieval Muslim scholars, which he narrowly regarded as accretions to the original teachings of Islam. With true reformist zeal, he also forbade the wearing of silk clothing, disapproved of music and singing, and destroyed a number of mosques and minarets. The Wahhabis expanded into Iraq and Syria until, in 1925, **King Ibn Saud,** descended from the Saudi family that had been consolidating power since the 18th century, captured the holy cities of Mecca and Medina and most of the Arabian peninsula. The Wahhabis rule Saudi Arabia today by the strict Hanbalite code, which forbids alcohol, tobacco, use of the rosary, and veneration of saints and punishes thieves by cutting off one of their hands and adultery by stoning to death (although these Quranically sanctioned measures are rarely enforced). Wahhabis also encourage polygyny at a time when the practice among Muslims is in decline (contrary to popular opinion, it is tolerated but disapproved of by the Quran) and extend the practice of unilateral divorce to a husband's merely declaring it verbally. The Wahhabi influence in American mosques is disproportionately strong, backed by generous Saudi funding, and its narrow interpretations may be pushing American Islam in an extremely conservative direction.

The **Ahmadiya** sect, founded in 1889 by the Punjabi **Mirza Ghulam Ahmad** (1835–1908), is also reform-minded. Ahmad taught that Jesus was taken down from the cross while still alive and lived out his days in Kashmir in northern India. He also claimed to be the messenger named Ahmad foretold (by Jesus) in the Quran (61:6), a reference which orthodox Muslims assume to be another name for the Prophet Muhammad. For good measure, he added that he was an avatar* of the Hindu god Krishna* and that his spirit had somehow merged with that of Muhammad. The Ahmadiyas split into two sects: the more radical **Qadiyanis** (named for Ahmad's birthplace in the Punjab), now based in Pakistan, and the **Lahoris,** who acknowledge Ahmad as a Muslim reformer rather than a prophet, a belief that allows them to remain closer to traditional Islam. The Ahmadiyas engage in extensive missionary work in the U.S. and elsewhere, misleadingly presenting themselves as mainstream Muslims.

The **Black Muslim** movement in the U.S. was founded by a traveling salesman named **Wallace Fard,** who arrived in the States from Arabia in 1930 and settled among the black community of Detroit. Fard disappeared in 1934, leaving his right-hand man **Elijah Muhammad** (formerly Elijah Poole, 1897–1975), in charge of the **Lost-Found Nation of Islam,** as it was called. Since then, the number of African American Muslims in America has risen to over a million, or roughly one-fourth of all American Muslims. Elijah Muhammad preached a mixture of heterodox Islam and black separatism, claiming that blacks were the "original" race and that Caucasians were "white devils" who derived from a botched experiment on subhuman creatures by an evil wizard named Yacub. **Malcolm X** (Malcolm Little, 1925–65), for ten years the major spokesman for Elijah Muhammad, became interested in authentic Islam and eventually broke with the Nation of Islam after making the hajj, which revolutionized his thinking about the racial separatism espoused by Elijah Muhammad. He took the name **al-Hajj Malik Shabaz** and was later assassinated by religious rivals. When Elijah Muhammad died in 1975, his seventh son, **Wallace Deen Muhammad,** now known as **Warith Deen Mohammed,** took charge of the Nation of Islam. Rejecting his father's teachings, he nonviolently returned the Black Muslims to conventional Sunni Islam. In 1985 he formally dissolved the movement, and its members became integrated with mainstream Islam, a continuing process referred to by African American Muslims as "the change" or "the second experience." Warith Deen Mohammed has upwards of 250,000 followers, to whom he communicates with a scholarly and inspiring weekly television program about Muslim life. He is considered by many as the most prominent and respected indigenous Muslim leader in the West. In 1992 he became the first imam ever to give the invocation before the U.S. Senate.

A new **Nation of Islam** was formed under **Louis Farrakhan** in 1978 as Warith Deen Mohammed was beginning his move to orthodox Islam.

Once Malcolm X broke with Elijah Muhammad, Farrakhan, who as Louis X had played a role at a Boston mosque similar to Malcolm's in Harlem, opposed and later replaced Malcolm at his Harlem mosque. He continued to embrace the heterodox teachings of Elijah Muhammad, and neither Farrakhan nor his splinter group has been acknowledged by orthodox Muslims in the Middle East. He has been widely criticized by non-Muslims for his promotion of racial separatism laced with anti-Semitism, although he has been quicker to advance women to the ministry, something that never occurs in traditional Islamic mosques. Farrakhan has only about 20,000 followers today. A one-time calypso singer and violinist, he has claimed to seek rapprochement with the Jewish community, in part by playing the violin concerto of Felix Mendelssohn*, a Jewish-born convert to Christianity, at a number of small concert venues.

Meanwhile, the hundreds of black mosques with no more connection to the Nation of Islam have become a strong presence in inner-city communities, their members openly opposing drug dealers, abstaining from alcohol, tobacco, and gambling, and promoting "conservative" attitudes toward dress, family life, sexual conduct, and religious worship. No longer strictly African American, these congregations are accepting members of all ethnic communities. Like most American Muslims, their mosques tend to be politically liberal but socially conservative. The best estimates of Islamic population in the United States range between 3 and 5 million, of whom approximately 25 percent are African American (the term Black Muslims no longer applies).

Sports figures like **Muhammad Ali** (formerly Cassius Marcellus Clay) and **Kareem Abdul-Jabbar** (formerly Lew Alcindor) are not the only prominent black Americans to have embraced Islam over recent decades. A modest national following has developed around **Jamil Abdullah Al-Amin,** who was known in the 1960s as H. Rap Brown, the civil rights leader and Black Panther. Of more than a dozen significant subgroups of black American Muslims, most are aligned with mainstream Islam, but some theological splinter groups have survived, including the **Moorish Science Temple** of Noble Drew Ali (Timothy Drew, 1886–1929), founded in Newark, N.J., in 1913, and a minor offshoot of Elijah Muhammad's Nation of Islam called the **Five Percenters,** which originated in Harlem in the 1960s. The latter are syncretists who combine an extremist political ideology with esoteric Eastern theology.

438

THE SUFIS: TRUE BELIEVERS OR WOOLGATHERERS?

> When the heart weeps for what it has lost, the spirit laughs for what it has found.
>
> —SUFI SAYING

The image of **Sufism** as a worldly or mystical element at odds with orthodox Islam is pretty much a Western confection, shiny on the surface but soft and gooey at the core. What may be true is that in the conquering

---

THE COLOR OF ISLAM

Not long after breaking with Elijah Muhammad and the Nation of Islam, Malcolm X decided to make the ritual hajj expected of all orthodox Muslims at least once. His experience in Mecca was to prove a turning point in his life and in his thinking about relations between the races in America, where he had at one time embraced Elijah's notions of black separatism and "white devils." Here is an excerpt from a letter which Malcolm wrote from Mecca in 1964 to members of his **Muslim Mosque, Inc.** in Harlem and which was carried in some of the American press. It is followed by an accepted hadith.

During the past 11 days here in the Muslim world, I have eaten from the same plate, drunk from the same glass, and slept in the same bed (or on the same rug)—while praying to the *same God*—with fellow Muslims, whose eyes were the bluest of blue, whose hair was the blondest of blond, and whose skin was the whitest of white. And in the *words* and in the *actions* and in the *deeds* of the "white" Muslims, I felt the same sincerity that I felt among the black African Muslims of Nigeria, Sudan, and Ghana.

There were tens of thousands of pilgrims, from all over the world . . . but we were all participating in the same ritual, displaying a spirit of unity and brotherhood that my experiences in America had led me to believe never could exist between the white and the non-white.

We were *truly* all the same (brothers)—because their belief in one God had removed the "white" from their *minds,* the "white" from their *behavior,* and the "white" from their *attitude.*

I could see from this that perhaps if white Americans could accept the Oneness of God, then perhaps, too, they could accept *in reality* the Oneness of Man—and cease to measure, and hinder, and harm others in terms of their "differences" in color.

With racism plaguing America like an incurable cancer, the so-called "Christian" white American heart should be more receptive to a proven solution to such a destructive problem. Perhaps it could be in time to save America from imminent disaster—the same destruction brought upon Germany by racism that eventually destroyed the Germans themselves.

> —MALCOLM X (WITH ALEX HALEY)
> *THE AUTOBIOGRAPHY OF MALCOLM X*

An Arab has no preference over a non-Arab, nor a non-Arab over an Arab; nor is a white one to be preferred to a dark one, nor a dark one to a white one.

> —THE PROPHET MUHAMMAD (HADITH)

sweep of Muslims into India and points north and east, the Sufis served as good cops, or mystical interpreters, to the sword-in-hand bad cops, or literalists, of Islam. Certainly as warriors spread the faith and were rewarded with piles of booty, the ruling elite of Islam grew ever more materialistic and its caliphs began to deviate from the teachings of the Quran and the Messenger. Much of the initial impetus of Sufism was a reaction to the luxury-loving superficiality developed in Islam under the caliphs—perhaps not surprising in a religion that abjured monkish celibacy. But Sufis also opposed the increasing literalism of Islamic legal interpretations, challenging the rulers and religious guides of their countries to be true to the essential spirit of that law rather than the letter, always seeking the hidden spiritual significance of the most common ritual or prayer. They sought deeper connections to the mystical core of the other great religious traditions as well, and so tended to be more tolerant than unreflective Muslims. In most cases, however, they were unable to affect the power of the largely corrupt dynastic caliphs, and they turned to inner contemplative practices and to elevating the spiritual life of the common people.

Still, the vast majority of Sufis remained first and foremost orthodox Muslims who performed the prayers and followed the sunna. One Muslim scholar put it this way: "Sufism is universalist and humanist Islam striving for spiritual purity." Rather than avoiding the worship practices of orthodox Islam, Sufis must do more of these practices even more carefully, contrary to the teachings of some American Sufi groups. Shaykh Fadhlalla Haeri, a Sufi born in Iraq and educated in Europe and America, writes that the basic laws of Muslim worship, the Five Pillars, are, "although necessary, not sufficient for most of the people who are sick in this vast hospital called the world." According to Fadhlalla, Sufism "starts with following the Islamic Law, . . . with acquiring the knowledge of the outer practices in order to develop, evolve, and enliven the inner awakened state."

From the earliest days of Islam's expansion in the mid to late 7th century, Sufis functioned as missionaries and spiritual masters, adding immeasurably to the richness of Islamic life, even though individual Sufis were sometimes accused of heresy much as great Christian mystics like John of the Cross* and Meister Eckhart* were. Muslims have a tradition based in the Quran that about four years before the death of the Prophet, he called together certain of his Companions under a tree to pledge themselves to him on a higher level than when they first joined Islam. (Initiations into Sufi orders often replicate this event in a ritual grasping of right hands, holding the shaykh's rosary, or some other form.) Seeking this higher pitch of commitment, Sufis read and interpret the Quran on several levels, finding esoteric, hidden, or subtle truths where the text appears to speak of external, earthly matters. For instance, in the passage describing the Companions' pledge, the Quran promises that those who pledged will receive the spoils of war, then adds, "God knows of other spoils which you have not yet taken, but which God encompasses"

(48:21). Sufis interpret this as a reference to the great treasure of union with the Infinite.

The term *Sufi* has been authoritatively traced to the root word *suf* ("wool"), reflecting the austere garments worn by some of the earliest Sufis and probably applied by extension to Islamic mystics generally. Wool was traditionally the clothing of the Prophet and of the Christian anchorites* whom the early Sufis encountered in the deserts of Syria, Arabia, and Egypt. However, the Christianity that was absorbed by Islam from the desert hermits and communities was less the orthodox religion of Rome than a mystical variant that had been influenced by both Gnosticism* and Neoplatonism*. Sufi prayer beads or rosaries were adapted from those used by Buddhist monks (and later borrowed by the Catholic church), along with much of the meditative orientation of the Buddhists and the Desert Fathers*. But although the Sufi spirit was an essential aspect of Islam from the beginning, and the Sufis ground their understanding in hadiths of the Prophet, the word *Sufi* was not used until at least 2 centuries after Muhammad. Certainly the earliest masters who can be identified as Sufi spoke in familiar ascetical-mystical terms that expressed a yearning for purification—e.g., **Abul Qasim al-Junayd** of Baghdad (d. 910), who defined Sufism as "adopting every higher quality and leaving every lower quality." Junayd was close enough to sober orthodoxy to be considered "safe," whereas the early master **Abu Yazid Taifur al-Bistami** (d. 874) was more openly ecstatic and spiritually intoxicated, having experienced a union with God so intense that he was able to exclaim, "Glory be to me! How great is my majesty!"

Sufism was one area in early Islam where women were granted full equality; a woman could become a master teacher, or **shaykh** (fem. **shaykha**), teaching in her own home or in a nonmonastic convent. The most prominent woman Sufi was **Rabia al-Adawiyya** (d. 801), the slave-girl of Basra, whose teachings emphasized ecstatic, devotional love of God to the exclusion of all else, including marriage and the material world. Rabia's insistence on worshiping God out of sheer love rather than because of any reward either on earth or in the afterlife set a standard for all other Sufis. When asked why she often carried a torch and a container of water, she replied, "To burn up Paradise and to quench the fires of Hell."

From *suf* comes the Arabic term **tasawwuf,** or "mysticism." Once again, we can define mysticism* as a reverence for the inner truth of a religious

442

tradition in addition to its formal or sacred law, or as a sense of wholeness, of incorporating spiritual experience into every facet of daily life and breath. But the most common understanding of the work of mystics is their search for direct and complete experience of God, not merely of interaction with God but, ultimately, divine union. That union is viewed by mystics of all creeds as having its pinnacle in the dissolution or extinction of the separative ego-self by merging with God, which the Sufis call fana. Yet Sufis seek a further step they call baqa: the reemergence of the dissolved soul as a ray from God. In the often used metaphor for fana, the individual soul becomes a drop of water that merges with the Ocean of Divine Love; the traditional image for baqa is a diamond in clear water.

Although most Sufis consider themselves fully Muslim, they have discovered ways of encountering God and expressing their spiritual being that are not common in mainstream Islam. Sufis emphasize the path of love by which the soul makes its journey to God. The search of the soul to return to its ultimate Source is often expressed, particularly in the poems of the 13th-century Persian mystic Jelaluddin Rumi, in the metaphor of a lover seeking out his beloved. Sufi poets also use the metaphor of wine in describing the soul's intoxication with God, usually making clear that it is merely a metaphor, as in the Quranic description of Paradise. Rumi sings:

Before garden, vine or grape were in the world
Our soul was drunken with immortal wine.

A SUFI MARTYR:
MANSUR AL-HALLAJ

The Persian Sufi mystic Husayn ibn Mansur is commonly known as **Mansur al-Hallaj,** or Mansur "the Wool Carder" (858–922). Like other notable Sufis, he took a nickname that had a double meaning. For example, al-Ghazzali ("the Spinner") and Attar ("the Chemist") reflect the inner spiritual work of refining coarse elements and transforming them into new products or essences. But Hallaj may be the most controversial figure in all of Muslim mysticism, having developed a belief that God fully manifested Himself through the perfect human being, such as Adam and Jesus. He followed the mystical path of union with God until he had become so absorbed in the Divine that he cried out publicly in ecstasy, *"ana 'l-Haqq"*—"I am the Truth." Haqq being one of the 99 names of Allah, this was equivalent to saying that he was God, a great heresy to the orthodox. Worse yet, Hallaj seemed to take literally the mystic's desire to die to earthly things so as to be alive to the spiritual, and actually asked his countrymen to kill him—an attitude shared by some Christian martyrs. But despite his "blasphemy" and his strange request, he was so revered in Baghdad as a holy ascetic by the court and the Queen Mother that he continued to preach with impunity for some time. When he was finally arrested and thrown into prison in 911, he was treated with great respect and allowed to preach to the other prisoners. But in 922, the Caliph, apparently for political reasons and in a drunken state, signed his execution papers and Hallaj was martyred.

Given the graceful way in which he accepted his brutal execution, Mansur al-Hallaj may have surpassed the early Christian martyrs for sheer nervy attitude. Arrested and condemned to death, he gently played with his executioners. After they cut off his hands and feet, he smiled, explaining, "With these feet I made an earthly journey. Other feet I have which even now are journeying through both the worlds. If you are able, hack off *those* feet!" Then he rubbed the bloody stumps of his wrists across his face, saying that his face had grown pale from loss of blood, and he didn't want his accusers to think his pallor was caused by fear. After cutting off his nose, ears, and tongue and plucking out his eyes, they beheaded him. According to legend, the following day when his limbs were burned, from his ashes came the cry "I am the Truth."

Finally, Sufis employ a variety of spiritual exercises and techniques along with the more common prayers and rituals of Islam to bring the aspirant to a direct knowledge or experience of the Divine. These contemplative methods are related to, although different in appearance from, the mystical techniques of Hindus, Buddhists, Taoists, Christians, and Jews.

The shaykh (also spelled *sheikh* or *shaikh* and pronounced "shake"), sometimes called a **Murshid** ("director"), is the individual's spiritual guide on the journey of the soul. Through his or her intervention, the student in dreams or visions may meet the **Pir,** usually considered the original founder of a particular order. Their conference takes place on the invisible, spiritual level, as do future meetings with the Prophet himself and finally with God. The aim is **marifa** ("gnosis," "knowledge"), an intuitive experience of ultimate Reality reached by passing through various ecstatic states of purification, unification, and illumination. Students must give themselves up to the shaykh and trust him or her implicitly—the metaphor that was often used, although originally applied to one's surrender to God, is that the student must be in the hands of the shaykh like a corpse in the hands of the person washing it, i.e., providing no resistance, no expression of separative ego.

Like Christianity, Islam, especially the Sufi orders, is replete with saints and martyrs as well as stories of their miracles and extraordinary abilities, including walking on water, flying, bilocation, clairvoyance, telepathy, telekinesis, and communing with animals and plants. These feats are often played down by mainstream teachers and Sufi masters themselves as unnecessary distractions and possibly even dangers to spiritual growth. The path proceeds through stages of repentance (**tauba**), faith (**tawakkul**), endurance (**sabr**), and the infamous Dark Night of the Soul (**gabd**) to spiritual knowledge or awakening (marifa). The next stage is **fana,** or self-eradication through merging with the Absolute and the extinction of all passions and wants. Fana is akin to Hindu samadhi* and Buddhist nirvana*, although it differs from nirvana because it involves **baqa,** the continuance of earthly existence while still in the enlightened awareness of unity with God. In fana, the individual ego-soul that previously saw itself in relation to the God it sought has been absorbed in God; it no longer exists as a separate identity. Sufis sometimes call this state Haqq ("reality" or "truth") for the same reason it made perfect sense for Hallaj, after having the experience of fana, to declare that he was Truth: he no longer saw a distinction between himself and the Divine Reality. Baqa is the spiritual station of serving the people—a parallel to the compassion of the bodhisattva* in Mahayana* Buddhism.

✳ FOLLOWING SUFI ORDERS

Although Sufis, like Muslims in general, eschewed the monastic life and were frequently allowed the use of the local mosque for their meetings and exercises, they did construct **khanaqas** where traveling Sufis could stay. Smaller or more specialized versions were called **ribats** or **zawiyas**, where instruction in a specific tariqa, or mystic order, was available, usually from a single shaykh. These often provided the first link in a chain of hereditary succession that developed into global Sufi orders. That

---

IN THE NAME OF GOD

Constant repetition of the name of God is a popular technique of religious practitioners to keep their attention on the Supreme Reality. In Hinduism it is called japa*; in Catholic and Orthodox Christianity it takes the form of litanies, the rosary*, or the Jesus prayer*. Muslims practice **dhikr** ("remembrance"), breathing silently, saying, or chanting Allah or any of "the 99 Beautiful Names of God" which appear in the Quran. Muslim converts often take one or more of these names, each of which represents a particular energy or attribute of Allah—e.g., **Jamil** ("strength"), **Rahim** ("compassion"), **Rahman** ("mercy"), **Kareem** ("generosity"), **Jabbar** ("compelling"), **Nur** ("light"), **Rashid** ("unerring"), or **Wahid** ("one"). The purpose of repeating the divine names is generally the same, as illustrated by this story from Sufi lore, which bears a remarkable resemblance to accounts of the Jesus prayer from Eastern Orthodox sources:

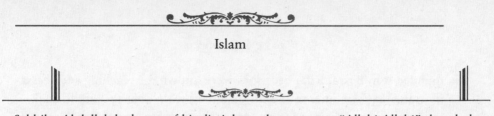

Sahl ibn Abdallah bade one of his disciples endeavor to say "Allah! Allah!" the whole day without intermission. When he had acquired the habit of doing so, Sahl instructed him to repeat the same words during the night, until they came forth from his lips even while he was asleep. "Now," said he, "be silent and occupy yourself with recollecting them." At last the disciple's whole being was absorbed by the thought of Allah. One day a log fell on his head, and the words "Allah, Allah" were seen written in the blood that trickled from the wound."

—REYNOLD A. NICHOLSON, *THE MYSTICS OF ISLAM*

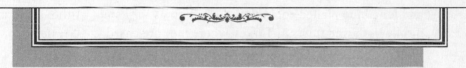

chain, known as a **silsila,** established the authority of a shaykh by tracing his or her lineage back from teacher to teacher, usually ending with the Prophet or one of his Companions, particularly Ali. By the 9th–11th centuries, specific Sufi orders began to take shape around the teachings of individual shaykhs. With some notable exceptions, these brotherhoods descended from Sunni founders. Structurally, the orders patterned themselves on the craft guilds that flourished in the Near East, with hierarchies, secret initiations, and oaths similar to those of the guilds, themselves often loosely connected to a Sufi tariqa. There are 400 major Sufi orders, of which the following are a few of the most renowned. A Sufi practitioner or **dervish** ("mendicant") may belong to more than one order and have more than one shaykh, since all of these orders share a commitment to Islam—much like the varying orders of Christian religions or of Tibetan Buddhists.

Reputed to be the first Sufi order, the **Qadiri** never achieved mass popularity but remains a significant cultural force. Founded by the Hanbali preacher and ascetic **Abd al-Qadir al-Jilani** (c. 1077–1166) in 12th-century Baghdad, it has since spread from the Arabian peninsula to much of Africa, southern Russia, and parts of India. Qadir, however, showed little evidence of having created a specific path or teaching, although later accounts credited him with being a miracle worker.

The **Rifai** order is named for **Ahmad ibn al-Rifai** (1106–82), who founded it in Basra. Rifai dervishes were known for reaching such ecstatic states in their intense dhikrs that they were able to handle snakes, sometimes biting their heads off, dance through fire, and pierce their bodies with swords without suffering any deleterious effects, a reputation that continues in modern times. A related order, the **Haidaris** of Khurasan, inserted iron rings in their hands, ears, and necks, and occasionally in their penises so that they couldn't have sexual intercourse.

The Turkish **Mevlevi** (Ar. **Mawlawi**) order, derived from the teachings of Jalaluddin Rumi, was renowned for its use of music in its spiritual exercises; its members came to be known in Europe as the **Whirling Dervishes.** They wore high, camel-hair hats shaped like inverted flower pots and long blue plaited robes that floated up as they spun. Although technically outlawed today in Turkey where they are based, the Mevlevis continue to meet there as a "historical society" and have branches in the U.S.

The **Shadhili** order is one of the largest worldwide, attributed to **Shaykh Abul Hasan Ali al-Shadhili** (1196–1258), but derived from **Abu Madyan Shuaib** (d. 1197). Popular in North Africa, Arabia, and Syria, it also gave rise to the **Burhani** order in Egypt.

The only Sufi sect that doesn't trace its lineage to the son-in-law of the Prophet, Ali, is the **Naqshbandi,** named for **Shaykh Muhammad Baha ud-Din Naqshband** of Bukhara (d. 1389), but actually based on the insights of two 12th-century shaykhs, including a silent dhikr. The Naqshbandis base themselves on the first caliph, Abu Bakr. They are noted for their use of breathing exercises that use the divine names and increase the flow of oxygen into the bloodstream, inducing ecstatic states through their concentration on divine energy (reminiscent of certain Taoist and yogic techniques).

The main order of India and Pakistan is the **Chisti,** now prominent in South East Asia. Founded by **Muin ad-din Hasan Chisti** (c. 1142–1236), it focuses largely on the recitation of the dhikr. Although Shaykh Chisti was influenced by the writings of **Dia ad-din Abu Njib al-Suhrawardi** (1097–1168), whose **Suhrawardi** order is also influential in India, the Chisti order is distinct from it. The Chisti was the first Sufi order to come to America, brought from India to Europe by Hazrat Inayat Khan in 1910 and then to the U.S.

The **Jerrahi** (or **Halveti-Jerrahi**) order derives from **Nur ud-Din Muhammad al-Jarrahi al Halveti** of Istanbul (d. 1720) and is limited mainly to Turkey, with prominent followings in Europe and the U.S., having been brought over from Istanbul in 1978 by **Sheikh Muzaffer** (1916–86).

❊ SUFISM ABIDES IN THE WEST

Sufism in America has sometimes taken a different shape from its Middle Eastern and Asian versions. The Indian-born Sufi master **Hazrat Inayat Khan** (1882–1927), the first major Sufi figure to come to the West, brought his teachings to the U.S. in the 1920s. Hazrat Inayat, who belonged to the Chisti order in India, later married the niece of Mary Baker Eddy*, the founder of Christian Science*; the offspring of that union was **Pir Vilayat Inayat Khan** (b. 1916). Pir Vilayat went on to become a promi-

RUMI AT THE TOP

Omar Khayyam may be more famous (at least in the popular 19th-century translations by Edward Fitzgerald), and Firdausi is probably more favored among Muslims, but no Islamic poet has received a warmer reception in modern America than **Jalal ud din** (or **Jelaluddin**) **Rumi** (1207–73). Considered by many the greatest poet writing in the Persian language, Rumi came from a Sufi family where his father, **Baha ud-din Walad,** began his son's spiritual training early. Born in Balkh (modern Afghanistan), Rumi left with his father for Anatolia (modern Turkey) to escape marauding Mongols, settling in Qonya in the province of Rum (hence his name), where he lived out his days. Rumi was fortunate enough while in Baghdad to encounter Ibn Arabi, the great Spanish Sufi master from Andalusia. But it was his brief relationship with a mysterious 60-year-old dervish named **Shams ad-din of Tabriz**, or **Shams-i-Tabriz**, in 1244 that changed Rumi from an accomplished, enlightened

Sufi master to an ecstatic visionary. Not much is known about Shams apart from his intersection with the life of Rumi. Anywhere from 15 months to 3 years after he met Rumi (accounts vary), Shams disappeared, leaving behind no writings. Yet he inspired Rumi to write voluminously, including a large volume that appeared as the *Diwan of Shams-i-Tabriz*. Tradition holds that Rumi's **murids,** or disciples, were so jealous of Shams that they plotted against him; one source claims that they murdered Shams with the help of one of Rumi's sons. Rumi's most famous work is simply titled *Mathnawi* ("Couplets") and consists of another massive agglomeration of apparently disconnected mystical lyrics, often in the form of love poetry, teachings, and allegorical tales composed over a 43-year span.

nent Sufi teacher in America and the formal spiritual successor of his father, founding a community known as the **Abode of the Message** in New Lebanon, New York, in 1974. The Abode is currently the national headquarters of the **Sufi Order in the West,** Pir Vilayat's universalist vision of Sufism that teaches respect for all the world's great religious traditions. Grounded in his father's teachings, Pir Vilayat's Sufism incorporates songs, chants, and scripture readings taken from the various traditions. But it does not embrace orthodox Islamic laws and practices, such as the daily prayers, and so is not considered to be genuine Sufism by many Muslims.

Besides learning Sufism from his father, Pir Vilayat studied with an American Sufi named **Samuel Lewis.** Heir to the Lee jeans fortune, Lewis had been disowned by his family, traveled the world, and studied Zen and Islam. He received the transmission of Hazrat Inayat Khan while Pir Vilayat was still a small boy, and he later became one of Pir Vilayat's collaborators, ultimately bringing Sufism back to his native San Francisco, where he was known as Sufi Sam (or SAM, for Sufi Ahmed Murad, his Sufi name). It was Sam who started the practice of **Sufi Dancing,** or Dances of Universal Peace, as they were originally known, combining elements of music and chants from various world traditions, including dervish and American Indian dances. When Lewis died in 1971, many of his students went with Pir Vilayat as he founded the Abode. Now there are two branches of the order, one under Sufi Sam's named successor, the American **Moineddin Jablonsky,** the other under Pir Vilayat.

THE ARABIAN HEIGHTS: GENIUS IN ISLAMIC ARTS AND SCIENCES

The influence of Muslim thinkers on Western science and culture is indicated partly by the number of terms that come to us from the Arabic: *alchemy, alfalfa, algebra, alkalai, almanac, amber, benzine, caliber, camphor, chemistry, cipher, coffee, elixir, sheriff, tariff,* and *traffic* are just a few. Muslim women, at least under the Umayyad and early Abbasid rulers, enjoyed a freedom and prominence in the fields of politics, scholarship, and the arts that surpassed those of Europe. Among the great figures of Islamic genius, many of whom are better known in the West by the Latinized names given them by medieval European writers, were **Abu Bakr al-Razi** (Rhazes, 864–925) who cataloged, among other things, 176 contraceptive and abortifacient techniques (in Islam for over 1,000 years, abortion in the first trimester has been permissible); **Abu Ali ibn Sina** (Avicenna, 980–1037), whose *Canon of Medicine* was at one time more widely used than the works of Galen and Hippocrates; and, perhaps most famous of all in the West, **Ibn Rushd** (Averroes, 1126–98), whose commentary on Aristotle influenced the medieval scholastics*, especially Thomas Aquinas*, and the German mystic Meister Eckhart*.

But of greater significance to Islam itself was **Abu Hamid al-Ghazzali** (1058–1111), a leading intellectual who was raised as a Sufi, abandoned Sufism early on, and returned to it in his later years. Although Ghazzali was the most brilliant theologian of his time, it has been said that in his early years he had no avocation for mystical theology and that his real interest was Islamic jurisprudence. But in his mid-30s, he suddenly underwent a period of intense inner turmoil and physical illness which led him to abandon his successful career as canon lawyer and theology teacher and, largely in response to the arid intellectualism of the orthodox Islam he witnessed, to revert to the Sufi practices he had learned as

451

a child. Ghazzali's integration of the theology, philosophy, and mysticism of the era, combined with his continuing respect for Islamic laws and traditional teachings, made him one of the largest figures of the Muslim religion, often referred to as the "Authority of Islam." Because of him, mainstream Muslims were able to accept Sufism as a legitimate aspect of Islam. Ghazzali favored using music to enhance spiritual states, as the Mevlevi order of Whirling Dervishes do. The famously repetitive melody of Ravel's *Bolero* is reputed to be an adaptation of such a piece of music.

Islamic poets writing in the Persian tongue, which had reasserted itself by the 10th century, include Jelaluddin Rumi and **Omar Khayyam** (1050–1123), whose *Rubaiyat* ("Quatrains") has long been popular in Edward Fitzgerald's translation. Although he is most famous in the West for his poetry, Omar was more notable in Persia as an astronomer and mathematician. The poet considered greatest by Muslims themselves is probably **Firdausi** (**Abul Qasim Mansur,** 935–1020), author of *Shah Nama ("Book of Kings")*.

Ibn al-Arabi (1164–1240) was known as "the Greatest Master" and "the Andalusian," since he came from that part of Spain. Like Rumi, he grew up in a Sufi family and deepened his knowledge of Sufism by associating with Sufi groups in Spain and writing poetry. His major works, *The Meccan Revelations* and *The Bezels of Wisdom,* are packed with startling statements unlikely to appear in the work of mainstream religious writers. "When a man loves a woman," he wrote, "he finds the most complete union in the act of love when all his senses are pervaded by desire. . . . The sight of God in woman is the most perfect of all, for in woman, man sees God in His active and passive principles, whereas when a man contemplates God in himself, he sees God in only His passive principle. For this reason Muhammad loved women, seeing in them the most perfect means to contemplate God." Arabi also advocated esoteric techniques similar to the dream yoga of the Tibetans, in which the sleeper seeks to "control his thoughts in a dream." This technique is known today as lucid dreaming*.

Sadly, Islamic politics did not fare as well as the arts and sciences. Three of the first four, "rightly guided" caliphs were assassinated while performing congregational prayers. The four scholars who largely shaped Islamic law during a 100-year period from the middle of the 8th to the middle of the 9th century were all beaten or imprisoned or both

452

WHERE DO WE GO FROM HERE?

Solving the afterlife dilemma in the popular mind proved invaluable to nascent Islam, as it had for the early Christian church in Europe. And, as with Christianity, converting to the new faith bore political and other practical advantages. These two factors combined to help Islam spread with explosive speed. Writes a Western Muslim scholar:

The reasons were not purely spiritual: the Prophet was . . . known as a dangerous and incalculable enemy and as a powerful, reliable and generous ally; by comparison, other alliances were beginning to seem less attractive and more hazardous. In many cases the political and religious motives were inextricably connected; but there was also a factor, slow-working yet powerful and profound, which had nothing whatsoever to do with politics, and which was also largely independent of the deliberate efforts made by the believers to spread the message of Islam. This was the remarkable serenity which characterized those who practiced the new religion. The Quran, the Book of God's Oneness, was also the Book of Mercy and the Book of Paradise. The recitation of its verses, combined with the teaching of the Messenger, imbued the believers with the certainty that they had within easy reach, that is, through the fulfillment of certain conditions well within their capacity, the eternal satisfaction of every possible desire. The resulting happiness was a criterion of faith. The Prophet insisted: "All is well with the faithful, whatever the circumstances.

—MARTIN LINGS, *MUHAMMAD: HIS LIFE BASED ON THE EARLIEST SOURCES*

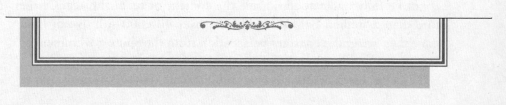

by corrupt Muslim rulers—which was at least a testimony to the scholars' unimpeachable honesty. As a leader, **Salah-al-din** (**Saladin**, 1138–93) was different. Known for his military exploits, his battles with Richard the Lionhearted of England, and his retaking of Jerusalem from the Crusaders* in 1187, Saladin was also famous for his generosity, civility, and sense of chivalry. But he was one of the few exceptions to a long string of caliphs who with each military victory charged further and further from the enlightened moral disciplines of Muhammad and the Quran.

Yet for all their reputation of converting by the sword (a tactic shared in essence by the European Christians), Muslims gained many more converts peaceably, as the inherent appeal of Islam to the masses began to grow exponentially. And they often avoided violence by a show of strength. According to the 9th–10th-century Muslim historian **Al Tabari** (whose history of the world fills 38 volumes today), the victorious general Khalid ibn Walid went so far as to send a written warning to the Persians before sweeping down on them. Khalid offered a choice of becoming Muslim or merely paying a tribute (**jizya**) that amounted to protection money. "If not," the noble general wrote, "I shall come against you with men who love death as you love to drink wine."

❋ HETERODOXY: THE BAHAI FAITH AND SUBUD

The **Bahai Faith**, as it is now known, is no longer thought of as a religion connected to Islam, and this is essentially accurate, even though its roots lie in the Islamic world of 19th-century Iran. The umbilical cord connecting the Bahai Faith to its Muslim origins has long since been cut; in recent times it has been embraced by a number of popular musicians from Dizzy Gillespie and Vic Damone to Seals and Crofts and Flora Purim, and its insistence on absolute equality between the sexes distinguishes it from other religions born in the Middle East. Still, the faith cannot be fully understood outside the context of its birthplace. Of the more than 5 million Bahais worldwide, over 400,000 still live in Iran, where they are under constant persecution from the Shiite government as that country's largest non-Muslim religious minority.

The Bahai Faith developed from the Persian sect of **Babism** begun in

1844 by **Siyyid Ali Muhammad** (1819–50), who believed in "progressive revelation." This doctrine, which bears some similarities to both the Hindu avatar* principle and to Islamic teachings, holds that God has sent a succession of divine messengers to educate and enlighten humanity. Against a background of early-19th-century Shiite esoteric and millenarian movements, Siyyid Ali Muhammad took the name **Bab** (Ar. "Door" or "Gate"), declaring on May 23, 1844, that he was Islam's promised Imam Mahdi, or Qaim ("He who will arise"), and pointing out that it had been 1,000 lunar years since the disappearance of the 12th or Hidden Imam. His major book of writings, called the **Bayan** ("Exposition"), forbade polygyny and concubinage, mendicancy, and slave trading and announced a new law of equality between men and women (one of the most prominent Babis was the poet and orator **Qurratu l'Ayn**, known as **Tahirih**, the first woman to be martyred for the cause). But the Bayan's main theme was the coming of a second Messenger or Prophet who would usher in the long-awaited age of peace and prosperity promised not only by Islam but also by Judaism and Christianity.

Despite their high levels of Muslim piety and scholarship, the Bab and his disciples, or **Babis**, were persecuted by Muslims, who found the promise of a prophet to come after Muhammad blasphemous. (Yet the "prophet" whose coming the Bab foretold was to be a manifestation of the returned Christ, a legitimate Islamic claim.) Because the Bab proclaimed that the scriptures he revealed superseded the Quran, he was imprisoned, tortured, and finally executed in 1850. An attempt by two Babi youths in Teheran to assassinate the Shah in 1852 led to further persecutions.

The prophet of whom the Bab spoke was **Husayn-Ali** of Nur, a contemporary who came to be known as **Baha'u'llah** ("Glory of God," 1817–92). The son of a wealthy government minister whose family was among Persia's oldest landed gentry, he was a householder and father of three children who devoted himself to philanthropic activities until 1844, when he became a leading advocate of Babism. Although he never met the Bab in person, he carried on a correspondence with him that continued up to the Bab's martyrdom. In 1852, Baha'u'llah himself was imprisoned for four months in the infamous "Black Pit" of Teheran, where he had profound mystical experiences during which he said he received a revelation from God to humanity. He described the experience in these terms: "Though the galling weight of the chain and the stench-filled air allowed me but little sleep, still in those infrequent moments of slumber I felt as if something flowed from the crown of my head over my breast, even as a mighty torrent that precipitates itself upon the earth from the summit of a lofty mountain. Every limb of my body would, as a result, be set afire. At such moments my tongue recited what no man could bear to hear."

Banished to Baghdad after his release from prison, Baha'u'llah began a 40-year period of solitary wandering, exile, and imprisonment, during which he taught his followers by eloquent epistles and other writings. His manifestation as the Christ foretold by the Bab did not take place until 1863, at which time Babis began to call themselves **Bahais**, or followers of Baha'u'llah. (The religion was originally referred to as Bahaiism, a name that was replaced by the Bahai Faith in the 1920s.) In the ensuing years, Baha'u'llah called not only for the healing of the world by "the union of all its peoples in one universal Cause, one common Faith," but also for the dissolution of nationalist conflicts and for the abrogation of the Islamic and Babi principle of jihad, advocating that it is better to be killed than to kill. Beginning in 1867, he wrote a series of letters to world leaders including Queen Victoria, Kaiser Wilhelm, Emperor Franz Josef, and Pope Pius IX, announcing the arrival of a new age that would be presaged by political and social cataclysms and calling for world disarmament and the formation of a world commonwealth to act collectively against war. "The earth is but one country," he wrote, "and mankind its citizens." During his last 24 years of exile at Acre, a penal city in Palestine, he wrote his most important book, the **Kitab-i-Aqdas** ("Most Holy Book"), outlining the laws and institutions for the new world order he envisioned. Among his other significant works is the **Kitab-i-Iqan** ("Book of Certitude"), the principal exposition of his doctrinal message.

Baha'u'llah's eldest son, **Abdul Baha** (1844–1921), succeeded his father in the Bahai lineage and is considered the authoritative interpreter of his teachings. From 1911 to 1913, he brought the Bahai message to Europe and North America. After his death in 1921, Abdul Baha was succeeded as Guardian of the Bahai Faith by his eldest grandson, **Shoghi Effendi Rabbani** (1897–1957). But Shoghi Effendi designated no successor, and in 1963 the notion of individual leaders was replaced by an elected governing body originally conceived by Baha'u'llah. It is called the **Universal House of Justice**, a group of nine believers of varied ethnic and national origins who govern the spiritual affairs of Bahais today.

Tolerance is one of the keynotes of the Bahai Faith, which has no formal creed, few rituals or ceremonies, no clergy, and nothing to exclude those holding other beliefs from participating, which may help explain its growing popularity in the West. Bahais believe in three fundamental principles: the oneness of God, the oneness of humanity, and the fundamental unity of religion. However, formal membership in the Bahai Faith—being what is called an "enrolled" Bahai—precludes formal membership in another religion. Baha'u'llah taught that God continues to intervene in human history through great spiritual messengers, whom he called "Manifestations of God"—Abraham, Moses, Krishna, Zoroaster, Buddha, Jesus, Muhammad, and so on. "These firmly established and mighty systems," he said of the religions they founded, "have proceeded from one Source and are the rays of one Light. That they differ from one another is to be attributed to the varying requirements of the ages in which they were promulgated." Bahai beliefs are merely the perfection of those teachers and traditions; according to one Bahai scholar, "to be a real Christian in spirit is to be Bahai, and to be a real Bahai is to be a Christian," the same going for all other religions. (The American Christian sect of Adventists*, through studying the prophecies in the Old Testament book of Daniel*, predicted that the Messiah would arrive on earth in 1844 and were disappointed when he failed to show. Some Bahais point out that in that very year, the Bab began his ministry and Abdul Baha was born—according to one Bahai scholar, "fulfilling the prophecy, but in a manner not anticipated by men.")

Bahai tolerance extends to gender, and some of the statements of Baha'u'llah and Abdul Baha seem well ahead of their time in this regard: "The world in the past has been ruled by force and man has dominated over woman by reason of his more forceful and aggressive qualities both of body and mind," Abdul Baha said in Paris in 1911. "But the scales are already shifting, force is losing its weight, and mental alertness, intuition, and the spiritual qualities of love and service, in which woman is strong, are gaining ascendancy. Hence the new age will be an age less masculine and more permeated with the feminine ideal, or, to speak more exactly, will be an age in which the masculine and feminine elements of civilization will be more properly balanced."

Along with its emphasis on tolerance and equality of the sexes, the Bahai Faith also calls for the union of religion and science, the adoption of an auxiliary international language, compulsory education for both men and women (where facilities are limited, women are to receive preference), and the abolition of extremes of wealth and poverty. Baha'u'llah's writings on world peace and one government reportedly influenced Woodrow Wilson's thinking that led to the founding of the League of Nations. Despite advocating global disarmament, universal suffrage, the unity of all religions, the creation of a global assembly and a world language, and the lowering of regressive taxes on the poor, Bahai law requires its members strictly to abstain from political involvement of any kind. Voting and holding nonpolitical government jobs are allowed, but partisan political action is seen as divisive and thus contrary to Bahai ideals. However, Bahais may express public positions on social and moral issues, such as racial and sexual equality, as long as they do not identify themselves with a particular political party.

The Bahai Faith encourages service to others, daily individual prayer and meditation, including a daily obligatory prayer and an annual 19-day dawn-to-dusk fast (from March 2 to 20) similar to the Muslim Ramadan; the faith supports marriage, strict monogamy, and complete equality for women, with no veiling or seclusion. Divorce is permitted but is strongly discouraged, as are all forms of criticism and backbiting. Like Islam, the Bahai Faith forbids the use of drugs and alcohol, strongly disapproves of tobacco as being injurious to health, yet discourages asceticism and celibacy. There are seven Bahai Houses of Worship, one on each of the six populated continents and Western Samoa, open to members of all religious traditions and to nonbelievers. Local communities, which are still rather small, hold a **Nineteen-Day Feast** on the first day of each Bahai month (the Bahai solar calendar, which originated with the Bab, consists of 19 months of 19 days each plus four intercalary days of additional celebration).

There are no sects or denominations of the Bahai Faith; it has remained free of serious dissension during the hundred years since its founder's death in 1892—something Bahais attribute to Baha'u'llah's **Covenant**, in which he laid out his vision for the continuity of the Bahai Faith, and the **Will and Testament of Abdul Baha**.

Subud bears some superficial resemblance to the Bahai Faith, most notably in that it espouses a "universal brotherhood" of spiritual consciousness, open to members of all races and religions; it has no hierarchy and preaches no creed or system of ideas that members must follow. Subud is not especially Islamic, except that its founder is a 20th-century Sufi from Java. The practices of **Bapak Muhammad Subuh** (b. 1901), have been adopted by members in over 60 countries, including more than 70 Subud Centers in the U.S. Although it reflects the name of its founder, Subud is said to be an acronym of three Sanskrit words: *susila* ("right living"), *budhi* ("inner force"), and *dharma* (which Subud translates with an Islamic tinge as "submission to divine power"). Its main practice is the **latihan** (Indonesian, "spiritual exercise"), a half-hour session engaged in twice weekly by members who have read about it and prepared for a period of about 3 months.

Subuh first experienced the latihan himself in 1925, when a ball of radiant light visibly entered his body through the crown of his head while he was in the company of some friends. He described the experience as a kind of "opening" to divine energy which continued to occur spontaneously, even during perfectly ordinary activities like shopping or watching television. It appears to have something in common with the ecstatic experiences of certain mystical schools, including Sufism, but is controllable and may be stopped at any time by an exertion of the conscious will. In 1933, Subuh began to transmit the experience to others, a process called **contact**. After growing slowly in Java, the movement began spreading to Europe and America by 1957. Muslims, Christians, Hindus, Jews, and Buddhists practice the latihan, but formal membership in Subud precludes formal membership in any other sacred tradition, including Islam.

✳ ISLAM IN THE MODERN WORLD

Confounding popular perception, Islam today is no more monolithic than communism was at its zenith. Yet with Marxism collapsing around the world, perhaps parallels with Christianity are more appropriate: Muslim countries regularly war with and attempt to invade each other, much as Christian nations in Europe have done. And, as in Christian history, varying sects of Islam fight to gain political control within Islamic nations, and minority sects are regularly persecuted. Libyan leader **Moammar Gaddafi** was recently found guilty of apostasy by a commission under the **Qadi,** or judge, of Medina, and most Islamic nations do not support Iran's death sentence against the author Salman Rushdie (Iran is, after all, Shiite rather than Sunni).

Modern Islamic nations also take very different approaches to interpreting Islamic law. Turkey, whose policy of Westernization under **Kemal Atatürk** in the 1920s virtually drove Sufi orders underground, follows the Swiss civil code. The Hanafite code, less strict than the Hanbalite, is followed in Lebanon and Syria and is influenced there and in Egypt and Tunisia by Turkey's more liberal laws, tending to do away with the right of jabr ("arranged marriage"), to allow women to initiate divorce, and to insist on formal procedures as opposed to verbal divorce by men. Beneath its pluralistic surface, though, a strong sense of a coherent Islamic worldview thrives, framed by relatively consistent moral and spiritual values. Most Muslim countries outside of the Arabian peninsula have accepted some degree of modification of traditional Islamic laws, either moderate, in the cases of Syria and Pakistan, or extreme, in Egypt and Turkey. This reflection of Western legal principles has in some cases sprung a backlash, as in Egypt, where fundamentalist Muslim groups have attempted to overturn the pro-Western government.

Islamic fundamentalism, epitomized by the Wahhabi movement, seeks to return to an ideal, "fundamental" form of Islam like that in the era of the **Rashidun,** or "rightly guided caliphs," as opposed to the worldly rule of the dynasties that followed and that were more concerned with amassing booty, building extravagant palaces, and living lives of luxuriant excess. Again like their Christian counterparts, Islamic fundamentalists selectively ignore some of their richest mystical traditions and some of the deepest implications of their scripture. As an added source of confusion for Westerners struggling to understand Muslim fundamentalism, its proponents may be Sunni or Shiite, may favor good relations with the West, as do the Wahhabis of Saudi Arabia, or be openly hostile, like the Hezbollah, the Amal, or the Islamic Group.

Hezbollah (Ar. *Hizb Allah,* "Party of God") is a fundamentalist Shiite sect that came into being after the Iranian revolution of 1979. Hezbollah has been associated with numerous terrorist acts but is only one of many such groups which, like fundamentalists of all religions around the world, seek to enforce their religious beliefs on others. (An extreme example of this in the U.S. was the murder by a member of the pro-life group Operation Rescue of a doctor who performed legal abortions.)

Amal ("Hope") is a Shiite group formed in Lebanon in 1974 by the late **Imam Musa al-Sadr.** Their militia, like the Druzes, figured prominently in the fighting in Lebanon during the 1980s, but they appear to have no special religious beliefs to make them worthy of note. The same can be said for the so-called **Islamic Group,** which has been tied to terrorist plots in the U.S. These cells (which qualify as neither cults nor sects) garner a disproportionate share of media attention, but their religious significance is virtually nil.

WHEN THE SMOKE CLEARS

Filtered though the baffling turmoil in the Middle East, the West's view of Islam has been grimly colored by the stridency of warring factions and

WHAT'S IN A SPELLING?

Many Muslim converts name themselves, as Muslim parents name their children, after the great prophets of Islam, beginning with Muhammad, the most popular Muslim name. Yet many common Muslim names are Arabic equivalents of names that are familiar to Christians and Jews from the Bible. Here are just a few, with the Arabic names in their most common transliterations.

Ibrahim	Abraham
Musa	Moses
Dawood	David
Ishaq	Isaac
Yaqub	Jacob
Yusuf	Joseph
Sulayman	Solomon
Jibril	Gabriel

terrorist groups that have little or nothing to do with the essence of Muslim spirituality. Imagine an observer from the East trying to evaluate Christianity based on reports of the continual bloody strife in Northern Ireland as delivered by unsympathetic foreign news media. That observer might conclude that Catholics are little more than bitter terrorists who randomly murder innocent civilians in the name of Jesus, while Protestants relish their role as a casually brutal occupying force to rival the Romans in ancient Judea. What all this misery might have to do with the mysteries of the Eucharist, the deep spiritual power of congregational hymns, or the transcendent love and compassion taught by Jesus 2,000 years ago our observer could only dimly surmise. And what relation might the violent conflicts bear to legitimate theological disagreements between sincere Catholics and Protestants over the nature of the Trinity or the Immaculate Conception?

These repeated parallels with Christianity are not gratuitous. The basic principles undergirding Islam are so similar in nature to those of the Christian faith that a disinterested observer—and to be genuinely disinterested in this context might mean to be from another galaxy—could have trouble seeing what all the antagonism is about. One God, demanding yet infinitely loving and merciful, calls humanity to worship Him and Him alone and offers a relatively simple ethical code based on submission to His will and compassion for one's neighbor. The same thumbnail sketch might also describe Judaism, whose relationship to Islam is implicit in these parallels through its enormous influence on Christianity. (Muhammad made the link explicit. "Never did I see a man who looked so much like me," the Prophet remarked when he encountered Abraham during his mystical Night Journey.)

Given the enormous size and influence of the Muslim world, Westerners at the very least owe it to themselves to explore the richness and diversity of Islam while shedding their stereotypes and preconceptions. With a little effort they can also learn from it, just as they have learned to enrich their lives through contact with Zen and Tibetan Buddhism, yoga, meditation, and other gifts of Eastern religion. Whether on a mystical or devotional level, or in terms of a cogent ethical code of living, Islam has at least as much to offer as its two sister religions. Only our misconceptions and prejudices, rooted in a complex tangle of political and economic agendas, prevent us from appreciating its underlying strength and nobility.

The interior of this elegant Mosque of Suleyman the Magnificent in Rhodes (rebuilt in 1808) may at first appear spare. But the genius of Islamic design is everywhere, from the framed calligraphy and the arabesques above the windows to the glorious carpets covering the floors. At the right is the minbar, or pulpit; set between two windows is the east-facing prayer niche known as a mithrab, with several small prayer rugs in front of it.

ALINARI/ART RESOURCE

✻ INSIDE A MOSQUE

An Islamic mosque can at first sight seem extremely bare to any Westerner used to churches or synagogues with their orderly rows of pews or chairs, stained-glass windows, choir lofts, organs, and statuary. Not that some Middle Eastern mosques are not as imposing and awe-inspiring in their architectural grandeur as any medieval European cathedral. But a traditional mosque has no raised seating of any kind. The entire floor may be covered with carpeting or may be bare stone; worshipers bring their own prayer rugs or not. The cycle of prayer called a raka involves a series of seven stages, each with its accompanying prayer and posture, which include standing, kneeling, and prostration. Traditionally, worshipers cover their heads, often with white caps known as **kufis**; today, though, some Muslim men dispense with the head covering. All footwear except cloth or leather socks must be left at the entrance to the mosque.

Because of the Prophet Muhammad's initial struggle against the worship of idols in Arabia, no statues or pictorial images of any kind are permitted, including picture windows. In their place are texts from the Quran or the names of certain caliphs written in Arabic calligraphy, sometimes as beautiful and radiant with gold leaf as any stained-glass window. The attention of worshipers is focused on two main structures common to every mosque, the minbar and mithrab. The **mithrab** is a prayer niche that worshipers face throughout the prayer service as they line up in orderly rows behind the prayer leader, or imam; it establishes the direction of the Kaaba in Mecca. Although women participated in Friday services in Muhammad's day, standing in back or off to the side (a tradition which is maintained in more liberal American mosques), in some Muslim countries they no longer do. Many mosques have a separate area or room for women to pray. The mithrab has written above it an ayat, or verse from the Quran. In many mosques, the verse concerns the Virgin Mary, and the niche itself represents the east-facing room in which the Annunciation of Gabriel to the Virgin Mary took place.

The **minbar,** or pulpit, is usually a handsomely carved wooden or stone structure with seven steps representing the seven heavens through which Muhammad ascended during his mystical Night Journey. During the traditional Friday service, the imam of the mosque will ascend the minbar following formal prayers and deliver a sermon, or **khutba,** which in some mosques can have a political, often inflammatory, content, although it was instituted by the Prophet to explore social, moral, and spiritual issues in the light of the Quran. Tradition states that Muhammad never raised his voice during his sermons or at any other time.

The two major Islamic religious festivals, which involve two rakas of congregational prayer in the mosque, are known as the Great Feast and the Little Feast. The **Feast of Sacrifice (Id al-Ahda),** or **Great Feast,** celebrating Abraham's substitute sacrifice of a sheep in place of his son Ishmael (not Isaac, as in the Hebrew Bible) is performed in conjunction with the annual hajj and requires the sacrifice of a lamb, cow, goat, or camel. The **Little Feast,** or **Id al-Fitr,** celebrates the end of the month-long Ramadan fast and lasts for three days. Among the Shiites, **Muhurram,** the normally joyful Muslim New Year's festival, is celebrated as a 10-day period of mourning for the martyrdom of Ali and his sons Hasan and Hussein. During the 10 days, Shiites dress in mourning and neither shave nor bathe. And during the celebration of the Shiites' holiest holiday, **Ashura,** which occurs annually on the date of Hussein's death, they celebrate their willingness to die as martyrs, seeking purification through beating themselves with chains and branches somewhat in the manner of medieval Christian Flagellants*.

Coming to Terms

Because Arabic plural forms are fairly complex, this glossary uses the standard English form instead. Also eliminated are all diacritical marks and the two Arabic letters *ayn* and *hamza,* transliterated as ' and ' respectively. As with any transliterated language, English spellings are approximations and often vary from source to source. The guiding premise here is simplicity and the most commonly used English version.

Abu Bakr (ah-*boo* bah-*keer*)   Closest friend of Muhammad, and the first caliph to succeed him.

Aisha (eye-*ee*-shuh)   Daughter of Abu Bakr and Umm Ruman, one of the first children born into Islam, and Muhammad's youngest wife.

Ali ibn Abi Talib, or simply **Ali**   Grandson of Abd al-Muttalib, son of Abu Talib, and cousin of Muhammad. The Prophet "adopted" Ali and took him into his household because Abu Talib had more children than he could afford to raise. Ali later married Fatima, Muhammad's daughter, and produced two sons, Hasan and Hussein. After Muhammad's death, Ali's nonelection as caliph led to the split between Sunni and Shiite Muslims.

Allah (uh-*lah*)   The Muslim name for God is a contraction of the Arabic term *al-ilah,* "the god." He was originally worshiped as a special Creator God in a class by Himself by some pre-Islamic Arabian hanifs. Muhammad's great breakthrough, based on the revelations he received, was to proclaim Allah as the *only* God at a time and place where many were worshiped. The Arabic is not far from the common Hebrew root for god, *El,* which also appears as *Eloah* (in the book of Job) and the mysterious plural *Elohim*. Arabic and Hebrew are both, after all, Semitic languages, in the same family as Aramaic, the language of Jesus.

Allahu Akbar (uh-*lah*-hu *ahk*-bar, "God is greater")   A cry of Muslim warriors, now an integral part of Muslim prayers, implying that the Divine is greater than any merely human conception.

angel (Ar. malak) Islam teaches that angels are incorporeal beings who are separated from heaven by 70 curtains of light. Their purpose is to praise, serve, and obey Allah, often in the form of messengers, such as the Archangel Gabriel, or as guardian angels who keep track of the good and evil deeds of humans. Some are mentioned by name besides Gabriel: **Israfil** will sound the trumpet on the Last Day; **Michael** (Ar. Mika'il) guards Islamic houses of worship; **Munkar** and **Nakir** are the Angels of the Grave who will be prominent in the afterlife.

as-Salamu alaykum (ah-sah-*lahm* uh-*lay*-kim) "Peace be on you," the greeting given to Muhammad by the Archangel Gabriel, now the standard greeting among Muslims. These are also the first words spoken by the risen Christ to his disciples and are quite similar to the traditional Jewish greeting, *Shalom aleichem.*

Baha'u'llah (bah-*hah*-uh-*lah*, "Glory of God") The key figure in the transition from Babism to Bahai.

Buraq White, winged beast ("between a mule and an ass") on which Muhammad rode, guided by Gabriel, from Mecca to Jerusalem and then through the seven heavens, in one night. This visionary experience is known as the Night Journey (al-Isra) and Ascension (al-Miraj).

calender (Pers. qalandar) Wandering Sufi dervish not attached to any particular order, especially one who disregards his appearance and flouts public opinion, reminiscent of the wandering ascetics of India.

caliph (Ar. khalifah, *kay*-lif, "vice-regent") Short for Khalifat Rasul Allah, or vice-regent for the Messenger of God, applied to rulers of the Muslim community following the death of Muhammad.

dervish (Pers. darwish, "mendicant") A member of a Sufi order; the original meaning of beggar, similar to Hindu sannyasin* or Christian friar*, no longer necessarily applies.

dhikr Allah (*zhick*-er, "remembrance of God") The chief Muslim voluntary practice, consisting of calling on the name of God with great devotion. In Sufi circles dhikr can involve prolonged chanting and ecstatic dance. Also spelled *zikr* or *zhikr* in Turkish, and possibly related to the Arabic word *sukr* ("intoxication").

faqir (fah-*keer*, "poor") A Muslim who has renounced worldly things. Faqirs sometimes acquired a reputation for working wonders. In India the term, spelled *fakir*, came to be associated with non-Muslim mendicants and yogis who performed superficially miraculous feats.

Fatima (*fah*-teh-mah) Muhammad's favorite daughter, and the only one of his children to have descendants. He said of her: "She is part of my prophecy."

fatwa (*fuht*-wah) A formal legal opinion given by a canon lawyer. The term has been applied to the death sentence announced by the Ayatol-

466

lah Khomeini against author Salman Rushdie for writing a book deemed blasphemous.

fiqh ("understanding") Canonical jurisprudence, which among the Sunnis is divided into four schools: Hanbalites, Malikhites, Hanafites, and Shafiites.

Hypocrites (Ar. Munafiqun) Early converts to Islam who held a superficial faith and sought only social and commercial advantages.

ijtihad (ihz-tih-*hahd)* Personal interpretation of Islamic law by the ulama, the knowledgeable and inspired scholars of the time.

imam (ih-*mahm)* The word has several distinct but related meanings. Primarily the imam is the leader of prayers in a mosque; since there are no priests in Islam and the imam is not ordained, any Muslim male may assume this role as the need arises. In upper case, Imam can also refer to one of the 7 or 12 early leaders, beginning with Ali, recognized by various Shiite sects. The title was sometimes applied to the early caliphs and is still generally used as an honorific today, as in the case of the Ayatollah Khomeini, who liked to be and often was addressed as Imam Khomeini.

inshallah (*in*-shah-*lah,* "God willing") The most common Muslim expression, indicating that all events are contingent upon the will of Allah.

Jibril (zhih-*breel)* The Archangel Gabriel, who transmitted the Quran from God to Muhammad. According to Islamic tradition, Jibril was active throughout history, showing Noah how to build his ark and luring Pharaoh's army into the Red Sea.

jinn Collective name (sing. **jinni,** jih-*nee)* for the beings on subtle planes, good and evil, who inhabit the Muslim worldview.

Kaffir (*kaff-*er) Contemptuous Arab term for any non-Muslim.

kaffiyeh (kuh-*fee*-yuh) A headdress, possibly of Bedouin origin, made up of a square cloth kerchief bound by a cord called an agal, worn so that a corner falls over each shoulder. It has become familiar in the West partly through its identification with PLO chairman Yasir Arafat and other Palestinian Arabs.

Karbala (kar-buh-*lah)* The central Iraqi city where Hussein ibn Ali met a martyr's death, it is now the site of his dome-shaped tomb and the most sacred spot on earth for Twelver Shiites.

kufi Simple white cap worn by Muslims, especially during prayer services in the mosque.

maktub ("what is written") The sense that God has ordained what is to happen, but not to be taken as an excuse for apathy or mere fatalism. In the famous words of Muhammad when asked by a Bedouin if faith in God precluded the need to tie up his camel, "Trust in God, and secure your camel."

masjid ("place of prostration") A mosque, generally a small, local one. A **masjid jami** is larger and may have a wider social function, especially for the Friday prayer when all the Muslims in a given area gather to receive special blessings from God.

Messenger (Ar. Rasul)   A name for Muhammad. His other titles include the Key of Mercy, the Key of Paradise, the Spirit of Truth, and the Happiness of God.

Promised Ten   The Companions of Muhammad whom he assured of entry into Paradise: Abu Bakr, Umar, Uthman, Ali, Abd ar-Rahman ibn Awf, Abu Ubayda, Talha, Zubayr, Sad of Zuhra, and Said the son of Zayd the Hanif.

Ridwan ("good pleasure")   God's final, absolute acceptance and taking to Himself of a human soul; the supreme Paradise, notwithstanding the usual perception of Paradise as a place of celestial delights. Also, the angel in charge of the Garden (**al-Janna**), as Paradise is most often referred to in the Quran.

shahada (shuh-*hah*-duh)   The single most important statement of Islamic faith; in Arabic, *La ilaha illallah. Muhammadun rasulullah.* ("There is no god but God. Muhammad is the Messenger of God").

sharia (shah-*ree*-uh)   The sacred law of Islam, encompassing both sunna and the revealed word of the Quran, which requires interpretation by the wise.

shaykh (shake, "old man," also sheikh or shaikh)   Originally, the head of an Arabic family, clan, or tribe; later, a title of respect, along the lines of imam; in Sufism, a master or teacher.

sura   A chapter of the Quran.

tariqa (tah-*ree*-kuh)   Path, specifically of the Sufis, and so by extension a Sufi order or brotherhood.

tauhid, tawhid (taw-*heed,* "unity")   The theology underlying belief in one God, called Allah and by many other names, revealed to all the prophets.

ulama (oo-luh-*mah,* sing. **alim**)   Religious scholars or doctors of sacred law.

umma   From the Arabic root meaning "mother," it is the name given to the international religious community of Muslims. One of Muhammad's great gifts was to create an Arab umma out of many disparate clans and tribes.

wali (wah-*lee,* pl. **awliya,** "nearness")   Muslim saint; a person near to God. According to the Sufi **al-Hujwiri** (d. c. 1075), there are 4,000 hidden saints, unknown to humanity and even to each other. The 4,000 make up an invisible hierarchy on which the whole world order depends, headed by a **Qutb,** or axis.

7

THE NEW AGE

❋ FALLING OUT OF THE CLOSET

Trying to define the New Age is a little like opening Fibber McGee's closet: the instant you get the door ajar, hundreds of disparate objects come tumbling out, threatening to overwhelm even the most interested and open-minded observer. In fact, the New Age has been forced to carry so much freight in the decades since it became popular that it's easier to make jokes about it than to define it. Having Shirley MacLaine as a spokesperson for the New Age is akin to calling Richard Gere a Buddhist role model—it raises more questions than it answers. And if it is problematic that a Hollywood star's best-selling books combine New Age wisdom with long descriptions of her love life, then how are we to look at J. Z. Knight, whose channeled entity, Ramtha, advised her clients to purchase expensive Arabian horses from her? And just what is a channeled entity, anyway?

The first thing we need to do when discussing the New Age is to agree that no one definition will cover all the sects, movements, techniques, and personalities that can be gathered under its roof—and further, that the name "New Age" itself is entirely inadequate. What we often mean when we speak of the New Age, apart from a lot of seemingly disconnected beliefs, is a mushrooming network of alternative learning centers that are slowly disseminating those beliefs into the mainstream of American (and international) life through a continuing series of classes, workshops, and retreats. From the Open Center and Omega Institute in New York and Esalen Institute in California to Alternatives in London and Findhorn in Scotland, hundreds of these centers large and small are introducing a growing clientele to the wealth of alternative spiritually along with the rudiments of various Eastern and Western mystical traditions.

The second thing needed in approaching the New Age is the same openness and respect with which one would approach the religious beliefs of an acquaintance who happened to be a Muslim or Buddhist. Some of those beliefs may seem incredible, preposterous, or superstitious to the conventional Western mind. But are they any more of a challenge to logic than the idea that God spoke to Moses from a burning bush or that an unleavened wafer can turn into the body and blood of Jesus Christ—beliefs firmly held by hundreds of millions of people around the world? For all the media coverage and financial success of the New Age, its underlying beliefs have often been subjected to contempt and even persecution of sorts. Fundamentalist religions are not generally accepting of the New Age, often mistaking, for instance, Goddess theology or Witchcraft for Satanism. At the same time, the secular humanist and scientific communities are eager to label the movement either gullible or downright fraudulent. But it now seems highly unlikely that the momentum impelling New Age assumptions and beliefs into popular consciousness can be held in check. The closet door is open and its contents are spilling out all around us.

As far as the popular press is concerned, the New Age began to take shape around 1970, when certain elements of Eastern spirituality and occultism which had been manifesting, often superficially, in the counterculture of the 1960s—and which had previously been tossed around with even less understanding by the Beats—began to merge with **transpersonal psychology.** That approach to therapy espoused the idea that psychological problems could be dealt with on a higher level than the purely mechanistic, atheistic approach taken by Freud-based therapies. Experimental treatments, like the work being done at the **Esalen Institute** in Big Sur, California, were often pioneered by therapists who had experience in Oriental practices such as Zen Buddhism and yoga. They were joined by others for whom psychedelic drugs had opened the doors to new forms of therapy based on insights similar to those of Eastern spiritual literature. Still others developed alternative forms of healing derived from Eastern medical/metaphysical techniques ranging from acupuncture and chi kung* to meditation*, visualization, and hypnosis. But what in the East are often viewed as interconnected systems—ayurvedic* medicine and yoga* as integral aspects of Hinduism in India, or acupuncture and t'ai chi ch'uan* as components of Taoism in China became separated and jumbled in the West by practitioners who either were not aware of the entire system or else cannibalized the system for one or more of its parts.

This severing of practices from their traditional moorings both necessitates and helps to explain the use of a catchall phrase like "New Age" to refer to apparently disparate techniques and worldviews. The full range of teachings and practices encompassed by the New Age includes not merely Eastern meditation and yoga covered in previous chapters, but also an increased awareness of nutrition and the value of preventive medicine, alternative approaches to healing, ecological concerns, an integration of business procedures with the common good, a reconsideration of the value of intuition as opposed to strictly logical thought, and, above all, an acknowledgment of the invisible realm of spirit. In the New Age, these generalities have been fleshed out in ways that may be enlightened, compassionate, and trustworthy or muddled, venal, and misleading, depending on who is purveying the teaching or treatment.

Criticism of New Age philosophies and techniques often targets the very newness that appeals to its adherents, charging that these techniques or belief systems have not been proven in the crucible of time. Conversely, much of what is termed New Age actually recycles old or even ancient practices such as shamanism, herbal remedies, Goddess worship, channeling, and astrology, which reach back to the dawning of metaphysical awareness. The fact that these approaches have been reconfigured in some ways—shamanic journeys carried out in a practitioner's office for a set fee may seem worlds apart from the work of an authentic American Indian or Siberian shaman—leads to further skepticism about the efficacy of certain New Age practices. In fact, popular New Age oversimplifications of complex Eastern concepts like karma and reincarnation threaten to strip them of their essential meaning.

To be fair, the New Age may receive more than its share of public contumely simply because it has no organizational structure with which to return fire. The media may hesitate even to criticize the Catholic church, Orthodox Jews, the Dalai Lama, or the local Islamic mosque. But channeling, homeopathy, astrology, and anything to do with crystals regularly come in for sarcastic, one-sided, and often misinformed treatments in the press and on TV news programs that have nothing to fear from Vatican or B'nai B'rith spokespeople.

And yet the very existence of so many alternatives to orthodoxy—whether in medicine, psychotherapy, or religion—begs the question of why large numbers of people are seeking them out. If the mainstream belief systems and therapeutic treatments were satisfying the needs of the population, would the New Age be so successful? Why exactly are so many people being drawn to New Age practices and beliefs? One compelling reason is the generally peaceful, nonjudgmental attitude of most New Age thought. Especially for those in the West who have been reared on rigorist, exclusionary belief systems, whether Christian or Jewish, the New Age offers a refreshing alternative.

What the New Age may lack in logical, sharply structured theory, it more than makes up for in openness and acceptance of diversity. More than almost any of the major belief systems, the New Age embraces women and women-centered teachings, minorities, homosexuals, and just about anyone else who doesn't feel comfortable or welcome in many mainstream religious institutions. This is not to say that the New Age doesn't have its share of narrow interpretations, parochialism, or charlatans. Sectarian rivalries created splinter groups within many of the New Age's first major components, including New Thought and Theosophy. The New Age has so far not succeeded, however, in launching a single religious war of note or slaughtering significant numbers of people in its name.

The greatest potential weakness of the New Age may be its confusing variety of beliefs, the often vague nature of their definition, and an overall lack of focus. Mainstream religions can also be confusingly divided into numerous sects and denominations, as this book has shown, but their strength generally comes from one set of underlying beliefs. Christianity, in all of its denominations, teaches that Jesus Christ, the Son of

THIS IS THE DAWNING OF THE EVE OF AQUARIUS

The New Age should not be confused with the **Age of Aquarius,** popularized by the 1970s Broadway musical *Hair!* That is an astrological designation referring to the period of time that will begin when the sun at the moment of the spring equinox is in the 30-degree arc of sky known as the sign of Aquarius. According to New Age theory, we are leaving the Piscean Age, characterized by the rise of Christianity, and entering the Aquarian Age, which will see the birth of a new, universalist religion. Unfortunately for this theory, the astrologically correct Age of Aquarius will not begin for roughly another 100 years, at which time the sun will be in the sign of Aquarius at the spring equinox.

God, died to redeem humanity; Muslims believe that Muhammad received the divine revelation of Allah to give to the world; Buddhism teaches that all human beings can solve the dilemma of suffering through their own efforts. Does the New Age offer any comparable set of firm beliefs that can unite all its disparate nestlings gathered under one brooding wing?

That question may have no simple answer. Still, it's possible to supply a working definition of the New Age movement—and for all its diversity and disparateness, it can be considered a movement—and to list a menu of beliefs, systems, and techniques that the movement encompasses. We've already mentioned its nonjudgmental attitude, and we might add, by implication, the sense that all forms of spirituality that are not violent or harmful to others and don't try to restrict other forms of belief or practice are acceptable. If the New Age may be said to have a preeminent goal, it is probably the evolution of a universal religion. This sometimes gets confused with the New Age principle that is most frequently challenged: the idea that everyone is God. On the face of it, that does sound terribly cloudy and self-absorbed. But the related teaching, often embraced by traditional spiritual masters, is that we need to discover the guru within each of us. One studies and follows teachers, this belief goes, only to be able ultimately to become one's own guru, shaman, channeler, healer. The inner guru can be another name for the Higher Self, or the Divine within, and to say that we are looking to realize and acknowledge our identity with the God within is vastly different from saying that we are all God. Or is it?

Some schools of Buddhism teach, for instance, that each of us is already a perfect Buddha, it's just that we don't realize it yet. The Indian philosophy of Vedanta* insists that there is no distinction between the individual Self (sometimes called the Atman* or Witness*) and Brahman*, the Absolute Godhead. How is that different from saying we are all God? It comes down to a question of the mindset of the person holding that belief. If it is said from a position of identifying with the individual ego, in the sense of being a separate, autonomous entity indifferent to the needs and suffering of others—a god in the Greek sense of Olympian impunity—then we are in a very different realm from the nondualistic teachings of the great spiritual traditions. Nondualism* proclaims the identity of each individual with every other one and impels compassion toward all. In that sense, saying that I am God may amount to nothing more than a very confused, egocentric statement of disconnection from the rest of humanity.

Other principles of the New Age apparent in many of its sects and teachings may seem downright American: individualism, practicality, and a commitment to social justice. But maybe the most commonplace New Age tenet is apocalypticism*—the expectation that the world as we know it is coming to an end. In some ways, New Age apocalypticism is similar

474

to the same strain in many of the great traditions. But its perspective is significantly different. Many New Agers believe that the apocalypse will take the form of a vast transformation in human consciousness, a move up to the next level of awareness, for which we all need to prepare. Although some New Agers envision this change as potentially explosive and destructive, most view it as an inevitable but benevolent event; preparing for it through meditation and other spiritual practices, they say, will help reduce the confusion and fear that some people may experience during the transition.

New Age absorption of other religious traditions may seem to make its practitioners difficult to distinguish from those of certain Eastern belief systems. The major difference is that people who identify themselves as New Age practitioners are less likely to belong actively and formally to a specific order of Tibetan Buddhism or Sufism or to follow its precepts and practices faithfully. Most New Agers are **syncretists:** they combine elements from many different traditions, tossing in techniques drawn from esoteric and occult practice for good measure.

From a historical perspective, the landscape leading up to the New Age of today can appear hopelessly cluttered. And yet a number of significant pathways crisscross and overlap within that landscape. By tracking a few of the major ones closely and seeing where they intersect each other, we may be able at least to get a feel for the territory.

WHO PUT THE "NEW" IN NEW AGE?

In purely etymological terms, the phrase "New Age" began to appear around 1914, when the **Freemasons,** an esoteric society said to be derived from the Sufi master builders of the Middle Ages, called their publication *New Age.* At about the same time, the British literary critic A. R. Orage published a pre–World War I weekly newspaper in London entitled *The New Age.* Orage's paper combined articles on spiritual, political, and psychological subjects by the likes of G. B. Shaw, T. S. Eliot, and H. G. Wells (back in the days when any real intellectual had at least two initials before his last name). The term has been tossed around rather casually ever since; but with no generally accepted founder and no specific core of followers, the New Age will probably always suffer from a lack of definition in the popular mind and from unfortunate associations with cultural spin-offs such as the dreaded New Age music.

But whether the New Age is qualitatively different from previous historical movements that have augured massive changes in human consciousness remains a fascinating question. In *Cosmic Consciousness,* one of the classic guidebooks to the coming era, published in 1901, Canadian psychiatrist **Richard M. Bucke** argued the case for an actual evolutionary change in humanity from self-consciousness to cosmic or spiritual consciousness. Bucke believed that this change would parallel the prior shift from animal consciousness to self-consciousness that had ratified our very identity as human beings. He based his theory on his own experience of a moment of illumination in 1872 as well as on the mystical experiences of over a dozen extraordinary individuals, including the Buddha, Jesus, St. Paul*, Plotinus*, Muhammad, Dante, St. John of the Cross*, William Blake*, Walt Whitman, Balzac, Spinoza*, Sri Rama-

GETTING COSMIC

Although Richard Bucke's brief account of his early life in *Cosmic Consciousness*—told entirely in the third person—is engaging, very little in it suggests the spontaneous experience that came over him one night in England. Born "of good middle class English stock" and raised "almost without education on what was then a backwoods Canadian farm," Bucke describes himself as an introspective youth who somehow developed a love for poetry, especially Shelley and Whitman. He says he never accepted Christian teachings and thought of Jesus as a great man but not divine. At 16, after the death of both parents, Bucke left Canada to wander the length and breadth of North America for five years, working to pay his way. He returned home, used his modest inheritance to get a college education, and continued reading. In his 36th year, after a night of reading his favorite poets with a couple of friends, he was riding in a hansom cab in a quiet, peaceful mood.

All at once, without warning of any kind, he found himself wrapped around as it were by a flame-colored cloud. For an instant he thought of fire, some sudden conflagration in the great city; the next, he knew that the light was within himself. Directly afterwards came upon him a sense of exultation, of immense joyousness accompanied or immediately followed by an intellectual illumination quite impossible to describe. Into his brain streamed one momentary lightning-flash of the Brahmic Splendor which has ever since lightened his life; upon his heart fell one drop of Brahmic Bliss, leaving thenceforward for always an aftertaste of heaven. . . . He saw and knew that the cosmos is not dead matter but a living Presence, that the soul of man is immortal, that the universe is so built and ordered that without any peradventure all things work together for the good of each and all, that the foundation principle of the world is what we call love and that the happiness of every one is in the long run absolutely certain. He claims that he learned more within the few seconds during which the illumination lasted than in previous months or even years of study, and that he learned much that no study could ever have taught.

—RICHARD M. BUCKE, *COSMIC CONSCIOUSNESS*

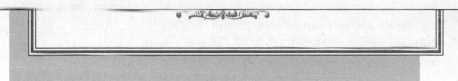

krishna*, and the 17th-century French mystic Madame Guyon. His evidence suggested that such a change was beginning to occur at an accelerating pace among humanity. But Bucke talked about "many thousands of generations" before this new consciousness would become a universal fact of human existence, present from birth in each human heart.

To step back further, we could look to earlier eras, such as the 6th century BC, when wholesale changes in the way humans related to each other, the world, and the notion of Divinity created a new paradigm of consciousness. Based on that assessment, we could say that the New Age of today is merely a term of convenience to characterize the modern implications of a chain of events begun thousands of years ago and held together tenuously under one ponderous logo.

We could also, of course, insist that the current situation represents a vast qualitative change, a surge of consciousness that will take us beyond the realm of scattered, individual faiths and traditions into a consensus of unified belief somewhat similar to the Perennial Philosophy, a term indicating that the same core elements underlie mystical experience in every tradition. We could further posit that Bucke's temporal estimate was too conservative and that the arrival of a critical mass of new consciousness is imminent. For alongside the massive turbulence of the modern world, with its mounting ethnic strife, impending ecological disaster, and the global plague of AIDS, is evidence of increasing awareness of the overwhelming need to change. But such a prediction could just as easily be seen as premature; judgments of such a vast scope are difficult to make from the eye of the maelstrom.

In the New Age classic *The Aquarian Conspiracy,* **Marilyn Ferguson** makes the case for speeding up Bucke's time frame. What in the past were isolated incidents of personal spiritual transformation, she writes, "in response to disciplined contemplation, grave illness, wilderness treks, peak emotions, creative effort, spiritual exercises, controlled breathing, techniques for 'inhibiting thought,' psychedelics, movement, isolation, music, hypnosis, meditation, reverie," have suddenly become commonplace. "These deceptively simple systems and their literature, the riches of many cultures, are available to whole populations, both in their original form and in contemporary adaptations."

New Age observer **Jon Klimo** uses the metaphor of lucid dreaming to explain the potential uses of some of these phenomena. What happens in the course of a normal dream to turn it into a lucid dream is usually that the dream ego becomes aware that something out of the ordinary has occurred. For example, the dreamer may suddenly realize that a relative or a celebrity to whom he is speaking is actually dead, and this will cause the dreamer to reflect that "this must be a dream." At that point the dreamer will become conscious within the dream—an extraordinary mixture of two presumably distinct states of consciousness—and can even learn to control the course of the dream. In a similar fashion, the occurrence of nonordinary reality in the form of a channeling phenomenon, clairvoyance, nonmedical healings, and the full range of experiences gathered in this chapter can function as stimulants to "wake up" the consciousness of individuals or of society as a whole to the realization that, on one level, what we are experiencing is a dream. The concomitant freedom to experiment, to have a sense of mind over matter, of the potential to direct the "dream" situation in ways not previously imagined possible, also applies. In the lucid dream, the dreamer can, if she chooses, fly through the air, visit faraway places, make love to the dream object of her choice, drink rare vintage wines, or merely revel in the increased light and awareness that comes with lucidity; in the state of awakened mind, one can do unimagined things of much greater magnitude than in the state of ordinary awareness.

Media-fed stereotyping of the New Age tends to accentuate high-profile areas open to both extravagant claims and showy debunking, such as psychic phenomena, the occult, Neo-Pagan religions, channeling, and apocalyptic prophecies. Yet the movement also deals with more pragmatic, less glitzy issues, including ecological restoration, socially responsible business ventures, alternative healing, preventive medicine and wellness care, and organic farming. And some of its concerns are closer to the major spiritual traditions than many people suspect. As New Age scholar David Spangler notes in his introduction to *The New Age Catalogue*, these issues include "the emergence of an awareness that we are all one people living upon one world that shares a common destiny. The New Age represents social, political, economic, psychological, and spiritual efforts to recognize and include all that our modern society has tended to exclude: the poor, the dispossessed, the feminine, the ecological, and, inwardly, all the painful, repressed and unintegrated material that Carl Jung called the Shadow." Acknowledging the self-empowerment orientation of so much New Age literature, its self-absorbed penchant to proclaim "I am God!," Spangler insists that "the essence of the New Age is the expression of a compassionate love and a social awareness and responsibility that reaches beyond the self to embrace and empower others."

Amid all this idealism, some critical voices have been raised not so much to condemn the New Age as to make crucial distinctions about its

479

underlying philosophies. One of the most consistently articulate commentators is **Ken Wilber,** a psychologist and philosopher who in his book *Transformations of Consciousness* has encapsulated his warnings in his theory of the **pre/trans fallacy,** which he defines as "a confusing of *pre*-rational structures with *trans*-rational structures simply because both are *non*-rational." In other words, prerational structures such as magic and myth may be elevated to the status of transrational states of genuine enlightenment because both are outside ordinary rationality; likewise, a genuinely ecstatic, mystical state may be misperceived as infantile or schizophrenic. Misperceptions in either direction can create difficulties. "Practitioners of meditation," Wilber continues, "often swimming in the rhetoric of transformation, may fail to recognize the regressive nature of much of their experience." This may result in "a mixture and confusion of pre-egoic fantasy with trans-conceptual insight, of prepersonal desires with transpersonal growth, of pre-egoic whoopee with trans-egoic liberation."

A student of both Wilber and the New Age, Chicago-based sociologist and former Catholic priest **Michael Ducey** sums up the problem this way:

"Higher consciousness" is an inner awareness. However, inner stillness is easily invaded by painful unconscious material. Meditation can turn into trance. The tricky part is that trance is essential to investigate certain deep parts of the inner self, but when trance is constructed to avoid pain, it can become a seductive state of mind that poses as permanent fulfillment.

Therefore a crucial skill in post-rational growth is to distinguish between being awake and being in trance. . . . Inner pain makes us extremely clever in confusing the two. Escapist trances form the foundation of cults and other totalitarianisms.

And so, in new-age circles you find everything from true mystics to real nut-cases, and it is not always easy to tell the difference.

—MICHAEL DUCEY, "SEA CHANGES: NEW AGE
SPIRITUALITY, TRADITIONAL VALUES, AND SOCIAL
PROBLEMS IN AMERICA" (1992, UNPUBLISHED ESSAY)

NEW AGE NETWORK

One of the most confusing aspects of the New Age is its eclecticism. The virtue of religious pluralism has been taken to extremes by many New Age practitioners, who spread their interests over so many fields as to render themselves uncategorizable. The following entry in a New Age reference work hints at a vast subcultural tapestry of alternative healing techniques, Neo-Pagan and ecological groups, and heterodox religious sects.

ANODEA JUDITH Anodea Judith, formerly named A. Judith Mull, is founder and director of Lifeways, a school for the study of consciousness and healing arts located in northern California. Judith is a professional healer and bodyworker who has studied acupressure, yoga, bioenergetics, psychic healing and reading, gestalt therapy, radical psychiatry, ritual magic, and shamanism. Currently living in Oakland, California, she serves as priestess and president of the Church of All Worlds (CAW), which was originally founded in St. Louis, Missouri, by Otter G'Zell (formerly Tim Zell), and she helps oversee CAW's subsidiary organizations, which include Forever Forests, Nemeton, the Ecosophical Research Association, and the Holy Order of Mother Earth (HOME). In addition, she is a priestess with Vortex, a Wicca coven. Judith is also an ordained minister and elder of the Covenant of the Goddess, and has served as one of its officers.

—J. GORDON MELTON, *NEW AGE ALMANAC*

❋ THE MIND-BODY CONNECTION

The interconnectedness of all levels of being (as we will see soon in a discussion of holism) is a primary tenet of the New Age. Body, mind, and spirit, according to this worldview, are intimately related, just as the ancient Hindu system of the chakras* connects the generative and survival organs with the heart, intellect, and spiritual consciousness; what happens on one plane affects the others. And so, as the psychotherapeutic profession was exploring the implications of spiritual awareness for personal psychological growth, the medical profession—at least along its most finely honed cutting edge—was delving into the long reported but frequently overlooked ability of the mind to heal the physical organism.

The implications of this linkage between mind and body have become familiar today through the works of a number of modern authors, some of whom come from conventional medical backgrounds. In the late 1970s, **Norman Cousins** wrote a popular article and then a best-selling book (*Anatomy of an Illness as Perceived by the Patient*) about overcoming a serious disease through a "program calling for the full exercise of the affirmative emotions as a factor in enhancing body chemistry." The program included, in part, watching episodes of *Candid Camera* and some Marx Brothers movies and reading books of humor. In the 1980s, **Bernie Siegel,** a surgeon and teacher, propounded the concept of unconditional love as the most effective stimulant for the immune system in his books *Love, Medicine and Miracles* and *Peace, Love and Healing*. He advocates the use of meditation and visualization in helping to heal diseases such as cancer and AIDS. At the same time, **Louise Hay** taught related procedures in best-sellers such as *Heal Your Body* and *You Can Heal Your Life*. Hay especially promoted the use of affirmations as an integral part of any healing process. And **Deepak Chopra,** an Indian-born endocrinologist, after establishing a successful practice in the U.S. returned to India to explore the ancient science of ayurvedic* medicine. Over the past two decades, he has written and lectured extensively about the remarkable kinship between the most modern developments in medicine and physics and the 6,000-year-old teachings of the Hindu Vedas*.

These are only a few of the most prominent names in a field of relationship that is rapidly expanding and gaining respect not only among the public but also with some of the world's leading physicians and sci-

THE MAGNETISM.

The bacquet was designed for multiple healings. The iron rods could be grasped by patients, many of whom were well-to-do ladies of Parisian society. In this drawing, probably intended to be satirical, the lady on the right is in the midst of a healing "crisis." In the background, another woman, seized with convulsions, is being carted off to a "crisis room" lined with mattresses, where she could thrash around without doing harm to herself. Other cartoons of the era depicted mesmerists with asses' heads, pockets stuffed with money, in the act of seducing "gullible" ladies.

COURTESY BIBLIOTHÈQUE NATIONALE

entists. And yet the concept of "mind over matter" has been around—in fact, has been a cliché—for so long that its exact origins are hard to discern. To some degree it derives from tales of yogic powers, the ability of certain yogis and lamas of the Himalayas and Tibet to slow the heartbeat and respiration virtually to a halt or to raise their body temperature in a cold environment so as to dry sheets dipped in ice-cold water and wrapped around them. These powers of mind over matter have been scientifically documented on several occasions, but because they have been exhibited by foreign ascetics with a lifetime of arduous practice behind them, they seem out of the reach of the average Westerner.

Nonetheless the Greeks, upon whose wisdom much of Western science and culture is presumably based, themselves believed in the suprarational healing powers of the mind, and their belief was shared by the secular, rationalistic Romans. The Greek physician **Aesclepiades of Bythynia** (fl.

483

100 BC) treated his patients with therapies including bathing, exercise, and change of diet and is said to have made systematic use of the "induced trance" in the cure of some diseases. At the Temple at Epidaurus, south of Corinth, the sick spent the night asleep, and the cure for their illness was revealed either to them or to a priest in dreams.

In the 16th century the Swiss physician and chemist known as **Paracelsus** (1493–1541) theorized that the universe asserted a magnetic influence over humans—somewhat reminiscent of the Taoist concept that the microcosm of the body mirrors the macrocosm of the universe. In the next century, Flemish physician **Jan Baptista van Helmont** (1577–1644) described the healing force of imagination as "an invisible fluid called forth and directed by the power of the human will," and **Sir Kenelm Digby** (1603–65) chronicled the power of the imagination not only to heal but also to cause disease. The German-born physician **Franz Anton Mesmer** (1734–1815), living in a time when gravitation and electromagnetism were hot topics, was intrigued by the concept that invisible forces influence the body at a distance. Picking up on the work of Paracelsus and others, Mesmer came to believe that the real agent of healing was a "universal fluid," influenced by the movement of the heavenly bodies, that passes through the earth and creates "tides" in the bloodstream and nervous system similar to the tides of the sea. This force he first called "animal gravitation" and later **animal magnetism,** likening it to the well-known effects of mineral magnetism.

Mesmer sought to cure certain illnesses by passing magnets over the body of the patient, then amended his procedure to passes made with bare hands, believing that he could in this way control the flow of animal magnetism himself. He later supplied animal magnetism to his patients from a **bacquet,** a large, battery-like wooden tub filled with water and iron filings—all magnetized by Mesmer's touching or pointing at them. Iron bars radiated from the bacquet, and each patient held a bar against an ailing body part. While music was played in the dimly lit room, Mesmer and his trained assistants would suggest that the patients be healed. Patients waited for their illness to intensify into a convulsive "crisis" that preceded the cure and during which their symptoms got worse before they got better. Mesmer did not attempt to cure organic illnesses in which bodily organs had suffered deterioration, but he was surprisingly successful at healing psychosomatic maladies with symptoms as dire as paralysis, deafness, blindness, insanity, and gout (although the underlying cause in many cases was some form of hysteria).

Needless to say, the medical establishment was not pleased. Even the many aristocrats, mainly women, who were among his most satisfied patients (and whose large fees subsidized his free treatment of the lower classes), could not save him. For his efforts, Mesmer was hounded out of Vienna, where he had been a friend and patron of the much younger Mozart, and Paris, where his work was discredited in 1784 by a committee of the Academy of Sciences whose members included Lavoisier, Ben Franklin, and Joseph Guillotin, largely on the grounds that they could find no physical explanation for the healings they observed. Mesmer retired to spend the last years of his life in small Swiss and German villages near the shore of Lake Constance, where he continued to practice healing and to write about his work.

In the course of developing his treatments, Mesmer had discovered that he could induce in his patients a state between sleep and waking, during which they would respond to commands and suggestions regarding their ailments. He found that he could, in effect, have the patient will himself or herself to be cured. Yet Mesmer still believed that animal magnetism was a physical principle and that by pointing his finger or waving a wand he could direct its flow into a patient. Over a period of many years, however, his followers determined that the physical props were not necessary for the process, which had come to be called **mesmerism**, nor was the belief in animal magnetism as a physical force. They found that an induced somnambulistic state—what is now referred to as a **hypnotic trance**—would work as well. Suggestion, combined with the creation of a high state of expectancy within the patient, was sufficient to effect cures, and suggestions given to the patient in this state would be carried out later (**posthypnotic suggestion**). An English physician and surgeon named **James Braid** (1795–1860), a student of mesmerism, applied the term *neurohypnotism,* later shortened to **hypnotism** (Gr. *hypnos,* "sleep"), to a condition of mind and body induced by gazing fixedly at an inanimate object. A Scottish surgeon living in India, **James Esdaile** (1808–59), used the techniques developed by Mesmer and his followers to help during the performance of over 300 major operations with an astonishingly low mortality rate—and without anesthesia or antibiotics.

Underlying much of this work was the notion of an "unconscious" or

TRIUMPH OF THE WILL

Franz Mesmer, born in Germany, educated in Vienna, was an accomplished musician who played the cello, clavichord, and glass harmonica (an old instrument that had recently been improved by Ben Franklin). A friend of German composer Christoph Willibold Gluck and a patron of Mozart (whose opera *Bastien et Bastienne* was produced at Mesmer's home and who later made reference to Mesmer and his magnetic techniques in a scene in *Così fan tutti*), Mesmer was a fascinating character whose contribution to the development of hypnosis, mental healing, and depth psychology may be vastly underrated. The fact that Mesmer himself may not have been fully aware of the implications of what he was doing should not detract from his accomplishments, as his biographer explains.

Mesmer understood full well that his will dominated the will of the patient, the cure coming about partly because he made the patient will the cure. He saw, moreover, that the subject in a trance could obey his commands because something deeper than ordinary consciousness was at work. He did not at once grasp the concept of the unconscious mind or realize that he was probing into deeply hidden parts of the psyche. Only after Mesmerism developed along unexpected lines, in his own hands and those of his followers, did he comprehend the meaning of the trance.

Years later he wrote, "Sleep is not a negative condition or simply the absence of wakefulness . . . the human faculties are not always quiescent but are actually as active as during wakefulness." By then he realized what he had been doing with his patients—he had been putting them into a special kind of sleep and then making them use their faculties in a special way. Today we would say that he had discovered controlled hypnotism.

—VINCENT BURANELLI, *THE WIZARD FROM VIENNA*

"subconscious" level to the mind, in which influential memories and impressions are stored, long forgotten but capable of determining one's actions and mental and physical health. Indeed, after a period of study in Paris in 1885 at Salpêtrière under the neurologist **Jean Martin Charcot** (1825–93), who used hypnotism and mental suggestion in his treatment of nervous and mental diseases including hysteria, a young **Sigmund Freud** (1856–1939) decided to change his area of study from the physical aspects of neurology to the psychological—or from the brain to the mind. For over a decade, Freud used hypnosis in his therapeutic work and declared the results "marvelous" in some cases. But when one female patient began to form a personal attachment to him and embraced him during a hypnotic session (an early example of transference), he changed to free association, and hypnosis lost a chance for much wider exposure.

For a time, even church groups began to look seriously at the possibilities of mental healing, to the extent of supplementing the usual physical and chemical means of medicine with mental and spiritual therapy, something which was known as the **Emmanuel Movement.** But medical science was growing more powerful by the day, and these alternatives to *materia medica* were given short shrift by the establishment. Nonetheless, they continued to develop as part of another strain of American belief that included New Thought and Christian Science*, which grew up alongside each other and which preached healing and preventing illness through mental and spiritual means. In the 1920s, a French chemist and student of hypnotism, **Emile Coué** (1857–1926), spearheaded the self-improvement movement with his famous **autosuggestion** formula, "Every day in every way, I am getting better and better." Hypnotism itself, meanwhile, entered a dormant phase during which it survived mainly in a rather debased form as a theatrical and carnival sideshow attraction. Only recently has it begun once again to be perceived by the mainstream as a potentially powerful force in healing.

✳ MIND-CURE OVER MATTER

Around the turn of the century, the great American philosopher and psychologist **William James** (1842–1910), in his landmark study of the psychology of belief entitled *The Varieties of Religious Experience,* identified a movement that can be seen as a clear forerunner of any number of New Age beliefs. James called it the "mind-cure movement" although its adherents referred to it as, among other things, the **New Thought;** it was promoted in writings with evocative titles like *Ideal Suggestion Through Mental Photography* and *Happiness as Found in Forethought Minus Fearthought*. According to James, mind-cure or New Thought had several doctrinal sources, including the Gospels, Emersonianism or New England Transcendentalism, idealism, and Hinduism. "But the most characteristic feature of the mind-cure movement is an inspiration much more direct," he wrote. "The leaders in this faith have had an intuitive belief in the all-saving power of healthy-minded attitudes as such, in the conquering efficacy of courage, hope, and trust, and a correlative contempt for doubt, fear, worry, and all nervously precautionary states of mind."

The sense of mild irritation running through James's remarks probably reflects his impatience with the blend of philosophical idealism and secular optimism that undergirded New Thought. The idealism of the day, with its roots in Plato, held that mind or intelligence is the ultimate principle behind the functioning of the world. By thinking and acting optimistically, one could overcome material barriers, from illness to financial need. At its core, this is a deeply spiritual philosophy, but in the context of late-19th-century Western life, it ran the danger of confusing issues of social advancement and prosperity with inner enlightenment.

NEW THOUGHT IN OLD BOTTLES

Just as the major spiritual traditions can be seen as responses to particular sets of problems endemic to specific times and places, so smaller movements like New Thought also tend to address particular historical and social developments. The following evaluation from a scholar of the New Age places New Thought in perspective as a product of turn-of-the-century America that "emerged in the context of, and was enriched by, what sociologists call the modernization process." But since

New Thought is less visible today than it was a century ago, much of its thunder stolen by the New Age movement, it may be helpful to read this sociological assessment in light of the enormously popular work of Norman Vincent Peale (discussed later) that regularly appeared on best-seller lists in the 1950s.

New Thought put an optimistic spin on advancing secularization, increasing industrialization, and rapid urbanization, and brought a new gospel of happiness and prosperity to a young but developing American culture that was seeking both. This was a secular culture, an emerging technological culture, and a culture developing, for the first time, a large and significant middle class. America's middle class found something of value in this new faith, which proclaimed that God was wholly good, evil was only error, ultimate reality was the mind, and one's life and one's world were predicated on one's thought. This was religious idealism packaged for popular consumption by an optimistic, self-confident, self-made society. The movement was given further appeal because it claimed to be a pragmatic philosophy of life that was based on scientific methods—a religious technology.

—J. GORDON MELTON, *NEW AGE ALMANAC*

Beyond its modest numbers, the New Thought movement popularized many of the themes and attitudes that are now familiar components of the New Age, primarily the idea that mind or consciousness is the force behind the material world. New Thought held, among other things, that "all life is one" and that God is omnipresent, a kind of vague pantheism foreshadowing the New Age assumptions of interconnectedness. New Thought adherents spoke of the "limitless self," which sounds like a loose translation of the Hindu concept of the Atman*. One of New Thought's progenitors, **Phineas Quimby** (1802–66) of Portland, Maine, began as a student of mesmerism but soon came to believe that the real source of cure was the patient's faith in the healer's remedies. He held that illness was merely a delusion that the suffering individual inflicted on himself or herself. If the mind of the patient could be changed, a cure would result, and so mesmerism itself was no longer necessary.

Quimby appears to have directly influenced the founder of Christian Science*, Mary Baker Eddy*. In 1859, three years before he met and healed her of a serious disease, he wrote, "Disease is what follows the disturbance of the mind or spiritual matter. . . . It is made up of mind diverted by error, and Truth is the destruction of this opinion," sentiments that foreshadow Eddy's own beliefs. Quimby was a gifted healer with clairvoyant abilities who cured thousands in the New England area; he even effected several cures while in a location distant from the patient, which were later verified anecdotally.

But although Quimby identified his healing technique as similar to that of Jesus in the Gospels, he did not base his conclusions on biblical beliefs. He often spoke in religious or spiritual terms but was vague about his understanding of God while seeming to despise institutional religion and "priestcraft" as much as he did physicians. "All the religion I acknowledge is God, or Wisdom," he wrote. "I will not take man's belief to guide my barque. I would rather stand at the helm myself." Likewise, the system of New Thought that Quimby presaged should not be confused with the Bible-based teachings of Christian Science, even if both emphasize the role of the mind in healing. For one thing, Christian Science teaches the finality of revelation in Mary Baker Eddy, whereas New Thought remains open to the ongoing revelation of Truth. New Thought never attached itself to any specific religious tradition, and in that as well as its generic principle of right thinking as a cure for illness, it predicted much of the holistic health movement of today. And unlike Christian Science, New Thought never categorically ruled out the partnership of conventional medicine in collaborative healing.

The popular spread of New Thought is usually traced to the writing and ministry of **Emma Curtis Hopkins** (1853–1925), a former Christian Scientist who at one time served as editor of Eddy's nascent *Christian Science Journal*. Fired for departing from Christian Science dogma, Hopkins continued to think of herself as a Christian Scientist for a time, although she eventually stopped using the name; in later articles she credits teachers other than Jesus, including the Buddha and the compiler of the Vedas*, with having imparted principles that were "essentially Christian Science teachings." Among the people she herself taught were the founders or co-founders of several New Thought groups still in evidence today from North America to Japan, including the **Unity School of Christianity,** the **United Church of Religious Science,** and **Divine Science.** These groups range from devotional to nonsectarian, occasionally incorporating Bible teachings with Eastern, Rosicrucian, and other beliefs in a nonjudgmental framework consistent with New Age values. They have tended to support the New Age teachings concerning *A Course in Miracles* (which purports to be the channeled teachings of Christ), crystals, and rebirthing.

Transcendentalism developed in New England around Ralph Waldo Emerson in the 19th century, defined by one scholar as "fundamentally an expression of a religious radicalism in revolt against a radical conservatism." Emerson's circle included **Henry David Thoreau** along with **Margaret Fuller,** the center of a circle of brilliant women in Boston and Cambridge, and **Sarah Ripley,** considered to be the most learned woman in New England. Emerson had read a translation of the *Bhagavad-Gita** and several other works of Eastern philosophy and evolved a composite philosophy of his own that blended aspects of Hinduism with the quintessentially American concepts of individualism, practicality, and social justice—a combination that can still be said to be at the heart of alternative spirituality in the U.S. Key to Transcendentalism was the concept of the **Over-Soul,** Emerson's rendering of the Hindu Brahman*. In his essay "History" Emerson wrote, "There is one mind common to all individual men. Every man is an inlet to the same and to all of the same. . . . Of the universal mind, each individual is one more incarnation."

The concatenation of neo-industrial optimism and religious idealism produced perhaps its greatest commercial success in the mid-20th century in the figure of a Protestant minister named **Norman Vincent Peale** (1898–1993). Best known for inspirational self-help books such as his 1952 best-seller *The Power of Positive Thinking,* Peale preached regularly in his Marble Collegiate Church on the corner of Fifth Avenue and 29th Street in Manhattan, attracting a large congregation. At the time, Peale's message seemed to embody the perfect marriage of the vaunted Protestant work ethic and the American dream, proclaiming that a positive attitude enabled one to achieve all one's goals and material desires.

Calling his approach "applied Christianity, a simple yet scientific system of practical techniques of successful living that works," Peale heartily recommends, without labeling them as such, creative visualization, positive affirmations in the form of biblical quotations, and silent meditation, all of which have become staples of the New Age approach to life. The first lines of Peale's book, in fact, sound as if they might be introducing the latest work on holistic healing or subliminal suggestion. "This book is written to suggest techniques and to give examples which demonstrate that you do not need to be defeated by anything," he begins, "that you can have peace of mind, improved health, and a never-ceasing flow of energy. In short, that your life can be full of joy and satisfaction."

In its practical applications, however, Peale's approach turned out to be considerably more materialistic than that. His examples focus on men who started with nothing and became millionaires or successful executives. The Christian Gospel is present in the form of scriptural quotations, but what he chooses to stress are the ingredients that facilitate material success. Nonetheless, something must be said for Peale's own applications of his theory, considering that he lived to age 95.

ALL GOD'S CHILLUN GOT RHYTHM

Norman Vincent Peale's *The Power of Positive Thinking* is not without its deft observations. Occasionally, Peale suggests that the reader break away from the hypnotic trance of modern industrial society with its speeded up rhythms and, almost literally, go back to the earth. In a passage that sounds Taoist, or at least Transcendentalist, he writes, "The solution is to get into the time synchronization of Almighty God. One way to do this is by going out some warm day and lying down on the earth. Get your ear close down to the ground and listen. You

492

will hear all manner of sounds. You will hear the sound of the wind in the trees and the murmur of insects, and you will discover presently that there is in all these sounds a well-regulated tempo. You cannot get that tempo by listening to traffic in the streets." But then, in the following passage, which epitomizes the industrial optimism of the New Thought that preceded him, Peale goes on to explain how you *can* catch the same rhythm in a factory:

A friend of mine, an industrialist in a large plant in Ohio, told me that the best workmen in his plant are those who get into harmony with the rhythm of the machine on which they are working. He declares that if a worker will work in harmony with the rhythm of his machine he will not be tired at the end of the day. He points out that the machine is an assembling of parts according to the law of God. When you love a machine and get to know it, you will be aware that it has a rhythm. It is one with the rhythm of the body, of the nerves, of the soul. It is in God's rhythm, and you can work with that machine and not get tired if you are in harmony with it. There is a rhythm of the stove, a rhythm of the typewriter, a rhythm of the office, a rhythm of the automobile, a rhythm of your job. So to avoid tiredness and have energy, feel your way into the essential rhythm of Almighty God and all His works.

—NORMAN VINCENT PEALE,
THE POWER OF POSITIVE THINKING

THE STORY OF THEOSOPHY

Probably the most fascinating and influential stream of thought that fed into the incipient New Age was a group that came to be known as the **Theosophical Society.** The term **theosophy** (Gr. "divine wisdom") can be applied to any of a number of historical approaches to direct experiential knowledge of God, including Gnosticism*, Neoplatonism*, Vedanta*, and Buddhism. In the 16th century, it referred to the disciples of Paracelsus, known as "fire philosophers" because they held the mystical belief that the soul and the divine spirit (which the Greeks generally distinguished from one another) are merely particles of a fire taken from the eternal ocean of Light. But the term *theosophy* is now generally associated with the Theosophical Society founded in New York City in 1875 by **Helena Petrovna Blavatsky, Henry Steele Olcott,** and **William Quan Judge.** The society put forth three main objectives that are in many ways still relevant to New Age practitioners, even if the society itself is somewhat outmoded:

1. To form a nucleus of the universal brotherhood of humanity, without distinction of race, creed, sex, caste, or color.
2. To encourage the study of comparative religion, philosophy, and science.
3. To investigate the unexplained laws of nature and the powers latent in man.

The modest numerical membership of the society during its heyday in the early 20th century was far outweighed by its influence over generations of spiritual seekers to come. Among the areas of knowledge which the society, and especially Helena Blavatsky, helped to codify and expose to the West in a major way were the occult, astrology, channeling, reincarnation*, yoga*, and theories concerning Atlantis and Lemuria and the Great White Brotherhood. The Society still accepts members of all religious persuasions and none, agreeing that the ancient Divine Wisdom has taken many shapes but remains basically the same.

The Ukrainian-born Madame Blavatsky (1831–91), as she is commonly known, experienced automatic writing and spiritualism and traveled to India and Tibet in her exploration of Eastern religious thought. Blavatsky said that she communicated with invisible adepts or masters, whom she called the **Mahatmas** (Skt. "great souls," a traditional Indian term for highly respected spiritual masters) and who she said belonged to a loose association called the **Great White Brotherhood.** These perfected beings are not of any specific religion, but they occasionally become incarnate to found new religions when and where necessary, along the lines

*Helena Petrovna
Blavatsky in her best-
known portrait, taken
by Enrico Resta in Lon-
don on January 8, 1889,
just two years before her
death.*
COURTESY
THEOSOPHICAL
PUBLISHING HOUSE

of the Hindu avatars*. Among the masters she said she had contacted were **El Morya** and **Koot Hoomi** (or **Kuthumi**). Distinct from angels, who have been created for the purpose of mediating between the human and divine levels, the Mahatmas are formerly incarnated humans who have completed their cycle of reincarnations and "ascended" to one of the dimensions of being above the earth plane. They are more commonly called **ascended masters.**

Blavatsky's claims were attacked by the **Society for Psychical Research,** which had been formed in 1882 in London to investigate psychic phenomena, and she was labeled a fraud. The charges and countercharges have never been adequately settled, but the impact of Blavatsky and the Theosophical Society on Western spirituality is irrefutable. In fact, Madame Blavatsky deserves a special place among forerunners of the New Age, probably beyond the contributions made by men like William James and Richard Bucke. She succeeded in either introducing to the West or reviving interest in a full panoply of mystical and occult teachings, in her great works *Isis Unveiled* (1877) and *The*

Secret Doctrine (1889). The former, a summary of occult phenomena up to her day, occasionally reflected misconceptions or incomplete knowledge but was nevertheless a remarkable achievement for its time, collating information on the Kabbalah*, Hinduism, Buddhism, and Jainism*, psychic phenomena, mesmerism, shamans*, yogis, Atlantis, and much more. Often reporting firsthand observations from the Orient shored up by prodigious reading and research, Blavatsky also helped standardize the use of the term *reincarnation**, in place of **metempsychosis** and **transmigration of souls,** which mean the same thing but are rarely employed today.

Madame Blavatsky's role was continued by the London-born **Annie Besant** (1847–1933), who served as international president of the Theosophical Society for almost 30 years. Besant met Blavatsky three years before the latter's death and became actively involved not only in the society but in the **Esoteric Section,** a subgroup of Blavatsky's disciples within the society who engaged in occult practices. Besant took over its leadership from Blavatsky and went on to speak at the **World Parliament of Religions** in Chicago in 1893, at which Swami Vivekananda* spoke on Hinduism and Soyen Shaku* introduced Zen Buddhism to America.

The Mahatmas had informed Madame Blavatsky of the coming of a world teacher, known as the **Lord Maitreya,** who would begin a higher evolutionary cycle in human development. Although the name Maitreya* is taken from the Buddhist title for the Buddha-to-come, in Theosophical and New Age thought the figure is actually believed to be that of Jesus, effectively combining the millennial expectations of Eastern and Western traditions. A close associate of Besant's, former Anglican clergyman **Charles W. Leadbeater,** discovered the person he believed to be this world teacher on a beach in India in 1909. Jiddu (better known as J.) Krishnamurti* (1895–1986) was quickly taken under Besant's wing as she toured the world during the 1920s and built the **Order of the Star of the East** to help promote his mission. But at the height of worldwide interest and rising membership in the Society, Krishnamurti resigned and disbanded the Order, saying that he had no wish to be a world religious leader, to teach formally, or to have followers.

Following the death of Madame Blavatsky, the Theosophical Society split into several branches, some based in America, but the splinter groups have remained small and relatively inconsequential. Branches such as the New York Theosophical Society are not directly involved in worship services but act as conduits for instruction on a spectrum of philosophical, theological, and practical knowledge, ranging from meditation, hatha yoga*, and Therapeutic Touch to the teachings of Spinoza, Madame Blavatsky, and others. The international society has its headquarters in Adyar, Madras, India, with a modest world membership.

One of the more significant spin-offs of the society is the **"I AM" Religious Activity,** founded by **Guy Warren Ballard** (1878–1939) and his wife **Edna Ballard.** Ballard claimed that in 1930, while walking near Mount Shasta in California, he met the **Comte de Saint Germain,** a notorious 18th-century nobleman and failed alchemist who claimed to have lived 2,000 years and whose occult adventures had been the subject of several recent books. Saint Germain now claimed that he was an ascended master and announced the beginning of the "I AM" Age of Eternal Perfection, appointing Ballard and his family as Accredited Messengers of the Ascended Masters. Over the ensuing years, Ballard wrote and published a series of books relating his continuing encounters with Saint Germain and other masters. After Ballard died and his wife assumed leadership of the group, they were charged and convicted of fraud; although the verdict was finally overturned by the Supreme Court, "I AM" dropped out of sight but continued to grow.

During this period of apparent dormancy, other members of "I AM" claimed to receive transmissions from the masters, notably **Mark Prophet** (1918–73) and his wife, **Elizabeth Clare Prophet** (b. 1940). Mark Prophet, who had been involved in two offshoots of the "I AM" Religious Activity (the **Bridge to Freedom** and the **Lighthouse of Freedom**) founded the **Summit Lighthouse,** which over time became the **Church Universal and Triumphant.** After his death in 1973, Elizabeth Clare Prophet took over the church and is its current head. The church, which draws on both Eastern religions and Catholicism (emphasizing the Bible, devotion to Mary and the saints, and the use of rosaries), considers itself Christian; it also teaches that Mark Prophet ascended immediately after dying and is now known as Ascended Master Lanello, the Ever-Present Guru. Prophet claims to channel Lanello along with a variety of ascended masters including Saint Germain, El Morya, Kuthumi, Djwhal Khul, Jesus, Mother Mary, and the Buddha.

APOCALYPSE NOW AND THEN

According to an often voiced New Age apocalyptic scenario, a change of consciousness, described as a general raising of the vibratory rate of humanity, is now imminent. Those who have prepared by gradually adapting themselves to these higher frequencies may ascend in "lightbodies" to new levels of consciousness, although what will happen to anyone who has failed to prepare is usually not explained. This New Age apocalypticism is typically less violent than that evinced by most fundamentalist Christians, yet some have hinted at more catastrophic events, including a massive redrawing of the map of the world, with much of the Western Hemisphere disappearing under water. Elizabeth Clare Prophet's Church Universal and Triumphant, which has been labeled apocalyptic, insists that it is just the victim of bad reportage. Around 1989, the church began arousing controversy by building nuclear-proof bomb shelters in an area of Montana known as Paradise Valley. Prophet warned that a period of dangerous times was beginning in April 1990 and invited followers to come to Paradise Valley to pray to avert possible nuclear war or other catastrophes. Some members of her church sold their homes, closed their bank accounts, and headed to the valley, where they began to stockpile food and survival gear in an elaborate underground system of concrete and steel bunkers built by the church on Grand Teton Ranch, its 33,000-acre property. Although the *New York Times* reported that Prophet had predicted a major cataclysm, she later asserted that the ascended master Saint Germain had said that the period between 1990 and 2002 is a dangerous time for Earth, marking the end of a 25,800-year cosmic cycle during which humans have sown hatred, war, and murder. But Prophet does not believe the year 2000 will usher in the end of life on the planet or the Second

Coming of Christ, as some have predicted; and she believes that prayer and change in consciousness can soften or cancel out the impending karma of destruction. Preparing physically for calamity by building fallout shelters, she maintains, is one way to turn back war and natural catastrophes. When April 1990 passed without event, Prophet's followers, who call her Guru Ma, claimed that their prayers had in fact helped avert disaster.

Apocalyptic groups that emphasize a specific date for the end time are primarily a feature of Western religion. Hinduism speaks of cycles of destruction and creation, saying that we are now in the Kali Yuga*, the last of four cyclical eras, at the end of which the world will be destroyed before being remade. At that time, **Kalki,** the future reincarnation of Vishnu*, will arrive on a white horse to liberate the world from strife. But the Kali Yuga, although relatively brief by Indian standards, still has over 350,000 years to run, give or take a millennium. Some Buddhists await the advent of Maitreya, the Buddha-to-come, but that, too, is in the distant future, tens of thousands of years away.

Muslims, on the other hand, expect the Imam Mahdi*, the Guided One, who will usher in 1,000 years of peace on earth before the actual end of history. Christians inherited the apocalyptic urge from the Jews, whose book of Daniel began the tradition, and many early Christians expected the end to come in their lifetime. Among the most disastrous later apocalyptics were the German Anabaptists*, who took control of Münster in the 1530s under Jan Matthys, claiming that he was Enoch preparing the way for the coming of Christ. He was succeeded by **Jan of Leyden,** who pronounced himself king and the city the New Zion. Socialist, antiauthoritarian, and fanatical, Leyden and his followers practiced polygyny, held property in common, and ruled the city with great cruelty and self-indulgence. In the end, Münster was laid siege and captured, and Leyden was tortured to death with red-hot pincers.

In the U.S., William Miller*, a Baptist, preached throughout the 1830s that Christ would return in 1843 or 1844. When Jesus didn't show, Miller admitted his error and quit preaching. However, his followers split into several splinter groups, including the Seventh-day Adventists*, who stopped setting dates. Charles Taze Russell*, a former haberdasher, later carried on the tradition, founding the sect now known as Jehovah's Witnesses* and predicting the end of the world in 1914. The Witnesses have since proclaimed the Second Coming for 1918, 1920, 1925, 1941, and 1975, without discernible results.

❋ THE HINDU INVASION

The influence of Eastern philosophy and practice on the New Age cannot be underestimated. Buddhism, especially Zen, and Chinese beliefs, through the *I Ching* and the *Tao Te Ching*, have made a substantial mark. But the body of beliefs and practices included under the heading of Hinduism has probably had the most profound effect on the New Age of any Eastern religion, encompassing yoga and meditation and the concepts of karma*, reincarnation*, and the chakras*. The impact of Indian religion in the U.S. came in several waves, beginning in the late 18th century with the translation into English of essential Hindu scriptures like the *Bhagavad-Gita*. These scriptures influenced not only Emerson and Thoreau but also Madame Blavatsky and the whole Theosophical movement. In the late 19th and early 20th centuries, a second wave brought in Swami Vivekananda*, who established the Vedanta Society* in New York in 1894, and Paramahansa Yogananda*, who founded a yoga institute in Los Angeles in 1925 and later established the Self-Realization Fellowship*. Yogananda's *Autobiography of a Yogi* (1946) continues to be widely read in the West.

Immigration barriers in place between 1917 and 1965 effectively curtailed the invasion, but as soon as restrictions were lifted, the third wave entered and is still entering. The most influential gurus to spearhead this incursion were undoubtedly Maharishi Mahesh Yogi*, the founder of Transcendental Meditation*, or TM, who counted the Beatles, Clint Eastwood, Mia Farrow, and Merv Griffin among his earliest Western devotees, and Swami Satchidananda*, who gave the invocation at the Woodstock Festival in 1969 and later established an ashram in Virginia. Swami Muktananda*, his co-successor Gurumayi Chidvilasananda*, and Sri Chinmoy*, among others, arrived later but have each made an important impact.

However, the popular Hinduism of India, with its rituals and festivals and pilgrimages, its competitive sectarian worship of Shiva*, Shakti*, or Vishnu*, and its connection to a still repressive social caste system, is largely unacceptable to modern America. The Indian religion that has so affected New Age belief, as modern scholars are quick to point out, is a somewhat idealized version that reflects a reverse image of everything that is wrong with the West: its materialism, its authoritarian structure, its institutionalized religions. We would be more realistic to acknowledge that Hinduism as it is actually practiced in India shares some of these traits. The Hinduism of Shankara* and Ramakrishna* (as different as those are from each other) or of Muktananda and Satchidananda (different again) are apparently more accessible to Western dispositions than the popular forms of the religion. This is not to say that one version is somehow more beneficial or "spiritual" than the other, but that each appeals to a different sensibility—just as born-again Christianity and the mysticism of Meister Eckhart* and John of the Cross* appeal to different Christian hearts.

Western students of Eastern gurus have rung some changes of their own on the ancient teachings of India. In Virginia, an American disciple of Swami Muktananda who took the name **Brother Charles** before changing it at the request of his community to **Master Charles** (b. 1945) has begun what he calls the "contemporization of the journey of enlightenment." Acknowledging Muktananda as a teacher with whom he spent 12 years, Charles does not consider himself to be associated with that teacher's tradition in any formal way but aims to make the same sorts of insights "accessible to the West in terms it can understand."

To that end he has developed a system of meditation based on a program of prerecorded audiotapes that rely on sophisticated "sound phasing" technology. The principle behind the tapes is similar to that behind

501

the use of drumming in shamanic cultures: to entrain the brain waves to the ranges associated with traditional meditation, thereby inducing a meditative state without spending years learning established techniques of meditation. Brain wave activity occurs in four major frequency ranges, from about .5 to 32 Hertz, or cycles per second. Although all four sets of frequencies are active in the brain at any given time, one set is usually dominant: beta (normal waking consciousness), alpha (relaxed, meditative, and creative states), theta (the "twilight learning" stage, the threshold to sleep), and delta (deep sleep). The last three states are associated with various depths of meditative absorption, as has been proven by monitoring the brain waves of trained meditators. Master Charles's tapes entrain the brainwaves by the use of sound waves set at differing vibratory rates, barely audible underneath music or chanting. On the early tape series, which entrain the brain to the alpha range, the sound phasing is combined with chants taken from all the major religious traditions. More advanced series entrain to the theta and delta ranges. Tapes are used by members of Master Charles's resident community in Faber, Virginia, as well as by individuals at home. His **Synchronicity Foundation** claims a "four-fold acceleration factor," meaning that, according to its own tests, those who have been using the tapes for 7 years show comparable brain wave activity to Zen monks with 20 to 40 years of experience.

The notion of "speeding up" the age-old process of enlightenment fits in with the New Age's apocalyptic bent. One of the most controversial of all the Indian teachers to come West was **Bhagwan Shree Rajneesh** (1931–90). In the mid-1970s, Rajneesh ran ashrams in Bombay and Poona, attracting a wide variety of Western seekers, including psychologists and therapists who had been at Esalen in California experimenting with new forms of therapy and new ways of expanding human potential. Rajneesh offered a unique synthesis of Eastern meditation practices and Western psychotherapeutic techniques, including encounter groups, on a larger scale than anywhere else in the world at that time. His format was based on a variation of Tantric* practice involving free indulgence in anger, violence, and sexuality as a way of working through attachment to those and other taboo-laden forms of expression. The idea was to take those expressions to the limit, exhaust their possibilities, and realize that in and of themselves they cannot satisfy.

In 1981, Rajneesh moved his operation to a 64,000-acre ranch in Oregon, later called **Rajneeshpuram.** There the experiments in Tantric living continued, although according to many accounts of people who participated, the spiritual community ran out of control. Rajneesh attracted unfavorable attention as word of machine-gun-toting bodyguards and his private fleet of 93 Rolls-Royces began to appear in the news media. ("So many religions look after the poor," he was quoted as saying. "Leave the rich to me!") Troubles with nearby townspeople and law enforcement officials escalated, and in 1985 Rajneesh was deported to India for violating U.S. immigration laws.

The reasons for the implosion at Rajneeshpuram have been debated by his former disciples, many of whom still regard Rajneesh as a highly realized teacher who allowed the ashram to be taken over by a cadre of deluded followers. Other disciples insist that Rajneesh deserves much of the blame. In any case, he returned to India and continued traveling and teaching until his death. One of his foremost disciples, who had been in charge of some of the most controversial encounter groups in which sex and violence were explored in depth, was an Englishman named **Paul Lowe** (b. 1933). Lowe had previously participated in groups at Esalen and established his own successful Esalen type growth center in London before joining Rajneesh in India. After the dissolution of Rajneeshpuram, Lowe took to the road, teaching his own distillation of Eastern and Western wisdom that stresses "waking up" without the accoutrements of formal meditation practice or connection with any specific tradition. In this sense he reflects the approach of teachers like Krishnamurti, who worked with individuals and groups but rejected institutionalized training systems to achieve enlightenment. In his lectures, Krishnamurti liked to ask, "Can you be instantaneously free?" insisting that this was the only way out of human misery. "When you are interested in something," he said, "you do it instantaneously, there is immediate understanding, immediate transformation. If you do not change now, you will never change, because the change that takes place tomorrow is merely a modification, it is not transformation."

Lowe continues traveling and teaching with his wife, Grace Lowe, largely offering workshops. **Ariel and Shya Kane,** a married couple who spent time briefly working with Lowe, have developed a different approach to awakening which they call "Instantaneous Transformation." Working very much as a team, they lead small groups at a variety of locations from New York City to Bali, where they have built a retreat center. The Kanes emphasize opportunities for growth and expansion in simply "being around" them. They work in an impromptu, unstructured format that does not make use of traditional "processes" such as meditation, visualization, or other established practices borrowed from Eastern religions, yet echoes the immediacy of Zen teaching.

✳ VOICES CARRY

Along with an affinity for Eastern religious practices and beliefs (albeit without the disciplined daily routines that are integral to those belief systems), the legacy of the Theosophical Society has included a New Age fascination with what is known as channeling. **Channeling** is the current name given to the process by which individuals access information that is not normally available to them, usually from an entity that may or may not identify itself by name but is considered to be **discarnate,** i.e., a spirit without a physical body. The premise behind all channeling—or **mediumship,** as it is sometimes known—is that entities of intelligence exist on several planes other than the physical and can communicate from one dimension to another. These entities include spirits of deceased humans residing in the after-death (or between-life) realms as well as ascended beings who have left the body but continue to work with individuals on the earth plane with the aim of helping them evolve spiritually. Some channeled sources are even said to be extraterrestrials—nonhuman beings from our solar system and beyond who are able to communicate with human mediums.

During the channeling process, the voice and physiognomy of the channeler often change, and in some cases his or her personal consciousness lapses, leaving no conscious memory of what occurred. The phenomenon of channeling appears to be as old as recorded history, although the format and terminology have changed frequently, the modern term coming from the language of UFO abductees. Channeled entities have described themselves variously as "the energy vortex" or "the higher and wiser level of energy," "an energy personality essence no longer focused in physical matter," and "a pinnacle of wisdom."

By the broadest definition, the shamans* of preliterate cultures, the rishis* of ancient India, and the prophets* of the Bible were all involved

504

in transmitting knowledge and wisdom from a source apparently outside themselves. In ancient Egypt, Greece, and the Orient, tales abound of communications between the spirit world and mortals, of advice and direction—and occasional trickery and deception—being received visually and auditorily. Some modern interpretations propose that Jesus and Muhammad were channeling wisdom directly from the Source of all being or from their Higher Selves, although orthodox adherents of their respective religions strongly disagree with that interpretation. The Bible identifies the source of extrahuman communications as God, but the appearances are remarkably congruent with modern accounts of channeling. In the book of Numbers, the God of the Hebrews speaks not only to Moses but to 70 elders of his people while they are wandering in the desert: "Then the Lord came down in the cloud and spoke to him, and took some of the spirit that was upon him and put it upon the seventy elders; and when the spirit rested upon them, they prophesied" (Num. 11:25). And later, Samuel anoints Saul king of the Israelites and informs him that he will encounter a band of prophets and that "the spirit of the Lord will come mightily upon you, and you shall prophesy with them and be turned into another man" (1 Sam. 10:6).

This state of being "turned into another man" is one point of commonality among the different kinds of transmissions. In trance mediumship, the medium acts as a conduit for a spirit from beyond the grave. Instances of mediumship appear in the Bible and throughout history, but the phenomenon became vastly popular in 19th century America. At gatherings called séances (Fr. "sittings"), mediums claimed to be able to contact the spirits of departed personalities, increasingly the relatives of those seeking contact, a practice that became known as spiritualism (spiritism in Europe). Spiritualism had a number of famous supporters, including Sir Arthur Conan Doyle and Abraham Lincoln, who was reportedly advised by channeled spirits not to delay action on the Emancipation Proclamation.

Because of the obvious opportunity for fraud in such situations, the procedure was abused, and the reputation of mediums and mediumship declined—despite the fact that many legitimate mediums were closely observed and their work evaluated by teams of scientists who could find no evidence of deception. Spiritualism has been attacked by many Christian churches even though much channeled material speaks a message consonant with that of Christianity itself: that we are much more than our mere physical bodies and that the ego, in the words of Seth as channeled by Jane Roberts, "is a jealous god and wants its interests served."

Perhaps because the modern channeling process bears a striking resemblance to trance mediumship, it has often been ridiculed or treated askance in the popular press. Unlike yoga and meditation, which have been scientifically tested and proven beneficial on at least a physiological level, no compelling objective evidence has emerged to prove the efficacy

OTHER PLANES OF BEING

The notion that the physical body has counterparts on other planes of existence can be traced to ancient Indian teachings. New Age belief systems from Theosophy to Eckankar use different nomenclatures for the planes, which have been described by clairvoyants who claim to see them as a series of cloudlike sheaths that surround the physical body. The levels vary from group to group; Theosophy gives seven, a number that has had a mystical resonance from time immemorial, probably based on the division of the lunar cycle into four seven-day weeks. But the following five appear to be generally accepted.

1. physical The plane of dense matter, corresponding to the physical body, and the only plane with a clearly visible aspect.

2. etheric The plane of vital energy surrounding and suffusing the body, known in Sanskrit and Chinese as prana* and ch'i*, respectively.

3. astral Sometimes called the desire or feeling plane or "Summerland," the level on which **astral travel** takes place, when the soul temporarily leaves the body. It is also the plane on which certain departed souls exist.

4. mental The level of thought-forms, which are said by

clairvoyants to be vibrantly colored patterns reflective of specific thoughts and emotions.

5. causal The plane, sometimes called the higher mental plane, that stores all karmic fruits, samskaras* and other vital energies, essences, and tendencies attaching to the individual during life. The causal body is the one that is said, in most theories of reincarnation, to carry over from one lifetime to another.

Annie Besant and Charles W. Leadbeater were both believed to be endowed with clairvoyant powers, including the ability to see human auras and thought-forms. Here they describe the mental body itself:

The mental body is an object of great beauty, the delicacy and rapid motion of its particles giving it an aspect of living iridescent light, and this beauty becomes an extraordinarily radiant and entrancing loveliness as the intellect becomes more highly evolved and is employed chiefly on pure and sublime topics. Every thought gives rise to a set of correlated vibrations in the matter of this body, accompanied with a marvelous play of color, like that in the spray of a waterfall as the sunlight strikes it, raised to the nth degree of color and vivid delicacy. The body under this impulse throws off a vibrating portion of itself, shaped by the nature of the vibrations—as figures are made by sand on a disk vibrating to a musical note—and this gathers from the surrounding atmosphere matter like itself in fineness from the elemental essence of the mental world.

—ANNIE BESANT AND C. W. LEADBEATER,
THOUGHT-FORMS

of channeling. Few modern channelers, or channels as they are also known, try to contact dead relatives but focus on discarnate entities seeking to dispense their wisdom and to prepare humanity for a spiritual transformation that many of the entities insist is imminent. Changes in posture and voice tone are part of the process, although varying degrees of trance state have been observed in modern channels. A distinction is usually made between a **full trance channel,** who goes unconscious while the entity speaks and who later has no recall of what has transpired, and an **open channel,** who is conscious throughout. Several degrees of **light trance** have also been observed; some channelers claim to see an image of their spirit guide or to hear a voice speaking in their mind (**clairaudience**). Still others find their hand spontaneously writing down material as if taking dictation, a process known as **automatic writing.**

In the late 19th century, Madame Blavatsky channeled the teachings of masters known as the Great White Brotherhood, some of whom claimed to shuttle between the discarnate spirit world and the physical plane. She may be considered the first of the modern channelers in that she emphasized the transmission of wisdom from more highly evolved "spirit guides" rather than communication with dead relatives. Blavatsky and her protégé Alice Bailey distinguished among as many as seven levels of existence, beginning with the physical and astral planes and ranging up to the divine, and cautioned against relying very heavily on transmissions from the lower planes. In other words, a medium or channel may not always know in which level of evolution the contacted spirit moves, and a certain degree of circumspection is advised. This may explain the variations in quality and relevance in the vast profusion of channeled material that has begun to accumulate in this century.

A variation on the mediumistic process was initiated by **Edgar Cayce** (1877–1945). While apparently sleeping, Cayce delivered in his normal speaking voice a body of wisdom not from a discarnate spirit guide but from a source he called the **akashic record.** The term derives from the Sanskrit word *akasha**, for the ether or all-pervading space, and refers to a complete record of all events that have occurred on the earth plane. (*The Aquarian Gospel of Jesus the Christ,* published in 1907 by **Levi Dowling,** also claimed to be channeled from the akashic record. Among other things, Dowling's book includes an account of Jesus' stay in India, where he studied the laws of Manu* and the Veda*, and his excursion to Tibet to study at a temple in Lhasa.) Cayce called himself a psychic diagnostician, beginning his career by diagnosing ailments in people who presented themselves. On several occasions he prescribed cures for himself, his wife, and son which led to their healing. He also transmitted esoteric information about the lost continent of Atlantis and the power of crystals.

The first popular channeled books of the modern era belong to **Jane Roberts,** who channeled an entity called **Seth** and placed several books of Seth's channeled wisdom, including *Seth Speaks* and *The Seth Material,* on the best-seller list. From 1963 until her death in 1984, she continued to channel Seth in trance and published book after book of transcriptions of those sessions.

One of the most popular channeled books today is *A Course in Miracles,* which came to **Helen Schucman** between 1965 and 1973. An associate professor of medical psychology at Columbia University's College of Physicians and Surgeons in New York, Schucman was at pains to retain her anonymity during the transmission and later publication of the 1,188-page tome. The course contains a text, a workbook of 365 lessons, and a manual for teachers. The channeled source is never named, but the text implies that it is the Jesus Christ of the Gospels. The essence of the course is to teach people to choose love rather than fear and to learn to forgive others. Although the course is written in language reminiscent of the New Testament, with references to God the Father and the Holy Spirit, it often sounds like an updated Christian Science* text when it refers to sin as an illusion. Many commentaries and interpretations of the text have appeared since its publication, some scholarly and studious, some popular simplifications, such as those by **Marianne Williamson.**

Other individuals have purported to channel Jesus, including **James Edward Padgett** (1852–1923) and **Virginia Essene,** in her book *New Teachings for an Awakening Humanity* (1986), which refers to "the Master known as The Christ."

One of the remarkable things about the channeling phenomenon today, and not readily explained, is the apparent ordinariness of most of the channels themselves. They are not, for the most part, monks or extremely devout religious personalities who have devoted years of their lives to meditation or contemplative prayer. In some cases they are agnostics who have previously shown no special psychic abilities, although some channelers *have* spent years in meditation or claim to have experi-

SEE IT THEN

A currently popular channel named **Kevin Ryerson** came to fame when he was highly touted by **Shirley MacLaine** in her book *Out on a Limb*. In the TV movie made from the book, Ryerson played himself and, not content to simulate a channeling session, reportedly went into an actual trance and channeled two of the entities whom he had first channeled for MacLaine years before. Ryerson and MacLaine claim that the channeled entities agreed to reproduce the essence of those earlier channeling sessions for the television cameras.

In Jon Klimo's authoritative work *Channeling* (from which the Schucman and Rodegast quotes are also taken), Ryerson describes the sources of his channeling sessions this way:

The guides and teachers who speak through me are primarily energy, and I act not unlike a human telephone or radio receiver. . . . The spirits who speak through me are human personalities who lived in another historical period. They are no different from you or me. They are merely in a discarnate state. . . . Their motivation to speak when I'm in the trance state is to help facilitate both individual and collective well-being.

enced religious feelings at an early age. No overall pattern obtains. Helen Schucman was an atheist psychologist with no belief in paranormal experiences when she began to channel *A Course in Miracles*. She reported with some alarm to a colleague that she'd been hearing an inner voice that wouldn't leave her alone. "It keeps saying, 'This is a course in miracles. Please take notes.' What am I supposed to do?" The colleague calmly suggested that Helen take notes in shorthand. "But what if it's gibberish?" Schucman said. "Then I'll *know* I'm crazy."

One trait the modern channelers seem to share, however, is their recognition of the necessity to give themselves over completely to the experience. **Pat Rodegast,** who channels **Emmanuel,** says it is necessary to remove her "active mind from its dominant role. . . . The more I am removed from my intellect, and the more I am clearly in the moment of Now surrounding what happens, the less I know before it's said. It's a willingness to simply say, I trust, I trust, I trust."

One explanation offered by some of the channeled entities themselves for the sudden proliferation of channeling is that the earth population is at the beginning of a major transition to a higher level of consciousness, which is often translated in energetic terms as a shift in "vibratory frequency." The channeled entity called Bartholomew put it this way: "This new energy is pouring into the earth and far past it. It is not just this little planet that is going to be engulfed with wonder. There is a vast area in this part of the universe that is going to be lifted and *is* being lifted into another state of understanding. Change is upon the face of this earth, and the outward manifestations of physical change mirror the inner changes that are occurring and will occur in the psyche and the physical body."

The criticism directed at channeling has to do partly with the unverifiable nature of the work and partly with a general perception that many of the pronouncements suffer from a kind of vagueness and repetitiveness. However, a reading of even a few of the numerous channeled books or attendance at channeling sessions reveals a much more complex field of possibilities regarding this work. It's probably fair to say that the majority of channeled entities offer the same kind of spiritual advice that is already available from any number of incarnate sources. It varies from generic wisdom about the nature of the universe to specific procedures for meditation and other practices. Some entities have even offered advice regarding very recent concerns, such as how to think of the explosion of the space shuttle *Challenger* in 1986 or whether the drug Ecstasy is safe to take.

In channeling sessions, the entities often answer the personal questions of those present (who have usually paid a fee of varying magnitude), and their responses range from the wise to the mundane. Sometimes the answers are rather specific, as when Emmanuel advised one man whose marriage was under enormous strain because he and his wife were unable to conceive a child to relax and stop focusing on conception—to forget about it entirely, in effect, and concentrate only on giving each other pleasure. Letting go of their attachment to conception might change the atmosphere enough to allow conception to take place. That kind of advice that might just as well have come from an experienced therapist or marriage counselor (who would probably have charged more than the channeler). At other times, the answers tend to sound vague and unrelated. Once again, since there is no licensing board or clerical structure in place, the potential for abuse is significant enough to serve as a warning to anyone who invests money in such sessions or in investments proposed by the channeled being. Nonetheless, the ratio of people complaining of fraud to those expressing satisfaction is no higher than with followers of most carnate gurus. The appeal of channeled teachings, in fact, may be that there is no human guru to obey, no priest class, no set of doctrines to learn or dogma to follow, no fixed place of worship, or any of the other trappings of established religions.

Possibly because of the free-form nature of channeling, literally hundreds of channeled entities have checked in during the last 30 or so years. Here are just a few of the more popular or interesting ones:

Ramtha, channeled in full trance by **J. Z. Knight** beginning in 1977, claims to be a discarnate 35,000-year-old warrior, which would make him a contemporary of Cro-Magnon man. In the book *I Am Ramtha,* the channeled entity begins his personal history as one of the survivors of the lost continent of Lemuria who fled to Atlantis and over time developed the ability to travel outside of his body and to alter its vibratory level to that of light. He evolved into the incarnate personality known and worshiped in India as Rama*. Knight herself developed a following of celebrities, most notably Shirley MacLaine, whose best-selling books have described her own adventures with various New Age phenomena. Because her large fees have enabled Knight, who was born Judith Darlene Hampton in 1946 and was living as a housewife in Tacoma when she began to channel Ramtha, to buy a large ranch for breeding Arabian horses, she attracted considerable notoriety. The notoriety increased when it was disclosed that Ramtha had advised some of Knight's clients to purchase Arabian horses from her. No criminal charges were filed, but Knight did reimburse several investors.

Lazaris has been channeled by **Jach Pursel** of Lansing, Michigan, in full trance since 1974. Unlike Ramtha, Lazaris says he has never taken on a human body, although he does have a personal identity. His books include *Lazaris: A Spark of Love* (1986) and *Lazaris Interviews* (1988), and he has developed a large industry around himself in Beverly Hills.

Mafu, channeled by **Penny Torres,** a Roman Catholic living in Los Angeles, describes himself as having incarnated 17 times over the last 32,000 years. This makes him roughly the same age as Ramtha, whom he resembles in some ways; he appeared just as Ramtha was gaining in popularity.

Bartholomew, channeled by **Mary-Margaret Moore,** has published *I Come as a Brother: A Remembrance of Illusions* (1984) and *From the Heart of a Gentle Brother* (1987). Bartholomew describes his own enlightenment experience while he was in human form and offers a variety of meditative and other spiritual practices to help people "wake up."

Michael, channeled in the New York area by **Shepherd Hoodwin** in light trance, claims to be a multiple entity, a collaboration of 1,050 beings who work together for greater efficiency.

Other channeled entities include **Ashtar** and the **Archangel Gabriel,** channeled by **Jo Ann Karl; Jonah,** by **Hassca Harrison; Raj,** by **Paul Tuttle;** and **Mika,** by **Julie Winter** of New York City.

Finally, **Christina Whited,** a New York City psychic experimenter and mother of three says that since 1987 she has been channeling **James Beard,** the late chef and dean of American cuisine. Beard, who died in 1985, has transmitted over 50 recipes to her. Whited reported that Beard appears younger and slimmer, and the recipes eschew the rich stuff for which Beard was famous in favor of health food; tofu pudding pie, rye sesame sticks, and carob cookies are among the new recipes.

If we approach channeling with a presumption of good faith on the part of at least a sizable percentage of channelers, we still are left with the question of whether the wisdom that comes through them actually originates in some discarnate being—the soul of a departed human, an ascended master, an extraterrestrial intelligence—or whether it comes from some part of the channeler's unconscious mind. Some observers lean toward the latter, interpreting "unconscious mind" as the Higher Self. The **Higher Self** is not to be confused with the superego of Freud, a merely moralistic traffic cop, but is viewed in New Age terms as the element of God-consciousness within every human being. This theory is not essentially different from the Upanishadic equation of Brahman*, the Absolute Reality or Godhead, with Atman*, the immortal Self that

513

dwells within each human heart and is identical with Brahman. In Christian terms, that relationship is plain in the statement of Paul* that "it is no longer I who live, but Christ who lives in me" (Gal. 2:20).

To access that Higher Self fully and with total clarity, as mystics are said to do in the unitive experience, would be to receive communication directly from the Absolute. The problem is that, just as mystics experience different levels or intensities of union with God, and Buddhists and Hindus speak of varying levels of enlightenment, so channelers may be in touch with any of a potentially infinite series of levels of consciousness, including the delusional. Because a channeler is accessing his or her Higher Self does not mean that he or she is in touch with its highest level or with the optimum clarity. In the end, we can add to the levels of that Self other sources, including the familiar ascended masters, departed souls, demigods, and all sorts of lesser spirits—the jinn* of the Muslims, the kuei* of the Taoists, the maggids* and golems* of the Hasidim, the Hindu asuras* and rakshasas*.

This brings up the question of good versus evil spirits. Just as folk cultures admit both sorts, so do most students of channeling or mediumship. There is a kind of consensus among channelers and psychic researchers that some departed souls—often those who were not highly evolved spiritually while on earth—may go through a long period of confusion after death. They may roam the earth or frequent old haunts, so to speak, and try to make contact with humans. In extreme cases, they may attempt to take over human bodies, resulting in spirit possession or (if the body is beyond repair) zombiism. Or they may merely try to communicate their confused and deluded awareness through an unsuspecting channel. All the more reason, channels say, to exercise great discrimination in evaluating the quality of what is presented as channeled wisdom.

✳ HOLY HOLISM

> You ought not to attempt . . . to cure the body without the soul. . . . This is the reason why the cure of many diseases is unknown to the physicians of Hellas, because they are ignorant of the whole which ought to be studied also; for the part can never be well unless the whole is well.
>
> —PLATO, "CHARMIDES, OR TEMPERANCE"

The adjective *holistic* is used in an often confusing welter of contexts, but it originally derives from the philosophical doctrine of **holism,** which has roots in ancient Greek, Egyptian, and Chinese teachings. Holism contends that the determining factors in nature, particularly in evolution, are whole organisms rather than their constituent parts. Not only is the whole more than the sum of its parts, but it is also qualitatively different from them.

The holistic principle was effectively brought into modern awareness by the South African general and statesman **Jan Christiaan Smuts** (1870–1950), who coined the term *holism* in his 1926 book *Holism and Evolution.* Smuts may seem an unlikely candidate for such a distinction: a guerrilla leader of the Boers (Dutch settlers) against the British in the Boer War, he went on to become prime minister of South Africa, later originated the concept of the British Commonwealth of Nations, and was a principal architect of both the League of Nations and United Nations. He succeeded in bringing South Africa into World War II against Hitler despite the presence of a strong pro-Fascist party there and was potentially reform-minded enough to have averted the racial conflict that was brewing in his country. But when Smuts lost the election of 1948 to the right-wing Nationalist party under D. F. Malan, South Africa began its disastrous descent into apartheid.

Nursing a lifelong interest in biology, Smuts managed in his spare moments to articulate a theory that has become a cornerstone of New Age thinking. "Taking a plant or an animal as a type of a whole," he wrote, "we notice the fundamental holistic character as a unity of parts which is so close and intense as to be more than the sum of its parts; which not only gives a particular conformation or structure to the parts, but so relates and determines them in their synthesis that their functions are altered; the synthesis affects and determines the parts, so that they function towards the whole; and the whole and the parts therefore reciprocally influence and determine each other, and appear more or less to merge their individual characters: the whole is in the parts and the parts are in the whole."

Although Smuts was primarily interested in biology and evolution, he understood the broader implications of his theory. "Wholes are not mere artificial constructions of thought; they point to something real in the universe," he wrote. "The idea of wholes and wholeness should therefore not be confined to the biological domain; it covers both inorganic substances and the highest manifestations of the human spirit."

This notion of wholeness as somehow sacred is crucial to the intersection of the holistic health movement and New Age spirituality. (The English words *holistic* and *holy,* although drawn from different languages, both have roots meaning "whole.") Perhaps the major contribution of Eastern spirituality to the West has been its understanding of nonduality*, the belief that all existence, simply put, is One Reality. The holistic approach, whether to medical or environmental concerns, insists that just as all parts of an organism are interrelated, so all organisms are also inextricably related to each other. Any action, no matter how small, must take into account its effects on other parts of the organism as well as on all other organisms.

Holistic health, which is probably the most common application of the term and concept, is less interested in treating an individual's symptoms with synthetic medicines or surgery than in understanding the functions of a healthy body and how the body can heal itself. Holistic health practitioners emphasize the value of a client's learning to interpret the body's signals and taking a personal role in staying healthy through nutrition, exercise, and stress management. Antibiotics, for instance, may serve a short-term purpose, but they also destroy helpful bacteria like acidophilus and can lead to long-term problems, just as pesticides may solve an isolated insect infestation but create hardier, pesticide-resistant mutations down the road, leave toxic residues on produce, and contaminate the groundwater. This sense of interconnectedness is part of what lends a spiritual character to holism and earns it a place at the New Age banquet table.

The same concept holds true for holistic approaches to everything from food and fitness to spiritual practice. A holistic attitude toward business, for instance, carries with it the understanding that every aspect of business has a bearing on the physical, social, and economic environments in which it is conducted. How workers are hired and treated, the integrity of the product, from organic apples to life insurance, the ways in which waste is disposed of, and how profits are invested all have to be taken into account. Holistic principles dictate that which foods are eaten and the way in which food is cultivated affect not only individual health but also the environment as a whole. For instance, some people have begun to reduce or eliminate red meat consumption for health reasons. But cattle grazing is also disastrous to the environment, entailing the clear-cutting of forests for pasture land and the pollution of the groundwater from an overabundance of cow manure, and is a highly inefficient use of increasingly scarce land resources.

The term *holistic* is, unfortunately, often applied lightly to businesses, products, or healing techniques that do not actually fit its meaning. In some encouraging ways, though, the concept of holism is sneaking into present-day consciousness without the word itself. In 1993, the Mutual of Omaha Insurance Company, the country's largest provider of health insurance for individuals, announced that it would reimburse patients who participate in a program developed by **Dr. Dean Ornish** to reverse heart disease. The program combines a vegetarian diet with exercise, yoga, meditation, and support groups. Ornish embraces vegetarianism for health and environmental reasons, but in best-selling books such as *Eat More, Weigh Less,* he clearly takes a spiritual approach to all aspects of health. Although his advice, conveyed in chapter subheadings such as "Eating with Awareness," reflects the insights of Eastern spiritual thought, he does not embrace or recommend a specific religious practice. Yet his approach is total, requiring his patients to change aspects of their living patterns that may seem unrelated to heart disease, and in that respect it is quintessentially holistic. With its acceptance by large insurance companies, holism has begun to enter the mainstream of American life.

On a larger scale, the earth can be seen as a whole organism of which humans are a small but crucial part. The **Gaia Hypothesis**, first proposed in the scientific journal *Icarus* in 1965, was later elaborated in several books, including **James Lovelock**'s *Gaia: A New Look at Life on Earth* (1979). Named for the Greek goddess of the Earth, the hypothesis holds that the planet is a single, complex organism made up of air, soil, water, plants, and animal and human life forms, all intricately interconnected and interdependent. The holistic view of life on Earth has obvious implications in the realm of ecology.

✳ WHAT'S THE ALERNATIVE?

Holism has been the source for a broad range of developments in the medical field that offer alternatives to standard practice. The number and kinds of alternatives that have grown from these roots, including some that preceded Smuts's development of the concept of holism, are far too vast to treat in detail here, and their connection to New Age spirituality is often tenuous. Perhaps the most significant conceptual shift has been the start of a movement away from the conventional militaristic model of medical intervention, which views disease as an enemy and seeks to attack its symptoms with a battery of drugs, chemicals, surgery, and other invasive procedures. The problem with this approach is that in a surprisingly high percentage of cases, these radical procedures produce **iatrogenic** (Gr. "physician-originated") illness and even death. It has been estimated that during the 1960s and '70s, for example, many more Americans died from iatrogenic illness than were killed in the Vietnam War.

The newer paradigm of healing relies much more extensively on the body's own innate defense systems against disease and, more significantly, on preventing disease by keeping the body free of toxins, including chemicals such as drugs and food additives. **Naturopathy,** a 20th-century name given to a movement that probably began in the late 18th century, sees disease as the body's own way of cleansing itself of toxins. Naturopaths, such as the 20th-century doctor **Max Warmbrand** and many others before and since, prescribe dietary changes, colon cleansing treatments, exercise, fasting, massage, and other "natural" methods of allowing the body to muster its own resources. German physician **Samuel Hahnemann** (1755–1843) discovered the modern principle of **homeopathy,** or treatment of an illness with extremely small amounts of the same substance that induces symptoms in a healthy person. He also coined the opposing term **allopathy** to refer to the kind of medicine that uses drugs and invasive procedures to produce "other" (Lat. *alius)* symptoms. Most modern medicine, despite paying lip service to holistic principles, is allopathic in its reliance on drugs, radiation, and surgery to treat both simple and serious ailments.

Natural treatments for illness extend to other modalities as well, including the use of aromatic oils, color, music, and possibly the most valuable, a reliance on unprocessed, organic foods from vegetable rather than animal sources. **Aromatherapy,** an ancient healing art that was largely discontinued in the 18th and 19th centuries, was revived in France in the 1920s and again in the 1960s by **Marguerite Maury.** It consists of the medicinal use of essential aromatic oils extracted from plants and incorporated into shampoos, conditioners, and cosmetics. These aromas, released when the oils are massaged into the scalp or body, are believed to be healing because of both their ability to kill germs and bacteria and their stimulating effect on the portion of the brain that controls emotion, memory, and libido. Maury claimed that the beneficial effects were caused by the activity of free electrons, which are more abundant in molecules of scent. **Chromotherapy** employs different-colored lights to stimulate glandular activity (red for liver, green for pituitary, blue for pineal) and to promote health and healing. **Colon cleansing** is based on the principle, voiced by nutritionists such as **V. E. Irons, Bernard Jensen,** and **Robert Gray,** that all disease and death begins in the colon. They all advocate removing the toxins that have built up over the years from eating processed, adulterated foods, meats and dairy products, refined grains and sugars, and other nutritionally dubious substances, and sometimes from the excessive consumption of otherwise healthful products like wheat. Among the tools of colon cleansing are regular colonic irrigation and the intake of psyllium husks and other fibers that keep the colon clean of impurities.

❋ THE BODY-MIND CONNECTION

By extending the holistic paradigm to the human organism, an entire field of therapists has developed an understanding of the interconnection of the external body with its internal organs, and of the entire body with the mind. Flipping the premise that the mind has the power to shape and heal the body, the therapies created in this field, known collectively as **body-work,** seek not only to heal the body of pain and to correct structural abnormalities and imbalances but also to relieve emotional and psychological dysfunctions through direct manipulation of tissue and joints. One classic example of the so-called **body-mind connection** is the work done by **Alexander Lowen** and his followers, known as **Bio-Energetic Analy-**

sis. Lowen developed a form of psychoanalysis that focuses on freeing up psychic energy by releasing energy blockages within the body through a system of physical exertion.

Many of Lowen's ideas derived from his years of study with the Austrian-born psychotherapist **Wilhelm Reich** (1897–1958). A one-time protégé of Freud, Reich explored the idea that illnesses are caused by a blockage in the natural flow of biological energies into and out of the body. He sought ways to dissolve these blockages through some combination of tissue manipulation and emotional release—especially by helping his patients develop the ability to achieve what he considered a healthy orgasm. Reich's theories about **orgone energy,** a force which he believed flows through the atmosphere and living organisms—a relative of prana*, ch'i*, and Mesmer's animal magnetism—were attacked and discredited, largely because of the emphasis he placed on the role of sexuality in releasing energy blocks. Reich was expelled from the Communist party in 1933, was forced to flee from Nazi Germany in 1935, and died in a U.S. federal prison where he was serving a sentence for contempt of court after refusing to cooperate with the Food and Drug Administration—an impressive record, to which must be added the fact that all three governments, at various times, burned Reich's books.

But even before Reich and Lowen, there was **chiropractic.** Now widespread, chiropractic was, little over half a century ago, not only out of the mainstream but held by the medical establishment to be positively dangerous. The conflict between medical doctors and chiropractors at that time is indicative of the differing approaches of allopathic and alternative healing in general: the former typically waits for a system within the body to become dysfunctional before intervening; the latter focuses on the healing potential within the body, sometimes referred to as the body's "innate intelligence." Specifically, chiropractic bases its system of healing on the theory that disease and disability are caused by interference with nerve function and can be treated by manipulation and adjustment of primarily the spinal column. The guiding principle of chiropractic, consonant with the underlying tenets of Reich and of Chinese medicine, is to remove any impedance to the flow of vital energy. Besides adjustment of the spine, the application of cold and heat, deep tissue massage, electrical muscular stimulation, considerations of diet and exercise, and stretching techniques similar to those employed in hatha yoga* also make up the chiropractic approach to natural health care.

Like just about everything else in the New Age, chiropractic traces its origins back to the early Egyptians, Indians, and Chinese—the Indian sages, for instance, called the body's innate intelligence prana* and used various forms of yoga to release energy blockages. Aspects of this ancient science were rediscovered, researched from age-old roots, and named *chiropractic* (Gr. "hand" + "effective") by Canadian-born **Daniel David Palmer** (1845–1913). Prior to this discovery, Palmer had practiced magnetic healing, a descendant of mesmerism and somewhat similar to today's **Therapeutic Touch** healing, which involves the use of the hands passing over various parts of the body to dissolve energy blockages and get the vital force moving again. Palmer founded a chiropractic teaching college in Davenport, Iowa, and published several books on the subject; his work was expanded by his son, **Bartlett Joshua Palmer** (1881–1961).

The senior Palmer found that manipulation of the vertebrae not only could relieve back pain and other muscular discomfort but sometimes could also cure seemingly unrelated symptoms such as hearing disorders, as long as the recuperative powers of the body were sufficiently strong to respond to treatment. Unfortunately, Palmer and many of his followers were arrested for practicing medicine without a license in the late 1920s and '30s. However, today chiropractic is accepted and widely practiced around the world. Medical doctors and chiropractors are increasingly coming to understand the need for both the preventive and the crisis intervention modes of healing.

Ida P. Rolf (1896–1979) created a system of bodywork that she called **Structural Integration** but that is now popularly known as **rolfing**; it is based on manipulation of the deep connective tissue, or **fascia**. After studying osteopathy, chiropractic, and yoga, Rolf created a method of realigning the body, which may have lost its natural alignment because of injury or psychological trauma, by reshaping the fascia through deep manipulation. Rolf's goal was to correct gravitational imbalances in the posture and movements of the body. Her system came to public attention when she began teaching at the Esalen Institute in Big Sur in the 1960s and is now commonly practiced across the country and in Europe. A rolfer named **Judith Aston** subsequently developed a method of main-

MILTON TRAGER,

M.D.

COURTESY OF THE
TRAGER INSTITUTE

taining the improvements brought about by rolfing, a process known as **Aston-Patterning.**

The **Feldenkrais Method** is named for **Moshe Feldenkrais** (1904–84), an Israeli scientist who healed himself of a debilitating knee injury with a blend of therapeutic techniques rather than surgery. Feldenkrais developed a method he termed Functional Integration, in which the key is learning to move more skillfully. Practitioners guide clients to become aware of differences between the routine ways they are accustomed to moving and more conscious and effective alternative modes. The system also uses a group technique called Awareness Through Movement in which clients learn series of repeated movements to help them discover the potential of Functional Integration. Feldenkrais, who worked on antisubmarine and sonar technology in England during World War II, had great success in treating Israeli Prime Minister David Ben-Gurion and violinist Yehudi Menuhin and taught at the Esalen Institute; his system is now in place worldwide, overseen by the Feldenkrais Guild.

Trager Psychophysical Integration and Mentastics, a system of body-work also called **Trager work,** was developed by **Dr. Milton Trager.** Trager workers induce a meditative state in their clients called the "hook-up," which facilitates connection with universal cosmic energy while the clients are led through a series of rhythmic motions. Mentastics, a sequence of dancelike movements, allows clients to continue to enjoy the benefits of the integration work.

Early in the 20th century, a New England surgeon named **William H. Fitzgerald** (d. 1925) discovered that by applying pressure to certain exterior areas of the body he could perform minor surgery without anesthesia. He developed a system of mapping the connections between external points in 10 areas or zones of the body, calling his system **zone therapy.** Applying pressure to one of these points, especially in the hands or feet, affects the whole zone, including its vital organs, not only for purposes of anesthesia but also for healing and general conditioning of the body. Fitzgerald's findings were taken up and modified by **Eunice Ingham** of Rochester, New York, who focused her attention on the bottom of the feet, using what she called the Ingham Reflex Method of Compression Massage, which came to be known as **reflexology.** Reflexologists have developed complex charts of the foot, relating precise areas or points of the foot to internal organs such as the kidneys, liver, lungs, and heart. They aim to heal disorders of specific organs and reduce overall stress or fatigue by working on the related area of the foot.

Many of the techniques and concepts that were developed in the West as bodywork ultimately derive from earlier, usually Eastern, sources, although in some cases there was no conscious linkage. Whether the developers of reflexology were aware of the Chinese medical techniques of acupuncture (which were present in the U.S. at the time but not widely known outside of Chinese immigrant communities) is not as significant as the fact that the two systems have much in common and tend to support each other's validity. The foot charts developed by reflexologists, on which each minute portion of the sole of the foot corresponds to a vital organ or area of the body, are very similar to those used by practitioners of acupressure, a variant of acupuncture. Likewise, charts of acupuncture meridians can often be found hanging in chiropractors' offices. As in so much of the New Age movement, bodywork techniques exhibit a good deal of synergy.

Acupuncture is several thousand years old; the earliest text on the subject, the *Nei Ching,* or *Yellow Emperor's Classic of Internal Medicine,* is believed to have been originally composed in the mid-3rd millennium BC. And so acupuncture is intimately tied in with the same principles that underlie Taoist thought, namely, yin-yang* and Five Element* cosmologies. In essence, the theory of acupuncture is based on an understanding of the role of ch'i*. Ch'i refers literally to the air we breathe and on a deeper level to the subtle environmental energy or essence, the life force, that is absorbed into our bodies through entry portals in the skin known as **acupuncture points.** The subtle energy of ch'i then circulates along 12 pairs of invisible pathways called **meridians** to the internal organs. Ch'i flows freely in healthy individuals; any blockage or imbalance in the flow of ch'i results in disease and debilitation. Blockages can be released and the flow of ch'i facilitated by the insertion of needles into the skin at one or more of the approximately 365 major acupuncture points located along the meridians.

Although acupuncture fell out of favor in China in the late 19th century, Mao Tse-tung returned it to prominence, and in the 1970s American journalists gave accounts of surgery being performed there for which the only anesthetic was acupuncture. With Richard Nixon's reopening of ties with China, the knowledge of this most effective healing art began to flow more freely to the West.

The Chinese also developed treatments that use the application of heat to the acupuncture points to achieve similar results. In **moxibustion,** the heat comes from smoldering balls or sticks of moxa (compressed wormwood leaves); in **cupping,** small heated jars are held in place over the acupuncture points through vacuum suction. And in **acupressure,** the acupuncture points are massaged by the practitioner's fingertips.

In **Shiatsu** (Jap. "finger pressure"), developed by **Tokujiro Namikoshi** in the 20th century, the practitioner applies deep finger pressure to certain muscles to relieve pain and heal internal disorders. **G-Jo** is a form of acupressure that requires the simultaneous application of pressure to pairs of acupuncture points with the fingertip or knuckles. **Jin Shin Jyutsu** works much the same way, except that pressure is applied to the paired points in a specific sequence of as many as 50 sets of points.

Reiki (also called the **Usui Shiko Ryoho System of Healing**) is the application of ch'i to the healing process through laying on of hands. Based on the discoveries of **Mikao Usui,** a Japanese Christian minister who in the 1880s became interested in Christ's healing practices, Reiki involves placing the hands on four points in each of three body areas: the head, front, and back.

✳ ENDGAME: DEATH AND DYING

With all the emphasis on health and healing, it was probably inevitable that the New Age would begin to explore new ways of coping with what happens when even the most efficacious remedies are exhausted and the process of dying begins. Social critics in this century have already made the point that, particularly in America, the gritty, unpleasant reality of death has largely been removed from public view. The terminally ill die in hospitals; the elderly are removed to nursing homes; few people ever have the experience of handling a corpse. Perhaps spurred on by mushrooming cancer rates and the AIDS epidemic on one hand and, on the other, advances in medical science that allow prolonging life beyond the bounds of a mercifully quick death, a few pioneers have developed ways to humanize and spiritualize the last days of life.

Largely through the work and writings of the Swiss-born physician **Elisabeth Kübler-Ross** (b. 1926) in the 1970s and '80s, the process of dying, which she referred to as "the final stage of growth," has become an area of serious study. Kübler-Ross identified and described five stages that most of the dying go through, beginning with denial and followed by anger and resentment, bargaining with God (for more time in exchange for certain virtuous behavior), and an acute sense of loss and depression, before arriving at acceptance and accommodation. Based on these insights and those of her student **Stephen Levine,** the practice of **hospice** (a word that used to refer to a place of refuge for weary travelers) was developed to help both the terminally ill person and members of the person's family recognize and cope with the stages of dying and receive many different levels of help and support during the process.

At the same time, accumulating accounts of people who had been pronounced clinically dead, whose vital signs had terminated but who were subsequently brought back to life following an accident, heart attack, or medical operation appear to provide graphic evidence that "the final stage of growth" may not be so final after all. Although accounts of returning from apparent death have been provided by historical figures as diverse as Plato, the Venerable Bede, and Carl Jung, recent advances in medical technology have created the circumstances for many more such experiences to occur. As documented by **Raymond Moody, Margot Grey, Kenneth Ring,** and others, people who have returned from these **near-death experiences** (or NDEs) report the beginnings of a transition to another stage of consciousness that incorporates many of the classical elements long associated with death in popular lore and religious belief. These authors have identified certain common experiences reported by their subjects: an all-enveloping sensation of peace and well-being at the outset of the NDE; out-of-body experiences in which the subjects seem to float above their bodies and can see and hear doctors and loved ones in the room without being able to communicate with them; movement through a tunnel toward a dazzling bright white or blue light; meeting with a guide or "being of light" who may conduct a kind of life review; the appearance of deceased friends and relatives (including individuals whose very recent deaths were not known to the subject at the time he or she reported the encounter); and visions of afterlife realms, often preternaturally beautiful and peaceful, but sometimes disturbingly chaotic and hellish.

As Moody and other writers have pointed out, many of these descriptions appear to coincide very closely with a body of Buddhist literature claiming to describe the transition in consciousness at the moment of death—a literature that culminated in the 8th-century *Tibetan Book of the Dead** (or *Bardo Thödol Chenmo*). Some modern Tibetan commentators insist that the near-death experience should not be equated with the experience of the bardos* (the Tibetan term for the stages between death and reincarnation described in the *Book of the Dead*), which applies to people who have actually died. (Tibet has a tradition of near-death experience itself, people known as deloks who undergo out-of-body experiences, meet spirits of the deceased, and return with messages for the living.)

People returning from NDEs often undergo profound transformations in their lives, most notably a new or heightened involvement in spirituality and a greatly reduced fear of death. In addition, the life review, in which subjects are shown scenes from their lives in rapid succession, with an emphasis on those occasions in which they acted or failed to act with compassion for others, seems to be a compelling expression of the laws of karma* as understood in Eastern spirituality or the heavenly judgment of Western afterlife beliefs. Some near-death experiencers tell of being informed by spirit guides of the necessity of infusing their lives with greater love and compassion—precisely the teachings of the great masters of all traditions, irrespective of the fact that many Westerners reporting NDEs considered themselves agnostics or atheists. The universal appeal of these experiences is difficult to overlook—a Gallup poll has reported that 1 in 20 Americans claims to have had some sort of NDE.

Furthermore, interest in NDEs and in the processes of death and dying seems to cross sectarian lines. In 1993, a book by a first-time author describing her near death after a hysterectomy, including an account of rising up to heaven to meet Jesus and scores of angels (*Embraced by the Light* by Betty J. Eadie), sold over half a million copies. At the same time, a book by a highly respected but little-known Tibetan lama that discusses the wisdom of the *Tibetan Book of the Dead* as it applies to helping the dying and preparing for death oneself (*The Tibetan Book of Living and Dying* by Sogyal Rinpoche) also became a surprise best-seller.

Western teachers like Kübler-Ross and Tibetan masters like Sogyal have at least one other principle in common, namely, that the insights that apply to the stages of death and passage into the afterlife realms also apply to day-to-day living. "What happens in our mind now in life is *exactly* what will occur in the bardo states at death," Sogyal writes, "since essentially there is no difference; life and death are one in 'unbroken wholeness' and 'flowing movement.' " Kübler-Ross says much the same thing in more secular language, noting, "Our purpose is to encourage people to view life as a series of challenging experiences from birth through death rather than a threatening and painful ordeal."

✳ ARCHETYPAL HEROES AND HEROINES

Since the New Age draws on the entire vocabulary of psychospiritual experience and scientific and technological developments, one never knows from what realm or in which configuration new emanations of ancient or modern wisdom will appear. The connections are seemingly boundless, as a perusal of almost any New Age catalog of books, tapes, or workshops will readily reveal: "Shamanism, Suffering, and Social Action,"

527

"Addiction as Spiritual Emergency," "Work as a Spiritual Path," "The Tao of Voice," "The Wisdom of Your Other Hand."

The past decade has seen the publication of a number of influential books based on the insights of the seminal Swiss psychiatrist and scholar **Carl Gustav Jung** (1875–1961). While still a medical student, Jung was fascinated by spiritualistic phenomena, including what appeared to be poltergeist activity occurring in his own home, and later made a study of some elements of the occult. In the early 1900s, Jung became a protégé of Sigmund Freud, who announced he was adopting Jung, 19 years his junior, "as an eldest son." They later collided over Freud's rejection of occultism and parapsychology and broke, according to Jung, because he "could not accept Freud's placing authority above truth."

From observations of his patients plus expansive readings in mythology and a familiarity with Eastern religious texts as well as with alchemy*, Gnosticism*, and other suprarational systems, Jung developed theories that assigned a far larger role to ancient myths and Eastern spiritual insights than Freud's system. Freud, influenced by the work of Mesmer, Charcot, and others, had developed his notion of the unconscious, a hidden layer of the mind formed from earliest childhood by repressing or otherwise disguising unacceptable wishes, drives, and impulses. Jung believed that, in addition to the personal unconscious acquired during each individual's lifetime, humanity shares what he called a **collective unconscious,** the contents of which are present in each individual from birth. Through this unconscious flows a stream of stock characters and images common to all humans, which he called **archetypes.** These terms, along with others like **synchronicity** (by which Jung referred to "the occurrence of meaningful coincidences which, in themselves, are chance happenings, but are so improbable that we must assume them to be based on some kind of principle, or on some property of the empirical world") and the shadow (repressed or "dark aspects of the personality"), have become part of the common currency of modern speech. But the reasons for Jung's increasing prominence—at least at the hands of an expanding number of popularizers—are more apparent in his concept of the "four functions of consciousness."

Jung posited that people primarily use either **Thinking** or **Feeling** as a guide to judgment, just as they experience the world chiefly through **Sensation** or **Intuition.** One of the four functions becomes predominant in an individual's life and is backed up by one from the other pairing. He observed that in the West, some combination of Thinking and Sensation generally seemed to dominate, leaving Feeling and Intuition underdeveloped or repressed. In some ways, the entire thrust of the New Age could almost be said to be an attempt to give Feeling and Intuition their due and, in so doing, integrate them with Thinking and Sensation. (To some observers, of course, the New Age has gone too far in the direction of Feeling and Intuition, leaving it deficient in logical thought and empirical information, but that is a matter of opinion.)

Jung spoke further of integrating the opposite aspects of personality, such as ego and the shadow, light and dark, male and female—a process he referred to as **individuation.** When in balance, these aspects produce an integrative principle called Self; this balance of opposites has its counterpart in Eastern philosophy, especially the yin-yang* of China, the Shiva-Shakti* of India, and the yab-yum* of Tibetan Buddhism. As the principle of transcendent integration of the personality, Self is experienced as divine Being in any number of images drawn from the world's religious iconography, from the Holy Grail and Christ and Buddha figures to the wise old man and wise old woman.

A major critique of the principle of Self was developed by **James Hillman,** who broke with the Jungian movement in the 1970s. Hillman attacked Jung's idea of Self as another variant of Western monotheism, challenging the implicitly Christian underpinnings of Jung's system and arguing for a pluralism of gods, myths, and archetypes. As he expressed it in his influential book *Re-visioning Psychology,* Hillman believes the psyche does not have a central unifying principle—a philosophy very similar to the core teaching of Buddhism known as anatman*. His school of thought has come to be called **archetypal psychology.**

As so often happens with revivals, the original has not been nearly so successful as the disciples and popularizers. The resurgence of interest in Jungian teachings does not always extend to Jung himself, whose writings are often rather erudite and abstruse. The major catalyst for the current fascination with Jung's ideas was probably the surprise success of a series of television interviews with the mythologist **Joseph Campbell** (1904–87) that took place very near the end of a long and productive life spent out of the spotlight. Shown on public television in the U.S., the interviews revealed Campbell as a living storehouse of archetypal myths and legends who could masterfully weave together material from Indian, Chinese, Egyptian, Christian, Native American, African, or Australian sources into coherent and beguiling segments built around a variety of themes. Chief among these legends was the Jungian archetype of the hero, who is called to embark on an adventure that may require doing battle with a dragon or fellow human and may even result in dismemberment or death. The hero, according to Campbell, journeys through a strange world of severe trials, "undergoes a supreme ordeal and gains his reward." He then returns from the kingdom of his journey, and the reward that he carries back with him restores the world.

The broad appeal of Campbell's storytelling came as no surprise to readers of his many books, including filmmaker George Lucas, whose *Star Wars* trilogy was inspired in part by Campbell's 1949 classic *The Hero with a Thousand Faces*. In fact, it was Lucas who lent his Skywalker Studio facilities to Campbell and interviewer Bill Moyers after PBS initially declined to fund the project, citing a low potential for viewer interest in a series of interviews about non-Christian religion. The huge success of the series and of video- and audiotapes and books based on it and other Campbell interviews helped create a market for Jungian-inspired teachers.

Jung believed that folktales are the collective dreams of certain peoples and that when one adjusts for the cultural or ethnic biases inherent in them, what remains are fairly pure archetypal stories—about the hero, the goddess, the witch as the dark mother, and others. Jung's study of fairy tales was developed and elaborated by **Marie-Louise von Franz** (b. 1915), one of his closest disciples, in a series of books based on lectures exploring the feminine principle in fairy tales. Von Franz's work has been taken up today by at least two familiar figures on the New Age book-and-lecture circuit, Robert Bly and Clarissa Pinkola Estés.

Robert Bly, a poet and mythologist (a "Feeling" rather than a "Thinking" type), is a successful popularizer of Jung's ideas and approaches who frequently teaches and lectures in tandem with Marion Woodman, a Jungian analyst. His book *Iron John* was a major best-seller that lifted Bly into mainstream media consciousness—and contumely, as his "Wild Man" weekends, during which men gather to drum, chant, dance, make masks, tell stories, and rediscover the fierce wild man within, were often ridiculed as superficial, drumbeating reactions to the women's movement. But according to Jungian analyst and scholar Roger Woolger, *Iron John* comes out of the tradition of Jung and von Franz of "using the fairy tale as a condensed picture of a psychological conflict and its potential resolution." And Bly is careful to warn against confusing "fierceness" with violence, saying that "violence and brutality toward women and children is not the function of fierceness, but evidence of the absence of it." Curiously, although Jung wrote very little about the masculine principle, Bly has been joined by a number of other Jungian analysts and storytellers, including James Hillman, **Sam Keen, Michael Meade,** and **Robert Moore,** in applying interpretations of folk tales and Jungian archetypes to the rediscovery of masculine identity.

Clarissa Pinkola Estés, a Jungian analyst with a great gift for storytelling, threads together traditional myths and fairy tales from Eskimo, American Indian, classical Greek, Assyrian, and Hispanic cultures dealing primarily with the feminine. Her best-selling book *Women Who Run with the Wolves* and a series of audiotapes based on her telling and interpreting of myths and folktales are among the most popular and highly respected works in the market. **Marion Woodman,** aside from her joint teachings with Robert Bly, has used myth and fairy tales to shine light on problems of creativity and addiction from a Jungian perspective. Jungian analyst and psychiatrist **Jean Shinoda Bolen** has also contributed a large body of work based on Jungian analysis of Goddess and Greek myths and the sacred dimension of the wise woman/crone archetype, exploring the wisdom that evolves in women following menopause.

Out of this emerging pool of trained Jungian analysts, scholars, and storytellers some unique and captivating syntheses have come into being. **Roger Woolger,** an English-born Jungian analyst who trained at Oxford and the Jung Institute in Zurich, has developed the theory that Jung's work with the collective unconscious forms a compelling basis for interpreting "past life" episodes. **Past life regression** has often been associated with bizarre, cinematic tales in which the subject may relive a grandiose existence as an Egyptian princess, a Renaissance painter, or perhaps Moses or Elijah, lending the technique an air of the sensational. Woolger's sessions, as recorded in his book *Other Lives, Other Selves,* now considered the definitive work on past life therapy, lead his clients to relive existences so unglamorous and frankly harrowing that nobody would undergo them for amusement or self-aggrandizement.

Nor does Woolger insist that the "memories" elicited correspond to historical past lives, holding instead that they represent significant states from the person's unconscious that have a bearing on his or her current life situation. The person need not take these experiences literally or even believe in reincarnation. "The unconscious mind will almost always produce a past life story when invited in the right way," Woolger says. "Even if the conscious mind is highly skeptical about the reality of past lives as historical memories, the unconscious is a true believer and is simply waiting to be asked."

Jung's understanding of the deficiencies of Western rational psychology and his appreciation for the value of Eastern religion (he wrote prescient introductions to some of the earliest translations of Eastern clas-

CROSSOVER DREAMS

Early Christians were . . . involved in some of the same things that the new age movement is interested in: prayer, meditation, dreams, afterlife, and healing by religious and metaphysical means. You can find most of the new age practices in the depth of Christianity. The gifts of the Spirit are mentioned throughout the Old and New Testaments. Clairvoyance and telepathy can be found in the Book of Acts. There are dreams at crucial times throughout the life of St. Paul. There is the ecstatic experience of speaking in tongues which gave people the same kind of experience that is described today as kundalini. We have all these things in the New Testament which modern Christianity has blocked out and ceased practicing except in some monastic traditions where there has been deep spirituality and prayer. These things are integral to the Christian tradition.
—MORTON KELSEY, EPISCOPAL PRIEST AND AUTHOR OF *THE OTHER SIDE OF SILENCE: THE GUIDE TO CHRISTIAN MEDITATION*

sics such as the *Tibetan Book of the Dead* and the Taoist *Secret of the Golden Flower*) make him a prime candidate for canonization by the New Age. More than anything, though, Jung's elucidation of a set of universal archetypes underlying, and common to, all of humanity strikes a chord that is dear to the New Age and essential to our understanding of it. The interconnectedness of humankind reflected in the holistic theory of health, in the sense of the earth as a single complex organism, and in the concept of the **Perennial Philosophy**—one universal set of spiritual realities running through all the world's religions—is implicit in Jung's teachings about the collective unconscious, described by Joseph Campbell as "a patterning force, which may, at various times and in places out of touch with each other, spontaneously put forth similar constellations of fantasy." As Jung himself wrote, "One could almost say that if all the world's traditions were cut off at a single blow, the whole mythology and the whole history of religion would start all over again with the next generation."

Expressed in myth and folktales, this notion of an underlying Oneness offers the New Age a rationale and a framework for its yearning toward a universal spirituality to counter the divisiveness and dogmatism of fundamentalist religion and, in fact, of all forms of separative consciousness. And modern-day storytellers such as Estés and Bly provide that framework in a way that, like the parables of Jesus or the tales of the Sufis, is more readily grasped and appreciated than complex theology or theoretical speculation.

Coming to Terms:
A Comprehensive New Age Glossary

More so than with any of the six major traditions, the multiplicity and disparateness of New Age beliefs make them resistant to inclusion in a neatly linear historical narrative. That is also partly because the movement itself has more of a mosaic form: connections extend from specific groups or submovements sideways to several other groups and backward

533

to one or more prototypes in the past. This complex structure, which reflects the modern character of the New Age, is also one of its strengths, allowing for more leeway than doctrinaire belief systems. And so, although most of the terms listed here have connections to one or more of the preceding sections, they are better understood on their own.

affirmations   An affirmation can be any statement that the speaker wishes to reify, such as "I am completely fulfilled in my spiritual practice," "I allow love to come into my life," or "My book is now on the *New York Times* best-seller list (and the film version starring Arnold Schwarzenegger is a box-office hit)." Based on the principle that the subconscious mind hears all statements uncritically and works to fulfill them, affirmations should always be made in the present tense and phrased in a positive way. Rather than saying, "I will not succumb to cancer," one should say, "I now enjoy perfect health." Affirmations made up a large part of the philosophy and practice of New Thought, were later appropriated, with a biblical tinge, by Norman Vincent Peale, were brought into the New Age movement by Sondra Ray and Leonard Orr, the pioneers of rebirthing, and were further popularized by Louise Hay and others.

Anthroposophy (Gr. "human wisdom")   In 1909, the Viennese-born philosopher and mystic **Rudolf Steiner** (1861–1925) founded the **Anthroposophical Society,** combining elements of Theosophy, Rosicrucianism, Christianity, and occultism with the scientific and spiritual theories of the German poet Goethe (whose works Steiner had edited). Steiner also pioneered a system of special schools for children established on the principle of equality of children with adults, a revolutionary concept even today. Over 100 Steiner schools are in existence worldwide, and a number of **biodynamic farms,** which use only natural fertilizers and are based on his principles, are still in operation in the U.S. An early explorer of the body-mind connection, Steiner developed a system known as **eurythmics** on the premise that the sounds of language are related to physical posture and movement and that therapists can heal certain ailments by prescribing the right combination of sounds and movements.

534

In theosophy there should really be a fresh feeling of what the Greeks understood by the word "Anthropos." If we would find a true modern rendering of the Greek word, we might say "one who looks up into the heights" . . . to find the source and origin of his life. To recognize man as a being of this nature is the very *raison d'être* of theosophy. Theosophy wants to rise above the details of sense existence and of the outer activity of life, into the heights of spiritual experience where we are able to learn whence man has come and whither he is going.

—RUDOLPH STEINER, *MAN IN THE LIGHT OF OCCULTISM, THEOSOPHY AND PHILOSOPHY*

Arica (uh-*reek*-uh) **Institute**   Spiritual school founded in 1970 by Bolivian-born visionary **Oscar Ichazo** (b. 1931) in Arica, Chile. Ichazo's father was a career army officer, and when Oscar was 9 years old, at the outbreak of World War II in the Pacific, a Japanese military officer visiting Bolivia was interned in the Ichazo household. The officer introduced Oscar to Zen meditation and the martial arts. In Buenos Aires, Ichazo studied with a group of mostly Oriental esoteric practitioners who taught him a number of techniques taken from Zen*, Sufism*, and Kabbalah*. He later traveled to Hong Kong, India, and Tibet, studying Buddhism, Confucianism*, alchemy, the *I Ching*, and other Oriental wisdom, discovering the same truth beneath the religions and esoteric practices of these different cultures. His unique achievement seems to lie in his discovery of the principles by which the mystical cosmology becomes logical, subject to certain "scientific" laws rather than based on faith; he forged those principles into a synthesis of Zen, Taoist, yogic, and Sufi disciplines. Many of the first 54 or so of Ichazo's students came to Arica in 1970 by way of Esalen, where they had been doing innovative work in psychology and human development. Moving the next year to New York City, the school immediately began to expand around the world, enrolling thousands of students in 40-day training sessions and influencing less sophisticated psychospiritual training systems like est. In the two decades since, as many as 250,000 people have taken part in various aspects of Arica training, although only a small core group has followed the elaborate 9-level curriculum developed by Ichazo, who lives in semiseclusion in a retreat on Maui. Arica proposes to teach "self-realization and clarification of consciousness," stressing techniques, meditations, and psychophysical exercises that facilitate experiences rather than dogma or beliefs. Perhaps Ichazo's most controversial teaching is the Enneagram (see later entry).

ascended masters The term generally applies to those beings who, having achieved a certain threshold of enlightenment while embodied, are continuing their evolution in disembodied form. They are said to teach and guide embodied humans through various means and are sometimes referred to collectively as the Universal or Great White Brotherhood, the Masters of Wisdom, and other names. They retain the option of reincarnating in human form if necessary to advance the spiritual growth of others.

astrology Tabloid horoscopes, Jeanne Dixon, and the come-on question "What's your sign?" have combined to lend astrology an air of meretriciousness that belies its ancient origins in the Babylonian Empire of the 7th century BC and probably earlier. In the early era, astrologers predicted the fortunes of entire nations or great rulers rather than individuals. The practice did not become popular in America until the mid-19th century, but even as late as 1917, **Alan Leo** (born William F. Allen, 1860–1917), a co-founder of the **Society for Astrological Research,** was arrested and tried for fortune telling under the Witchcraft Act of 1736. No definitive scientific studies have either proved or disproved the efficacy of astrological predictions, but a number of studies have established surprising correspondences between birth times, occupation, and temperament, especially those published by French researcher **Michel Gauquelin** (b. 1928).

Atlantis First mentioned in the *Timaeus* and the *Critias* of Plato (who heard about it from Solon, the Athenian lawgiver, who got it from an Egyptian temple priest), Atlantis was said to be an island nation somewhere in the **Atlantic** Ocean which at its peak was destroyed by geological cataclysms. The myth has been elaborated and popularized in the last century or so by a number of writers, including **Ignatius Donnelly** (1831–1901) in *Atlantis: The Antediluvian World* (1882), Madame Blavatsky in *The Secret Doctrine* (1889), **Lewis Spence** (1874–1955), and Edgar Cayce (1877–1945). In recent years, Atlantis lore has been augmented by volumes of channeled material. During this time, the Atlantis myth shifted noticeably. Atlantis itself evolved from being an island to an entire continent; its civilization went from being somewhat more advanced than the Greece of Plato to being technologically superior to the modern West; and its destruction is now said to have been caused not by natural upheavals but by some kind of unspecified technological disaster touched off by the Atlanteans' overreaching or misuse of advanced science. About 50 years ago, a Greek archaeologist put forth a somewhat more credible theory supported by recent geological evidence. **Spyridon Marinatos** proposed that the great Minoan civilization, considered to have been one of the most artistically and culturally advanced of all time, came to an end after Crete and its surrounding islands were severely weakened by earthquakes and tidal waves, allowing invaders from the north to finish the Cretans off. He suggested that the legend of Atlantis sinking into the sea was a clouded memory of this event.

The existence of **Lemuria,** a similar but otherwise unrelated hypothetical lost continent in the Pacific Ocean, was posited in the mid-19th century by British zoologist **Philip L. Schattler** and furthered by biologist **Ernst Haeckel** (1834–1919). Schattler surmised the prior presence of a land bridge linking Madagascar and southern India to explain the presence of certain animal species in southern Africa and southern India but not on the land between them. One such species, the lemur, thought by some to represent the ancestral primate form, lent its name to the hypothesized landmass. Once again, Madame Blavatsky played a seminal role in introducing Lemuria into occult lore. Theories about Lemuria's size, exact location, and causes of destruction proliferated through further writings and the inevitable channeled input. In 1882, a spiritualist named **John Newbrough** produced a mammoth channeled work entitled in part *OAHSPE: A New Bible in the Words of Jehovih and His Angel Ambassadors,* which contained a description and map of the lost continent of Pan (which some readers identified with Lemuria), locating it in the North Pacific from the Aleutian Islands to the southern coast of California. (The notion that California might have once been part of a mysterious lost continent could, in itself, be said to be one of the underlying principles of the New Age.) Ramtha, the 35,000-year-old warrior channeled by J. Z. Knight, claims to have been a refugee from Lemuria who moved to Atlantis when his homeland was destroyed. He puts forth the theory that Lemurians were more advanced spiritually than technologically and that their descendants inhabited Tibet, Nepal, and India, areas known for their highly developed spiritual teachings and fairly primitive living conditions.

creation spirituality Developed by **Matthew Fox** (b. 1940), a Roman Catholic priest of the Dominican order, this theology is based on an appreciation of the creation stories in Genesis that is resonant with the Jewish interpretation of them. After each act of creation, according to Genesis, "God saw that it was good." Although humanity committed the "original sin"* through Adam and Eve, creation itself remains blameless, a concept Fox labeled, in his controversial book of the same name, the Original Blessing. Although many Roman Catholic theologians find Fox's work biblical and not heretical, he has been pursued relentlessly by **Cardinal Joseph Ratzinger,** head of the Sacred Congregation for the Doctrine of the Faith, the theological enforcement arm of the Vatican (and the direct descendant of the Inquisition). Under pressure from Ratzinger, in 1993 Father Fox was expelled from his order; he remains a priest but is prohibited from celebrating mass or administering the sacraments in public. Besides his teaching of creation spirituality, Fox attracted the ire of the Vatican by his embrace of Eastern spiritual-

---

aura   Often portrayed in Buddhist and Christian art as a circle of light surrounding the head of a sacred being, the aura or nimbus is a sort of energy envelope composed of various layers and colors, made up of elements from primarily the etheric and astral planes and said to reflect the emotional and spiritual state of an individual. Trained clairvoyants claim to see auras not only around the head but also around the seven chakras* as described in Eastern systems of knowledge. Widely subject to skepticism, the auric field has nonetheless been studied scientifically. At UCLA between 1974 and 1979, the ability of the clairvoyant healer **Rosalyn Bruyere** to see different-colored auras was found to correlate exactly with readings taken from EMG electrodes (ordinarily used to measure the electrical potential of muscles), described here by an American medical doctor with metaphysical leanings.

The electrodes were connected to telemetry equipment that transmitted data to a recording booth, where various types of physiograph systems recorded energetic fluctuations from these points [chakras] on the body. Most interestingly, [researcher Dr. Valerie Hunt] found regular, high frequency, sinusoidal electrical oscillations coming from these points that had never previously been recorded nor reported in the scientific literature. . . . The readings from the chakras usually lay in a band of frequencies between 100 and 1600 cps [cycles per second], figures far higher than what has traditionally been found radiating from the human body. . . .

[Dr. Hunt] found that Bruyere's auric observations, relating to color changes in the subject's energetic field, correlated *exactly* with the EMG electrode recordings. Over time, Hunt discovered that each color of the aura was associated with a different wave pattern recorded at the chakra points on the skin of her subjects. . . . When Bruyere would describe red in a subject's aura, unbeknownst to her the recording equipment always displayed the wave pattern later associated with red, and so on with other colors. Most interestingly, when colors such as orange were seen in the auric field, the recording equipment picked up the wave forms of yellow and red—two primary colors that when mixed form orange—from different chakras at the same time.

—RICHARD GERBER, M.D., *VIBRATIONAL MEDICINE*

ity, feminism, and environmentalism and by his hiring of the Wiccan Priestess Starhawk to teach at his Institute in Culture and Creation Spirituality in Oakland, California.

creative visualization The practice of seeing in the mind's eye results that one wants to bring about. Visualization as a healing technique may date back to the legendary **Hermes Trismegistus.** (Best known by the Greek name for the Egyptian god Thoth, Hermes ruled the moon, time, measurement, and human intelligence; all the early Egyptian writings on science, mathematics, astronomy, music, and medicine are attributed to him and are known as the **Hermetic Books.**) In more recent times, healing visualization was advocated by the German physician **J. H. Schultz** (1870–1936) as what he called **autogenic training** and by Norman Vincent Peale as part of his "positive thinking." It was developed into a virtual cottage industry by a woman known as **Shakti Gawain,** whose 1979 book *Creative Visualization,* workshops, and audiocassettes are a mainstay of New Age culture. A number of allopathic physicians who have remained open to alternative healing methods have embraced visualization, including Dr. Bernie Siegal, the surgeon who wrote two best-sellers about the value of love in the doctor-patient relationship, and **Carl Simonton,** who has used visualization successfully in the treatment of cancer patients.

539

crystals   The distinctive, multifaceted shapes of crystals are a reflection of their internal molecular structure. For instance, the most abundant form of natural crystals, those made of quartz, are formed from the interaction of water and silicon under pressure and heat and are generally six-sided with a point at one end (single-terminated) or both (double-terminated). Most are clear, but they may vary in color from rose or yellow to blue, green, and black. Over 2,500 known crystals, composed of 25 of the 92 elements in the periodic table, have been discovered. The oldest known amulets using crystals are more than 20,000 years old, although crystals were probably used in jewelry and totems well before that. Prior to the 18th century, it was believed that crystals could cure the sick by being placed over the ailing part of the body, left in the room with the patient, or ground up and administered as powder. Modern media pundits look askance at the notion that crystals might have the power to heal physical or spiritual malaise or transform consciousness, and, to be sure, virtually no scientific or medical study of this use of crystals has been undertaken. And yet a vast range of modern technology is already based on the exploitation of crystals and their unique properties.

When electricity is applied to a properly prepared quartz crystal, it vibrates at a very precise frequency that depends on the thickness of the crystal. This property has led to the extensive use of quartz in radios and electronic watches. The extreme precision and reliability of crystal vibration is also at the heart of most modern computer and telecommunication technologies, which are guided by millions of artificially produced crystals. Is there a connection between these fabulous-seeming properties of crystals and their long-touted role as metaphysical facilitators and healing agents? A possible link appears in the writings of Edgar Cayce (1877–1945), who is largely responsible for the New Age "rediscovery" of crystals as a healing force. During his sleeping trances, Cayce transmitted information about, among other things, Atlantis and the role that crystals played in the putative lost continent. According to Cayce, a large "firestone," which sounds very much like a gigantic crystal, was used by Atlanteans to power their flying machines. In his book *Edgar Cayce: The Sleeping Prophet,* Cayce's most popular biographer, Jess Stern, likens the power of the firestone to that of modern lasers: "The firestone, or ruby of its time, was housed in a dome-covered building with a sliding top. Its powerful rays could penetrate anywhere; just as the laser beam, it could be either a death ray or a constructive energy source. It was hard to conceive that which Cayce put into words: 'The influences of the radiation that arose in the form of the rays were invisible to the eye but acted upon the stones themselves as set in the motivating forces, whether aircraft lifted by gases or guiding pleasure vehicles that might pass along close to the earth, or the crafts on or under the water.' "

The popular belief that precious stones with distinctive crystal lattice structures, such as emerald, ruby, and garnet, could cure diseases was recorded as early as the 1st century by the Roman naturalist Pliny the Elder (c. AD 23–79). Yet the New Age understanding of the healing function of crystals relies on an essentially Eastern paradigm of how life energy flows throughout the body. The vital force which the Indians call prana* and the Chinese call ch'i* is said to move like electricity through the seven energy centers, or chakras*. When the body is free of tension and fear, the theory goes, it is in balance, and the life energy moves freely. But once the system goes out of balance, energy may become obstructed or blocked at one or more of the chakras, and this blockage may manifest as disease. The body itself is surrounded by an electromagnetic field, a principle that we can easily discern by moving close to or away from a radio with an indoor antenna and observing the changes in strength or clarity of reception. The theory of crystal healing holds to a similar principle, in line with the belief promulgated by Madame Blavatsky, among others, that the human body is surrounded by a number of energy sheaths corresponding to the physical, mental, etheric, and other planes. The energy field of a crystal, according to this theory, can help to align the distorted energy fields surrounding the body and clear blockages in the chakras. In addition, many New Age practitioners believe that crystals store and can transmit energy—in the form of metaphysical or paranormal spiritual abilities—to humans.

As far back as the book of Exodus (39:10–14), 12 precious gems set in the breastplate of the high priest were associated with the 12 tribes of Israel. In the book of Revelation (21:18–21), the foundations of the heavenly city of Jerusalem were adorned with 12 precious stones. Eventually these or similar stones came to represent the 12 apostles* and the 12 astrological signs. As the modern calendar replaced astrological months, these gems, known as **birthstones,** shifted accordingly. The birthstones corresponding to the 12 calendar months are generally said to be, respectively: garnet, amethyst, aquamarine (or bloodstone), diamond, emerald, pearl (or moonstone), ruby (or turquoise), sardonyx, sapphire (or peridot), tourmaline (or opal), topaz, and lapis lazuli (or ruby).

Eckankar Although Eckankar was founded around 1965 by a Kentuckian named **Paul Twitchell,** it claims to be "the most ancient religious philosophy known to man," also calling itself "the Ancient Science of Soul Travel" and, currently, "the Religion of the Sound and Light of God." Twitchell wrote that he received instruction on the art of Soul

Travel, or extended out-of-body experiences, from his older sister when he was 3 years old and subsequently studied with the Sikh* master **Sudar Singh** of Allahabad, India (about whom little is known) and, on the "inner plane," with an adept named **Rebazar Tarzs,** a Tibetan master whose physical existence is not recorded anywhere outside of Eckankar. Through a lifetime of Soul Travel, Twitchell charted a whole series of trips to invisible worlds which he described as a series of distinct planes situated above the visible one, roughly analogous to the planes charted by Madame Blavatsky and others. Eckankar teaches a variety of meditation techniques and offers workshops in Soul Travel and dream work. The ultimate goal of Soul Travel is to reach the highest heavens where the **Sugmad** (God) dwells.

Eck theology holds that a **Living Eck Master** has always been physically present somewhere on the earth throughout history. The 1st-century Greek philosopher, ascetic, and thaumaturge **Apollonius of Tyana,** the 13th-century Sufi mystic Shams-i-Tabriz*, and his student Jelaluddin Rumi* are said to have been among them. Following Twitchell's death in 1971, the Eck leadership passed to **Darwin Gross,** who was later discredited, and eventually to the current Living Eck Master, an unassuming-looking man who grew up on a farm in Wisconsin, **Harold Klemp** (whose name is often preceded by the Hindu honorific Sri).

Twitchell claimed that he was initiated as the 971st Living Eck Master, sometimes called the **mahanta.** Much of the terminology of Eckankar appears to derive from Sikh, Hindu, Sufi, Buddhist, and other religious traditions, with their meanings somewhat altered. For example, the symbol **Ek Oankar** ("There is One God") is displayed on the canopy over the Sikh holy scripture, known as Guru Granth Sahib*. Eckists seek to experience the **Sound and Light of God,** a practice that is remarkably similar to that of a small international Sikh offshoot called **Radhasoami,** which developed toward the end of the 19th century and spread to the U.S. early in the 20th.

Enneagram   A system of nine habitual patterns (or "fixations") of being and behavior developed by Oscar Ichazo, the founder of the Arica Institute, who also calls it the Enneagon. Each of the nine types or fixations is interrelated with two other fixations in complex ways. Ichazo stresses that the fixation is not a personality type but an inflexible approach to life, developed during childhood, which produces internal contradictions and stress. Discovering it (usually based on anatomical features) can catalyze self-understanding and give new perspectives on one's strengths and weaknesses. The Enneagram supposedly had its origins in the 6th-century BC Greek mystic Pythagoras* and, according to Ichazo, passed into Judaism by way of Philo Judaeus* and into Christianity through a Greek abbot known as Pseudo-Dionysius*. The image of a circle with nine points connected by intersecting lines was described by the Russian-born mystic G. I. Gurdjieff, but without the elaborate behavior patterns outlined by Ichazo. In 1989 and 1990, Ichazo and Arica sued Jesuit priest Pat O'Leary and, in a separate case, **Helen Palmer,** whose best-selling book *The Enneagram* is the standard reference work on the subject, for infringement of copyright, claiming that both parties had misinterpreted his system. But a U.S. Circuit Court of Appeals ruled essentially against Ichazo, saying that the Enneagram was, as Ichazo himself had claimed, "an unalterable fact of nature which is not entitled to copyright protection." Enneagram study and interpretation has spread rapidly, especially among Catholics, through the work of O'Leary and others who continue to teach without Ichazo's imprimatur.

Esalen Institute Founded by **Michael Murphy** (b. 1930) and **Richard Price** (1930–85) in 1962, Esalen occupies a 300-acre tract of land at Big Sur on the California coast that had been in Murphy's family for generations. (Neither Murphy nor Price had any special credentials when they founded Esalen; they had done undergraduate work in philosophy and psychology at Stanford University and Murphy had spent 18 months at Sri Aurobindo's* ashram in India.) Esalen has figured prominently in many of the innovations in psychotherapy and Western-style consciousness expansion in the past 30 years, including Gestalt psychology, encounter groups, psychodrama, and bodywork. Located in an idyllic setting overlooking the Pacific, Esalen featured an astonishing faculty representing many of the major achievements in modern Western thought: Aldous Huxley, Buckminster Fuller, psychologist Rollo May, Gestalt founder Fritz Perls, political activist-turned psychic and Enneagram interpreter Helen Palmer, influential Zen author Alan Watts, Ida Rolf, mythologist Joseph Campbell, Ram Dass, Abraham Maslow, Alexander Lowen, and B. F. Skinner, among many others.

est Less a spiritual teaching than a kind of psychological assertiveness training course, est has played a part in the development of a surprising number of spiritual seekers, beginning around 1971. The name is an acronym, generally written in lowercase, for Erhard Seminar Training, although its developer, former used-car salesman **Werner Erhard,** has acknowledged that he borrowed the initials, lowercase and all, from a book by L. Clark Stevens called *est: The Steersman's Handbook* (where they stand for "electronic social transformation"). Born Jack Rosenberg in 1935, Erhard became enamored of the work of German philosopher Friedrich Nietzsche (1844-1900) and later chose to assume a new identity with a German name: *Werner* from either rocket scientist Werner von Braun (as est literature claims) or physicist Werner Heisenberg (as others assert), and *Erhard* from German economist Ludwig Erhard. Werner Erhard experimented with various psychospiritual techniques and systems, including Subud*, Gestalt psychology, Silva Mind Control, Scientology, and Zen Buddhism, before experiencing a kind of enlightenment experience in which, he says, he "got it." The "it," in Zen fashion, was never specified. But during his two-weekend-long workshops, Erhard and his associates sought to spark the realization on the part of participants that they are fully responsible for their experiences, that they, in essence, create their own reality (a concept with philosophical links to New Thought). Like Scientology and TM*, est had its share of celebrity enrollees, including Diana Ross and John Denver. The workshops at first were highly charged and confrontational, characterized by some participants as harassing and intimidating, and often involving intense verbal abuse. The stated intention was to break down some of the participants' ego defenses to facilitate the experience of "getting it." However, in the wake of media criticism, the workshops were softened somewhat and renamed **The Forum.** Erhard himself has long been the center of controversy. In 1991, he was sued by his former wife for physical abuse and by the IRS for millions in back taxes. The est Hunger Project has been attacked for doing little to help the poor or distribute food to the hungry. The Forum, however, continues to have a large following.

Gurdjieff The Russian-born mystic George I. Gurdjieff (1874–1949) developed his unique system of spiritual practice from years of travel and learning in the Middle East during the early part of the 20th century. He absorbed the teachings of many individuals and groups, most notably certain Sufis*, but his own teaching could not be categorized as specifically Sufi. By all accounts, his teaching methods, as he employed them at his **Institute for the Harmonious Development of Man** at Fontainebleau in France and elsewhere, were extremely rigorous physically, psychologically, and spiritually. He combined hard physical labor with practices such as a sequence of exacting dances, or "movements," which were derived from the so-called Whirling Dervishes* of Sufism. Often he had his students perform arduous tasks for days at a time, only to have them undo their work arbitrarily. His training, referred to as **the Work,** was conducted in secret, and not until shortly before his death were any of his writings published, beginning with *All and Everything, or Beelzebub's Tales to His Grandson.* The Work continues in a loose network of Gurdjieffian teachers and schools around the world.

From the Sufis he met, Gurdjieff adapted a practice termed the **Way of Malamat,** or the method of Blame. By this practice, Gurdjieff often went out of his way to put himself in a bad light, so as to put people off rather than draw them to him. According to the Gurdjieff scholar J. G.

Bennett, the Sufis did this "partly in order to avoid attracting praise and admiration" and "partly as personal protection," to avoid "attracting to [themselves] the wrong kind of hero-worship that verges on idolatry. The power of personal attraction is a terrible temptation that few can resist." The following story, taken from Gurdjieff's best-known work, *Meetings with Remarkable Men,* published posthumously and later turned into a feature film, may be an expression of the Way of Malamat, or it may represent another aspect of his often paradoxical teachings.

While staying in the town of New Samarkand in southeastern Russia, Gurdjieff hit upon a novel way of making some money. Knowing that the local townsfolk were fond of canaries, he contrived to trap a sparrow, clip its feathers into the shape of a canary, and then color it "fantastically" with some aniline dyes. "I took this sparrow to Old Samarkand," he writes, "where I immediately sold it, claiming that it was a special 'American canary.' I charged two rubles for it. With the money, I at once bought several simple painted cages and from then on began selling my sparrows in cages. In two weeks I sold about eighty of these American canaries."

Not one to take the Way of Malamat to dangerous extremes, Gurdjieff decided not to risk wearing out his welcome in Samarkand. "I was afraid the devil would play a joke, and that my sparrows might suddenly get wet in the rain, or that some American canary in its cage might take a fancy to bathing in its drinking trough, and then indeed there would be a great uproar, as my American canaries would be turned into disfigured, clipped and miserable sparrows. So I hastened to get away with my skin whole."

homeopathy A method of combating disease and illness by giving the patient small (sometimes microscopic) doses of a substance which is known to create symptoms of the same disease in a healthy person. The principle was introduced to the modern world by German physician Samuel Hahnemann in the 1790s. After being greeted with great hostility by other physicians in Leipzig, where Hahnemann practiced, it was later accepted during the 19th century in Europe, then fell out of favor in the early 20th century. Homeopathy is now practiced by a growing number of Americans, although the process of intensive shaking and dilution of the remedies (called **succussion**) has been attacked by some critics as producing no more than a glorified placebo effect. Science has yet to disprove authoritatively, however, the efficacy of either homeopathy or the placebo effect.

lucid dreams Simply put, a lucid dream is one in which the dreamer becomes aware that he or she is dreaming and continues in the dream with that awareness without waking up. Although much has been written about this phenomenon in the 20th century, its roots extend at least as far back as the 1st millennium BC. Aristotle mentioned it in the 4th century BC; Augustine* described a lucid dream in detail in the 5th century AD; Tibetan Buddhists practice a form of yoga aimed at preserving full awareness during dreams; and in the 12th century, the great Sufi adept Ibn el-Araby* advocated training oneself to "control [one's] thoughts in a dream." More recently, books by **Stephen LaBerge, Patricia Garfield,** and others have presented case histories and techniques to help develop the ability to dream lucidly, adding a new dimension to the standard Freudian view of the dream process. Garfield, for instance, writes that she could not experience orgasm in her waking life but developed the ability to do so during a series of lucid dreams and was ultimately able to carry the experience back with her to waking existence. Lucid dreams have sometimes been likened to out-of-body experiences or to the Soul Travel of Eckankar, and the distinctions among the three are not entirely clear.

New Age Music This term can refer to instrumental or vocal sounds, including chants, bird calls, and nature recordings, that have less to do with accepted notions of music as a popular or fine art form than with sound as a facilitator of relaxation, meditation, bodywork, or trance. New Age music is best not judged by standards applied to European classical music, American jazz, or other serious musical forms based on variations in rhythm, timbre, dynamics, melody, and harmony, since it often seeks to bypass altogether the normal intellectual functions of aesthetic appreciation. What may serve wonderfully well in relaxing or entrancing (some would say numbing) the psyche can easily be experienced as boring, repetitious, and flavorless if listened to with any expectation of musical development.

occultism The term *occult* (Lat. "concealed, hidden") once referred to secret practices ranging from trance mediumship, dowsing, numerology*, and divination to exceptional psychic abilities such as clairvoyance, clairaudience, telepathy, and precognition. But it has lost much of its meaning as these practices and capacities not merely have been openly discussed and scientifically studied and verified but also have become downright commonplace. When books on numerology can be purchased in shopping mall chain stores and Midwestern farmers employ professional dowsers to help them find water, the root meaning of *occult* is lost. The term is now often pejoratively applied to practices that appear threatening to the American Christian mainstream, such as satanic rites or Witchcraft. To the extent that these practices remain largely concealed from public knowledge or view, however, they can rightly be labeled occult.

out-of-body experience Simply put, during an OBE or OOBE, as it is sometimes called, the body remains in a state of dormancy while the mind and spirit are awake and alert, endowed with the ability to travel long distances and to see and hear without being able to interact with physical reality. It is possible while out of the body, however, to communicate with other disembodied beings. Many people have commented on this experience under a variety of names: it is sometimes likened to lucid dreaming, near-death experiences, and the Soul Travel of Eckankar. Some of the most compelling accounts are those of **Robert A. Monroe,** who runs the Monroe Institute of Applied Sciences in Virginia, which is devoted to the exploration of OBEs and related phenomena. In his books, Monroe describes a series of personal interactions with a wide range of other beings while in the spirit state.

rebirthing Sitting in a sauna one day, Leonard [Orr] noticed a sign that said: "It is recommended that you stay in the sauna no more than fifteen minutes." Typically, he decided to stay there longer and find out why there was a suggested limit. His experiment ended when he crawled from the sauna and almost passed out. Later he came to believe that he had gotten "plugged in" to the memory of life in the womb, and the memory had blocked out his consciousness. About this time he noticed that he was having trouble getting out of the bathtub; he would get all kinds of insights into infancy if he stayed in the bath for a very long time. He started to do this regularly. He even learned to sleep in the tub. And so Leonard began the long process of unraveling his birth trauma, which led to his creation of the rebirthing technique, in his own bathtub.

—LEONARD ORR AND SONDRA RAY,
REBIRTHING IN THE NEW AGE

Following the events described here, **Leonard Orr** became convinced that much of our psychic pain and sense of disconnection and our negative beliefs about life originate in the trauma of birth, particularly as experienced in modern medical practice. The bright lights and antiseptic ambience of the hospital room, the immediate cutting of the umbilical cord, slapping the baby to make it breathe, and separating newborn and mother all give the preverbal infant the unforgettable tactile message that the world is a hostile and painful environment in which it is not especially welcome. In Orr's words, "Original sin is transmitted through birth trauma which invalidates a child's divinity, and rebirthing is a scientific method of regeneration," providing a reconnection to what he calls "Divine Energy."

In an effort to help others overcome the deleterious effects of birth trauma, Orr developed a technique of allowing adults to reexperience birth in a safer, warmer, more welcoming environment. He began rebirthing clients by having them float face down in a hot tub wearing a snorkel and nose plug. While being held in place by the rebirther and an assistant, clients were directed to breathe deeply and rapidly in an attempt to liberate the breath from inhibitions created during the birth trauma. When Orr discovered that it was not the immersion in water but the act of breathing and relaxing in the presence of a trained rebirther—defined as "someone who has worked out his or her own birth trauma"—he devised a system of **dry rebirthing** in which the rebirthee experiences several sessions simply lying on a bed or mat before going on to the hot tub or bathtub. The standard procedure now involves a series of ten sessions. The client lies on his or her back and breathes deeply into the upper chest (rather than the abdomen, as with most forms of yogic breathing). The hyperventilation that results is considered desirable as a "cure for subventilation, commonly called *normal* breathing."

To facilitate the process and alleviate the fear associated with the birth trauma, Orr and **Sondra Ray** rely heavily on the use of positive affirmations reminiscent of those fostered by the New Thought movement, e.g., "I am glad I was born. I have a right to be here" or "I am safe, protected by Infinite Intelligence and Infinite Love."

Many of Orr's observations about the unnecessarily harsh birthing process were simultaneously arrived at by French obstetrician **Frederic LeBoyer,** whose book *Birth Without Violence* had an effect on Orr and the rebirthers he trained and who himself was rebirthed by Orr. LeBoyer's techniques of delivering babies in dim light, with few sounds, of waiting to cut the umbilical cord until after the baby has begun breathing on its own, and of holding the child gently in a tub of warm water have gradually begun to be embraced by some parents and doctors.

Rosicrucianism   A secret society whose members are sometimes called **Rosy-Cross Knights** or **Brothers of the Rosy-Cross.** The sect's creation was attributed to a 15th-century German knight named **Christian Rosenkreutz,** as revealed in two pamphlets published in Germany c. 1614 and believed to have been written by Lutheran theologian **Johann Valentin Andrea.** Rosenkreutz was purportedly adept in Eastern, Arabic, and Kabbalistic esoterica, although he is commonly believed to be a fabricated figure. The Rosicrucian symbol is a cross with a rose in the center, emblematic of "man's soul unfolding and evolving." More recent manifestations include the California-based **Rosicrucian Fellowship,** founded in 1907 by **Carl Louis von Grasshof (Max Heindel),** which concentrates on astrology and astrological reference works, and the **Ancient and Mystic Order of the Rosae Crucis (AMORC),** founded in 1915 in New York City by **H. Spencer Lewis** (1883–1939). Lewis had been involved with the British occult group **Ordo Templi Orientis** and its leader, **Aleister Crowley,** the famous magician. During the 18th century, the so-called Golden Age of Secret Societies, the Rosicrucians along with Freemasons and the Illuminati preserved in the West a combination of Eastern mystical practices and certain Western mysteries and occult rituals, although their exact nature is unclear precisely because of the secrecy these societies treasured. As a result, the term *Rosicrucian* today has become synonymous with arcane or occult circles whose teachings are obscure. In an earlier day, they had good reason to guard their secrets zealously. In her ground-breaking book *Isis Unveiled* (1877), Madame Blavatsky detailed some of the persecution such societies faced in Europe at the hands of the Roman Catholic Church, although, she added, "No one could ever lay hands on the Rosicrucians, and notwithstanding the alleged discoveries of 'secret chambers' . . . and of fossil-knights with ever-burning lamps, this ancient association and its true aims are to this day a mystery. Pretended [Knights] Templars and sham Rose-Croix, with a few genuine Kabbalists, were occasionally burned, and some unlucky Theosophists and alchemists sought and put to the torture; delusive confessions even were wrung from them by the most ferocious means, but yet, the true Society remains today as it has ever been, unknown to all, especially to its cruelest enemy—the Church."

shamanism The Russian Tungusic tribe's word for a medicine man, *saman,* may be derived from the Sanskrit *shramana* ("striver"), applied to the wandering ascetics of the first millennium BC who were probably skilled in yoga and possibly in certain practices that are similar to shamanism. The connection is not unwarranted, as the Indian shramanas* represent an ancient tradition that may have preceded the Vedic* religion of India's Aryan* invaders. Shamanism may be just as ancient if not more so. Images of people identified as shamans appear in the cave paintings of France dating back at least 20–30,000 years. The tradition is also in evidence all over the globe, from Africa to Australia to the Amazon, in many places where indigenous peoples survive the encroachments of more modern cultures. The term *shaman* is now used by anthropologists to refer to individuals within those cultures who used to be called medicine men, witch doctors, witches, sorcerers, wizards, and magicians—all words that may imply slightly different functions but that also carry a heavy burden of Western condescension and a distinct aroma of Hollywood B movies. **Michael Harner,** one of the foremost Western practitioners and students of shamanism defines *shaman* as "a man or woman who enters an altered state of consciousness at will to contact and utilize an ordinarily hidden reality, in order to acquire knowledge, power, and to help other persons. A shaman usually has at least one, and usually more, 'spirits' in his personal service. As [religious historian] Mircea Eliade observed, the shaman is distinguished from other kinds of magicians and medicine men by his use of a state of consciousness which Eliade, following Western mystical tradition, calls 'ecstasy.' "

Shamans such as those of northern and central Asia and the Arctic, for instance, conduct rituals to facilitate contacting spirits for the purposes of divination, prophecy, and healing. They may have begun by seeking to heal themselves of their own maladies, learning to self-induce trance states through various combinations of drumming, dance, drugs, meditation, or fasting. During trance, the shaman's spirit is believed to travel out of his or her body, visiting the upper, middle, or lower world—levels roughly corresponding to the heavens, the earth plane, and belowground, where various spirits are said to reside. The shaman seeks help from the spirits in healing the malady with which he or she has been presented, either, according to Harner, "by restoring beneficial or vital power, or extracting harmful power."

The shamanic tradition which flourished in Siberia and northern China probably crossed to North America when it was still connected to Asia and is alive today among Eskimos and North American Indian tribes, as well as many native South American peoples. Shamanism has also become familiar to New Age practitioners who have learned the ancient techniques from the books and workshops of Harner, **Joan Halifax,** and other modern shamans. These New Age authorities, in turn, have learned their skills from authentic shamans of various primal cultures. In fact, because these cultures are for the most part still preliterate, the most accomplished shamans on earth may be known only to their own clan members and perhaps a few outsiders. In whichever culture the shamanic initiate appears, the goal is similar: to learn how to enter a trance state, during which one's spirit travels either below, on, or above the earth plane, and to encounter and become acquainted with power animals, spirit guides, or other entities, including deceased relatives and spiritual masters, to find help in various matters. Reasons for seeking such help vary widely: to heal psychological, spiritual, or physical ills, correct environmental, community, or planetary imbalances, or answer questions about one's path in life. Initiates also seek to obtain guidance in dealing with relationships, work, or any significant matter for which help is specifically sought.

tarot   A deck generally consisting of 22 Major cards and 40 Minor cards divided into four suits of wands, cups, swords, and coins. Sometimes believed to have derived from Hellenistic Egypt because of a loose correlation between the Major cards and the significant deities of the Mystery cults of Egypt and Greece, the tarot may also have been influenced (in the Minor suits, at least) by Celtic myth. Secrets of the Egyptian priests were hidden in the symbology of the cards, which were used primarily for gaming until about 18th-century France. There the modern 52-card game decks of today emerged, as the four suits evolved into spades (swords), hearts (cups), diamonds (coins), and clubs (wands). But at the same time, occult associations that may or may not have corresponded to the original Egyptian secrets were developed by a French Huguenot* pastor named **Antoine Court de Gebelin** (1719–84). Gebelin also apparently originated the idea of using the tarot for a form of divination called **cartomancy.** Two members of an English occult circle called the **Hermetic Order of the Golden Dawn,** scholar **Arthur Edward Waite** (1857–1942) and artist **Pamela Coleman Smith,** created the 78-card tarot deck that remains the most popular today and that can be purchased in almost any New Age bookstore.

transpersonal psychology   A recent development in the field of psychology that takes into account the spiritual dimension as an essential element in mental well-being. This school of psychology took shape around the work of **Abraham Maslow** (1908–70), an American psychologist who explored the realm of the transpersonal (Lat. "beyond the self"), based on his study of **peak experience,** the efflorescence of joy, expanded consciousness, or energy flow that can occur in spiritual, artistic, or even athletic contexts. What distinguished transpersonal from conventional psychology was its emphasis not on helping the patient "adjust" to life but in seeking realization and fulfillment, in Maslow's words, in "the farther reaches of human nature." The best-known modern exponent of transpersonal psychology in America is probably **Ken Wilber** (b. 1949), author of *Transformation of Consciousness* and many other books in the field. The leading form of transpersonal psychology today is **psychosynthesis,** a school founded by **Roberto Assagioli** (1888–1974) that seeks to help the patient establish contact with the Higher Self. Assagioli rejected both the Freudian and Jungian outlines of consciousness as too limiting. He posited a Higher Self, a reflection of the Divine Reality, which he distinguished from the ego and superego of Freud and the collective unconscious of Jung. Transpersonal therapists combine traditional therapeutic techniques with meditation, guided visualization, and other spiritually based approaches. A goal of the treatment process may not be merely for the patient to become "well adjusted" but rather the advancement of his or her spiritual development.

ufology   The belief that UFOs not only exist but have been contacting humanity over a long period of time. Ufologists accept the presence of **extraterrestrials** not as metaphor but as a physical reality, although explanations of their nature vary—from alien beings originating in distant galaxies to high-level intelligences or "energies" from within the earth plane. A large circle has developed consisting of those who believe they have been abducted by UFOs and therapists who, like **Budd Hopkins,** help UFO abductees through hypnotic regression to recall and come to terms with what they describe as the traumatic aftereffects of their abductions.

The Urantia Book   Transmitted through automatic writing in the 1930s (the channeler has remained anonymous) from extraterrestrial sources, this nearly 2,100-page book details an elaborate spiritual ruling structure of the universe, in which the planet Earth, called **Urantia,** is merely one of many similar inhabited planets constituting the local universe of Nebadon in the superuniverse of Orvonton. The book also gives a detailed historical overview of human civilization focusing mainly on Judeo-Christian theology, the development of the concept of Yahveh, and a lengthy section on the life of Christ. The celestial authors make a significant distinction between the teachings of Jesus and the concept of Christianity, which they feel was created largely by Paul*. "Jesus founded the religion of personal experience in doing the will of God and serving the human brotherhood," the book concludes. "Paul founded a religion in which the glorified Jesus became the object of worship and the brotherhood consisted of fellow believers in the divine Christ. In the bestowal of Jesus these two concepts were potential in his divine-human life, and it is indeed a pity that his followers failed to create a unified religion which might have given proper recognition to both the human and the divine natures of the Master as they were inseparably bound up in his earth life and so gloriously set forth in the original gospel of the kingdom." This understanding of Jesus vis-à-vis Pauline Christianity is somewhat consonant with New Age interpretations, and yet *The Urantia Book* speaks almost entirely in terms of a male God the Father and the Son of God, with little or no mention of a feminine principle.

BEYOND THE NEW AGE

✳ THE RETURN OF THE NATIVE AMERICAN

For some time, surveys of the world's religious traditions have tended to leave out altogether the spirituality of cultures that existed before the development of sophisticated systems of written language. This generalization has a particular bearing on two extremely important developments in the study of religious traditions: the reemergence of Native American spirituality and the wholesale rediscovery of the role of the Goddess in ancient cultures that preceded the historical religions already described in this book.

The reasons for avoiding a detailed analysis of primal or preliterate cultures (sometimes referred to as indigenous peoples) are not completely arbitrary; although racial and cultural biases have played some role, these traditions present specific problems that are not easily addressed in survey books. Since the cultures have lacked written language systems, information on the evolution of beliefs has been hard to come by, depending to a large extent on relatively recent accounts of Western anthropologists studying the cultures, with all the limitations and room for error inherent in that format. However, as members of these cultures have begun to write about their own traditions and experiences, some reliable inside views have emerged. This is especially true of the North American Indian. Their proximity to the dominating white cultures of the United States and Canada—which for some time had suppressed the spiritual traditions of Indian life—has probably sharpened their ability to address the members of the dominant culture in language they can appreciate. The names of Native American sages and spokespeople have begun to be familiar from the books and workshops that are increasingly available to non-Indian spiritual seekers through a growing network of New Age bookstores and learning centers—names like **Lame Deer, Dhyani Ywahoo, Luther Standing Bear, Joseph Rael (Beautiful Painted Arrow), Twylah Nitsch, Sun Bear,** and **Hyemeyohsts Storm.**

But this unprecedented exposure of Indian voices through the New Age network, and the enthusiastic response of many non-Indians to those voices, has raised a sensitive issue among the Native American community. As American Indians in this century have emerged from the controlling influence of Christian missionaries on the reservations, they have struggled to reclaim their religious heritage and to guard it from distortion by the dominant culture of North America. Some Native Americans have expressed the feeling that their religion is not appropriate for use by outsiders and that non-Indians have no business participating in Indian rituals such as the sweat lodge and vision quest. Other Indians have taken a different stance, saying that there is no reason why non-Indians should not participate in and learn from Native American rituals and beliefs in much the same way they have benefited from the practices of Zen,

Sufism, and other non-European belief systems. In fact, these Indian teachers and spokespeople argue, the world has never before been so deeply in need of what their tradition has to offer.

New Age bookstores and cultural centers have also attracted the ire of some Indian tribal leaders who oppose the sale of Indian cultural artifacts by non-Indians. Many Indians see this as part of a growing trend to distort Indian culture for profit or to reduce it to a kind of secular mysticism. Some of the objects in question are not authentic; others are designed for use in sacred rituals and are no more meant to be sold in the marketplace than Catholic chalices or Jewish Torah scrolls. Realistically, of course, statues and paintings of the Buddha and Kuan-yin* created by non-Buddhists have long been available, not only in New Age emporia but also in stores that sell lawn furniture and pool accessories. The deeper issue, according to some supporters of Indian causes, is one of sensitivity. Having been stripped of most of their land and having had their culture suppressed for so long, many Indians feel that their religious traditions are among the little they have left. The idea that members of the dominant culture are now beginning to appropriate that aspect of their heritage is infuriating to much of the Indian community. Reports of some non-Indians charging high fees for admission to naked, mixed-sex sweat lodges during which caviar is served have not helped to allay the fears of the traditionalists. This issue is not likely to be settled easily or quickly.

But despite the collateral commercialism, many New Age practitioners have shown a serious and respectful interest in Native American spiritual traditions. That interest is consistent with the New Age inclination to re-explore ancient spiritual forms and traditions in a seemingly endless quest to expand the modern understanding of what constitutes spiritual practice. It is hard to argue against either the Indians' desire to control their own traditions or the New Age interest in the valuable spiritual resources those traditions offer. Native American leaders are rightfully the final authority on their rituals and traditions, but if they wish to share those traditions with non-Indians, as many of them have generously done, there seems to be no good reason not to explore an offering of such profundity.

We should acknowledge that similar issues have arisen within the world's other spiritual traditions as they have begun to interact with

Western culture. Most Sufi Muslims disapprove of the Americanized versions of Sufism, such as the Sufi Order in the West*, which do not follow orthodox Islamic practices like the daily prayers. And Japanese and Tibetan Buddhist orders jealously guard their lineages in the West, overseeing closely the way in which sacred knowledge is transmitted and how rituals and practices are performed.

In that context, it's essential to emphasize that American Indian religion should in no way be viewed as a subset of the New Age. As a tradition whose very vitality and earth-centeredness has made it so attractive to a generation of non-Indian Americans, it merits consideration apart from its compelling interest to some New Age practitioners.

WHERE IT ALL BEGAN

> The historical religions now pretty much blanket the earth, but chronologically they form only the tip of the religious iceberg; for they span less than four thousand years as compared with the three million years or so of the religions that preceded them. During that immense time span people lived their religion in an importantly different mode, which must have shaped their sensibilities significantly. . . . This mode of religiosity continues in Africa, Australia, Southeast Asia, the Pacific Islands, Siberia, and among the Indians of North and South America.
>
> —HUSTON SMITH, *THE WORLD'S RELIGIONS*

At one time, archaeologists propose, a somewhat uniform culture stretched around the northernmost regions of the globe from Greenland and Scandinavia across northern Russia to Siberia. The peoples of this circumpolar or circumboreal culture shared a common history and many religious beliefs and practices including animism, shamanism, and ceremonies centered around hunting and animals. Their culture reached down into China (where it influenced the development of Taoism) and as far as Tibet (whose shamanistic Bon* culture interacted with Tibetan Buddhism). Over thousands of years, and beginning as long ago as 60,000 BC, the peoples of northern Europe and Asia migrated across what is now the Bering Sea to Alaska and Canada and then down through the Great Plains of North America to Mexico and Central and South America, reaching the southern tip of the continent by 9000 BC.

As with the Neolithic and Bronze Age cultures of Europe and the Middle East, the culture of the North American Indians incorporated elements of religions based on nomadic hunting, with their mountain and sky gods, and those based on agriculture, with their earth goddesses, shrines, and temples. Less dualistic than most institutional religions, Indian spirituality is this-world-oriented. As in many Goddess religions, the universe is divided into heaven, earth, and underworld. Distinctions between spirits, divinities, humans, and animals are often blurred. Animals, places, even stones and trees can possess spirits that interact with human beings in a kind of cosmic harmony, similar to the ancient concept of kami* that informs the Shinto* religion of Japan. This belief, known as **animism,** is common to many primal religions which hold that personal, intelligent spirits inhabit almost all natural objects, from stones, plants, and rivers to insects, birds, animals, trees, and mountains. Indians regard some but not all places as sacred—certain places and animals are singled out as manifestations of the supernatural, including those seen in dreams or visions.

The native religions of North America, like those of other continents, by and large rely on oral rather than written transmission, which is why they are sometimes called *preliterate.* They are also called *primal,* acknowledging their ancient status (but the term *primitive* is no longer applied, because of its pejorative connotation). These traditions have no written counterpart, nor any one founder or central charismatic figure or figures. In the truest sense, they make up a communal religion, many tribes and members contributing to a tradition which is basically the same for most Indians, with a wide range of regional and tribal variations.

Indians have a different orientation toward the physical world from most of the historical religions. Indigenous peoples look on the cosmos as a living womb that nurtures their lives, and so they generally don't try to destroy or reshape it as more technologically developed cultures do (although they are sometimes capable of abuse of the land and livestock—romanticizing the indigenous is as foolish as patronizing them). Their goal could be described as achieving harmony in the personal, social, and cosmic realms, rather than gaining personal salvation or liberation as historical religions aim to do.

✳ INDIAN GIFTS

The terms **Native American** and **American Indian,** or just Indian, are both used by various North American tribes and tribal representatives to refer to their people. Some insist on Native American; others say that only white liberals use that term, and they prefer the traditional, respectful title American Indian. In fact, though, most spokespeople use the phrases interchangeably with little concern for political correctness. Further, the terms actually used by tribes such as the Comanche, Hopi, and Lakota Sioux to refer to themselves in their native languages can be translated as "the People." What is undeniable is that the culture of American Indians, Native Americans, or the People has so thoroughly influenced the cultural history of the United States that we are often unaware of its true extent.

To begin with the obvious, hundreds if not thousands of American place names are taken from Indian words or tribal names, most memorably those of the Missouri, Alabama, Delaware, Iowa, Illinois, Biloxi, Taos, Mohave, Yuma, Shasta, Spokan, Wallawalla, Chinook, Wichita, Miami, Mobile, Catawba, Erie, Conestoga, and Winnebago tribes. More fundamentally, though, the very principles of American democracy are clearly descended from the egalitarian governance models of the native inhabitants of the land whom the European settlers found here when they landed at Plymouth Rock and elsewhere.

According to historians who have studied the relations between the Indians and the early colonists, the men we call our Founding Fathers were profoundly influenced by their contacts with the land's inhabitants. The idea of uniting the 13 American colonies came originally from the Indian leader Chief Canassatego of the Iroquois League. In that historic confederation, founded between AD 1000 and 1400, five and later six member nations had equal voices irrespective of their numbers or seniority—a forerunner of the Continental Congress and the Senate. The Iroquois League also had provisions for initiative, referendum, and recall. Even the concept of a democratic open meeting in which citizens exercised an equal voice in decision making was borrowed from the Indians, along with the Algonquian word for it: *caucus.* The Indian tradition of having separate leaders for war and peace was also adopted by the Americans; unlike England and many African and Latin American democracies, the U.S. does not allow military leaders to serve in the government unless they first resign their commissions.

Benjamin Franklin, Tom Paine, Thomas Jefferson, and John Adams, among others, openly acknowledged their debt to Native Americans for the structure of the democracy they erected. The same revolutionary concepts of government they learned from the Indians were later exported to Europe, beginning with France, where they were carried directly by Paine. Paine had negotiated with the Iroquois during the American Revolution, tried to learn their language, and sought to incorporate their social structure into the Constitution. Franklin often expressed his frustration at the colonists' halting efforts to learn from the example of the Iroquois League. "It would be a very strange thing," he wrote sarcastically in 1751, "if Six Nations of Ignorant Savages should be capable of forming a Scheme for such an Union and be able to execute it in such a manner, as that it has subsisted Ages, and appears indissoluble, and yet a like Union should be impracticable for two or a dozen English colonies."

✳ EARTH AND SKY

Indian religion is interwoven into your life. Everything, the way you live, the way you sleep. Indian religion is a way of life. To call it a "religion" is misleading. Everything is close to Mother Earth, in accordance to the way we are taught.

—RON BARTON, QUOTED IN *THE SACRED*

That the indigenous inhabitants of North America were able to inspire the civilized, educated colonists with their sophisticated, egalitarian system of government was no accident. To begin with, Indian spirituality is remarkably free of dogma and hierarchy, centering instead around a collection of similar beliefs shared by most tribes, with variations in details, rituals, and ceremonies. Distinctions are often made, for example, between the Plains Indians of the Midwest, the Pueblo Indians of the Southwest, and the Northern Woodland tribes. Yet almost all tribes practice a

DEMOCRATIC CONVENTIONS

Contrary to popular perception, the Western concepts of egalitarian democracy and liberty did not derive entirely from a Greco-Roman ideal, handed down to America from our European forebears. According to historians and anthropologists such as Bruce Johansen and Jack Weatherford, the accepted conventions of modern democracy (extended to women as well as men) were already embodied in the practices and attitudes of American Indians when the first European immigrants arrived here. Even before the American Revolution, visitors to the New World observed the ways of the "savages" and reported these radical notions back to Europe, influencing the work of Voltaire, Rousseau, and John Locke. The egalitarian philosophies of Europe's most radical thinkers, inspired largely by the example of the Native American social order, were then packaged into theories that the colonists later used to justify their rebellion.

America's settlers from Europe knew little of democracy. The English came from a nation ruled by monarchs who claimed that God conferred their right to rule and even allowed them to wage wars of extinction against the Irish. Colonists also fled to America from France, which was wandering aimlessly through history under the extravagances of a number of kings named Louis, most of whom pursued debauched and extravagant reigns that oppressed, exploited, and at times even starved their subjects.

Despite the government sketched by Plato in *The Republic,* and the different constitutions analyzed by Aristotle in his *Politics,* the Old World offered America few democratic models for government. . . . Despite the democratic rhetoric that came into fashion in eighteenth-century Europe, no such systems existed there at that time.

—JACK WEATHERFORD, *INDIAN GIVERS*

The Iroquois' extension of liberty and political participation to women surprised some 18th-century Euro-American observers. An unsigned contemporary manuscript in the New York State Library reported that when Iroquois men returned from hunting, they turned everything they had caught over to the women. "Indeed, every possession of the man except his horse & his rifle belong to the woman after marriage; she takes care of their Money and Gives it to her husband as she thinks his necessities require it," the unnamed observer wrote. The writer sought to refute assumptions that Iroquois women were "slaves of their husbands." "The truth is that Women are treated in a much more respectful manner than in England & that they possess a very superior power; this is to be attributed in a very great measure to their system of Education." The women, in addition to their political power and control of allocation from the communal stores, acted as communicators of culture between generations. It was they who educated the young.

—BRUCE JOHANSEN, *FORGOTTEN FOUNDERS*

modified monotheism—belief in the **Great Spirit** alongside an animistic belief in individual spirits residing in animals and forces of nature, none of which are seen as higher than the Great Spirit. As a result, Native American spirituality is nature-based, growing out of a strong sense of interrelation with the earth; shared communal ritual and sacred traditions are accompanied by the teaching of morals and ethics. This is especially true of North American Indians; Indians of Central and South America follow somewhat different belief systems. The Aztecs of Mexico, for example, who built much of their knowledge and belief on that of the Mayas and other Mezo-Americans (the Toltecs and Olmecs) worshiped over 100 gods, ranked hierarchically and somewhat bureaucratically like the deities of ancient China, whose celestial organization reflected Chinese government bureaucracy.

Furthermore, most tribes, especially among the Northwest Coast and Plains Indians, have traditionally practiced some form of **potlatch,** or giveaway, ceremonies highlighted by the lavish distribution of goods and food to members of other clans, villages, or tribes. The potlatch symbolizes a basic value of communal responsibility reaching back to aboriginal times, and the tradition is tied in with the democratic beliefs of the People. Whenever anyone was elected to a leadership position, he was expected to give away all his possessions so as not to be able to profit materially from his new position (except in the sense that inspired leadership would profit the entire tribe or clan). Even less conceivable by Western standards, debts were traditionally not meant to be repaid, since the ability to bestow possessions and favors on others was a sign of great social standing, and repaying them would be considered a dishonor to the creditor.

Finally, Indians believe in stewardship rather than ownership of the land. This proved difficult for the Europeans who settled America to comprehend as they kept trying to buy land from the Indians. The famous letter of **Chief Seattle** (or Seathl) of the Suwamish tribe to President Franklin Pierce in 1854 states this dilemma eloquently. "The Great Chief in Washington sends word that he wishes to buy our land," Chief Seattle wrote. "How can you buy or sell the sky, the warmth of the land? The idea is strange to us. If we do not own the freshness of the air and the sparkle of the water, how can you buy them? Every part of this earth is sacred to my people. Every shining pine needle, every sandy shore, every mist in the dark woods, every clearing, and every humming insect is holy in the memory and experience of my people. The sap which courses through the trees carries the memories of the red man. So, when the Great Chief in Washington sends word that he wishes to buy our land, he asks much of us."

Indian myths tell of a time when all beings were essentially human. Some of them were changed to animals or birds, but those who resisted the change now make up the human population of the earth. For this reason, the Indians feel a brotherly affinity for animals, whom they respect, with the exception of some domesticated animals like dogs.

The Great Spirit is sometimes conceptualized as **Father Sky** or **Mother Earth** or both, echoing the Neolithic Goddess culture in which women were essentially equal partners with men and the feminine principle was openly acknowledged as the great source of human, animal, and vegetable life. Indian culture also shows the impact, however, of the warlike post-Goddess era, with its violence and its masculine hierarchies, so any attempt to see Native American religion as a direct descendant of Goddess culture is bound to be awkward at best. And yet the male and female principles appear to be far more equitably balanced in most American Indian traditions than in Western historical religions. North American Indian culture is divided between primarily hunting and primarily agrarian tribes, patrilineal and matrilineal descent. Women are given a place of respect and influence rarely acknowledged in either the East or the West.

TRANCES WITH WOLVES

Shamanism is one of the most widely shared components of Indian life. As in the ancient cultures of China, Tibet, and northern Russia, North American shamans induce trance states in themselves to facilitate contacting the spirit world and to help in the work of healing the afflicted. During these trance contacts, they may communicate with spirits of the dead or other spirits, including the spirits of birds and animals, and learn what they need to know to help heal the body, mind, or soul of a patient, to locate game, or to predict the future. Shamanic trances can be induced through a variety of techniques, including chanting or drumming, fasting, and in some cases using psychotropic drugs, the mildest of which might be tobacco. Because in many tribes almost all men went on a vision quest and were said to have contacted the supernatural, sometimes the only difference between shamans and the rest of the tribe was the number or relative power of the spirit guides or helpers they contacted.

White anthropologists have often used the name **medicine man** (even though many of them were women) to indicate a mixture of shamanic and priestly capacities—in this context, *priestly* implies the use of rituals, songs, and verbal formulas learned from other priests in the manner of the brahmans of India. Although the term *medicine man* may have acquired a derogatory overtone from countless bad Hollywood westerns, it does reflect that many tribal shamans were also knowledgeable and astute in the use of hundreds of herbal remedies known to the Indians. The

562

WOMEN OF HONOR

The position of women in Native American social and religious life is extraordinary by Western standards, perhaps reflecting an indirect survival of the Goddess cultures of Old Europe and Asia. Here an Oglala Sioux lawyer, writer, and lecturer describes the role played by women in his own culture.

The older a woman becomes among the Sioux, the more powerful she is regarded to be, because her acquired wisdom is listened to and respected by all. It is women who sit in the place of honor, holding the sacred pipe in the Spirit-calling Ceremony, because it was, after all, a woman who brought the sacred pipe and the seven ceremonies to the people. It is a woman who will make the first cut on the Sun Dance tree, so that it can be felled later and brought to the dance arena. A woman must also be the first to open the Sun Dance arena. In this day of dangerous atomic weapons, womankind is the peaceful segment of humanity; therefore, women's importance and leadership should advance and be recognized, both spiritually and politically.

—ED MCGAA, EAGLE MAN, *MOTHER EARTH SPIRITUALITY*

16th-century French explorer Jacques Cartier, for example, had lost 25 of his men to scurvy when a band of Iroquois cured the rest by administering a decoction of pine bark and needles, a source of Vitamin C.

Native American concepts of life after death appear to be varied and sometimes contradictory, incorporating elements of reincarnation* (either as human or animal), a heavenly afterlife, and ghosts. The often disputed Indian belief in a "happy hunting ground" is consistent with nomadic hunting cultures in Scandinavia and Asia (such as the Aryans*), for whom the afterlife holds an abundance of game. Agrarian cultures, on the other hand, often saw the afterlife as a subterranean land from which the Mother Earth Goddess generated new life and vegetation.

Indian concepts of God may also appear contradictory at times, probably because they derive from different religious traditions with their roots in different sources. For example, **Wakan Tanka,** the Lakota Sioux name for Great Spirit, Great Mystery, or Supreme Being, is sometimes seen as an amalgamation of the Indian concepts of a dominant Father Sky god, Mother Earth, and numerous spirits who control the elements as well as human life. And so Wakan Tanka can refer to either a personal God or a collection of 16 spirits. Other Indian nations since ancient times have believed in a Supreme Being whom they called Father and thought of as a man or as an animal—especially a wolf—with human thoughts and speech. This Creator god is addressed by the Shoshone, for instance, as **Tam Apo** ("Our Father") and is the recipient of certain ritual practices. The apparent dichotomy between a personal Creator God the Father and anthropomorphic animals derived from Indian mythology should seem no more inappropriate, however, than the behavior of Christians at Christmastime who adore the Infant Jesus and erect a Christmas tree derived from an ancient pagan festival.

✳ SEVEN RITUALS

As noted, most North American tribes share a similar frame of reference but differ among themselves as to specific rituals and ceremonies. According to Sioux tradition, for instance, seven ceremonies were taught to tribal elders by the **Buffalo Calf Woman,** who appeared to two members of the Sioux tribe in a vision and explained that the sacred pipe was to be used in seven rituals. She also taught the seven ceremonies to the tribe, the first in person and the other six in visions granted after she departed, leaving behind her sacred bundle, which is still kept on one of the Sioux reservations. The **medicine bundle** remains a significant element of Indian religion, a collection of sacred objects carried by Native American males of any importance in their community. The bundle's "medicine" consists of various sacred objects that facilitate interaction with the supernatural, especially a pipe and tobacco, which are smoked whenever the bundle is unwrapped and used for religious purposes. Some of the bundle's contents are incorporeal, such as songs and rituals, which go with it when the bundle is bought or sold. Historically, one man could own more than one bundle, a sign of his wealth or importance within the tribe.

The Sioux rituals are shared by many North American tribes, especially the sweat lodge and vision quest, which are becoming increasingly familiar to non-Indians as well. The purpose of all the rituals is to bring

BLACK ELK'S REVISION

Nicholas Black Elk (1863–1950) witnessed the defeat of Lieut. Col. George A. Custer by Lakota Sioux warriors at the Little Big Horn in 1876 and survived the massacre of the Lakota, including women and children, at Wounded Knee in 1890. His story, recorded and published by Nebraska poet John Neihardt in 1932 as *Black Elk Speaks,* and his recollection of the seven rites of the Oglala, reported by Joseph Epes Brown (*The Sacred Pipe,* 1953) have made Black Elk one of the best-known names in American Indian culture. (At Carl Jung's suggestion, *Black Elk Speaks* was translated into German in the 1950s.) Black Elk's great vision of the Six Grandfathers, a classic told in language reminiscent of biblical apocalyptic writings, has long been read and revered by Indians and non-Indians alike.

What has only begun to be common knowledge over the last few years, however, is the fact that Black Elk, a convert to Roman Catholicism since 1904, spoke only part of what appears as his own words in those books. Recent scholarship has revealed the extent to which the two previous authors changed or interpreted Black Elk's original remarks (which had been taken down stenographically and later typed up by Neihardt's daughter) and completely invented much of the text—including some of the most widely quoted and admired passages.

Indian and non-Indian commentators often speak of the devastation wrought on Indian culture by Christian missionaries who for a time forbade the practice of traditional rituals like the sun dance and vision quest. And yet Black Elk himself now appears, through the accounts given by his only surviving child, to have been a devout Catholic lay missionary who preached and taught the catechism to young children. (The difference may be that, as a Native American convert, he did not disavow or try to eradicate his people's own sacred traditions.) According to Michael Steltenkamp's *Black Elk: Holy Man of the Oglala* (1993), Black Elk not only succeeded in integrating his Indian beliefs with his newfound Catholicism but based much of the famous vision that he related to Neihardt on the picture catechism that he and other Indian missionaries used to help instruct the young in Christianity.

the participants closer to Mother Earth and the powers that reside in her, creating an experience of unity with all of creation. The **sweat lodge** ceremony (Lakota Inipi) traditionally takes place in an outdoor structure made of saplings bent to a central point and tied together in the shape of a dome 8 to 12 feet in diameter, covered with animal hides, although a tarp or heavy blankets are used today. Heated rocks are placed in a pit dug in the middle; water is poured over the rocks, generating steam. Participants sit in the dark interior and, as they sweat profusely from the steam, pray to the Great Spirit, drum, sing songs, and view images that may appear in the hot stones. Traditionally held with males only, the sweat lodge is increasingly open to both sexes; of the seven rituals, it is the one in which non-Indians most frequently participate.

Vision Quest (Lakota Hanblecheyapi) is perhaps the most common connecting link among the native religions of North America, except for the Pueblo Indians of the Southwest. An individual goes off alone for from 2 to 5 days of fasting to receive a vision, often on a mountain, near a river, in a cave, or in some other isolated place in the wilderness. Orig-

inally associated with rites of passage for young men and for luck in hunting, the quests are undertaken by adult Indians more than once. The vision may be of an animal or any guardian spirit that the seeker needs to help guide him or her and can be of special help to someone who wants to be a shaman. The vision may take place while the quester is asleep, but it will seem as if he or she were awake.

The **Sun Dance ceremony** (Lakota Wiwanyag Wachipi) is an annual tribal thanksgiving to the Great Spirit held in late summer. The ritual usually lasts through 4 days of dancing around a cottonwood tree. Tribal members who choose may be "pierced"—a wooden peg is run through two slits made in the skin above the breastbone, attached to a rope that in turn is connected to the cottonwood. The participants form a circle around the tree and lean back until the peg rips through the outer skin.

The other rituals include **making relatives** (entering a relationship with a nonrelative that is stronger than kinship), **preparing a girl for womanhood, throwing the ball** (a ritual that evolved into a game on which lacrosse is based), and the **spirit-calling ceremony** (called **shaking tent** or **longhouse** by some tribes) in which a holy man or woman acts as a medium in calling on the spirit world for help in healing, finding missing persons, or giving thanks. The sacred pipe, ritually filled with tobacco or tobacco substitute, but never with any psychotropic substance as is often mistakenly believed, is passed among participants at all sacred ceremonies (inhaling is not required of nonsmokers).

Some Native American rituals are peculiar only to certain tribes or regions. One of the most controversial of these is **Peyotism.** Based on a pre-Columbian ritual, the use of peyote as a sacrament (first described in Spanish records in 1560) began as part of a tribal dance ceremony and evolved into a smaller group ritual involving singing, prayer, and contemplation. Peyote (from the Nahuatl word *peyotl,* "caterpillar," referring to the downy center of the peyote button) is a spineless cactus with strong psychotropic properties that grows along the Rio Grande in Texas and south into Mexico. Originally used by a small number of North American tribes in the area where it occurs naturally, since the 19th century peyote has spread north through the Great Plains and west to California. Taken in appropriate quantities, the substance induces visions, long a crucial element in American Indian spirituality. Along the way, Peyotism absorbed elements of Catholic rituals and beliefs, much like Santería* and other indigenous belief systems that have come in contact with a dominant, colonial culture.

At the suggestion of a white man named James Mooney, who had been sent from Washington to investigate peyote use among the Cheyenne and Arapaho in the early part of the 20th century, Indians formed the **Native American Church** for the purpose of formalizing the use of peyote as a sacrament. In a 1990 decision popularly known as the *Smith* case, the U.S. Supreme Court ruled against two Oregon members of the Native American Church who were fired as alcohol and drug abuse counselors and denied jobless benefits because they used small amounts of peyote as part of their church service. At the time, 23 states allowed the use of peyote in some religious ceremonies, although Oregon does not. Citing the "war on drugs" (now generally deemed to be a failure in any event), the Court alarmed even conservative religious organizations by ruling that, in a religiously diverse society, religious freedom is not constitutionally protected in all cases.

Participants familiar with the peyote ceremony point out that the substance is taken under strict supervision of a tribal leader in relatively small amounts in a ceremony that lasts from evening until sunup the next day and is about as far from the modern conception of a drug party as the Christian consumption of the bread and wine of the Eucharist* is from a gourmet dinner. Religious leaders of many mainstream denominations have now joined forces to overturn the *Smith* case because of the dangers it poses to their own practices (including the serving of wine to minors at Christian and Jewish services).

❋ BACK TO THE LAND

The United Nations declared 1993 the Year for the World's Indigenous Peoples, acknowledging the role of native peoples around the globe in environmental management and development, based on their knowledge and traditional practices. Like many other indigenous cultures, American Indians have become valued for their development over many generations of a holistic attitude toward the land and their place in it, an attitude that is rapidly becoming indispensable for the entire population of the earth. More than any specific spiritual practices or rituals, including the sweat lodge and vision quest, this awareness of the interrelationship between the natural environment and its sustainable development may be the greatest single gift of the Native Americans and other indigenous peoples to the dominant Western culture.

❋ THE RETURN OF THE GODDESS

> In most "traditional religions" the supreme or only deity is male. But what we are now learning is that our most ancient traditions are traditions in which both men and women worshiped a Great Mother, a Great Goddess who was the mother of both divine daughters and divine sons.
>
> —RIANE EISLER, "RECLAIMING OUR GODDESS
> HERITAGE: THE FEMININE PRINCIPLE
> IN OUR PAST AND FUTURE"

If the major religious traditions outlined in this book have one dubious element in common, it is probably their complicity, at least on the institutional level, in relegating women to secondary status. It can be argued that the political and economic suppression of women in the larger society draws its authority and rationale from their suppression within the religions that dominate the earth. This raises the question of how great religious founders like the Buddha, Jesus, or Muhammad could be genuinely enlightened and still treat women as inferiors.

The short answer is that those spiritual leaders did just the opposite. If anything, their attitudes toward women were extraordinarily open and compassionate, even if their followers didn't always get the message or, for a variety of reasons, chose to ignore it. Having experienced profound inner openings, the great spiritual radicals looked on women in ways that were startling and discomfiting to their contemporaries, so much so that their support of women contributed to the resistance they experienced—in Jesus' case from the Jews and Romans, in Muhammad's from his fellow Arabs. So strong were the social predispositions and surrounding political pressures on their followers, moreover, that no sooner had these enlightened leaders disappeared from the world than those left to structure and administer their teachings did their best to void their egalitarian treatment of women by erasing it from their sacred scriptures and traditional practices.

According to the testimony of mystics of all religions, anyone who has undergone a genuine enlightenment experience no longer sees others in terms of race, class, gender, or nationality, but simply as reflections of the One. In the case of spiritual teachers who have been accused of sexually exploiting their disciples, one would have to question the level and authenticity of their supposed enlightenment or the extent to which self-delusion may have set in. In modern times, the mainstream religions have struggled to rectify their historical wrongs by finding room for women in their clergies and hierarchies, some more successfully than others. The Catholic church, Orthodox Judaism, and traditional Islam lag far behind; most forms of Buddhism as practiced in America have done much better. But the New Age appears to be well ahead of all the major traditions in this regard. One area in which this is most clearly apparent is its open embrace of the concept of the Goddess, whose proponents are calling for a thorough reenvisioning of the paradigm of social and spiritual experience.

But who precisely is this Goddess they're talking about, and where has she been all our lives?

Long ago, some 20,000 years ago and more, the image of a goddess appeared across a vast expanse of land stretching from the Pyrenees to Lake Baikal in Siberia. Statues in stone, bone and ivory, tiny figures with long bodies and falling breasts, rounded motherly figures pregnant with birth, figures with signs scratched upon them—lines, triangles, zigzags, circles, nets, leaves, spirals, holes—graceful figures rising out of rock and painted with red ocher—all these have survived through the unrecorded generations of human beings who compose the history of the race.

—ANNE BARING AND JULES CASHFORD,
THE MYTH OF THE GODDESS

Largely from recent archaeological discoveries and more sophisticated dating techniques, a number of scholars now posit a time before the appearance of the warlike, male-dominated, and hierarchical societies that rule the earth today, an era when the Goddess was worshiped as the primary Deity, the Source of all life, the Creator. They point to the rather obvious fact that our early forebears, when first asking their eternal questions about their origins, would have looked on women as the bearers of new life and would have envisioned the cosmic Source of the universe as female. Ancient figurines of broad-hipped women with prominent breasts and small heads or no faces, like the so-called Willendorf Venus, have been turning up by the thousands in new archaeological digs. They are no longer viewed as mere fertility symbols or as the fevered excrescences of primitive male imagination—"an ancient analogue for today's *Playboy* magazine," as one scholar put it—but as loving depictions of the Mother Goddess as the great life-giver.

Goddess culture was a blend of monotheism and polytheism whose closest parallel among the major religious traditions is probably classical Hinduism, with its concept of an Absolute Godhead and many, many particular forms and manifestations of the Godhead. From the Paleolithic, or Old Stone, Age (which ended around 10,000 BC), the Goddess appears to have been universally worshiped across a wide geographical swath of civilization, from southern Europe to Siberia, around the Mediterranean rim to Egypt and down to the Fertile Crescent of Mesopotamia. But she took on numerous manifestations, including birds as diverse as the crane, duck, goose, dove, and owl, as well as the bull, bear, doe, butterfly, and bee. She was identified with life-giving waters in

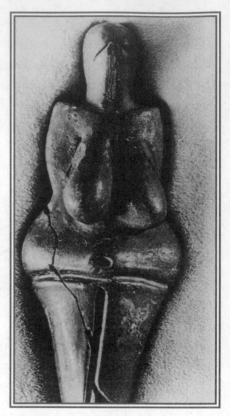

Found near a hearth in Dolni Vestonice in Czechoslovakia and dated at about 20,000 BC, this figurine made of clay and powdered bone is less than five inches tall. Exhibiting the classic swollen hips, belly, and breasts of the Goddess, and tapered at the bottom, it was probably meant to be placed in the ground or held in the hand during rituals. "The flowing breast is the essential image of trust in the universe," write Baring and Cashford. "The faintest pattern of stars was once seen as iridescent drops of milk streaming from the breast of the Mother Goddess: the galaxy that came to be called the Milky Way."
WERNER FORMAN/ART RESOURCE

the form of rain or river, with vegetation of all kinds, and with the moon, whose cycles determined the lunar calendar essential to agriculture. We have no idea what she was called in the earliest cultures, which left no decipherable written records. With the advent of writing in about the 4th millennium BC, she was called **Inanna, Ishtar, Astarte,** or **Asherah** in the Fertile Crescent, **Isis** in Egypt, **Gaia, Artemis, Aphrodite, Demeter,** and **Hera** in Greece, **Cybele** in Anatolia and Rome.

As the Great Mother, the Goddess originally embodied both male and female characteristics. Those little figurines with the swelling hips often have long, phallic necks. But during the 7th and 6th millennia, separate phallic figures began to appear, often in the form of a serpent or bull. Human male figures also appear, occasionally in tandem with the Goddess, in what is referred to as the **sacred marriage.** Male gods later appear in Egyptian and Mesopotamian culture as the son and/or lover of the Goddess, but not yet as the dominant Creator God of later times.

572

The culture that produced these artifacts was not so much one in which women dominated and ruled (although the society was most likely matrilineal, i.e., descent was traced through the mother rather than the father as it generally is today). But it was one in which women enjoyed a high degree of importance and esteem, in which the roles of the sexes were balanced in a way that they have not been in any large measure since. Their society left no artwork depicting weapons, warriors, warfare, or captives, no signs of military fortifications, nor any indication of great discrepancies in wealth, rank, and status. The sacred and the secular were more intimately interconnected than in later "religious" societies, including medieval Christian Europe or modern Muslim states, and their social structure was egalitarian and communal rather than authoritarian and hierarchical. The arts flourished then; in fact, the arts were largely developed during this long, peaceful summer following the last ice age—in all likelihood, by women.

PALE RIDERS

Yet sometime between 6,000 and 8,000 years ago—which is to say, just before the dawn of written records—the balance shifted. Two millennia or more of agrarian tranquility were shattered by traumas and anarchy; a period of violent upheaval followed. Marauding men riding on horseback or driving horse-drawn chariots thundered across Europe and Asia. The number of pastoral nomads, animal herders with no fixed abode, had been growing for centuries along the fringes of the stable agricultural societies of the Middle East, the Indus Valley, and Old Europe (a designation covering most of modern Italy, Greece, Crete, western Turkey, and southeastern Europe). Descended from the Paleolithic hunters of the steppes, they had become warriors; now they began to disrupt the peaceful civilization that worshiped the Mother Goddess.

Known today as Indo-Europeans or Aryans* (the same people Nietzsche and Hitler proclaimed the master race), they were not necessarily Nordic in appearance and were neither Indian nor European, originating somewhere in Asia and northeastern Europe. Archaeologist **Marija Gimbutas** (1921–94) of UCLA, whose ground-breaking work over the last 20 years is responsible for many of the new insights concerning this transition, calls these nomadic tribes **Kurgans** and believes that they began invading in three major onslaughts dated at approximately 4300, 3400, and 3000 BC. The impact of the Aryans or Kurgans on Indian life and religion is discussed in the chapter on Hinduism; but the Kurgans also overran Anatolia (Turkey), Greece, and eastern Europe, irrevocably

WHOLE EARTH MOTHER

At the dawn of the Neolithic, or New Stone, Age, somewhere between 10,000 and 6000 BC, agriculture was discovered, and humanity began moving from life in the caves—a slapdash affair of constant migration, following the wild herds, hunting and gathering—to a stable life of growing crops and domesticating animals. People gathered in villages and communities, which were based on a relatively predictable food supply and the means to store it (particularly grains, which could be eaten through the winter); with that, the beginnings of civilization as we know it took shape. Women, who tended the hearth while the men hunted, most likely had discovered and maintained agriculture; as farming flourished and displaced the age-old occupation of hunting, the power of women increased. Here two English Jungian analysts with backgrounds in art and mythology comment on this axial period in world history and the devotion to the Mother Goddess that underlay it:

The movement of consciousness in the Neolithic is one of differentiation and proliferation, but there is no loss of the original sense of unity, which is now explicitly explored through the myth of the goddess. The Mother Goddess in the Neolithic age is an image that, more obviously than before, inspires a perception of the universe as an organic, alive and sacred whole, in which humanity, the earth, and all life on earth participate as "her children." As the Great Mother, she presides over the whole of creation as the goddess of life, death and regeneration, containing within herself the life of plants as well as the life of animals and human beings. There is the same recognition of an essential relationship between an invisible order, governing the revolving phases of the moon, and a visible earthly order, embodied earlier in the cycles of human and animal life, and now in the cycles of seasons and the agricultural year.

—ANNE BARING AND JULES CASHFORD,
THE MYTH OF THE GODDESS

transforming cultures that had been in place for millennia. In the Middle East, the Semites, a similar group that developed in the large, arid desert west of Mesopotamia and stretching south from Syria into the Arabian peninsula, swept over the more fertile lands of Sumeria and what later became known as Canaan and Palestine.

These nomadic invaders were characterized by male hierarchies of priests and warriors (and sometimes warrior-priests), worshiping not the Goddess but male gods of war and sky and mountains. The Hebrews, a Semitic tribe who probably got their name from one of the Habiru*, or nomadic tribes from the south of Canaan, fit this mold; the accounts of their invasion, conquest, and subjugation of the Canaanites in the early books of the Bible are replete with the massive destruction and slaughter that invariably accompanied the appearance of the nomadic invaders. What the Hebrews and other Semites, including the Arabs, had in common with the Aryans or Kurgans who invaded northern India, Greece, and Old Europe was something the scholar Riane Eisler, in her seminal book *The Chalice and the Blade,* terms a "dominator model of social organization" as opposed to the "partnership model" of the previous Goddess culture.

Gimbutas's controversial theories have recently been corroborated by an Italian-born genetics professor at Stanford University Medical School, **Luigi Luca Cavalli-Sforza.** By analyzing patterns of geographic variation and distribution of genes, using rapid methods for decoding the chemical sequences of genes developed in only the last decade, Cavalli-Sforza has independently arrived at a similar picture of the spread of agriculture from its introduction in the Middle East in about 8000 BC. Replacing the original hunter-gatherers of Paleolithic times, he says, the Neolithic farmers reached across Europe to the Pyrenees. Their sole direct survivors are believed to be the Basques, a mysterious and fiercely independent people living in the western Pyrenees who are genetically and linguistically distant from other Europeans and have long been thought to represent a pre-Aryan race.

One thing archaeologists have not been able to explain fully is what gave rise to the violence and blood lust of the nomadic tribes that eventually overran and dominated all the Neolithic cultures they encountered. Certainly their nomadic existence itself, necessitated by the herding of cattle, sheep, and goats and the constant search for water and pasture land, precluded any kind of stable life that might have allowed the arts or a taste for beauty to flourish. For the most part, the nomads seem to have come from arid, unproductive lands—the steppes of central Asia or the deserts of Arabia—and to have worshiped warlike sky gods, especially gods of the storm, wind, lightning, sun, and fire. The harshness of the conditions under which they lived would have dictated the reliance on superior might that shaped their culture. From a life characterized by dominance over other tribes, it was a logical step to the pillaging of stable agrarian cultures settled in the more fertile lands of Old Europe or Canaan ("a land flowing with milk and honey"), who could offer relatively little resistance. The contrast between these violent nomadic herders and the peaceful farmers they rode roughshod over seems to be echoed in our own recent past, in the conflicts between cattlemen and sodbusters in the American West that have formed the basis for endless Hollywood westerns. One other possibility that has not been suggested may be the contrast in diets. The Neolithic peoples relied for only a small portion of their food on the hunting or slaughter of animals; their most plentiful sources of food were the grains and other edible plants they farmed. The nomads, in contrast, must have depended to a much larger extent on the slaughter of herd animals and a meat-centered diet that may have stoked their aggressiveness.

Aided by the use of copper, bronze, and iron for making weapons and the domestication of the horse into an implement of battle, the invaders initiated a new culture based not on production but on conquest. The armed man on a horse, writes Gimbutas, "in its time must have had the impact a tank or an airplane has among primitives in ours." The beginnings not only of warfare but also of slavery, subjugation, and plundering, of social stratification with the warrior strongman at the top, the amassing and concentration of wealth, large-scale human and animal sacrifices, and the custom of killing the wives, concubines, and slaves of powerful men to be buried with them can all be traced to this shift in civilizations. At the same time there was a precipitous decline in the level of art and culture—what we might almost call today "quality of life." Warriors had little use for art, decoration, and the mystical rites of the Mother Goddess; even the use of vivid colors virtually disappeared. The Kurgans typically killed off the men and took possession of the women for slaves or concubines, the beginning of a long tradition of degrading and disempowering women that has only recently begun to be addressed by society at large.

And so the theory put forth by the proponents of the Goddess—and the mounting archaeological and genetic evidence shows it to be less an anthropological theory than a fairly accurate historical model—links the dominant religions of the West today to the wrathful, warlike Semite male deity who ultimately came to be worshiped as Yahveh in Judaism, God the Father in Christianity, and Allah in Islam. During the pre-invasion "golden age," once thought to be myth but now proposed as a dim memory of a historical era, the Goddess reigned in peace, and women served not only as her chief priestesses and oracles but also as lawgivers, judges, and agricultural overseers, creators of the arts of pottery, weaving, dyeing, spinning, stone carving, shrine building, and probably writing. According to **James Mellaart,** the archaeologist who discovered the Neolithic site of Catal Huyuk in Anatolia, which flourished from 7000 to 5000 BC, evidence suggests that the inhabitants had already developed the art of weaving kilims, beautiful knotted rugs that are still woven in Turkey and that add color and warmth to thousands of modern homes around the world. There is also evidence that the great megalithic cultures that produced so many impressive monuments, of which Stonehenge is only the most famous and most nearly intact, were Goddess cultures with extraordinarily advanced knowledge of astronomy and geometry, not to mention architectural abilities.

NO MORE MISTER RICE GUY

The impact of the successive waves of Kurgan invasion cannot, in the view of Gimbutas and many other scholars, be underestimated. What they didn't eradicate outright they transformed. An entirely different paradigm of life began to take shape. The world today has inherited both the vestigial memories and cultural advances of the earlier Goddess culture and the warlike, dominance-oriented pattern of the Kurgans, as described here by a feminist scholar and peace activist:

The power to dominate and destroy through the sharp blade gradually supplants the view of power as the capacity to support and nurture life. For not only was the evolution of the earlier partnership civilizations truncated by armed conquests; those societies that were not simply wiped out were now also radically changed.

Now everywhere the men with the greatest power to destroy—the physically strongest, most insensitive, most brutal—rise to the top, as everywhere the social structure becomes more hierarchic and authoritarian. Women . . . are now gradually reduced to the status they are to hold hereafter: male-controlled technologies of production and reproduction.

At the same time the Goddess herself gradually becomes merely the wife or consort of male deities, who with their new symbolizations of power as destructive weapons or thunderbolts are now supreme. . . . The story of civilization, of the development of more advanced social and material technologies, now becomes the familiar bloody span from Sumer to ourselves: the story of violence and domination.

—RIANE EISLER, *THE CHALICE AND THE BLADE*

✴ FATHER GOD KNOWS BEST

The implications of these discoveries could potentially revolutionize current understanding of history and human development. According to the new theories, the mythologies of the Middle East gradually replaced the Mother Goddess with a Father God, originally warlike, who creates a world of matter separate from himself. The Goddess *was* the world, with her sacred groves and animals and her identification with the earth itself (a notion that survives in Gaia, the Greek goddess of earth, and our own image of Mother Nature). The Father God of Mesopotamia went on to become the patriarchal God of the Israelites, Christians, and Muslims; He evolved into an ethical deity characterized by mercy and compassion, but He remains apart from his creation. The roots of the dualistic split between spirit and matter that has wracked Western culture and theology for thousands of years can now be seen in this distance between Creator and creation. Concomitantly, the Goddess model of relationship between all aspects of creation devolved to the model of a male deity ruling by mastery and control, dominating what he has created. That domination is even passed on to man in the language of Genesis, when Yahveh tells Adam, "Fill the earth and subdue it; and have dominion over the fish of the sea and over the birds of the air and over every living thing that moves upon the earth" (1:28).

The power to control the environment was echoed in the power to amass territory and wealth through war and conquest rather than through peaceful cultivation. Heroism, physical strength, and aggressiveness became the highest values, and, by extension, the duality implicit in opposition and conflict became the new way of visualizing life. Over time, the Father God in the sky became associated with light and good, and the Mother Goddess of the earth with darkness and evil. Even before the exaltation of Yahveh and Allah, the peoples of the Middle East had begun downgrading their goddesses, making them the consorts of male gods, turning them into war deities, or replacing them altogether. And so the triumph of the Father God over the Goddess resulted in a celestial hierarchy, a God of gods—in Baring and Cashford's words, "not the One that is an image of unity, but the One who stands above and alone."

We should note here that the mystical traditions underlying the mainstream institutional religions, especially in the West, have sought to restore the original sense of the One as "an image of unity" rather than of separation or dominance. Having experienced directly the One-ness of all existence, mystics have little use for intrinsically dualistic notions of power or dominance. This is probably the main reason that Western mystics have always been somewhat suspect within their own traditions, why John of the Cross* and Meister Eckhart* were all but excommunicated by the Christian church, why the great Sufi saint Mansur al-Hallaj* was martyred by fellow Muslims, why the Kabbalah* and Hasidism* were originally resisted by the Judaic establishment.

The onset of continual warfare and bloodshed, the domination of strong men over weaker men and most women, also brought with it the first depictions of a dismal afterlife and the possibility of hellfire for the damned. As the tide of violence rose in the world, humankind became convinced of its own evil nature. Sin, guilt, punishment, and eternal damnation were the logical corollaries of a life of conquest and slaughter. According to the Goddess scholars, these developments have left their mark on civilization in general and on the great religious traditions in particular, especially Western monotheism.

However, like a plant that pushes its way up through a patch of macadam, the Goddess continues to reappear even after she has been suppressed and paved over by male-dominant theologies. And so today, the feminine principle can be identified even in religions that do not recognize a specifically female deity. Hinduism does acknowledge the feminine manifestations of its male gods in the shakti*, or energizing force of the deities; the Absolute Godhead from which all the deities proceed, Brahman*, is considered neuter. In China, Taoism has always embraced the feminine principle through its yin-yang* philosophy, in which yin represents the dark, cool, feminine elements and yang the light, hot, masculine ones. Lao-tzu in the 6th century BC speaks of a time when yin was not yet ruled by yang, when the Goddess was the original Source of the universe. Kuan-yin*, the bodhisattva* of compassion in Chinese Buddhism, has from about the 10th century AD been depicted as feminine, reflecting the Taoist influence on Buddhism. Like the Christian Mary*, Mother of God, she is often the one to whom childless women turn for help. In Mahayana* Buddhism we find not only Prajnaparamita*, known as "the Mother of the Buddhas," the embodiment of one of the greatest Buddhist sutras*, but also Tara*, an emanation of Avalokitesh-vara*, the bodhisattva of compassion whose Chinese counterpart is Kuan-yin. Tara, a savior goddess of about the 2nd century, is a popular deity in Tibetan Buddhism, appearing in 21 forms of different colors, postures, and iconographies.

Although the feminine is more suppressed in Judaism, it still appears in the figures of Shekhinah and Hokhmah. Shekhinah* is the name for the manifestation of the divine presence on earth in the tabernacle of the Ark of the Covenant*, the burning bush, and other Biblical images. **Hokhmah** is the Hebrew embodiment of Wisdom (like the Greek Sophia, feminine in gender) who shows up in the Wisdom writings (Ketubim*) of the Bible, e.g., in the book of Proverbs, where she says:

The Lord created me at the beginning of his work,
　the first of his acts of old.
Ages ago was I set up,
　at the first, before the beginning of the earth.
When there were no depths I was brought forth,
　when there were no springs abounding with water.
Before the mountains had been shaped. . . .
When he marked out the foundations of the earth,
　then I was beside him, like a little child,
and I was his daily delight,
　rejoicing before him always,
rejoicing in his inhabited world,
　and delighting in the sons of men. (8:22–25, 29–31)

This sense of a feminine principle that existed before the creation of the earth and humanity is consistent with the much older Neolithic conception of the Goddess as the preexisting, self-sufficient Creator of all life. In Christianity, especially Catholicism, the figure of Mary, barely mentioned in the Gospels, gradually took on greater significance and power over the centuries, along with many of the roles once played by the great Mother Goddess: Blessed Mother, Queen of Heaven, source of fertility and child-birth, protectress of grain and farming and animals. Especially among peasant women in the same areas in which the Neolithic Goddess culture of Old Europe flourished, thousands of shrines to Mother Mary are visited and venerated annually. Some, like Our Lady of Czestochowa in

Poland, are the sites of massive annual pilgrimages of a million or more, which neither Hitler nor the Communist governments were able to stop.

The significance for the New Age of the new passion about the Goddess is manifold. For one thing, it represents a turn toward intuition, the "feminine" way of knowledge needed to balance the "masculine" mode of knowledge through the intellect. The Goddess offers humanity an alternative to the principles of competition and domination which continue to plague international politics and threaten society with economic and ecological destruction. On another level, the Goddess principle is tied into the Gaia Hypothesis, the notion that the earth is an organic whole possessing a kind of sacred consciousness, much the way the Goddess was originally envisioned and worshiped.

Most proponents of the Goddess do not see the movement as a pendulum swing back to matriarchal society but as an attempt to balance the genders and their characteristics, avoiding a preponderance of one or the other. This approach is consistent with the Taoist concept of yin-yang*, the Tantric Buddhist image of the yab-yum* (Father-Mother), and the Hindu Shiva-Shakti*. (Unfortunately, although these concepts appear to be more available in Eastern theologies, in practice Indian and Chinese culture elevate men and suppress women as ruthlessly as Western society. The practice in India of sati*, or widow-burning, is a direct descendent of the Kurgan practice of killing the wives and concubines of great military leaders to be buried with them. And in both countries, large numbers of girl children are still either killed at birth or aborted beforehand once their sex is known.)

Much of the Goddess movement, if it can be called that, is intertwined with the feminist movement in the West. Yet many of its proponents make the case that male-dominant religions and cultures are potentially as debilitating for men as they are for women. The concept of spirituality as an inner war (which the Prophet Muhammad characterized as the "lesser jihad," or holy war against the ego) tends to set men against themselves; they then feel a need, in Western terminology, to "conquer" sin and evil impulses or, in Eastern thought, to "extinguish" the ego as represented by passionate craving, or what the Buddha called trishna* ("thirst"). The same model may lead us to experience God as someone utterly other, outside of ourselves, who rules the world. But rather than ruling the world, the Goddess is one with the world, containing the possibilities for light and dark, good and evil, feminine and masculine, creation and destruction within the continuity of her being. The respected English Buddhist scholar Edward Conze has proposed that the Buddha was responding as much to the specific temporal problem of massive, uncontrolled violence in civilization as to humanity's timeless dilemma. Seen from that perspective, Buddhism, along with Taoism and the Upanishads of India, can appear as an attempt to return to an understanding of the individual's place in the cosmos that had once been prevalent but had been lost through centuries of shattering warfare.

According to its own tradition, Witchcraft reaches back to the Paleolithic Age and the dawn of the Goddess tradition, more than 30,000 years ago. One theory suggests that after the Kurgan invasions upset the Neolithic Goddess cultures, some refugees fled the fertile valleys for the hills and mountains, where they were sometimes called fairies, pixies, or the "little people." **Covens,** or small groups, were formed to preserve the mystical knowledge and rituals of the Goddess culture; and these came to be known generically as **Wicca** or **Wicce** (Anglo Saxon for "witch"). They became the healers, herbalists, midwives, and mystics of many European communities.

During the witch-hunts and persecutions of the Middle Ages, referred to in the Craft as the Burning Times, they were rooted out, accused of non-Christian worship and practices, and executed in the hundreds of thousands (some put the figure into the millions). Most of them were women, as the church's fear of rampant Goddess worship turned to focus on women themselves, often identifying female sexuality with evil. According to the infamous *Malleus Maleficarum* ("Hammer of Witches," 1484), a Dominican* book on witch beliefs that stressed the importance of eradicating witches, "All witchcraft stems from carnal lust, which is in women insatiable" (a statement that may have represented wishful thinking on the part of its author).

❋ BRINGING IT ALL BACK HOME AGAIN

One thing the Goddess literature can teach anyone willing to listen is that what scholars thought they knew about the origins and evolution of the world's religious traditions is far sketchier than most would probably like

THAT OLD WHITE MAGIC

The applications of Goddess research are many and varied, ranging from social action networks and study groups to the implementation of its ancient principles in modern **Witchcraft**. Unfortunately, the Craft, as its followers prefer to call it, suffers from an even worse image than the New Age in general. Ira Levin's best-seller *Rosemary's Baby* and the film made from it have probably done more to shape the popular conception of the Craft than any other element in our culture, with the possible exception of the television sitcom *Bewitched*. Between these extremes of incarnate evil and interminable silliness, there hasn't been much room in the modern imagination for an understanding of the Craft as a serious and benevolent force. Here a modern-day Witch (a term she uses to include men and women) discusses Witchcraft as a form of Goddess religion.

On every full moon, rituals . . . take place on hilltops, beaches, in open fields and in ordinary houses. Writers, teachers, nurses, computer programmers, artists, lawyers, poets, plumbers, and auto mechanics—women and men from many backgrounds come together to celebrate the mysteries of the Triple Goddess of birth, love, and death, and of her Consort, the Hunter, who is Lord of the Dance of life. The religion they practice is called *Witchcraft*.

Witchcraft is a word that frightens many people and confuses many others. In the popular imagination, Witches are ugly, old hags riding broomsticks, or evil Satanists performing obscene rites. Modern Witches are thought to be members of a kooky cult, primarily concerned with cursing enemies by jabbing wax images with pins, and lacking the depth, the dignity, and seriousness of purpose of a true religion.

But Witchcraft is a religion, perhaps the oldest religion extant in the West. Its origins go back before Christianity, Judaism, Islam—before Buddhism and Hinduism as well, and it is very different from all the so-called great religions. The Old Religion, as we call it, is closer in spirit to Native American traditions or to the shamanism of the Arctic. It is not based on dogma or a set of beliefs, nor on scriptures or a sacred book revealed by a great man. Witchcraft takes its teachings from nature, and reads inspiration in the movements of the sun, moon, and stars, the flight of birds, the slow growth of trees, and the cycles of the seasons.

—STARHAWK, *THE SPIRAL DANCE*

to admit. What's more, theories will be subject to further revision as excavations continue and refinements in research technologies accelerate geometrically. Nobody knows for certain what new revelations may come from sites like Catal Huyuk in Turkey, where archaeologists have quite literally only scratched the surface of a culture that precedes the dawn of writing and of historical religion as we know it.

Recent discoveries appear, at least, to be headed in the direction of locating a common source for spiritual beliefs. On a purely subjective level, an observer could choose to interpret events in the world as backing up the theory that the earth's religions, so long divided by bitter bloody warfare and irreconcilable doctrinal differences, are edging perceptibly closer to each other. Of course, another observer could just as easily look at the same events and find the roots of widening conflict.

What is harder to dispute is the observation that the last 100 years or so have brought about unprecedented developments toward the interconnection of world religions, so much so that, looking back from some future vantage point, this century, and perhaps the next, could be seen as in some ways parallel to the 6th century BC. The remarkable efflorescence of spiritual insight and growth that appears to have taken place in that century is a matter of some speculation. But if traditional dates are accepted, both the Buddha and Mahavira* (the latter is credited with establishing Jainism* as a religious community) were teaching their radical

585

departures from conventional Brahmanism in India at about the same time in the 6th century BC—a period during which other Indian sages were developing the mystical insights recorded in the Upanishads. In China, Lao-tzu* was writing the *Tao Te Ching* (or at least evolving the teachings that were later expressed in it), and Confucius* was almost simultaneously creating a system of ethics that would direct public life in China for the next 2,500 years. The Greek Pythagoras* meanwhile was propounding a mystical school of philosophy (including a belief in reincarnation) unlike any that had preceded him in the West. And in Iran, Zarathustra* was reforming the religion of his forebears into what would become known as Zoroastrianism, an all but disappeared teaching that nonetheless had a profound influence on both Judaism and Christianity.

The century that is currently coming to a close has seen a different kind of expansion of spiritual wisdom, perhaps not as laden with great names and radically new ideas, and more diffuse than concentrated, but with impressive implications for the future just the same. Beginning almost exactly 100 years ago, the West began to receive vital transmissions from the East: waves of Hindu and Zen masters have brought over the essence of their wisdom traditions from India and Japan; Tibetan lamas fleeing the Communist invasion have carried their unique dharma with them; and a surge of interest in Chinese medicine and Taoist ways of looking at the physical world have subtly begun to infiltrate the Western mindset. The components of the Western triad of Judaism-Christianity-Islam have each haltingly begun to expand their own internal boundaries, giving new power and influence to women and engaging in dialogues with each other that a few centuries ago would have seemed unthinkable.

And the New Age, for all the mistrust, animadversion, and sheer skepticism directed toward it, has managed to serve a syncretistic function alongside this other activity. In ways that the major religions may not even be aware of, New Age proponents have begun to integrate spiritual principles—fuzzy and incompletely formed though they sometimes may be—into the mainstream of Western life. Health and healing, food and nutrition, sex and love, business and industry, death and dying—areas that have generally been given short shrift by the big institutional religions—continue to be subjected to deep exploration in the New Age.

SELECTED BIBLIOGRAPHY
AND
RECOMMENDED READING

I hold it is the duty of every cultured man or woman to read
sympathetically the scriptures of the world. If we are to respect others'
religions as we would have them respect our own, a friendly study of the
world's religions is a sacred duty.

Mahatma Gandhi

To what is One, sages give many a title.
Rig Veda I, 164, 46

When it comes to religion, there is no such thing as total objectivity. Few
authors write books about religion, their own or anyone else's, without
evincing some kind of predilection. The case could be made that the
most insightful commentators on a given spiritual tradition are those
who have been through its rigors personally; yet such writers in many
cases are prone to biases that an outsider might not carry. The occupa-
tional hazard of writing about one's chosen path may be the firm belief
that that path is the best, or only, approach to God or enlightenment.
Despite the wisdom articulated so clearly in the epigraph, some believers
find the title more compelling than the One Truth, or at least feel that
their particular truth is perceptibly truer than any other.

Some of the books in this listing reflect the preferences of their au-
thors, whether toward Theravada Buddhism, the Ramakrishna order of
Vedanta, mystical Judaism, radical feminist Catholicism, or Shia Islam.
Others are more broad-based and inclusive. What they all share, though,

is an ability to state their cases effectively, from the heart, and with a minimum of obfuscating rhetoric. Even the most opinionated, I believe, radiate a gentle tolerance for the rest of humankind who have not quite seen what they have seen.

And who would have it otherwise? Why should it be, as an Irish mystic poet once proposed, that only the worst are full of passionate intensity while the best lack all conviction? My own bias toward religious pluralism in general and the nondualistic substratum common to all the great traditions in particular should be obvious. But I have tried to do justice to as many other viewpoints as I could fit into such a relatively small volume. Some of those whom I may have left out or served poorly can be found in the following books, along with the many who helped to inform me and to shape my understanding of the world's beliefs.

Overall

Abhayananda, S. *History of Mysticism: The Unchanging Testament.* Naples, Fla.: Atma Books, 1987.

Eliade, Mircea. *A History of Religious Ideas.* 3 vols. Trans. Willard R. Trask. Chicago: University of Chicago Press, 1978.

Finegan, Jack. *The Archaeology of World Religions: The Background of Primitivism, Zoroastrianism, Hinduism, Jainism, Buddhism, Confucianism, Taoism, Shinto, Islam, and Sikhism.* Princeton: Princeton University Press, 1952.

Great World Religions: Beliefs, Practices, Histories. 5 vols. Audiotape series. Springfield, VA.: The Teaching Company, 1994.

James, William. *The Varieties of Religious Experience: A Study in Human Nature.* 1902; New York: Modern Library, 1936.

Hixon, Lex. *Coming Home: The Experience of Enlightenment in Sacred Traditions.* Los Angeles: Jeremy Tarcher, 1989.

Huxley, Aldous. *The Perennial Philosophy.* New York: Harper & Row, 1944.

Jung, Carl G. *Psychology and the East.* Trans. R. F. C. Hull. Princeton: Princeton University Press, 1977.

Smith, Huston. *The World's Religions: A Completely Revised and Updated Edition of* The Religions of Man. San Francisco: HarperSanFrancisco, 1991.

Hinduism, Sikhism, Zoroastrianism

Basham, A. L. *The Origins and Development of Classical Hinduism.* Ed. Kenneth G. Zysk. New York: Oxford University Press, 1991.

Boyce, Mary. *Zoroastrianism: Its Antiquity and Constant Vigour.* Costa Mesa, Calif.: Mazda Publishers, 1992.

Embree, Ainslie T., ed. *The Hindu Tradition: Readings in Oriental Thought.* New York: Vintage, 1972.

How to Know God: the Yoga Aphorisms of Patanjali. Translated with commentary by Swami Prabhavananda and Christopher Isherwood. New York: New American Library, 1953.

The Kama Sutra of Vatsayana. Trans. Sir Richard F. Burton. New York: Arkana, 1991.

Klostermaier, Klaus K. *A Survey of Hinduism.* Albany: State University of New York, 1989.

Knipe, David M. *Hinduism: Experiments in the Sacred.* San Francisco: HarperSanFrancisco, 1991.

Koller, John M. *The Indian Way.* New York: Macmillan, 1982.

Krishna, Gopi. *Kundalini: The Evolutionary Energy in Man.* Boston: Shambhala, 1985.

Lemaitre, Solange. *Ramakrishna and the Vitality of Hinduism.* Translated by Charles Lam Markmann. Woodstock, N.Y.: Overlook Press, 1984.

Muktananda, Swami. *Play of Consciousness.* South Fallsburg, N.Y.: SYDA Foundation, 1978.

Murthy, T. S. Anantha. *The Life and Teachings of Sri Ramana Maharshi.* Clearlake, Calif.: Dawn Horse Press, 1990.

The Rig Veda: An Anthology. Trans. Wendy O'Flaherty. New York: Penguin, 1981.

Textual Sources for the Study of Zoroastrianism. Ed. and trans. Mary Boyce. Totowa, N.J.: Barnes & Noble, 1984.

Worthington, Vivian. *A History of Yoga.* New York: Arkana, 1989.

Buddhism and Shinto

Burtt, Edwin A., ed. *The Teachings of the Compassionate Buddha.* New York: Mentor, 1955.

Conze, Edward. *A Short History of Buddhism.* Oxford: Oneworld, 1993.

The Diamond Sutra and the Sutra of Hui-Neng. Trans. A. F. Price and Wong Mou-lam. Boston: Shambhala, 1990.

Evans-Wentz, W. Y., ed. *The Tibetan Book of the Dead.* 3rd ed. London: Oxford University Press, 1957.

Holtom, D. C. *The National Faith of Japan: A Study in Modern Shinto.* New York: Paragon, 1965.

Kapleau, Roshi Philip. *The Three Pillars of Zen: Teaching, Practice, and Enlightenment.* New York: Doubleday, 1989.

Ono, Sokyo. *Shinto: The Kami Way.* Rutland, Vt.: Charles E. Tuttle, 1962.

Parrinder, Geoffrey. *The Wisdom of the Early Buddhists.* New York: New Directions, 1977.

Rahula, Walpola. *What the Buddha Taught*. Rev. ed. New York: Grove Weidenfeld, 1974.

Reps, Paul, and Nyogen Senzaki. *Zen Flesh, Zen Bones: A Collection of Zen and Pre-Zen Writings*. New York: Anchor Books, 1961.

Robinson, Richard H., and Willard L. Johnson. *The Buddhist Religion: A Historical Introduction*. 3rd ed. Belmont, Calif.: Wadsworth, 1982.

Ross, Floyd Hiatt. *Shinto: The Way of Japan*. Boston: Beacon Press, 1965.

Sogyal Rinpoche. *The Tibetan Book of Living and Dying*. San Francisco: HarperSanFrancisco, 1992.

Stevens, John. *Lust for Enlightenment: Buddhism and Sex*. Boston: Shambhala, 1990.

Suzuki, Shunryu. *Zen Mind, Beginner's Mind*. Tokyo: Weatherhill, 1970.

Trungpa, Chögyam, as told to Esmé Cramer Roberts. *Born in Tibet*. Boston: Shambhala, 1985.

Tworkov, Helen. *Zen in America: Profiles of Five Teachers*. San Francisco: North Point Press, 1989.

Taoism

Blofeld, John. *Taoism: The Road to Immortality*. Boston: Shambhala, 1985.

Chia, Mantak, with Michael Winn. *Taoist Secrets of Love: Cultivating Male Sexual Energy*. Santa Fe: Aurora Press, 1984.

Chia, Mantak, and Maneewan Chia. *Healing Love Through the Tao: Cultivating Female Sexual Energy*. Huntington, N.Y.: Healing Tao Books, 1986.

Chuang Tsu: Inner Chapters. Trans. Gia-fu Feng and Jane English. New York: Vintage, 1974.

Overmyer, Daniel L. *Religions of China: The World as a Living System*. New York: HarperCollins, 1986.

Saso, Michael. *Blue Dragon White Tiger: Taoist Rites of Passage*. Washington, D.C.: The Taoist Center, 1990. (Distributed by the University of Hawaii Press, Honolulu.)

Smith, D. Howard. *The Wisdom of the Taoists*. New York: New Directions, 1980.

Tao Te Ching. Trans. Stephen Mitchell. New York: HarperCollins, 1991.

Welch, Holmes. *Taoism: The Parting of the Way*. Boston: Beacon Press, 1966.

Wing, R. L. *The Illustrated I Ching*. New York: Doubleday, 1982.

Judaism

Ausubel, Nathan. *The Book of Jewish Knowledge*. New York: Crown, 1964.

Buber, Martin. *Tales of the Hasidim: Early Masters*. New York: Schocken Books, 1975.

Encyclopaedia Judaica. 17 vols. Jerusalem: Keter Publishing House, n.d.

Goldberg, David J., and John D. Rayner. *The Jewish People: Their History and Their Religion.* New York: Viking, 1987.

González-Wippler, Migene. *A Kabbalah for the Modern World.* St. Paul, Minn.: Llewellyn Publications, 1987.

Hertzberg, Arthur. *Judaism: The Key Spiritual Writings of the Jewish Tradition.* New York: Simon & Schuster/Touchstone, 1991.

Johnson, Paul. *A History of the Jews.* New York: Harper & Row, 1987.

Scholem, Gershom. *Major Trends in Jewish Mysticism.* 1946; New York: Schocken Books, 1988.

Strassfeld, Michael. *The Jewish Holidays: A Guide and Commentary.* New York: Harper & Row, 1985.

Telushkin, Rabbi Joseph. *Jewish Literacy: The Most Important Things to Know About the Jewish Religion, Its People and Its History.* New York: William Morrow, 1991.

———. *Jewish Humor: What the Best Jewish Jokes Say About the Jews.* New York: William Morrow, 1992.

Christianity

Butler's Lives of Patron Saints. Ed. Michael Walsh. San Francisco: Harper & Row, 1987.

Charlesworth, James H. *Jesus Within Judaism: New Light from Exciting Archaeological Discoveries.* New York: Doubleday, 1988.

Crossan, John Dominic. *The Historical Jesus: The Life of a Mediterranean Jewish Peasant.* San Francisco: HarperSanFrancisco, 1991.

Dowley, Tim, ed. *The History of Christianity.* Batavia, Ill.: Lion Publishing, 1990.

Erikson, Erik. *Young Man Luther: A Study in Psychoanalysis and History.* New York: W. W. Norton, 1962.

González-Wippler, Migene. *The Santería Experience.* Englewood Cliffs, N.J.: Prentice-Hall, 1982.

Johnson, Paul. *A History of Christianity.* New York: Atheneum, 1976.

Kersten, Holger. *Jesus Lived in India: His Unknown Life Before and After the Crucifixion.* Longmead, Eng.: Element Books, 1986.

La Barre, Weston. *They Shall Take Up Serpents: Psychology of the Southern Snake-Handling Cult.* Minneapolis: University of Minnesota Press, 1962.

Larson, Martin A. *The Story of Christian Origins: Or the Sources and Establishment of Western Religion.* Tahlequah, Okla.: Village Press, 1977.

Levi, Peter. *The Frontiers of Paradise: A Study of Monks and Monasteries.* New York: Weidenfeld & Nicholson, 1988.

Mead, Frank S., and Samuel S. Hill. *Handbook of Denominations in the United States.* New 9th ed. Nashville: Abingdon Press, 1992.

Meier, John P. *A Marginal Jew: Rethinking the Historical Jesus*. New York: Doubleday, 1991.

Mitchell, Stephen. *The Gospel According to Jesus: A New Translation and Guide to His Essential Teachings for Believers and Unbelievers*. New York: HarperCollins, 1991.

Murphy, Joseph M. *Working the Spirit: Ceremonies of the African Diaspora*. Boston: Beacon Press, 1994.

The Oxford Illustrated History of Christianity. Ed. John McManners. New York: Oxford University Press, 1990.

Pagels, Elaine. *The Gnostic Gospels*. New York: Random House, 1979.

Ranke-Heinemann, Uta. *Eunuchs for the Kingdom of Heaven: Women, Sexuality, and the Catholic Church*. Trans. Peter Heinegg. New York: Penguin, 1990.

Schaberg, Jane. *The Illegitimacy of Jesus: A Feminist Theological Interpretation of the Infancy Narratives*. New York: Harper & Row, 1987.

The Secret Teachings of Jesus: Four Gnostic Gospels. Trans. Marvin W. Meyer. New York: Random House, 1984.

Smith, Morton. *Jesus the Magician*. New York: Harper & Row, 1978.

The Unvarnished Gospels. Trans. Andy Gaus. Putney, Vt.: Threshold, 1988.

Islam

Ahmed, Akbar S. *Discovering Islam: Making Sense of Muslim History and Society*. New York: Routledge & Kegan Paul, 1988.

Attar, Farid al-Din. *Muslim Saints and Mystics: Episodes from the Tadhkirat al-Auliya (Memorial of the Saints)*. Trans. A. J. Arberry. New York: Arkana, 1966.

Dermenghem, Emile. *Muhammad and the Islamic Tradition*. Woodstock, N.Y.: Overlook Press, 1981.

Haeri, Shaykh Fadhlalla. *The Elements of Sufism*. Longmead, Great Britain: Element Books, 1990.

Hatcher, William S., and J. Douglas Martin. *The Bahá'í Faith: The Emerging Global Religion*. San Francisco: Harper & Row, 1984.

Hixon, Lex (Nur al Jerrahi). *Atom from the Sun of Knowledge*. Westport, Conn.: Pir Publications, 1993.

The Koran. Trans. N. J. Dawood. 5th rev. ed. New York: Penguin, 1990.

Lings, Martin. *Muhammad: His Life Based on the Earliest Sources*. Rochester, Vt.: Inner Traditions International, 1983.

Momen, Moojan. *An Introduction to Shi'i Islam: The History and Doctrines of Twelver Shi'ism*. New Haven: Yale University Press, 1985.

Nicholson, Reynold A. *The Mystics of Islam*. New York: Arkana, 1989.

Nigosian, Solomon. *Islam: The Way of Submission*. Great Britain: Crucible, 1987.

Payne, Robert. *The History of Islam*. New York: Dorset Press, 1990.

Rumi, Jelaluddin. *The Ruins of the Heart*. Trans. Edmund Helminski. Putney, Vt.: Threshold, 1981.

———. *Unseen Rain*. Trans. John Moyne and Coleman Barks. Putney, Vt.: Threshold, 1986.

Shah, Idries. *The Sufis*. New York: Doubleday, 1964.

The New Age and Beyond

Anderson-Evangelista, Anita. *Hypnosis: A Journey into the Mind*. New York: Arco Publishing, 1980.

Baring, Anne, and Jules Cashford. *The Myth of the Goddess: Evolution of an Image*. New York: Viking, 1991.

Bartholomew. *"I Come as a Brother": A Remembrance of Illusions*. Taos, N. Mex.: High Mesa Press, 1986.

Beck, Peggy V., Anna Lee Walters, and Nia Francisco. *The Sacred: Ways of Knowledge, Sources of Life*. Tsaile, Ariz.: Navajo Community College Press, 1992.

Besant, Annie, and C. W. Leadbeater. *Thought-Forms*. 1901; Wheaton, Ill.: Theosophical Publishing House, 1980.

Blavatsky, H. P. *Isis Unveiled: A Master-Key to the Mysteries of Ancient and Modern Science and Theology*. 2 vols. 1877; Pasadena, Calif.: Theosophical University Press, 1972.

Braden, Charles S. *Spirits in Rebellion: The Rise and Development of New Thought*. Dallas: Southern Methodist University Press, 1963.

Bucke, Richard Maurice. *Cosmic Consciousness: A Study in the Evolution of the Human Mind*. 1901; New York: E. P. Dutton, 1923.

Bullis, Douglas. *Crystals: The Science, Mysteries, and Lore*. New York: Crescent Books, 1990.

Campbell, Joseph. *The Hero with a Thousand Faces*. Princeton: Princeton University Press, 1949.

Eisler, Riane. *The Chalice and the Blade: Our History, Our Future*. San Francisco: HarperSanFrancisco, 1987.

Ferguson, Marilyn. *The Aquarian Conspiracy: Personal and Social Transformation in the 1980s*. Los Angeles: Jeremy Tarcher, 1980.

Garfield, Patricia. *Creative Dreaming*. New York: Ballantine, 1976.

Harner, Michael. *The Way of the Shaman*. San Francisco: Harper & Row, 1990.

Klimo, Jon. *Channeling: Investigations on Receiving Information from Paranormal Sources*. Los Angeles: Jeremy Tarcher, 1987.

LaBerge, Stephen. *Lucid Dreaming: The Power of Being Awake and Aware in Your Dreams*. New York: Ballantine, 1985.

Lewis, James R., and J. Gordon Melton, eds. *Perspectives on the New Age*. Albany: State University of New York Press, 1992.

McGaa, Ed (Eagle Man). *Mother Earth Spirituality: Native American Paths to Healing Ourselves and Our World*. San Francisco: HarperSanFrancisco, 1990.

Melton, J. Gordon, Jerome Clark, and Aidan A. Kelly. *New Age Almanac*. New York: Visible Ink Press, 1991.

Monroe, Robert A. *Far Journeys*. New York: Doubleday, 1985.

Moody, Raymond A., Jr., M.D. *Life After Life*. New York: Bantam, 1986.

Needleman, Jacob. *The New Religions*. New York: Crossroad, 1987.

Needleman, Jacob, and George Baker, eds. *Understanding the New Religions*. New York: Seabury Press, 1981.

Orr, Leonard, and Sondra Ray. *Rebirthing in the New Age*. Berkeley, Calif.: Celestial Arts, 1977.

Peale, Norman Vincent. *The Power of Positive Thinking*. New York: Prentice-Hall, 1952.

The Portable Jung. Ed. Joseph Campbell. Trans. R. F. C. Hull. New York: Penguin, 1976.

Roberts, Jane. *The Seth Material*. New York: Bantam Books, 1970.

Smuts, Jan Christiaan. *Holism and Evolution*. New York: Viking, 1961.

Starhawk [Miriam Simos]. *The Spiral Dance: A Rebirth of the Ancient Religion of the Great Goddess*. 10th anniversary ed. San Francisco: HarperSanFrancisco, 1989.

Steltenkamp, Michael. *Black Elk: Holy Man of the Oglala*. Norman: University of Oklahoma Press, 1993.

Stern, Jess. *Edgar Cayce: The Sleeping Prophet*. New York: Bantam, 1968.

Twitchell, Paul. *Eckankar: The Key to Secret Worlds*. Minneapolis: Eckankar, 1969.

Weatherford, Jack. *Indian Givers: How the Indians of the Americas Transformed the World*. New York: Fawcett Columbine, 1988.

Wilber, Ken, Jack Engler, and Daniel P. Brown. *Transformations of Consciousness: Conventional and Contemplative Perspectives on Development*. Boston: New Science Library, 1986.

Woolger, Roger J. *Other Lives, Other Selves: A Jungian Psychotherapist Discovers Past Lives*. New York: Doubleday, 1987.

Specialized Reading,
Including Some Out-of-Print and Hard-to-Find Books

Angus, S. *The Mystery-Religions: A Study in the Religious Background of Early Christianity*. 1928; New York: Dover, 1975.

Ballou, Robert O. *Shinto, the Unconquered Enemy: Japan's Doctrine of Racial Superiority and World Conquest*. New York: Viking, 1945.

Bunce, William K. *Religions in Japan: Buddhism, Shinto, Christianity*. Rutland, Vt.: Charles E. Tuttle, 1955.

Selected Bibliography and Recommended Reading

Buranelli, Vincent. *The Wizard from Vienna: Franz Anton Mesmer.* New York: Coward, McCann, & Geoghegan, 1975.

Gerber, Richard, M.D. *Vibrational Medicine: New Choices for Healing Ourselves.* Santa Fe: Bear & Company, 1988.

Gimbutas, Marija. *The Goddesses and Gods of Old Europe, 7000–3500 B.C.* Berkeley: University of California Press, 1982.

————. *The Language of the Goddess: Images and Symbols of Old Europe.* San Francisco: HarperSanFrancisco, 1989.

Hultkrantz, Ake. *Native Religions of North America: The Power of Visions and Fertility.* San Francisco: HarperSanFrancisco, 1987.

Interviews with Oscar Ichazo. New York: Arica Institute Press, 1982.

Johansen, Bruce E. *Forgotten Founders: Benjamin Franklin, the Iroquois, and the Rationale for the American Revolution.* Ipswich, Mass.: Gambit, 1982.

Lalljee, Yousuf N. *Know Your Islam.* Elmhurst, N.Y.: Tahrike Tarsile Qur'an, n.d.

The New Age Catalogue: Access to Information and Sources. By the Editors of *Body, Mind, and Spirit* Magazine. New York: Doubleday, 1988.

Nicholson, Shirley, ed. *The Goddess Re-awakening: The Feminine Principle Today.* Wheaton, Ill.: Theosophical Publishing House, 1989.

Paglia, Camille. *Sexual Personae: Art and Decadence from Nefertiti to Emily Dickinson.* New Haven: Yale University Press, 1990.

Palacios, Miguel Asin. *Islam and the Divine Comedy.* Translated and abridged by Harold Sutherland. London: Frank Cass, 1968.

Remey, Charles Mason. *The Bahai Movement.* Washington, D.C.: J. D. Milans & Sons, 1912.

Rhie, Marilyn M., and Robert A. F. Thurman. *Wisdom and Compassion: The Sacred Art of Tibet.* New York: Harry N. Abrams, 1991.

Spalding, Baird T. *Life and Teaching of the Masters of the Far East.* 5 vols. Marina Del Rey, Calif.: DeVorss, 1964.

Spong, John Shelby. *Born of a Woman: A Bishop Rethinks the Birth of Jesus.* San Francisco: HarperSanFrancisco, 1992.

The Urantia Book. Chicago: Urantia Foundation, 1955.

Wilber, Ken. *Grace and Grit: Spirituality and Healing in the Life and Death of Treya Killam Wilber.* Boston: Shambhala, 1991.

Woodward, Kenneth L. *Making Saints: How the Catholic Church Determines Who Becomes a Saint, Who Doesn't, and Why.* New York: Simon & Schuster, 1990.

INDEX

Defining references of terms and names, which appear in boldface in the text, can be found by looking up the page number listed in boldface below.

Index

Index

Index

Index

Brown, Joseph Epes, 565
Bruderhof, 346
Bruno, 328
Bruyere, Rosalyn, 538
Bubba Free John, 67
Buber, Martin, 249
Bucke, Richard M., 476–78
Buddha, the, xxii, xxv, 12, 83–86, 87–93, 102, 106–7, 142, 146, 188, 276–77, 283, 294, 475, 582, 585
    as historical personage, 87–93, 127, 146
Buddha-nature, 122, 198
Buddhism, xxiv, xxv, 83–146, 494, 496
    Confucianism and, 178–79
    Taoism and, 107, 149, 151, 152, 160, 167, 168, 178–79, 184, 188–90, 192
    See also Pure Land Buddhism; Tibetan Buddhism; Zen Buddhism
Buffalo Calf Woman, 564
Bukhari, Muhammed ibn Ismail al-, 410
Bulgars, 325
Bull, papal, 338
Bunyan, John, 348
Buranelli, Vincent, 486
Buraq, 412, 466
Burhani, 448
Burnouf, Eugène, 277
Bushido, 112
Bussho, 122
Butsudan, 142
Butterfly dream, 161

Cabala. See Kabbalah
Caduceus, 31
Calendars, 260, 379–80
Calenders (dervishes), 466
Caliphs, 418–19, 430, 432, 434, 452, 466
Calvin, John, 346, 390
Calvinism, 346
Campbell, Joseph, 529–30, 543
Canaan, 215–16, 575, 576
Candomblé, 360–61
Canon, 223
Canonical hours, 330
Canonization, 382–83
Canon law, 320
Capital punishment, 305, 326
Capuchins, 329
Carmelites, 329, 338
Carpocratians, 385
Carradine, David, 108
Carthusians, 328, 333
Cartier, Jacques, 563
Cartomancy, 551
Cashford, Jules, 317, 571, 575, 579
Caste, 4, 10–12, 14, 26
Casuistry, 331
Catal Huyuk (Turkey), 577, 585

Catechism, 385
Catechumen, 386
Cathars, 325
Cavalli-Sforza, Luigi Luca, 575
Cayce, Edgar, 508, 536, 540
Celestial Masters, 183
Celibacy
    Bahai and, 458
    in Buddhism, 102
    in Christianity, 299–300, 324, 332, 344, 350, 354, 355
    in Judaism, 230, 262
    in Taoism, 188
Celsus, 302, 304
Cenobitism, 327
Chadwick, Henry, 300
Chai (fasting), 195
Chaitanya, 54–55
Chakras, 6–7, 88, 198, 482, 538–39, 541
Chalcedon, Council at, 322
Ch'an Buddhism, 107, 111, 112, 122, 141
    See also Zen Buddhism
Chancel, 378
Chandi, 53
Chandogya Upanishad, 22, 24, 25, 43
Chang Chueh, 183
Ch'ang Ch'un, 189
Chang Kuo Lao, 177
Chang Lu, 183
Chang Po-tuan, 189
Chang Tao-ling (Chang Ling), 153, 182
Channeling, 240, 504–14
Cha no ya, 112
Charcot, Jean Martin, 487, 528
Charismatic movements, 369
Charlemagne, 310, 318, 320
Charles, Master (Brother Charles), 67, 501
Charles Martel, 420
Charvaka, 28
Charya tantra, 117
Chastity, vow of, 340
Chaturvarga, 5, 29
Chaturvarnashramadharma, 77
Chaucer, Geoffrey, 313
Chela, 77
Cheng-i tao, 182
Chenrezi, 141, 197
Chen T'uan, 189
Chen-yen, 123
Ch'i, 153, 175, 191, 195, 524, 541
Chia, Mantak, 185
Chiao (festival), 194
Chidvilasananda, Gurumayi, 66, 501
Chien ai, 198
Chih (wisdom), 157
Chih-i, 122
Chikhai, 106
Ch'i-kung, 107, 195

Index

Children's Crusade, 337
Chin-ch'ueh yu-ch'en t'ien-tsun, 180
Chinese dynasties, 174
Chinese language, 105, 184, 194
Ching, 175, 195
Ch'ing-t'an, 181
Chin-lien, 188
Chinmoy, Sri, 67, 501
Chi-rho, 310
Chiropractic, 520–21
Chisti, Muin ad-din Hasan, 448
Chiu-ko, 170
Chödrön, Pema, 121
Chonyid, 106
Chopra, Deepak, 66, 482
Chosen people, Jews as, 203
Chou, Duke of, 164
Choudhury, Bikram, 37
Christ, 270, 298. *See also* Jesus of Nazareth
Christendom, 320
Christian Church, 372
Christianity, xxiv, xxv, 267–304, 309–57,
    362–93, 532
  Hinduism and, 59–62
  Islam and, 303, 335–37, 395–96, 400,
    408–9, 416, 422–24, 462
  Judaism and, 232, 236–37, 271, 279, 303,
    311–12, 335, 343
  Zoroastrianism and, 73–74
  See also Protestantism; Roman Catholic
    Church
Christian Science, 137–38, 364–66, 449, 490
Christmas, 304, 378
Christopher, 384
Chromotherapy, 519
Ch'uan-chen tao, 188–89
Chuang-tzu, 148, 151, 161–62, 181
Chu Hsi, xxiii, 191
Chu-lin ch'i-hsien, 181
Chumash, 224
Ch'un Ch'iu, 169
Chung Li-ch'uan (Han Chung-li), 177
Chung-yang, 188
Chung Yung (The Doctrine of the Mean),
    156, 169
Chun-tzu, 157
Churches of Christ, 347 373
Church of England, 347, 385
Church of God, 369, 374
Church of God in Christ, 369, 374
Church of Jesus Christ of Latter-Day Saints,
    362–64, 375
Church Taoism, 153–54
Church Universal and Triumphant, 497
Circumcision, 222, 262, 296–97, 414, 429
Cistercians, 328
Clairaudience, 508
Clairvoyance, 532, 538

Classic on Converting the Barbarians, 167
Cold Food Festival, 193
Collective unconscious, 528, 531
Colon cleansing, 518
Coltrane, John, 357
Communism
  Chinese, 120, 143, 147, 183, 190, 191
  Eastern European, 324, 582
Companions (of Muhammed), 403, 407,
    410, 417–18, 430, 441, 447, 468
Complete Reality School, 195
Compline, 330
Composite things, 93
Concubines, in Islam, 404
Confession
  in Christianity, 320, 378
  in Taoism, 183–84
Confessors, 382
Confucianism, 122, 123, 128, 134, 169,
    190–91, 198
  Buddhism and, 178–79
  Taoism and, 161–63, 178–79, 181, 188,
    190–91
Confucius, 149, 154–58, 273, 586
Congregationalists, 348, 374, 386, 393
Connor, Charles, 67
Conservative Judaism, 253
Constantine the Great, 310
Constantinople, 310, 322, 337
  Second Council of, 301
Contact (in Subud), 459
Continuous revelation, 363
Conze, Edward, 583
Coptic (Egyptian) language, 300
Coptic Orthodox Church, 322–23
Coryell, Larry, 67
Cosmic egg, 10
Coué, Emile, 487
Councils, Christian, 297, 301, 303, 310,
    313, 320, 350, 352, 378, 385
Counter Reformation, 349–51
Cousins, Norman, 482
Covenant, of Baha'u'llah, 458
Covens, 583
Cow-worship, Hindu, 12, 41
Creation
  by the Goddess, 581
  in Hinduism, 9–10
  in Judaism, 204–7, 241
  in Taoism, 147–48
  Ussher's dating of, 379–80
Creationism, 367
Creation spirituality, 537
Creative visualization, 539
Creole language, 359
Crossan, John D., 288
Crowley, Aleister, 548
Crucifix, 378

Index

Index

605

Index

Gregory I the Great (Pope), **328**, 343
Gregory VII (Pope), **335**
Gregory IX (Pope), **332**
Grey, Margot, **526**
Grihasthya, 5, 28
Groote, Gerhard (Geert), **340**
Gross, Darwin, **542**
Gunas, 7, 42, 77, 150
Gurdjieff, G. I., 543, **544–45**
Guru, **56–57**, 77, 98
Guru Granth Sahib, **57**, 542
Guru Rinpoche. *See* Padmasambhava
Gutenberg Bible, **341**
Guyon, Madame, **477**
Guzman, Dominic, **329**

Hachiman, **135**
Hadhoxt Nask, 73
Hadith, 273, 404, 408, **410**, 415, 418, 426, 432, 440
Hadith nabawi, **411**
Hadith qudsi, **410**
Haeckel, Ernst, **537**
Haeri, Shaykh Fadhlalla, 421, 441
Hafsa, **403**, 407
Hagar, xxv, **398**, 428
Hahnemann, Samuel, **518**, *545*
Haidaris, **448**
Haile Selassie, **357**
Hail Mary (prayer), 27, **359**
Hajj, **427–29**, 432, 439–40
Hakim, **406**
Hakim, al- (Caliph), **434**
Halakhah, **236**
Halifax, Joan, **550**
Halima, **400**
Hallaj, Mansur al-, xxiii, **443–44**, 580
Halveti-Jerrahi, **448**
Hanafites, **431**, 460
Hanbal, Ahmad ibn Muhammed, **422**, 431
Hanbalites, **431**, 436, 460
Han Chung-li (Chung Li-ch'uan), **177**
Han Fei, **196**
Han Hsiang-tzu, **178**
Hanifs, **401**
Hanina ben Dosa, **292**
Hanukkah, 227, 259, **260–61**
Hanuman, 14, 41
Han Wen Ti, **160**
Han Wu Ti (Wu-ti), 157, 174
Haoma, **70**
Happy hunting ground, **563**
Haqiqa, **430**
Haqq, **406**, 444, 445
Hara, **53**
Hardenberg, Baron Friedrich von (Novalis), 246
Hare Krishnas, 35

Hargobind, Guru, 58
Hari, **54**
Harijan. *See* Untouchables
Harner, Michael, **549**
Harrison, Hassca, **513**
Hasan ibn Ali, 418, **432**, 465, 468
Hasegawa Kakugyo, **136**
Hashim clan, 399, 400, 402
Hashish users, **435**
Hasidim, xviii, **226**, **247–50**, 251, 253, 580
Haskalah, **251–52**, 254
Hatha yoga, 5, 30, 32, 35, 65, 497, 521
Hatha Yoga Pradipika, 30
Havurah movement, **254**
Hay, Louise, 482, **534**
Hazrat Inayat Khan, **449**
Healing
    Christian, 271, 276–77, 292–93, 318, 364–66, 369, 371
    Native American, **562**
    New Age, 482–93, 514–25, 539, 540, 541
    shamanistic, **549–50**
    See also Medicine
Healthy, Happy, Holy Organization (3HO), **55**
Heaven
    in Christianity, 309, 320
    in Greek religion, 307
    in Islam, 412, 424–25, 466, 468
    in Judaism, 231
    in Pure Land Buddhism, **123**
    in Taoism, 171
    in Vedic Hinduism, 17, 25
    in Zoroastrianism, 71
Hebrew language, 226, 233, 239, 241, 465
Hebrews, 207, 214–15, 575. *See also* Judaism
Hegira, **414**
Heian period, **122**
Heine, Heinrich, **254**
Hekhalot, **238**
Helena, **310**
Hell, **580**
    in Buddhism, 171, 199
    in Christianity, 334
    in Greek religion, 307
    in Islam, 424
    in Judaism, 231
    in Taoism, 171, 185–86
    in Zoroastrianism, 71
Helwys, Thomas, **348**
Henotheism, **208**
Hensley, G. W., 370
Hera, **572**
Heresy, **324–27**
Hermes, 31, **539**
Hermetic Order of the Golden Dawn, **551**
Herod the Great, **227–28**

Index

Index

Jesus of Nazareth (Jesus Christ), xviii, xxii, xxv, 46, 73, 84, **230**, 268–95, 304, 366, 378, 379, 388, 476, 509, 552
    as avatar in Hinduism, 62
    in Islam, xxv, 395–96, 409, 412, 422, 423, 433, 437
Jesus prayer, 388, 446
Jewish Theological Seminary, 253
Jezebel, 219
Jibril, 467
Jihad, **409**, 415, 456
Jikaku Daishi. *See* Ennin
Jikko Kyo, 136
Jilani, Abd al-Qadir al-, **447**
Jimmu Tenno, 133
Jinas, 49, 50
Jinja, 134, 135–36
Jinn, 399, 467
Jin Shin Jyutsu, 524
Jivanmukta, 77
Jizya, 454
Jnana yoga, 4, **34**, 78
Job, 409
Jodo Shin, 125
Jogues, Isaac, 314–15
Johanen ben Zakkai, 225
Johansen, Bruce, 559, 560
John, Gospel of, 74, **284**, 307, 402
John of the Cross, xix, 338, 441, 476, 580
John Paul II (Pope), 383
John the Baptist, 230, 270–71, 274, 280, 383, 409
John the Divine, 286
Jojitsu, 122
Jonah, 513
Jones, Franklin, 67
Joseph, 211, 270, 288, 289
Josephus, 216, 263, 292
Joshua, 215, 234
Juan Chi, 182
Juan Hsien, 182
Judah, 214
Judah Halevi, 239
Judah Ha-Nasi, 234
Judah Maccabee, 227, 260
Judaism, xxiv, xxv, 201–66
    Christianity and, 232, 236–37, 271, 279, 303, 311–12, 335, 343
    Islam and, 224, 395, 400, 402, 409, 414–16, 423, 438, 461–62
    Zoroastrianism and, 73–74
Judas Iscariot, 278, 280
Judeo-Christian tradition, 312–13
Judge, William Quan, 494
Judges, 215
Judgment. *See* Last Judgment
Judith, Book of, 287
Jukai, 101

Julian of Norwich, 339, 392
Jumpers, 354
Junayd, Abul Qasim al-, **442**
Jung, Carl Gustav, 169, 479, 526, **528–30**, 531–32, 565
Justification by faith and works, 344, 350
Justin Martyr, 299, **388**
Just war, 336

Kaaba, 398–400, 402, 409, 415, 427, 428, 464
Kabbalah, xviii, 231, **238–44**, 261, 301, 496, 548, 580
Kabir, 55, 58
Kach, 58
Kaffir, 467
Kaffiyeh, 467
Kagura, 139
Kagyu, 117, 118, 120
Kali, 20, 53, 61, 63, 78
Kali Yuga, **78**, 499
Kalki, 499
Kalpa, 78
Kalpa Sutras, 23
Kama, 5, 29, 78
Kamakura period, 124–25
Kama Sutra, 42–43
Kami, 131, 143, 556
Kan Chi, 199
Kane, Ariel, 503–4
Kane, Shya, 503–4
Kangha, 58
Kaplan, Mordecai M., 253
Kapleau Roshi, Philip, 113
Kara, 58
Karbala, 467
Kareem, 446
Karim, Prince, 434
Karl, Jo Ann, 513
Karma, 78, 527
    in Buddhism, 85, 86, 143
    in Hinduism, 26–28, 48, 143
    in Jainism, 49–50
    in Sikhism, 57
Karma Kagyu, 118, 120
Karmapa, 120
Karma yoga, 4, 34
Kashrut, 264, 297
Katha Upanishad, 22, 29, 30
Kaur, 58
Kauravas, 38, 39, 41
Kaushitaki Upanishad, 22
Kautilya, 24
Keen, Sam, 531
Kegon, 122
Kelippot, 265
Kellogg, John Harvey, 391
Kelsey, Morton, 532

Index

Kempo, 112
Kena Upanishad, 22
Kendo, 112
Kennett Roshi, Jiyu, 113
Kensho, 112, 143
Kes, 58
Kesakambalin, Ajita, 28
Ketubim, 225
Kevala (kevalin), 49–50
Khadija, 401–3, 411, 418
Khalid ibn al-Walid, 418, 454
Khalifat Rasul Allah, 418
Khalistan, 58
Khalsa, 58
Khalsa, Harbhajan Singh, 55
Khanaqas, 446
Kharijites, 431
Khatvanga, 116
Khomeini, Ayatollah Ruhollah, 408, 433, 467
Khuddaka nikaya, 103
Khutba, 464
King, Franzo, 357
Kingdom of God, 274–75, 292–94, 297
King James Bible, 239, 287–88
Kings, Book of, 215
Kings, divine right of, 134
Kirpan, 58
Kirtan, 35, 58, 78
Kitab-i-Aqdas, 456
Kitab-i-Ighan, 456
Kitchen God. *See* Tsao-chun
Klemp, Harold, 542
Klimo, Jon, 478, 510
Klostermaier, Klaus, 8, 56
Knight, J. Z., 469, 512, 537
Knights Templar, 328, 549
Knipe, David M., 69
Knox, John, 346
Koans, 109–12
Kobo Daishi. *See* Kukai
Kodashim, 235
Ko Hung, 182, 185, 196, 199
Kojiki, 131, 133, 140
Konko Kyo, 136
Koot Hoomi (Kuthumi), 495
Koran. *See* Quran
Koresh, David, xxx, 392
Koseva, 232
Kosher, 263–64
Koshitsu, 135
Kripalu Yoga, 37
Kripalvanandiji, Swami, 37
Krishna, 4, 45–46, 51, 54, 78, 436
  in *Bhagavad-Gita,* xxiii, 27, 39, 42
Krishna Dvaipayana, 38
Krishnamurti, Jiddu, 65, 496, 503
Krisjnajayanti, 75

Kriyananda, Swami, 37
Kriyas, 30, 32
Kriya tantra, 117
Kriya Yoga, 36–37, 66
Kshatriya caste, 4, 11–12, 28, 42, 78
Kuan Ti (Kuan Kung), 196
Kuan-yin, 124, 140, 143–44, 193, 197, 581
Kübler-Ross, Elisabeth, 525, 527
Kuei, 171, 172
Kufi, 463, 467
Kukai, 123, 135
Kumbha Mela, 78
Kundalini yoga, 6, 36, 54, 67, 243
K'ung Chi, 156
Kung fu, 107
K'ung-tzu (K'ung Fu-tzu). *See* Confucius
K'un-lun mountains, 196
Kuo Hsiang, 181
Kuo P'o, 195
Kurgans, 13, 574–78, 582, 583
Kurozumi Munetada, 137
Kusha, 122
Ku tao, 197
Kwong, Jakusho Bill, 114
Kyoba, 135, 136
Kyosaku, 111, 112

La Barre, Weston, 371
LaBerge, Stephen, 117, 546
Lacrosse, 567
Ladino language, 265
Lahoris, 437
"La ilaha illallah," 402
Lakshmana, 40
Lakshmi, 20
Lalla Yogishwari, 51, 78
Lamas, 37, 114, 120
Lamedvovnik, 142
Lanello, Ascended Master (Mark Prophet), 497
Lan Ts'ai-ho, 178
Lao Chun, 179–80
Lao-tzu, xix, xxii, xxiv, 147–49, 151, 156, 158–59, 166, 167, 179–80, 194, 198, 586
Lares, 305
Larger Catechism, 385
Last Judgment (Last Day)
  in Egyptian religion, 228
  in Greek religion, 307
  in Islam, 396, 422–24
  in Judaism, 228
  in Zoroastrianism, 73, 228
Lat, al-, 399, 408
Latihan, 459
Latin language, 352–53, 392
Latria, 382
Lauds, 330

610

Index

612

Index

Index

Index

Pretas, **145**
Pre/trans fallacy, **480**
Price, Richard, 543
Priests
  in African diasporan religions, 359–61
  in Christianity, 279, **302**, 311, 312, 324,
    363
  Gnostic, 301
  in Hinduism, 10–11, 21, 22, 68
  in Judaism, 223, 273, 278
  Native American, 563–64
  in Shinto, 134
Prime, **330**
Prisca, **302**
Promised Land, **208**, 210, 214, 215
Promised Ten, **468**
Prophet, Elizabeth Clare, 497–98
Prophet, Mark, **497**
Prophets, Judaic, 218–20, 504
Protestantism, 287–88, 311, 340–51, 372
Protestant work ethic, 347
Proverbs, Book of, 581
Psalms, 396, 410
Pseudepigrapha, **229**, 265, 287
Psyche, 307
PTI, 369
P'u, **198**
Publicans, 325
Puja, **16**, 79
Pulpit, **378**
Puranas, 20, **24**, 79
Pure and Bright Festival, **193**
Pure Land Buddhism, 27, **123**–25, 127, 184
Purgatory, 342
Puri, 19
Purim, **261**
Puritans, 347–48
Pursel, Jach, **512**
Purusha, **32**–34, 241
Purushamedha, **16**
Purusharthas, **5**
Purusha sukta, 10, 16
Purva-Mimamsa, **6**, 79
Pythagoras, **26**, 239, 308–9, 542

Q source, **284**, 300
Qadi, **459**
Qadiri, **447**
Qadiyanis, **437**
Qarmatians, 399, **434**, 436
Qaswa, 413
Qlipot, **265**
Quakers, 351–54, 374
Queen Mother of the West (Hsi Wang Mu),
    177, 192, **195**, 196
Quimby, Phineas, 364, **489**–90
Quinn, Michael, 363
Qumran community, **226**, 229, 282, 295

Quran, xxvi, 202, 224, 395–98, 404, **405**–7,
    418, **422**–24, 441, 453, 467
Quraysh tribe, 399, 400, 402, 408, 413,
    415–16
Qurratu l'Ayn, **455**
Qutb, **468**

Rabbinic Judaism, 233
Rabbis, **223**
Radewijns, Florens, 341
Radha, **39**
Radhakrishnan, Sarvepalli, 65
Radhasoami, **542**
Rahim, **401**, 407, 446
Rahman, **401**, 407, 446
Rahula, 87
Raihana, 403
Raj, **513**
Rajas, 7, 150
Raja yoga, **4**–5, 30, **35**–36
Rajneesh, Bhagwan Shree, 502–3
Raka, **425**, 463
Rakshasa, 79
Rama, **40**–41, **54**–55, 512
Ramadan, 401, 414, **427**
Ramakrishna, Sri, xiii, xix, **61**–62, 474,
    476–77, 501
Ramakrishna Mission, 63
Ramakrishna Order, 63, 70
Ramananda, 55
Ramanuja, 20, 46, 54, 68
Ramayana, 4, 10, 19, 20, 38, **40**–41, 54, 68,
    82
Rambam. *See* Maimonides
Ram Dass, Baba, 67, 543
Rameses II, 205, 211
Ramthu, **469**, **512**–13, 537
Ranade, Mahadev, 60
Rancé, Armand de, 329
Ranke-Heinemann, Uta, 289
Rashid, **446**
Rastafarianism, 356–57
Ratha, 19
Rationalism, Jewish, 244–45
Ratnasambhava, 142
Ratzinger, Joseph, 538
Ravana, 40
Ravel's *Bolero*, 452
Ray, Sondra, 534, 548
Rebazar Tarzs, 542
Rebbe, **248**
Rebirthing, 547–48
Rechabites, 265
Reconstructionist Judaism, 253–54
Reflexology, 523
Reformation, Protestant, 340–48
Reformed churches, **347**, 377
Reform Judaism, 252

617

Index

Reich, Wilhelm, 520
Reiki, 524–25
Reincarnation
  in ancient Greece, 26, 308
  in Buddhism, 85, 94, 96, 120, 123, 135
  in Christianity, 388–89
  in Hinduism, xxiii, 16, 25–29, 48
  in Jainism, 49
  in Judaism, 231, 238, 241
  in New Age, 493–96
  in Sikhism, 57
Relics, 313, 344
Religious Right, 368
Religious Taoism, 153–54
Reorganized Church of Latter Day Saints,
  363
Reps, Paul, 109–10
Resurrection, 278, 378
Revelation (book of the Bible), 228, 286,
  302, 385, 391, 424
Revised Standard Version, 287
Revivalism, 390
Reza Pahlavi, Shah, 433–34
Rhazes (Abu Bakr al-Razi), 451
Ribats, 446
Richards, Mira, 64
Ridwan, 425, 468
Rifai, 447–48
Righteous, the, in Islam, 424
Rigpe Dorje, 120
Rig Veda, 3, 9–10, 14, 17–21, 78–79, 587
Rigzin Karma Lingpa, 105
Ring, Kenneth, 526
Rinzai, 111–13, 141
Ripley, Sarah, 491
Rishis, 3, 8, 38, 40, 80, 504
Rita, 12, 19
Ritsu, 122
Ritual. *See* Worship
River Brethren, 353, 373
Roberts, Jane, 506, 509
Roberts, Oral, 368, 371
Robertson, Pat, xviii, 369
Rodegast, Pat, 511
Rolf, Ida P., 521, 543
Rolfing, 521–22
Roman Catholic Church, 284, 287, 311,
  323–24, 349–51, 369, 377, 381, 549,
  565
Roman religion, 304–5, 309
Rosaries. *See* Prayer beads
Rosenkreutz, Christian, 548
Rosh Hashanah, 222, 260
Roshi, 110
Rosicrucianism, 548–49
Ross, Floyd H., 133
Roth, Philip, 258
Rousseau, Jean-Jacques, 386, 559

Roy, Ram Mohan, 59–60, 61, 80
Rudra, 19, 40, 79
Rumi, Jalal-ud-din (Jelaluddin), xix, 443,
  449–50, 452, 542
Rushdie, Salman, 408, 460, 467
Russell, Charles Taze, 355, 500
Russian Orthodox Church, 324, 353, 376
Ruth, Book of, 240
Ryerson, Kevin, 510
Ryobu Shinto, 135, 137

Sabaeans, 422–23
Sabbah, Hasan ibn al-, 435
Sabbath, 205, 222, 259–60, 275, 278,
  279–80, 397
Sabians, 389
Sabr, 445
Sabur, 406
Sacramentals, 390
Sacraments, 350, 390. *See also* Baptism;
  Eucharist
Sacred embryo, 189
Sacred marriage, 572
Sacred pipe, 567–68
Sacrifices
  in Bon, 142
  in Hinduism, 16, 17, 19, 21, 48
  in Islam, 429
  in Judaism, 230
  in Santería, 361–62
  in Taoism, 172
Sacristy, 378
Sadaqa, 425
Saddam Hussein, 432
Sadducees, 226, 227, 230, 265, 277, 279,
  296
Sadhana, 80
Sadhus, 67, 70, 80, 248
Sad of Zuhra, 468
Sadr, Musa al-, 461
Safa, al-, 428
Safiya, 403
Sahasrara chakra, 7
Sai Baba of Shirdi, 65
Saicho, 122, 124
Said (son of Zayd the Hanif), 468
Saint Germain, Comte de, 497, 498
Saints, 142, 381–84, 468
Sakya, 120
Salabhasana, 32
Saladin (Salah-al-din), 454
Salat, 330, 425
Salinger, J. D., 111
Salman the Persian, 416
Salvation Army, 390–91
Samadhi, 36, 80, 113
Samantabhadra, 94, 118, 119
Sama Veda, 3, 20, 21

618

Index

Sambandar, **51**
Samhitas, **3**, 20, 80
Sampradaya, **9**
Samsara, **26**, 27, 48, 49, 80, 96, 97
  in Buddhism, 85, **144–45**
Samskaras, **26**, 60, 80, 507
Samson, 264
Samuel (judge and prophet), **217**, 505
Samuel, King, 264
Samuel, Book of, **215**, 505
Sanatana dharma, **2**, 80
San-chiao kuei-i, **178–79**
San Ch'ing, **179**
San-ch'ung, **187**
Sangha, **90**, 101, 104, 145
Sangye nyipa, 116
Sanhedrin, **227**, 278
San I, **170**, 187, 192
Sankhya, **6**, 8, 32–34, 42
Sannyasins (sannyasa), **5**, 29, 70, 80
Sanron, **122**
Sanskrit language, **2**, 68–69, 75–76, 93,
  102–3
Santana, Carlos, 67
Santería, **361–62**
Sants, **55**
Saoshyant, **72**
Sarah, 398
Sarasvati, **20**
Saraswati, Dayananda, **61**
Saso, Michael, 186
Satan, **391**, 429
Satanael, **326**
Satanic Verses, The, **408**
Satanism, **470**
Satchidananda, Swami, 37, 65, **66**, 76, 501
Sati, **59**, 60, 69, 80, 582
Satmar, 250
Satori, **112**, 115, 145
Sattva, **7**, 150
Saturnalia, **304**, 379
Satyagraha, **65**
Saul, King, **205**, 217, 505
Saul of Tarsus. *See* Paul
Savikalpa samadhi, **36**
Savonarola, Girolamo, **341**, 391
Sawda, **403**
Sawm, **427**
Schaberg, Jane, 289
Schattler, Philip L., 537
Schneerson, Menachem M., 250
Scholastica, 328
Scholasticism, **391**
Scholastics, **391**, 451
Scholem, Gershom, 241, 246
School of Force. *See* Legalism
Schucman, Helen, **509**, 510
Schuller, Robert, 371

Schultz, J. H., **539**
Scientology, **544**
Scribes, Jewish, **265**, 271, 277, 279
Scriptoria, **331–32**
Scriptures
  Buddhist, **102–6**, 122, 125
  Christian, **268–91**, 295–96
  Confucian, 156, 169
  Hindu, **3–4**, 8, 20–24, 38–43, 53
  Islamic, **395–96**, 405–11
  Jain, **51**
  Judaic, **23**, 224–26, 229, 232–36
  Shinto, **131**, 140
  Sikh, **57–58**
  Taoist, **159–61**, 163–69, 170, 187
  Zoroastrian, **72–73**
Séances, **505**
Seattle (Seathl), Chief, **561**
Sebastian, 314
Second Coming of Christ, **299**, 354, 367,
  385, 387, 396, 423, 498–99, 500
Secret Book of John, **300**
*Secret of the Golden Flower, The (T'ai I
  Chin Hua Tsung Chih)*, **168–69**, 189,
  533
Sects
  Christian, **344**, 370–77, 490–91, 500
  Hindu, **9**, 151
  Islamic, **430–39**
  Jewish, **226–30**
  mystery, **307**
  Taoist, **150–51**, 190
  use of term, **xxix–xxx**
Seder, **278**
Sefer ha Zohar, **240–41**
Sefir Yetzirah, **239**
Self-Realization Fellowship (SRF), **66**, 500
Sen, Keshub Chandra, 60
Seneca, 305
Sensation, **528–29**
Sensei, **110**
Separatists, 348
Sephardim, **265**
Sephirot, **240–41**, 243, 265
Septuagint, **225–26**, 239, 287, 312
Serbian Orthodox Church, 324, 376
Sermon on the Mount, 304
Seth, **506**, 509
Seveners, **433**, 434
Seven Sages of the Bamboo Grove, **181–82**
Seventh-day Adventism, **355**, 372, 391–92,
  500
Sext, **330**
Sexuality
  in Buddhism, 87–88, 98–99, 117, 119
  Christian witch-hunts and, 583
  in Hinduism, 42, 54, 99. *See also* Lingam;
  Yoni

Index

Index

Index

Index

Index

Index